D1643431

LANGUAGE PROCESSING

Language processing

edited by

Simon Garrod and Martin J. Pickering
University of Glasgow, UK

Psychology Press Ltd, Publishers
27 Church Road
Hove
East Sussex, BN3 2FA
UK

British Library Cataloguing in Publication Data

A catalogue record for this book is available from the British Library

ISBN 0-86377-836-4 (hbk)

ISSN 1369-0183

Cover painting *Sculptural Study 2* (Tempera) by Ian Hopton

Typeset by Acorn Bookwork, Salisbury, Wilts
Printed and bound in the UK by Biddles Ltd, Guildford & King's Lynn

Contents

List of contributors

David A. Balota, Department of Psychology, Washington University, St Louis, MO 63130, USA

Kathryn Bock, Beckman Institute for Advanced Science and Technology, University of Illinois at Urbana-Champaign, 405 N. Mathews, Urbana, IL 61801, USA

Nick Chater, Department of Psychology, University of Warwick, Coventry, CV4 7AL, UK

Morten H. Christiansen, Department of Psychology, Southern Illinois University, Carbondale, IL 62901-6502, USA

Matthew W. Crocker, Computational Linguistics, Saarland University, Saarbrücken, D-66041, Germany

Julie A. Foertsch, The LEAD Center, 1402 University Avenue, University of Wisconsin-Madison, Madison, WI 53706-1611, USA

Alan Garnham, Laboratory of Experimental Psychology, University of Sussex, Falmer, Brighton, BN1 9QG, UK

Simon Garrod, Human Communication Research Centre, Department of Psychology, University of Glasgow, Florentine House, 53 Hillhead Street, Glasgow G12 8QF, UK

M. Gareth Gaskell, MRC Cognition and Brain Sciences Unit, 15 Chaucer Road, Cambridge, CB2 2EF, UK

Morton Ann Gernsbacher, Department of Psychology, University of Wisconsin-Madison, 1202 W. Johnson Street, Madison, WI 53706-1611, USA

John Huitema, Beckman Institute for Advanced Science and Technology, University of Illinois at Urbana-Champaign, 405 N. Mathews, Urbana, IL 61801, USA

William Marslen-Wilson, MRC Cognition and Brain Sciences Unit, 15 Chaucer Road, Cambridge, CB2 2EF, UK

Helen E. Moss, Department of Experimental Psychology, University of Cambridge, Cambridge, CB2 3EB, UK

Stephen T. Paul, Psychology Department, PO Drawer 6161, Mississippi State University, Mississippi State, MS 39762, USA

Martin Pickering, Human Communication Research Centre, Department of Psychology, University of Glasgow, Florentine House, 53 Hillhead Street, Glasgow, G12 8QF, UK

Anthony J. Sanford, Human Communication Research Centre, Department of Psychology, University of Glasgow, Florentine House, 53 Hillhead Street, Glasgow, G12 8QF, UK

Daniel H. Spieler, Department of Psychology, Jordan Hall, Stanford University, Stanford, CA 94305-2130, USA

Paul Warren, School of Linguistics and Applied Language Studies, Victoria University of Wellington, PO Box 600, Wellington, New Zealand

Series preface

Over the past 20 years enormous advances have been made in our understanding of basic cognitive processes concerning issues such as: What are the basic modules of the cognitive system? How can these modules be modelled? How are the modules implemented in the brain? The book series "Studies in cognition" seeks to provide state-of-the art summaries of this research, bringing together work on experimental psychology with that on computational modelling and cognitive neuroscience. Each book contains chapters written by leading figures in the field, which aim to provide comprehensive summaries of current research. The books should be both accessible and scholarly and be relevant to undergraduates, postgraduates, and research workers alike.

Glyn Humphreys

Studies in Cognition Series
Published Titles

Series Editor
Glyn Humphreys, University of Birmingham, UK

Cognitive Models of Memory
Martin A. Conway (Ed.)
Language Processing
Simon Garrod & Martin Pickering (Eds.)
Knowledge, Concepts, and Categories
Koen Lamberts & David Shanks (Eds.)
Attention
Harold Pashler (Ed.)
Cognitive Neuroscience
Michael D. Rugg

CHAPTER ONE

Issues in language processing

Simon Garrod and Martin J. Pickering
Human Communication Research Centre, University of Glasgow, UK

This book is about human language processing: what happens in the mind when someone speaks, listens, reads, or converses. A reader unfamiliar with the subject might well ask what makes language processing such a special topic; why does it deserve its own volume in a series on cognitive science? The simple answer is that language is our principal intellectual faculty and yet it is only recently that we have begun to understand how it is processed. Like vision, language processing is something we can all do with great skill and speed, but analysis of what is involved reveals deep complexity. In the words of a computational linguist, "If it were not for the brute fact that the world contains more than five billion primates that are demonstrably able to produce and comprehend natural languages, mathematical linguists would long ago have been able to present convincing formal demonstrations that such production and comprehension was impossible" (Gazdar, 1995). The book sets out to explain how humans make it possible and, as we shall see, much hinges on the efficiency with which we can integrate multiple sources of information.

What is it about language that presents such a processing challenge? Perhaps the most important thing is the number of levels involved and the ambiguity inherent in all of them. Initially, there is the problem of how people can extract structure from speech. Given a sound wave that we would hear as *recognise speech*, an automatic speech recognition device would come up with *wreck a nice beach* or *reckon ice peach* or *wreck on ice beach*, all of which are possible alternatives on the basis of the sound alone. However, in the right context human listeners experience no difficulty and are not aware of any ambiguity. Then there is the problem of how to establish the particular meaning of each word: *Speech* can mean the human faculty of speech, but it can also mean a presentation in front of an audience or the thing that contrasts with writing. Beyond this there is the problem of establishing the structure of the sentence as a whole. For example, sentence (1) is open to a number of quite different structural interpretations:

(1) Time flies like an arrow

Altmann (1997) illustrates at least 47 quite different readings for the written version and over 100 for the spoken. These come about because each word can play different grammatical roles in the sentence and have different meanings. *Time* can be a noun or a verb (i.e. something recorded by a watch or the process of measuring it), *flies* can be a noun with one of at least two different meanings (insects or a zipper) or a form of the verb *to fly*, and so on. In general, the longer the sentence, the more ambiguous it can be. Some 12 word sentences have literally hundreds of thousands of different interpretations. Computer systems collapse under the weight of all these alternatives, whereas human language processors are not even aware of the problem.

Further problems emerge when we consider how to interpret texts. A particularly important problem is with the interpretation of referential expressions, such as pronouns, which link one sentence to another through common reference to things in the world. Pronouns present a processing challenge because they are almost always multiply ambiguous. For example, the *they* below could in principle refer to a number of different groups of people on the basis of what has already been said.

(2) Mary, John, and the lodger went for a walk with the children.
They . . .

(3) . . . came back cold and exhausted.
(4) . . . always kept the children in sight.
(5) . . . did not often see him.

In (3) it probably refers to all of them, in (4) to Mary, John, and the lodger, in (5) to Mary and John. It is not difficult to generate other examples where the pronoun would refer to different groupings. Yet any piece of normal discourse is packed with such pronouns, and language users, unlike computer systems, rarely encounter problems.

Thus, language is full of complexity. Yet we use it with great speed and efficiency. For example skilled readers interpret words at the rate of about three per second, as fast as they can count out loud. Similarly, we are able to perform the equally complex problem of producing intelligible utterances, and, moreover, to hold conversations when we have to shift repeatedly from production to comprehension and vice versa. The field of language processing investigates how it is that we can perform such tasks.

In all issues concerned with comprehension, it becomes apparent that information provided by the utterance is insufficient on its own to allow the comprehender to obtain the intended interpretation. People must therefore draw upon additional information to assist them. For instance, the signal heard as *recognise speech* may get that interpretation in part because it is sensible, whereas *wreck on ice beach* is not. This suggests some role of background knowledge in comprehension. More locally, the first two words of *time flies like an arrow* cannot both be verbs, because such an utterance would be ungrammatical. The relevant knowledge here is specifically linguistic, but it is grammatical knowledge rather than knowledge concerned with the recognition of individual words. Perhaps the most fundamental issue in language comprehension is understanding how "top-down" knowledge, not provided by the relevant aspect of the stimulus, is accessed and used. Similar issues are raised by production, where theories differ on how knowledge is employed when generating utterances.

As in the understanding of other complex systems, the appropriate research strategy appears to be to separate language processing into different components, to investigate them individually, and to determine how they interact. The first level we consider consists of words, the smallest independent meaningful elements in a language; these can then be combined according to grammatical rules to form phrases and sentences, the last being the most complex linguistic forms with a clearly definable meaning. We also consider aspects of processing that involve integrating multiple sentences. Therefore, a standard psycholinguistic approach is to break down the comprehension or production process according to the structural levels of analysis that it has to deal with. Some of the book is organised in this way. Hence there are parts on Lexical Processing, Syntactic Processing, and Semantic and Discourse Processing. However, there are also parts that follow a somewhat different organisation: There is a part on Language Production and Dialogue Processes and another on Computational Issues in Language Processing.

This particular organisation leaves many areas of psycholinguistics uncovered. Nothing is said about language acquisition, neurolinguistics, or low-level speech processing. We have chosen to concentrate on core psychological issues that relate directly to semantic interpretation—the process of relating speech or writing to meaning. A key issue, reflected in all the contributions to this volume, is that of the speed and accuracy of this process. As yet, research on acquisition of language or its neural substrate says little about this issue, and research on speech perception is more directly concerned with perceptual than cognitive issues. Thus, from the point of view of cognitive science, the topics considered here form the areas most central to the understanding of language processing.

The first part on Lexical Processing consists of three chapters, which consider various aspects of how and when the meaning of each word is recovered during normal comprehension. All of these chapters agree that the central issue is the special status or otherwise of words as units of processing, but they address this issue in slightly different ways. According to linguists, words, or more precisely their component morphemes, constitute the smallest units of meaning. So it is natural to ask how lexical and morphological interpretation fit into language understanding as a whole. On the basis of a structural linguistic analysis, an attractive hypothesis is that interpretation should proceed sequentially, starting with basic units such as words or morphemes, and then moving on to sentences, followed ultimately by whole segments of text or dialogue. A subsidiary issue, also considered here, concerns precisely what the basic unit should be: Should it be a word, a morpheme, or something else?

There are also theoretical reasons for splitting the process into components that might be associated with these different levels of analysis. Thus, Fodor (1983) has produced influential arguments for what he calls modularity, whereby, among other things, different processing domains are treated as autonomous and computationally encapsulated from each other. This is one approach to the computational problem highlighted by Gazdar. However, others have taken a somewhat different approach which focuses on the speed and efficiency of language processing. Thus, Marslen-Wilson and Tyler (1987) take the view that the only way in which we can manage to operate so efficiently is by throwing all available resources into the task as soon as possible. This means that lexical processing, for example, should call on semantic, syntactic, and pragmatic sources of information as soon as they become available—hence the question about the special nature of the word in processing. If processing is modular then it should be possible to find an encapsulated process for word recognition that cannot depend upon processes operating at other levels.

The opening chapter, by Balota, Paul, and Spieler, explores some of the implications of this debate in relation to written words and how these are processed during reading. It addresses two main issues: the methodological question of how much we can learn about language processing in general by studying lexical processing in isolation; and the more theoretical question of whether lexical processing represents a clearly defined stage of comprehension in itself. The authors express reservations on both points. Their review of the area suggests that different word processing tasks tend to highlight different aspects of interpretation, and that focusing on any particular one may lead us to draw over-restrictive conclusions about the nature of lexical processing during normal comprehension. For example, in certain tasks the orthographic patterns (i.e. sequences of letters) predict processing ease or difficulty irrespective of the semantic properties of the words being processed. However, in other tasks it seems to be the syntactic or semantic properties of the words that are the major determinates of processing difficulty. In yet others, plausibility—how the word fits into its overall context—is crucial. Hence any conclusion about the fundamental nature of lexical processing drawn on the basis of one particular experimental technique may overstate the case that lexical processing depends upon that one particular information domain.

The chapter by Moss and Gaskell (Chapter 3) concentrates on the special nature of words in relation to speech processing. In reading, a whole word may normally be processed as a result of a single eye fixation (Rayner & Pollatsek, 1989). This is not the case in listening: spoken words are encountered as part of a transient speech stream with the component sounds heard in a temporal sequence. So a central issue in understanding the efficiency of spoken language comprehension is determining how processing synchronises with the temporal sequence in which the information occurs. This problem led to the formulation of what is called the cohort model of spoken word recognition (Marslen-Wilson & Welsh, 1978). The basic idea is that all words consistent with the pattern of speech segments encountered so far are activated. Recognition only occurs when this cohort is reduced to one, and all other words have been eliminated. This account raises interesting questions about the time-course of semantic interpretation. In a truly modular system we would not normally expect to find evidence of activation of the meanings of all the words in the initial cohort (i.e. all those words consistent with the first segment or two of the speech pattern) before the word itself has been recognised. However, in an interactive system that has access to higher levels of linguistic representation, meaning (and context) may also be activated before the word has been recognised. In other words, one would expect not just the forms but also the meanings of the cohort members to be available during the course of speech comprehension. The evidence tends to support this interactive view (Zwitserlood, 1989). Moss and Gaskell's chapter centres around these issues, some of which are also taken up in Sanford's chapter on semantic interpretation of sentences and discourse (Chapter 10).

The final chapter in this part is by Marslen-Wilson (Chapter 4). It addresses the question raised earlier of what is the basic semantic unit in language processing. Marslen-Wilson concentrates on the contrast between purely word-based accounts of semantic analysis and those based on morphemes. As he points out, our obsession with the word is very much a literary one, and the use of spaces to segment words is a recent historical development. In psycholinguistics, the concentration on the word may also reflect the fact that so much psycholinguistics is carried out in English, which has an uncommonly simple morphological structure. Hence, it might be more natural for the morpheme to be the basic unit. The chapter considers a range of evidence that suggests a morphological as opposed to lexical basis for early semantic analysis. This is an important and controversial move towards a more linguistic treatment of lexical meaning than that adopted by most cognitive psychologists.

We introduced this first part of the book in the context of a historical debate between modularists and interactionists. In fact, as becomes apparent in most of the chapters, the current debate has moved a long way from any simple contrast between modular and interactional processing. The current issue is very much one of precisely how the different sources of information are brought to bear in language processing. This same concern is central to the two chapters in the next part of the book, which are on syntactic processing.

The chapters in Part 2 start with the assumption that lexical processing has occurred and consider the way in which words are combined together to produce complete sentences. Most work on parsing has investigated how the processor resolves syntactic ambiguities (Bever, 1970; Frazier & Rayner, 1982). Sometimes these ambiguities continue throughout the sentence, but often they are only local, with the complete sentence not being ambiguous. For example, in *The florist sent the flowers was very pleased*, the verb *sent* is used as a past participle modifying *the florist* (cf. *the florist who was sent the flowers*). But after reading *the florist sent the flowers*, another analysis is also possible, in which the fragment corresponds to a simple transitive sentence. Under some circumstances, people experience difficulty when the continuation makes it clear that this simple transitive analysis is incorrect. In such a case, it appears that the processor changes its favoured analysis. Researchers in parsing ask whether it considers one analysis at a time or whether it can consider multiple analyses in parallel, and how it changes between different analyses. Perhaps the most basic question, however, is why the processor initially favours one analysis over another. For example, does it adopt the simplest analysis, the most plausible analysis, or the most frequent analysis? Put another way, what sources of information does the processor draw upon in selecting or favouring an analysis?

Pickering (Chapter 5) provides a general overview to these questions. He begins by discussing the clear evidence that sentence comprehension is generally extremely incremental. In other words, both syntactic analysis and associated semantic interpretation normally take place as soon as every new word is encountered. Pickering then considers the question of how the processor chooses which analysis to favour, and provides an overview of the sources of information that appear to be relevant to this question. He then considers current accounts of sentence processing in detail. The basic contrast is between unrestricted accounts, in which all sources of information can be used immediately, and restricted accounts, in which initial parsing decisions are based on some sources of information but not others. Pickering explores this distinction with reference to a number of different types of syntactic ambiguity.

Warren (Chapter 6) investigates a specific and, until recently, somewhat neglected topic in sentence comprehension: the role of prosody. The main reason for this neglect is certainly that most research has involved written language comprehension. Written comprehension is "self-paced", so that the experimenter can identify points of difficulty by the fact that the reader experiences disruption at those points; but the rate of spoken comprehension is entirely fixed by the speaker. One interesting aspect of Warren's chapter is, therefore, to highlight different innovative methods that have been used to explore the role of prosody in spoken language comprehension. Warren provides a detailed discussion of the nature of prosody and its relation to syntax. He then considers studies that investigate the role of prosody in syntactic disambiguation and semantic interpretation, and relates them to the question of how prosodic information is integrated with other sources of information within the processor.

Part 3, on computational processes considers some of the ways in which aspects of language processing can be described at a more computational level. Recent research makes it very clear that a detailed understanding of the system is simply not possible without a considerable understanding of the computational issues that underlie it. We include two chapters here: one that specifically relates to syntactic processing, an area where explicit computational models are having a considerable impact on theoretical development and experimental work; and one that is much more general, and is concerned with the impact of connectionism on different areas of language processing.

Crocker (Chapter 7) provides an account of the computational mechanisms that underlie syntactic processing. He begins with a theoretical discussion about the relationship between grammars and parsers, and assumes that the parser makes use of grammatical knowledge in its operations; this is known as the "competence hypothesis" (Chomsky, 1965). The chapter then considers various mechanisms that might be employed in the construction of syntactic analyses, and relates these to the problem of ambiguity in parsing. It then provides a computational perspective on accounts of syntactic ambiguity resolution discussed in Part 2.

Chapter 8, by Chater and Christiansen, begins by providing background about connectionist modelling in general, and then describes and evaluates connectionist models of different aspects of language processing. It first considers visual word recognition and naming in detail, and shows how these processes can be modelled using different kinds of connectionist networks. The next section looks at speech, and considers both recognition and production. The section on morphological processing focuses on learning, generally regarded as one of the major strengths of connectionist modelling in general, and concentrates on attempts to model the acquisition of the past tense. Finally, the chapter considers the difficult issue of whether connectionism can provide an account of syntax and parsing, in light of the common observation that natural language syntax is particularly hard to model without explicit rules. The authors remain fairly agnostic about whether connectionist accounts of language processing are to be preferred over traditional symbolic ones, and suggest that each application needs to be assessed on its individual merits.

Part 4, Semantic and Discourse Processing, considers some of the deeper levels of language processing. Human language processing is not exhausted by the identification of words, lexical–semantic processing and syntactic processing. Full understanding involves relating what is in the text to the world; in other words, it is concerned with reference. It also involves refining the interpretation of each individual sentence in relation to the message that the speaker or writer is trying to convey, thereby establishing what is sometimes called the significance of the sentence. Each of these operations can affect the interpretation of the words themselves. For instance, whether a word is to be taken literally or as part of an idiom or metaphor often depends upon its overall discourse context (Recanati, 1995).

The three chapters in this part address all of these issues. Gernsbacher and Foertsch, in Chapter 9, begin with a general review of theories about the integration of sentence interpretations into the broader discourse representation. One of the key issues raised here is the extent to which processing at these deeper levels is specific to language and the extent to which it reflects more general cognitive processes that are used in the understanding of, for example, pictorial representations or films. Gernsbacher and Foertsch emphasise some of the general cognitive constraints that apply to higher level comprehension of language. In particular, they argue that the processor makes use of principles that they call structure building, conceptual enhancement, and suppression.

In Chapter 10 Sanford concentrates on the linguistic details of semantic and pragmatic processing. Pragmatic processing goes beyond semantic processing, and relates to establishing the significance of what is being said. In the past there has sometimes been a tendency to ignore pragmatic processing and to assume that sentence interpretation involves little more than accessing the literal meanings of words and combining them via parsing. In contrast, Sanford illustrates how the interpretation of words, as well as more complex expressions, is intimately tied up with the broader context in which they are processed. Figurative language illustrates this particularly well. For example when we say *London has gone to sleep* we are clearly not making a literal statement, since cities cannot literally sleep. However, there are at least two figurative interpretations of the sentence, which are based on different interpretations of the individual words. If we take *London* to refer metonymically to its inhabitants, then *sleep* can be taken literally; but we could also take *London* literally and assign a metaphorical interpretation to *sleep*, with the meaning that the city has ceased to be an exciting place to be. This kind of ambiguity presents fascinating problems in understanding the time-course of semantic and pragmatic processing. So, whereas Gernsbacher and Foertsch concentrate on general discourse processing issues, Sanford focuses on the details of the interpretation process as it applies beyond the isolated sentence.

The final chapter in this part considers a particularly important aspect of higher-level interpretation. Garnham (Chapter 11) concentrates on the problem of reference—how different linguistic expressions relate to things in the world. The chapter begins with a review of the theoretical issues surrounding reference that have mainly been discussed in the philosophical literature. Garnham then considers how these referential links might be computed during comprehension. Of particular interest are links between expressions in different sentences that are co-referential, for example, the problem with *they* in sentence (2). Establishing such links makes it possible to integrate information between sentences in a discourse. Again, one of the main issues concerns the precise time course of this process and its consequences for resolving ambiguity. Garnham shows that, as with other aspects of language processing, we are extraordinarily efficient at co-reference resolution.

The final part is called *Production and Dialogue Processing*. These chapters are concerned with particular types of language processing, rather than with the relationship between processing and a particular level of linguistic or cognitive structure. Clearly we spend about as much time producing language as listening to it, and a great deal of time in conversation. However, researchers have paid much less attention to production and, especially, dialogue than they have paid to comprehension. One important reason for this is that it has, until recently, appeared more difficult to investigate these processes in controlled experiments. Chapter 12 by Bock and Huitema illustrates the considerable advances (due largely to the ingenuity of experimenters in the study of language production) in the last 10 years or so. They first discuss evidence from speech errors and dysfluencies that has traditionally formed the basis of models of production. They then discuss a model of language production that incorporates message-level (roughly, semantic), syntactic, and phonological processing. They use this model to illustrate recent experimental work on language production that considers the time-course of processing in detail.

The reasons why dialogue processing has received so little attention are both methodological and theoretical. First, it is extremely difficult to have any experimental control over normal conversation and this makes it difficult to investigate dialogue in a rigorous way. Second, from a theoretical point of view, the language of dialogue is disorderly compared to the straightforward grammatical sentences of monologue. In the last chapter by Garrod (Chapter 13), these issues are discussed in relation to recent experimental work on dialogue. The central question is whether the study of dialogue uncovers aspects of language processing not revealed by the study of either language comprehension or language production in isolation. Garrod comes to the conclusion that it does. What seems to be particularly important in conversational processing is the intimate interaction between the process of producing an utterance and its concurrent interpretation in the dialogue context. Thus, production is constantly being modified by feedback from the listener; and the listener's subsequent production process is strongly influenced by what he or she has just interpreted as a listener. However, as the chapter indicates, this area of language processing, as in the case of production, is still ripe for investigation.

Overall, we believe that the chapters in this volume point towards an integrated, general picture of language processing. Perhaps most strikingly, language processing is clearly very efficient and incremental. Different sources of information are rapidly drawn upon and integrated, in such processes as determining the appropriate meaning of a word, syntactic analysis of a string of words, or antecedent of an anaphor. Similar evidence for incrementality occurs in language production and in the integration of production and comprehension that is necessary in dialogue. We believe that there are some key outstanding questions, which can perhaps be framed in terms of the question of how precisely to specify these sources of information. For instance, is the word or the morpheme the basic unit of lexical processing? when, during discourse processing, do these sources of information cease to be linguistic and become more generally cognitive?, and, what kind of computational architecture is used to represent this information and allow it to be employed during processing? Research in language processing has developed many important theories about the kinds of representation we employ and the ways that we integrate these representations; future research will, we believe, help to determine the precise structure of this extraordinarily complex and efficient part of cognition.

REFERENCES

Altmann, G.T.M. (1997). *The ascent of Babel: An exploration of language, mind and understanding*. Oxford, UK: Oxford University Press.

Bever, T.G. (1970). The cognitive basis for linguistic structures. In J.R. Hayes (Ed.), *Cognition and the development of language*. New York: Wiley.

Chomsky, N. (1965). *Aspects of a theory of syntax*. Cambridge, MA: MIT Press.

Fodor, J.A. (1983). *The modularity of mind*. Cambridge, MA: Bradford Books/MIT Press.

Frazier, L., & Rayner, K. (1982). Making and correcting errors during sentence comprehension: Eye movements in the analysis of structurally ambiguous sentences. *Cognitive Psychology*, *14*, 178–210.

Gazdar, G. (1995). Paradigm merger in natural language processing. In R. Milner & I. Ward (Eds.), *Research directions in computer science*. Cambridge, UK: Cambridge University Press.

Marslen-Wilson, W.D., & Tyler, L.K. (1987). Against modularity. In J.L. Garfield (Ed.), *Modularity in knowledge representation and natural language understanding*. Cambridge, MA: MIT Press.

Marslen-Wilson, W.D., & Welsh, A. (1978). Processing interactions during word recognition during continuous speech. *Cognitive Psychology*, *10*, 29–63.

Rayner, K.A., & Pollatsek, A. (1989). *The psychology of reading*. Englewood Cliffs, NJ: Prentice-Hall.

Recanati, F. (1995). The alleged priority of literal interpretation. *Cognitive Science*, *19*, 207–232.

Zwitserlood, P. (1989). The locus of the effects of sentential-semantic context in spoken-word processing. *Cognition*, *32*, 25–64.

PART ONE

Lexical processing

CHAPTER TWO

Attentional control of lexical processing pathways during word recognition and reading

David A. Balota
Department of Psychology, Washington University, USA

Stephen T. Paul
Psychology Department, Mississippi State University, USA

Daniel H. Spieler
Department of Psychology, Stanford University, USA

The focus of the present chapter is on the primary meaning bearing element in reading, i.e. the word. There are certainly many different aspects of words that play crucial roles during word recognition (see Balota, 1994 and Henderson, 1982 for reviews). In the present chapter, we have decided primarily to emphasise research contributing to our understanding of *five* principal factors that have been shown to modulate word identification performance. Specifically, we will review some of the current word recognition research examining the influences of orthography, phonology, and meaning, along with syntactic- and discourse-level context effects. The first three factors are important in that each factor has been shown to affect processing of words both in isolation and in linguistic contexts, and each has yielded impressive amounts of data and controversy. The latter two factors are somewhat different in that discourse-based syntactic and semantic information do not contribute to isolated word recognition, but, of course, are fundamental in our use of words in the vast majority of language processing contexts.

In our discussion of each of the five factors, we will expand on some methodological and stimulus issues that we believe are crucial to our understanding of research in the area. For example, as outlined by Rayner and Pollatsek (1989), there are issues associated with the experimental paradigms involved in word recognition research that may not generalise to normal reading. Obviously, we rarely find ourselves reading with the tachistoscopic staccato frequently employed in word recognition research. Nor is it usual to have each word of a text masked, or presented via rapid serial visual presentation (RSVP) methods. In addition, unless the text is particularly dense with unfamiliar or misspelt words, we don't normally find ourselves performing lexical decisions as we progress through paragraphs of a text in a book. We will emphasise in the present chapter that perhaps the most critical difference between isolated word recognition and normal reading is the direction of attention to relatively distinct processing pathways.

The present chapter involves three sections. In the first section, we shall provide an overview of the processing pathway approach to lexical processing, which will be the unifying theme across aspects of this chapter. The second section will provide a brief overview of some of the theoretical approaches to word recognition and hence provide a foundation for interpreting the empirical literature that will be reviewed. The third and major section will provide a review of the five previously mentioned factors, with special emphasis on the manner in which the processing pathway perspective will help elucidate our understanding of the manner in which these factors influence word processing across a variety of tasks.

ATTENTIONAL SELECTION AND LEXICAL PROCESSING

One of the intriguing aspects of lexical processing is the multiplicity of internal representations and processes which may be used when a reader encounters a string of letters. For example, the deep semantic form of analysis which a reader of a classic Russian novel emphasises is quite different from the unusual mixture of orthographic and lexical information required when the same individual attempts to solve a crossword puzzle. Although there is clearly overlap in the nature of cognitive operations involved in each of these situations, the fact that a single individual may excel in such distinct situations highlights the importance of the highly flexible nature of the human language processing system.

When considering the types of codes that are available for stimuli, there are few stimuli that have such diverse codes as words. For example, a visually presented word can be queried at a number of quite distinct levels: Does it have the letters E and S (orthography)? Does it rhyme with the word SAVE (phonology)? Does it represent an animate object (semantics)? Is it a noun (syntax)? We believe that one of the key features of the human language parser is its flexibility in engaging each of these processing pathways based on the current task demands. We would argue it is precisely this flexibility that needs to be taken into consideration in developing adequate models of word recognition.

Unfortunately, the flexible nature of processing has not always played a crucial role in theories of lexical processing. A theory that incorporates processing flexibility would seem to be necessary in order to provide a complete picture of word processing in humans. Part of the problem may be the implicit notion that experiments are performed primarily to elucidate underlying cognitive architectures. The problem with the architecture metaphor is that it lends an image of a relatively static set of constraints that remain constant within and across experimental paradigms. In fact, in reviewing the work in word recognition, it appears that a fundamental goal has been to identify which codes or pathways are obligatorily processed upon lexical presentation. Consider, for example, the work on the processing of word meaning. Researchers have argued from semantic priming studies (Neely, 1977) and Stroop studies (Stroop, 1935) that meaning is automatically accessed when a word is visually presented. Thus, there appears to be automatic and autonomous access of meaning. However, as we shall see, even this fundamental observation about lexical processing can come under the influence of attentional selection and such results appear to depend upon the processing pathways that subjects select as a function of task demands. Indeed, we will entertain the possibility that there are no obligatory processing pathways engaged for words, and that the available evidence suggests that the cognitive system has the remarkable ability to select distinct processing pathways in response to a given task demand, thereby minimising the role of alternative unselected pathways. The ability to shift between reading a novel and solving a crossword puzzle or analysing a word for meaning versus orthography/phonology are a few examples of such flexibility. With this in mind, perhaps a better metaphor in which to couch experimental studies of word recognition is a quest for the specification of a cognitive "toolbox" in which, for any given task, only a subset of the available tools are brought to bear. Thus, in the spirit of using "the right tool for the right task", subtle changes in experimental context may lead individuals to employ different cognitive tools to accomplishing the goals of a given task.

In the context of the present chapter, the "cognitive tools" are psychological pathways (see also Posner, 1978) which are devoted to the processing of particular forms of information. These processing pathways might be analogous to neural pathways, such as the ventral and dorsal visual pathways, which are devoted to the processing of different forms of visual information (Ungerleider & Mishkin, 1982). Indeed, part of the motivation behind the emphasis on processing pathways is the involvement of different regions of the brain in processing different dimensions of a single stimulus. For example, in processing words, Petersen, Fox, Posner, Mintun, and Raichle (1990) have demonstrated through the use of positron emission tomography that vastly distinct areas of the brain are engaged when participants watch visually presented words (occipital), read aloud visually presented words (temporal), and generate verbs to nouns (frontal). The role of attention is to modulate processing along multiple pathways in a manner consistent with optimal performance of a task. The degree to which a pathway contributes to performance is continuously valued and dependent upon task instructions, strategies the subject might adopt, stimulus contexts, and a host of other factors.

A processing pathway approach emphasises two points which should be kept in mind throughout the present chapter (and possibly others in this volume). The first point concerns the frequently discrepant and often contradictory findings in the literature. A particular experimental design, combined with the stimuli used and the instructions given to individual participants, will result in the individual choosing some subset of available processing pathways and weighing the information from these pathways in a particular fashion. The combined contribution of information from each of these pathways will yield some pattern of performance. The highly flexible control which the attentional system has on the implicated pathways suggests that a different set of instructions, different lexical processing task, or even changes in list configuration could lead to a differential involvement of processing pathways, and hence, a different pattern of performance. Obviously, careful experimental design and task analyses must be applied to reveal differential involvement of processing pathways and to interpret the results of particular experiments.

The second point which we feel deserves emphasis is that theories and models of language processing cannot afford to ignore the central role played by attention. Researchers in the area of visual word recognition have formulated a number of elegant models of word processing in which attentional influences on processing have typically been ignored or have fallen outside the purview of the model. Clearly such simplifications by omission are to some extent necessary in any research endeavour. However, neglect of the role of attentional processes may not always serve to simplify the theoretical questions. In particular, such neglect runs the risk of asking comparatively inflexible models to account for data from highly flexible cognitive systems. In this light, we believe that an adequate model of visual word recognition must reflect the type of attentional selection that occurs during reading. Therefore, we believe that it is paramount to keep in mind the goal standard of developing a model of lexical processing in which task demands direct attentional selection to meaning level information.

Of course, in order to appreciate the role of attentional selection in lexical processing, we must first review the elegant theoretical and empirical work that has been developed in the lexical processing literature. Thus, we now turn to a brief overview of some of the extant theoretical perspectives on lexical processing.

OVERVIEW OF THEORETICAL PERSPECTIVES

In lieu of attempting to provide an overview of the rich theory that has developed in word recognition research, we will simply highlight a few theoretical perspectives that provide a foundation for the later discussion of the empirical literature. The goal here is simply to mention a few of the approaches to word processing, not to provide a detailed evaluation of any single model. In pursuit of this goal, we have selected Forster's search model (1976), the Seidenberg and McClelland (1989) parallel distributed processing (PDP) model, and Coltheart's (1978) dual-route model. At the onset, one should note that a goal of this modelling endeavour is to develop a task-independent model of word recognition. It is precisely this assumption that we believe will need to be substantially modified by the constraining influence of attentional selection.

Forster's serial search model

In general, serial search models (e.g. Becker, 1979, 1980; Norris, 1986; Paap, Newsome, McDonald, & Schvaneveldt, 1982; Taft & Hambly, 1986) propose that, based on a preliminary visual analysis of a stimulus, an assortment of lexical possibilities becomes available. The input stimulus is compared with each member of some candidate set, one at a time, until a match is found. The search set is typically assumed to be organised so that more frequent words are checked before less frequent words. Thus, search models have an easy way to handle a principal finding in word recognition literature, i.e. low-frequency relatively uncommon words are processed more slowly and less accurately than high-frequency relatively more common words (see Balota & Chumbley, 1984, 1985, 1990; Balota & Spieler, 1999; Monsell, Doyle, & Haggard, 1989, for a discussion of the role of word-frequency in word recognition tasks).

Forster's (1976) autonomous search model includes a number of distinct access bins to the master lexicon. These access bins correspond to orthographic codes (reading), phonological codes (speech perception), and semantic/syntactic codes (speech production). Most of the work by

Forster and colleagues has dealt with the orthographic access file. The notion is that when a word is visually presented, an orthographically defined bin is created and then searched according to frequency of occurrence until a match is found. Then, based on a pointer from the matched item, the reader can access the plethora of lexical information available with that item in the mental dictionary.

Although much of Forster's work has dealt with the orthographic access file, other search models, such as Becker's (1979) verification model nicely demonstrate why one might wish to hypothesise other access routines, such as one based on semantic access files. Becker used the serial search framework to account for another principal finding in word recognition, the semantic priming effect. The semantic priming effect refers to the finding that readers are faster and more accurate to process a visually presented word (DOG) when it follows a semantically related word (CAT) compared to when it follows a semantically unrelated word (PIN). Becker simply argues that in addition to an orthographically defined search bin, subjects also have a semantically defined bin, which is a generated set of target candidates made available based on the meaning of the prime item. These related candidates are compared with the stimulus item before unrelated items, and hence, one finds a semantic priming effect.

The emphasis in Forster's original search model is on an autonomous word recognition device that is relatively uninfluenced by attentional control. In fact, such a model was quite consistent with modular views of lexical processing, in which visual lexical presentation drives the search through orthographic bins independent of attentional control. However, the primary data base that was used to test aspects of this model where speeded naming and lexical decision performance; both are tasks that place relatively minimal load on meaning processing, at least compared to reading comprehension. Moreover, work by Glanzer and Ehrenreich (1979) and Becker (1980), both advocates of the serial search framework, have demonstrated that the two fundamental aspects of word recognition, word frequency effects and semantic priming effects, can be modulated by probability manipulations across different lists. Interestingly both Glanzer and Ehrenreich and Becker have suggested that list probability manipulations influence the strategic control of different types of search processes. Thus, these studies are quite consistent with the processing pathway approach in suggesting that attentional control can modulate the manner in which access files are searched.

Coltheart's (1978) dual-route model

This model is motivated by a logical analysis of the problem facing a reader of English. Namely, that while there exists a degree of consistency of mapping spelling to sound correspondences (e.g. MINT) there are many words which violate these "standard" spelling to sound rules (e.g. PINT). In order to address such problems, Coltheart (1978) suggested that there may be two routes through which a word may be named (see Coltheart, Curtis, Atkins, & Haller, 1993, for a more recent computational version). One route entails a direct look-up of the pronunciation in the lexicon (i.e. the lexical route). Presumably, any word that has been learned by the reader is stored in memory along with its correct pronunciation. Whenever the word is subsequently encountered during reading, the visual form is used to access the lexical entry for the word. Once accessed, the correct pronunciation of the word may be retrieved directly from memory. This direct route is frequency modulated and is quite similar to Morton's (1970) logogen model. The second route computes the pronunciation based on general letter-to-sound rules (i.e. the assembled route). Use of this route is necessary at least for cases in which unfamiliar or new words are encountered, as well as to account for the relative ease with which non-words (pronounceable letter strings such as BLANT and PLATAMARG) may be pronounced (see, however, Marcel, 1980 for an alternative view of non-word naming). Because this route makes use of fairly consistent rules for translating groups of letters into sounds, it will deliver incorrect pronunciations for words that do not comply with these spelling-to-sound rules (e.g. "pint" as a rhyme for "lint"). In this way, the model nicely accounts for the frequency by regularity interaction (e.g. Seidenberg, Waters, Barnes, & Tannenhaus, 1984). Specifically, low-frequency words that have inconsistent spelling to sound correspondences (e.g. PINT) produce slowed response latencies compared to low-frequency words that have consistent spelling-to-sound correspondences (e.g. LINK). Because high-frequency words have a relatively fast lexical route, there is relatively little competition from the slower sublexical route and so one finds little or no consistency effect for high frequency stimuli (e.g. SAME vs. HAVE).

One of the more powerful lines of support for the dual-route model has come from studies of acquired dyslexics, wherein there is evidence of a double dissociation between the two processing pathways. Specifically, for one type of acquired dyslexic (surface dyslexics) there appears to be a breakdown in the lexical processing pathway. Hence, these individuals are fine at pronouncing non-words and regularly spelled words. However, when confronted with an irregularly spelled word these individuals are likely to regularise it, i.e. pronounce BROAD such that it rhymes with the non-word BRODE (see Marshall & Newcombe, 1980; Shallice, Warrington, & McCarthy, 1983). On the other hand, there is a second class of acquired dyslexics, phonological dyslexics, who appear to have an intact lexical route but an impaired phonological route. These individuals can pronounce irregular words and other familiar words that have lexical representations; however, when presented with a non-word that does not have a lexical representation, there is a considerable breakdown in performance (Patterson, 1982; Shallice & Warrington, 1980). Of course, the question that we would be interested in is the extent to which the output from these different processing pathways are under attentional control. In fact, Balota and Ferraro (1993, 1996) have reported evidence that populations that appear to have a breakdown in attentional control (individuals with senile dementia of the Alzheimer's type) appear to produce leakage from the non-selected pathway. Specifically, for a task that demands the lexical processing pathway (naming) there is an increased influence of the sublexical route, as reflected by regularisation errors (see also Patterson, Graham, & Hodges, 1994), whereas, for a task that demands the sublexical processing pathway (rhyme judgements) there is an increased influence of the lexical route, as reflected by word-frequency effects.

Seidenberg and McClelland's (1989) PDP model

An important alternative to the classic dual-route framework is the Seidenberg and McClelland parallel distributed processing approach to word recognition. In this model, information concerning features, letters, and words is distributed across an array of elements, as opposed to being represented "locally" by single units (e.g. McClelland & Rumelhart, 1981). The model consists of three layers of distributed units. In the original model there were 400 orthographic input units that were connected to 200 hidden units, which in turn were connected to 460 phonological units. The weights (connection strengths) between the input units and the hidden units and the weights between the hidden units and the phonological units do not initially represent any organised mapping (i.e. starting weights are given random values). During training, the model is presented an orthographic string which produces some output that initially is very dissimilar to the correct output. The output is compared with the correct output and the weights are then adjusted, via the back propagation algorithm, in order to gradually reduce the discrepancy between the correct pronunciation and the observed pronunciation.

The model was trained on a total of 2884 unique orthographically represented words. The probability of training a given word was monotonically related to its estimated frequency in the language. Thus, high-frequency words had a greater influence on training than low-frequency words. The result of this training regime yielded an impressive ability of the model to encode many aspects of the statistical regularity of the mapping of orthography to phonology even in a language with such variable mapping as English. In fact, Seidenberg and McClelland nicely demonstrated that the model can capture the frequency by regularity interaction that is found in human behaviour with the same set of stimuli. Moreover, the model did a reasonable job in predicting naming performance on items that it was not trained on and also on non-words (see, however, Besner, Twilley, McCann, & Seergobin, 1990).

Interestingly, when the Seidenberg and McClelland model first introduced the model it was couched in terms of a single-route alternative to the dual-route account. However, recent discussions have acknowledged the contributions of multiple information processing pathways (see Plaut, McClelland, Seidenberg, & Patterson, 1996). Perhaps indicating progress in the word recognition literature, it appears that the question has shifted from a single/dual-route dichotomy to a question of what are the relative contributions of different sources of information to performance. For example, do certain words place particular emphasis on visual analyses (bare and bear) or phonological analyses (e.g. lead as in the metal or what a leader does). The central goal at this stage might be to determine the "division of labour" across multiple processing pathways (Seidenberg & Harm, 1995). We would argue here that the division of labour will not be a static aspect of the processing architecture of the model, but rather will ultimately depend upon attentional direction that is driven by task goals. For example, the influence of semantics might be much larger if attention is directed towards understanding message-level information in reading than if it is directed more towards phonology in a task such as naming or orthography in a task such as lexical decision. Thus, we would suggest that even within a connectionist system, there needs to be a role of attentional modulation of the overall influence of the various components (see Cohen, McClelland, & Dunbar 1990, for an example of the role of attentional selection on the output from individual modules within a connectionist framework).

REVIEW OF THE LITERATURE

As noted earlier, our goal in this section was to simply sketch a few of the major processing assumptions that are available in models of word recognition. We believe that it is quite important to note here that the development of each of these models is based on data obtained in large part from studies of isolated word recognition. Hence, we shall now turn to the extant literature regarding the available evidence concerning the five targeted variables (orthography, phonology, meaning, syntax, and semantics) for this chapter. The organisation of each section involves first providing an overview of the data that have been instrumental in developing the extent models of word processing and then reviewing the relevant literature from on-line measures of reading performance (e.g. eye-fixation duration data) to determine if in fact the findings generalise to situations where attentional selection drives processing pathways relevant to message level information, the major goal of reading.

Isolated word recognition

Obviously the visual/orthographic make-up of a word remains an important "initial" influence on identification whether the word occurs in a context or is encountered in isolation. For instance, it is this visual/orthographic form that supplies the visual system with information that determines where eye fixations will occur during reading. Rayner (1979) showed that readers tend to fixate between the first and middle letters of words, regardless of word length. Before an accurate eye movement can be made from a preceding word to a given location within the next word, readers must have some information about the word shape when it initially appears in the parafovea.

A second source of information that can be extracted from a word and still be considered independent of surrounding context is phonology. A word's meaning may change as a function of its contextual setting, whereas its pronunciation is relatively context-independent with the exception of certain types of ambiguous words such as WIND, BASS, TEAR, DOVE, and LEAD (i.e. heteronyms). In fact, some have argued that the phonology of a word provides a more reliable source of information for recognition than either orthography or meaning (e.g. Van Orden, 1991). Therefore, although this chapter deals primarily with reading rather than pronouncing words, it will be important to discuss recent evidence suggesting that phonology plays an important role in visual word recognition.

Finally, there are issues regarding whether meaning-level information (e.g. context availability, number of meanings, concreteness/imageability) can influence identification (see Balota, Ferraro, & Connor, 1991 for a review). To the extent that the activation of meaning-level information assists in the recognition of a word, it may be possible to determine whether the process of recognising a word likely involves the simultaneous extraction of meaning or whether meaning activation is a by-product of (i.e. follows) word recognition. This issue has received recent attention with regard to the number of meanings ("NOM") effect, in which words having multiple meanings such as BANK are identified more quickly than words having fewer meanings (Kellas, Ferraro, & Simpson, 1988; Millis & Button, 1989; Rubenstein, Garfield, & Millikan, 1970). Despite the fact that a word is usually read for meaning, most models of word recognition (e.g. those mentioned previously) do not consider the possible early contribution of its meaning to recognition. Of course, this will be a central issue in our discussion of this literature.

Orthographic neighbourhoods. In English, there are 26 unique letters (ignoring capitalisation alternatives) which can be used in various numbers and combinations to produce words or word-like forms. Assuming reasonable restrictions on length, the number of possibilities is almost limitless. However, in English there are constraints on what combinations can occur among groups of letters in order to be considered word-like. Even with rules governing how these letters can or cannot occur (or are likely to occur) together, there are many possibilities. What is interesting, then, is that we are able to quickly recognise or identify a randomly presented word in isolation. Somehow, we are capable of isolating a single word from the population of stored possibilities. Intuitively, it seems unlikely that recognition could occur as rapidly as it does during reading if we had to search through memory checking each word with all stored words one at a time until a match is found. However, matches *are* obviously found during reading; therefore, there must be some way of speeding the word retrieval process.

One possibility for speeding a memory search would be to organise memory so that words used more frequently are evaluated before less frequently used words. Searching for most words typically encountered during reading will not require an exhaustive or extended search and so access will be relatively quick on the average. This organisation captures the finding that high-frequency words are identified more quickly than low-frequency words (Balota & Chumbley, 1984). Of course, as noted previously, each of the models presented has no difficulty capturing the word-frequency effect.

Another way to make word retrieval more efficient would be somehow to capitalise on the visual similarities among words. Havens and Foote (1963) were one of the first studies to demonstrate that the orthographic similarity of a given word to other words can modulate early aspects of word processing. They showed that words such as CASE, that under tachistoscopic exposures may be confused with a number of similar words (e.g. CANE, BASE, CARE, etc.), were identified less accurately than words less likely to be confusable with alternative words such as OVER. Interestingly, this outcome was found to be independent of word frequency. These results would appear to support the notion that there is parallel activation of a set of orthographically related words, and that word identification involves the pruning of orthographically similar candidates as perception of the stimulus unfolds across time.

Of course, one might be concerned about the possibility that individuals are using partial information to guess what the stimulus word is under the degraded presentation conditions of the Havens and Foote study. Thus, Coltheart, Davelaar, Jonasson, and Besner (1977) extended the Havens and Foote observation in a seminal study of lexical decision performance (speeded word/non-word discriminations). Coltheart et al. (1977) evaluated lexical decision tasks ("LDT") latencies to both words and non-words that varied in how many English words could be produced by replacing a single letter with some other letter of the alphabet (but without changing letter positions). Coltheart et al. called this the N of a letter string, and it has since become known as the neighbourhood of a word or non-word. It was found that words which had many neighbours were identified as quickly as words with few neighbours. Non-words, on the other hand, were more quickly identified as such when they had fewer neighbours than when they had many neighbours. Because there was no influence of neighbourhood size for words, the authors concluded that access to a word occurred directly.

Coltheart et al.'s failure initially to find neighbourhood size effects with words is inconsistent with more recent accumulation of evidence that neighbourhood size *can* affect word processing performance (e.g. Andrews, 1989, 1992; Grainger, 1990; Pugh, Rexer, Peter, & Katz, 1994). However, even within this body of research, results are inconsistent with words having large neighbourhoods producing inhibition under some circumstances (e.g. lexical decision in Grainger, 1990), and facilitation under other conditions (e.g. lexical decision and naming for low-frequency words, Andrews, 1989; see Andrews, 1997, for a recent review).

Grainger's view (Grainger, O'Regan, Jacobs, & Segui, 1989) with regard to neighbourhood effects is that neighbourhood frequency, rather than neighbourhood size, is what drives response latencies. Controlling for bigram frequency, Grainger et al. (1989) demonstrated with both lexical decision and visual gaze durations (sum total of all fixations on a word during reading) that performance was slowed on words that had at least one neighbour of a higher frequency than the stimulus itself. Orthographic neighbourhood size was not found to affect performance. Grainger (1990) further demonstrated that the neighbourhood frequency effect had opposite results for lexical decision and naming tasks. Controlling neighbourhood size, Grainger found that, as neighbourhood frequency increased, performance was slowed for lexical decisions but speeded for naming. Although Andrews (1992) did not directly manipulate neighbourhood frequency, she did examine bigram frequency and concluded that it had no effect on either lexical decision or naming performance. In accounting for the apparent discrepancy between the effects of neighbourhood frequency (i.e. inhibition) and neighbourhood size (i.e. facilitation) in LDT, Andrews (1992) proposed that Grainger et al.'s

(1989) manipulation of neighbourhood size was not strong enough to detect neighbourhood size effects (ranging only from 2.2 to 7.9 neighbours compared with her 3.4 to 12.0 range). Andrews proposed that the neighbourhood frequency effects observed when neighbourhood size was restricted (Grainger, 1990), along with her results showing neighbourhood size effects, indicates that it is likely that both processes affect word recognition. However, Andrews also argued that because the inhibitory effects due to frequency have only been demonstrated with LDTs, it might be that the locus of such effects is in the decision stage of the task, rather than a reflection of earlier affects on lexical access. This conclusion has received more recent support by Pugh, Rexer, Peter, and Katz (1994), who suggested that the inhibitory effects of neighbourhood frequency observed by Grainger (1990) were likely due to strategic, or post-access processes associated with the LDT. Interestingly, Perea and Pollatsek (1998) have recently reported data from an eye-tracking study which suggests that the frequency of neighbours influencing relatively late processes in reading (i.e. regressions and fixation durations on the subsequent word). These results are also consistent with a post access locus of neighbourhood frequency.

It is important to note that the facilitatory effects observed for increases in neighbourhood density have proved to be troublesome for serial search models of word recognition. For example, according to Forster's autonomous search model, if neighbourhoods are collected together in single search bins ordered by frequency, then, on average, a serial search would result in slower identification times for large neighbourhood items. This is because more time would be required to search larger bins (dense neighbourhoods) than smaller bins (sparse neighbourhoods). This is precisely the opposite pattern found by Andrews (1992) and Pugh, Rexer, Peter, and Katz (1994). On the other hand, if a letter string produces parallel activation of many neighbours then one might expect larger neighbourhoods to produce overall more familiarity than smaller neighbourhoods; that this might drive a "word" response in lexical decisions, and possibly slow a non-word response (see Balota & Chumbley, 1984; Besner, 1983; Besner & Swan, 1982, for familiarity-based interpretation of lexical decision performance). Such a pattern would not necessarily extend to reading performance wherein the task demands should direct attention to message level information that requires a unique identification of the target word. Thus, we shall now turn to studies of on-line reading and orthographic neighbourhood effects.

Bohemier (1994) conducted a series of experiments that were designed to directly address the role of orthographic neighbourhoods across naming, lexical decision, and on-line reading tasks. In the first three experiments, Bohemier reported evidence of neighbourhood density effects in both naming and lexical decision tasks. More importantly, for the present chapter is the pattern observed in Exp. 4: Bohemier found that there was no evidence of a density effect when the same stimulus words were embedded in short sentences and eye-fixations were measured. In fact, Bohemier cites the results from three eye-tracking studies that have failed to find neighbourhood density effects in on-line measures of reading (Bohemier, 1991; Bohemier & Inhoff, in prep., Exps. 3 and 4; Grainger et al., 1989, Exp. 2). Hence, it appears that, when attentional selection is directed towards message-level pathways, one finds a reduced influence of a code (reflected by orthographic neighbourhood effects) that appears quite useful in isolated word processing tasks. Thus, the nature of the word recognition architecture appears to be highly influenced by where attention is directed. In making lexical decisions, overall activation of many candidates is likely to lead to increased familiarity thereby increasing the ease of making lexical decisions. Also, it is possible that when there are many candidates that converge on a similar spelling to sound correspondence, naming latencies will be facilitated as observed by Andrews (1992). Both of these benefits may be somewhat minimised when attention is directed towards message-level pathways and there is a clear demand to integrate the unique word into on-going comprehension processes, as in reading text.

Phonology. Much of our linguistic experience (especially during language acquisition) is with the sounds of words. Our experience with how words sound is obviously critical to learning to read (Perfetti, Beverly, Bell, & Hughes, 1987). Moreover, there is considerable evidence that phonological recoding is a critical component of reading comprehension (see Rayner & Pollatsek, 1989 for a review), and hence there is little debate concerning the importance of phonological coding during reading. The question that has received considerable attention is whether phonological information plays an early role in word identification, and hence we can simplistically divide this literature into two camps: First, according to the phonology-is-necessary camp, all word identification must go through some transformation of orthography to phonology for identification to occur. There are a number of proponents of this view that have varying commitments to this extreme position (e.g. Lukatela & Turvey, 1994a,b; Perfetti, Bell, & Delaney, 1988; Rayner, Sereno, Lesch, & Pollatsek, 1995; Van Orden & Goldinger, 1994). Second, according to the multiple route camp, there is a number of distinct routes in early lexical processing; one that is primarily mediated by orthography to phonology transformations and one that is more directly available from the mapping of a visual stimulus onto a lexical representation. Of course, the classic model within this camp is the dual-route model (Coltheart, 1978; Coltheart et al., 1993) reviewed earlier. We would simply argue that the role of phonology in word recognition depends upon the direction of attention to distinct processing pathways. The extent to which phonology is demanded by task goals will at least in part modulate the role of phonological processing. We shall now turn to a review of such evidence.

Interestingly, there are a number of findings that are quite consistent with the role of attention (modulated by task demands) in the degree of influence of the phonological processing route in word recognition. First, consider the classic consistency effect that is observed in naming performance. As noted earlier, readers are relatively slow to name low-frequency words that have inconsistent spelling patterns (e.g. PINT) compared to low-frequency words that have consistent spelling patterns (e.g. PARK). However, one might ask that because the response is overt naming, possibly there is an increased reliance on phonological information. Consistent with this argument, one finds relatively little influence of spelling to sound correspondence when one uses the same stimuli in a lexical decision task (see Andrews, 1982; Seidenberg, Waters, Barnes, & Tanenhaus, 1984). This would be expected according to the processing pathway perspective because overt naming may place a heavier load on a phonological pathway compared to lexical decision, in which there may be more emphasis on a visually based pathway.

An interesting set of experiments by Monsell, Patterson, Graham, Hughes, and Milroy (1992) has recently indicated that, even in naming performance, one can find strategic control of different processing routes. Monsell et al. were motivated in part by an observation by Midgley-West (1979). In the Midgley-West study, subjects were asked to name a series of 24 non-words, followed by an irregularly pronounced word. The interesting pattern was that subjects often regularised the last word (e.g. if the last word was WOLF, the subjects would name it as if it was pronounced like GOLF after naming 24 non-words). The argument is that, because non-words primarily demand the sublexical spelling to sound pathway, participants decreased their reliance on the lexical pathway and hence regularised the irregular word. Thus, these results are quite consistent with the notion that there is attentional control of processing pathways even in naming. Monsell et al. (1992) extended this finding to situations where subjects either received lists of only non-words, only exception words, or mixed lists of non-words and exception words. Subjects named exception words faster and made fewer regularisations when they were not also prepared to name non-words. Thus, Monsell et al. argued that subjects controlled, via attentional direction, the role of the sublexical spelling to sound pathway. Although there has been an alternative interpretation of the Monsell et al. results (see Lupker, Brown, & Colombo, 1997), there also is converging evidence across a number of distinct paradigms and languages for attentional control of these pathways (e.g. Baluch & Besner, 1991; Frost, Katz, & Bentin, 1987; Paap & Noel, 1991; Pugh, Rexer, Peter, & Katz, 1994; Simpson & Kang, 1994; Zevin & Balota, 1999).

Of course, there are other data that have been taken as strong support for an early role of phonology in lexical processing. Consider the important work of Perfetti et al. (1988). They reported the results from a series of masking studies in which a stimulus word was presented (MAIL) and then followed by one of three different types of mask: a graphemically and phonologically unrelated mask (e.g. FLEN), a graphemically related and phonologically unrelated mask (e.g. MARL), or a graphemically related and phonologically related mask (e.g. MAYL). The results clearly indicated that performance was best in the graphemically and phonologically related condition, which was better than in the graphemically related and phonologically unrelated condition, which in turn was better than the graphemically and phonologically unrelated condition. Thus, there appears to be some benefit from a phonologically related mask above and beyond simple visual similarity. Interestingly, however, Verstaen, Humphreys, Olson, and d'Ydewalle (1995) have recently reported evidence that, even under these conditions, there may be strategic control of the output from these different pathways. Specifically, Verstaen et al. found that the influence of phonology was eliminated under conditions in which all target items were homophones. Verstaen et al. argued that subjects modulated, via attentional control, the influence of the phonological pathway, minimising its role when the target stimuli could not be discriminated based on sound. Clearly, it appears that the role of phonological information in early aspects of lexical processing is not independent of attentional control.

A more important question concerns the role of spelling to sound correspondences in a task in which attention is directed towards message-level information, as in reading. There is some evidence of an early role for phonology during reading in a study by Pollatsek, Lesch, Morris, and Rayner (1992). Pollatsek et al. used the parafoveal preview paradigm. In this study, individuals' eye movements were monitored while reading a sentence. In the critical sentences, a homophonic word (e.g. reins) or a visually similar word (e.g. ruins) was replaced with a homophone (e.g. rains). Pollatsek et al. found that fixation duration was shorter on the target when it was preceded by the homophone word compared to the visually similar word (see also Folk & Morris, 1995).

Inhoff and Topolski (1994) examined fixations while subjects were reading words that either had consistent or inconsistent spelling to sound correspondences. These words were embedded in short neutral sentence contexts. The results indicated that there was no evidence of neighbourhood consistency on either first fixation data or gaze durations and only small effects of spelling to sound regularity on first fixations, despite the fact that this same set of stimuli yielded quite striking consistency and regularity effects in speeded naming performance. These results suggest that the demands of the naming task may in fact exaggerate the role of phonological codes, and that such effect of spelling to sound consistency effects may not be strong in the early analysis of words in on-line reading as the strong versions of mandatory phonological processing would demand. This is not to say that there is no role for phonology early in the processing of lexical information during reading. Rather, the point is that phonological influences appear to be attenuated when attention is directed towards message-level processing pathways. This contrasts with processing during single word naming studies in which attention is directed toward the production of a phonological output (e.g. Lukatela & Turvey, 1994a,b). We believe that further work is necessary to determine whether the same factors that strongly modulate naming performance, and have had a striking influence in theory development, also produce a strong influence in on-line measures of reading (see Folk & Morris, 1995, for one such study).

In the previous two sections we have reviewed evidence that addresses the influence of both orthographic and phonological information on the routes to word recognition. Clearly, these two types of information have dominated work in word processing. We shall now turn to a third factor that has been relatively ignored in word processing. That is, the extent to which the ease of accessing meaning for a word influences the speed to recognise that word.

Meaning. A word's meaning(s) must be retrieved from memory to understand the message conveyed by the text. It would appear that some translation of an auditory or visual presentation of a word is necessary in order to locate the meaning of the word in memory. That is, the process appears to require that the lexical or phonological status of a word be determined prior to meaning activation. This intuition, is captured in the notion of a modular word recognition system (e.g. Fodor, 1983; Forster, 1976).

Fodor (1983) elaborated a modular view of processing whereby the various processes associated with language use are delegated to several modules. According to this view, for example, accessing a representation of a word in the mental lexicon proceeds the same whether it is encountered in a context or in isolation (presuming that the quality of the inputs are equivalent). No influences external to the lexicon will affect the speed with which the word is located. Once it is located, however, the lexical processor provides the lexical information to the next module in the series for processing (e.g. context integration, elaboration). It is at these later modules that aspects of a word such as its syntax, phonology, and meaning may be observed to affect performance. The modular position contrasts with a strong interactive and cascadic processing view (McClelland, 1987; McClelland & Rumelhart, 1981) in which information is shared among operations throughout the recognition process (including meaning). In this case, a word's meaning(s) could be useful for recognition processes because lower level information about the input will become available to higher level processes prior to identification. These higher level processes (e.g. at the meaning-level) will provide useful information to lower level processes (e.g. lexical level) thereby aiding identification or lexical access.

The extent to which the meaning-level characteristics of a word have been shown to influence isolated word recognition has varied (see Balota et al., 1991 for a review). For example, the concreteness of a word's meaning has been shown to influence lexical decision in that more-concrete words have an advantage over less-concrete words (e.g. Day, 1977; Kroll & Mervis, 1986). However, there is also evidence suggesting that concreteness may *not* affect lexical decision (e.g. Richardson, 1976) when potentially confounding factors (e.g. familiarity, context availability) have been controlled (Schwanenflugel, Harnishfeger, & Stowe, 1988). It is noteworthy that these potentially confounding factors are themselves likely to be correlated with semantic characteristics of a word. Thus, it is therefore not clear from this literature that meaning-level influences on isolated word recognition are non-existent. Interestingly, Strain, Patterson, and Seidenberg (1995) have recently reported evidence that the imageability of a word (abstract versus concrete) can produce an influence on word naming for words that are relatively low in frequency and spelling to sound regularity. Specifically, subjects were slower to name exception words with abstract meanings (e.g. scarce) compared to abstract regular words (e.g. scribe) or highly imageable exception words (e.g. soot). This pattern is quite intriguing and suggests that there may be a trade-off between high-level semantic information and the clarity of the translation between orthography and phonology, precisely as an interactive architecture might predict (see also Cortese, Simpson, & Woolsey, 1997).

The concreteness or imageability of a word seems intuitively to tap some semantic aspect of meaning which probably varies from word meaning to word meaning. In addition to this semantic variable, a second variable that has received considerable attention in the literature is the number of meanings that are available for a word. For example, the word "bank" can refer to a number of distinct unrelated meanings (something an aeroplane does in a turn; the land immediately adjacent to a river; a financial institution). It is possible that if there is increased semantic support for both phonological and orthographic information then number of meanings may lead to facilitated lexical decision and naming performance. There have been a number of demonstrations of such effects in both word naming and lexical decisions (Balota et al., 1991; Fera, Joordens, Balota, & Ferraro, 1992; Jastrzembski, 1981; Jastrzembski & Stanners, 1975; Kellas et al., 1988; Millis & Button, 1989; Rubenstein et al., 1970; Rubenstein, Lewis, & Rubenstein, 1971). Unfortunately, however, there have also been a number of concerns raised about this observation. For example, Clark (1973) found that the number of meanings ("NOM") effect observed by Rubenstein et al. (1970) in their analysis by subjects was not significant when analysed by stimuli. In addition, a later study by Gernsbacher (1984) demonstrated that the NOM effect observed by Jastrzembski (1981; Jastrzembski & Stanners, 1975) could be attributed to an uncontrolled variable confounded with number of meanings (i.e. familiarity). As noted earlier, it is unclear what dimensions of a stimulus are tapped in unspeeded familiarity judgements, and so it is possible that familiarity ratings actually include meaning-level dimensions of a stimulus. Moreover, the NOM effect observed by Kellas et al. (1988) was obtained using stimuli that were controlled along many dimensions, including familiarity, in lexical decision performance.

A recent series of experiments by Borowsky and Masson (1996) replicated the NOM effect in lexical decision performance under conditions in which the non-words were orthographically legal, and failed to find a NOM effect with orthographically illegal non-words. In addition, Borowsky and Masson did not find any consistent effect of number of meanings in naming performance (although there was an effect found in Exp. 1 by subject means). Borowsky and Masson accounted for the general discrepancy between their results (failure to show NOM effects in naming) and previous naming results showing NOM effects (Fera et al., 1992) as possibly being due to a differential sensitivity of the subject populations to factors confounded with number of meanings (e.g. word length, neighbourhood density). When Borowsky and Masson matched these possible differences between ambiguous and unambiguous items, there was no trace of a NOM effect in naming (Exp. 2).

As Borowsky and Masson (1996) pointed out, NOM effects rely on between-stimuli comparisons of performance, and so will always be vulnerable to the possibility that observed differences are due to some uncontrolled variable that happens to vary between stimulus sets (e.g. the familiarity account of the NOM effect proposed by Gernsbacher, 1984). Borowsky and Masson proposed that matching stimuli on as many extraneous variables as possible, as well as partialling out such influences using multiple regression techniques, will maximise the validity of the NOM effect. Because the number of meanings metric typically involves either counting meanings in a dictionary, or asking subjects to provide an estimate of number of meanings, the final meaning tally associated with individual items represents a fairly continuous, but potentially skewed dimension. Simply splitting such items into two groups (ambiguous and unambiguous) for subsequent analyses does not seem ideal for representing the nature of potential relationships between NOM and other variables of interest. Indeed, this seems especially problematic if items classified as unambiguous according to such splits are actually ambiguous. This is illustrated more concretely in that a word such as "force" can be classified as ambiguous by Millis and Button (1989) but classified as unambiguous by Borowsky and Masson (1996). Although regression techniques were employed by Borowsky and Masson (1996), it is possible that the range of NOM across the 64 ambiguous and 64 unambiguous items used in this study was too variable to provide a sensitive test of meaning effects in naming.

We have examined the NOM effect more closely using the full set of 360 stimuli (see Kellas et al., 1991), which have a fairly large range for rated number of meanings. Based on the concerns raised by Borowsky and Masson (1996), we used regression analyses to examine contributions of variables known to have been (or may have been) confounded with number of meanings. Most importantly, we obtained the settling times from a recent model of word naming (Plaut, McClelland, Seidenberg, & Patterson, 1996) to partial out the regularities of various spelling to sound correspondences. The results of this study indicated that there were clear number of meaning effects that occur in word naming beyond what can be accounted for by frequency number of neighbours, and the settling times obtained from the Plaut et al. model, $t(352) = 4.09$, $P < .01$. Obviously, this pattern suggests either that (1) the Plaut et al. model does not capture some components of orthographic to phonological computations involved in naming (see Balota & Spieler, 1998; Besner & Bourassa, 1995; Seidenberg & Plaut, 1998; Spieler & Balota, 1997, for further discussion), or (2) a level that takes into account number of meanings needs to be added to the model.

It appears then that there may be some relatively small beneficial effect of NOM on word naming and a stronger effect on lexical decision performance. Within the present chapter, we are interested in what sorts of processing dimensions engaged by both naming and lexical decision might produce such a facilitatory effect of polysemous words. With respect to the lexical decision task, one might argue that because words and nonwords can be discriminated on the amount of meaning that is available, subjects may direct attention to the overall activation available in meaning-level pathways, thereby producing the beneficial effect of words with multiple meanings. Turning to naming performance, it is possible that multiple meanings that converge on the same phonological output may have a stabilising force for that phonological output.

If the previous accounts of NOM effects in naming and lexical decision are correct, then one might ask what would be expected if one examined the influence of NOM in reading. Based on the processing pathways approach, one might expect just the opposite influence of NOM in on-line reading measures. Specifically, because in reading attention is directed towards message-level processing pathways, one cannot integrate two unrelated meanings simultaneously with a previous context and so one might expect a slowdown in resolving ambiguity. Interestingly, this is precisely what Duffy, Morris, and Rayner (1988) and Rayner and Frazier (1989) have found. In both of these studies, gaze durations were longer on ambiguous words compared to unambiguous words in neutral context. When the number of meanings available for a word can increase either the ability to discriminate words from non-words (lexical decision) or possibly provide converging evidence for a phonological representation (naming), one finds evidence of a benefit from the availability of multiple meanings, whereas, when attention is directed towards message level information (and hence meaning selection must occur), one finds some decrement in performance.

It is important to note here that a number of recent models of word processing have placed considerable importance on the difference in the NOM effects in naming, lexical decision, and reading performance. For example, Borowsky and Masson (1996) have interpreted such effects (assuming no effect of NOM in naming) within Masson's (1991) distributed model of semantic priming and word processing. Borowsky and Masson argued that such effects may simply fall from different criteria used across naming, lexical decision, and gaze durations. In addition, Kawamoto, Farrar, and Kello (1994) have presented a connectionist model that also has been directed towards handling the opposite effects of number of meanings in lexical decision and in gaze durations. Kawamoto et al. suggest that such differences naturally follow from differences in monitoring information from different sets of units in the network. In fact, the notion of a monitor directed towards output of different processing modules is quite consistent with the notion of the current processing pathway approach. We believe that an important distinction that may eventually need to be made in this area is whether the results are best captured by differences in criteria or in monitoring the output from different modules; both of these approaches do not change the parameters influencing the activation across units within a module. The alternative possibility is that there is a module that maintains task demands and this module actually can control a gain parameter that modulates the activation processes within the relevant and irrelevant processing modules ("pathways" in keeping with the present jargon). This is the approach taken in the architecture described in the Cohen, Dunbar, and McClelland (1990) model of Stroop performance.

Contextual constraints in word recognition

Heretofore, we have reviewed evidence that effects of traditional variables that have been investigated in isolated word processing tasks such as lexical decision and naming can sometimes have quite different influences when attention is directed to message-level information such as in on-line reading measures. We shall now turn to a discussion of the results from studies that directly address the influence of context on word processing. Obviously, it is relatively rare that words are read in isolation. When processing words in context, there are at least two major types of information that play an important role: syntax and message-level semantic information. However, there is considerable controversy concerning how and when such information plays a role. There are at least three ways in which discourse-level information would likely be useful to reading: Syntactic and semantic information may serve to facilitate *initial* word processing, *subsequent* integration processes, or *both*. If these context-based sources of information are useful for initial word processing, it becomes less clear whether examinations of isolated word recognition generalise to normal reading processes. On the other hand, if word recognition proceeds uninfluenced by sentence-level (or more complex) sources of information, then it would suggest that discourse information is only important for later or higher level processes. If both early recognition and late comprehension processes are influenced by syntactic and semantic information, then examinations of either isolated word recognition or of discourse comprehension alone are incomplete.

Syntactic contextual constraint. It seems reasonable (and many theories of syntactic processing hold) that a word's syntactic classification is determined very rapidly in order for it to be integrated with the grammatical structure of a sentence. This view suggests that, at least under some conditions, syntactic/contextual information may actually be useful in the early aspects of word processing.

The early investigations of the role of syntax on initial word recognition processes involved minimal syntactic priming manipulations along with lexical decision and naming responses as the dependent measures. For example, Goodman, McClelland, and Gibbs (1981) examined syntactic priming in a lexical decision task. Part of the reason for examining relatively impoverished syntactic (priming) contexts was that the authors wanted to reduce the likelihood that their results could be interpreted as semantically based rather than syntactically based (a possible interpretation of the results of Fischler & Bloom, 1979 and Schuberth & Eimas, 1977). It is difficult, for example, to manipulate the syntactic constraint of a sentence without also affecting semantic constraint. Goodman et al. reasoned that the use of carefully constructed minimal priming contexts could serve to address this potential problem if a syntactic prime made the target syntactically predictable but not semantically predictable (e.g. whose-planet; the-tree; he-sent).

Goodman et al. (1981) demonstrated effects of both syntax and semantics on lexical decision times (see also Wright & Garrett, 1984). When semantic and syntactic prime conditions were blocked, words were identified more quickly when they were syntactically or semantically primed (e.g. FRUIT-APPLE, YOUR-OVEN) than when they were incongruently primed (e.g. THREAD-APPLE, THEY-OVEN). However, when semantic and syntactic primes varied from trial to trial, priming effects were observed only for semantic primes. Goodman et al. concluded that subjects' utilisation of syntactic information in the blocked but not the mixed conditions indicated that syntactic priming is likely to be the result of conscious or strategically driven processes (cf. Posner & Snyder, 1975). On the other hand, because semantic effects were observed regardless of changes in stimulus presentation (mixed versus blocked), Goodman et al. hypothesised that semantic effects result from automatic structural characteristics of the lexical processing system. Consider these results within the processing pathway approach. It is possible that in the blocked conditions, subjects were able to selectively focus attention to information most beneficial to performance (syntactic elements in the HE-SENT conditions and semantic information in the FRUIT-APPLE conditions). Under mixed conditions, semantic information apparently wins out over syntactic information, possibly because more information is typically conveyed via semantic routes than syntactic routes in relatively impoverished conditions (two words) such as those used by Goodman et al. (1981).

Seidenberg, Waters, Sanders, and Langer (1984) extended the results of Goodman et al. (using the identical stimuli) by contrasting performance on the LDT with naming performance (see also Sereno, 1991). Syntactic effects were observed only for the LDT, which was interpreted as support for the view that syntactic processing is under strategic control. Although the conclusions among these studies tend to converge, it is worth considering whether single-word syntactic primes actually reflect the full engagement of syntactic analyses that are necessary when reading sentences. Studies which have examined syntactic influences using sentence contexts have shown syntactic effects which seem to support the hypothesis that one-word contexts do not fully engage syntactic processes (e.g. Nicol & Swinney, 1989; West & Stanovich, 1986; Wright & Garrett, 1984). Unfortunately, one must temper the conclusions of these studies because it is possible that some of the effects were due to a type of post-lexical checking process, described earlier, that is engaged by the demands of the lexical decision task. Thus, we again need to look at converging evidence from on-line measures of reading when attention is directed to message-level information.

The influence of syntax on early word processing in reading was addressed in a classic study by Frazier and Rayner (1982). In this study subjects were presented one of the following two sentences:

(1) *Since Jay always jogs a mile this seems like a short distance to him.*
(2) *Since Jay always jogs a mile seems like a short distance to him.*

Frazier and Rayner (1982) were interested in, among other strategies, a syntactic parsing strategy called late closure. According to late closure, readers attempt to attach new items to the phrase or clause currently being processed. The critical issue in these two sentences is that in (1) the subject can attach the word *mile* as the object of *jogs* (consistent with late closure), whereas in (2) subjects may attempt to attach *mile* to *jogs* but then when they encounter the word *seems* it is syntactically incorrect and so subjects will need to reparse the sentence. Interestingly, Frazier and Rayner found that subjects increased their first fixation on the word *seems* in (2) compared to (1). Given that eye fixations on the target word were on the order of 250 ms, it appears that subjects detected the incorrect syntactic interpretation very early on in processing, thereby suggesting a strong influence of syntactic constraint on early lexical processing. This of course is quite reasonable given the importance of the direction of attention to message-level information, and the immediate loss of such information if the sentence is misparsed.

The power and independence of the syntactic parser on lexical processing in reading was also elegantly demonstrated in a set of experiments by Britt, Perfetti, Garrod, and Rayner (1992), Ferreira and Clifton (1986), Rayner, Carlson, and Frazier (1983), and Rayner, Garrod, and Perfetti (1992). In general, these studies indicate that there is very little influence of contextual constraint on the initial stages of strong syntactic preferences. For example, Rayner et al. (1983) found that readers tend to favour a particular syntactic structure when given an ambiguous initial clause such as, "The performer sent the flowers...". Here, readers tend to initially process this as a simple active clause which would be inconsistent with the grammatically acceptable reduced-relative completion, "...*was very* pleased with herself." Rayner et al. (1983) found that readers slowed down their reading considerably at the point of disambiguating of the sentence (*was very*) for the reduced-relative version of the sentence compared with the consistent simple-active version of the sentence (i.e. "...and *was very* pleased with herself." These findings are in agreement with either the view that the influence of certain types of syntactic processes act prior to pragmatic considerations or independent of higher level semantic operations (Fodor, 1983; Forster, 1976, 1979; Oden & Spira, 1983; Seidenberg, Tanenhaus, Leiman, & Bienkowski, 1982).

Unfortunately, there has been considerable recent controversy concerning the influence of contextual constraints on syntactic parsing. For example, there have been a number of studies that have demonstrated an influence of context on reading times for reduced relatives (MacDonald, 1994; Pearlmutter & MacDonald, 1992; Trueswell & Tanenhaus, 1991; Trueswell, Tanenhaus, & Garnsey, 1994). In an attempt to reconcile the differences across these two sets of studies, MacDonald, Pearlmutter, and Seidenberg (1994) argued that some of this discrepancy may be accounted for by differences in the frequency of the morphological forms of ambiguous verbs. It appears that when context effects were found on initial syntactic parsing, verbs were used that made the reduced relative a more viable option, whereas when context effects were not found it was more likely that verbs were used that did not have a reduced relative reading as a likely option. MacDonald et al. argue from these results that the reader will use whatever information that is available to constrain a particular interpretation. This again suggests a non-static processor of information that takes into account multiple sources of information that are relevant to accomplish the goals of the task. Possibly, the more important question is not whether the syntactic parser acts independent of contextual constraints but how does the reader modulate the activation amongst a number of relevant processing pathways that are necessary to achieve the goal of reading, i.e. abstract message-level information. We shall now turn to a second type of constraint which for simplicity we label as semantic contextual constraint.

Semantic contextual constraint. At the onset of this subsection, it is important to note that we shall use the term "semantic" contextual constraint rather loosely here, and shall be discussing a number of distinct levels of constraint in this section. Possibly, a better label would be non-syntactic interword constraints. However, because of the prominent role semantic priming research has played in this area, we will retain this label, and attempt to indicate the precise nature of the constraint in the reviewed literature.

The influence of semantic context on word recognition has been a central area of research within a number of distinct areas of cognitive psychology. For example, a considerable amount of work in this area has dealt with semantic priming effects (see Neely, 1991 for a review). As noted earlier, the semantic priming effect refers to the finding that subjects are faster and/or more accurate to make a response to a target stimulus when it follows a related prime compared to when it follows an unrelated prime. There has been considerable evidence in this literature that the nature of priming effects are quite dependent upon the task constraints (see Balota & Lorch, 1986; Neely, 1991; Sereno, 1991; Stanovich & West, 1983). This is quite consistent with the processing pathway approach because the tasks determine what sorts of pathway are most useful for making a given response.

In order to illustrate the powerful role of task constraints in interpreting priming effects, we shall briefly review a set of experiments by Balota and Paul (1996). This study addressed the issue of whether two associatively related primes produce additive, underadditive, or superadditive effects on target word processing. Balota and Paul were interested in the influence of multiple primes, because in natural sentence processing there are multiple constraints (semantic, syntactic, global constraints) on target word processing. In this study, there were two major classes of stimuli that differed with respect to whether the primes converged on the same semantic representation of the target (e.g. LION-STRIPES-TIGER) or diverged onto distinct semantic representations (e.g. MUSIC-KIDNEY-ORGAN). The results of the first five experiments yielded clear additive effects of related primes (i.e. the beneficial effect of two related primes was the algebraic sum of the independent effects of each of the single primes). This pattern was found in both naming and lexical decision tasks, across varying stimulus onset asynchronies, and for degraded targets. More importantly, the additive effects were observed equally for conditions in which the primes converged onto the same semantic representation (e.g. LION-STRIPES-TIGER) and conditions in which the primes diverged onto distinct semantic representations (e.g. MUSIC-KIDNEY-ORGAN). Because there was no influence of the type of semantic representation that was being primed (i.e. no difference between convergent and divergent semantic conditions), Balota and Paul suggested that the locus of the observed additive effects is most consistent with the notion that the subjects were primarily relying on lexical processing pathways in both the naming and lexical decision tasks. In the sixth experiment, subjects' attention was directed to select a semantic processing pathway by requiring a relatedness judgements between the target word and the primes. Now, the results differed dramatically between convergent and divergent target conditions. Specifically, for targets in which the primes converged onto the same semantic representation there were clear additive effects of the primes; however, for targets that included primes that diverged onto distinct semantic representations, there was no additional benefit of two primes related to different semantic interpretations of the target over a single prime. These results suggest that when the priming task demands selection of meaning-level pathways, one will observe very different patterns of data compared to when the task primarily emphasises lexical processing pathways. This pattern of dissociation across different types of tasks that place more or less emphasis on lexical level representations compared to meaning-level representations is quite consistent with the data reviewed previously on meaning-level effects on isolated word processing. Specifically, in naming and lexical decision, there appears to be a benefit of multiple-meaning representations, whereas, in reading, there appears to be a deleterious effect when multiple meanings are available. A similar pattern is found in Balota and Paul's multiple priming studies when attention is directed towards meaning level representations via the relatedness judgements. The question that we now turn to is what is the influence of different types of message-level constraint in our target task, reading.

Hess, Foss, and Carroll (1995) discussed three fundamental models that have evolved to account for effects of sentence context on word processing. According to the first view, associative priming accounts of context effects typically rely on automatic spreading activation from one word in the mental lexicon to all other related words. Because the spread of activation is assumed to be automatic, there is no mechanism for preventing multiple meanings of ambiguous words, for example, from becoming activated even when the ambiguous word is embedded in a biasing context such as, "We carved our initials into the *bark*" (Seidenberg et al., 1982; Swinney, 1979). As Hess et al. point out, a clear advantage of this model is that it can handle context effects independently of the contextual setting in which words occur (i.e. single- or multiple-word primes). According to the second view, there is a direct influence of discourse-level representations on lexical processing (e.g. Auble & Franks, 1983; Foss & Ross, 1983; Hess et al., 1995; Sharkey, 1990; Sharkey & Sharkey, 1992; Vu, Kellas, & Paul, 1998). Here, the notion is that context effects in reading are a reflection of the extent to which a given target word fits a higher level representation that has been extracted from the earlier text. Finally, there are hybrid models in which context effects are argued to result from multiple sources within a text. One source is a fast-acting automatic spread of activation from a single word of a text to related words within the lexicon. The other source occurs later and represents a more global process of integration.

The available evidence from on-line reading measures suggests that there are clear influences of contextual constraint during reading. For example, consider two early studies by Ehrlich and Rayner (1981) and

Zola (1984). Both studies found clear effects of *predictability* of a target word on fixation durations. Of course, there is some question about where in the system such effects of predictability are occurring. For example, in the Zola study subjects were presented with a strong contextual adjective (e.g. *buttered* before *popcorn* versus *adequate* before *popcorn*). As noted previously, the effect of predictability may be due to more local intralexical priming or possibly due to higher level discourse congruity effects.

Given that there appear to be clear influences of constraint on word recognition, let us now consider three distinct ways in which researchers have attempted to delineate the locus of such constraint, i.e. more intralexical effects versus higher level text integration effects. For example, Schustack, Ehrlich, and Rayner (1987) manipulated both global contextual constraint (distance of previous mention of the target item in the text) and local contextual constraint (via a preceding associatively related verb). The results indicated that in naming performance there was only an effect of the local context, with no influence of global constraint. On the other hand, when one considers on-line reading measures, one finds clear influences of both variables on eye fixation measures. Schustack et al. interpreted this pattern as indicating that the effect of local information in both naming performance and as reflected in eye initial fixations on target words may reflect a type of intralexical priming; however, the more global discourse effect of distance on eye-fixations is more likely to reflect integration processes that are not engaged in speeded naming. Thus, based on this pattern it appears that the hybrid model may be most applicable to the reading situation.

Morris (1994) also attempted to distinguish between local and global context effects during reading. In the Morris study, readers were presented sentences such as *The gardener watched as the barber trimmed the moustache*. Here, one can see that there are two words related to *trimmed* (i.e. *gardeners trim hedges* and *barbers trim hair*). A change in the sentence such as *The gardener who watched the barber trimmed the moustache*, results in a mismatching of the message-level context and the lexical relationships among the words. According to a lexical view of context effects, fixation times on "*moustache*" should not be affected by message-level shifts as long as the lexical components have not been altered (as in the previous sample sentences). A discourse model, on the other hand, requires that the inconsistency between what *gardeners trim* and the message of the second sentence (*a gardener trimming a moustache*) will increase fixation times while readers attempt to resolve the apparent conflict. Morris found that fixation times on *moustache* were significantly shorter when it was presented in a sentence that contained the words *barber*, *gardener*, and *trimmed* but only when the overall sentence context was consistent with the *barber trimming the moustache*. No facilitation was observed when changes in the context made *barber* inconsistent with *moustache trimming*. Although these results tend to imply that it is overall context (discourse) which affects word processing, Morris also found *lexical* influences on word processing in which gaze durations on the critical verb in the sentence (e.g. *trimmed*) were unaffected by the overall message. Specifically, when either *barber* or *gardener* appeared alone in the sentence (the other replaced by a neutral word such as *person*), gaze durations were shorter compared to when both were replaced by neutral words. Thus, based on these on-line measures of reading, it appears that both types of constraint are powerful determiners of lexical integration (see also Duffy, Henderson, & Morris, 1989; O'Seaghdha, 1989).

The second approach to determine the locus of the influence of predictability on word recognition versus integration processes is to orthogonally manipulate variables related to the two factors. This was done in a study by Balota, Pollatsek, and Rayner (1985) in which predictability of a target word was crossed with the visual similarity of a parafoveal preview word. For example, participants would read sentences such as the following: *Since the wedding was today, the baker rushed the wedding cake/pies to the reception*. The high-constraint target was *cake* whereas the low-constraint target was *pies*. In addition, when subjects were fixated before a critical boundary (within the second occurrence of the word *wedding* in this example), there were a number of distinct types of previews that were crossed with predictability of the target (e.g. identical previews, *cake*, *pies*; visually similar previews *cahc picz*; visually dissimilar preview, *bomb*). The results indicated that there was an interaction between contextual constraint and parafoveal preview. Specifically, subjects apparently benefited more from visually related parafoveal information for high constraint targets (cake) than for low-constraint targets (pies). Because the extraction of parafoveal information should be relatively early in word processing, one might argue that the influence of predictability in this case is on word identification processes. In further support of this observation, subjects were also more likely to skip the high-constraint targets than the low-constraint targets, again supporting a relatively early influence of context. A similar pattern was reported by Schustak, Ehrlich, and Rayner (1987). Finally, it should be noted that predictability also appeared to have had a later effect in the Balota et al. (1985) study because there was some evidence of a spill-over effect of predictability onto fixations after the target word was processed. This later effect may be more likely to reflect an influence at global text integration processes than more local processing constraints (i.e. lexical information).

The third approach to distinguishing between the influence of local and global contexts is to examine the influence of context on reading polysemous words (e.g. *mint*, *bear*, *top*, etc.). Because ambiguous words have multiple possible semantic interpretations in isolation, embedding them in a constraining context and probing for meaning activation (e.g. using naming or lexical decision) provides information about the relative success of the context in determining which meaning is activated (or received the greatest activation). The basic positions have been either that context *can* affect initial meaning activation (context dependent view), or that context *does not* affect initial meaning activation (context independent view). The context-dependent view is more consistent with a discourse view of priming, whereas the context-independent view is in line with lexical accounts of context effects.

There is a relatively large literature examining context effects in resolving ambiguity for polysemous words (e.g. Conrad, 1974; Dooling, 1972; Foss, 1970; Foss & Jenkins, 1973; Holmes, Arwas, & Garrett, 1977; Kellas, Paul, Martin, & Simpson, 1991; Neill, Hilliard, & Cooper, 1988; Oden & Spira, 1983; Onifer & Swinney, 1981; Paul, Kellas, Martin, & Clark, 1992; Schvaneveldt, Meyer, & Becker, 1976; Seidenberg et al., 1982; Simpson, 1981; Swinney, 1979; Swinney & Hakes, 1976; Tabossi, 1988; Till, Mross, & Kintsch, 1988). The results from such studies have typically been viewed as supporting the context-independent (lexical) view of initial processing. As mentioned earlier, this outcome is also consistent with accounts of single prime word recognition (see Simpson, 1984, 1994, for reviews) and so can be captured within similar theoretical frameworks without positing involvement from higher levels of processing (i.e. discourse effects). Although there appears to be converging evidence across different tasks for lexical-level effects, there has also been some evidence to support discourse-level effects (Kellas et al. 1991; Paul et al., 1992; Simpson, 1981; Tabossi, 1988; Tabossi, Columbo, & Job, 1987; Van Petten & Kutas, 1987; Vu et al., 1998).

One possibility that might account for both previous failures and successes to show discourse-level effects relies on the processing pathways approach we have attempted to develop throughout this chapter. Specifically, the extent to which evidence will be found for lexical or discourse influences on word processing depends on the information subjects utilise in order to perform the task. This can presumably be manipulated in a number of different ways. One way we have already considered concerns the particular task subjects are required to perform (e.g. lexical decision, naming, relatedness judgements). A second possibility is that there may be differences in the goals of the reading task. For example, one may approach the materials differently if one is required to later recall the gist of the material versus recognise the details of what was earlier read. In the latter case, it is possible that subjects would be more likely to emphasise lexical-level pathways, whereas in the earlier case it is more likely that individuals will emphasise semantic-level integration-based information. Of course, this is an important possibility when one considers on-line reading measures to examine word processing effects, under different levels of instructions. Again, the notion is that the task demands should drive the pathways that are crucial in achieving the goals of the task.

Another possible means by which subjects may be directed to use different sources of information to perform a task may be particularly subtle. Specifically, a manipulation of contextual constraint might be sufficient to direct subjects to multiple sources of information. If this is the case, then researchers interested in estimating context effects on lexical processing would first be required to consider carefully the appropriateness of their stimuli for assessing context effects (for additional discussions of such concerns see Kellas et al., 1991; Oden & Spira, 1983; Olson, 1970; Tanenhaus & Donnenworth-Nolan, 1984). This point may be made more salient by considering contexts which contain ambiguous words. Such contexts can be constructed with varying levels of constraint. That is, context preceding an ambiguous word can range from making only a single interpretation of the homograph sensible to making no particular interpretation any more sensible than another. When no interpretation is biased by the context, it would not be surprising to find that multiple interpretations of the homograph are initially activated. Hence, this would be interpreted as support for a lexical view of processing. What *would* be surprising from a lexical (or context-independent) view of processing is if a constraining context resulted in *only* the contextually appropriate meaning becoming activated. Consider that, in most experiments, subjects do not typically receive only one or two contexts. Rather, sentence primes are presented, as is also typical of most single word prime studies, one after another as separate and unrelated from one another. It is likely that this is atypical of most common or normal reading situations. However, the degree to which the sentences, as a group, are similar to one another may be readily picked up by subjects. If a substantial proportion of the sentences are not sufficiently constraining, subjects may become biased to process all sentences (whether constraining or not) at a lexical level. This would probably result in findings inconsistent with discourse views of processing.

One of the most frequently cited examples of context-independent processing may be found in Swinney (1979). Although Swinney presented context stimuli auditorially, subjects responded to visually presented targets (i.e. lexical decision). Ignoring, for the sake of argument, any potential concerns with the task used (after all, lexical decisions were, at the time, widely held to accurately reflect initial processing), there is an aspect of the study that suggests the contexts used may not have been adequately constraining. Consider the Swinney (1979) study in light of a distinction made by Hess et al. (1995) between local and global context, reviewed above (see also Foss & Speer, 1990). Given the following stimulus: *Rumour had it that, for years, the government building had been plagued with problems. The man was not surprised when he found several spiders, roaches, and other bugs in the corner of his room*, it could be argued that there is a clearly biasing local context that favours the "insect" meaning of *bugs*. Indeed, Swinney found that responses to "ant" were facilitated relative to responses to an unrelated word (i.e. "sew"). Swinney also reported, however, that responses to words related to the contextually inappropriate sense of *bugs* (e.g. "spy") were facilitated as well. One might argue that the "spy" sense of the ambiguous word may also be related to the global context which includes government buildings, problems, and covert listening devices. Given that responses to "spy" were no longer facilitated when presented three syllables following the presentation of *bugs,* the conclusion that multiple meanings were initially activated independent of context seems as likely as the alternative conclusion that all meanings relevant to the global and local context of *bugs* were initially facilitated, as a *result* of context. The reason that the "insect" meaning of *bugs* was maintained for a longer duration may be due to a specific interpretation of the *type* of problems which plagued the government building (that is, the "spy" interpretation of "plagued with problems" was made less likely by later context). Although this was only one stimulus of many used by Swinney (1979), it is worthwhile to note that the notion of priming from local and global sources of context has been investigated for unambiguous words (e.g. Foss & Ross, 1983; Hess et al., 1995).

In sum, there appears to be converging evidence for two loci of contextual constraint during reading: one locus is more locally driven and may result from intralexical processes, and a second locus appears to involve a higher level text integration process. Thus, when attention is directed toward message-level processing pathways in reading, it appears that readers do not merely rely on a single source of constraint but rather will capitalise on any source that increases the efficiency of extracting message-level information.

Conclusions

One of the goals of word recognition research is to uncover the processes involved from the journey from visual features to meaning. Clearly, the evidence that has accumulated from isolated word recognition has been highly influential in a number of distinct areas of cognitive science. Moreover, there have been considerable theoretical advances that have led to important insights into the processes involved in language processing.

We believe that now that researchers are armed with this battery of observations and theoretical perspectives, it is time to more closely tune models of word recognition to processes involved in the common use of words in language processing tasks, i.e. as the core building blocks of message-level information. Hence, we have adopted a processing pathway approach in this chapter which emphasises the pathways that are engaged by the reader in pursuit of a given task's goals. In an attempt to illustrate the importance of attentional selection of appropriate processing pathways, we have reviewed a number of the important issues in word recognition research, which included orthographic neighbourhood effects, spelling to sound correspondence effects, number of meaning effects, syntactic context effects, and discourse-level context effects. In each of these sections, we have attempted to demonstrate that one may find quite different patterns of data depending upon the types of goals engaged by a given task. The relevance of certain classes of variables apparently come to the forefront when a given task places high priority on those variables.

Figure 2.1 presents a possible way to conceptualise the manner in which attentional control might influence different characteristics of the lexical processing system. As shown, there are a number of distinct processing modules that deal with computations involved in orthography, phonology, meaning, syntax, and higher level discourse integration. The goals of the task drive attention to relevant processing dimensions. For example, in naming, the attentional control system would increase the influence of the computations between orthography and phonology. On the other hand, the demands of lexical decision performance might place a high priority on the computations between orthographic and meaning level modules. Finally, if the goal of the task is reading comprehension, then attentional control would increase the priority of computations of the syntactic-, meaning-, and discourse-level modules. It is important to note that we do not intend to argue that attention *totally* controls the output of a given set of task relevant processing modules. Rather, we believe that the *degree of influence* of these different processing modules will be affected by attentional control. Moreover, we would argue that the degree of control will be dependent upon such factors as (1) the ability to maintain a representation of experimental task demands across time, and also (2) the prepotent strength of the pathways between the modules. For example, with respect to this later factor, although participants can avoid naming the stimulus word in a Stroop study, it is very difficult, but not impossible (see Besner, Stoltz, & Boutilier, 1997), to completely eliminate the influence from the relatively strong pathways that compute meaning from orthography.

In conclusion, we would like to argue for a flexible lexical processing system in which attentional systems modulate the importance of the

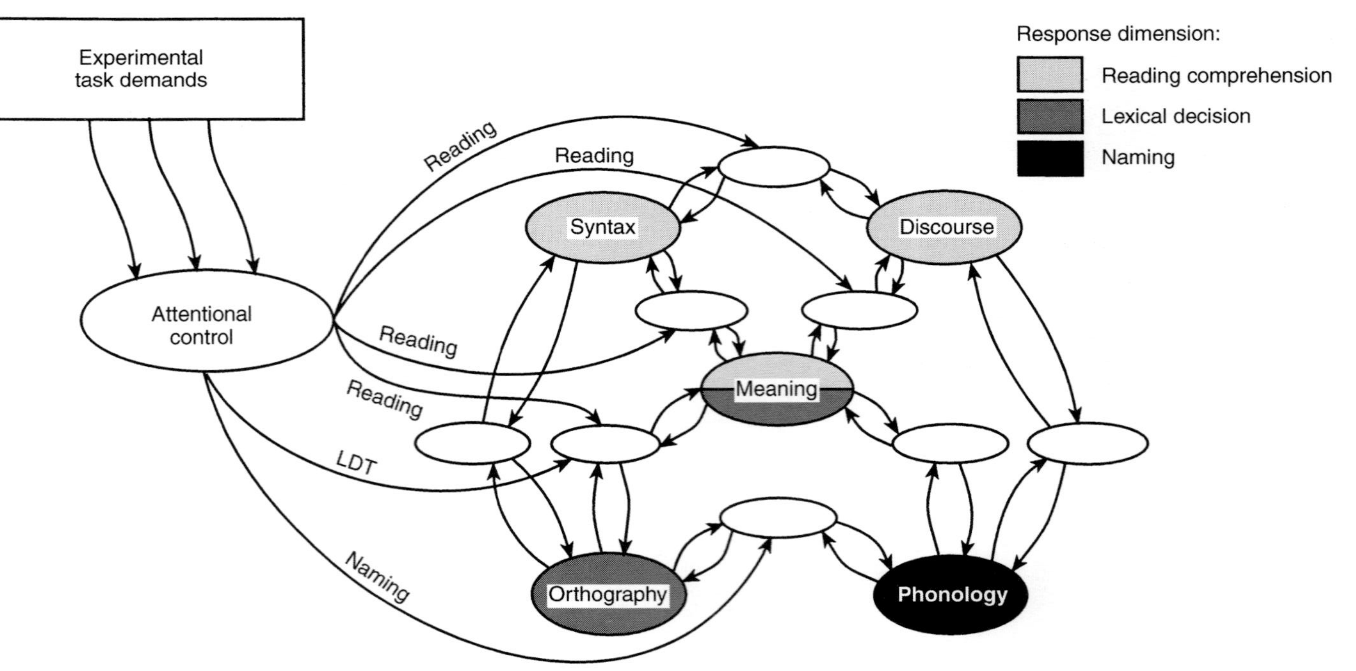

FIG. 2.1 An attentional control framework for lexical processing tasks.

numerous codes available for a given word. Until this flexibility is acknowledged and eventually implemented, we believe that one may be misled by the relevance of a given set of results to the goal of this enterprise, i.e. to understand how words serve as vehicles for communication.

REFERENCES

Andrews, S. (1982). Phonological recoding: Is the regularity effect consistent? *Memory and Cognition, 10*, 565–575.

Andrews, S. (1989). Frequency and neighbourhood effects on lexical access: Activation or search? *Journal of Experimental Psychology: Learning, Memory, and Cognition, 15*, 802–814.

Andrews, S. (1992). Frequency and neighbourhood effects on lexical access: Lexical similarity or orthographic redundancy? *Journal of Experimental Psychology: Learning, Memory, and Cognition, 18*, 234–254.

Andrews, S. (1997). The effect of orthographic similarity on lexical retrieval: Resolving neighborhood conflicts. *Psychonomic Bulletin & Review, 4*, 439–461.

Auble, P.M., & Franks, J.L. (1983). Sentence comprehension processes. *Journal of Verbal Learning and Verbal Behavior, 22*, 395–405.

Balota, D.A. (1994). Visual word recognition: The journey from features to meaning. In M. Gernsbacher (Ed.), *Handbook of psycholinguistics*. San Diego, CA: Academic Press.

Balota, D.A., & Chumbley, J.L. (1984). Are lexical decisions a good measure of lexical access? The role of word frequency in the neglected decision stage. *Journal of Experimental Psychology: Human Perception and Performance, 10*, 340–357.

Balota, D.A., & Chumbley, J.L. (1985). The locus of word frequency effects in the pronunciation task: Lexical access and/or production? *Journal of Memory and Language, 24*, 89–106.

Balota, D.A., & Chumbley, J.L. (1990). Where are the effects of frequency in visual word recognition tasks? Right where we said they were! Comments on Monsell, Doyle, and Haggard (1989). *Journal of Experiment Psychology: General, 119*, 231–237.

Balota, D.A., & Ferraro, F.R. (1993). A dissociation of frequency and regularity effects in pronunciation performance across young adults, older adults, and individuals with senile dementia of the Alzheimer type. *Journal of Memory and Language, 32*, 573–592.

Balota, D.A., & Ferraro, F.R. (1996). Lexical, sublexical, and implicit memory processes in healthy young and healthy older adults and in individuals with dementia of the Alzheimer type. *Neuropsychology, 10*, 1–14.

Balota, D.A., Ferraro, F.R., & Connor, L.T. (1991). On the early influence of meaning in word recognition: A review of the literature. In P.J. Schwanenflugel (Ed.), *The psychology of word meanings* (pp. 187–222), Hillsdale, NJ: Lawrence Erlbaum Associates Inc.

Balota, D.A., & Lorch, R.F. (1986). Depth of automatic spreading activation: Mediated priming effects in pronunciation but not in lexical decision. *Journal of Experimental Psychology, Learning, Memory, and Cognition, 12*, 336–345.

Balota, D.A., & Paul, S.T. (1996). Summation of activation: Evidence from multiple primes that converge and diverge within semantic memory. *Journal of Experimental Psychology: Learning, Memory, and Cognition, 22*, 827–845.

Balota, D.A., Pollatsek, A., & Rayner, K. (1985). The interaction of contextual constraints and parafoveal visual information in reading. *Cognitive Psychology, 17*, 364–390.

Balota, D.A., & Spieler, D.H. (1998). The utility of item-level analyses in model evaluation: A reply to Seidenberg and Plaut. *Psychological Science, 9*, 238–240.

Balota, D.A., & Spieler, D.H. (1999). Word frequency, repetition, and lexicality effects in word recognition tasks: Beyond measures of central tendency. *Journal of Experimental Psychology: General, 128*, 32–55.

Baluch, B., & Besner, D. (1991). Visual word recognition: Evidence for strategic control of lexical and nonlexical routines in oral reading. *Journal of Experimental Psychology: Learning, Memory, and Cognition, 17*, 644–652.

Becker, C.A. (1979). Semantic context and word frequency effects in visual word recognition. *Journal of Experimental Psychology: Human Perception and Performance, 5*, 252–259.

Becker, C.A. (1980). Semantic context effects in visual word recognition: An analysis of semantic strategies. *Memory and Cognition, 8*, 493–512.

Besner, D. (1983). Basic decoding components in reading: Two dissociable feature extraction processes. *Canadian Journal of Psychology, 37*, 429–438.

Besner, D., & Bourassa, ?. (1995). *Localist and parallel processing models of visual word recognition: A few more words.* Paper presented at the Brain, Behavior, and Cognitive Science Society, Halifax, Canada.

Besner, D., Stolz, J.A., & Boutilier (1997). The Stroop effect and the myth of automaticity. *Psychonomic Bulletin & Review, 4*, 221–225.

Besner, D., & Swan, M. (1982). Models of Lexical access in visual word recognition. *Quarterly Journal of Experimental Psychology, 34A*, 313–325.

Besner, D., Twilley, L., McCann, R., & Seergobin, K. (1990). On the connection between connections and data: Are a few words necessary? *Psychological Review, 97*, 432–446.

Bohemier, G.L. (1991). *Neighborhood and frequency effects on word recognition in a foveal presentation of text.* Unpublished master's thesis, State University of New York at Binghamton, NY.

Bohemier, G.L. (1994). *Neighborhood effects and the role of neighborhood rhyme.* Unpublished dissertation, State University of New York at Binghamton, NY.

Bohemier, G.L., & Inhoff, A.W. (in prep.). *Effects of neighborhood density and dominance on lexical access measured across tasks.*

Borowski, R. & Masson, M.E.J. (1996). Semantic ambiguity effects in word identification. *Journal of Experimental Psychology: Learning, Memory, and Cognition, 22*, 63–85.

Britt, M.A., Perfetti, C.A., Garrod, S., & Rayner, K. (1992). Parsing in discourse: Context effects and their limits. *Journal of Memory and Language, 31*, 293–314.

Clark, H.H. (1973). The language-as-a-fixed-effect fallacy: A critique of language statistics in psychological research. *Journal of Verbal Learning and Verbal Behavior, 12*, 335–359.

Cohen, J.D., Dunbar, K., & McClelland, J.L. (1990). On the control of automatic processes: A parallel distributed processing account of the Stroop effect. *Psychological Review, 97*, 332–361.

Coltheart, M. (1978). Lexical access in simple reading tasks. In G. Underwood (Ed.), *Strategies in information processing* (pp. 151–216). San Diego, CA: Academic Press.

Coltheart, M., Curtis, B., Atkins, P., & Haller, M. (1993). Models of reading aloud: Dual-route and parallel distributed processing approaches. *Psychological Review, 100*, 589–608.

Coltheart, M., Davelaar, E., Jonasson, J.T., & Besner, D. (1977). Access to the internal lexicon. In S. Dormic (Ed.), *Attention and performance VI* (pp. 535–555). Hillsdale, NJ: Lawrence Erlbaum Associates Ltd.

Conrad, C. (1974). Context effects in sentence comprehension: A study of the subjective lexicon. *Memory and Cognition, 2*, 130–138.

Cortese, M.J., Simpson, G.B., & Woolsey, S. (1997). Effects of association and imageability on phonological mapping. *Psychonomic Bulletin & Review, 4*, 226–231.

Day, J. (1977). Right-hemisphere language processing in normal right-handers. *Journal of Experimental Psychology: Human Perception and Performance, 3*, 518–528.

Dooling, D.J. (1972). Some context effects in the speeded comprehension of sentences. *Journal of Experimental Psychology, 93*, 56–62.

Duffy, S.A., Henderson, J.M., & Morris, R.K. (1989). The semantic facilitation of lexical access during sentence processing. *Journal of Experimental Psychology: Learning, Memory and Cognition, 15*, 791–801.

Duffy, S.A., Morris, R.K., & Rayner, K. (1988). Lexical ambiguity and fixation times in reading. *Journal of Memory and Language, 27*, 429–446.

Ehrlich, S.F., & Rayner, K. (1981). Contextual effects on word perception and eye movements during reading. *Journal of Verbal Learning and Verbal Behavior, 20*, 641–655.

Fera, P., Joordens, S., Balota, D.A., & Ferraro, F.R. (1992, November). *Ambiguity in meaning and phonology: Effects on naming.* Poster presented at the annual meeting of the Psychonomic Society, St Louis, MO.

Ferreira, F., & Clifton, C. (1986). The independence of syntactic processing. *Journal of Memory and Language, 25*, 348–368.

Fischler, I., & Bloom, P.A. (1979). Automatic and attentional processes in the effects of sentence contexts on word recognition. *Journal of Verbal Learning and Verbal Behavior, 18*, 1–20.

Fodor, J.A. (1983). *Modularity of mind.* Cambridge, MA: MIT Press.

Folk, J.R., & Morris, R.K. (1995). Multiple lexical codes in reading: Evidence from eye movements, naming time, and oral reading. *Journal of Experimental Psychology: Learning, Memory & Cognition, 21*, 1412–1429.

Forster, K.I. (1976). Accessing the mental lexicon. In E. Walker & R.J. Wales (Eds.), *New approaches to language mechanisms* (pp. 257–287). Amsterdam: North-Holland.

Forster, K.I. (1979). Levels of processing and the structure of the language processor. In W.E. Cooper & E.C.T. Walker (Eds.), *Sentence processing: Psycholinguistic studies presented to Merrill Garrett* (pp. 27–85). Hillsdale, NJ: Lawrence Erlbaum Associates Inc.

Foss, D.J. (1970). Some effects of ambiguity upon sentence comprehension. *Journal of Verbal Learning and Verbal Behavior, 9*, 699–706.

Foss, D.J., & Jenkins, C.M. (1973). Some effects of context on the comprehension of ambiguous sentences. *Journal of Verbal Learning and Verbal Behavior, 12*, 577–589.

Foss, D.J. & Ross, J.R. (1983). Great expectations: Context effects during sentence processing. In G.B. Flores d'Arcais & R.J. Jarvella (Eds.), *The process of language understanding* (pp. 169–191). New York: John Wiley.

Foss, D.J. & Speer, S.R. (1990). Global and local context effects in sentence processing. In R.R. Hoffman & D.S. Palermo (Eds.), *Cognition and the symbolic processes: Applied and ecological perspectives* (pp. 115–139). Hillsdale, NJ: Lawrence Erlbaum Associates Ltd.

Frazier, L., & Rayner, K. (1982). Making and correcting errors during sentence comprehension: Eye movements in the analysis of structurally ambiguous sentences. *Cognitive Psychology, 14*, 178–210.

Frost, R., Katz, L., & Bentin, S. (1987). Strategies for visual word recognition and orthographical depth: A multilingual comparison. *Journal of Experimental Psychology: Human Perception and Performance, 13*, 104–115.

Gernsbacher, M.A. (1984). Resolving 20 years of inconsistent interactions between lexical familiarity and orthography, concreteness, and polysemy. *Journal of Experimental Psychology: General, 113*, 256–281.

Glanzer, M., & Ehrenreich, S.L. (1979). Structure and search of the internal lexicon. *Journal of Verbal Learning and Verbal Behavior, 18*, 381–398.

Goodman, G.O., McClelland, J.L., & Gibbs, R.W. (1981). The role of syntactic context in word recognition. *Memory and Cognition, 9*, 580–586.

Grainger, J. (1990). Word frequency and neighbor frequency effects in lexical decision and naming. *Journal of Memory and Language, 29*, 228–244.

Grainger, J., O'Regan, J.K., Jacobs, A.M., & Segui, J. (1989). On the role of competing word units in visual word recognition: The neighborhood frequency effect. *Perception and Psychophysics*, *45*, 189–195.

Havens, L.L. & Foote, W.E. (1963). The effect of competition on visual duration threshold and its independence of stimulus frequency. *Journal of Experimental Psychology*, *65*, 6–11.

Henderson, L. (1982). *Orthography and word recognition in reading*. London: Academic Press.

Hess, D.J., Foss, D.J., & Carroll, P. (1995). Effects of global and local context on lexical processing during language comprehension. *Journal of Experimental Psychology: General*, *124*, 62–82.

Holmes, V.M., Arwas, R., & Garrett, M.F. (1977). Prior context and the perception of lexically ambiguous sentences. *Memory and Cognition*, *5*, 103–110.

Inhoff, A.W., & Topolski, R. (1994). Use of phonological codes during eye fixations in reading and in on-line and delayed naming tasks. *Journal of Memory and Language*, *33*, 689–713.

Jastrzembski, J.E. (1981). Multiple meanings, number of related meanings, frequency of occurrence, and the lexicon. *Cognitive Psychology*, *13*, 278–305.

Jastrzembski, J.E., & Stanners, R.F. (1975). Multiple word meanings and lexical search speed. *Journal of Verbal Learning and Verbal Behavior*, *14*, 534–537.

Kawamoto, A.H., Farrar, W.T., & Kello, C.T. (1994). When two meanings are better than one: Modeling the ambiguity advantage using a recurrent distributed network. *Journal of Experimental Psychology: Human Perception and Performance*, *20*, 1233–1247.

Kellas, G., Ferraro, F.R., & Simpson, G.B. (1988). Lexical ambiguity and the timecourse of attentional allocation in word recognition. *Journal of Experimental Psychology: Human Perception and Performance*, *14*, 601–609.

Kellas, G., Paul, S.T., Martin, M., & Simpson, G.B. (1991). Contextual feature activation and meaning access. In G.B. Simpson (Ed.), *Understanding word and sentence* (pp. 47–71). Amsterdam: North-Holland.

Kroll, J.F., & Mervis, J.S. (1986). Lexical access for concrete and abstract words. *Journal of Experimental Psychology: Learning, Memory, and Cognition*, *12*, 92–107.

Lukatela, G., & Turvey, M.T. (1994a). Visual lexical access is initially phonological: 1. Evidence from associative priming by words, homophones, and pseudohomophones. *Journal of Experimental Psychology: General3*, *123*, 107–128.

Lukatela, G., & Turvey, M.T. (1994b). Visual lexical access is initially phonological: 2. Evidence from phonological priming by homophones and pseudohomophones. *Journal of Experimental Psychology: General*, *123*, 331–353.

Lupker, S.J., Brown, P., & Colombo, L. (1997). Strategic control in a naming task: Changing routes or changing deadlines? *Journal of Experimental Psychology: Learning, Memory, and Cognition*, *23*, 570–590.

MacDonald, M.C. (1994). Probabilistic constraints and syntactic ambiguity resolution. *Language and Cognitive Processes*, *9*, 157–201.

MacDonald, M.C., Pearlmutter, N.J., & Seidenberg, M.S. (1994). Lexical nature of syntactic ambiguity resolution. *Psychological Review*, *101*, 676–703.

Marcel, A.J. (1980). Surface dyslexia and beginning reading: A revised hypothesis of pronunciation of print and its impairments. In M. Coltheart, K. Patterson, & J.C. Marshall (Eds.), *Deep dyslexia* (pp. 227–258). London: Routledge & Kegan Paul.

Marshall, J.C., & Newcombe, F. (1980). The conceptual status of deep dyslexia: An historical perspective. In M. Coltheart, K. Patterson, & J. C. Marshall (Eds.), *Deep dyslexia* (pp. 1–21). London: Routledge & Kegan Paul.

Masson, M.E.J. (1991). A distributed memory model of context effects in word identification. In D. Besner & G.W. Humphreys (Eds.), *Basic processes in reading: Visual word recognition* (pp. 233–263). Hillsdale, NJ: Lawrence Erlbaum Associates Inc.

McClelland, J.L. (1987). The case for interactionism in language processing. In M. Coltheart (Ed.), *Attention and performance XII* (pp. 3–36). Hove, UK: Lawrence Erlbaum Associates Ltd.

McClelland, J.L., & Rumelhart, D.E. (1981). An interactive activation model of context effects in letter perception: 1. An account of basic findings. *Psychological Review, 86*, 287–330.

Midgley-West, L. (1979). *Phonological encoding and subject strategies in skilled reading.* Unpublished dissertation, Birkbeck College, University of London.

Millis, M.L., & Button, S.B. (1989). The effect of polysemy on lexical decision time: Now you see it now you don't. *Memory and Cognition, 17*, 141–147.

Monsell, S. (1990). Frequency effects in lexical tasks: Reply to Balota and Chumbley. *Journal of Experimental Psychology: General, 119*, 335–339.

Monsell, S., Doyle, M.C., & Haggard, P.N. (1989). Effects of frequency on visual word recognition tasks: Where are they? *Journal of Experimental Psychology: General, 118*, 43–71.

Monsell, S., Patterson, K.E., Graham, A., Hughes, C.H., & Milroy, R. (1992). Lexical and sublexical translation of spelling to sound: Strategic anticipation of lexical status. *Journal of Experimental Psychology: Learning, Memory, and Cognition, 180*, 452–467.

Morris, R.K. (1994). Lexical and message-level sentence context effects on fixation times in reading. *Journal of Experimental Psychology: Learning, Memory, and Cognition, 20*, 92–103.

Morton, J. (1970). A functional model for memory. In D.A. Norman (Ed.), *Models of human memory*. New York: Academic Press.

Neely, J.H. (1977). Semantic priming and retrieval from lexical memory: Roles of inhibitionless spreading activation and limited-capacity attention. *Journal of Experimental Psychology: General, 106*, 226–254.

Neely, J.H. (1991). Semantic priming effects in visual word recognition: A selective review of current findings and theories. In D. Besner & G. Humphreys (Eds.), *Basic processes in reading: Visual word recognition* (pp. 264–336). Hillsdale, NJ: Lawrence Erlbaum Associates Inc.

Neill, W.T., Hilliard, D.V., & Cooper, E.A. (1988). The detection of lexical ambiguity: Evidence for context-sensitive parallel access. *Journal of Memory and Language, 27*, 279–287.

Nicol, J., & Swinney, D. (1989). The role of structure in coreference assignment during sentence comprehension. *Journal of Psycholinguistic Research, 18*, 5–19.

Norris, D. (1986). Word recognition: Context effects without priming. *Cognition, 22*, 93–136.

Oden, G.C., & Spira, J.L. (1983). Influence of context on the activation and selection of ambiguous word senses. *Quarterly Journal of Experimental Psychology: Human Experimental Psychology, 35*, 51–64.

Olson, D.R. (1970). Language and thought: Aspects of a cognitive theory of semantics. *Psychological Review, 77*, 257–273.

Onifer, W., & Swinney, D.A. (1981). Accessing lexical ambiguities during sentence comprehension: Effects of frequency of meaning and contextual bias. *Memory and Cognition, 9*, 225–236.

O'Seaghdha, P.G. (1989). The dependence of lexical relatedness effects on syntactic connectedness. *Journal of Experimental Psychology: Learning, Memory, and Cognition, 15*, 73–87.

Paap, K., & Noel, R. (1991). Dual route models of print to sound: Still a good race horse. *Psychological Research, 53*, 13–24.

Paap, K.R., Newsome, S.L., McDonald, J., & Schvaneveldt, R.W. (1982). An activation-verification model for letter and word recognition: The word-superiority effect. *Psychological Review, 89*, 573–594.

Patterson, K.E. (1982). The relation between reading and phonological coding: Further neuropsychological observations. In A.W. Ellis (Ed.), *Normality and pathology in cognitive functions* (pp. 77–111). San Diego, CA: Academic Press.

Patterson, K.E., Graham, N., & Hodges, J.R. (1994). Reading in dementia of the Alzheimer's type: A preserved ability? *Neuropsychology, 8*, 395–407.

Paul, S.T., Kellas, G., Martin, M., & Clark, M.B. (1992). The influence of contextual features on the activation of ambiguous word meanings. *Journal of Experimental Psychology: Learning, Memory, and Cognition, 18*, 703–717.

Pearlmutter, N.J., & MacDonald, M.C. (1992). Plausibility and syntactic ambiguity resolution. In *Proceedings of the 14th annual conference of the Cognitive Science Society* (pp. 498–503). Hillsdale NJ: Lawrence Erlbaum Associates Ltd.

Perea, M., & Pollatsek, A. (1998). The effects of neighborhood frequency in reading and lexical decision. *Journal of Experimental Psychology: Human Perception and Performance, 24*, 767–780.

Perfetti, C.A., Bell, L.C., & Delaney, S.M. (1988). Automatic (prelexical) phonetic activation in silent word reading: Evidence from backward masking. *Journal of Memory and Language, 27*, 59–70.

Perfetti, C.A., Beverly, S., Bell, L.C., & Hughes, C. (1987). Phonemic knowledge and learning to read: A longitudinal study of first grade children. *Merrill-Palmer Quarterly, 33*, 283–319.

Petersen, S.E., Fox, P.T., Posner, M.I., Mintun, M., & Raichle, M.E. (1990). Positron emission tomographic studies of the processing of single words. *Journal of Cognitive Neuroscience, 1*, 153–170.

Plaut, D., McClelland, M.L., Seidenberg, M.S., & Patterson, K.E. (1996). Understanding normal and impaired word reading: Computational principles in quasi-regular domains. *Psychological Review, 103*, 56–115.

Pollatsek, A., Lesch, M., Morris, R., & Rayner, K. (1992). Phonological codes are used in integrating information across saccades in word identification and reading. *Journal of Experimental Psychology: Human Perception and Performance, 18*, 148–162.

Posner, M.I. (1978). *Chronometric explorations of the mind.* Hillsdale, NJ: Lawrence Erlbaum Associates Inc.

Posner, M.I., & Snyder, C.R.R. (1975). Attention and cognitive control. In R. Solso (Ed.), *Information processing and cognition: The Loyola symposium* (pp. 55–85). Hillsdale, NJ: Lawrence Erlbaum Associates Inc.

Pugh, K.R., Rexer, K., Peter, M., & Katz, L. (1994). Neighborhood effects in visual word recognition: Effects of letter delay and nonword context difficulty. *Journal of Experimental Psychology: Learning, Memory, and Cognition, 20*, 639–648.

Rayner, K. (1979). Eye guidance in reading: Fixation locations within words. *Perception, 8*, 21–30.

Rayner, K., Carlson, M., & Frazier, L. (1983). The interaction of syntax and semantics during sentence processing: Eye movements in the analysis of semantically biased sentences. *Journal of Verbal Learning and Verbal Behavior, 22*, 358–374.

Rayner, K., & Frazier, L. (1989). Selection mechanisms in reading lexically ambiguous words. *Journal of Experimental Psychology: Learning, Memory, and Cognition, 15*, 779–790.

Rayner, K., Garrod, S., & Perfetti, C.A. (1992). Discourse influences during parsing are delayed. *Cognition, 25*, 109–139.

Rayner, K. & Pollatsek, A. (1989). *The psychology of reading.* Englewood Cliffs, NJ: Prentice-Hall.

Rayner, K., Sereno, S.C., Lesch, M.F., & Pollatsek, A. (1995). Phonological codes are automatically activated during reading: Evidence from an eye movement priming paradigm. *Psychological Science, 6*, 26–32.

Richardson, J.T.E. (1976). The effects of stimulus attributes upon latency of word recognition. *British Journal of Psychology*, *67*, 315–325.

Rubenstein, H., Garfield, L., & Millikan, J.A. (1970). Homographic entries in the internal lexicon. *Journal of Verbal Learning and Verbal Behavior*, *9*, 487–494.

Rubenstein, H., Lewis, S.S., & Rubenstein, M.A. (1971). Homographic entries in the internal lexicon: Effects of systematicity and relative frequency of meanings. *Journal of Verbal Learning and Verbal Behavior*, *10*, 57–62.

Schuberth, R.E., & Eimas, P.D. (1977). Effects of context on the classification of words and nonwords. *Journal of Experimental Psychology: Human Perception and Performance*, 73, 27–36.

Schustack, M.W., Ehrlich, S.F., & Rayner, K. (1987). Local and global sources of contextual facilitation in reading. *Journal of Memory and Language*, *26*, 322–340.

Schvaneveldt, R.W., Meyer, D.E., & Becker, C.A. (1976). Lexical ambiguity, semantic context, and visual word recognition. *Journal of Experimental Psychology: Human Perception and Performance*, *2*, 243–256.

Schwanenflugel, P.J., Harnishfeger, K.K., & Stowe, R.W. (1988). Context availability and lexical decisions for abstract and concrete words. *Journal of Memory and Language*, *27*, 499–520.

Seidenberg, M.S., & Harm, M. (1995, November). *Division of labor and masking in a multicomponent model of word recognition*. Paper presented at the 36th annual meeting the Psychonomic Society, Los Angeles, CA.

Seidenberg, M.S., & McClelland, J.L. (1989). A distributed, developmental model of word recognition and naming. *Psychological Review*, *96*, 523–568.

Seidenberg, M.S., & Plaut, D.C. (1998). Evaluating word-reading models at the item level: Matching the grain of theory and data. *Psychological Science*, *9*, 234–237.

Seidenberg, M.S., Tanenhaus, M.K., Leiman, J.M., & Bienkowski, M. (1982). Automatic access of the meanings of ambiguous words in context: Some limitations of knowledge-based processing. *Cognitive Psychology*, *14*, 489–537.

Seidenberg, M.S., Waters, G.S., Sanders, M., & Langer, P. (1984). Pre- and postlexical loci of contextual effects on word recognition. *Memory and Cognition*, *12*, 315–328.

Seidenberg, M.S., Waters, G.S., Barnes, M.A., & Tanenhaus, M.K. (1984). When does irregular spelling or pronunciation influence word recognition? *Journal of Verbal Learning and Verbal Behavior*, *23*, 383–404.

Sereno, J.A. (1991). Graphemic, associative, and syntactic priming effects at a brief stimulus onset asynchrony in lexical decision and naming. *Journal of Experimental Psychology:. Learning, Memory, and Cognition*, *17*, 459–477.

Shallice, T., & Warrington, E.K. (1980). Single and multiple component central dyslexic syndromes. In M. Coltheart, K. Patterson, & J.C. Marshall (Eds.), *Deep dyslexia* (pp. 119–145). London: Routledge & Kegan Paul.

Shallice, T., Warrington, E.K., & McCarthy, R. (1983). Reading without semantics. *Quarterly Journal of Experimental Psychology: Human Experimental Psychology*, *35*, 111–138.

Sharkey, N.E. (1990). A connectionist model of text comprehension. In D.A. Balota, G.B. Flores d'Arcais, & K. Rayner (Eds.), *Comprehension processes in reading* (pp. 487–514). Hillsdale, NJ: Lawrence Erlbaum Associates Inc.

Sharkey, A.J.C., & Sharkey, N.E. (1992). Weak contextual constraints in text and word priming. *Journal of Memory and Language*, *31*, 543–572.

Simpson, G.B. (1981). Meaning dominance and semantic context in the processing of lexical ambiguity. *Journal of Verbal Learning and Verbal Behavior*, *20*, 120–136.

Simpson, G.B. (1984). Lexical ambiguity and its role in models of word recognition. *Psychological Bulletin*, *96*, 316–340.

Simpson, G.B. (1994). Context and the processing of ambiguous words. In M. Gernsbacher (Ed.), *Handbook of psycholinguistics* pp. 359–374). San Diego, CA: Academic Press.

Simpson, G.B., & Kang, H. (1994). The flexible use of phonological information in word recognition in Korean. *Journal of Memory and Language, 33*, 319–331.

Spieler, D.H., & Balota, D.A. (1997). Bringing computational models of word naming down to the item level. *Psychological Science, 8*, 411–416.

Stanovich, K.E., & West, R.F. (1983). On priming by a sentence context. *Journal of Experimental Psychology: General, 112*, 1–36.

Strain, E., Patterson, K.E., & Seidenberg, M.S. (1995). Semantic effects in single-word naming. *Journal of Experimental Psychology: Learning, Memory, & Cognition, 21*, 1140–1154.

Stroop, J.R. (1935). Studies of interference in serial verbal reactions. *Journal of Experimental Psychology, 18*, 643–661.

Swinney, D.A. (1979). Lexical access during sentence comprehension: (Re)consideration of context effects. *Journal of Verbal Learning and Verbal Behavior, 18*, 645–659.

Swinney, D.A., & Hakes, D.T. (1976). Effects of prior context upon lexical access during sentence comprehension. *Journal of Verbal Learning and Verbal Behavior, 15*, 681–689.

Tabossi, P. (1988). Accessing lexical ambiguity in different types of sentential contexts. *Journal of Memory and Language, 27*, 324–340.

Tabossi, P., Colombo, L., & Job, R. (1987). Accessing lexical ambiguity: Effects of context and dominance. *Psychological Research, 49*, 161–167.

Taft, M. & Hambly, G. (1986). Exploring the cohort model of spoken word recognition. *Cognition, 22*, 259–282.

Tanenhaus, M.K., & Donnenworth-Nolan, S. (1984). Syntactic context and lexical access. *The Quarterly Journal of Experimental Psychology, 36A*, 649–661.

Till, R.E., Mross, E.F., & Kintsch, W. (1988). Time course of priming for associate and inference words in a discourse context. *Memory and Cognition, 16*, 283–298.

Trueswell, J.C., & Tanenhaus, M.K. (1991). Tense, temporal context and syntactic ambiguity resolution. *Language and Cognitive Processes, 6*, 303–338.

Trueswell, J.C., Tanenhaus, M.K., & Garnsey, S.M. (1994). Semantic influences on parsing: Use of thematic role information in syntactic ambiguity resolution. *Journal of Memory and Language, 33*, 285–318.

Ungerleider, L.G., & Mishkin, M. (1982). Two cortical visual systems. In D.J. Ingle, M.A. Goodale, & R.J.W. Mansfield (Eds.), *Analysis of visual behavior* (pp. 549–580). Cambridge, MA: MIT Press.

Van Orden, G.C. (1987). A ROWS is a ROSE: Spelling, sound and reading. *Memory and Cognition, 15*, 181–198.

Van Orden, G.C. (1991). Phonologic mediation is fundamental to reading. In D. Besner & G. Humphreys (Eds.), *Basic processes in reading: Visual word recognition* (pp. 77–103). Hillsdale, NJ: Lawrence Erlbaum Associates Inc.

Van Orden, G.C., & Goldinger, S.D. (1994). Interdependence of form and function in cognitive systems explains perception of printed words. *Journal of Experimental Psychology: Human Perception and Performance, 20*, 1269–1291.

Van Petten, C., & Kutas, M. (1987). Ambiguous words in context: An event-related potential analysis of the time course of meaning activation. *Journal of Memory and Language, 26*, 188–208.

Verstaen, A., Humphreys, G.W., Olson, A., & d'Ydewalle, G. (1995). Are phonemic effects in backward masking evidence for automatic prelexical phonemic activation in visual word recognition? *Journal of Memory and Language, 34*, 335–356.

Vu, H., Kellas, G., & Paul, S.T. (1998). Sources of sentence constraint on lexical ambiguity resolution. *Memory & Cognition, 26*, 979–1001.

West, R.F., & Stanovich, K.E. (1986). Robust effects of syntactic structure on visual word processing. *Memory and Cognition, 14*, 104–112.

Wright, B., & Garrett, M. (1984). Lexical decision in sentences: Effects of syntactic structure. *Memory and Cognition, 12*, 31–45.

Zevin, J.D., & Balota, D.A. (1999). *Priming and attentional control of lexical and sublexical pathways during naming.* Manuscript submitted for publication.

Zola, D. (1984). Redundancy and word perception during reading. *Perception and Psychophysics, 36*, 277–284.

CHAPTER 3

Lexical semantic processing during speech comprehension

Helen E. Moss
Department of Experimental Psychology, University of Cambridge, UK

M. Gareth Gaskell
MRC Cognition and Brain Sciences Unit, Cambridge, UK

INTRODUCTION

In order to understand spoken language the listener must be able to identify the sequence of words in the speech stream and to access a range of different kinds of information about each of those words from the mental lexicon, allowing them to be interpreted and combined with other words to build up a representation of the utterance. The kinds of information that are made available by lexical access include, at least, morphological structure, syntactic structure, and meaning. In this chapter we focus on the latter; the processes by which the meanings of words, or their *semantic representations*, are activated as we hear them; processes that are at the heart of language comprehension.

Our study of the activation of meanings by spoken words must take into account the special, temporal characteristics of speech. Words must be recognised rapidly and efficiently—at a rate of several words a second in normal speech—because the signal fades quickly and the acoustic information for each word is immediately overwritten by the next word (Crowther & Morton, 1969). The speech signal is also inherently variable; the realisation of most sound segments varies as a function of the surrounding phonological context, and background noise is the norm rather than the exception (Repp, 1978; Warren & Marslen-Wilson, 1987). Speech is also continuous, and therefore, segmentation is a fundamental problem;

how do we tell when one word ends and the next begins (e.g. Cutler & Norris, 1988). In all these ways, spoken language differs from written text, where the signal is clear, less variable, and remains in view for as long as the reader wishes, and where word boundaries are conveniently marked by white spaces. Thus, although we assume that the target of lexical access is the same, whether the input is spoken or written (or, indeed, Braille or sign language), the mapping process from sound to meaning may differ in important ways from that from text to meaning, especially in terms of its time-course and the range of competitor words that are activated (see Holcomb & Anderson, 1993).

The study of the processes by which word meanings are activated provides a bridge between two bodies of psycholinguistic research. On the one hand, several models of spoken word recognition have been developed. However, these models are primarily concerned with the way in which the speech signal activates lexical form representations rather than with the access of word meanings. A second area of research has focused on the interpretation of words in discourse contexts (e.g. Garrod & Sanford, 1981). Such studies do not, however, address the issue of how the meanings initially become available for interpretation and combination. These two areas of research have largely been carried out in isolation from each other and one of the aims of this chapter is to bring together research that provides a basis for greater integration of the two sets of issues.

FRAMEWORK

Models of spoken word recognition

Before beginning the discussion of how the meanings of words are accessed during speech, we first need to consider briefly the nature of spoken word recognition in general. Most current models describe the process of spoken word recognition in terms of activation of processing units within a mental store or "lexicon". Each processing unit corresponds to a specific word in the vocabulary. A processing unit increases in activation as a function of the degree of match between its phonological form and the incoming speech signal. At a certain point, one processing unit will reach a criterial level of activation, allowing that word to be recognised. On these models, there will be an initial phase during which many words in the lexicon are a potential match for the input, and so many processing units will be activated simultaneously. These words are all candidates for recognition, and the competition among them is resolved as further speech input is heard, which will continue to match some words, so increasing their activation, but will mismatch other words so reducing their activation or allowing it to fade away (e.g. Luce, Pisoni & Goldinger, 1990; Marslen-Wilson, 1987; McClelland & Elman, 1986; Norris, 1994). The Cohort model (Marslen-Wilson, 1987; Marslen-Wilson & Welsh, 1978), which has perhaps been the most influential of these, claims that a set of word candidates is activated on the basis of approximately the first 100–150 ms of the speech input. This word-initial cohort consists of all the words with onsets consistent with the acoustic input. As the speech continues, words which continue to match the input are increasingly activated, while those words that mismatch the input at any point experience a sharp drop-off in their activation level. At a certain point in any word—its *recognition point*—the input will be consistent with only one candidate, and this word will be recognised. For example, as the speech input/tre/ is heard, this will activate a word initial cohort including, *tress*, *trestle*, *tread*, *trend*, *trek*, and *trespass*. When the following /s/ is heard, only *tress*, *trestle*, and *trespass* will continue to be activated, while the activation of the mismatching candidates (*tread*, *trend* and *trek*) will quickly start to decline. Then when the /p/ is heard, only the single word, *trespass*, continues to match and it can be recognised at this point. For many words the recognition point will be before the acoustic offset (as in the case of *trespass*), although this will not always be the case, especially for monosyllables, and following context will sometimes be necessary for identification (e.g. Bard, Shillcock, & Altmann, 1988). Other models such as TRACE (McClelland & Elman, 1986) and the Neighbourhood Activation Model (NAM; Luce et al., 1990) have similar processing assumptions to the Cohort model, but differ in a number of details. For example, NAM places less emphasis on the onset of the word, with the activation of candidates being a function of total degree of phonological overlap regardless of initial match (e.g. *mountain* would be a strong competitor of *fountain*, whereas on the Cohort model *mountain* would not enter the word-initial cohort and so would not be activated at all). TRACE also treats the beginnings and ends of words in similar ways, although competition still depends more strongly on overlap early on in the word. This is because TRACE implements competition in terms of a "rich get richer" mechanism. Words with a low activation value are subject to strong competition effects from their neighbours, whereas words with higher activations are more resilient to competitor effects. Since activations build up as speech comes in, this means that word-initial speech is more important in determining the final activation level of a word.

Although these models make detailed predictions about which words will be activated at any point in the duration of a word, these are primarily claims about the activation and identification of the phonological forms of words, rather than access to semantic information. For example, in TRACE, the top-most level of representation consists of nodes corresponding to each word in the model's lexicon, but these simply identify the word as a specific phonological form, rather than its meaning(s). In general these models do not focus on when in the recognition process the meaning of a word is accessed, or whether the meanings of its competitors are also activated. Nevertheless, the Cohort model makes one crucial claim about the access of word meanings: that there is early activation of multiple semantic representations (Marslen-Wilson, 1987). What this means is that the meanings of all the words in the initial cohort will start to be activated in parallel, as soon as the first 100–150 ms of the word has been heard. So, for example, on hearing the initial sequence /tre/ the meanings of *trespass*, *trestle*, *trend*, *trek*, and so on will all begin to be activated, as well as their phonological forms. This is an essential premise for one of the other major claims of the model, which is that when a word is heard in context, sentential semantic constraints interact with the word recognition process to allow the appropriate word to be selected more rapidly than when the same word is heard in isolation. In order for this to be possible, the meanings of the words in the candidate set must be available for evaluation against the prior context. Any kind of interactive activation model must make a similar claim in order for higher level context to have an effect early in the word recognition process. This contrasts with accounts in which semantic information only becomes available for the correct candidate after it has been recognised, such as Forster's Search model, in which the meaning of a word is looked up in a master file only after it has been uniquely identified on the basis of its orthography (Forster, 1976) and Morton's logogen model, in which a processing unit has to reach a pre-set threshold before its meaning is accessed (Morton, 1969).

In this chapter we will consider the available evidence with respect to the issues of when semantic information becomes available during word recognition, and whether the meanings of competitor words are activated or not. We will also examine experimental data concerning more detailed questions about the structure and contents of the meanings accessed, whether there are differences in the time-course with which different kinds of semantic information become available, and whether all competitor meanings are fully activated, in order to start developing a more complete model of lexical semantic activation. We will then turn to the question of how the data can be accounted for in models of word representation and processing. In particular we will consider the claims of a new kind of model in which word forms and their meanings are not represented as single processing units, as in the models outlined earlier, but are distributed over patterns of activation across many processing nodes (Gaskell & Marslen-Wilson, 1997b). This kind of distributed, connectionist model offers interesting new ways of thinking about how the meanings of words are activated during speech (see also Chapter 8 in this volume by Chater & Christiansen). Due to space limitations the main part of our discussion will focus on the recognition of single words heard in isolation. Although this simplifies the nature of the problem, a full consideration of lexical semantic access during speech must take into account the fact that words are not heard as single units but as part of larger discourse contexts, and therefore their meanings must be interpreted with respect to the meanings of both preceding and subsequent words. We return to this point at the end of the chapter, where we outline some of the ways in which the issues concerning single word recognition interact with the demands of semantics processing in context.

WHAT?

In this investigation of how word meanings are accessed we will start with the question of *what* it is that is actually being accessed: What is the nature of the semantic information that becomes available when we hear a word? One approach to this question is to try to map out the contents of the mental representations of word meanings that are the goal of the access process. The question of how the meanings of words are represented in our minds has taxed linguists, philosophers, and psychologists for centuries and has generated a huge body of debate and research (e.g. Locke, 1690/1981; Lyons, 1977). Almost all theories of semantic representation share the assumption that word meanings are componential; that is, they are made up of a collection of semantic attributes or features, rather than being unanalysable wholes. The majority of psychological evidence supports the componentiality claim, and we will assume that it is correct (see McNamara & Miller, 1989 for a review of this issue). The major debate over the years has been between "classical" theories of word meaning, in which the lexicon contains only the most rarefied of information, that is, the necessary and sufficient conditions for application of the meaning of a word (e.g. *bachelor* would be represented by the features [+human, +male, +adult, +unmarried] and nothing more; Katz, 1972), and theories in which a word's meaning is made up of a richer set of information, including characteristic or typical as well as defining features. This class of account includes prototype and exemplar-based theories (see Smith & Medin, 1981 for a review). On the classical view there is a sharp dividing line between the meaning of a word that is stored in the mental lexicon, and other "encyclopaedic" information that lies outside the lexicon and is part of our general knowledge store. This distinction is not made so clearly on the other views, where certain semantic properties may be more or less central to the meaning of the word, but they may all be part of the same kind of representation or "cut from the same cloth" (Jackendoff, 1983).[1]

In spite of the enormous interest in word meanings, the true nature of our semantic representations remains elusive. Traditionally, psychologists have asked questions about people's knowledge of word meanings by asking them to define words, list their properties, or make judgements about their properties (e.g. McNamara & Sternberg, 1983). The problem with this approach is that it relies on subjects' metalinguistic judgements about meanings. Although these reflections tell us something about what people know, they do not necessarily correspond to the mental representations of word meaning that are involved in normal, automatic language comprehension. The idea that our mental lexicons contain static definitions of words, which can be the objects of introspection, is an appealing one, but is probably no more than an artifact of our literacy and familiarity with written dictionaries and encyclopaedias. Canonical definitions may have no part in language comprehension, but rather can be explicitly learned as a result of metalinguistic education. A study of definition generation described by Barsalou (1993) demonstrates the opacity of the relationship between our explicit generation of "meanings" and the underlying semantic representations. This study showed that there was a great deal of variability in the semantic properties listed for a word, both across subjects, and within subjects on different occasions. Although it is possible to interpret this as a result of variation and fuzziness in the representations themselves, a more plausible explanation is that, even if our semantic representations are available to conscious awareness, their format is unlikely to be a list of propositions that can simply be read out. Therefore there must be some kind of translation and construction process to produce a list of properties, and the variability may be located in these processes.

In the light of these problems, we need to try to find out about the nature of semantic representations in a way that does not involve explicitly asking people to reflect on the meanings of words. This can be done using a class of experimental procedures known as "on-line" tasks. These tasks require subjects to make a speeded reaction time response as close in time as possible to the process we are interested in investigating. The attention of the subjects is directed away from the process of interest because they are concentrating on the reaction time task. The speeded, implicit nature of these tasks enables them to tap into the fleeting,

---

[1] Some authors have distinguished between *word meanings* and *conceptual representations*. In line with most psychologists, we do not distinguish between the two, and use the terms interchangeably. For a discussion of how meaning and concepts could differ, see Murphy (1991).

automatic and largely unconscious processes that underlie language comprehension, rather than explicit, metalinguistic knowledge, so avoiding many of the problems associated with traditional methods of studying the mental representations of word meanings (Marslen-Wilson & Tyler, 1980; Tyler, 1992). The most valuable on-line paradigm for this purpose is semantic priming (e.g. Fischler, 1977; Meyer & Schvaneveldt, 1971; see Neely, 1991 for a review). In a priming task, subjects make a speeded response to a target word (e.g. lexical decision or naming), and reaction times are measured as a function of the preceding word. When the preceding prime word is related (e.g. *cat–dog*) subjects' reaction times are significantly shorter than when it is unrelated (e.g. *pen–dog*). The majority of priming studies have focused on the issue of how contextual factors affect word recognition, by exploring the influence of the prime on recognition of the target word. However, by manipulating the nature of the relationship between prime and target, we can exploit the same task to chart the range of semantic information that becomes available when the prime word is heard. For example, if the prime *canary* facilitates responses to *bird*, we can infer that the semantic information that a canary belongs to the *bird* category was accessed when *canary* was heard. Likewise, if canary primes *yellow* and *wings*, this suggests that these perceptual attributes about what canaries look like were made available, and if *canary* primes *sing*, or *cage*, this shows that certain pieces of information about what canaries typically do, and where we see them, are also being activated (Hodgson, 1991; Moss, Ostrin, Tyler, & Marslen-Wilson, 1995a).

It is important to note here that the priming task can tell us about the information automatically accessed when a word is heard in isolation. If we assume that the full semantic representations of words are exhaustively accessed whenever a word is heard, then this is equivalent to a direct view onto the nature of the underlying semantic representation. This view of exhaustive, context-independent lexical semantic access has often been implicitly assumed in psycholinguistic research, and has been labelled the *standard position* by Williams (1988). However, it is possible that the semantic information made available when a word is heard is not the same on every occasion, and may not always correspond to the sum total of information that is represented in the lexicon (cf. Gerrig, 1986). We return to the issue of how variable this information may be in different contexts in the discussion at the end of this chapter. For the moment, the point is that we cannot necessarily treat the semantic information accessed for a word in isolation as an exhaustive or invariant reflection of the meaning stored in the lexicon. A more appropriate way to characterise the information activated for a word in isolation is as a set of *default* information that is generally made available when there is no supporting context. On some accounts, this corresponds to a core meaning, with other more peripheral properties of the semantic representation being made available only when specifically relevant in a given context (Barsalou, 1982; Greenspan, 1986).[2]

Most of the numerous priming studies that have been carried out over the last 20 years suggest that a wide range of semantic information is made available when a word is heard (or read).[3] Reliable priming has been shown for words that belong to the same semantic category (category coordinate), such as *cat–dog*, *chair–table* (e.g. Hines, Czerwinski, Sawyer, & Dwyer, 1986; Moss et al., 1995a), words that stand in a superordinate–subordinate category relationship, such as *bird–robin*, *table–furniture* (e.g. Neely, Keefe, & Ross, 1989), antonym pairs such as *hot–cold* (e.g. Colombo & Williams, 1990), and pairs of words that share functional properties and relations such as *bee–hive*, *broom–floor* (e.g. Chiarello, Burgess, Richard, & Pollack, 1990; Moss et al., 1995a) or perceptual properties, like cherry–ball (Schreuder, Flores d'Arcais, & Glazenborg, 1984). Given this pattern of results we might want to conclude that as we hear or read a word, a rich set of default information rapidly and automatically becomes available to us, including considerably more than the restricted set of defining features identified by classical theories of word meaning. The meaning activated within a few milliseconds of hearing a word includes, at least, information about the semantic category the word belongs to, and some kind of link or connection to members of the same category, as well as information about its perceptual and functional properties.

There are, however, two important methodological points that need to be borne in mind in interpreting the results of these priming studies. The first important point is that we need to be certain that the priming task is measuring the effect of the semantic relationship between the prime and target word, rather than some other kind of relationship between them. A possible problem here is that many priming studies have confounded semantic relations with an *associative* relationship. By associative relationship, we mean the probability that subjects will give the target as a response to the prime in a free association test (e.g. Moss & Older, 1996). For example, *cat* and *dog* are strongly associated, whereas *pig* and *horse*

[2] However, the term *core meaning* is not always used to refer to the properties that are automatically activated in language comprehension. McNamara and Miller (1989) call such properties the *immediate level* of meaning, and use the term core meaning to refer to additional information that people may be able to retrieve in order to make fine judgements about the real nature of referents.

[3] Most priming studies have looked at written rather than spoken words. However, because we have assumed that the semantic representation accessed by the written and spoken word is the same, we can consider evidence from both modalities at this point. It is when we move onto the time-course of activation and the role of the competitor environment, in the following sections, that the two modalities diverge.

are not, even though both pairs share the same kind of semantic relations of category co-membership. If we assume that the mental lexicon contains a representation of the phonological form of each word (i.e. what it sounds like) as well as of its meaning, it is possible that associated words are linked not only semantically, but also at the level of their phonological forms. These form-level links may build up because of the likelihood of hearing the words together in the language (Chiarello et al., 1990; Shelton & Martin, 1992; Tanenhaus & Lucas, 1987). For example, the word *dog* often follows shortly after *cat*, as has been demonstrated in several studies of large language corpora (e.g. Spence & Owens, 1990). This high probability of co-occurrence may lead to facilitation of recognition of a word when preceded by an associated word (e.g. *dog* preceded by *cat*). Priming between a pair of words that are strongly associated does not necessarily reflect the activation of the meanings of the prime and target, as indicated by the fact that words that often occur together but which have little semantic relation prime each other significantly (e.g. *pillar–society*, *stork–baby*; Moss, Hare, Day, & Tyler, 1994). However, several studies have now shown that semantic priming does hold across the range of relations described previously, even when any associative connection is deliberately avoided (Chiarello et al., 1990; Fischler, 1977; Lupker, 1984; Moss, Ostrin, Tyler, & Marslen-Wilson, 1995a; Shelton & Martin, 1992; Zwitserlood & Schreifers, 1995). Therefore, we conclude that associative priming between pairs of words that frequently occur together may be a separate mechanism that can operate in addition to priming at the semantic level (Moss et al., 1994), but that semantic priming also exists in its own right, and provides a window onto the semantic information that is activated when a word is heard.

The second, perhaps more problematic point is that priming may involve non-automatic processes in addition to the implicit effect of activation of the meaning of the prime on the recognition of the target, and that certain tasks are more susceptible to these strategic effects than others (e.g. Neely, 1991). For example, priming of lexical decision involves a component of *semantic matching* (also termed *coherence checking*) of the target's meaning against that of the prime, after both words have been recognised (Neely et al., 1989). However, this does not undermine the use of the task to probe the meaning activated by the prime, as long as the target can only be matched against the semantic information initially made available when the prime was heard. Indeed, the semantic matching process may be an integral part of normal language comprehension, in which the meaning of each word is evaluated against the meanings of the previous words, rather than a conscious strategy that is peculiar to the priming paradigm (Hodgson, 1991). A more difficult possibility to address is that the facilitation of the target could be due to *backward priming* (Koriat, 1981). This may operate if the prime has not been fully processed when the target is presented, and the target can act as a context for the prime as well as *vice versa*. If this is the case, then priming may not reflect the information that is automatically accessed by default for the prime heard in isolation, but may be a product of activation of its meaning in the context of the following target word, which may or may not be the same thing. For example, the information "used to sweep floors" may not always be accessed when we hear the word *broom*, but may be activated by backward priming when we heard *broom* followed by the target context *floor*. However, backward priming has only been demonstrated for associative relations and it is not clear that it applies to purely semantically related primes and targets.

One of the problems in evaluating the role of purely automatic semantic priming is that there is debate as to which paradigms are susceptible to strategic priming and which are not. Although it is generally thought that a low proportion of related pairs and a short interval between prime and target is effective in minimising strategic effects, Shelton and Martin (1992) have recently argued that any paradigm in which prime and target are presented to explicit pairs encourages post-lexical matching and backward priming. They advocate a version of the priming task in which the primes and targets are presented in a continuous list without gaps between each prime–target pair. However, this paradigm is not without its own problems (Moss et al., 1995a). The issue of the extent to which different tasks pick up a purely automatic priming effects remains an open one. A related issue is whether different tasks reflect different processing pathways or levels within the recognition system (see Balota, Paul, & Spieler, Chapter 2). For example, a lexical decision task may focus attention on the semantic level to a greater extent than a naming task. However, it is not yet clear whether this account applies to spoken word recognition in the same way as visual word recognition. Reading is a task that is learned relatively late in life, and there is an extensive literature detailing the possible different "routes" that may be available to the reader (e.g. sounding out from orthography to phonology, recognition of whole words, or direct semantic access). There is no evidence that speech recognition has the same potential for dissociable pathways. Therefore, priming paradigms provide our most transparent window onto the activation of lexical semantic information, although it will probably never be possible to eliminate strategic effects entirely.

Lexical semantic ambiguity

The discussion so far has concerned the semantic information that is retrieved in the case of words that have a single meaning. An additional set of questions arises when we extend our investigation to those words which have two or more separate meanings, such as *bank*, *plane*, and *rose*. Are all the possible meanings of these ambiguous words automatically accessed when we hear them, or is only one of the meanings made available on any given occasion? This is an important question, since a surprisingly large proportion of words (at least in the English language) are ambiguous in this way, and it is one that has received a great deal of attention in psycholinguistic research.

Several experiments have suggested that both meanings of an ambiguous word are activated when it is heard in isolation. For example, Holley-Wilcox and Blank (1980) presented subjects with an ambiguous word as a prime, followed by a target related to one of its two meanings. Lexical decisions to both targets were facilitated as much as when the prime was a related unambiguous word. However, the activation level appears to be modulated by the relative frequency of use of the alternative meanings. When the meanings are polarised, such that one is much more frequently used than the other, priming was observed for the higher frequency (or dominant) meaning but not for the lower frequency (subordinate) meaning (Simpson, 1984). More recently, Simpson and Burgess (1985) have argued that the subordinate meaning is activated, but to a lesser extent and with a slower time-course than the dominant meaning. The results of these experiments indicate that when we encounter an ambiguous word, in the absence of any other information, all possible meanings are made available, with the degree of activation determined by relative frequency. However, the limitations of these studies are first, that they have been carried out with visually presented materials, so that we cannot determine the time-course of activation of the meanings during a spoken word, and, second, that associative priming has not been ruled out, so that we cannot be sure that the results reflect simultaneous access to multiple conceptual semantic representations rather than the co-occurrence of ambiguous primes with target words related to both meanings.

Most of the interest in ambiguous words has centred around the activation of their meanings when heard in context, rather than in isolation. The key question is whether the exhaustive activation of all possible meanings is automatic and context-independent, or whether the biases and constraints of the prior semantic context can guide access such that only the appropriate meaning is activated. This is just one aspect of the broader debate about whether the language comprehension system operates in a purely bottom-up, data-driven fashion, or whether contextual information can interact with lower level processes (e.g. Tanenhaus & Lucas, 1987). A number of early studies using a sentential cross-modal priming paradigm suggested that access of the meanings of an ambiguous word is not guided by context. For example, Swinney (1979) presented an ambiguous word in a spoken context which biased towards one of the meanings. Visual targets for lexical decision were presented shortly after the offset of the ambiguous prime. Targets related to both the context-appropriate and context-inappropriate meanings were facilitated, indicating automatic exhaustive access. However, when a longer delay (e.g. 100 ms) is introduced between prime and target, only the relevant meaning supports priming, indicating rapid decay or suppression of the meaning that does not fit with the semantic context (see Simpson, 1984 for a review). More recently, however, several researchers have pointed out some of the weaknesses of the earlier studies, and shown that the picture is more complex. Most importantly, the nature of contextual bias was not well controlled in the earlier studies (Tabossi, Colombo, & Job, 1987). Tabossi et al. found that when the sentential semantic contexts biased towards specific semantic features of one of the meanings of an ambiguous prime word rather than making one meaning more plausible in a general way, only targets related to the appropriate meaning primed significantly, at least for the subordinate meanings. Simpson and Krueger (1991) also found context-dependent activation of meaning when contexts were strongly constraining. Thus, the nature of the semantic context, as well as meaning dominance, appears to determine the degree to which alternative meanings will be activated when an ambiguous word is heard.

Summary

Results of priming experiments do not support the view that only necessary and sufficient features of a word's meaning are activated when it is heard in isolation. Rather, it seems that a wider range of information is made available although confirmation of this awaits further experiments in which possible associative relations and strategic backward priming are completely eliminated. One interesting finding that is emerging from our recent research is that *functional* properties of meaning support particularly robust priming effects, suggesting that they may be especially salient in the mental representations of word meanings. By "functional properties", we mean information about what a thing typically does, how it behaves, what it is used for, and where it is found, and so on (for example, *bee–honey*, *desk–work*, *broom–floor*). These relations support priming across a wide range of paradigms, including the continuous list version of the lexical decision task, claimed by Shelton and Martin (1992) to eliminate strategic priming effects (Moss et al., 1995a). Further evidence for the central role of functional information comes from neuropsychological studies of patients with semantic impairments. We studied a patient, PP, who had a profound semantic deficit known as semantic dementia (Moss, Tyler, Hodges, & Patterson, 1995b). PP showed robust normal priming for functionally related word pairs (e.g. *hammer–nail*, *broom–*

floor), but no priming for category coordinates (e.g. *cat–dog*, *spade–rake*). At the time of testing, this patient had little or no conscious awareness of the meanings of words, and so would have been unable to carry out any kind of strategic processing (for example, when asked what was her favourite kind of food, she replied, "*food, food, I wish I knew what that was*..."). The implicit facilitation of functionally related words in this case suggests strongly that this information is automatically activated when words are heard, and may be more resistant to brain damage than other kinds of information. We have found that several patients with semantic processing deficits show the same pattern of effects, with a tendency for greater priming for functional relations of various kinds than for other more formal kinds of semantic relation such as category coordinates or super-ordinates (Moss & Tyler, 1995).[4] A related finding is that young children also weight the importance of functional properties of objects more heavily than that of form-based properties (Nelson, 1974; although see Flores d'Arcais, Schreuder, & Glazenborg, 1985 for an alternative account).

The robustness of functional property priming suggests that the information activated is that which is most relevant to the use of a word's referent. This is plausible, given that when we are listening to spoken language we are generally trying to interpret it in terms of its relevance to ourselves. For example, in talking about chairs and tables, we are generally considering their use for sitting on or eating from, rather than the fact that they belong to the category *furniture*, or *artificial object*, or that they are in the same category as beds and sideboards. This claim is consistent with McNamara and Miller's (1989) view that one of the major determinants of the salience of semantic properties is their "goal-relevance". It is also unsurprising that function should have a special status when we consider how word meanings fit into larger scale mental representations of world knowledge. Many theories of knowledge representation stress the importance of scripts or schemata, that encode information about the nature and structure of the events and situations we encounter in the world (e.g. Garrod & Sanford, 1981; Schank & Abelson, 1977). Within such scripts, the functional role of each individual element is represented. Script elements will often correspond to the meanings of single words. If the aim of language comprehension is to interpret the incoming message with reference to the background knowledge we have stored as scripts, then the

[4] This emphasis on functional properties runs counter to a widely held view in the neuropsychological literature that when semantic memory is impaired, superordinate information is less vulnerable to damage than detailed semantic properties (including functional properties, e.g. Warrington & Shallice, 1984). However, these conclusions are based on data from off-line tasks, and so may be probing knowledge in a different way from implicit semantic priming studies (Moss & Tyler, 1995).

crucial semantic information that we need about the meaning of each word is that which allows us to determine its functional role (or more correctly, the functional role of its referent in the world).

However, at this stage we have not yet determined whether the centrality of functional information generalises to all types of word. So far, all of the prime words that we have tested in our functional relation condition have been artifacts such as furniture, vehicles, and so on, rather than natural kinds such as animals and birds. It has been argued that functional information is at the core of our concepts for artifacts, in a way that is not true of natural kinds such as living things (e.g. Atran, 1989; Keil, 1986). For natural kinds, category membership may be more central. There is also a body of neuropsychological and developmental literature that suggests that perceptual properties may be especially important for living things (Keil, 1986; Warrington & Shallice, 1984). Therefore, we might expect that when prime words refer to living things, we will not see automatic activation of functional information. On the other hand, although living things rarely have well-defined functions or purposes in the same sense as artificial objects, we have recently started to investigate the "biological" functional properties of living things (such as *breathing*, *moving*, *eating*, for animals). These have been argued to be central to our representations (e.g. Keil, 1986) and appear to be well-preserved for patients with semantic impairments (Tyler & Moss, 1997; Moss, Tyler, Durrant-Peatfield & Bunn, 1998). Another limitation of all of this priming research is that the vast majority of primes are concrete nouns; it is possible that different semantic properties will be activated for abstract words (e.g. *truth*, *luck*) and for words from other syntactic classes, such as verbs and adjectives. However, these have only rarely been studied, especially in the current context of investigating the nature of semantic properties that are activated as the words are heard.

WHEN?

The previous section gives us some idea of the kinds of semantic information that are activated for a word at, or shortly after, its offset. However, it has been demonstrated in a variety of different psycholinguistic paradigms that the lexical access process starts considerably earlier than the end of a spoken word, at around 100–150 ms from word onset (e.g. Marslen-Wilson & Tyler, 1980; Tyler & Wessels, 1983). We now need to examine whether the *meanings* of words also start to be activated at this early stage (as claimed on the Cohort model), or whether there is a delay between activation of a word's phonological form and access to its meaning, such that meanings only become available after the word has been uniquely identified. It is important to examine the time-course of the activation of word meanings because the nature of speech recognition is fundamentally constrained by the fact that speech is distributed in time and is fast-fading. The question of how early lexical semantic information becomes available also has important consequences for the nature of language comprehension. If the meaning is available before a word is recognised, this would allow the semantic properties of a word to be evaluated against the prior context, and may speed recognition of a word that is highly congruent, and/or hinder the recognition of a word that is unexpected or anomalous. Early semantic activation would in turn lead to rapid integration of the word into the ongoing message-level representation, so providing contextual constraints that can help recognition of the *next* word along. Thus, the earliness of semantic activation in spoken word processing is closely related to the possible nature of contextual influences on word recognition.

One source of evidence that the meanings of words are made available at an early stage in the recognition process comes from studies demonstrating the influence of semantic variables on the latency of reaction times in word recognition tasks such as naming and lexical decision (Balota, Ferraro, & Connor, 1991). For example, several studies have shown that words with concrete meanings (i.e. whose referents can be experienced through the senses, e.g. *table*, *dog*, *helicopter*) are recognised more quickly than those with more abstract meanings (e.g. *truth*, *luck*, *attitude*; de Groot, 1989; James, 1975). Although most of the studies in this area have concerned the recognition of written words, we have demonstrated the same effect for spoken words using both naming and lexical decision tasks (Tyler, Voice, & Moss, 1996). This suggests that meanings are available before a word has been uniquely identified, and can influence the time course of recognition. The fact that concrete words are recognised more quickly is explained in different ways according to different models of word meanings. On some accounts, concrete words have dual semantic representations (both visual and verbal), whereas abstract words have only the single verbal representation (Paivio, 1986); on other accounts the difference between abstract and concrete words is quantitative rather than qualitative, with concrete words having more semantic properties than abstract words (Jones, 1985; Plaut & Shallice, 1993). The key point for all of these accounts is that there is a richer semantic representation for concrete words, which starts to be accessed early in the recognition process and facilitates the identification of the word.[5] A similar claim has been made for the facilitatory effect of

[5] Gernsbacher (1984) argued that the concreteness effect in lexical decision was confounded with rated word familiarity. However, a number of studies have now shown a concreteness effect when familiarity is controlled (as well as written word frequency), at least for low-familiarity words (e.g. Strain, Patterson, & Seidenberg, 1995).

multiple meanings. Some studies have demonstrated faster reaction times for words with many meanings (e.g. Kellas, Ferraro, & Simpson, 1988). Although this effect is less well documented, and appears to be less reliable (Rueckl, 1995) than the concreteness effect, the proposed basis for the effect is similar. The faster recognition times for semantically ambiguous words are thought to be a result of a richer set of semantic information becoming available early in the course of recognition, and so speeding identification of the word. Although the exact mechanism behind the facilitatory effects of a richer semantic representation is not clear, the general claim is that there is feedback of activation from the semantic level to the lexical form level, and more semantic information means more activation (the *more is better* principle, Balota et al., 1991). We return to this question later in the chapter.

A second source of support for the view that semantic information becomes available early in the duration of spoken words comes from studies that measure event-related brain potentials (ERPs). This technique uses electrodes placed on the scalp to record electrical activity in different areas of the brain while subjects are engaged in a cognitive task. The advantage of ERP studies is that they measure a response over which subjects have no voluntary control, and so cannot be affected by people's conscious strategies or metalinguistic knowledge. Several studies have identified a consistent "N400 effect", which appears to reflect the ease with which a word can be integrated into the prior context. The effect is that words that are consistent or predictable in their context (which may be a sentence or a one-word prime as in the semantic priming experiments described earlier) produce a smaller negative-going ERP, which peaks at approximately 400 ms after the onset of the stimulus, than do context-inconsistent or unprimed words (e.g. Brown & Hagoort, 1993).[6]

Holcomb and Neville (1990) examined the time course of the N400 effect for words presented in either the visual or auditory modality, as a function of whether the target word was preceded by a related or unrelated prime. The N400 reduction was found for both modalities, but it could be detected sooner after the onset of the target for spoken words. The effect could be detected as early as 200 ms from stimulus onset (as

---

[6] These authors have argued that the N400 priming effect reflects post-lexical integration of the meaning of the target with the meaning of the prior context, rather than automatic activation of lexical items. This is comparable to Neely's semantic matching account of semantic priming discussed earlier. This appears to be consistent with the view that post-lexical semantic integration should be seen as one of the automatic processes involved in normal language comprehension rather than as a task-specific conscious strategy (Hodgson, 1991), although this is not the conclusion reached by Brown and Hagoort (1993) who state that integration is a controlled process that can be guided by the subjects' awareness of the information content of the discourse.

opposed to about 300 ms from onset for written words). Given that the duration of all of the spoken word targets was more than 200 ms, and that semantic information about the target word must be available for comparison with the prior context to produce the N400 effect, this indicates that semantic information is available before the acoustic offset of the target words.

Perhaps the most striking evidence for the early activation of spoken word meanings comes from a series of cross-modal priming studies described by Marslen-Wilson (1987). Subjects listened to primes that were either complete words (e.g. *captain*) or fragments of words that have been cut off before they become unique (e.g. /kapt.../). The fragment prime facilitated subjects' lexical decisions to target words related to the complete word (e.g. *ship*), which suggests that the meaning of *captain* has been activated when only part of the word has been heard. The same fragment /kapt.../ is also consistent with the cohort competitor, *captive*, and Marslen-Wilson (1987) found that targets related to this competitor (e.g. *guard*) were also significantly primed. But when the prime was the complete word, *captain*, *ship* was strongly facilitated, but *guard* was not. This indicates that early in the duration of the word, the semantic representations of multiple cohort competitors are activated, but as soon as further acoustic input is heard, which mismatches with any of those candidates (the final /n/ segment in the *captain/captive* example) the activation of the competitor meaning rapidly decays. In a further cross-modal priming study, Zwitserlood (1989) showed that multiple activation can be detected as early as 130 ms from the onset of the prime word. This suggests that semantic information starts to be activated as soon as lexical access begins.

One potential problem with the Marslen-Wilson and Zwitserlood studies is that the target words in each case were associates of the primes (e.g. *captive-guard*, *captain-ship*). It is possible that the early automatic priming observed in these studies is form-based associative priming, and does not reflect activation of semantic representations by the word-initial fragment. However, in a more recent study, Zwitserlood and Schriefers (1995) found priming as early as 3.6 phonemes from the onset of the prime for targets which were non-associated category coordinates such as *pig-horse*, ruling out a purely form-based explanation of the results.[7] We

[7] Zwitserlood and Schriefers (1995) also reported priming for non-associated targets for shorter prime fragments (mean 2.6 speech segments), but only when a delay of approximately 100 ms was introduced between prime and target. Although the authors claim that this is due to the time taken for activation to build up within the system, it is also possible that the inter-stimulus interval allows second-pass processes to operate (cf. Marslen-Wilson, Moss, & van Halen, 1996).

have also demonstrated significant priming for non-associated targets at the Isolation Point of words.[8] The mean duration of the fragment from onset to Isolation Point was 331 ms, approximately half the duration of the complete words (mean 622 ms). In one experiment we carried out a direct contrast between associated and non-associated category coordinates, and we found that non-associated pairs such as *silver-bronze* prime as well as strongly associated pairs (*silver-gold*) (Moss, McCormick, & Tyler, 1997). Therefore, we can conclude that the results from the cross-modal priming experiments reflect early activation of semantic information rather than associative priming.

Taken together, the studies described provide compelling evidence that at least some semantic information is made available very early in the duration of a spoken word. We turn now to an additional question concerning the time course of activation of semantic information. Does the full semantic representation of the word start to be accessed at the same time, or is there earlier activation of some kinds of information than others? Given our earlier argument that functional properties are especially salient aspects of word meanings that play a central role in interpretation, we might also predict that this kind of information will be activated more rapidly than other semantic properties, at least for artificial objects.

However, in one of the few sets of studies to address this issue, Schreuder and colleagues have claimed that perceptual properties are the first to become available, at least for concrete nouns (Flores d'Arcais et al., 1985; Schreuder et al., 1984). They carried out visual priming experiments, in which the target shared either a "perceptual property" with the prime (e.g. *cherry-ball*, which share the property of being round), or a "conceptual property" (e.g. *cherry-banana*, sharing the property of being fruit), or both (*cherry-apple*, which are both round and fruit). Schreuder et al. (1984) found that when subjects were asked to name the targets, there was significant facilitation in the perceptual condition, but not in the conceptual condition, but when the reaction time task was lexical decision, targets sharing conceptual relations were significantly facilitated, but those sharing perceptual relations showed a reduced effect. The assumption is that word naming reflects activation at an earlier point in time than the lexical decision task, and therefore that perceptual properties undergo a

[8] The Isolation Point is the point in the duration of a spoken word where people start to recognise what the word is going to be, but are not yet confident because there are still one or two other possible candidates available. It can be identified empirically in a gating task, where subjects are played out increasingly long fragments of a word from its onset, and asked to indicate what they think the word is and how sure they are that they are right (e.g. Tyler & Wessells, 1983).

process of rapid activation and decay when the prime is processed, whereas conceptual properties are accessed more slowly. This finding was extended by Flores d'Arcais et al. (1985). The authors claim that these results support their model of semantic representation in which concepts include two distinct kinds of properties—perceptual elements and knowledge-based or functional elements. Perceptual elements are based on our direct experience of objects in the world, and therefore their activation is also more direct and more rapid than that of functional elements, which are not apparent in the world but have to be learned or inferred.

Although this study suggests an intriguing insight into the time course of activation of semantic information it is not clear what kind of semantic information underlies the "conceptual property relation". The word pairs in this condition are all members of the same semantic category and many are probably strongly associated. Flores d'Arcais et al. (1984) describe the properties as "functional" when implementing the results in their model, but priming for these word pairs could be supported by information other than functional properties, such as category links via the superordinate (e.g. *cherry-fruit-apple*) or form-based associative co-occurrence. Another problem is that the targets were presented following a visual prime at an SOA of 400 ms. Thus, although naming may tap into an earlier stage of processing than lexical decision, it is still the case that subjects have seen the whole of the prime word by the time they start to respond to the target, and so the results cannot tell us about the activation of different semantic properties that may take place throughout the duration of a spoken word.

We undertook a cross-modal priming study to investigate the time-course of activation of different kinds of semantic information, that avoids the problems of the Schreuder et al. (1984) study (Moss, McCormick, & Tyler, 1995). We presented subjects with spoken prime words, which were played out either to their offset or up to the Isolation Point. Visual targets were displayed for lexical decision at one of these two points. The targets corresponded to either a perceptual property (e.g. *spade-handle*, *aeroplane-wing*) or a functional property (e.g. *rifle-shoot*, *helicopter-fly*) of the prime word.[9] In both cases, the target describes a property without introducing the additional possible semantic connections that are involved in category relations. Moreover, the target words were not strong associates of the primes. All of the prime words were artificial

[9] In common with the majority of other psychological studies the materials in our perceptual condition refer only to the visual sense modality (e.g. colour, shapes, visible parts) and do not include auditory or olfactory properties. The latter are clearly important attributes of many objects, but most are unsuitable for a priming study because they cannot be described with a single word.

objects. If Schreuder et al.'s claim is correct, and perceptual properties are always activated more rapidly than functional properties, then we should see priming for the perceptual properties at an earlier point in the duration of the prime. However, if functional properties are more salient than perceptual properties for artificial objects, as suggested by our earlier priming results, and by developmental (e.g. Keil, 1986) and neuropsychological evidence (e.g. Warrington & Shallice, 1984), this would be more consistent with functional properties becoming available more quickly and so showing priming at the earlier point.

The results supported the latter hypothesis. Functional properties showed significant priming both when presented at prime offset and at the Isolation Point of the prime. This indicates that functional properties are activated early in the duration of a word referring to an artificial object—before the word has been uniquely identified—and continue to increase in activation as the rest of the word is heard. Perceptual properties, in contrast, showed no facilitation at the Isolation Point, although a priming effect emerged by the acoustic offset of the prime word. This shows a slower activation function for semantic information about what an object looks like than about what it is used for (see Fig. 3.1), and is not consistent with Schreuder et al.'s model on which perceptual elements of the

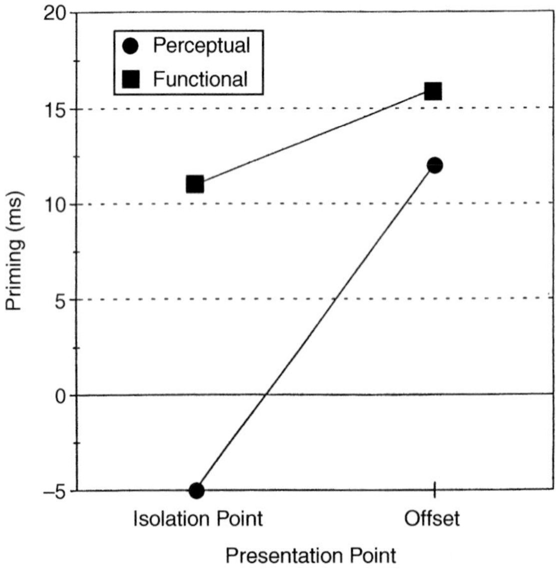

FIG. 3.1 Priming effects for perceptual and functional properties of words referring to artificial objects (Moss, McCormick, & Tyler, 1997). Reprinted with permission.

semantic representation are activated before other kinds of information. The results are, however, consistent with our conclusions concerning the role of functional semantic information in language comprehension, as outlined in the previous section. The early availability of this kind of information allows the rapid assignment of functional roles to the elements in the discourse and provides an additional source of contextual constraint for the interpretation of upcoming words. However, as in our previous discussion, we have to bear in mind that the results to date all concern the time-course of semantic activation for artificial objects and will not necessarily extend to other classes of word.

WHICH?

The data presented in the previous section indicate that the meaning of a word becomes available very early in the duration of the speech input. In the introduction we highlighted the point that on most current models of word recognition, a set of potential word candidates are activated, not just the single word that is eventually recognised. It is therefore possible that semantic activation begins to be activated for a whole range of competitor words, as the speech input begins to be heard. However, the different models of word recognition differ with respect to which words will be activated as competitors. While the Cohort model claims that only words that overlap at the onset will be activated, other models such as the Neighbourhood Activation Model (Luce et al., 1990) and the TRACE model (McClelland & Elman, 1986) claim that the activation of competitor words will be a function of overall phonological overlap between the speech input and the phonological form of the word, regardless of whether there is a complete match at word onset. Therefore, a third set of important questions about lexical semantic processing is whether the meanings of all competitor words are activated and, if so, which words count as competitors.

Turning first to the claims of the Cohort model, there is good evidence that the meanings of at least some word-initial competitors are activated early in the duration of a word. It has already been mentioned that, in Marslen-Wilson's (1987) study, word-initial fragments supported priming not only for targets related to the word that was actually being spoken, but also for targets related to competitors that overlapped at the onset. For example, */kapt.../* primed *ship* (related to *captain*) as well as *guard* (related to *captive*). This effect was also demonstrated in a later study by Zwitserlood (1989) in which the fragments were embedded in a range of sentential semantic contexts. In this study, Zwitserlood found that even when fragments such as */kapt.../* were heard in sentences that made one of the candidates more plausible than the other, both targets were still facilitated until after the Isolation Point of the word, indicating activation of the meanings of competitor words, even when they were inappropriate in the current context. However, context effects did start to operate before the offset of the prime, by facilitating the selection of the correct word from the set of candidates activated on the basis of the sensory input. These findings are consistent with the claim of the Cohort model, that the semantic representations of multiple lexical items are activated as the first 150 ms or so of the input is heard, and that the meanings of these competitor candidates can then be evaluated against the context. This will allow the correct word to be recognised more quickly if it fits in well with the contextual constraints. Notice, however, that the prior context does not have any effect on whether the meanings of competitors are initially activated, but only on the process of selection among those meanings.

Although Marslen-Wilson and Zwitserlood's experiments show that the meanings of at least two word-initial competitor words are activated, further research is needed in this area before we can determine whether meanings are activated for the full set of cohort candidates. To go back to the example of *captain*, is it the case that the meanings of *cat*, *catapult*, *cap*, *cab*, *character*, and so on, are all activated in addition to *captain* and captive when the input */ka.../* has been heard, or is a greater amount of sensory information required before semantic information starts to be activated for the full range of competitors? Two factors which might influence the activation of competitor meanings are: (1) the relative frequency of competitors, and (2) the total number of competitors in the cohort. There is some evidence that relative frequency modulates the activation of multiple-word candidates. For example, Marslen-Wilson (1990) used cross-modal priming to examine the activations of word pairs such as *road* and *robe*, which diverge on their final segment. When these words were presented auditorily with the word-final consonants cut off, the amount of time by which the visual target word was facilitated depended on its frequency; so high-frequency words such as *road* were primed more strongly than their low-frequency competitors. This frequency effect diminished when the prime words were presented in unambiguous form (i.e. with their final segments intact). Even though Marslen-Wilson's experiments measured the activation levels of the forms rather than the meanings of competitor pairs, it is plausible that the meanings of high-frequency competitor words will show a similar head-start in the time-course of activation. In fact, Zwitserlood (1989) found a similar transient effect of relative frequency in the cross-modal priming study discussed previously; that is, at the earlier presentation points, prime words that were of higher frequency than their cohort competitor facilitated the associatively related targets more than did those primes that were lower in frequency than their competitor. By the later points this difference had disappeared. However, the number of items in each frequency band was very small and the effect was not statistically significant. No effect of the relative frequency of the prime word to its competitors was found in the study by Moss, McCormick, and Tyler (1997), although the earliest presentation point was the Isolation Point of the prime, by which time such frequency effects may have passed. These results suggest that any effects of relative frequency of words in their competitor sets on the activation of word meanings are small and short-lived.

The number of competitors in a cohort may also affect the activation of the meanings of the members. Whereas it is plausible that all the meanings of a small cohort may be activated in parallel (e.g. *squid* and *squint*), the same may not be true when the cohort contains hundreds of words (e.g. *cat*, *cab*, *can*, *captain*, *catapult*, *catalogue*, *catch*, *character*, *cancel*, etc.). There is little empirical evidence relating to this issue, since most studies so far have examined quite small cohort neighbourhoods. However, Zwitserlood and Schriefers' (1995) experiments showed semantic priming for short fragments of words, which were consistent with a cohort of 12.7 words on average, although only when a delay of approximately 100 ms was introduced between prime and target.

We now turn to the question of whether there is activation of competitor words that overlap with the speech input but which mismatch at the onset, as predicted by the Neighbourhood Activation and TRACE models of spoken word recognition. The usual definition of a competitor (or neighbour) on these models is any word that diverges by only one phoneme in any position. So, for example, the competitors of *cat* would include *bat*, *rat*, *pat*, *cot* and *cut* as well as *cab* and *cap*. Several studies have examined the activation of competitors that do not overlap at onset by looking at the effectiveness of rhyme-primes (i.e. words that share all their phonological information with the exception of the initial phoneme; e.g. Connine, Blasko & Titone, 1993; Marslen-Wilson et al., 1996; Milberg, Blumstein & Dworetzky, 1987). For example, when we hear the word *cattle*, is the meaning of *battle* activated? This has been tested in priming experiments where the target is a word related to a rhyme of the prime. If the meaning of *battle* is activated by the input *cattle*, then hearing the prime *cattle* should facilitate the target *war* (related to *battle* but not to *cattle*). Although there have been some apparently conflicting results, the conclusion appears to be that there is no immediate activation of the meanings of rhyming competitors, even when the rhymes are different only by one phonetic feature of the initial segment (e.g. *blank* does not prime *wood*, even though it differs from *plank* by only the voicing feature of the first phoneme). In fact, the meaning of a word does not appear to be activated even if the input differs by less than a full phoneme at the onset, but is ambiguous between two possible phonemes (e.g. an input *p/blank* that has a voicing value half way between a /p/ and a /b/ does not prime *wood* (related to *plank*) or *page* (related to *blank*; Marslen-Wilson et al., 1996). The lack of activation for rhyme competitors has been shown in experiments where the visual target for lexical decision is presented immediately at the offset of the auditory prime, so reflecting the activation state of competitors immediately after the word has been heard. In other studies, where the target has been presented at a delay from the offset of the prime, or where subjects' reaction times have been particularly slow, some facilitation by rhyme primes has been found (Connine et al., 1993; Milberg et al., 1987). A direct comparison between immediate and delayed priming was carried out by Andruski, Blumstein, and Burton (1994). They found an immediate inhibitory effect of a subphonetic manipulation of the initial consonants of words on recognition of a related target. However, this effect disappeared when the target was presented at a delay of 250 ms. This suggests some kind of recovery process, which operates when the initial comparison between speech input and lexical forms fails. This may be similar to a backward priming effect; subjects try to reinterpret the prime input, partly on the basis of the target which hints towards a meaning other than that which may have been initially activated on the first pass (Marslen-Wilson et al., 1996). Therefore, while there is good evidence for activation of the meanings of at least some word-initial cohort competitors, there is no evidence for immediate activation of the meanings of competitors that mismatch at word onset.[10]

A third type of potential competitor comprises words that are embedded in longer words. In the case of words that are embedded at the onset of a longer word (e.g. *cat* in *catapult*), we can assume that the meanings of both would be activated in the same way as any other cohort competitors, since both are consistent with the first part of the input. However, when a word is embedded in the middle or at the end of a longer word, the situation may be more complicated. There is good evidence of this kind of competition from word-spotting tasks, where subjects have to press a button as soon as they recognise a word. For example, McQueen, Norris, and Cutler (1994) showed that subjects are

[10] Because these studies were primarily concerned with the access of lexical form representations by competitor inputs, the targets for lexical decision were strong associates of the prime as well as being semantically related. As argued earlier, this may confound co-occurrence based associative priming with activation of semantic information in the mental lexicon. However, in this case, targets which are both semantically and associatively related to the competitor word are failing to prime, and therefore it is unlikely that targets which are semantically related only would prime either.

slower to monitor for a short word such as *mess* when it is embedded in another word (e.g. *domestic*) than when it is embedded in a non-word. But does this imply that the meaning of the embedded word is activated as the speech is heard? Evidence from a cross-modal priming study (Shillcock, 1990) suggests that it is: When a target related to the embedded word *bone* (e.g. *rib*) was presented for lexical decision at the offset of *trombone* there was a small but significant priming effect. This suggests that listeners continue to access additional possible word meanings, even though when the /b/ is heard, the input is still consistent with a word from the onset (*trombone*). Although this effect is predicted by models such as TRACE (McClelland & Elman, 1986) and Shortlist (Norris, 1994), in which lexical access procedures are initiated by each incoming phoneme, it is not consistent with the Cohort model, which claims that lexical access is initiated only at word onset and that one of the major cues to the onset of a word is the identification of the end of the previous word (so the /b/ in *trombone* should not be treated as a word onset, because *trom* is not a complete word). However, this finding should be treated with some caution, since a replication of Shillcock's result using cross-modal repetition priming found no facilitation of the embedded word target (Marslen-Wilson, Tyler, Waksler, & Older, 1994).

In summary, the set of competitors for which semantic information is made available seems to depend on an exact (if transient) match between the available sensory evidence and lexical form representations. The meanings of word-initial cohort competitors are activated simultaneously for as long as they match the speech input. There is also some evidence that competing meanings are activated for embedded words that do not share word onsets. However, the meanings of words that rhyme with, or possess a global resemblance to, the input do not appear to be activated during first-pass processing, although they can be recovered quite rapidly with a second pass. We cannot yet be sure whether the meanings of all members of the initial cohort are accessed as soon as the beginning of the word is heard, or whether only a subset of the most frequent words start to be activated at the earliest point. The results of our cross-modal priming study (Moss, McCormick, & Tyler, 1997) suggest that the answer to this question may be modulated by the kind of semantic information concerned. Functional properties of artifacts seem to be activated by the Isolation Point of a word, regardless of the relative frequency of the word in its cohort, but perceptual properties are not activated until the offset of a word. Although there is some evidence that the relative frequency within its competitor set may affect the rise time of activation, this seems to be a small and fleeting effect.

HOW?

Having considered the evidence concerning the nature of semantic information accessed, when it is accessed and the activation of competitor meanings, we turn to the task of developing a model of lexical representation and processing that can accommodate these findings. As a first step the data argue strongly against any model of word recognition in which semantic information is activated for only a single word following the point of recognition. It is clear that at least some aspects of the meanings of words are available before recognition point, perhaps as early as 130 ms from the acoustic onset, and that meanings of at least some competitor words are also activated. This rules out Forster's search model and Morton's logogen model as adequate accounts of semantic activation processes during spoken word recognition, because both of these claim that the meaning of a single word is accessed only after the point at which it has been uniquely recognised on the basis of its match to the speech signal (see Introduction).[11] Rather, we need a model that allows early activation of multiple semantic representations. The evidence also suggests that the range of meanings activated is largely determined by word-initial match to the acoustic input, and not just overall phonological overlap. This is more consistent with the Cohort model in which the competitor set is determined by the onset of the word, than with models like TRACE and NAM, where a word-initial match is not crucial.

As outlined earlier, neither the Cohort model, nor the other activation/competition based models of word recognition, have considered the semantic representation of words in any detail. There are two different approaches to semantic representation (and to representation within the cognitive system in general) that could be adopted. The first is a localist approach, as exemplified by Collins and Loftus's (1975) semantic network model, in which the meaning of each word in the lexicon is represented by a single processing node. These nodes are connected by activation links to nodes corresponding to word forms, which in turn are activated by the acoustic input. The nodes within the semantic level are connected to other nodes for words which are related. This kind of localist connectionist approach is very similar to that adopted for the phonetic feature, phoneme and word-form levels in the TRACE model, and would be a natural extension of such a model. More recently, however, several researchers have rejected localist representation in favour of distributed models. In these models, a unit within the language system, such as the

---

[11] These models were originally proposed to account for written rather than spoken word recognition, and it is a separate question whether they can account for activation of meanings during reading.

meaning of a word, is not represented by a single node within a network, but by a pattern of activation across a large set of nodes. These nodes may correspond to smaller units within the system (e.g. semantic features) or there may be no one-to-one correspondence between any node and any identifiable element of the system. In the following sections we discuss the interpretation of the data concerning lexical semantic activation according to a localist and distributed model, and the differences between them.

Localist models. The structure of a localist semantic network and its relation to the levels of representation generally believed to be involved in word recognition are shown in Fig. 3.2. When lexical form nodes start to be activated by the acoustic input, this activation passes on to the semantic level to activate the corresponding meaning node. To account for the earliness of semantic activation this activation must propagate in a cascaded fashion on the basis of partial activation at the form level, rather than requiring a threshold to be reached first. To account for the activation of meanings of multiple competitors, we can also assume that activation passes in parallel from the form to the meaning nodes of all words that are consistent with the speech input so far. On this model even the largest cohort of words could be activated in parallel because each node is separately represented and has no adverse effects of the

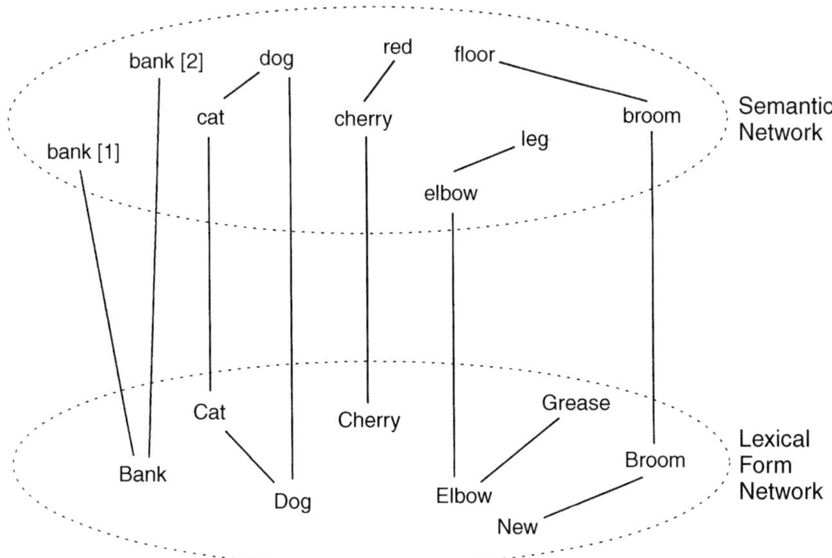

FIG. 3.2 Representation of semantic and associative relations in a localist network.

activation of other meaning nodes. Finally, to account for the apparent influence of meaningfulness on word recognition, there must also be feedback of activation from the meaning to the form levels, in the same way as feedback is assumed to operate at other levels of the system.

In the semantic network model, activation also spreads out from the semantic nodes to other words with related meanings. For example, if the meaning of *cat* is activated, activation will spread to the models for *dog*, *kitten*, *tiger*, *animal*, *purr* and so on. This automatic spread of activation has been one of the most influential accounts of semantic priming effects, such as those described in earlier sections. If spread of activation is the basis of semantic priming, then the links that exist between nodes must include many different kinds of semantic relation. In particular, the links between words that are related by functional properties (at least for artificial objects) should be particularly strong. In terms of the network, this would mean that pairs of words like *broom* and *floor* or *party* and *music* would be more strongly linked than pairs with other kinds of relation such as perceptual relations. In this model, associative priming is captured by activation links between nodes at the lexical form level rather than within the semantic level (see Fig. 3.2). The basis for the formation of these links would be the frequent co-occurrence of the words in the language.

Although the basis for the formation and strengthening of links between associated words is sound and can be implemented easily using simple learning mechanisms (e.g. Hebbian learning; Hebb, 1949), it is not clear what principles encapsulate the linkage between purely semantically related words. The pattern of priming effects we find for perceptual and functional properties of artificial objects suggests that contextual relevance is an important factor: Functional properties are most relevant for the integration of the word's meaning with its utterance context. It follows that the formation or strengthening of links in a semantic network should be based in part on this relevance, so that the immediately useful properties of a word are swiftly retrieved when a word is activated.

The effects of semantic properties on the time-course of word recognition are interpretable as top-down facilitation from the semantic network to the word-form level in a model such as TRACE. For example, the effect of semantic ambiguity on recognition time (Kellas et al., 1988) can be accommodated as an effect of strength of feedback from the semantic level. A word with multiple meanings is connected to more than one node in the semantic network. If, as activation propagates through the network, these nodes feed back activation to the word-form level, then their facilitatory effect should be proportional to the number of meanings, producing a small advantage for semantically ambiguous words (Balota et al., 1991; Kellas et al., 1988). The effect of concreteness on word recognition can also be explained in terms of feedback, based on the assumption that concrete words are represented twice—in a verbal system and an image-based system—whereas abstract words are only represented verbally (Bleasedale, 1987; Paivio, 1986).

In summary, a localist implementation of semantic representations in a word recognition model could account for many of the empirical findings concerning the activation of word meanings. The separable effects of associative and semantic priming are explained neatly in terms of a two-level spreading activation system. Similarly, an advantage for words with multiple meanings in lexical decision is easily accommodated in the localist framework. However, the localist approach, although tenable, seems less productive when we focus on effects of semantic structure, such as concreteness effects or functional/perceptual distinctions. In these cases, it seems somewhat clumsy to represent fine details of the structure of word meanings purely in terms of their links to other words. It may be more profitable instead to turn to distributed models of word recognition, which stress the componential nature of word meaning and allow partial activations of selected properties to develop.

Distributed models. Several distributed connectionist models of language comprehension mechanisms have been developed. These models share the common representational assumption that elements of the language system are captured as patterns of activation over large numbers of processing units, rather than in a single node. This system of representation makes processes such as generalisation to novel elements and pattern completion simple to perform (Hinton, McClelland, & Rumelhart, 1986). A further advantage of distributed systems is that when damage is simulated (by removing units or connections between units) performance degrades gradually, as is generally found in brain-damaged patients (e.g. Plaut & Shallice, 1993).

The distributed representation approach seems particularly appropriate in the case of semantic representations. As we outlined earlier, most theories of word meanings claim that meanings are not stored as unanalysable wholes, but rather are composed of a range of different kinds of information and semantic features. In a distributed account, it is possible to model a word's meaning over a set of processing nodes which each correspond to an individual semantic property. However, by assigning each node of the network to a labelled "microfeature", there is still an element of localist representation in the system; it has simply been moved from one level of representation (word meanings) to a more fine-grained level (semantic features). It is conceivable that even this level of localism is unrealistic and that there is in fact no level of representation at which single units have a fixed meaning (Clark, 1993).

A number of connectionist models have demonstrated aspects of lexical processing within the distributed framework (e.g. Joordens & Besner, 1994; Kawamoto, Farrar, & Kello, 1994; Masson, 1995; Plaut & Shallice, 1993). Microfeatural accounts of distributed representations ensure that words with similar meanings will have similar representations. For example, the words *teapot* and *coffeepot* might share such features as [container], [handle], [spout], and differ on relatively few features. Distributed models of lexical processing exploit these similarities in modelling semantic priming data. Masson (1995) modelled access to semantic information during word recognition in terms of a mapping from a set of perceptual (orthographic) nodes onto a set of semantic nodes, which encoded the distributed semantic representations of the words. The network employed a simple learning algorithm to memorise the semantic patterns, allowing the network to develop "attractors" for each word. The time taken to access the meaning of a word could then be modelled in terms of the number of processing cycles needed to settle into the correct semantic state. Priming occurs when a word with a similar semantic representation is presented before the target. The network settles into the semantic state corresponding to the prime word and when the target is presented the network is quick to settle into the semantic state for the target, due to the close proximity of the prime's semantic state.

Although representational similarity may provide a good basis for explaining purely semantic priming, it cannot easily be extended to cover associative priming. This can occur even when there is little or no similarity between the meanings of the two words, as in *pillar* and *society* or *elbow* and *grease*. In addition, priming based on representational similarity is necessarily symmetrical, whereas associative priming is often highly asymmetrical. Associative priming has, however, been modelled within the distributed framework using recurrent networks which exploit co-occurrence statistics in order to reduce output error (Moss et al., 1994; Plaut, 1995). In these models, associative priming is based on the assumption that associatively related words often co-occur in sentence contexts, as in the phrases *elbow grease* and *pillar of society* (Fischler, 1977). These co-occurrences can be learned by a network and then employed in the prediction of incoming words. The associative priming effect is then realised as an advantage in the recognition of a contextually predictable word over a contextually unpredictable word. Moreover, there is some doubt as to whether representational similarity alone can be the full explanation of purely semantic priming. If priming results from the representations of prime and target involving similar patterns of activation over semantic units, then we should see the most robust effects for those word pairs that have the most similar meanings, that is, synonyms and close category coordinates. However, our research suggests that word pairs connected by goal-relevant functional properties may in fact prime more strongly. The degree of semantic overlap between functionally related word pairs such as *broom-floor* or *shampoo-hair* intuitively seems to be less than that between close category coordinates such as *broom-mop* or *shampoo-conditioner*. The explanation of such effects within a distributed model will depend on more sophisticated accounts of the structure of the semantic representations of words such as *broom*, and how the functional properties are captured within them.

Distributed representations are convenient for modelling partial activations and so are able to explain why some properties of a word become active more quickly than others (Borowsky & Masson, 1996; Kawamoto, 1993). Such behaviour is particularly valuable in the explanation of the differential time-course effects found in the activation of perceptual and functional properties of artificial objects (Moss, McCormick, & Tyler, 1997). This can be explained as an example of pattern completion from a partial representation in an attractor-type network (e.g. Masson, 1995). As a word is heard, a partial semantic activation develops, consisting, in the case of an artificial object, of its functional properties. The partial nature of this representation is transient, since the network quickly fills in the remaining features to complete the pattern, activating both perceptual and functional properties. However, as in the localist description of this kind of effect, we need to ask what drives the initial activation for functional properties. Somehow, contextual relevance must be built into the learning phase of such a model to allow functional properties of artificial object words to be activated more quickly.

The concrete–abstract distinction has been captured in distributed systems as a qualitative representational difference. Plaut and Shallice (1993) used a microfeatural semantic representation for which concrete words had roughly four times as many features as abstract words. The psychological motivation for this difference was based on the finding that the number of predicates subjects can generate for a word is highly correlated with its imageability (Jones, 1985).[12] In addition, the meanings of concrete words are believed to be more stable across contexts than abstract words (Saffran & Schwartz, 1994). These findings were used to argue that the context-independent semantic representation generated when an isolated word is read or heard is richer for concrete than for abstract words. Plaut and Shallice's objective was to simulate the neuropsychological data on deep dyslexia by examining network performance under damage. However, this representational system may also be able to explain the effect of concreteness found on lexical decision time for both spoken and written words. This is because there is greater redundancy in

[12] Imageability is, in turn, highly correlated with concreteness.

the richer semantic representation used for concrete words. This redundancy makes a full semantic representation easier to construct given the partial information that develops during the time-course of perception of a word.

The fact that words often have multiple meanings is more troublesome for distributed models. Each meaning is represented as a pattern over all the processing units, which implies that only one meaning can be properly represented at any one time. A distributed model of semantic ambiguity could easily choose to activate only one meaning for an ambiguous word, based on frequency or contextual factors. However, the experimental evidence suggests that in many cases two or more meanings are activated simultaneously (Simpson, 1984). The only way to accommodate this in a distributed model is to construct a blend of the meanings, which is broadly similar to both meanings, by settling into a pattern that is somewhere between the two, and so shares some properties of both meanings (Joordens & Besner, 1994). It is, as yet, unclear whether modelling ambiguity in this way allows the lexical decision advantage for ambiguous words to be simulated. Recent attempts to simulate this effect have had mixed results (e.g. Borowsky & Masson, 1996; Joordens & Besner, 1994; Kawamoto et al., 1994), with attention focusing on the representational basis required in order to make a lexical decision. A deeper understanding of the lexical decision task is necessary in order to resolve this debate.

A distributed model of speech perception. The models just described have all employed a static form representation as input in order to model the lexical processing involved in word recognition. However, in the case of speech perception we have argued that a more realistic representation is needed, which captures the transient nature of the incoming speech. Gaskell and Marslen-Wilson (1997b) have recently developed a model which incorporates many of the key processing claims of the Cohort model into a distributed connectionist architecture, and which includes a level of semantic representation (see Fig. 3.3). The model employs a simple recurrent network architecture (Elman, 1991) to map from a stream of phonetic features, representing incoming speech, to distributed lexical representations. The recurrent connections allow the network to recognise patterns entering the network over time, meaning that internal representations of words can be learned by the network.

In comparison to the speech perception models we have discussed earlier on in this chapter, such as TRACE and Cohort, the scope of the model is extended: It captures the time-course of activation of meaning and other lexical knowledge rather than simply the identification of word forms. Indeed, the model no longer incorporates a representation of form that is separable from the lexical entry. Both form and meaning are

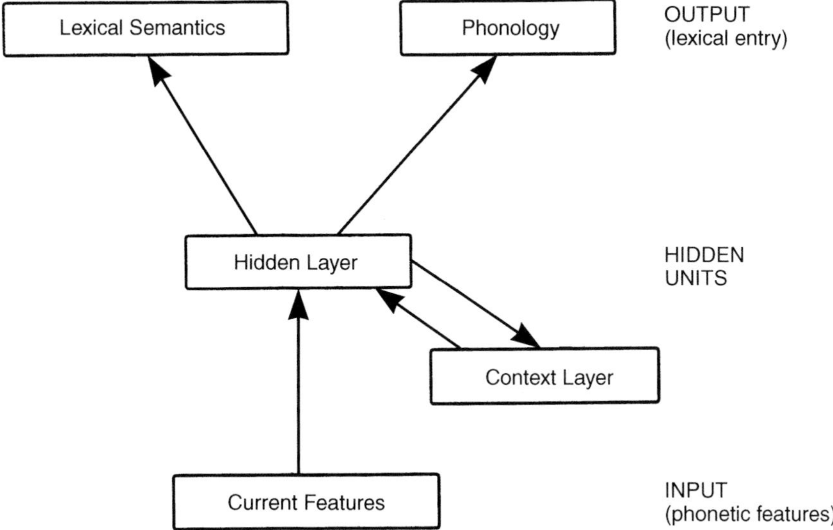

FIG. 3.3 Distributed model of lexical representation (Gaskell & Marslen-Wilson, 1997b). Reprinted with permission.

products of the perceptual process and are represented at essentially the same level in the system.

Nonetheless, many of the properties of earlier models of speech perception are retained, but implemented in a distributed framework. A crucial feature of the model is the early activation of multiple semantic representations, as in the Cohort model. As we have discussed, Cohort predicts that once a small amount of word-initial speech has been processed, the meanings of all words matching so far are activated, allowing contextual information to influence the process of selection from the remaining candidates. Because Cohort is a localist model, employing independent word-form representations, these meanings can also be accessed independently. For example, given the onset /fr/, the meanings of the words *freeze* and *frost* would be activated, making elements such as *cold* available for integration with the sentential context. However, the meanings of *fry* and *frazzle* would also be activated, whose semantic representations would include the feature *hot*. According to Cohort, both these (and many other) concepts would be simultaneously active during the presentation of the speech.

However, in the distributed model all these meanings must be encoded in the same distributed representational space. As we have seen, this implies that when many meanings are activated simultaneously they will interfere, producing a semantic blend of the different features. Obviously, the details of this interference depend on the theory of semantic representation chosen, but, as a general rule, its strength depends on the number of competing words and their relative frequency. This gives a rather different picture of the time-course of activation of word meaning. Instead of many meanings being activated early on, with a gradual filtering process as subsequent information eliminates candidates, the activation of semantics increases as the number of matching candidates drops. The distributed model predicts that at the beginning of a word, the semantic representations of the thousands of word candidates interfere strongly, cancelling out any semantic activation. As speech eliminates mismatching candidates, the interference between the remaining candidates decreases, increasing the potential for priming of related words. The recognition point of a word is marked by the isolation of a single coherent semantic representation.

The distributed model of Gaskell and Marslen-Wilson does not predict that multiple meanings cannot be accessed in parallel, but it does suggest that their informativeness depends strongly on the number of meanings being represented. Thus, we may well get semantic priming for speech tokens before recognition point (e.g. Zwitserlood & Schriefers, 1995), but the strength of the priming should depend strongly on the number of word candidates remaining and their relative frequencies. Evidence for this pattern of semantic activation was found in a study by Gaskell and Marslen-Wilson (1997a) using a cross-modal semantic priming.

The integration of semantic processing and lexical access also offers the potential for explaining a wider range of data. The differences we find in the time course of activation of different types of semantic knowledge (Moss, McCormick, & Tyler, 1997) can be explained in terms of the influence of semantic *structure* on the interference between semantic patterns. Broad semantic distinctions such as between perceptual and functional properties or between concrete and abstract words should be reflected in the distributed semantic structure of the words and are therefore able to affect the blending and interference between semantic representations during lexical access.

DISCUSSION

In this chapter we have examined evidence concerning the nature of semantic information activated when a word is heard, the time-course of its activation and the activation of meanings of competitors for recognition. The major conclusions are that: (1) a wide range of information is automatically activated when a word is heard in isolation—certainly more than defining features, and with functional attributes being particularly salient, at least for concrete artifact nouns; (2) word meanings start to be activated early in the word's duration, probably on the basis of the first CV or CCV (this means that there is no delay between the activation of lexical forms and the activation of semantic contents; moreover, it may be possible to chart different activation curves for different properties of the word's meaning); and (3) the meanings of a number of candidates for word recognition are all activated as a word starts to be heard. The available evidence suggests that the competitor space is determined mainly by the onset of the word, with less evidence for the activation of meanings of competitors that do not overlap at word onset.

Next we examined how these characteristics of lexical semantic access could be accounted for in a model of word recognition and semantic representation. We argued that the data are consistent with the main processing claims of the Cohort model but that these claims can be implemented in two different kinds of architecture—either localist or distributed representation. These approaches both capture the claims about multiple semantic access, activation, and competition, but the different representational assumptions have important consequences for how these processes operate. This highlights the important point that issues concerning lexical semantic processing are intricately bound up with issues concerning lexical semantic representation, and the two cannot be considered in isolation. We have discussed how such an integrated model could accommodate these findings, considering both localist and distributed representations. However, we are not yet in a position to reject one of these approaches to semantic representation in favour of the other. Indeed it is slightly disturbing that two such dissimilar theories are proving so difficult to distinguish experimentally (although see Masson, 1995 for a step in this direction).

In concluding, it is important to emphasise that we have only been able to discuss the access of the meanings of words heard in isolation. However, the goal of language comprehension is, of course, not to understand individual unconnected words, but to interpret the meanings of words as they are heard in sentential and discourse contexts. We have, however, referred to the interaction of lexical semantic processing and the higher level context at a number of points. For example, claims about the earliness of activation of semantic information clearly have implications for the ability of contextual constraints to influence the word recognition process. Also, the apparently central role of functional properties of word meaning are readily accounted for by the important part they play in the integration of word meanings into larger knowledge structures such as scripts.

Contextual constraints on the processing of word meanings probably have their most noticeable role in the disambiguation of words that have more than one meaning. But the role of context is ubiquitous, and applies to unambiguous, just as much as to ambiguous words. Indeed, we should probably think of ambiguity as a matter of degree, rather than an all-or-none state, ranging from subtle variations on a single meaning, through words with different senses and metaphorical extensions, to the classical homophones that have two unrelated meanings attached to a single sound sequence. Even in the former case—words with a single meaning—the constellation of semantic properties activated for the word in any given utterance may differ according to the nature of the context. The relevance of different properties in different contexts has been clearly demonstrated in a number of experimental studies. For example, Barclay, Bransford, Franks, McCarrell, and Nitsch (1974) showed that different properties of a word like *piano* were more or less effective in cueing recall depending on whether *piano* had been read in the context of playing a piano (*piano as a musical instrument*) or lifting a piano (*piano as a heavy wooden object*). The important question is how such "semantic flexibility" comes about; does the prior context guide the access process such that only relevant properties are activated, or are all default properties automatically activated, followed rapidly by a process of selection? Both of these positions have been argued in the literature with some experimental support for both views; for example, Whitney, McKay, Kellas, and Emerson (1985) argued in favour of the automatic context-independent view on the basis of a priming experiment in which target words were facilitated whether they were related to a contextually relevant or irrelevant semantic property of the prime in different sentences. In contrast, Tabossi (1988) found priming only for relevant semantic features in a similar paradigm, but with better controlled and more strongly constraining sentence contexts. An alternative account is that in certain kinds of semantic contexts, the level of access is "deeper" with more properties being activated than in other contexts, although not necessarily limited to relevant properties only (Moss & Marslen-Wilson, 1993). Thus, the debate about the processes by which context modulates the meanings of words continues. However, the consideration of the representation and processing of words in isolation provides an essential framework against which to study these contextual effects.

ACKNOWLEDGEMENTS

This research was supported by a British Academy Postdoctoral Research Fellowship to Helen Moss and a programme grant from the Medical Research Council of Great Britain to William Marslen-Wilson and Lorraine K. Tyler.

REFERENCES

Andruski, J.E., Blumstein, S.E., & Burton, M. (1994). The effects of subphonetic differences on lexical access. *Cognition, 52,* 163–187.

Atran, S. (1989). Basic conceptual domains. *Mind and Language, 4,* 7–16.

Balota, D.A., Ferraro, F.R., & Connor, L.T. (1991). On the early influence of meaning in word recognition: A review of the literature. In P.J. Schwanenflugel (Ed.), *The psychology of word meanings* (pp. 187–222). Hillsdale, NJ: Lawrence Erlbaum Associates Inc.

Barclay, J., Bransford, J., Franks, J., McCarrell, N. & Nitsch, K. (1974). Comprehension and semantic flexibility. *Journal of Verbal Learning and Verbal Behavior, 13,* 471–481.

Bard, E.G., Shillcock, R.C., & Altmann, G.T.M. (1988). The recognition of words after their acoustic offsets in spontaneous speech: Effects of subsequent context. *Perception and Psychophysics, 44,* 395–408.

Barsalou, L.W. (1982). Context-independent and context-dependent information in concepts. *Memory and Cognition, 10,* 82–93.

Barsalou, L.W. (1993). Flexibility, structure and linguistic vagary in concepts: Manifestations of a compositional system of perceptual symbols. In A.C. Collins, S.E. Gathercole, M.A. Conway, & P.E.M. Morris (Eds.), *Theories of memory* (pp. 29–102). Hove, UK: Lawrence Erlbaum Associates Inc.

Bleasedale, F.A. (1987). Concreteness-dependent associative priming: Separate lexical organization for concrete and abstract words. *Journal of Experimental Psychology: Learning, Memory, and Cognition, 13,* 582–594.

Borowsky, R., & Masson, M.E.J. (1996). Semantic ambiguity effects in word identification. *Journal of Experimental Psychology: Learning, Memory, and Cognition, 22,* 63–85.

Brown, C., & Hagoort, P. (1993). The processing nature of the N400: Evidence from masked priming. *Journal of Cognitive Neuroscience, 5,* 34–44.

Chiarello, C., Burgess, C., Richard, L. & Pollack, A. (1990). Semantic and associative priming in the cerebral hemispheres: Some words do, some words don't ... sometimes, some places. *Brain and Language, 38,* 75–104.

Clark, A. (1993). *Associative engines: Connectionism, context and representational change.* Cambridge, MA: MIT Press.

Collins, A.M., & Loftus, E.F. (1975). A spreading activation theory of semantic processing. *Psychological Review, 82,* 407–428.

Colombo, L., & Williams, J.N. (1990). Effects of word- and sentence-level context on word recognition. *Memory and Cognition, 18,* 153–163.

Connine, C.M., Blasko, D.G., & Titone, D. (1993). Do the beginnings of spoken words have a special status in auditory word recognition? *Journal of Memory and Language, 32,* 193–210.

Crowder, R.G., & Morton, J. (1969). Precategorical acoustic storage (PAS). *Perception and Psychophysics, 5,* 365–373.

Cutler, A., & Norris, D. (1988). The role of strong syllables in segmentation for lexical access. *Journal of Experimental Psychology: Human Perception and Performance, 14,* 113–121.

De Groot, A.M.B. (1989). Representational aspects of word imageability and word frequency as assessed through word associations. *Journal of Experimental Psychology: Learning, Memory, and Cognition, 15,* 824–845.

Elman, J.L. (1991). Distributed representations, simple recurrent networks, and grammatical structure. *Machine Learning, 7,* 195–225.

Fischler, I. (1977). Semantic facilitation without association in a lexical decision task. *Memory and Cognition, 5,* 335–339.

Flores d'Arcais, G.B., Schreuder, R., & Glazenborg, G. (1985). Semantic activation during recognition of referential words. *Psychological Research, 47,* 39–49.

Forster, K.I. (1976). Accessing the mental lexicon. In R.J. Wales & E. Walker (Eds.), *New approaches to language mechanisms* (pp. 257–287). Amsterdam: North Holland.

Garrod, S., & Sanford, A. (1981). Bridging inferences in the extended domain of reference. In J. Long & A. Baddeley (Eds.), *Attention and performance IX* (pp. 331–346). Hillsdale, NJ: Lawrence Erlbaum Associates Inc.

Gaskell, M.G., & Marslen-Wilson, W.D. (1997a). Discriminating local and distributed models of competition in spoken recognition. *Proceedings of the 19th Annual Conference of the Cognitive Society*. Mahwah, NJ: Lawrence Erlbaum Associates Inc.

Gaskell, M.G., & Marslen-Wilson, W.D. (1997b). *Integrating form and meaning: A distributed model of speech perception. Language and Cognitive Processes, 12*, 613–656.

Gernsbacher, M.A. (1984). Resolving 20 years of inconsistent interactions between lexical familiarity and orthography, concreteness and polysemy. *Journal of Experimental Psychology: General, 113*, 256–280.

Gerrig, R. (1986). Process and products of lexical access. *Language and Cognitive Processes, 1*, 539–557.

Greenspan, S.L. (1986). Semantic flexibility and referential specificity of concrete nouns. *Journal of Memory and Language, 25*, 539–551.

Hebb, D.O. (1949). *The organization of behavior*. New York: John Wiley & Sons.

Hines, D., Czerwinksi, M., Sawyer, P.K., & Dwyer, M. (1986). Automatic semantic priming: Effect of category exemplar level and word association level. *Journal of Experimental Psychology: Human Perception and Performance, 12*, 370–379.

Hinton, G.E., McClelland, J.L., & Rumelhart, D.E. (1986). Distributed representations. In J.L. McClelland & D.E. Rumelhart (Eds.), *Parallel distributed processing: Explorations in the microstructure of cognition* (Vol. 2, pp. 77–109). Cambridge, MA: MIT Press.

Hodgson, J. (1991). Informational constraints on pre-lexical priming. *Language and Cognitive Processes, 6*, 169–205.

Holcomb, P.J., & Anderson, J.E. (1993). Cross-modal semantic priming: A time-course analysis using event-related brain potentials. *Language and Cognitive Processes, 8*, 379–411.

Holcomb, P.J., & Neville, H.J. (1990). Auditory and visual semantic priming in lexical decision: A comparison using event-related potentials. *Language and Cognitive Processes, 5*, 281–312.

Holley-Wilcox, P., & Blank, M.A. (1980). Evidence for multiple access in the processing of isolated words. *Journal of Experimental Psychology: Human Perception and Performance, 6*, 75–84.

Jackendoff, R. (1983). *Semantics and cognition*. Cambridge, MA: MIT Press.

James, C.T. (1975). The role of semantic information in lexical decisions. *Journal of Experimental Psychology: Human Perception and Performance, 1*, 130–136.

Jones, G.V. (1985). Deep dyslexia, imageability and the ease of predication. *Brain and Language, 24*, 1–19.

Joordens, S., & Besner, D. (1994). When banking on meaning is not (yet) money in the bank: Explorations in connectionist modelling. *Journal of Experimental Psychology: Learning, Memory, and Cognition, 20*, 1051–1062.

Katz, J.J. (1972). *Semantic theory*. New York: Harper & Row.

Kawamoto, A.H. (1993). Nonlinear dynamics in the resolution of lexical ambiguity: A parallel distributed processing account. *Journal of Memory and Language, 32*, 474–516.

Kawamoto, A.H., Farrar, W.T., & Kello, C. (1994). When two meanings are better than one: Modeling the ambiguity advantage using a recurrent distributed network. *Journal of Experimental Psychology: Human Perception and Performance, 20*, 1233–1247.

Keil, F.C. (1986). The acquisition of natural kind and artifact terms. In W. Domopoulos & A. Marras (Eds.), *Language learning and concept acquisition* (pp. 133–153). Norwood, NJ: Ablex.

Kellas, G., Ferraro, F.R., & Simpson, G.B. (1988). Lexical ambiguity and the time course of attentional allocation in word recognition. *Journal of Experimental Psychology: Human Perception & Performance, 14*, 601–609.

Koriat, A. (1981). Semantic facilitation in lexical decision as a function of prime-target association. *Memory & Cognition, 9*, 587–598.

Locke, J. (1981). *An essay concerning human understanding*. Glasgow, UK: William Collins Sons & Co. (Original work published 1690).

Luce, P.A., Pisoni, D.B., & Goldinger, S.D. (1990). Similarity neighborhoods of spoken words. In G.T.M. Altmann (Ed.), *Cognitive models of speech processing* (pp. 122–147). Cambridge, MA: MIT Press.

Lupker, S.J. (1984). Semantic priming without association: A second look. *Journal of Verbal Learning and Verbal Behavior, 23*, 709–733.

Lyons, J. (1977). *Semantics*. London/New York: Cambridge University Press.

Marslen-Wilson, W.D. (1987). Functional parallelism in spoken word recognition. *Cognition, 25*, 71–102.

Marslen-Wilson, W.D. (1990). Activation, competition, and frequency in lexical access. In G.T.M. Altmann (Ed.), *Cognitive models of speech processing: Psycholinguistic and computational perspectives* (pp. 148–172). Cambridge, MA: MIT Press.

Marslen-Wilson, W.D., Moss, H.E. & van Halen, S. (1996). Perceptual distance and competition in lexical access. *Journal of Experimental Psychology: Human Perception and Performance, 22*, 1376–1392.

Marslen-Wilson, W.D., & Tyler, L.K. (1980). The temporal structure of spoken language comprehension. *Cognition, 6*, 1–71.

Marslen-Wilson, W., Tyler, L. K., Waksler, R., & Older, L. (1994). Morphology and meaning in the English mental lexicon. *Psychological Review, 101*, 3–33.

Marslen-Wilson, W.D., & Welsh, A. (1978). Processing interactions and lexical access during word recognition in continuous speech. *Cognitive Psychology, 10*, 29–63.

Masson, M.E.J. (1995). A distributed memory model of semantic priming. *Journal of Experimental Psychology: Learning, Memory, and Cognition, 21*, 3–23.

McClelland, J.L., & Elman, J.L. (1986). The TRACE model of speech perception. *Cognitive Psychology, 18*, 1–86.

McNamara, T.P., & Miller, D.L. (1989). Attributes of theories of meaning. *Psychological Bulletin, 106*, 335–376.

McNamara, T.P., & Sternberg, R.J. (1983). Mental models of word meaning. *Journal of Verbal Learning and Verbal Behavior, 22*, 449–474.

McQueen, J.M., Norris, D., & Cutler, A. (1994). Competition in spoken word recognition—spotting words in other words. *Journal of Experimental Psychology: Learning, Memory, and Cognition, 20*, 621–638.

Meyer, D.E., & Schvaneveldt, R.W. (1971). Facilitation in recognizing pairs of words: Evidence of a dependence between retrieval operations. *Journal of Experimental Psychology, 90*, 227–235.

Milberg, W., Blumstein, S., & Dworetzky, B. (1987). Phonological factors in lexical access: Evidence from an auditory lexical decision task. *Bulletin of the Psychonomic Society, 26*, 305–308.

Morton, J. (1969). Interaction of information in word recognition. *Psychological Review, 76*, 165–178.

Moss, H.E., Hare, M.L., Day, P., & Tyler, L.K. (1994). A distributed memory model of the associative boost in semantic priming. *Connection Science, 6*, 413–427.

Moss, H.E., & Marslen-Wilson, W.D. (1993). Access to word meanings during spoken language comprehension: Effects of sentential semantic context. *Journal of Experimental Psychology: Learning, Memory, and Cognition, 19*, 1254–1276.

Moss, H.E., McCormick, S. & Tyler, L.K. (1997). The time course of activation of semantic information during spoken word recognition. *Language and Cognitive Processes*, *12*, 695–731.

Moss, H.E., & Older, L. (1996). *Birkbeck word association norms*. Hove, UK: Lawrence Erlbaum Associates Inc.

Moss, H.E., Ostrin, R.K., Tyler, L.K. & Marslen-Wilson, W.D. (1995a). Accessing different types of lexical semantic information: Evidence from priming. *Journal of Experimental Psychology: Learning, Memory, and Cognition*, *21*, 1–21.

Moss, H.E., & Tyler, L.K. (1995). Investigating semantic memory impairments: The contribution of semantic priming. *Memory*, *3*, 359–395.

Moss, H.E., Tyler, L.K., Durrant-Peatfield, M., & Bunn, E.M. (1998). 'Two eyes of a see-through': Impaired and intact semantic knowledge in a case of selective deficit for living things. *Neurocase*, *4*, 291–310.

Moss, H.E., Tyler, L.K., Hodges, J., & Patterson, K. (1995b). Exploring the loss of semantic memory in semantic dementia: Evidence from a primed monitoring study. *Neuropsychology*, *9*, 16–26.

Murphy, G.L. (1991). Meaning and concepts. In P.J. Schwanenflugel (Ed.), *The psychology of word meanings* (pp. 11–35). Hillsdale, NJ: Lawrence Erlbaum Associates Inc.

Neely, J.H. (1991). Semantic priming effects in visual word recognition: A selective review of current findings and theories. In D. Besner & G. Humphreys (Eds.), *Basic processes in reading: Visual word recognition* (pp. 264–336). Hillsdale, NJ: Lawrence Erlbaum Associates Inc.

Neely, J.H., Keefe, D.E., & Ross, K.L. (1989). Semantic priming in the lexical decision task: Roles of prospective prime-generated expectancies and retrospective semantic matching. *Journal of Experimental Psychology: Learning, Memory, and Cognition*, *15*, 1003–1019.

Nelson, K. (1974). Concept, word and sentence: Interrelations in acquisition and development. *Psychological Review*, *81*, 267–285.

Norris, D. (1994). Shortlist: A connectionist model of continuous speech recognition. *Cognition*, *52*, 189–234.

Paivio, A.U. (1986). *Mental representations: A dual coding approach*. New York: Oxford University Press.

Plaut, D.C. (1995). Semantic and associative priming in a distributed attractor network. In J.D. Moore & J.F. Lehman (Eds.), *Proceedings of the 17th Annual Conference of the Cognitive Science Society* (pp. 37–42). Hillsdale, NJ: Lawrence Erlbaum Associates Inc.

Plaut, D.C., & Shallice, T. (1993). Deep dyslexia: A case study of connectionist neuropsychology. *Cognitive Neuropsychology*, *10*, 377–500.

Repp, B.H. (1978). Perceptual integration and differentiation of spectral cues for intervocalic stop consonants. *Perception and Psychophysics*, *24*, 471–485.

Rueckl, J.G. (1995). Ambiguity and connectionist networks: Still settling into a solution—comment on Joordens and Besner (1994). *Journal of Experimental Psychology: Learning, Memory, and Cognition*, *21*, 501–508.

Saffran, E.J., & Schwartz, M.F. (1994). Of cabbages and things: Semantic memory from a neuropsychological point of view: A tutorial review. In C. Umilta and M. Moscovitch (Eds.), *Attention & Performance XV* (pp. 507–536). Cambridge, MA: MIT Press.

Schank, R.C., & Abelson, R.P. (1977). *Scripts, plans, goals and understanding*. Hillsdale, NJ: Lawrence Erlbaum Associates Inc.

Schreuder, R., Flores d'Arcais, G.B., & Glazenborg, G. (1984). Perceptual and conceptual similarity effects in semantic priming. *Psychological Research*, *45*, 339–354.

Shelton, J.R., & Martin, R.C. (1992). How automatic is automatic semantic priming? *Journal of Experimental Psychology: Learning, Memory & Cognition*, *18*, 1191–1210.

Shillcock, R.C. (1990). Lexical hypotheses in continuous speech. In G.T.M. Altmann (Ed.), *Cognitive models of speech processing*. Cambridge, MA: MIT Press.

Simpson, G.B. (1984). Lexical ambiguity and its role in models of word recognition. *Psychological Bulletin, 96*, 316–340.

Simpson, G.B., & Burgess, C. (1985). Activation and selection processes in the recognition of ambiguous words. *Journal of Experimental Psychology: Human Perception and Performance, 11*, 28–39.

Simpson, G.B., & Krueger, M.A. (1991). Selective access of homograph meanings in sentence context. *Journal of Memory & Language, 30*, 627–643.

Smith, E.E., & Medin, D.L. (1981). *Categories and concepts*. Cambridge, MA: Harvard University Press.

Spence, D.P., & Owens, K.C. (1990). Lexical co-occurrence and association strength. *Journal of Psycholinguistic Research, 19*, 317–330.

Strain, E., Patterson, K. & Seidenberg, M.S. (1995). Semantic effects in single-word naming. *Journal of Experimental Psychology: Learning, Memory, and Cognition, 21*, 1140–1154.

Swinney, D.A. (1979). Lexical access during sentence comprehension. *Journal of Verbal Learning and Verbal Behavior, 18*, 645–659.

Tabossi, P. (1988). Effects of context on the immediate interpretation of unambiguous nouns. *Journal of Experimental Psychology: Learning, Memory, and Cognition, 14*, 153–162.

Tabossi, P., Colombo, L., & Job, R. (1987). Accessing lexical ambiguity: Effects of context and dominance. *Psychological Research, 49*, 161–167.

Tanenhaus, M.K., & Lucas, M.M. (1987). Context effect in lexical processing. *Cognition, 25*, 213–239.

Tyler, L.K. (1992). *Spoken language comprehension: An experimental approach to normal and disordered processing*. Cambridge, MA: MIT Press.

Tyler, L.K., & Moss, H.E. (1997). Functional properties of concepts: Studies of normal and brain-damaged patients. *Cognitive Neuropsychology, 14*, 426–486.

Tyler, L.K., Voice, J.K., & Moss, H.E. (1996). The interaction of semantic and phonological processing. In G.W. Cottrell (Ed.), *Proceedings of the Cognitive Science Society* (pp. 219–222). University of California, San Diego.

Tyler, L.K., & Wessels, J. (1984). Quantifying contextual contributions to word-recognition processes. *Perception and Psychophysics, 34*, 409–420.

Warren, P., & Marslen-Wilson, W.D. (1987). Continuous uptake of acoustic cues in spoken word-recognition. *Perception and Psychophysics, 41*, 262–275.

Warrington, E.K., & Shallice, T. (1984). Category-specific semantic impairment. *Brain, 107*, 829–853.

Williams, J. (1988). Constraints upon semantic activation during sentence comprehension. *Language & Cognitive Processes, 3*, 165–206.

Whitney, P., McKay, T., Kellas, G., & Emerson, W. (1985). Semantic activation of noun concepts in context. *Journal of Experimental Psychology: Learning, Memory, and Cognition, 11*, 126–135.

Zwitserlood, P. (1989). The locus of the effects of sentential-semantic context in spoken-word processing. *Cognition, 32*, 25–64.

Zwitserlood, P., & Schriefers, H. (1995). Effects of sensory information and processing time in spoken-word recognition. *Language and Cognitive Processes, 10*, 121–136.

CHAPTER FOUR

Abstractness and combination: The morphemic lexicon

William Marslen-Wilson
MRC Cognition and Brain Sciences Unit, Cambridge, UK

Modern psycholinguistics, like modern linguistics, has been deeply influenced by the fact that English is its mother tongue. The properties of English have set the research agenda for the discipline, influencing not only the kinds of question we ask, but also the kinds of answer we expect to find. This is clear to see in conventional views of the "mental lexicon"; of the way cognitive systems represent the words of a language. The framework here has not only been English, but the classic print dictionary of English, organised in word-based units, with the entries accessed either by their spelling or by their citation phonetic form.

I will argue in this chapter that this model is incorrect and misleading in almost every respect; that it fails not only as a general model for the world's languages, but even as a model for English itself. I will conduct this argument on three fronts, examining first the issue of units of representation at the lexical level, second, the issue of abstractness in lexical representation; and, third, issues in the architecture of the system.

UNITS OF REPRESENTATION: WORDS AND MORPHEMES

The design and organisation of a dictionary can be viewed as an exercise in applied folk psychology. The dictionary designer, or lexicographer, has to find a way of organising the language so that sound/meaning relations can be displayed in a way that makes them easily accessible to the ordinary user. One of the crucial decisions that has to be made concerns the primary unit of representation: Is it the word or the morpheme? In English, the word is generally defined as the graphical word; the element customarily written with a space on either side of it (cf. Grosjean & Gee, 1987). However, the word so defined may be made up of a number of smaller elements, known as *morphemes*, where the morpheme is the smallest meaning-bearing element in the language. Thus, the word *happy* is morphologically simple, being made up of the single morpheme {happy}.[1] Words like *happiness* or *unhappily*, in contrast, are morphologically complex, being analysable into two or more individual morphemes, as in {happy} + {-ness} and {un-} + {happy} + {-ly}, where *-ness*, *-ly*, and *un-* are derivational morphemes in English.

For English dictionaries, the choice has always been clear. The primary organisational unit is the word, where the dictionary word corresponds to the graphical word. The question we have to ask for the mental lexicon is whether this is the right kind of account of how the lexical knowledge of a language should be stored and accessed. Is the internal world of lexical representation just a mirror of the external world of apparently discrete and separable word forms? Are lexical representations indeed word based, or are they organised along morphological lines, so that the morpheme rather than the phonetic word is the primary unit of representation?

To answer these questions, it is necessary to study the representation and access of morphologically complex words, made up of two or more constituent morphemes. These allow us to dissociate word- and morpheme-based theories of representation, as well as their associated theories of lexical access. In particular, are morphologically complex words represented as unanalysed full forms, or does the representation reflect their morphological structure? In the psychological literature, these two possibilities correspond to *full-listing* and *morphemic* (or *decompositional*) approaches to lexical representation. Both views are well represented in the literature, but the evidence for them has been conflicting and inconclusive.

Full listing of polymorphemic words has been argued by, among others, Bradley (1980), Butterworth (1983), Fowler, Napps, and Feldman (1985), Kempley and Morton (1982), and Lukatela, Gligorijevic, Kostic, and Turvey (1980), whereas morpheme-based theories of representation have been proposed, for example, by Jarvella and Meijers (1983), MacKay (1978), Taft (1981) and Taft & Forster (1975). Going along with these conflicting proposals about representation are equally conflicting proposals

[1] Curly brackets are used here to indicate reference to a morphemic element.

about access. On a morphemic view, affixes are stripped away from base forms (Kempley & Morton, 1982; Taft, 1981), and the base form is used to access the lexicon. On a full-listing account, morphologically complex words are not decomposed into their constituent morphemes prior to access (Henderson, Wallis, & Knight, 1984; Manelis & Tharp, 1977; Rubin, Becker, & Freeman, 1979). Intermediate between these two camps are the mixed models, claiming that complex words can be represented—at least for the purposes of lexical access—both as full forms and in terms of their constituent morphemes (e.g. Caramazza, Laudanna, & Romani, 1988; Frauenfelder & Schreuder, 1992; Schreuder & Baayen, 1995).

A strong full-listing account is certainly not universally tenable. Hankamer (1989), for example, points out that such an account for languages like Turkish would place not only utterly impractical demands on learning but even on storage, with the language allowing hundreds of millions of possible complex forms. More recent research allows us to make the case that such an account is also wrong for English, with clear evidence for decompositional representation of morphologically complex words, and, more generally, for a dynamic view of the lexicon as based on the combinatorial manipulation of underlying morphemic, rather than lexical, elements.

Combination and decomposition

This argument is based on a series of priming experiments, where we have used an immediate cross-modal repetition priming task to probe the structure and properties of lexical representations (e.g. Marslen-Wilson, Tyler, Waksler, & Older, 1994). In this task, the listener hears an auditory prime word (for example, *happiness*), which is immediately followed by a visual prime word (for example, *happy*), to which the subject must make a lexical decision response ("Is this a word or not?"). The reason for using a cross-modal task, with prime and target being presented in different sensory modalities, is that this forces the processing interaction between prime and target to take place at a supra-modal level of the system. We locate this at the level of the *lexical entry*, the central abstract representation of a word's semantic, syntactic, and morphological properties. This is the aspect of the system we are primarily interested in here, and the fortunate property of a cross-modal immediate repetition task is that priming in this task, whether facilitatory or inhibitory, seems to depend on repeated access to the same underlying lexical representations, and is relatively unaffected by low-level overlap in the phonological properties of primes and targets (cf. Marslen-Wilson et al., 1994).

A first set of experiments looked at English derivational morphology, both suffixes and prefixes, and asked whether words like *happiness* did indeed prime their stems, and under what conditions (Marslen-Wilson et al., 1994). The general answer is very clear. We reliably get priming between derived words and their stems—between *happiness* and *happy*, or between *rebuild* and *build*—but only for cases where the relationship between the pairs is semantically transparent. Pairs like *apartment/apart* or *release/lease*, which historically are just as morphologically related as pairs like *government/govern*, do not prime at all (see Fig. 4.1). In fact, pairs like this prime no better than pairs like *bulletin/bullet* or *tinsel/tin*, where the relationship between prime and target is purely phonological.

We attribute this effect not to semantic priming between primes and targets but to the implicit structural decisions that the listener makes during language acquisition. A word like *apartment*, for example, cannot be stored as {apart} + {-ment} because this would give the wrong meaning. An apartment is a kind of living place, not the abstract noun

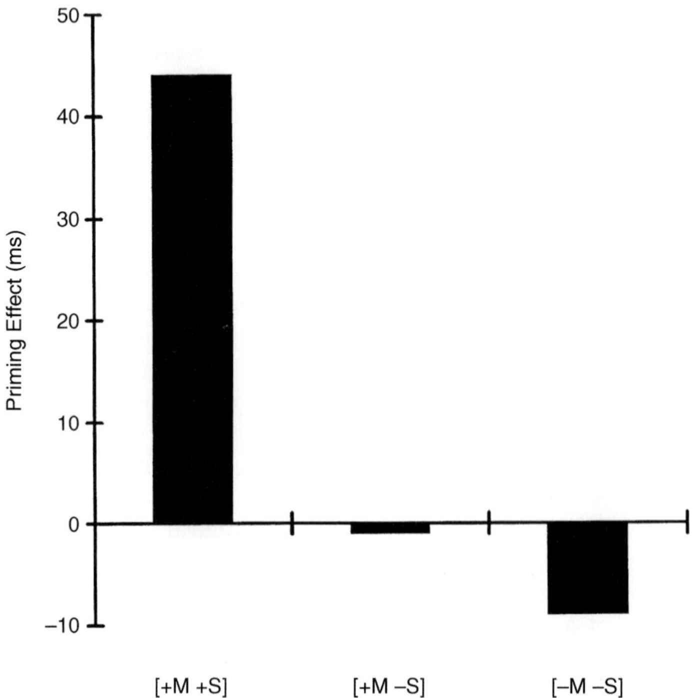

FIG. 4.1 Derivational morphology: Cross-modal priming between (i) morphologically and semantically related [+M +S] pairs, such as *happiness/happy*, (ii) morphologically but not semantically related [+M -S] pairs, such as *apartment/apart*, and (iii) unrelated [-M -S] pairs such as *bulletin/bullet*.

meaning the state of being apart. On the other hand, a transparent form like *happiness* or *decidable* can be stored in decomposed form, as {decide} + {-able} or {happy} + {-ness}, because the primary meanings of these forms are still compositional, the product of the combination of the meaning of the stem with the meaning of the affix.

We capture this, in a metaphorical representation of the functional relations between morphemes, in the kind of *stem + affix* format displayed in Fig. 4.2. This is intended to reflect, while making no commitments to the nature of the underlying computational realisation of these arrangements, the finding that the same morpheme—for example {happy}—can function both as a lexical item on its own, as the word *happy*, and as part of the underlying representation of the complex words *happiness*, *happily*, *unhappy*, and so on. It also implies that the meanings of these complex forms are not directly stored in the lexical system; they need to be computed, on the fly, when the word is heard or seen.

Semantic priming?

To establish this kind of claim we need to rule out a number of other possibilities, the most salient of which is that the reason we observe priming between semantically transparent forms but not between semantically opaque forms is because this simply *is* semantic priming, with no morphological component. On this account, *happiness* primes *happy* in the same way and for the same reasons as *cello* primes *violin* or *lion* primes *tiger*. In each case we have separate lexical representations, but because of shared semantic features these representations can prime each other through spread of activation, in the classical mould of semantic priming effects.

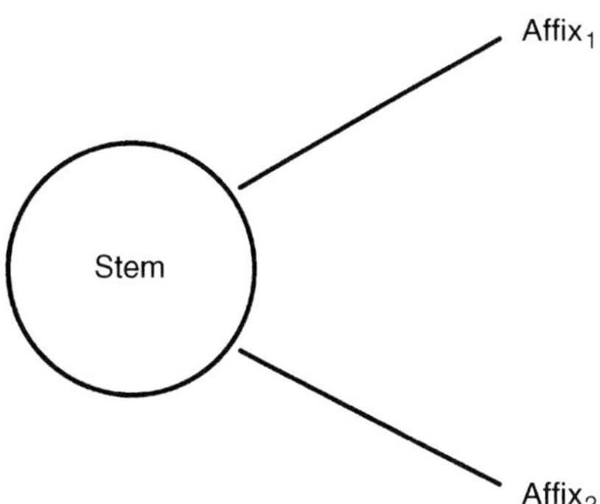

FIG. 4.2 Schematic view of morphologically decomposed lexical representation, with the same stem participating in different complex forms.

The general problem with an account along these lines is that it leads to implausible claims about lexical organisation. It requires not only that *happiness* and all its morphological relatives (*happily*, *unhappy*, *unhappily*, etc.) are separately represented from *happy* as individual word-forms, but also that each form has its own copy of the semantic and syntactic properties of the stem in question. These are cumbersome and uneconomical assumptions about representation, they fail to capture the fact that some words are morphologically as well as semantically related, and they provide no account of the ways in which morphological and semantic priming differ in their properties. We believe it is much more straightforward to assume that pairs like *happiness* and *happy* show priming because they are both linked to the same underlying morpheme in the lexical entry.

Furthermore, an increasing amount of evidence is now accumulating, which shows not only that morphological effects are separable from semantic effects, but also that the specific effects in our experiments are indeed morphologically and not semantically based. One type of evidence, which I discuss in more detail later, is the demonstration of reliable cross-modal priming between derivational affixes (Marslen-Wilson, Ford, Older, & Zhou, 1996). Affixes like {-ness} and {de-} do not have clearly definable semantic identities. They are fundamentally morphological entities, functioning in productive linguistic processes of word formation, and it is hard to see how priming between them can be accounted for in anything other than morphological terms.

The second type of evidence is the finding that semantic relatedness between morphologically related prime/target pairs does not by itself guarantee priming. As we report in Marslen-Wilson et al. (1994), suffixed pairs sharing the same stem, as in *excitement/excitable*, do not prime each other reliably, despite the fact that the two words are highly semantically related. We attribute this to competition between suffixes attached underlyingly to the same stem. On a full-listing, semantically based account, there should be no reason for them not to prime. A comparable dissociation has been obtained for English inflectional morphology, where, as I discuss below, pairs like *gave/give* or *built/build*, with irregular past tense forms as primes and their stems as targets, fail to show reliable priming (Marslen-Wilson, Hare, & Older, 1993; Marslen-Wilson, Hare, Older, & Ford, 1995), whereas regular past tenses and their stems, as in *jumped/jump*, prime very effectively. All these pairs are strongly semantically related, and should prime equally well on a semantic interpretation of morphological priming.

A final type of evidence is that semantic and morphological priming have markedly different time-courses, with semantic priming being more short-lived (e.g. Henderson et al., 1984). We have recently confirmed this in auditory–auditory delayed repetition priming experiments (Marslen-Wilson & Zhou, 1993, 1996). At short delays (one intervening item), priming is equally strong for morphologically related (*excitement/excite*) and semantically related (*cello/violin*) items, at 39 and 31 ms respectively. At longer delays (eight intervening items), morphological priming is undiminished (at 30 ms) but semantic priming has disappeared (at 1 ms). This clearly points to different representational substrates for the two types of priming.

Inflectional decomposition

The evidence for morphological decomposition extends very readily to English inflectional morphology, where there is anyway a generally greater acceptance that inflected forms are not stored as full forms—that, for example, the mental lexicon does not contain separate listings of *jumps*, *jumped*, *jumping*, and *jump*, each with its own copy of the semantics and syntax of the verb *jump*. Apart from a few linguistically driven claims (e.g. Segui & Zubizarreta, 1985), it is generally assumed that only the stem needs to be stored. In our own experiments, which have exhaustively explored the properties of English inflectional morphology, we have found plenty of evidence for decomposition in representation. As Fig. 4.3 shows, there is strong priming between regular inflected forms and their stems.

What Fig. 4.3 also shows, however, is that there are conditions under which inflected forms do not prime effectively. This is when the stem is preceded by an irregular past tense form, as in pairs like *crept/creep*, *gave/give*, *sent/send*, and so on. But this too is also consistent with a decompositional, combinatorial approach. The consistent property of English irregular past tense forms is that they are unpredictable, idiosyncratic, and not decomposable. A form like *taught* has to be learnt as a complete form; there is no plausible way of computing it from the regular combination of the stem *teach* with some phonological expression of the past tense operator. If, for regular inflectional and derivational complex forms, priming reflects repeated access to the same underlying morphemic representation (of the stem), the reduction in priming for the irregular forms may well reflect the disruption of these links by the unpredictability of the representations involved.

Affixes as processing structures

A final line of evidence for a dynamic, combinatorial view of lexical representation comes from some more recent work (Marslen-Wilson et al., 1996) focusing on the processing properties of *affixes*. This type of combinatorial approach assigns a crucial role not just to stem morphemes

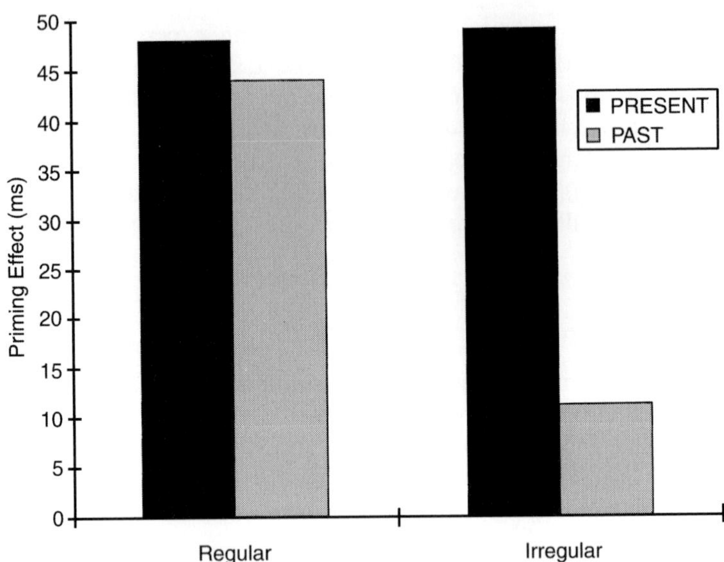

FIG. 4.3 Inflectional morphology: Cross-modal priming between regular and irregular verb-forms and their stems. Regular stems (e.g. *jump*) are preceded by regular present (*jumps*) and past tense (*jumped*) forms. Irregular stems (e.g. *give*) are preceded by regular present (*gives*) and irregular past tense (*gave*) forms.

but also to affixes; the derivational suffixes and prefixes which combine with stems to form new words, often with very different syntactic and semantic properties. These are powerful operations, and any morphologically based theory of lexical representation will have to accommodate them. But although linguistic accounts of morphology have had a lot to say about affixes, there has been very little experimental work on their mental representation. Psycholinguistic work, ours included, has been much more interested in the properties of stems. But until we understand more about affixes, and about how they fulfil their key role in lexical representation and processing, any theory of the mental lexicon will be incomplete; especially any theory arguing for a morphemically decomposed lexicon organised around combinatorial operations.

As a first step in this direction, we addressed the question of whether derivational affixes are independent entities in the lexical system. These are all *bound* morphemes. This means that they cannot, unlike free morphemes, stand alone as words in English. There are no words *ness* or *re*, corresponding to the *-ness* in *darkness* or the *re-* in *rebuild.* These are all morphemes that can only occur in conjunction with a stem. But does this also mean that they cannot stand alone as cognitive elements, represented separately from the stems to which they apply?

It follows from our decompositional approach to lexical representation that this should be the case; that affixes are independently represented as morphemic elements. On a combinatorial view, the *-ness* in *happiness* should be the same as the *-ness* in *darkness*; the *re-* in *refill* the same as the *re-* in *rebuild*, and so on. This predicts that we should be able to get priming between these forms. *Darkness* should prime *happiness*, in much the same way, and for the same reasons, as two forms sharing the same stem. Furthermore, any such effects should interact with *productivity*—whether an affix is still being used in ordinary speech to form new words. Productive affixes like *-ness* or *re-* are more likely to be independently represented—and therefore primable—than affixes like *en-* (as in *enslave*) or *-th* (as in *depth*) which are no longer productive in the language.

This is exactly what we found. As Fig. 4.4 shows, there is strong priming between productive affixes, averaging over 30 ms. This is just as strong as priming between stems in the same experiment, and much stronger than priming in the control condition, where an affixed prime such as *darkness* is followed by a pseudo-affixed target like *harness*, where the final syllable *ness* is not the morpheme {-ness). The unproductive affixes, in contrast, do not differ from their pseudo-suffixed control targets. The prime word *adjustment*, for example, using the unproductive suffix *-ment*, does not prime the target *government* significantly more than it primes the pseudo-suffixed target *garment*.

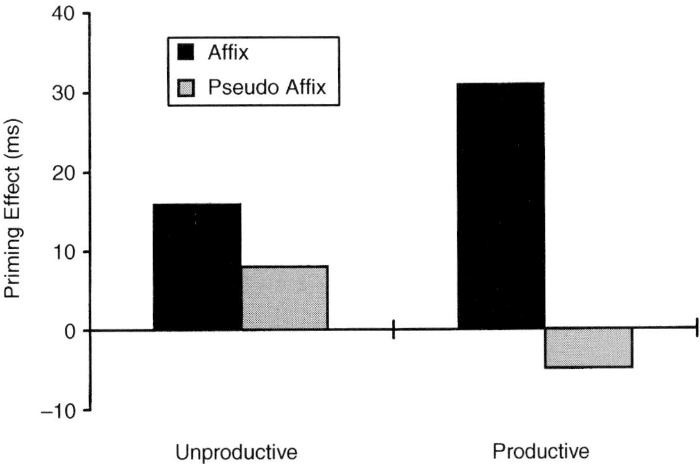

FIG. 4.4 Affix priming: Cross-modal priming between affixed primes (e.g. *darkness*) and affixed (*toughness*) and pseudo-affixed (*harness*) targets, broken down by the productivity of the affixes involved.

This is clear evidence that bound morphemes—in this case English derivational affixes—can be isolable and independent processing structures in the mental lexicon. We find priming across the board for prefixes and suffixes, under the same conditions and at the same level that we find priming between words sharing the same stem. It is hard to see how this can be explained except in terms of a combinatorial, morphemically decomposed view of the mental lexicon, where the representation and access of morphologically complex forms involves computational processes that combine stems and affixes, and where both partners in these computations—free and bound morphemes—have underlyingly equal status as processing agents.

The picture is strengthened by the effects of productivity. Affix productivity is a gradient phenomenon, but none the less priming is consistently stronger for productive affixes like *-ness*, *re-*, and *-able*. These are the affixes that are currently in productive use in forming new words in the language, and they could not perform this function, either for the speaker coining a new form or for the listener interpreting it, unless they had an independent cognitive status. As new words come into the language (like *microwaveable* and *downloadable* in the 1980s), their interpretability depends on the availability to the perceiver of the syntactic and semantic properties of the affix, and on the successful combination of these properties with those of the stem morpheme.

These are also results, as I have noted, that are hard to explain on any simple semantic story, which seeks to explain priming between morphologically related words as a form of semantic priming between listed full forms. The bound morphemes that prime here do not have clearly definable semantic identities. They are fundamentally morphological entities, functioning in productive combinatorial linguistic processes, and it is unlikely that priming relations between them can be accounted for in terms which do not take into account their role as part of a linguistic, morphological system.

ABSTRACTNESS IN LEXICAL REPRESENTATION

The second aspect of the dictionary metaphor is its implication not just that the unit of internal representation is the word, but also that these words are internally represented in much the same way as they appear on the surface, as fully specified phonetic objects. The representations of the forms of words in a print dictionary are representations of the word's surface form, whether orthographically or phonologically coded. These are, furthermore, representations of citation forms, of the word's standard form when it is produced in isolation.

If we move to a view of the mental lexicon where it is not a static list of surface words, but a more dynamic system, where the processing representations for complex forms are created as needed, rather than precompiled in fixed full-listing format, then we have to take a different view about the way the building blocks of these operations are represented at the level of the lexical entry. The issue here is not simply that complex forms cannot be assumed to be internally represented as full forms, but also how the phonological forms of the constituent morphemes themselves are represented.

Are we ultimately still dealing with entities like the entries in a print dictionary—strings of sounds or letters representing the surface form of a morpheme—or are we dealing with something much more abstract, and, indeed, much more dynamic? I will summarise here some of our recent claims for the *abstractness* of the mental representation of lexical form, and for the essentially constructed nature of these representations, which leads in turn to the more radical proposals in the final section of the chapter, where I review an approach to lexical architecture which questions the entire concept of stored representation of phonological form (Gaskell & Marslen-Wilson, 1995; Marslen-Wilson & Warren, 1994).

Abstractness and variation

The problem of abstractness in lexical representation is posed most directly by the phenomena of phonological and allomorphic *variation*. These are processes whereby the surface form of a word—the phonetic shape actually produced by a speaker—varies as a function of the phonological and morphological environment in which the word (or morpheme) finds itself. The word *hand*, for example, spoken as [hænd] in isolation (its citation form), may be produced as [hæm] in the context "Hand me the book", where the final [d] is deleted and the [n] assimilates in place to the following labial consonant. Alternatively, it may surface as [hæn] in the context "Hand Tony the book", where just the [d] deletes; as [handʒ] in the context "Did he hand you the book", where the final [d] is palatalised in the context of the final glide, and so on. These phonological processes of assimilation and deletion are extremely pervasive in natural speech, but do not seem to interfere with ordinary perceptual interpretation. Adult listeners appear not to notice these changes, nor does lexical access seem disrupted. The sequence [hæm], in the context "Hand me the book" is successfully interpreted as a token of *hand* and not of *ham*, despite clear phonetic evidence to the contrary.

How is the system organised to allow this, to prevent *hand* from being rejected and *ham* from being accepted? In particular, what implications does this have for the way lexical form is mentally represented? In earlier research, I argued for a primarily representational account where surface variations could map directly onto an *abstract* underlying lexical representation which was underspecified for the feature dimension that was varying (Lahiri & Marslen-Wilson, 1991; Marslen-Wilson, Nix, & Gaskell, 1995). Consider, for example, alternations such as "sweep boy" and "sweek girl", where underlying *sweet* is articulated either as [swip] or [swik], depending on whether it is followed by a labial or a velar consonant. We can resolve this by assuming that the word-final /t/ in *sweet* is unspecified for place of articulation, so that surface [k] or [p] do not create mismatch with the underlying specifications of the lexical form in question. This also means that no intermediate processing step is required, where surface [swik] maps onto an access representation of /swik/, which subsequently connects to the lexical entry for {sweet}.

In subsequent research (Marslen-Wilson et al., 1994) we proposed a similar kind of analysis to explain how listeners represent and perceive instances of *allomorphic* variation—that is, where phonological changes in the form of a stem are morphologically triggered. These are cases where the phonetic realisation of a stem morpheme, such as *sane* or *decide*, is changed when it is followed by certain derivational morphemes, as in forms like *sanity* or *decision*. In both cross-modal and intra-modal (auditory–auditory) repetition priming experiments we found that phonologically divergent prime/target pairs, such as *sanity/sane* or *decision/decide*, primed each other just as effectively as pairs like *happiness/happy*, where prime and target are phonologically much more similar (Marslen-Wilson et al., 1994; Marslen-Wilson & Zhou, 1996). To explain this we again proposed a representational account, where phonetically divergent surface forms of the same stem could map directly onto an abstract phonological representation at the level of the lexical entry.

On this account, the underlying representation of the morpheme {sane} would be something like /sÆn/, where the capitalised vowel symbol (Æ) denotes a vowel segment unspecified for the phonological feature of *tenseness* (Myers, 1987).[2] In the appropriate environment this abstract, underspecified vowel is realised as either [ey] or [æ], as in the surface forms [seyn] and [sæn't']. The crucial point, from the perceptual side, is that because the lexical representation is underspecified for this particular feature, both surface forms will match to it. Underlying [sÆn] will match equally well to surface [seyn] and to surface [sæn], but is not itself a representation of any specific surface form.

---

[2]The alternation here between pairs like [ey] and [æ] in pairs like *sane/sanity* or *vain/vanity* is typically characterised as a variation in the tense/lax feature.

Abstractness and inference

The representational hypothesis I have outlined so far seeks to explain the system's response to variation purely in terms of the presence or absence of specified information in abstract underlying representations. It turns out, however, that to explain fully the system's response to phonological variation we have to postulate additional machinery, able to relate featural cues and abstract representations to their broader prosodic context.

Evidence for this comes from a set of experiments in which we looked at the perception of assimilated words when they occur in sentence context (Gaskell & Marslen-Wilson, 1993, 1996). The subjects heard pairs of sentences which contained either an intact word or a potentially assimilated version of this word—as in *lean/leam*, *wicked/wickeb*, *clown/clowm*, etc.—where the assimilated form is always a non-word. These sentential contexts were constructed so that the assimilated form was either phonologically *viable* or *non-viable*, as in these examples:

(1a) We have a house full of fussy eaters. Sandra will only eat *lean/leam* bacon.
(1b) We have a house full of fussy eaters. Sandra will only eat *lean/leam* game.

In (1a) the non-word *leam* ([lim]) occurs in a phonologically viable context, since it is followed by the labial consonant [b], which provides the appropriate source for the assimilation (to [m]) of the place of articulation of the underlying /n/. This contrasts with (1b), where the right context is the velar consonant [g], which does not provide a potential source for the assimilation of /n/ to [m].

In the experiment, the target word *lean* is visually presented at the offset of the prime word (*lean* or *leam*) and the subjects are required to make a lexical decision response to the visual target. Priming effects are measured relative to responses to the same targets following an unrelated prime word (e.g. "Sandra will only eat *brown/browm* loaves"). If *leam* is being treated as a token of *lean*, then it should be equally effective as a prime.

The important result (Fig. 4.5) is that we see a strong contrast between the phonologically viable contexts (such as *leam bacon*) and phonologically unviable contexts (such as *leam game*). In the unviable condition, responses following the assimilated prime (*leam*) are 40 msec slower than responses to the identity prime (*lean*), indicating that the string [lim] is indeed not being treated as a token of the word *lean*. But in the viable condition, responses are equally fast to assimilated and identity primes, and both are faster than the relevant baseline conditions. This is

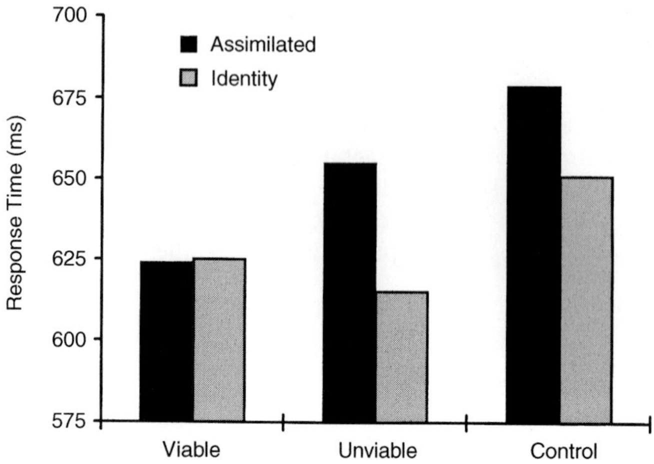

FIG. 4.5 Phonological regularity effects in lexical access: Cross-modal priming by assimilated and non-assimilated (identity) primes, for phonologically viable contexts (*lean/leam bacon*), phonologically unviable contexts (*lean/leam game*), and control contexts (*brown/browm loaves*).

consistent with our ordinary experience of speech, where variable forms are accepted and perceived without causing any apparent disruption of lexical access and perceptual experience.

But what this task also implies—as do comparable results using the quite different task of phoneme-monitoring (Gaskell & Marslen-Wilson, 1994)—is that this ordinary experience of speech is the product of dynamic, constructive processes. The phonological representation that we compute, as we hear the speech stream, is neither directly constructed from information in the speech signal, nor simply looked up in some stored citation form.

LEXICAL ARCHITECTURE AND COGNITIVE ARCHITECTURE

We need, finally, to consider how all this fits together in a processing system. What are the appropriate architectures here? Previous models have, almost without exception, approached lexical processing from the perspective of the dictionary metaphor, assuming a stable central store of lexical representations, with phonological (or orthographic) forms acting as the access code, and with the scientific problem of lexical access defined in terms of how these access procedures are conducted. This is the classical view, illustrated in Fig. 4.6 and I will focus on two of the core assumptions it embodies about the nature of the system.

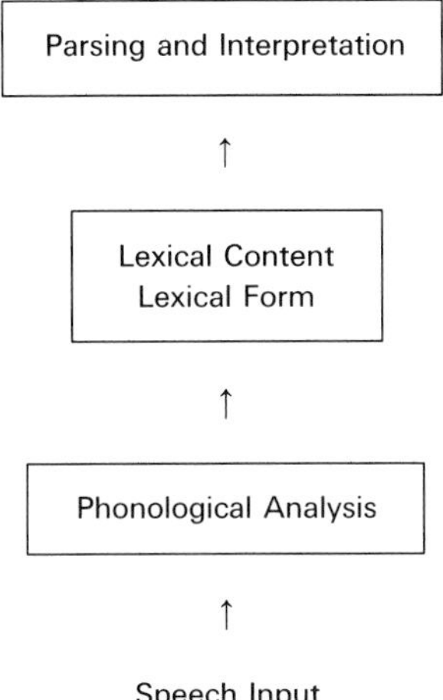

FIG. 4.6 The classical hierarchical model of lexical representation and lexical access.

The first is that there is a separate pre-lexical level of representation of the speech signal. This is the phonological input to the system, computed on the basis of the acoustic-phonetic information in the speech input. This level is computationally and perceptually independent, and it forms the basis not only for the subsequent processes of lexical access, but also for the listener's perceptual experience of speech.

The second major assumption is that successful access to meaning requires a prior successful solution to the problem of identifying the word's phonological form. This is the core of the dictionary metaphor: that the mental lexicon contains explicit stored representations of lexical form, and lexical access is the process of matching to these internal targets. It is this matching process which mediates the system's access to meaning.

These assumptions lead to the ubiquitous, and in many ways highly plausible view of lexical architecture summarised in Fig. 4.6. The point I want to make here is that there are alternative approaches to lexical (and indeed cognitive architecture) which lead to quite different views of how the system is organised, and which embody quite different basic assumptions.

The alternative I will focus on is a recently developed connectionist learning model (Gaskell & Marslen-Wilson, 1995, 1997), building on some architectural suggestions made by Marslen-Wilson & Warren (1994). This model assumes a distributed computational infrastructure, organised along the lines illustrated in Fig. 4.7. Featural inputs project,

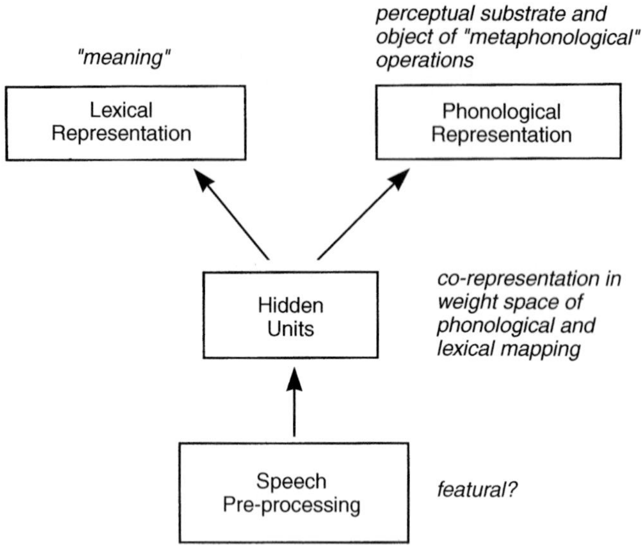

FIG. 4.7 The Distributed Cohort model (Gaskell & Marslen-Wilson, 1995).

via a hidden unit layer, onto two output layers, one reflecting the semantic representation and the other the phonological representation computed by the system as it responds to speech inputs.

The relevant feature of this model for the current discussion is that it allows us to depart from both of the key assumptions underpinning the dictionary metaphor. First of all, the listener's phonological representation of the speech input is assumed to be an *output* of the system, the perceptual end-point of processing rather than its starting point. There is no computationally and perceptually independent pre-lexical level of representation of the speech input. The phonological representation that is constructed is not itself part of the pathway to meaning, and its properties are not necessarily co-extensive with whatever acoustic-phonetic/phonological cues the system uses to map onto meaning/lexical representations.

This leads to the second main point about this architecture—that access to word meaning does not require prior access to word form. There are no stored phonological representations, functioning as a first-level perceptual target, which the system accesses in order to reach the semantic output layer. What the system has learnt is the mapping between preliminary, probably featural analyses of the speech input, and the representations of word meaning on the output. Phonological representations are indeed computed, but these are, again, an output of the system, and not part of the input sequence leading to meaning.

It is clear even from this brief sketch that a model of this type suggests a quite different perspective on how we should think about the mental representation of lexical form and lexical content. It offers a quite radical departure from the dictionary metaphor, especially where the relationship between phonological representation and meaning representation is concerned. It also offers a different approach to the problems of abstractness and variation—an appropriately trained network (e.g. Gaskell, Hare, & Marslen-Wilson, 1995) can simulate human responses to phonological variation, but without any need for intervening abstract representations of the classical type. More generally, like any distributed learning model, such an approach should deal very naturally with the variety of gradient and context-sensitive phenomena that are typical of language, and of the computation of phonological and semantic representations from the incoming speech signal.

The major challenge, and the major question-mark for this approach, remains its ability to deal with the combinatorial properties of language function, displayed for the lexical domain in the research we reviewed earlier in this chapter. Under the assumption that the computational infrastructure for human language processing is indeed distributed and subsymbolic, then how does a system of this type, exposed to the complex pattern of phonological and semantic regularities and irregularities in the language input, convert this into a form of internal representation with the morphological and combinatorial properties that seem to characterise human performance?

REFERENCES

Bradley, D. (1980). Lexical representation of derivational relation. In M. Aronoff & M.-L Kean (Eds.), *Juncture* (pp. 37–55). Saratoga, CA: Anma Libri.

Butterworth, B. (1983). Lexical representation. In B. Butterworth (Ed.), *Language production* (*Vol. 1*, pp. 257–294). London: Academic Press.

Caramazza, A., Laudanna, A., & Romani, C. (1988). Lexical access and inflectional morphology. *Cognition, 278*, 297–332.

Fowler, C.A., Napps, S.E., & Feldman, L. (1985). Relations among regular and irregular morphologically related words in the lexicon as revealed by repetition priming. *Memory and Cognition, 13*, 241–255.

Frauenfelder, U.H., & Schreuder, R. (1992). Constraining psycholinguistic models of morphological processing and representation: The role of productivity. In G.E. Booij & J.V. Marle (Eds.), *Yearbook of morphology 1991* (pp. 165–183). Dordrecht, The Netherlands: Kluwer Academic Publishers.

Gaskell, M.G., Hare, M., & Marslen-Wilson, W.D. (1995). A connectionist model of phonological representation in speech perception. *Cognitive Science, 19*, 407–439.

Gaskell, M.G., & Marslen-Wilson, W.D. (1993). Match and mismatch in phonological context. *Proceedings of the 15th annual meeting of the Cognitive Science Society*. Princeton, NJ: Lawrence Erlbaum Associates Inc.

Gaskell, M.G., & Marslen-Wilson, W.D. (1994, August). *Inference processes in speech perception*. Paper presented at the 16th annual conference of the Cognitive Science Society, University of Georgia, Atlanta, CA.

Gaskell, G., & Marslen-Wilson, W. (1995). Modeling the perception of spoken words. In J.D. Moore & J.F. Lehman (Eds.), *Proceedings of the 17th Annual Conference of the Cognitive Science Society* (pp. 19–24). Mahwah, NJ: Lawrence Erlbaum Associates Inc.

Gaskell, M.G., & Marslen-Wilson, W.D. (1996). Phonological variation and inference in lexical access. *Journal of Experimental Psychology: Human Perception and Performance*, *22*, 144–158.

Gaskell, M.G., & Marslen-Wilson, W.D. (1997). Discriminating form and meaning: A distributed model of speech perception. *Language and Cognitive Processes*, *12*, 613–656.

Grosjean, F., & Gee, J.P. (1987). Prosodic structure and spoken word recognition. In U.H. Frauenfelder & L.K. Tyler (Eds.), *Spoken word recognition* (pp. 135–155). Cambridge, MA: MIT Press.

Hankamer, J. (1989). Morphological parsing and the lexicon. In W.D. Marslen-Wilson (Ed.), *Lexical representation and process* (pp. 392–408). Cambridge, MA: MIT Press.

Henderson, L., Wallis, J., & Knight, K. (1984). Morphemic structure and lexical access. In H. Bouma & D. Bouwhuis (Eds.), *Attention and performance X: Control of language processes* (pp. 211–226). Hove, UK: Lawrence Erlbaum Associates Ltd.

Jarvella, R., & Meijers, G. (1983). Recognising morphemes in spoken words: Some evidence for a stem-organised mental lexicon. In G.B. Flores d'Arcais & R. Jarvella (Eds.), *The process of language understanding* (pp. 81–112). Chichester, UK: John Wiley & Sons.

Kempley, M., & Morton, J. (1982). The effects of priming with regularly and irregularly related words in auditory word recognition. *British Journal of Psychology*, *73*, 441–454.

Lahiri, A., & Marslen-Wilson, W.D. (1991). The mental representation of lexical form: A phonological approach to the recognition lexicon. *Cognition*, *38*, 243–294.

Lukatela, G., Gligorijevic, B., Kostic, A., & Turvey, M. (1980). Representation of inflected nouns in the internal lexicon. *Memory and Cognition*, *8*, 415–423.

MacKay, D. (1978). Derivational rules and the internal lexicon. *Journal of Verbal Learning and Verbal Behaviour*, *17*, 61–71.

Manelis, L., & Tharp, D. (1977). The processing of affixed words. *Memory and Cognition*, *5*, 690–695.

Marslen-Wilson, W.D., Ford, M., Older, L., & Zhou, X.-L. (1996). The combinatorial lexicon: Priming derivational affixes. *Proceedings of the 18th annual conference of the Cognitive Science Society*.

Marslen-Wilson, W.D., Hare, M., & Older, L. (1993). Inflectional morphology and phonological regularity in the English mental lexicon. *Proceedings of the 15th annual meeting of the Cognitive Science Society*. Princeton, NJ: Lawrence Erlbaum Associates Inc.

Marslen-Wilson, W.D., Hare, M., Older, L., & Ford, M. (1995, January). *Priming and blocking in English inflectional morphology*. Paper presented to the Experimental Psychology Society, London, UK.

Marslen-Wilson, W.D., Nix, A., & Gaskell, G. (1995). Phonological variation in lexical access: Abstractness, inference, and English place assimilation. *Language and Cognitive Processes*, *10*, 285–308.

Marslen-Wilson, W.D., Tyler, L.K., Waksler, R., & Older, L. (1994). Morphology and meaning in the English mental lexicon. *Psychological Review*, *101*, 3–33.

Marslen-Wilson, W.D., & Warren, P. (1994). Levels of perceptual representation and process in lexical access: Words, phonemes, and features. *Psychological Review*, *101*, 653–675.

Marslen-Wilson, W.D., & Zhou, X.-L. (1993, November). *Auditory morphological priming for English derived words*. Paper presented at the 34th annual meeting of the Psychonomic Society, Washington, DC.

Marslen-Wilson, W.D., & Zhou, X. (1996, January). *Modality specificity in lexical access?* Paper presented to the Experimental Psychology Society, London, UK.

Myers, S. (1987). Vowel shortening in English. *Natural Language and Linguistic Theory*, *5*, 487–518.

Rubin, G.S., Becker, C.A., & Freeman, R.H. (1979). Morphological structure and its effects on visual word recognition. *Journal of Verbal Learning and Verbal Behaviour*, *8*, 399–412.

Schreuder, R., & Baayen, H. (1995). Modeling morphological processing. In L.B. Feldman (Ed.), *Morphological aspects of language processing* (pp. 131–154). Hillsdale, NJ: Lawrence Erlbaum Associates Inc.

Segui, J., & Zubizarreta, J. (1985). Mental representation of morphologically complex words and lexical access. *Linguistics*, *23*, 759–774.

Taft, M. (1981). Prefix stripping revisited. *Journal of Verbal Learning and Verbal Behaviour*, *20*, 289–297.

Taft, M., & Forster, K. (1975). Lexical storage and retrieval of prefixed words. *Journal of Verbal Learning and Verbal Behaviour*, *14*, 638–647.

PART TWO

Syntactic processing

CHAPTER FIVE

Sentence comprehension

Martin J. Pickering
Human Communication Research Centre, University of Glasgow, UK

Language is clearly extremely complex at all kinds of different levels. Hence, it is very striking that language comprehension is in general so efficient. People can read, listen to a speaker or hold a conversation, and, except on rare occasions, understand most of what the writer or speaker intends to convey. One aspect of language comprehension is what I call sentence comprehension: determining the meaning of a sentence as a whole on the basis of a sequence of words. If we can understand the processes and mechanisms that underlie sentence comprehension, we will have taken one step forward in understanding how people can master the use of language.

Let us first try to provide a fairly precise delimitation of the area that the term *sentence comprehension* refers to. I assume that words have been recognised, so that the processor has access to their lexical properties. Sentence comprehension is concerned with how people obtain a particular syntactic analysis for a string of words and assign an interpretation to that analysis. Thus, it is not principally concerned with word recognition, morphological processing, anaphoric resolution, figurative language, discourse coherence, and inferencing in general (see other chapters). Very roughly, it concentrates on those aspects of language comprehension that draw upon the rules and representations that are studied within generative grammar. However, it is important to stress that the goal of this process is to obtain an interpretation for a string of words, not simply to obtain a syntactic analysis. Hence, I call this chapter *sentence comprehension* rather than simply *parsing*, which is sometimes employed in the narrow sense of syntactic analysis.

Probably the most striking and uncontroversial finding in this area is that sentence comprehension is highly incremental. In both spoken and written language, words are encountered sequentially. Experimental evidence indicates that a great deal of processing occurs immediately, before the next word is encountered (e.g. Just & Carpenter, 1980; Tyler & Marslen-Wilson, 1977). Thus, word recognition is not normally delayed (e.g. Marslen-Wilson, 1987; Rayner & Duffy, 1986), even if disambiguation occurs after the ambiguous word (e.g. Rayner & Frazier, 1989). This is a necessary precondition for incremental sentence comprehension. More importantly, there is normally no measurable delay before syntactic analysis and some aspects of semantic interpretation begin (though it is impossible to be sure that there are no circumstances under which delay occurs).

Evidence for incremental syntactic analysis comes from the vast literature showing "garden-path" effects. For example, the sentence *The horse raced past the barn fell* (Bever, 1970) is hard (in part, at least) because people assume that *raced* is an active past-tense verb, and hence that *the horse raced past the barn* is a complete sentence. When they encounter *fell*, they realise this is impossible, and reinterpret *raced* as a past participle in a "reduced relative" construction (cf. *The horse that was raced past the barn fell.*), or fail to understand the sentence entirely. In other words, they are "led up the garden path" by such a sentence. Hence, they have performed incremental syntactic analysis before reaching *fell*. Experimental evidence strongly supports this conclusion for many different sentence types, and suggests that syntactic analysis begins very rapidly (e.g. Altmann & Steedman, 1988; Frazier & Rayner, 1982; Rayner, Carlson, & Frazier, 1983; Trueswell, Tanenhaus, & Garnsey, 1994).

Evidence also supports the intuition that people start to understand sentences as they hear or read them. Most famously, Marslen-Wilson (1973, 1975) showed that participants' errors in shadowing (i.e. immediately repeating) a text at a lag of only 300 ms were constrained by semantic context. This demonstrates that the meaning of what is heard can be rapidly integrated with general knowledge, though it is conceivable that integration occurs during production rather than comprehension. Data from eye-tracking gives more direct evidence for incremental interpretation. For instance, Traxler and Pickering (1996b) found that readers were disrupted as soon as they read the word *shot* in (1):

(1) That is the very small pistol in which the heartless killer shot the hapless man yesterday afternoon.

Hence, they must have semantically processed the sentence fragment up to *shot* when they first encounter the word. Many other experiments also provide good evidence for incremental semantic processing using various methods (e.g. Boland, Tanenhaus, Garnsey, & Carlson, 1995; Clifton, 1993; Garrod, Freudenthal, & Boyle, 1994; Holmes, Stowe, & Cupples, 1989; Swinney, 1979; Trueswell et al., 1994; Tyler & Marslen-Wilson, 1977). We can conclude that the language processing system must very rapidly construct a syntactic analysis for a sentence fragment, assign it a semantic interpretation, and make at least some attempt to relate this interpretation to general knowledge.

These experiments suggest that any delays in either syntactic analysis or associated aspects of semantic interpretation must be extremely subtle. Hence, models that assume a major delay component (e.g. Marcus, 1980) cannot be accurate. In contrast, there may sometimes be delays in other aspects of interpretation, such as anaphoric resolution (Greene, McKoon, & Ratcliff, 1992; though cf. Garrod et al., 1994; Marslen-Wilson, Tyler, & Koster, 1994) or clausal integration (e.g. Millis & Just, 1994; though cf. Traxler, Bybee, & Pickering, 1997).

A very important consequence of incrementality is that the processor often makes decisions about syntactic and semantic analysis when a sentence fragment is syntactically ambiguous. Most experimental research in sentence comprehension in the 1980s and 1990s has focused on such "local" ambiguities. Through this research, psycholinguists have attempted to understand the organisation of the language processor.

The rest of this chapter discusses both experimental research on syntactic ambiguity resolution and theoretical models of sentence comprehension. I first ask whether the processor can consider only one analysis at a time, or whether it can consider different analyses at the same time. I then outline different sources of information that are relevant to parsing, and argue that the core question in parsing research is how the processor manages to integrate them. Current accounts can broadly be split into two types: restricted accounts, in which the processor can draw upon some sources of information during initial processing but not others; and unrestricted accounts, in which the processor can draw upon all relevant sources of information without delay. I interpret different restricted and unrestricted accounts in light of a range of empirical data. I then discuss a special topic, the processing of unbounded dependencies, within this general framework, and draw some conclusions.

Given the large amount of recent work on sentence comprehension, this review is necessarily selective and incomplete. A fuller review would not focus so overwhelmingly on initial stages of analysis. There is now considerable interest in the question of how the parser performs reanalysis if the initial analysis turns out to be wrong (Ferreira & Henderson, 1991;

Gorrell, 1995; Inoue & Fodor, 1995; Pickering & Traxler, 1998; Pritchett, 1992; Rayner et al., 1983; Sturt & Crocker, 1996; Sturt, Pickering, & Crocker, 1999). I have also entirely ignored formal aspects of semantic processing, such as the resolution of quantifier-scope ambiguities, as such topics have largely been neglected (though see Kurtzman & MacDonald, 1993). The review is probably biased towards research in reading rather than listening, in part because evidence concerning the role of prosody in ambiguity resolution is reviewed by Warren (Chapter 6). Finally, I have ignored individual differences in sentence comprehension (e.g. Just & Carpenter, 1992; MacDonald, Just, & Carpenter, 1992; Pearlmutter & MacDonald, 1996; Waters & Caplan, 1996).

PARALLEL AND SERIAL MODELS OF PROCESSING

When a fragment of a sentence is compatible with only one syntactic analysis, the evidence for incremental processing suggests that the analysis is computed and interpreted. But what happens when a fragment is compatible with more than one analysis? Does the processor compute all analyses in parallel? If so, does it retain all of these analyses or does it drop some? Does it foreground some analyses and background others? Or, alternatively, does it only compute one analysis initially, but have the capacity to reanalyse? These questions are fundamental to determining the strategy that the processor uses in resolving ambiguity. They also help us address the even more fundamental question of the basic architecture of the language processor. Unfortunately, this question has not been resolved, and it is very hard to imagine that a particular series of experiments will provide conclusive evidence on this question.

In a serial model, one analysis is selected. In Bever's sentence, the processor normally adopts the main clause analysis for *The horse raced past the barn*. If this analysis becomes impossible (e.g. following *fell*), then the processor must abandon this analysis and start again. Serial accounts are therefore broadly compatible with data demonstrating the existence of garden-path effects.

A parallel account can consider multiple analyses at the same time. Consider first what we can call *pure unrestricted parallelism*, whereby the processor initially constructs all possible syntactic analyses in parallel, and regards all analyses as being of equal importance (e.g. Forster, 1979). For instance, after *The horse raced* in Bever's sentence, the processor would represent both the main clause and the reduced relative analyses. After *The horse raced past the barn fell*, the processor would drop the main clause analysis, and would continue with the reduced relative analysis, without experiencing any difficulty. However, we know that this account cannot be correct, because the reduced relative analysis causes a garden-path effect. It therefore could not have been as available as the main clause analysis.

In a *ranked-parallel* model, one analysis is foregrounded, and any others are backgrounded. In Bever's sentence, the main clause analysis is foregrounded, and the reduced relative analysis backgrounded. If the main clause analysis becomes impossible, then the parser must change its ranking of analyses. In this case, it will foreground the reduced relative analysis; the main clause analysis may be dropped entirely. Like serial accounts, ranked parallel accounts are broadly compatible with current evidence.

Parallel models differ in many other respects, depending on how many analyses are maintained, what kind of ranking is employed, how long the different analyses are considered for, or whether parallelism is only employed under certain conditions or with certain constructions. Currently, however, the most influential kind of parallel model is the constraint-based account (e.g. MacDonald, Pearlmutter, & Seidenberg, 1994; Trueswell et al., 1994; Trueswell, Tanenhaus, & Kello, 1993), discussed in detail later. According to this account, different analyses are weighted on the basis of how compatible they are with a range of constraints. For example, an analysis will be foregrounded if it is highly frequent, highly plausible, highly compatible with the prosody employed, and so on. As the sentence progresses, new information will cause analyses to change their weightings, and so a different analysis may be foregrounded.

Alternatives to this kind of continuous competition of alternative analyses have been proposed. For instance, Gibson (1991) proposed a "beam search" mechanism in which analyses which are close enough in complexity to the simplest analysis are retained. Analyses are then dropped if their complexity, measured in a way proposed by Gibson, exceeds the complexity of the simplest analysis by some threshold value (cf. Jurafsky, 1996).

These accounts assume that different analyses are retained for an extended period. Other accounts assume momentary parallelism. The "referential" or "incremental-interactive" account of Altmann and Steedman (1988; cf. Crain & Steedman, 1985) is of this latter kind. Here, alternative analyses are proposed in parallel, and contextual information chooses between them immediately, on the basis of how felicitous the analyses are with respect to discourse context (see later for discussion of the actual model). After an initial parallel stage, processing becomes serial. Momentary parallel accounts are similar in spirit to many models of lexical ambiguity resolution (e.g. Swinney, 1979), where all alternative meanings of a word are proposed, but all but the most contextually appropriate (or frequent) meaning is rapidly abandoned. Empirically, it has proved extremely difficult to distinguish between serial and different kinds of ranked-parallel accounts. Though this issue is absolutely central to the development of processing models, it has in a sense remained behind the front line; most of the conflicts in this area have focused on the role of different information sources in parsing.

MODULARITY AND INFORMATION SOURCES

Traditionally, researchers have asked whether language comprehension is *modular* or not. This interest stems largely from J.A. Fodor's (1983) book, *The modularity of mind.* In it, he argued that certain mental faculties, basically consisting of the senses and aspects of language, were modules. Modules are specialised components of the mind, separate from general cognition or "central processes". Fodor defines a number of properties that he claims that all modular systems share; for instance, they are innate and employ a fixed neural architecture. Perhaps their most important property is that they are *encapsulated*: The internal workings of a module cannot be affected by anything external to the module. The output of a module is dependent on the input to the module and the internal structure of the module, and is unaffected by central processes or other modules. Fodor claimed that aspects of language comprehension constituted a module (see also Forster, 1979). Opponents of this position have argued that there are no modules, or that language comprehension in particular is not a module (e.g. Tyler & Marslen-Wilson, 1977; see Garfield, 1987).

Psycholinguists often still ask whether language comprehension is a modular process, but the current emphasis is rather different from Fodor's. In particular, the focus is entirely on encapsulation; few claims are made about, for instance, the developmental or neuroscientific status of the language processor. The main question is whether there is an encapsulated language processor, and, if so, precisely what aspects of language are contained within it.

It is worth distinguishing *representational modularity* from *processing modularity* (Trueswell et al., 1994). Representational modularity claims that sources of information like syntactic and semantic knowledge are represented separately. This assumption is standard to most generative grammars (e.g. Chomsky, 1965, 1981; Pollard & Sag, 1993), though it is not universally accepted (e.g. Lakoff, 1986). Similarly, it is assumed in the great majority of psycholinguistic research (though cf. McClelland, St. John, & Taraban, 1989). Some experimental evidence may bear on this question. For example, it is possible to prime syntactic structure in a manner probably independent of semantic factors, but the best evidence for this comes from language production (Bock, 1986). Also, evidence from event-related brain potentials (where electrical activity from the brain is measured as participants perform a task) provides some evidence that syntactic and semantic processing are distinct. Semantically anomalous words elicit a negative-going brain wave about 400 ms after the stimulus (Kutas & Hillyard, 1980; see also Garnsey, Tanenhaus, & Chapman, 1989). After *I drink my coffee with cream and*, the wave for the anomalous *dog* is negative compared with the wave for *sugar*. In contrast, syntactically anomalous words produce a positive-going wave around 600 ms after the stimulus, whether the anomaly is due to ungrammaticality or a garden-path construction (Hagoort, Brown, & Groothusen, 1993; Osterhout & Holcomb, 1992; Osterhout, Holcomb, & Swinney, 1994; Osterhout & Mobley, 1995; see Osterhout, 1994). (However, it is important to note that wave-forms for different kinds of syntactically anomalous sentences may also differ.) Thus, there is experimental as well as linguistic evidence for representational modularity.

Most researchers in sentence processing follow standard linguistic theory in assuming representational modularity. The main debate concerns the status of processing modularity. The central question is whether all potentially relevant sources of information can be employed during initial processing or not. Let us now outline some of these sources of information. The first two of these are particularly problematic, as theories differ on how they are organised and the relationship between them.

Syntactic category information. We assume that category information forms part of the lexical entry for each word. For example, the entry for *loves* states that it is a verb and that it is transitive (i.e. it takes both a subject and an object). An important question is whether this constitutes two different sources of information: (major) category (e.g. verb, noun, adjective) and subcategory (e.g. transitive verb, intransitive verb). If so, then the processor might base initial processing decisions on major category information alone (e.g. Ferreira & Henderson, 1990; Mitchell, 1987). But if there is no distinction between category and subcategory, then this option would not be available to the processor.

Many words are ambiguous as to their category (e.g. *rose* can be a noun or a verb) or their subcategory (e.g. *eat* can be transitive or intransitive). The frequency with which each category or subcategory is used affects processing, and therefore forms part of this source of information. For example, people have less difficulty with a sentence that employs a verb used with a more frequent subcategory than a verb used with a less frequent one (e.g. Mitchell & Holmes, 1985). One important current debate is whether this information affects initial parsing decisions (e.g. Trueswell et al., 1993); see below.

Syntactic rules. Traditionally, syntactic rules perform most of the work of determining possible sentences of a language and their structure (e.g. Chomsky, 1965). For instance, a syntactic rule might indicate that a sentence can consist of a noun phrase (e.g. *Mary*) followed by a verb phrase (e.g. *loves John*). In such accounts, a clear distinction is made between syntactic information and lexical category information, as discussed previously. More recent linguistic theories have reduced the syntactic component of the grammar and included more information in lexical entries (e.g. Chomsky, 1981; Pollard & Sag, 1993). In psycholinguistics, attempts to reduce the distinction between syntax and lexicon are found in constraint-based theories (e.g. MacDonald et al., 1994). Another issue is whether the grammar contains a listing of syntactic rules, or whether, as some recent theories assume, the rules arise as a consequence of the interaction of more basic components of the grammar, concerned with anaphora, thematic roles, and so on (Chomsky, 1981). The precise nature of the distinction between syntactic rules and syntactic category information may affect the organisation of the processor and hence its behaviour.

Grammatical features. These include person, number, gender, and case. In English, some pronouns, for instance, are marked for case (*she* vs. *her*), gender (*she* vs. *he*), person (*she* vs. *I*) and number (*she* vs. *they*). Such information can affect parsing (e.g. Traxler & Pickering, 1996a). Grammatical features play a much smaller role in English than in many other languages.

Information about discourse focus. In a text like *Tom was going to meet his uncle. He was slightly nervous.* Tom is the focused character (or thematic subject), not the uncle. Hence, the pronoun *he* preferentially refers to Tom. It may be that the processor makes use of this information to direct processes in parsing (e.g. Britt, Perfetti, Garrod, & Rayner, 1992), though its impact has perhaps been most clearly demonstrated in the resolution of anaphora (e.g. Garrod et al., 1994; Marslen-Wilson et al., 1994).

Prosody and punctuation. Some patterns of accent, intonation, and timing can convey information about syntactic structure and about the relation of an utterance to a discourse. Newly introduced information, for instance, is likely to receive a pitch accent, and a phonological break can sometimes signal the boundary between two syntactic constituents. In written language, punctuation plays something of the same role. In *While the plane flew the man watched*, a comma can be placed before *the man*. No comma would be placed there if *the man* were the object of *flew*. I do not consider the effects of prosody in this chapter (see Warren, Chapter 6).

"Sense-semantic" information. Some analyses are plausible, some implausible. This kind of semantic information may be useful to the process of syntactic ambiguity resolution. The earlier example, *While the plane flew the man watched* contains a local ambiguity: *flew* can be intransitive (as it turns out to be) or transitive. However, the transitive analysis is implausible: A plane is unlikely to be the agent of an act of flying. The parser might use this plausibility information to determine that *flew* is probably intransitive. It might come to a different conclusion if the sentence began *While the man flew* (cf. Trueswell et al., 1994). One type of sense-semantic information is due to "selection restrictions" (Katz & Fodor, 1963): Certain verbs normally require arguments of a particular semantic type (e.g. animate subjects) to be felicitous. This information might conceivably be independent of general knowledge; but this cannot be the case for other aspects of sense-semantic information.

Another way of looking at sense-semantic information is in terms of *thematic relations.* Thematic relations are broad semantic categories, usually thought to include agent, patient (or theme), goal, instrument, location, etc. Thus, the active verb *killed* takes an agent and a patient; it is only felicitous with an animate patient, though it can have an animate or an inanimate agent (e.g. *Mary killed John* or *The avalanche killed John*).

Discourse context information. Sometimes a particular analysis is only likely in a particular context. Altmann and Steedman (1988) argued that *Mary saw the man with the binoculars* is most likely to mean that Mary used the binoculars if only one man has been mentioned previously, but that the man had the binoculars if more than one man has been mentioned, since the additional information is only necessary if we need to distinguish between different men. The processor appears to be sensitive to this information (see later). Liversedge, Pickering, Branigan, and Van Gompel (1998) argued that other aspects of discourse context can also affect interpretation.

ACCOUNTS OF PARSING

How does the processor employ these sources of information? We distinguish two basic positions, which we call *unrestricted* and *restricted* accounts. Restricted accounts propose that the processor initially draws upon some sources of information but not others, even when they are potentially relevant (e.g. Ferreira & Henderson, 1990; Frazier, 1987a; Mitchell, 1987, 1989). Such models in practice always assume serial processing. Parsing is a "two-stage" process, with different principles accounting for initial decisions and ultimate decisions.

Unrestricted accounts propose that all sources of information can be employed in initial parsing decisions. This position is adopted by constraint-based models of parsing, as well as by other closely related accounts (e.g. MacDonald, 1994; MacDonald et al., 1994; Taraban & McClelland, 1988; Trueswell et al., 1993, 1994; Tyler & Marslen-Wilson, 1977). Current models assume ranked-parallel processing. Parsing is a "one-stage" process, with no principled distinction between initial parsing decisions and later decisions.

There is a great deal of overlap between parallel and unrestricted accounts on the one hand, and between serial and restricted accounts on the other. It is unclear to what extent this is necessary. It is certainly possible to have a parallel restricted account, where different analyses, for example, are weighted on the basis of construction frequency alone. A serial unrestricted account is harder to envisage, because some sources of information cannot be employed until the analysis has been constructed. In order to conclude that *The man read the air* is implausible, the processor must first decide that *the air* is the object of *read*, not the subject of a subordinate clause (e.g. *was of poor quality*). To do this the processor must have computed the object analysis. But since plausibility information is not available while computing the analysis, the processor could not be unrestricted. It is impossible to get round this without computing analyses in parallel.

Later I discuss restricted and unrestricted accounts in turn, in light of a range of experimental evidence. Throughout this review, it is worth considering the general question of why the processor might initially ignore potentially relevant information. Is the goal of the processor to determine the speaker or writer's intended interpretation of the sentence? If so, why ignore some information? Or is the processor faced with computational limitations that require it to ignore some sources of information?

All restricted accounts assume that some syntactic information is employed initially; and all assume that sense-semantic information and discourse context are not employed. However, they vary in other ways, often relating to the syntactic framework that they assume. By far the best known restricted account is the so-called "Garden-Path" model proposed by Frazier (1979), and discussed in many other places (e.g. Clifton, Speer, & Abney, 1991; Ferreira & Clifton, 1986; Ferreira & Henderson, 1990; Frazier, 1987a, 1990; Frazier & Rayner, 1982; Rayner et al., 1983; cf. Frazier & Fodor, 1978; Gorrell, 1995; Kimball, 1973). I therefore build the following discussion around this model, and introduce alternative accounts in relation to it. (Note that the name is perhaps confusing in that it is not the only theory that assumes the existence of garden paths.)

The Garden-Path model assumes that initial parsing is directed by two fundamental principles, defined by Frazier (1979) as follows:

- *Minimal attachment.* Attach incoming material into the phrase marker being constructed using the fewest nodes consistent with the well-formedness rules of the language.
- *Late closure.* When possible, attach incoming material into the clause or phrase currently being parsed.

The model assumes that all rules are applied in parallel to new material, in a kind of race, and the analysis that is obtained first will be the analysis that relates new material to the most available old material, using the smallest number of new nodes. Minimal attachment takes precedence if there is a conflict between the principles.

I now illustrate these principles using some classic experimental work, and present some challenges to the principles, where these challenges relate to the use of syntactic information. First consider the object/complement (or "NP/S") ambiguity in (2):

(2) The criminal confessed his sins harmed too many people.

After *the criminal confessed his sins*, the sentence is ambiguous, in that the noun phrase *his sins* might be the object of *confessed* or the subject of a complement clause, as in fact turns out to be the case. The garden-path model makes a straightforward prediction: The object analysis requires the postulation of fewer nodes than the complement analysis, so minimal attachment predicts that it is initially adopted. But after encountering *harmed*, it becomes clear that the object analysis cannot be correct, and reanalysis is necessary.

Unlike "reduced relatives", the intuitive evidence that people misanalyse sentences like (2) is not particularly strong. However, experimental evidence suggests that misanalysis can occur. For example, Rayner and Frazier (1987) monitored participants' eye movements as they read ambiguous sentences like (2) and unambiguous sentences like (3):

(3) The criminal confessed that his sins harmed too many people.

This sentence does not contain the object/complement ambiguity, because the word *that* renders the object analysis impossible. Hence people should immediately adopt the complement analysis, and should not have to reanalyse after encountering *harmed*. In accord with this, Rayner and Frazier found that readers were disrupted after reaching *harmed* in (2) relative to (3).

Many other experiments have confirmed that people can misanalyse such sentences (Ferreira & Henderson, 1990; Frazier & Rayner, 1982; Pickering & Traxler, 1998). However, the Garden-Path model makes the stronger prediction that people *always* misanalyse such sentences. This claim is much more controversial: Trueswell et al. (1993) argued that people misanalysed if the main verb (e.g. *confessed*) was more frequently used with an object than a complement, but not if the complement analysis was more frequent. This (unresolved) debate highlights a crucial aspect of the Garden-Path model: Its predictions are based on structural characteristics of different analyses, and cannot be affected by their frequency in the language. If the theory is correct, the processor will sometimes initially adopt analyses that are highly infrequent.

Next consider the ambiguity found in (4):

(4a) The spy saw the cop with binoculars but the cop didn't see him.
(4b) The spy saw the cop with a revolver but the cop didn't see him.

The phrase *with binoculars* in (4a) can attach "high" to *saw*, so that the spy saw with the binoculars, or "low" to *cop*, so that the cop had the binoculars. (The terms "high" and "low" refer to attachment sites within a phrase structure tree, with subordinate clauses or phrases being "lower" sites than main clauses. The main verb *saw* constitutes a high attachment site, whereas an argument of *saw*, such as *the cop*, constitutes a low attachment site.) In contrast, *with a revolver* in (4b) can attach high or low; but this time only low attachment is plausible (as seeing with a revolver is not possible). According to Frazier's assumptions about phrase structure, high attachment involves one fewer node than low attachment. Hence the processor initially attaches the prepositional phrase high, to *saw*. In (4a), this analysis is plausible, so the parser should encounter no problems. But in (4b), this analysis is implausible, and so the parser should have to change its analysis to low attachment. However, this prediction only holds if Frazier's syntactic assumptions are correct. Under other syntactic assumptions, (4a) and (4b) employ the same number of nodes (e.g. Kayne, 1984). If these assumptions are correct, then late closure predicts a low attachment preference. This makes the important point that the Garden-Path model, like other syntax-based accounts, depends critically on the syntactic assumptions that are made.

In accord with Frazier's predictions, Rayner et al. (1983) found that (4b) became harder to process than (4a) after readers encountered the disambiguating prepositional phrase. Many studies have confirmed this preference (Clifton et al., 1991; Frazier, 1979; Rayner, Garrod, & Perfetti, 1992). But again, there have been contradictory findings: Taraban and McClelland (1988) found a low-attachment preference with one set of materials, and argued that semantic factors guide initial attachment. Spivey-Knowlton and Sedivy (1995) found that the semantic category of the verb and the definiteness of the noun phrase affected processing difficulty, and argued that there was no need to appeal to minimal attachment. The major concern, however, has been demonstrations that contextual factors affect the processing of such sentences, as discussed later.

Finally, minimal attachment makes interesting predictions for verb-final constructions. Frazier (1987b) found that Dutch participants read (5a) faster than (5b). I include only the crucial subordinate clause, together with a literal gloss and translation:

(5a) dat het meisje van Holland houdt
that the girl Holland likes
"that the girl likes Holland"
(5b) dat het meisje van Holland glimlachte
that the girl from Holland smiled
"that the girl from Holland smiled"

The prepositional phrase *van Holland* can serve as an argument of the forthcoming verb, as in (5a), or as a modifier of the noun phrase *het meisje*. Frazier's finding is predicted by minimal attachment in combination with her assumptions about phrase structure (though cf. Scheepers, Hemforth, & Konieczny, 1994, who found the opposite pattern of results in German). If Frazier is right, another interesting point is that the processor does not wait until a verb is reached before attaching its argument into a syntactic representation, contrary to "head-driven" models (Abney, 1989; Pickering, 1994; Pritchett, 1992). There is in fact other evidence against head-driven accounts, based on cases where the processor encounters two noun phrases which might or might not be arguments of the same yet-to-be-encountered verb (e.g. Inoue & Fodor, 1995; cf. Bader & Lasser, 1994; Sturt & Crocker, 1996).

Late closure predicts that (6) causes people to misanalyse:

(6) As the woman edited the magazine amused all the reporters.

After *the magazine*, this noun phrase might serve as the object of *edited*, or as the subject of a new clause. According to late closure, the parser chooses the former because *the magazine* forms part of the current clause. This analysis turns out to be wrong when the parser reaches *amused*. Experimental studies have found processing difficulty after disambiguation (Clifton, 1993; Ferreira & Henderson, 1991; Frazier & Rayner, 1982; Pickering & Traxler, 1998; Warner & Glass, 1987). Indeed, Mitchell

(1987) made the dramatic claim that people initially misanalyse even if the subordinate verb is intransitive, as in (7):

(7) After the child sneezed the doctor prescribed a course of injections.

Since *sneezed* is intransitive, the object analysis should be grammatically impossible. If he is correct, the parser ignores subcategorisation information entirely during initial parsing. However, many of his verbs do occasionally allow an object (e.g. *sneezed a big sneeze*). Even so, his results suggest that subcategorisation preferences are ignored. Mitchell's findings are, of course, consistent with the Garden-Path model, but they have been subsequently questioned (e.g. Adams, Clifton, & Mitchell, 1998; Trueswell et al., 1993). However, the preference to adopt the object analysis with genuinely ambiguous verbs like *edited* in (6) has not been convincingly challenged.

Late closure has much greater difficulty with data concerning the modification of complex noun phrases:

(8) The spy shot the daughter of the colonel who was standing on the balcony.

The relative clause can modify either *daughter* or *colonel*; but late closure predicts low attachment to *colonel*. However, Cuetos and Mitchell (1988; Carreiras & Clifton, 1993) found high attachment preference in equivalent sentences in Spanish. In English, there appears to be little preference either way (Carreiras & Clifton, 1993; Mitchell & Cuetos, 1991). There may be a preference for high attachment in sentences with three possible attachment sites for a relative clause (Gibson, Pearlmutter, Canseco-González, & Hickok, 1996), though some evidence supports an initial low attachment preference in Italian (De Vincenzi & Job, 1995). However, there is certainly no universal low attachment preference. This is a very serious problem for late closure.

However, there is evidence for low attachment with some complex noun-phrase modification, for instance if the preposition is *with*. Gilboy, Sopena, Clifton, and Frazier's (1995) questionnaire studies showed that people interpreted *The steak with the sauce that tasted so good* as involving low modification, in contrast to other structurally identical constructions. Traxler, Pickering, and Clifton (1998) provide eye-tracking evidence in support of this finding.

Although late closure may well not be correct, there is considerable agreement about the need to explain a general "recency" or "locality" preference. Since Kimball (1973), an undisputed observation is that sentences like *Fred said Bill left yesterday* show a preference for associating *yesterday* with the most recent verb *left*, so that Bill left yesterday (e.g. Altmann, van Nice, Garnham, & Henstra, 1998). One explanation of such preferences is that there is a conflict between a bias towards the most recent attachment site and a bias towards the "highest" attachment site, which is resolved in different ways in different kinds of construction (Gibson et al., 1996).

Frazier and Clifton (1996) acknowledged that ambiguities like (8) provided the Garden-Path model with a very serious problem. However, they assumed that some kind of locality preference did exist. Their solution was to distinguish two kinds of parsing operation, *attachment* and *construal*. In this theory, attachment occurs with so-called "primary" relations which are found between verbs and their core arguments. It obeys the principles of minimal attachment and late closure, as before. However, "non-primary" relations are not initially attached, but are instead construed in relation to the current thematic processing domain, which is defined in terms of the last constituent which introduced a thematic role. In *the steak with the sauce*, the preposition *with* introduces a thematic role, so the domain is *with the sauce*. In this case, the only attachment site for the modifier is *the sauce*, so low attachment is predicted. But in (8) above, *the servant of the actress* constitutes the current thematic processing domain, because *of* does not introduce a thematic role. In this case, the relative clause is construed in relation to the whole domain. Hence, we see that the construal operation incorporates a locality principle.

Within this theory, the resolution of non-primary relations is strikingly incompatible with the assumptions of the Garden-Path model. A non-primary phrase eventually has to be attached, in order that a complete syntactic analysis can be constructed. After construing the relative clause *who was standing on the balcony* in relation to *the servant of the actress*, the processor has to decide whether to adopt high or low attachment. The point is that this attachment now takes place in an unrestricted manner; the only limit is that the attachment must occur within the current thematic processing domain. Hence, Frazier and Clifton (1996) proposed a model that is restricted for some constructions, but unrestricted for others. Perhaps the most important development, however, is that the model incorporates a well-defined locality assumption.

Pickering (1994) proposed another mixed account. His model does not employ phrase-structure grammar, but rather assumes the theory of dependency categorial grammar (Pickering & Barry, 1993), in which the fundamental linguistic notion is that of a *dependency constituent*, which can consist of, for example, a verb and any individual argument. Sentence processing involves the formation of these units in an incremental manner (cf. Ades & Steedman, 1982). Pickering proposed the Principle of

Dependency Formation, under which the processor initially constructs an analysis that forms a dependency constituent in preference to one that does not. This part of the account is restricted, and makes the same predictions as Frazier (1979) for (2) and (6) above, though the opposite prediction for (5). But if two different analyses both form a single dependency constituent, as in (4) and (8) above, then the parser makes its decision in an unrestricted manner.

Another group of models assumes that initial decisions are determined by differences in terms of thematic relations (Abney, 1989; Crocker, 1995; Gibson, 1991; Pritchett, 1992). Abney proposed that the processor initially resolves syntactic ambiguities in favour of an analysis under which a thematic relation can be assigned, and the other accounts are similar in this respect. On most accounts, thematic-role assigners like verbs assign roles to arguments but not to adjuncts, so the models also assume a preference for argument over adjunct attachment. Abney's account often makes the same predictions as the Garden-Path model, but not for (9):

(9) The doctor delivered a lecture on heart disease but he feared that his warnings would go unheeded.

This sentence is structurally similar to (4b) (assuming the plausible analyses for both sentences), but thematically distinct, in that *a lecture* assigns a thematic role to *on heart disease*. Clifton et al. (1991) contrasted (9) with other sentences in which the prepositional phrase was an adjunct of the noun, or an argument or adjunct of the verb. They found an initial preference for high attachment to the verb, but a later preference for argument attachment. This is more compatible with minimal attachment than with Abney's account, and suggests that structural preferences may not always be overridden by thematic strategies. However, Liversedge et al. (1998) found immediate preferences for argument over adjunct attachment of ambiguous *by*-phrases, which suggests that thematic processing need not be greatly delayed, at least if there is no structural ambiguity.

It is perhaps a surprise that there has been so little work concerned with the on-line assignment of thematic relations. In part, this may be because thematic processing is often treated as essentially a semantic rather than a syntactic issue, and has therefore not been the focus of many of the debates about parsing strategies. Also, some researchers have concentrated on the role of discourse in the assignment of thematic relations (e.g. Carlson & Tanenhaus, 1988). However, the undisputed preference for argument over adjunct interpretations indicates that the processor is eager to assign thematic roles whenever possible. Future research will undoubtedly build on Clifton et al. (1991) and investigate the precise relationship between thematic role assignment and structural preferences during initial processing.

Some evidence suggests that grammatical feature information has rapid effects on parsing. Traxler and Pickering (1996a) manipulated case-marking in complement sentences like (10):

(10a) I recognised you and your family would be unhappy here.
(10b) I recognised she and her family would be unhappy here.

People often initially misanalyse sentences like (10a) by treating the noun phrase *you and your family* as the object of *recognised* (see above). This is not possible in (10b), because *she and her family* is in the nominative case. Traxler and Pickering found that readers were disrupted while reading this noun phrase in (10b) compared with (10a) and other controls. This suggests that case-marking information is used extremely rapidly, though it is not clear whether it is used immediately or not (see also Brysbaert & Mitchell, 1996; Trueswell et al., 1993).

Let us now focus more directly on unrestricted accounts. These accounts propose that all potentially relevant sources of information can be employed during initial processing. Hence, such information as syntactic preferences, grammatical features, semantic plausibility, and prosody or punctuation can affect initial parsing decisions. By not respecting processing modularity, the parser is able to take into account whatever information is likely to determine which analysis should be favoured. Processing decisions are therefore affected by statistical information, derived from prior experience, about the frequency of analyses. As noted earlier, the currently most important unrestricted accounts are called "constraint-based": within a ranked-parallel account, all relevant sources of information or *constraints* are available immediately and can lead to continuous changes in the rankings assigned to different analyses. The strength of these constraints can be determined by various off-line pre-tests. For example, a group of participants might rate the plausibility of different analyses, or complete syntactically ambiguous sentence fragments in order to determine the frequency of the different possible analyses. These accounts do not normally determine where these preferences originate.

Constraint-based accounts developed from earlier interactive accounts. Marslen-Wilson and Tyler (Marslen-Wilson, 1973, 1975; Tyler & Marslen-Wilson, 1977) proposed interactive accounts in which different sources of information are employed immediately within an entirely non-modular architecture. Another non-modular antecedent is found in McClelland et al. (1989), in the context of a connectionist model. However, constraint-based accounts normally assume representational modularity (see above). These accounts also incorporate some of the claims of earlier models that proposed that one particular source of information could affect initial processing (contra the Garden-Path model). Thus, Ford, Bresnan, and Kaplan (1982) proposed that the processor adopts the most frequent analysis by accessing the most highly activated subcategorisation frame; and Referential Theory proposed that it made immediate reference to discourse context in selecting an initial analysis (Altmann & Steedman, 1988; Crain & Steedman, 1985) (see later). Such models employ one source of information alone and are therefore much less general than constraint-based accounts.

In practice, constraint-based theorists isolate various constraints and show that they have rapid effects on processing. The major assumption is that there is no earlier stage in parsing that ignores these constraints. I have already discussed some constraints, such as frequency information (Trueswell et al., 1993). Later, I focus on the issue of whether sense-semantic information or discourse context affect initial processing. As we shall see, there is good evidence that semantic factors can have very rapid effects on ambiguity resolution. If a restricted account is correct, then the initial stage that ignores these factors must be very brief indeed (though see McElree & Griffith, 1995).

With respect to sense-semantic information, Trueswell et al. (1994) used "reduced-relative" ambiguities (Bever, 1970):

(11a) The defendant examined by the lawyer turned out to be unreliable.
(11b) The evidence examined by the lawyer turned out to be unreliable.

After *examined*, both sentences could continue as a simple past-tense sentence. However, only (11a) would be plausible: Defendants can examine things, but evidence cannot examine anything. However, they are both "reduced relatives", as becomes clear when the *by*-phrase is reached. In this experiment, the plausibility depends on selection restrictions due to animacy. Trueswell et al. also employed unambiguous "unreduced relatives" containing the disambiguating words *that was* after *examined*, and different sentences containing unambiguous verbs like *drawn*. Sentence (11a) produced processing difficulty at *by the lawyer*, suggesting that the parser had adopted the main clause analysis. This is predicted by all accounts. However, no difficulty ensued in (11b), where animacy made the main clause analysis implausible. This is inconsistent with minimal attachment (so long as the processor had not reanalysed before reaching the *by*-phrase), and suggests that syntactic and semantic constraints can be applied at the same time during processing. The results are incompatible with Ferreira and Clifton (1986), who used very similar materials (and with Rayner et al., 1983). Trueswell et al. argued that there is a strong preference for main-clause constructions over reduced relatives in most cases (due to frequency), and that the preference can only be removed by strong competing constraint such as animacy (see also Trueswell, 1996). McRae, Spivey-Knowlton, and Tanenhaus (1998) replicated these results, but manipulated plausibility independently of animacy. The evidence for rapid effects of plausibility on syntactic ambiguity resolution is therefore very strong.

Discourse context affects the interpretation assigned to an ambiguous anaphoric noun phrase. Following Crain and Steedman (1985), Altmann and Steedman (1988) measured reading times on sentences like (12):

(12a) The burglar blew open the safe with the dynamite and made off with the loot.
(12b) The burglar blew open the safe with the new lock and made off with the loot.

These sentences are formally ambiguous, in that the prepositional phrase *with the dynamite/new lock* can modify either the noun phrase *the safe* or the verb phrase *blew open the safe*, but Altmann and Steedman used prior context to pragmatically disambiguate them. A context sentence referred to either one or two safes. If only one safe had been mentioned, then the complex noun phrase *the safe with the new lock* is redundant, and hence the prepositional phrase in (12b) took comparatively long to read. If two safes had been mentioned, then the simple noun phrase *the safe* fails to pick out a particular safe, and hence the prepositional phrase *with the dynamite* in (12a) took comparatively long to read.

In Altmann and Steedman's (1988) *Referential Theory*, the parser constructs different analyses in parallel and uses discourse context to provide immediate disambiguation. This immediate disambiguation distinguishes it from the constraint-based model. More generally, referential theory only applies to ambiguities that involve ambiguity between a simple and a complex noun phrase. For instance, it does not apply to (2) and (6) above. Hence it cannot serve as a complete account of initial parsing decisions. However, the fundamental insight about the felicity of noun phrases has been incorporated into constraint-based accounts (e.g. Spivey-Knowlton, Trueswell, & Tanenhaus, 1993). Such accounts allow for the possibility of other discourse context effects. In this respect, Liversedge et al. (1998) found that a sentence like *The man was wondering where to plant the shrubs* made a target phrase that specified a location easier to process; however, their results were not entirely consistent with constraint-based models.

A considerable amount of experimental work has attempted to determine whether discourse context can affect initial stages of processing.

Altmann and Steedman (1988) found their effect as the prepositional phrase was read, using self-paced reading. Some studies have failed to find such early effects (Clifton & Ferreira, 1989; Ferreira & Clifton, 1986; Mitchell, Corley, & Garnham, 1992; Rayner et al., 1992). However, a number of studies have replicated Altmann and Steedman's pattern of results, on a range of constructions, using self-paced reading and eye tracking (Altmann, Garnham, & Dennis, 1992; Altmann, Garnham, & Henstra, 1994; Britt, 1994; Britt et al., 1992; Spivey-Knowlton et al., 1993; Trueswell & Tanenhaus, 1991). The weight of the evidence therefore suggests that context can have effects that show up as soon as the processor encounters a critical word or phrase. This suggests, but does not prove, that context can affect initial parsing decisions.

Context may be more likely to have effects in cases where other constraints produce a fairly weak preference for one analysis over another, such as attachment ambiguities like (12), than in cases where there may be a strong initial preference, such as reduced relatives like (11). In Britt (1994), participants read sentences containing verbs like *put* that take an obligatory prepositional-phrase argument:

(13a) He put the book on the chair before leaving.
(13b) He put the book on the battle onto the chair.

She contrasted these with similar sentences in which the prepositional phrase was optional, more similar to (12) above. She found that discourse context could remove the preference for high attachment when the verb did not require a prepositional-phrase argument (as in 12), but not when it did require such an argument (as in 13). The verb's desire to fill its obligatory arguments took precedence over contextual influences. Notice, however, that Britt found no contextual override, merely contextual neutralisation of preferences in isolation. Other studies also show neutralisation (Altmann et al., 1992; Britt et al., 1992; Liversedge et al., 1998), though Altmann and Steedman (1988) did show override. The finding of neutralisation may merely reflect the strength of the biases in the items employed; but, alternatively, they may suggest that the effects of context are more limited than constraint-based models predict. Many of the results do, however, support the general conclusion that discourse context can affect initial processing, but not to the exclusion of other influences.

UNBOUNDED DEPENDENCIES

Let us now consider one particular type of construction that has been fairly extensively studied, the unbounded dependency, in order to shed further light on the issue of how the processor makes initial parsing decisions. In an unbounded dependency, closely associated constituents are separated from each other:

(14) Which girl do you believe John loves a lot?

In this sentence, *the girl* is a long way from *loves*, even though *the girl* is (roughly) the object argument of *loves*. In most other types of sentence, *the girl* would appear in its "canonical" location immediately after *loves*. Following psycholinguistic terminology, we say that *the girl* is the *filler* associated with the verb *loves*. In most constructions, verbs are very close to their arguments, but in unbounded dependencies, there is no limit to the number of words or clauses that may separate them. A theory of sentence comprehension must explain how the processor associates the verb and the filler, so that the filler is interpreted as the argument of the verb.

One issue concerns the representations employed by the processor. In classical transformational grammar, unbounded dependencies are assumed to involve a transformation, with the filler being in its "canonical" location at a level of "deep structure", and then moving to its surface structure position via a transformation. In more recent transformational grammar, surface structure contains a trace or gap (represented by *Ø* below) at the canonical location of the moved element. Thus, (14) above has the structure:

(15) [Which girl]$_i$ do you believe John loves $Ø_i$ a lot?

Many researchers assume that these representations and transformations correspond to processes that occur in sentence comprehension (e.g. Bever & McElree, 1988; Clifton & Frazier, 1989; J.D. Fodor, 1978, 1989; McElree & Bever, 1989). On these accounts, forming the unbounded dependency involves the process of *gap filling*, by which the filler is associated with the gap. Other aspects of sentence processing take place as if the filler had not been moved.

Pickering and Barry (1991) challenged this account, by arguing that the processor associated the filler with the verb directly, as represented in (16):

(16) [Which girl]$_i$ do you believe John [loves]$_i$ a lot?

In sentence (14), the gap location is adjacent to the critical verb *loves*, so it is hard to see how experimental evidence could distinguish between the two accounts. This is the case for all experimental evidence that has been interpreted in terms of gap-filling (see Pickering, 1993). In an eye-tracking experiment discussed earlier, Traxler and Pickering (1996b) found processing difficulty immediately *shot* was read:

(1) That is the very small pistol in which the heartless killer shot the hapless man yesterday afternoon.

The gap location is after *man*, because the canonical order of words would be *shot the man with the garage yesterday afternoon*. This demonstrates that the unbounded dependency is formed before the gap location is reached. Indeed there was no sign of any processing effect around the gap location. However, it is possible that the parser postulates gaps and performs gap-filling as soon as the verb is reached in a predictive or top-down manner (Crocker, 1995; Gibson & Hickok, 1993; see Crocker, Chapter 7). The processing evidence is therefore *compatible* with gaps, but provides no reason to assume their existence.

Unbounded dependencies provide a way to distinguish restricted and unrestricted accounts, as they contain a considerable amount of local ambiguity (J.D. Fodor, 1978). For instance, (14) is locally ambiguous at *believe*, because *which girl* could be the noun-phrase object of *believe* (e.g. if the sentence finished at that point). On one restricted account, the parser might never form the unbounded dependency immediately, but rather wait for disambiguating material so that it never misanalyses. This "cautious" delay account sits ill with the evidence for incremental processing, and is in fact ruled out by experimental evidence. Consider (17):

(17a) We like the book that the author wrote unceasingly and with great dedication about while waiting for a contract.
(17b) We like the city that the author wrote unceasingly and with great dedication about while waiting for a contract.

Both sentences are plausible, but (17b) contains an implausible misanalysis, under which the author wrote the city; whereas (17a) contains a plausible misanalysis, under which the author wrote the book. Traxler and Pickering (1996b) found that readers spent longer reading *wrote* in (17b) than (17a), indicating that they formed the unbounded dependency immediately (see also Boland et al., 1995; Garnsey et al., 1989; McElree & Griffith, 1998; Nicol & Swinney, 1989; Stowe, 1986; Stowe, Tanenhaus, & Carlson, 1991; Tanenhaus, Carlson, & Trueswell, 1989).

Another restricted account is much more plausible, and does involve incremental processing. Here, the parser always forms the unbounded dependency, and is prepared to reanalyse if necessary. This is a *first-resort* strategy, sometimes called the *active filler strategy* (Clifton & Frazier, 1989; Frazier & Clifton, 1989; Frazier & Flores d'Arcais, 1989; cf. De

Vincenzi, 1991; Pickering, 1994). Alternatively, the parser might form the unbounded dependency if all the information available suggests that this analysis is more likely than the alternative or alternatives. This is an unrestricted account compatible with constraint-based theory. It incorporates lexical guidance (J.D. Fodor, 1978; cf. Ford et al., 1982): For example, the parser might form the dependency between *which girl* and *believes* in (14) if *believes* more often takes a noun-phrase object than a complement clause. However, as discussed earlier, unrestricted accounts are more general than this, and take into account any other available and relevant factors (e.g. Boland et al., 1995).

The experimental evidence does not clearly distinguish between first-resort strategies and unrestricted strategies. For example, Stowe et al. (1991) found no plausibility effect in self-paced reading for sentences similar to (16) but with preferentially intransitive verbs (e.g. *hurried*). However, this null effect might be due to lack of sensitivity of the technique or the small number of items per condition. Frazier and Clifton (1989) found evidence suggesting the opposite conclusion, but their critical regions differed considerably between conditions (see also Boland et al., 1995; Clifton & Frazier, 1989). Thus, this question has not been convincingly resolved for unbounded dependencies. It may well be the case that unbounded dependencies and other constructions do not differ with respect to the way in which different sources of information are integrated. If anything, the tendency in recent work is to treat them as less distinct from other sentence types than previously (Boland et al., 1995; Traxler & Pickering, 1996b).

CONCLUSIONS

The field of sentence comprehension has reached an interesting point. On the one hand, largely incompatible theories compete to explain research results; but on the other hand, the number of clear findings is rapidly increasing. For example, we know that language comprehension is normally highly incremental. Thus, for example, both "sense" and discourse semantic factors have very rapid effects on comprehension. Moreover, they appear to affect the process of syntactic ambiguity resolution (e.g. Altmann & Steedman, 1988; Trueswell et al., 1994). We also know that other factors, such as frequency of an analysis, grammatical features, and focus are rapidly brought to bear. The emerging picture is of a system that integrates different sources of information on-line, in order that its choice of interpretation is based on all the sources of evidence that are available.

It is much less clear whether the processor integrates all sources of information in the manner that constraint-based accounts predict. I shall raise a couple of issues in relation to a recent study (Traxler et al., 1998). One concern for constraint-based accounts is that there is not always a good correspondence between processing difficulty and the results of completion norms that should determine the strength of the constraints in favour of one or other analysis (e.g. Clifton, Kennison, & Albrecht, 1997; Trueswell, 1996). In one experiment, Traxler et al. found a preference to complete fragments like *The driver of the car that had the*... with a modifier attaching to the second noun phrase *the car* (e.g. *puncture*) than the first noun phrase (e.g. *strange voice*). A new set of participants then read sentences like:

(18a) The driver of the car that had the moustache was pretty cool.
(18b) The car of the driver that had the moustache was pretty cool.
(18c) The son of the driver that had the moustache was pretty cool.

In (18a) the modifier *that had the moustache* attaches to the first noun phrase; in (18b), it attaches to the second noun phrase; in (18c), it can attach to either noun phrase. Contrary to the prediction of the constraint-based account, there was no preference for (18b) over (18a); in other words, the constraints determined by the completion norms did not determine attachment preferences.

However, the experiment had an even more interesting finding. Participants found the ambiguous sentence (18c) easier to read than either of the disambiguated sentences. The lack of a difference between (18a) and (18b) provides good evidence that the available constraints favoured neither analysis. Hence, constraint-based accounts predict that (18c) ought to lead to a considerable degree of competition between the two analyses, and therefore should cause processing difficulty, relative to the other two sentences (e.g. Spivey-Knowlton & Sedivy, 1995). The fact that the results showed the opposite pattern creates problems for current constraint-based accounts.

One possibility is that the processor does draw upon the full range of information during initial processing, as unrestricted accounts predict. However, it may not always integrate that information in a manner that leads it to favour the analysis that completion tasks (or other off-line tests of preferences) would predict. Ultimately adopting this analysis may be beneficial in helping the reader or listener access the interpretation intended by the writer or speaker. But in order to do this, the processor may benefit initially from focusing on a different analysis—perhaps one that it can rapidly decide whether it is likely to be correct or not (e.g. Chater, Crocker, & Pickering, 1998). One consequence of this may be the existence of structural factors, such as locality preferences, that continue to exist within an unrestricted processor. In conclusion, the evidence appears to support rapid use of different sources of information, though the manner in which the processor draws upon these sources of information may not correspond to the assumptions of current constraint-based accounts.

READINGS

For surveys of current theories of sentence comprehension and experimental evidence, see Mitchell (1994), Tanenhaus and Trueswell (1995), Altmann (1998), and Gibson and Pearlmutter (1998). For computational background, see Crocker (Chapter 7) and references therein. After this, it is best to jump into the primary literature. For restricted accounts, try Frazier (1987a) and classic "garden-path" papers like Frazier and Rayner (1982) or Rayner et al. (1983); also see Mitchell (1987). The main statement of Referential Theory is Altmann and Steedman (1988); Britt (1994) provides a clear experimental investigation of this approach. Important constraint-based papers include MacDonald et al. (1994), McRae et al., (1998), Trueswell et al. (1993), and Trueswell et al. (1994); and see also Taraban and McClelland (1988). For unbounded dependencies, see J.D. Fodor (1989) and Traxler and Pickering (1996b). A number of good review papers appear in volumes edited by Altmann (1989), Clifton, Frazier, and Rayner (1994), and Crocker, Pickering, and Clifton (in press), and in CUNY conference editions of the *Journal of Psycholinguistic Research.*

REFERENCES

Abney, S.P. (1989). A computational model of human parsing. *Journal of Psycholinguistic Research, 18*, 129–144.

Adams, B.C., Clifton, C., & Mitchell, D.C. (1998). Lexical guidance in sentence processing? *Psychonomic Bulletin & Review, 5*, 265–270.

Ades, A., & Steedman, M.J. (1982). On the order of words. *Linguistics and Philosophy, 4*, 517–558.

Altmann, G.T.M. (Ed.) (1989). *Parsing and interpretation.* Special issue of *Language and Cognitive Processes, 4*.

Altmann, G.T.M. (1998). Ambiguity in sentence processing. *Trends in Cognitive Sciences, 2*, 146–152.

Altmann, G.T.M., Garnham, A., & Dennis, Y.I.L. (1992). Avoiding the garden path: Eye-movements in context. *Journal of Memory and Language, 31*, 685–712.

Altmann, G.T.M., Garnham, A., & Henstra, J.-A. (1994). Effects of syntax in human sentence parsing: Evidence against a structure-based parsing mechanism. *Journal of Experimental Psychology: Learning, Memory, and Cognition, 20*, 209–216.

Altmann, G.T.M., & Steedman, M.J. (1988). Interaction with context during human sentence processing. *Cognition, 30*, 191–238.

Altmann, G.T.M., van Nice, K.Y., Garnham, A., & Henstra, J.-A. (1998). Late closure in context. *Journal of Memory and Language, 38*, 459–484.

Bader, M., & Lasser, I. (1994). German verb-final clauses and sentence processing: Evidence for immediate attachment. In C. Clifton, Jr., L. Frazier, & K. Rayner (Eds.), *Advances in sentence processing* (pp. 225–242). Hillsdale, NJ: Lawrence Erlbaum Associates Inc.

Bever, T.G. (1970). The cognitive basis for linguistic structures. In J.R. Hayes (Ed.), *Cognition and the development of language* (pp. 279–362). New York: John Wiley & Sons.

Bever, T.G., & McElree, B. (1988). Empty categories access their antecedents during comprehension. *Linguistic Inquiry*, *19*, 35–45.

Bock, J.K. (1986). Syntactic persistence in language production. *Cognitive Psychology*, *18*, 355–387.

Boland, J.E., Tanenhaus, M.K., Garnsey, S.M., & Carlson, G.N. (1995). Verb argument structure in parsing and interpretation: Evidence from wh- questions. *Journal of Memory and Language*, *34*, 774–806.

Britt, M.A. (1994). The interaction of referential ambiguity and argument structure in the parsing of prepositional phrases. *Journal of Memory and Language*, *33*, 251–283.

Britt, M.A., Perfetti, C.A., Garrod, S.C., & Rayner, K. (1992). Parsing in context: Context effects and their limits. *Journal of Memory and Language*, *31*, 293–314.

Brysbaert, M., & Mitchell, D.C. (1996). Modifier attachment in sentence parsing: Evidence from Dutch. *Quarterly Journal of Experimental Psychology*, *49A*, 664–695.

Carlson, G., & Tanenhaus, M.K. (1988). Thematic roles and language comprehension. In W. Wilkins (Ed.), *Syntax and semantics: 21. Thematic relations* (pp. 263–288). San Diego, CA: Academic Press.

Carreiras, M., & Clifton, C., Jr. (1993). Relative clause interpretation preferences in Spanish and English. *Language and Speech*, *36*, 353–372.

Chater, N., Crocker, M.J., & Pickering, M.J. (1998). The rational analysis of inquiry: The case of parsing. In M. Oaksford & N. Chater (Eds.), *Rational models of cognition* (pp. 441–469). Oxford, UK: Oxford University Press.

Chomsky, N. (1965). *Aspects of the theory of syntax*. Cambridge, MA: MIT Press.

Chomsky, N. (1981). *Lectures on government and binding*. Dordrecht, The Netherlands: Foris.

Clifton, C., Jr. (1993). Thematic roles in sentence parsing. *Canadian Journal of Experimental Psychology*, *47*, 222–246.

Clifton, C., Jr., & Ferreira, F. (1989). Ambiguity in context. *Language and Cognitive Processes*, *4*, 77–104.

Clifton, C., Jr., & Frazier, L. (1989). Comprehending sentences with long distance dependencies. In G. Carlson & M. Tanenhaus (Eds.), *Linguistic structure in language processing* (pp. 273–317). Dordrecht, The Netherlands: Kluwer.

Clifton, C., Jr., Frazier, L., & Rayner, K. (Eds.) (1994). *Perspectives on sentence processing*. Hillsdale, NJ: Lawrence Erlbaum Associates Inc.

Clifton, C., Jr., Kennison, S.M., & Albrecht, J.E. (1997). Reading the words her, his, him: Implications for parsing principles based on frequency and on structure. *Journal of Memory and Language*, *36*, 276–292.

Clifton, C., Jr., Speer, S., & Abney, S.P. (1991). Parsing arguments: Phrase structure and argument structure as determinants of initial parsing decisions. *Journal of Memory and Language*, *30*, 251–271.

Crain, S., & Steedman, M.J. (1985). On not being led up the garden-path: The use of context by the psychological processor. In D. Dowty, L. Kartunnen, & A. Zwicky (Eds.), *Natural language parsing* (pp. 320–358). Cambridge, UK: Cambridge University Press.

Crocker, M.W. (1995). *Computational psycholinguistics: An interdisciplinary approach to the study of language*. Dordrecht, The Netherlands: Kluwer.

Crocker, M.W., Pickering, M.J., & Clifton, C., Jr. (Eds.) (in press). *Architectures and mechanisms for language processing*. Cambridge, UK: Cambridge University Press.

Cuetos, F., & Mitchell, D.C. (1988). Cross-linguistic differences in parsing: Restrictions on the use of the late closure strategy in Spanish. *Cognition, 30*, 73–105.

De Vincenzi, M. (1991). *Syntactic parsing strategies in Italian.* Dordrecht, The Netherlands: Kluwer.

De Vincenzi, M., & Job, R. (1995). A cross-linguistic investigation of late closure: The role of syntax, thematic structure, and pragmatics in initial and final interpretation. *Journal of Experimental Psychology: Learning, Memory, and Cognition, 21*, 1–19.

Ferreira, F., & Clifton, C., Jr. (1986). The independence of syntactic processing. *Journal of Memory and Language, 25*, 348–368.

Ferreira, F., & Henderson, J. (1990). Use of verb information in syntactic parsing: Evidence from eye movements and word-by-word self-paced reading. *Journal of Experimental Psychology: Learning, Memory, and Cognition, 16*, 555–568.

Ferreira, F., & Henderson, J. (1991). Recovery from misanalyses of garden-path sentences. *Journal of Memory and Language, 30*, 725–745.

Fodor, J.A. (1983). *The modularity of mind.* Cambridge, MA: MIT Press.

Fodor, J.D. (1978). Parsing strategies and constraints on transformations. *Linguistic Inquiry, 9*, 427–473.

Fodor, J.D. (1989). Empty categories in sentence processing. *Language and Cognitive Processes, 4*, 155–209.

Ford, M., Bresnan, J.W., & Kaplan, R.M. (1982). A competence based theory of syntactic closure. In J.W. Bresnan (Ed.), *The mental representation of grammatical relations* (pp. 727–796). Cambridge, MA: MIT Press.

Forster, K. (1979). Levels of processing and the structure of the language processor. In W.E. Cooper & E. Walker (Eds.), *Sentence processing: Psycholinguistic studies presented to Merrill Garrett.* Hillsdale, NJ: Lawrence Erlbaum Associates Inc.

Frazier, L. (1979). *On comprehending sentences: Syntactic parsing strategies* (PhD thesis, University of Connecticut). West Bend, IN: Indiana University Linguistics Club.

Frazier, L. (1987a). Sentence processing: A tutorial review. In M. Coltheart (Ed.), *Attention and performance XII* (pp. 559–586). Hove, UK: Lawrence Erlbaum Associates Ltd.

Frazier, L. (1987b). Syntactic processing: Evidence from Dutch. *Natural Language and Linguistic theory, 5*, 519–559.

Frazier, L. (1990). Exploring the architecture of the language processing system. In G.T.M. Altmann (Ed.), *Cognitive models of speech processing* (pp. 409–433). Cambridge, MA: MIT Press.

Frazier, L., & Clifton, C., Jr. (1989). Successive cyclicity in the grammar and parser. *Language and Cognitive Processes, 4*, 93–126.

Frazier, L., & Clifton, C., Jr. (1996). *Construal.* Cambridge, MA: MIT Press.

Frazier, L., & Flores d'Arcais, G.B. (1989). Filler driven parsing: A study of gap filling in Dutch. *Journal of Memory and Language, 28*, 331–344.

Frazier, L., & Fodor, J.D. (1978). The sausage machine: A new two-stage parsing model. *Cognition, 6*, 291–326.

Frazier, L., & Rayner, K. (1982). Making and correcting errors during sentence comprehension: Eye movements in the analysis of structurally ambiguous sentences. *Cognitive Psychology, 14*, 178–210.

Garfield, J. (Ed.) (1987). *Modularity in knowledge representation and natural language processing.* Cambridge, MA: MIT Press.

Garnsey, S.M., Tanenhaus, M.K., & Chapman, R. (1989). Evoked potentials and the study of sentence comprehension. *Journal of Psycholinguistic Research, 18*, 51–60.

Garrod, S.C., Freudenthal, D., & Boyle, E. (1994). The role of different types of anaphor in the on-line resolution of sentences in a discourse. *Journal of Memory and Language, 33*, 39–68.

Gibson, E. (1991). *A computational theory of human linguistic processing: Memory limitations and processing breakdown.* Unpublished doctoral dissertation, Carnegie-Mellon University, Pittsburgh, PA.

Gibson, E., & Hickok, G. (1993). Sentence processing with empty categories. *Language and Cognitive Processes, 8*, 147–161.

Gibson, E., & Pearlmutter, N. (1998). Constraints on sentence comprehension. *Trends in Cognitive Sciences, 2*, 262–268.

Gibson, E., Pearlmutter, N., Canseco-González, E., & Hickok, G. (1996). Recency preference in the human sentence processing mechanism. *Cognition, 59*, 23–59.

Gilboy, E., Sopena, J., Clifton, C., Jr. & Frazier, L. (1995). Argument structure and association preferences in Spanish and English compound NPs. *Cognition, 54*, 131–167.

Gorrell, P. (1995). *Syntax and perception.* Cambridge, UK: Cambridge University Press.

Greene, S.B., McKoon, G., & Ratcliff, R. (1992). Pronoun resolution and discourse models. *Journal of Experimental Psychology: Learning, Memory, and Cognition, 18*, 266–283.

Hagoort, P., Brown, C.M., & Groothusen, J. (1993). The syntactic positive shift as an ERP-measure of syntactic processing. *Language and Cognitive Processes, 8*, 439–483.

Holmes, V.M., Stowe, L., & Cupples, L. (1989). Lexical expectations in parsing complement-verb sentences. *Journal of Memory and Language, 28*, 668–689.

Inoue, A., & Fodor, J.D. (1995). Information-paced processing of Japanese. In R. Mazuka and N. Nagai (Eds.), *Japanese sentence processing.* Hillsdale, NJ: Lawrence Erlbaum Associates Inc.

Jurafsky, D. (1996). A probabilistic model of lexical and syntactic access and disambiguation. *Cognitive Science, 20*, 137–194.

Just, M.A., & Carpenter, P.A. (1980). A theory of reading: From eye fixations to comprehension. *Psychological Review, 87*, 329–354.

Just, M.A., & Carpenter, P.A. (1992). A capacity theory of comprehension: Individual differences in working memory. *Psychological Review, 99*, 122–149.

Katz, J.J., & Fodor, J.A. (1963). The structure of a semantic theory. *Language, 39*, 170–210.

Kayne, R. (1984). *Connectedness and binary branching.* Dordrecht, The Netherlands: Foris.

Kimball, J. (1973). Seven principles of surface structure parsing in natural language. *Cognition, 2*, 15–47.

Kurtzman, H., & MacDonald, M.C. (1993). Resolution of quantifier scope ambiguity. *Cognition, 48*, 243–279.

Kutas, M., & Hillyard, S.A. (1980). Reading senseless sentences: Brain potentials reflect semantic incongruity. *Science, 207*, 203–205.

Lakoff, G. (1986). *Women, fire, and dangerous things: What categories tell us about the nature of thought.* Chicago: University of Chicago Press.

Liversedge, S.P., Pickering, M.J., Branigan, H.P, & Van Gompel, R.P.G. (1998). Processing arguments and adjuncts in isolation and context: The case of *by*-phrase ambiguities in passives. *Journal of Experimental Psychology: Learning, Memory, and Cognition, 24*, 261–475.

MacDonald, M.C. (1994). Probabilistic constraints and syntactic ambiguity resolution. *Language and Cognitive Processes, 9*, 157–201.

MacDonald, M.C., Just, M.A., & Carpenter, P.A. (1992). Working memory constraints on the processing of syntactic ambiguity. *Cognitive Psychology, 24*, 56–98.

MacDonald, M.C., Pearlmutter, N.J., & Seidenberg, M.S. (1994). Lexical nature of syntactic ambiguity resolution. *Psychological Review, 101*, 676–703.

Marcus, M.P. (1980). *A theory of syntactic recognition for natural language.* Cambridge, MA: MIT Press.

Marslen-Wilson, W.D. (1973). Linguistic structure and speech shadowing at very short latencies. *Nature, 244*, 522–523.

Marslen-Wilson, W.D. (1975). Sentence perception as an interactive parallel process. *Science, 189*, 226–228.

Marslen-Wilson, W.D. (1987). Functional parallelism in spoken word recognition. *Cognition, 25*, 71–102.

Marslen-Wilson, W.D., Tyler, L.K., & Koster, C. (1994). Integrative processes in utterance resolution. *Journal of Memory and Language, 33*, 657–666.

McClelland, J.L., St. John, M., & Taraban, R. (1989). Sentence comprehension: A parallel distributed processing approach. *Language and Cognitive Processes, 4*, 287–335.

McElree, B., & Bever, T.G. (1989). The psychological reality of linguistically defined gaps. *Journal of Psycholinguistic Research, 18*, 21–36.

McElree, B., & Griffith, T. (1995). Syntactic and thematic processing in sentence comprehension: Evidence for a temporal dissociation. *Journal of Experimental Psychology: Learning, Memory, and Cognition, 21*, 134–157.

McElree, B., & Griffith, T. (1998). Structural and lexical constraints on filling gaps during sentence comprehension: A time-course analysis. *Journal of Experimental Psychology: Learning, Memory, and Cognition, 24*, 432–460.

McRae, K., Spivey-Knowlton, M.J., & Tanenhaus, M.J. (1998). Modeling the influence of thematic fit (and other constraints) in on-line sentence comprehension. *Journal of Memory and Language, 38*, 283–312.

Millis, K.K., & Just, M.A. (1994). The influence of connectives on sentence comprehension. *Journal of Memory and Language, 33*, 128–147.

Mitchell, D.C. (1987). Lexical guidance in human parsing: Locus and processing characteristics. In Coltheart, M. (Ed.), *Attention and performance XII* (pp. 601–618). Hove, UK: Lawrence Erlbaum Associates Ltd.

Mitchell, D.C. (1989). Verb guidance and lexical effects in ambiguity resolution. *Language and Cognitive Processes, 4*, 123–154.

Mitchell, D.C. (1994). Sentence parsing. In M.A. Gernsbacher (Ed.), *Handbook of psycholinguistics*. San Diego, CA: Academic Press.

Mitchell, D.C., Corley, M.M.B., & Garnham, A. (1992). Effects of context in human sentence parsing: Evidence against a discourse-based proposal mechanism. *Journal of Experimental Psychology: Learning, Memory and Cognition, 18*, 69–88.

Mitchell, D.C., & Cuetos, F. (1991). *The origin of parsing strategies*. Unpublished manuscript. University of Exeter, UK.

Mitchell, D.C., & Holmes, V.I. (1985). The role of specific information about the verb in parsing sentences with local structural ambiguity. *Journal of Memory and Language, 24*, 542–559.

Nicol, J., & Swinney, D. (1989). The role of structure in coreference assignment during sentence comprehension. *Journal of Psycholinguistic Research, 18*, 5–19.

Osterhout, L. (1994). Event-related brain potentials as tools for comprehending language comprehension. In C. Clifton Jr., L. Frazier, & K. Rayner (Eds.), *Advances in sentence processing* (pp. 15–44). Hillsdale, NJ: Lawrence Erlbaum Associates Inc.

Osterhout, L., & Holcomb, P.J. (1992). Event-related brain potentials elicited by syntactic anomaly. *Journal of Memory and Language, 31*, 785–806.

Osterhout, L., Holcomb, P.J., & Swinney, D.A. (1994). Brain potentials elicited by garden-path sentences: Evidence of the application of verb information during parsing. *Journal of Experimental Psychology: Learning, Memory, and Cognition, 20*, 786–803.

Osterhout, L., & Mobley, L.A. (1995). Event-related brain potentials elicited by failure to agree. *Journal of Memory and Language, 34*, 739–773.

Pearlmutter, N., & MacDonald, M.C. (1995). Individual differences and probabilistic constraints in syntactic ambiguity resolution. *Journal of Memory and Language, 34*, 521–542.

Pickering, M.J. (1993). Direct association and sentence processing: A reply to Gorrell and to Gibson and Hickok. *Language and Cognitive Processes*, *8*, 163–196.

Pickering, M.J. (1994). Processing local and unbounded dependencies: A unified account. *Journal of Psycholinguistic Research*, *23*, 323–352.

Pickering, M.J., & Barry, G. (1991). Sentence processing without empty categories. *Language and Cognitive Processes*, *6*, 229–259.

Pickering, M.J., & Barry, G. (1993). Dependency categorial grammar and coordination. *Linguistics*, *31*, 855–902.

Pickering, M.J., & Traxler, M.J. (1998). Plausibility and recovery from garden paths: An eye-tracking study. *Journal of Experimental Psychology: Learning, Memory, and Cognition*, *24*, 940–961.

Pollard, C., & Sag, I.A. (1993). *Head-driven phrase structure grammar*. Stanford, CA & Chicago, IL: CSLI/University of Chicago Press.

Pritchett, B. (1992). *Grammatical competence and parsing performance*. Chicago: University of Chicago Press.

Rayner, K., Carlson, M., & Frazier, L. (1983). The interaction of syntax and semantics during sentence processing: Eye movements in the analysis of semantically biased sentences. *Journal of Verbal Learning and Verbal Behavior*, *22*, 358–374.

Rayner, K., & Duffy, S.A. (1986). Lexical complexity and fixation times in reading: Effects of word frequency, verb complexity, and lexical ambiguity. *Memory & Cognition*, *14*, 191–201.

Rayner, K., & Frazier, L. (1987). Parsing temporarily ambiguous complements. *Quarterly Journal of Experimental Psychology*, 39, 657–673.

Rayner, K., & Frazier, L. (1989). Selection mechanisms in reading lexically ambiguous words. *Journal of Experimental Psychology: Learning, Memory, and Cognition*, *15*, 779–790.

Rayner, K., Garrod, S.C., & Perfetti, C.A. (1992). Discourse influences in parsing are delayed. *Cognition*, *45*, 109–139.

Scheepers, C., Hemforth, B., & Konieczny, L. (1994). Resolving NP-attachment ambiguities in German verb-final constructions. In B. Hemforth, L. Konieczny, C. Scheepers, & G. Strube (Eds.), *First analysis, reanalysis, and repair* (pp. 51–76) (IIG-Bericht No. 8/94). Freiburg, Germany: Universitaet Freiburg, Institut für Informatik und Gesellschaft.

Spivey-Knowlton, M., & Sedivy, J. (1995). Resolving attachment ambiguities with multiple constraints. *Cognition*, *55*, 227–267.

Spivey-Knowlton, M., Trueswell, J., & Tanenhaus, M.K. (1993). Context and syntactic ambiguity resolution. *Canadian Journal of Experimental Psychology*, *47*, 276–309.

Stowe, L.A. (1986). Parsing WH-constructions: Evidence for on-line gap location. *Language and Cognitive Processes*, *1*, 227–245.

Stowe, L.A., Tanenhaus, M.K., & Carlson, G.M. (1991). Filling gaps on-line: Use of lexical and semantic information in sentence processing. *Language and Speech*, *34*, 319–340.

Sturt, P., & Crocker, M.W. (1996). Incrementality and monotonicity in syntactic parsing. *Language and Cognitive Processes*, *11*, 449–494.

Sturt, P., Pickering, M.J., & Crocker, M.W. (1999). Structural change and reanalysis difficulty in language comprehension. *Journal of Memory and Language*, *40*, 136–150.

Swinney, D.A. (1979). Lexical access during sentence comprehension: (Re)consideration of context effects. *Journal of Verbal Learning and Verbal Behavior*, *15*, 681–689.

Tanenhaus, M.K., Carlson, G., & Trueswell, J.C. (1989). The role of thematic structures in interpretation and parsing. *Language and Cognitive Processes*, *4*, 211–234.

Tanenhaus, M.K., & Trueswell, J.C. (1995). Sentence comprehension. In J. Miller & P. Eimas (Eds.), *Speech, language, and communication* (Vol. 11, pp. 217–262). San Diego, CA: Academic Press.

Taraban, R., & McClelland, J.R. (1988). Constituent attachment and thematic role assignment in sentence processing: Influence of content-based expectations. *Journal of Memory and Language*, *27*, 597–632.

Traxler, M.J., Bybee, M.D., & Pickering, M.J. (1997). Influence of connectives on language comprehension: Evidence for incremental interpretation. *Quarterly Journal of Experimental Psychology*, *50A*, 481–497.

Traxler, M.J., & Pickering, M.J. (1996a). Case-marking in the parsing of complement sentences: Evidence from eye movements. *Quarterly Journal of Experimental Psychology*, *49A*, 991–1004.

Traxler, M.J., & Pickering, M.J. (1996b). Plausibility and the processing of unbounded dependencies: An eye-tracking study. *Journal of Memory and Language*, *35*, 454–475.

Traxler, M.J., Pickering, M.J., & Clifton, C., Jr. (1998). Adjunct attachment is not a form of lexical ambiguity resolution. *Journal of Memory and Language*, *39*, 558–592.

Trueswell, J. (1996). The role of lexical frequency in syntactic ambiguity resolution. *Journal of Memory and Language*, *35*, 566–585.

Trueswell, J., & Tanenhaus, M.K. (1991). Tense, temporal context, and syntactic ambiguity resolution. *Language and cognitive processes*, *6*, 303–338.

Trueswell, J., Tanenhaus, M.K., & Garnsey, S. (1994). Semantic influences on parsing: Use of thematic role information in syntactic disambiguation. *Journal of Memory and Language*, *33*, 285–318.

Trueswell, J., Tanenhaus, M.K., & Kello, C. (1993). Verb-specific constraints in sentence processing: Separating effects of lexical preference from garden-paths. *Journal of Experimental Psychology: Learning, Memory, and Cognition*, *19*, 528–553.

Tyler, L.K., & Marslen-Wilson, W.D. (1977). The on-line effects of semantic context on syntactic processing. *Journal of Verbal Learning and Verbal Behavior*, *16*, 683–692.

Warner, J. & Glass, A.L. (1987). Context and distance-to-disambiguation effects in ambiguity resolution: Evidence from grammaticality judgments of garden path sentences. *Journal of Memory and Language*, *26*, 714–738.

Waters, G., & Caplan, D. (1996). The capacity theory of sentence comprehension: Critique of Just and Carpenter (1992). *Psychological Review*, *103*, 761–772.

CHAPTER SIX

Prosody and language processing

Paul Warren
School of Linguistics and Applied Language Studies, Victoria University of Wellington, New Zealand

INTRODUCTION

The focus of this chapter is the role played by prosody in language processing and the relationship of prosodic organisation to other aspects of utterance structure. The main emphasis will be on the use of prosody in sentence comprehension, particularly its relationship to aspects of syntactic parsing, but I will consider also aspects of the production of prosodic distinctions and the use of prosody in marking other, non-syntactic properties of utterances, such as topic focus. Two main themes run through the chapter. One is that the prosody of an utterance provides a rich and important source of information for language processing, a fact that is reflected in a recent upsurge in research interest in this area. The other is that the most appropriate characterisation of prosody is not in terms of specific measurable features of the speech waveform, but as a phonological system, i.e. a set of oppositions that can be realised by a range of possible features or feature combinations. These oppositions constitute the contrasts that are used by speakers and hearers in the interpretation of utterances.

The chapter is set out as follows. As a preliminary to the study of prosody and language processing, the first section provides some background information on prosodic features and systems, including some explanation of terminology that may be less familiar to the non-linguist.

The next section then presents a range of experimental findings concerning the role of prosody in language processing, including studies of production and comprehension, the latter including off-line studies of the use of prosody in judgements about the structural properties of sentences, on-line studies showing the immediate use of prosody in syntactic structural analysis, and research investigating the use of prosody in other types of structural analysis, such as informational structure and sentence focus. A synthesis of some of these findings is made in the following section, which discusses a set of theoretical issues concerning the relationship of prosody and the language processor. The final section provides some conclusions and points out directions for further research.

THE PHONETICS AND PHONOLOGY OF PROSODY

Prosody has been described as the "sauce" of the sentence (Cutler & Isard, 1980, p. 245); as with the ingredients of a good sauce, it is in practice often not possible to isolate completely the individual components that make up the prosody of an utterance. Indeed, there is a wide range of prosodic features that can be used in isolation or in various combinations to realise a particular flavour of the prosodic sauce. Of these, the chief features are *length*, *loudness*, and *pitch*, which are combined in various ways to mark a number of prosodic distinctions, such as stressed versus unstressed syllables, or questions vs. statements, and so on.

In the following, I describe these basic prosodic features and their perceptual and physical acoustic properties, along with some of the distinctions marked by these features. Subsequently, I present some details of one specific phonological framework, and its use in a transcription system for prosody, providing a frame of reference for the studies presented later in the chapter.

Prosodic features

Prosodic features have often been characterised as "suprasegmentals", i.e. length, loudness, and pitch make special use at some higher level of features that form part of the phonetic description of speech segments. For example, the simple presence of vocal cord vibration is one of the distinguishing properties of certain sound segments known as "voiced" sounds, while the rate of this vocal cord vibration, known as fundamental frequency (abbreviated to F0), is the primary acoustic correlate of pitch. Likewise, as well as being a suprasegmental prosodic feature, length is also a segmental property, with different speech sounds having different intrinsic durations. Of course, the term "suprasegmental" need not mean that the prosodic feature extends over more than one speech segment, since it is for instance possible to realise pitch patterns on a single speech segment, as in the various possible realisations of "ah" or "mm" signalling surprise, agreement, etc.

It is clear that prosodic features cannot be adequately described in terms of acoustic segmental properties. Not least, this is because prosodic features are in practice primarily perceptual parameters. For example, pitch refers to what listeners hear as "high" or "low" tonal properties, rather than to absolute F0 values. The mediation of the perceptual system is seen in a number of ways. First, while faster vocal cord vibration generally leads to higher pitch being perceived, a doubling in the rate of vibration results in less than a doubling of pitch, since the perceptual scale for pitch is not linear. Second, different vocal tracts (i.e. different speakers) have different F0 ranges; most noticeably, females have a higher range than males, and children have a higher range than adults. Our perceptual systems adjust for this—a F0 value of 200 Hz (Hertz, or cycles per second) is usually heard as a high pitch for an adult male speaker, but not for an adult female, and is low for a child. Third, judgements of differences in pitch between two syllables depend not only on a range of further prosodic parameters, such as on the duration and intensity of the syllables and on whether pitch is level or changing across the syllables (for further details, see e.g. 't Hart, Collier, & Cohen, 1990), but also on segmental factors, for instance on which vowel or other voiced sound carries the pitch information, or on whether the consonant preceding a vowel is voiced or voiceless (for a review of these and many other aspects of suprasegmental properties, see Lehiste, 1970).

The primary acoustic correlate of length is duration, usually reported in milliseconds in studies of segment or syllable durations. Perceived duration, or length, is also dependent on other properties of the signal, such as the position of a word in a phrase, the word's prominence, or the overall rhythm or rate of speech (Lehiste, 1970), factors which must be taken into consideration when comparing durations. A further important temporal feature of prosody is pausing, which may be a very brief break in rhythm, and may not in fact correspond to any measurable silence at all; a perceived pause may result simply from the lengthening of sound segments before the "pause" site (cf. further Warren, 1985).

The third primary prosodic feature, loudness, is related to the force of breath used by a speaker. Its main acoustic correlate is amplitude or intensity, determined by the amount of energy present in a sound or sequence of sounds. Again, though, there are additional factors influencing intensity and its perception, such as inherent differences between segments (e.g. open vowels, i.e. those with a larger distance between the tongue and the roof of the mouth, typically have greater intensity than close vowels). Once more, differences in measurable intensity do not bear a straightforward linear relationship to contrasts in perceived loudness, as reflected in the use of a logarithmic decibel (dB) scale for intensity.

Prosodic distinctions

Since they are auditory perceptual features dependent on the interaction of a number of factors, the prosodic parameters outlined previously are already somewhat removed from easily measurable physical characteristics of the speech waveform. The distance between the phonetics (realisation) and phonology (system) of prosody is in fact greater even than this, since the features of pitch, duration, and loudness themselves combine to form a range of prosodic distinctions. Two examples provide a relevant focus here; *stress* and *intonation*.

Stress. There is much terminological confusion in studies of prosody (as discussed for instance by Cruttenden, 1997; Cutler & Ladd, 1983), not least in the use of the terms *stress* and *accent*. Both refer to the relative prominence of syllables, which can be signalled by each of the prosodic features of length, loudness, and pitch, but they have not always been used in the same way by different researchers. In this chapter I will follow Cruttenden (1997: 13–14) in using *stress* as a general term for the relative prominence of a syllable, and *accent* for those cases where this prominence involves pitch marking (hence, also *pitch accent*).

Differences in stress can be noted at a number of levels. For instance, word or lexical stress distinguishes pairs such as *ímport* and *impórt*, or *bíllow* and *belów*. The stress contrast may also involve differences in segmental quality (vowel type) such as the contrast of full and reduced vowels in the first syllables of *résearch* and *reséarch*. Dialects differ in the realisation of many such words, with differences in stress patterns noticeable in the comparison, for example, of British and American English (cf. Kingdon, 1958). Languages also differ in the patterning of word stress; English, as we have seen, uses the possibility of variable stress placement to distinguish between lexical items, but Finnish, Welsh, and French have more fixed stress positions, with word stress on initial, penultimate, and final syllables respectively (Cruttenden, 1997). This difference has implications for the use of stress information in word recognition in different languages, as discussed by Cutler and colleagues (Cutler, 1990; Cutler & Butterfield, 1992; Cutler, Mehler, Norris, & Segui, 1986; Cutler & Norris, 1988; and cf. also Grosjean, 1985). This chapter will have little to say on the role of prosody in the segmentation and access of word forms.

Within larger utterances than the single word, it is clear that there are further differences in prominence, giving rise to degrees of stress. As well as the contrast between *unstressed* and *stressed* syllables, where the former are usually weak, reduced syllables with a central vowel (/ə/ as in the first syllable of *reséarch*) or no vowel at all (as in the use of a "syllabic" nasal in the second syllable of *bútton* /bʌtn̩/), further distinctions are made between types of stressed syllable. For English, three levels of stressed syllable have been proposed. The weakest of these (tertiary stress) involves marking of length and/or loudness; such syllables are often grouped with the unstressed syllables as types of *unaccented* syllables, since they have no pitch marking. The remaining stressed syllables are those that also receive accentual (pitch) prominence, as a result either of the accented syllable having higher or lower pitch than surrounding syllables or of pitch movement across the accented syllable. Within an intonation group (to be defined below), there will be a *primary* pitch accent that is more prominent than other *secondary* accents; this primary accent is frequently referred to as the *nuclear* accent. In English the nuclear accent can be described (rather simplistically) in terms of a starting pitch (high, low), an initial movement from this starting point (rise, fall), and a possible second (and even third) direction of movement (resulting in fall-rise or rise-fall-rise patterns, for example). This movement may also extend from the nucleus onto following syllables within the same intonation group.

These stress levels are demonstrated in (1), which gives a schematic prosodic transcription of a short declarative utterance, with the upper and lower lines representing the speaker's pitch range, and the size of the dots showing the stress level of each syllable.

(1) She's leaving Wellington tomorrow

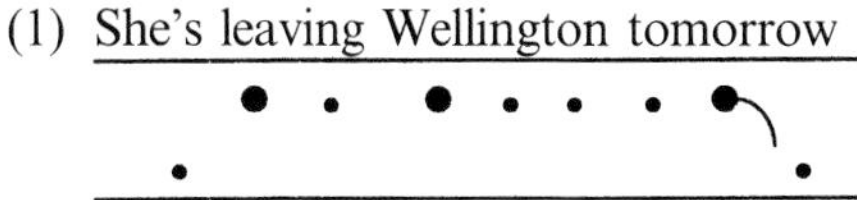

Primary stress or nuclear accent is marked by the fall in pitch on *-mo-*, which is the lexically stressed syllable of *tomorrow*, and this fall continues onto (and through) the final unstressed syllable. Secondary stress is found on *lea-*; here the step up in pitch from the preceding unstressed syllable results in pitch prominence. All other syllables are unaccented, and their pitch level is determined by that of the surrounding accented syllables. Of the unaccented syllables, only *We-* carries tertiary stress, i.e. has lexical stress (marked by length, intensity and/or vowel quality) without having pitch accent prominence.

Just as the same sequence of syllables within a word can be given different interpretations as a result of differences in relative prominences (as in *ímport* vs. *impórt*), so a phrase or sentence can be given a different structure or meaning as a consequence of the type and placement of pitch accents. Thus, the contrast between (1) and (2) depends on the location of the primary or nuclear accent.

(2) She's leaving Wellington tomorrow

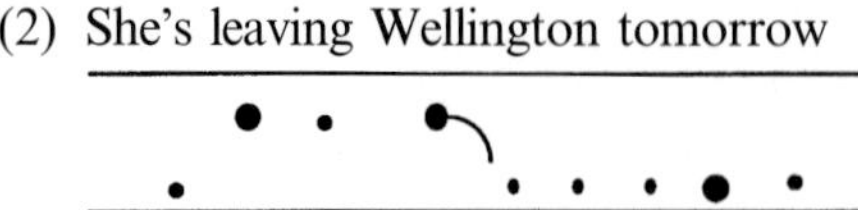

In (2) it is earlier, on the first syllable of *Wellington*, signalling perhaps a correction of the erroneous belief that the subject of the sentence is tomorrow leaving Hamilton.

Intonation. Clearly, as examples (1) and (2) have shown, stress levels and nuclear accent placement form a key aspect of the prosody of an utterance. Additional related aspects are the structuring of an utterance into a set of intonation groups and the intonation tunes associated with each such group. (These groups are also known variously as sense-groups, breath-groups, tone-groups, tone-units, intonational phrases, amongst others.) Intonation groups have a variable domain, and can include grammatical constituents of any level up to the sentence and beyond. They are notoriously difficult to determine within an utterance, not least because many styles of speech are littered with hesitations, interruptions, incomplete sentences, etc. Typically, both internal and external criteria are used to determine boundaries between such units (cf. Cruttenden, 1997).

The internal criteria relate to a judgement that the unit is a complete intonation group with an acceptable complete intonation pattern. Thus, each intonation group typically contains one or more pitch accents, including minimally a nucleus, along with a number of unaccented syllables. The overall pattern of intonation within the intonation group forms the pitch contour or *tune* of that group. Tunes contribute to the meaning of an utterance. For instance, a rising contour on the word string given as a statement in the example in (1) is likely to cause it to be interpreted as a question. This is demonstrated in (3), which also shows how intonation can break an utterance into syntactically non-standard parts—here the utterance has two intonation groups *She's leaving Wellington* and *tomorrow*, each carrying a rising tune. The intended meaning could be a questioning of both her departure from Wellington and her doing it tomorrow.

(3) She's leaving Wellington tomorrow?

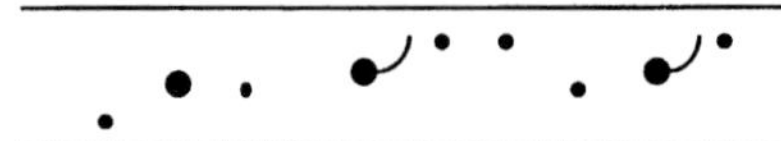

Whereas some pitch patterns recur with relatively constant meanings in any given language, many are often hard to characterise since they include affective and attitudinal as well as linguistic meanings. Indeed, there is disagreement among analysts concerning which possible combinations of pitch levels and movements constitute the most significant tunes and nuclear tones, as well as concerning the meanings attributed to each. Although intonational differences in meaning are not a primary concern of this chapter, it is clear that detailed analyses of the interpretation of utterances will have to recognise the meanings conveyed in this way. One factor that is relevant to syntactic structural analysis is the use of different tunes and/or nuclear tones to mark completion vs. continuation, with rising tunes at the end of an intonation group often signalling that a constituent is incomplete (cf. Warren, Grabe, & Nolan, 1995). We have also seen in (2) how prosody can mark aspects of meaning through the placement and type of pitch accents used to signal *focus* (Fowler & Housum, 1987). Focus can indicate that a constituent (a word or a phrase) is either new in the context or is being used contrastively, and listeners appear to be sensitive to the appropriate use of accent in marking informational structure—new information must be accented, whereas old or given information can only be accented if in contrast (Eefting & Nooteboom, 1991).

The external criteria for determining intonation groups concern the marking of boundaries through pauses and other markers. These include the lengthening of final syllables in an intonation group; changes in the pitch level of unaccented syllables across a boundary, with a step-up from a low final unaccented syllable to a higher initial unaccented syllable, and vice versa; the non-incidence of "connected speech processes", such as deletions and assimilations of speech sounds (e.g. flapping of /t/ to [ɾ] in ... *met Anne* ... , cf. Scott & Cutler, 1984); and anacrusis, which is the speeding-up and often elision of syllables at the beginning of an intonation group. Some of these features would most likely be found after *Wellington* in (3). It is the nature and presence of these boundary markers that has been the focus of many psycholinguistic studies of the use of prosody in language processing, primarily investigating the use of prosodic or intonational phrasing to mark syntactic constituency in otherwise structurally ambiguous word strings (see the next section).

Prosodic systems

The previous description of some key features and distinctions illustrates the richness and complexity of prosodic analysis. Many attempts have been made to provide a characterisation of these features in terms of a phonological prosodic system. From the point of view of language processing, the significance of a phonological analysis of prosodic features is that it acknowledges the fact that perceptually relevant distinctions in prosody often involve the combination of more than one acoustic parameter. Cutler and Isard's reference to prosody as the sauce of the sentence shows clearly that the realisation of prosody is often a complex blend of a number of ingredients. By taking a phonological view of prosody, researchers may be released from the shackles of determining specific contrasts in their materials in terms of hertz, milliseconds, or decibels, while still acknowledging the relevance of each of these to the realisation of prosodic structure.

The previous description of prosodic distinctions is based largely on a traditional "British" analysis of prosody, which divides an utterance into intonation groups, each containing a nuclear tone (Crystal, 1969; O'Connor & Arnold, 1961). The intonation groups may correspond to syntactic clauses, but the location of nuclear tones and the subsequent structuring of utterances into intonation groups may depend also on other factors such as informational focus. A number of alternative prosodic systems have been proposed, each of which contain at best a loose correspondence between prosodic and syntactic structure. One is embodied in the theoretical approaches of Metrical Phonology (Liberman & Prince, 1977; Nespor & Vogel, 1983; Selkirk, 1984), which takes as its basis the distinction between weak (unstressed) and strong (stressed) syllables. Further prosodic constituents are arranged in a hierarchical system, ranging from the syllable through phonological phrases (consisting of a phrasal head and its dependent elements, e.g. a noun with its determiners and adjectives) and intonational phrases (roughly corresponding to intonation groups) to the utterance.

The particular prosodic system to be used as a frame of reference for some of the experimental work reported in later sections is one that has been developed partly out of Metrical Phonology by Pierrehumbert and her colleagues (e.g. Pierrehumbert, 1980; Pierrehumbert & Beckman, 1988; Pierrehumbert & Hirschberg, 1990). This framework has provided the basis of a prosodic labelling system, known as ToBI (for *To*nes and *B*reak *I*ndices), which has been proposed as a standard for the transcription of large speech corpora (Beckman & Ayers, 1994; Silverman et al., 1992), and so the following description incorporates aspects of this system. The significance of a standard transcription system such as ToBI for psycholinguistic as well as phonetic and phonological research is that it allows researchers to be explicit about the prosody of the utterances they study, resulting in greater comparability, replicability and accountability of research.

Pierrehumbert's framework highlights the organisational structure of prosody as a quasi-independent system. That is, rather than being seen as a set of suprasegmental phonetic features, prosody is regarded as a hierarchically organised structure of phonological units, with its own "grammar". One consequence of this view, as pointed out by Beckman (1996), is that prosody, like syntax, has to be "parsed". In other words, a structure and interpretation can be derived from prosodic aspects of an utterance. However, while certain "meanings" can be ascribed to particular prosodic forms (Ladd, 1980), the interpretation of a particular prosody will depend also on the segmental and lexical text with which it is aligned.

The primary features of the system are stress, tune, phrasing, and pitch range. *Pitch range* is, simply, the distance between a speaker's highest and lowest F0 in a contour, which can be manipulated by a speaker for affective reasons or to highlight information. It also varies with discourse structure, with a greater range found at the beginning of a new topic, and a narrower, lower range at the end of an utterance (Brazil, Coulthard, & Johns, 1980).

Stress and *tune* have already been described, but note that tunes in Pierrehumbert's system are abstract patterns of F0, determined by sequences of low and high tones, transcribed in ToBI with L and H respectively. Tunes can be related to a number of other properties of utterances, including contrasts between sentence types, such as that between a statement and a question. Pitch accents in this system are tones that are aligned with stressed syllables, giving prominence within the tune to the lexical item with which they are associated; they are marked in the transcription by placing an asterisk with the tonal marking (e.g. H*), and can be simple or bitonal, the latter involving a movement in pitch (e.g. L + H* shows a rising tone, centred on the high).

Two further accent types are phrase accents and boundary tones, which contribute to the hierarchical *phrasing* of the utterance into intermediate and intonational phrases respectively (Beckman & Pierrehumbert, 1986). Phrase accents are indicated in ToBI transcriptions by "-" (i.e. H– or L–), and boundary tones by "%" (H% or L%).

Boundaries between intonational phrases are also marked by pausing, pre-boundary lengthening and other segmental effects, i.e. the "boundary markings" that form the external definition of intonation groups. These are indicated in ToBI by the "Break Index"—there is a tier in the transcription system specifically for marking the strength of a boundary, or, conversely, the degree of coherence between adjacent words. In the ToBI system the break index ranges from 0 (highest level of coherence) to 4 (least coherent), with 1 as the default for clause-internal word boundaries (0 marks connected speech processes across word boundaries, such as "wanna" contraction, i.e. realisation of "want to" as "wanna").

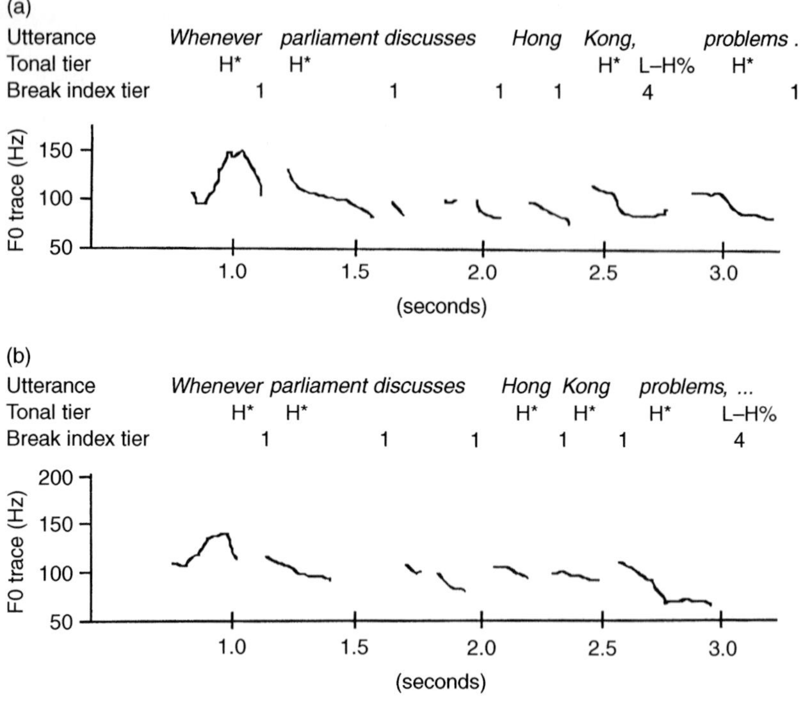

FIG. 6.1 ToBI transcription and pitch trace of two versions of the utterance fragment "Whenever parliament discusses Hong Kong problems...", with a clause boundary before or after "problems" in (a) and (b) respectively.

Figure 6.1 gives example transcriptions of two utterance fragments (based on Warren, Grabe, & Nolan, 1995). Traces of their pitch contours are also included, since ToBI transcriptions are typically based on a combination of pitch traces and auditory judgement. The tonal tier marks the high and low tones, including pitch accents, phrase accents and boundary tones. The phrase accents and boundary tones, together with the break indices on the line below, show that there is a prosodically marked boundary in each fragment that coincides with the clause boundary—before and after *problems* in (a) and (b) respectively. This prosodic boundary is marked by a low phrase tone (L–, reached via a falling contour from the preceding H*) and high boundary tone (H%); together these correspond to what is heard as a falling-rising tone, or a fall-rise nucleus. (Note that while the ToBI system does not explicitly acknowledge the special role of the nucleus, the latter is in most cases recoverable from a ToBI transcription.) As noted earlier, a falling-rising tune is often taken, as here, to show continuation after the clause boundary. Notice also the abstract nature of the H and L tones. For instance, the H* of *Whenever* is clearly higher in absolute F0 terms than that of *problems*, but both are heard as high pitch accents, marked as such by excursion from a pattern which is typical of many languages, including English, namely a downward drift in F0 across the utterance (often referred to as the *declination line*).

In summary, an utterance is realised as a series of intonational phrases, each of which may contain more than one intermediate phrase. The overall tune of an intonational phrase is determined by a sequence of (L and H) pitch accent(s), phrase accent(s), and a boundary tone. Intonational phrase boundaries may also be marked by durational and segmental effects.

EXPERIMENTAL FINDINGS ON THE ROLE OF PROSODY

Prosody and language production

The previous linguistic description of prosody suggests that any single prosodic distinction will often not correspond uniquely to a specific difference in acoustic features. However, the advocacy of a phonological descriptive framework for prosody should not be taken to imply any diminution of the many studies that have focused on the relationship between syntactic structure and the specific phonetic exponents of prosody. Such studies have provided us with a wealth of information on the realisation of sentence structure in spoken language. At the forefront of much of this research has been the work of Cooper and his colleagues (Cooper, 1976; Cooper & Paccia-Cooper, 1980; Cooper & Sorensen, 1981; Danly & Cooper, 1979), building on earlier work by Goldman-Eisler (1968), Klatt (1975), Lehiste (1972), and others.

This type of research has started from the assumption that differences in syntactic structure will be related to differences in the realisation of sentences, in terms of the acoustic features described above, i.e. pausing, speech segment durations, F0 modulation, and amplitude, as well as the incidence of phonological processes such as between-word assimilations or reductions of speech sounds. Investigation of a range of syntactic contrasts allows the development of a production model (e.g. Cooper & Paccia-Cooper, 1980), in which various factors, such as the syntactic complexity of the boundaries between words and the overall rate of speech, feature as variables in an algorithm that makes predictions about the acoustic speech features that will be found in subsequent data.

As a psycholinguistic model, this framework has often been used as a test-bed for the relative complexity and psychological plausibility of differing syntactic theories. For example, Cooper (1976) compared alternative syntactic representations of complement structures such as example (4) below. One analysis places *Kate* in subject position in the complement clause, as in (5), while the other raises it to object position in the higher clause, equivalent to (6). These analyses correspond to Chomsky (1973) and Postal (1974) respectively.

(4) John expected Kate to be at the party
(5) John expected Kate would be at the party
(6) John expected Kate at the party

On the basis of speech data from recordings of sets of such sentences, showing pre-boundary segment lengthening of the verb (*expected*) in both (4) and (5), Cooper claims support for Chomsky's view of complements, with *Kate* as the first word of a new clause.

This approach has considered a range of structural ambiguities predicted to result in distinctions in prosodic features. For example, durational properties of sentences reflect the level of attachment of the prepositional phrase *with a stick* in (7) as a modifier of the noun phrase *the cop* or of the verb *hit*.

(7) Jeffrey hit the cop with a stick

Increases in the duration of words in the position of *cop* and of the following pause are found when the prepositional phrase modifies the verb (Cooper & Paccia-Cooper, 1980; Warren, 1985).

Approaches such as this have their problems, such as the fact that the accuracy of prediction of a syntax-to-phonetics coding algorithm is dependent both on the computational assumptions of the algorithm itself and on the theory of syntax that is assumed for the input structures. Relatively minor adjustments in syntactic assumptions have been shown to result in major differences of prediction of prosodic features (Warren, 1985). Nevertheless, systematic studies of this type have shed considerable light on the relationship between syntactic structure and speech phenomena, and are therefore relevant to the study of the use of prosody in language comprehension. Among the basic findings of this approach are that stronger syntactic boundaries are more likely to be associated with the tonal and break index properties of an intonational phrase boundary, namely: more marked F0 movement (falls or fall-rises) on pre-boundary syllables; stepping-up in F0 across the boundary, often corresponding to a re-setting of pitch range at the beginning of a new constituent; a higher incidence of pausing (variously defined), together with longer individual pauses and greater pre-boundary lengthening of the segments and/or syllables of a word. Changes in amplitude across boundaries are also reported, though these are generally less reliable. When boundaries between words are weak, i.e. the break index is low, there is also a greater tendency for certain phonological processes to occur, such as between-word assimilations (/d j/ to [dʒ] in "did you"; /s/ to [ʃ] in "drinks champagne") and reductions (/t/ to the flap [ɾ] in "met Anne"; "want to" to "wanna") (see Cooper & Paccia-Cooper, 1980; Holst & Nolan, 1995; Scott & Cutler, 1984; Warren, Nolan, Grabe, & Holst, 1995). In other words, these studies have largely revealed patterns that correspond to the presence vs. absence of a phrase accent or a boundary tone at key sites in the utterances.

The differences in duration and fundamental frequency found in production studies are often statistically reliable but can also be small and possibly not detectable by listeners (Cooper & Paccia-Cooper, 1980). Detectability is not an immediate issue for the "syntax and speech" approach, which regards the study of comprehension as a secondary task, following the development of a clear model for production data. Clearly, though, the consideration of prosody in sentence comprehension depends on there being detectable differences between alternative readings of a sentence. We saw earlier that one advantage of considering prosody as a phonological system rather than as a set of individual phonetic features is that these relatively small distinctions in single features can be seen as components of a more salient difference at the phonological level. Treating prosody as a phonological system also reflects the common observation that speakers may use different phonetic parameters to make particular distinctions. Cutler and Isard (1980) report a study of the prosodic marking of boundaries in the same sentences by two speakers. While one speaker relied heavily on lengthening, the other used more marked pitch changes with no consistent durational effects, showing how cues from different aspects of the speech wave may potentially signal a single contrast in syntactic structure. As one author has put it, "normal speech is clearly a redundant multi-cue signalling system" (Henderson, 1980, p. 199).

A further advantage of a phonological approach has been demonstrated in a study of production data carried out by Gee and Grosjean (1983). These authors found that an algorithm based on phonological prosodic structure (using a model from Metrical Phonology) provided better predictions of pausing than the syntactically driven model of Cooper and Paccia-Cooper. The disparity results from the fact that syntactic and prosodic structures, although similar in many respects, are not isomorphic; prosodic structure is influenced by performance factors such as breathing, by aspects of the utterance that are not always closely linked to the syntactic structure, such as focus and informational structure, and by other interpretative differences associated with different tunes and pitch accent placements.

Prosody and comprehension

Syntactic processing—off-line studies. Speech production data have shown reliable prosodic marking of a range of syntactic distinctions, and further studies have aimed to determine whether listeners can use the available prosodic cues to assign a structural interpretation to an utterance (e.g. Lehiste, 1973; Streeter, 1978; Wales & Toner, 1979). These are mostly off-line studies, requiring an untimed decision or judgement after a stimulus has been presented. Some have used natural recordings of structurally ambiguous sentences; others have used editing, (re)synthesis, and other manipulations in an attempt to control certain parameters in the utterances.

In an early study, Lehiste (1973) used non-manipulated data in a judgement task, to determine which acoustic cues correlated most clearly with perceived boundary distinctions. She tested a range of different ambiguity types, including those in (8) and (9), and found that the sentences most clearly disambiguated were those with more than one possible surface bracketing, such as *[Steve or Sam] and Bob* or *Steve or [Sam and Bob]* for (8).

(8) Steve or Sam and Bob will come
(9) German teachers visit Greensboro

Lehiste also found that durational cues, i.e. pausing and pre-boundary lengthening, were the most reliable. F0 was not systematically used, but was more useful in those cases where the ambiguity lay not in alternative bracketing but in labelling, e.g. *German teachers* in (9) as N+N or Adj+N, corresponding to the difference between compounds and phrases. For a linguistic analysis of this, see Chomsky and Halle (1968); for further psycholinguistic considerations, see Grabe, Warren, and Nolan (1994), Warren (1995). As Lehiste points out, greater reliance on durational features to signal structure is unsurprising given the use that is made of intonational (primarily F0) patterns to mark other distinctions involving meaning and affect.

In a task using sentence materials which had been digitally analysed and then resynthesised, Warren (1985) manipulated duration and F0 cues independently. Subjects heard sentence fragments and chose the most likely continuation. Durational properties (pausing and lengthening) provided powerful cues to syntactic structure even in the absence of F0; the strength of the cue depended on the syntactic contrast involved, with clause closure ambiguities such as (10) less dependent on additional F0 cues than complement ambiguities like (11) or category ambiguities such as (12) (fragments heard by subjects are given in italics).

(10a) *Before the king rides his horse* it takes ages to groom.
(10b) *Before the king rides his horse* is groomed for him.
(11a) *The actor learnt the text* amused the cast.
(11b) *The actor learnt the text* and knew his role.
(12a) *The media report said that the talk shows* handsomely the government's aims.
(12b) *The media report said that the talk shows* had an educational slant.

A different source of variability in the use of a cue is reported by Scott and Cutler (1984). These researchers considered the use in sentence processing of the phonological modifications resulting from flapping (of /t/ to [ɾ]) and palatalisation (/d j/ to [dʒ]) across word boundaries. These processes were found to occur in the speech of Chicago Americans when the boundary between the two words was not a strong syntactic one (compare the sequence "met Anne" in "The last time we met Anne, she..." and "The last time we met, Anne..."). The effects of such processes were also readily used as cues in phrase-boundary judgements by subjects from the same population, but not by British English speakers, and inconsistently by British English speakers resident in Chicago. Scott and Cutler point out that dialect differences and the association of assimilated forms with certain socio-economic groups in the United Kingdom could have affected British listeners' relative unwillingness to interpret the cues as structural rather than sociolinguistic.

Other research has considered whether syntactic or prosodic structure is the best predictor of disambiguation, on a parallel to Gee and Grosjean's (1983) prediction for speech production features. Like Lehiste (1970), Nespor and Vogel (1983, 1986) compared ambiguities involving either syntactic constituency or syntactic labelling, but their materials contrasted also in prosodic structure, in terms of intonational and phonological phrases (see earlier). They predicted that syntactic ambiguities will only be resolved if their prosodic structures also contrast. Indeed they found that (Italian) sentences differing in syntactic constituency or labelling but not in prosodic structure were correctly identified only at chance level, whereas those with differences in prosodic phrasing were reliably disambiguated.

Price, Ostendorf, Shattuck-Hufnagel, and Fong (1991) also link syntactic disambiguation to intonational phonology rather than directly to specific correspondences between syntax and phonetic features. Their results distinguish prosodic phrasing and tonal cues, with break index strength a major cue to syntactic disambiguation, while differences in intonational cues (e.g. pitch accent placement) were, as in Lehiste's (1973) study, more closely related to semantic distinctions.

As suggested earlier, the indirect linking of syntax and speech features through a prosodic phonological system is attractive to considerations of language processing since it allows a greater degree of generalisation when specifying the prosodic events that signal syntactic structure. A contrast in syntactic analysis may thus correspond to a particular phonological distinction, which can have alternative realisations in terms of contrasts in duration, F0, amplitude or a combination of these features.

A question which arises from this approach concerns the relationship between the prosodic features, and how listeners interpret feature combinations. Beach (1991) used synthesised speech materials containing local complement ambiguities, such as (13), where the ambiguity is resolved morphosyntactically into a transitive or complement structure by the choice of material in braces:

(13) Jay believed the gossip about the neighbours {right away/wasn't true}

The key manipulations carried out by Beach involved the duration of the verb and the extent of F0 fall on that word (*believed* in the example), which were independently varied in steps on continua from extreme "transitive" forms to extreme "complement" realisations. With greater durations and more marked falls, subjects were more likely to choose the interpretation in which *the gossip* starts a complement clause. Interestingly, the two phonetic features stood in a cue-trading relationship, such that the importance of one of these cues increased when the other was in the middle of its range and was therefore assumed to be ambiguous between the two structural interpretations. This suggests that the phonetic cues to syntax are integrated into some kind of a (probabilistic) boundary percept. At the very least it confirms that the individual cues are not interpreted independently of one another.

Syntactic processing—on-line studies. While the studies discussed above show that prosodic cues can in many cases be used by listeners to determine the intended reading of a spoken sentence, they do not show that such distinctions are *necessarily* used in the immediate interpretation of utterances. As off-line studies, they are unable to do more than demonstrate a capacity for prosody to disambiguate.

In recent years researchers have begun to use on-line (e.g. reaction time) techniques to examine the use of prosodic cues in sentence interpretation. For instance, Tyler and Warren (1987) assessed listeners' use of syntax, prosody, and semantics with a word-monitoring task, previously shown to be sensitive to the developing syntactic and semantic interpretation of sentences (Marslen-Wilson, Tyler, & Seidenberg, 1978). Tyler and

Warren compared local and global disruptions both to syntactic and to prosodic organisation, for both meaningful and syntactically well-formed but anomalous utterances. They found that the strongest and most consistent effects were for local disruptions of either type (syntactic or prosodic). Global prosodic disruptions had significant effects for both meaningful and anomalous utterances, whereas global disruptions in syntactic organisation only affected meaningful prose. The results suggested that prosody has both a local role, helping listeners construct local relationships between words as they interpret an utterance, and a global role, relating phrases together. It was suggested that the prosodic organisation of a sentence, possibly into a hierarchical phonological structure, determines listeners' ability to detect a target word more rapidly later in an anomalous utterance than earlier (Marslen-Wilson & Tyler, 1980). In fact, it appears (Grosjean & Hirt, 1996) that subjects are able to make good use of the accumulating rhythmic properties of an utterance (which might be taken to arise from a hierarchical prosodic structure) in order to make predictions about its continuation, although this is dependent on the importance of rhythm to the language concerned; French speakers can predict only whether an utterance has finished, whereas English speakers can predict how much material is to come.

Further on-line studies have focused on the use of prosodic cues in the resolution of the kinds of ambiguity examined in research on parsing strategies. For instance, Marslen-Wilson, Tyler, Warren, Grenier and Lee (1992) and Warren, Grabe and Nolan (1995) show in cross-modal priming experiments that structural preferences are blocked or modified by prosodic information. Thus the strategy of minimal attachment (based on processing of visual text, e.g. Rayner & Frazier, 1987) expects the noun phrase *the last offer from the management* to be interpreted as object of the verb *considered* in the fragment in (14):

(14) The workers considered the last offer from the management.

However, Marslen-Wilson et al. (1992) found that when an auditory version of this fragment was taken from a recording of a non-minimal attachment sentence (continuing ... *was a real insult*), it provided a better prime of the visual naming probe *WAS* (appropriate to the non-minimal attachment reading) than a fragment taken from a minimal attachment version. Although they did not carry out a prosodic analysis of their materials, Marslen-Wilson et al. claimed that the utterance contains prosodic phonological information that influences the structural interpretation.

Warren, Grabe, and Nolan (1995) present acoustic and auditory analyses of their materials, as well as cross-modal naming latencies that show that subjects are sensitive to the appropriate prosodic distinctions in making a structural interpretation. The materials investigated the parsing operation of Late Closure (Frazier, 1979), which expects incoming material to be included in the current syntactic constituent where possible, thus predicting that *problems* in unpunctuated versions of (15) will be interpreted as part of a noun phrase with *Hong Kong*.

(15a) When parliament discusses Hong Kong problems, they take ages to solve.
(15b) When parliament discusses Hong Kong, problems are solved instantly.

Warren, Grabe, and Nolan considered the prosodic marking of clause boundaries, corresponding to the position of the commas in (15). In addition, they investigated the role of accent placement on words and phrases like *Hong Kong* in (15). In some contexts in English, including the citation context, such items have two full vowels and a late accent, i.e. on *Kong*. When the same items are immediately followed by an accented syllable, the accent will often be placed earlier; thus *Hong Kóng* becomes *Hóng Kong próblems* (cf. Durand, 1990; Giegerich, 1985; Hogg & McCully, 1987; Liberman & Prince, 1977). In addition to a strong effect on interpretation from sentence-level prosody, the cross-modal naming study found that early accent placement could be used to signal an immediately following accented item, i.e. as further evidence that the current constituent was not yet complete. However, the use of this cue was sensitive to whether early stress might be acceptable even when the following item was not accented, as determined in a separate test for the items used. Possible alternative interpretations of early accent include contrastive emphasis (*NAVY-blue*) and the lexicalization of early-accent forms (*HEATHrow*).

Using resynthesised materials to control prosodic cues, Nagel, Shapiro, Tuller and Nawy (1996) kept F0 constant and explored the role of the duration of the verb (*promised*) and following pause in complement ambiguities like (16), similar to those studied by Marslen-Wilson et al. (1992):

(16a) The company owner promised the wage increase to the workers.
(16b) The company owner promised the wage increase would be substantial.

Subjects made a lexical decision to a visual probe word presented during the (morphosyntactically) disambiguating region at the end of the sentence (i.e. after *increase*). Response times were significantly affected by whether the material in the disambiguating region matched the structure indicated by the prosody of the utterances, showing that subjects assign constituent structure on the basis of prosodic information in their immediate interpretation of such utterances.

In an experiment combining prosodic break location and verb argument structure, Pynte and Prieur (1996) considered the attachment site of prepositional phrases (PPs) in sentences such as (17) and (18), where the material in braces shows the choice between a PP modifying the verb phrase (VP) or the noun phrase (NP).

(17) The spies informed the guards {of the conspiracy/of the palace}
(18) The student chose a flat {with care/with a balcony}

Pynte and Prieur manipulated the position of prosodic breaks, marked by lower F0 and increased segment durations as well as by a pause (which the authors standardised to 150 ms). Using word monitoring tasks, Pynte and Prieur found that the presence of such a break after the verb resulted in response times that seemed to reflect a preference for NP attachments: *of the palace* in (17); *with a balcony* in (18). A second break before the PP, however, appeared to neutralise the effect of the first break, resulting in faster monitoring times for VP attachments, and markedly longer latencies for NP attachments. This last effect was particularly marked for verbs which expect two arguments, such as *inform* in (17), where a second break matches the preferred argument structure and forces the listener initially to contemplate a higher but, it turns out, inappropriate attachment of the PP (*of the palace*). Though their experiment was conducted in French, Pynte and Prieur found it fruitful to discuss their findings in the context of Selkirk's prosodic analysis of English syntax (Selkirk, 1984), pointing out that the patterning of acceptable prosodic break locations reflects the phrasings permitted by that analysis. I shall return to this discussion of possible prosodic phrasing and verb-argument structure in the next section.

Further experiments have used dichotic switch monitoring, which, unlike certain of the cross-modal techniques, avoids the premature cessation of the auditory sentence and does not require the listener to focus on a second modality for the test stimulus. Instead, the test sentence is presented at a lower volume in one headphone channel than in the other, and this difference in volume is switched across channels at a key point in the sentence. The subject's task is to press a response button on detecting the switch, and this has been shown to be sensitive to a number of general syntactic and prosodic characteristics of sentences (Briscoe & Warren, 1983; Flores d'Arcais, 1978; Warren, 1985). Dobroth and Speer (1995) measured response times to switches occurring immediately after morphosyntactic disambiguation in closure ambiguities such as (19) (i.e. before *closed*).

(19) Before the detective investigates the crime scenes {are/they're} closed off to reporters.

Prosodic boundaries marked either early closure (at *investigates*) or late closure (*scenes*). When morphosyntactic ambiguity resolution conflicted with these prosodic cues, switch monitoring latencies were significantly slower, echoing a similar disruptive effect of inappropriate prosody on switch monitoring reported in Warren (1984).

These studies reveal a recent accumulation of evidence for the use of prosody in on-line sentence processing. However, not all the data which have appeared support the influence of prosody on parsing, since there are a few studies that have failed to find prosodic effects, and these will clearly also need to be accounted for in any coherent theory that emerges of the use of prosody in parsing. For example, Watt & Murray (1996) fail to replicate the findings for attachment sentences reported by Marslen-Wilson et al. (1992). Using a range of experimental paradigms (cross-modal naming and cross-modal lexical decision with differing secondary tasks, as well as mispronunciation detection), they find no evidence that prosodic information is being used to guide parsing decisions.

One possibility that is suggested to account for these findings (Watt & Murray, 1996) is that previous research (e.g. Marslen-Wilson et al., 1992) has used materials with particularly marked prosodic contrasts between tokens. Although this is obviously a hazard in any experiment involving an explicit contrast between prosodic forms has been set up, there are other cases where this possibility is less likely. In the study by Warren, Grabe, and Nolan (1995), for instance, the nature of the experimental materials was based on systematic auditory and acoustic analysis of larger sets of speakers and materials who read the different versions of experimental materials on separate occasions and so would be less likely to produce over-emphasised distinctions (Grabe & Warren, 1995). Inconsistency of findings between experimenters, even using the same paradigms, is a strong motivation for clear and precise documentation and transcription of the experimental materials used.

Processing of other kinds of information. As already indicated, prosody is not linked solely to the syntactic structure of sentences, but also reflects various aspects of the meaning of an utterance. One aspect mentioned was the use of different *tunes* to realise different sentence types, such as declaratives and questions. This is clearly an area in which much psycholinguistic research is still to be done—how do listeners respond to these different tune types, and what are the implications for theories of sentence parsing? That is, what construal is made of the prosody of a sentence such that the surface word order of a statement, such as (20), is interpreted as a question?

(20) You really expect me to believe that?

Tune interpretation may also depend on dialect. One tune that is becoming increasingly common in many varieties of English, and not just in New Zealand and Australia (cf. Cruttenden, 1995), is the final high rise (HRT—high rising terminal). To the outsider or relative newcomer, this tune—perhaps because of its association with question forms—seems to suggest uncertainty or deference, but studies show that this is not how it is more generally distributed or perceived (Britain, 1992; Britain & Newman, 1992). However, reaction to such forms may also depend on a similar acclimatisation to that discussed by Scott and Cutler (1984) in the context of phonological processes in Chicago English (see earlier).

It was noted previously that accent placement can be varied to alter the focus of an utterance. A clutch of psycholinguistic studies have investigated such focus effects in the interpretation of sentences. Speer, Crowder, and Thomas (1993) manipulated both prosodic boundary placement and the prosodic marking of focus, and argued from paraphrase and sentence recognition tasks that both these aspects of the prosodic organisation of an utterance affect its interpretation and subsequent representation in memory. Whereas Price et al. (1991) suggest that focus may not have a direct role to play specifically in syntactic disambiguation, Schafer, Carter, Clifton, and Frazier (1996) present data which suggest that the point of attachment of a relative clause may be determined by the position of focus within a preceding complex NP. Thus in (21) the relative clause beginning with *that* will be interpreted as a modifier of either *propeller* or *plane*, depending on which of these carries a pitch accent (usually a H* accent in the ToBI transcription system).

(21) The sun sparkled on the propeller of the plane that the mechanic was so carefully examining.

Schafer et al.'s data, from questions asked about the interpretation of each sentence after it is presented, also show that this "focus attraction" does not depend on the prosodic status of the relative clause itself, i.e. an accented (new) clause is no more likely to be attached to the focused noun than an unaccented (given) clause.

These off-line studies of focus provide little information on the time-course of the use of prosodic information in establishing antecedent relations. Clearly, further research should determine whether there is an immediate processing advantage for structural decisions such as relative clause attachment that might result from the appropriate use of prosodic marking of focus.

PROSODY AND THE LANGUAGE PROCESSOR

The preceding sections have addressed some of the "what", "why", and "how" questions concerning the role of prosody in language processing. We have seen that prosody includes the durational and intonational properties of utterances, as well as segmental features such as assimilations, and that these various parameters can be viewed as components of a phonological prosodic system. We have also seen that prosody is used to indicate syntactic structure as well as discourse-level relations and other interpretative functions, but we have not delved at all into further meaning-related areas of the use of prosody, such as the expression of affective or attitudinal meanings. The "how" questions have included discussion of the notion that prosody may be interpreted as a phonological structure rather than as a set of distinct phonetic features, and the suggestion that these features may be integrated pre-linguistically in a cue-trading relationship, with the significance of one feature increasing as the interpretation of another becomes ambiguous.

There is a broader aspect to the question of how prosody is used in language processing, and this involves discussion of where and when prosodic information is used in relation to other information available to the language processor. In effect, it is very difficult to keep apart these two questions (where and when), since it is rather like taking two perspectives on one issue, namely the extent and nature of the interaction (or modularity) of prosodic and other information sources.

Where

Under the "where" rubric I will focus on the question of whether prosody should be regarded as a separate stream in the initial input to the language processor, or whether instead it is simply another aspect of one integrated input, taken to also include at least syntactic information.

There are a number of reasons why one might conjecture that prosody might constitute a separate processing component, providing a separate input stream. Prosody has its own grammatical or phonological structure, which is not totally isomorphic with syntactic structure. It can be used to convey non-structural aspects of communication, such as attitude and affect. Furthermore it shows right-hemispherical specialisation while other speech-related functions show left-hemisphere advantage (e.g. Grosjean & Hirt, 1996). Although such observations clearly involve a number of separate motivations for proposing a module specifically for prosodic analysis, they show nevertheless that there may be more than just some intuitive basis for such a proposal. We must distinguish, however, between the hypothesis that a prosodic component completes its own structural analysis of the input, which is then compared with the output of other grammatical analysers (at various stages of analysis, to be discussed later), and the suggestion that such a component recognises prosodic primitives much in the way that the word recognition system identifies candidate words, and presents these to the language processor as part of an integrated input stream.

Although most of this research makes little explicit comment on this issue, there is often an implicit assumption in this work that prosody somehow provides a separate strand of input that can be called on when required. For example, Stirling and Wales (1996) ask the question of whether prosody directs or supports sentence processing, that is, they ask whether prosody plays a pro-active role in determining the parse of an utterance, or provides confirmatory evidence for a syntactic analysis. Either of these functions implies that prosodic analysis is a separate component of analysis, rather than part of the initial structural input itself.

There is, however, a modular approach (in the sense of a modular syntactic component) of a somewhat different type and which is compatible with much of the experimental data. This is one in which the initial input to the syntactic processor, in the analysis of *spoken* language, is a representation that has been enriched by the inclusion of prosodic information as part of the structural description of words and phrases. Such a thesis is very much in the spirit of Frazier's discussion (1990) of "pseudoencapsulated" modules, where a task is defined in advance (in this case processing spoken language), allowing the specification of the input information relevant to that task (here, prosodic information). While this approach is initially rather attractive, in practice I suspect it will turn out to be somewhat problematic. This is because of the non-isomorphism of syntactic and prosodic structure mentioned earlier, and the fact that the prosodic structure (the tune and its associated tones) can be aligned with the syntactic structure in a number of different ways. (These and related issues are discussed further by Beckman, 1996.)

Steedman (e.g. 1991) has attempted to derive an explicit grammar of prosody and to link this to a model of sentence parsing in which prosody and syntax form two aspects of the same structural description. Steedman uses Pierrehumbert's system of prosodic analysis in conjunction with a parser based on Combinatory Categorial Grammar. One of the aims of his approach is to characterise interpretations of utterances that are not predicated simply on syntactic structure, but which depend on questions of presupposition and focus, or theme and rheme, and which have their correlates in prosodic structure. For example, the phrase "Fred ate the beans" has the same syntactic analysis but differing propositional structure when used as an answer to the two questions in (22) and (23)

(22) Well what about the BEANS? Who ate THEM?
(23) Well what about FRED? What did HE eat?

In response to (22), "ate the beans" would constitute the Theme (background) and "Fred" the Rheme (answer), whereas in answer to (23), the Theme is "Fred ate" and the Rheme is "the beans". This second propositional structure marks a division of the sentence that does not correspond to a traditional syntactic grouping into subject and predicate, although it does constitute an acceptable prosodic structuring (obeying Selkirk's, 1984, "sense unit condition"). A likely prosodic realisation of the two answers is given in (24) and (25), based on Steedman (1991) and using the ToBI transcription framework outlined earlier.

(24) (FRED) (ate the BEANS)
H* L- L+H* L–H%

(25) (FRED ate) (the BEANS)
L+H* L–H% H* L–L%

In the grammar fragment that Steedman presents, pitch accents are associated with specific propositional functions in an utterance. For instance, the L+H* pitch accent characterises a background focus. When it is combined with a following L–H% intonational phrase boundary, it forms an intonational phrase constituting a Theme. On the other hand, a Rheme is formed by an "answer" focus, represented by a H* pitch accent, combining with a low-tone boundary. Steedman extends his grammar to include rules governing the combinatory possibilities of such prosodic categories. For instance, if a Rheme carries a boundary tone (the L–L% in (25), i.e. a full intonational phrase boundary), then the Rheme needs to be combined with a preceding Theme. If it only has a phrase accent (the L– in (24), an intermediate phrase boundary), it combines with a following Theme. Steedman also introduces a "prosodic constituent condition", which prohibits a syntactic analysis if the combinatory analysis of the prosodic structure does not allow the same combination of constituents, and vice versa. In this way, certain parses of the utterance are blocked by the prosodic structure. Although the presentation treats syntactic and prosodic structure separately, and though the model on which he bases his prosodic analysis highlights the independent semantic possibilities of prosodic structure (Pierrehumbert & Hirschberg, 1990), Steedman sees syntactic and prosodic categories as two aspects of the same structural input, using the same principles of combination and composition, and collapsing together the "informational structure" of prosody, syntax, and semantics.

Marcus and Hindle (1990) also collapse prosodic information together with other aspects of the input to the parsing process. In their case, however, this is achieved by regarding just one component of the prosodic organisation of utterances, namely certain obligatory intonational boundaries, as a specific type of lexical item. These are then parsed along with other lexical items in the input string by a deterministic parser, i.e. one which cannot easily revise a structural analysis once it is made. This parser produces "chunks" of phrase structure description containing theta-role information such as verb-argument structure. Marcus and Hindle illustrate their views of the role of intonation with the example in (26), from Frazier and Rayner (1982).

(26) After you drank the strange looking water was discovered to be polluted.

In eye movement studies, this sentence leads to an inappropriate late closure analysis, with *the strange looking water* interpreted as the object of *drank*. Marcus and Hindle claim that this is because *drank* subcategorises for NP complements (i.e. expects a direct object) like *water*. When an intonational boundary intervenes between *drank* and the potential object NP, the theta-role assignment is prevented. In text, commas fulfil the same function (cf. also Mitchell, 1994). The mechanism proposed by Marcus and Hindle to account for the use of intonation in parsing is simple and attractive, but it is limited to the use of obligatory intonational boundaries, defined as further lexical items in the parse stream. It is not clear, therefore, how it would explain the use of other prosodic information such as that discussed by Steedman (1991), or the accent placement in "stress-shift" items, which Warren, Grabe, and Nolan (1995) show is used by listeners in processing closure ambiguities similar to the example discussed by Marcus and Hindle.

Both Steedman's and Marcus and Hindle's analyses represent attempts to integrate prosodic information into existing models of structural parsing at the input stage. Both are incomplete analyses, and both would have difficulty in dealing with some of the naturally occurring variation in prosodic realisations that results in the ambiguities of prosodic parsing discussed by Beckman (1996). The latter specifically discusses one problem for Steedman's analysis, namely the finding in her data that the boundary after a Rheme such as that in the first part of (24) above can in fact be a full intonational phrase boundary, which in Steedman's grammar would result in positing a backward- rather than forward-looking Rheme. Such (possibly minor) problems apart, it is clear that these models merit further serious consideration and development as frameworks that acknowledge the key role that prosody can play in language processing.

When

The "when" question concerns the point or points in the analysis of the spoken input at which prosody is used. It considers as it were the granularity of the use of prosodic information in interpretation—how much of the utterance is processed before prosody has a role to play? This issue is largely tangential to the question of where in the input the influence of prosody is exerted, since Steedman's and Marcus and Hindle's models discussed in the preceding section both propose the inclusion of prosodic information in the initial input to the parser, but the latter model only includes major (obligatory) intonational boundaries, while the former has a wider range of boundaries and pitch accents in the input description.

At one extreme, it might be envisaged that prosody provides a continuous supply of information to the parser, either as part of the parser's input (as approximated in Steedman's model), or as a highly interactive system of informational components. At the other extreme, a more modular approach could be taken, in the sense that prosody might only affect processing once the syntactic parse is completed. In considering her off-line ambiguity resolution data, Beach (1991) suggests that either framework (modular or interactive) can be modified to include prosodic information. A modular approach (e.g. the syntax-driven parser of Frazier, 1979, 1987) might allow the use of prosody along with other non-syntactic information sources in the verification and possible subsequent revision of an already-completed syntactic parse. In an interactive model (Marslen-Wilson, 1987; Marslen-Wilson & Tyler, 1987), prosody would serve as a further source of information constraining the initial interpretation of the utterance. Between these two positions, as Beach points out, there lie a number of "weak modular" and "weak interactive" models, which allow interaction between information sources at certain points in the parse, such as at phrase boundaries (e.g. Altmann & Steedman, 1988; Tanenhaus, Carlson, & Trueswell, 1989).

Extreme modular and interactive approaches can perhaps be distinguished by considering the timed response data from the studies presented earlier. For instance, the cross-modal naming studies of Marslen-Wilson et al. (1992) and Warren, Grabe, & Nolan (1995) demonstrate that subjects use prosodic information to derive an interpretation that differs from that expected by a "default" parsing operation, and that they do this before morphosyntactic information becomes available that might resolve the ambiguity. For example, Warren, Grabe, and Nolan (1995) used a probe word compatible with the early closure interpretation of sentence fragments such as (27), and found faster response times following early closure prosody than after late closure prosody.

(27) When parliament discusses Hong Kong problems.

This approach could be criticised for only testing the use of prosody in overriding a "default" parse, and for failing to demonstrate that prosody is used as a necessary part of all spoken sentence comprehension. In terms of the architecture of a parsing system, this could mean that prosody serves as a kind of checking system, providing additional information to guide the parser away from a default when necessary (cf. Briscoe, 1987). However, Nagel et al. (1996) found effects of inappropriate prosodic information for both object and complement versions of (28), and Dobroth and Speer (1995) similarly found effects of mismatch between prosodic and morphosyntactic ambiguity resolution in both readings of closure ambiguities such as (29).

(28) The company owner promised the wage increase {to the workers/ would be substantial}

(29) Before the detective investigates the crime scenes {are/they're} closed off to reporters.

Such results suggest that prosody is used on-line in all structural assignments, though they are still interpretable in terms of a weak interactive framework in which prosodic information is checked at potential boundary sites. Since these sites are almost always the points at which the use of prosodic information has been tested in these experiments, it is not possible to distinguish weak interactive models from fully interactive ones, nor indeed from models in which prosody might be assumed to take a more active and directive role.

A weak interactive approach to the use of prosody in parsing is suggested by Pynte and Prieur (1996) in their study of prosodic breaks in PP attachment. These authors propose in fact that prosody helps to group low-level syntactic constituents in a way that matches a verb's argument structure. When the grouping is inappropriate, as when prosodic breaks favour a NP attachment of the PP but the verb expects the PP as one of its arguments, or when the prosody supports a verb attachment but the verb only requires the NP as argument, then subjects' processing of the sentences is disrupted. Pynte and Prieur suggest an interpretation of this result in the context of Perfetti's (1990) restrictive interactive model of parsing. This model breaks the parsing process into stages, where low-level phrasal constituents are built (NPs, PPs, etc.), before then being integrated into a verb-argument structure. The prosodic breaks in Pynte and Prieur's experiments serve to confirm (or otherwise) the initial "chunking" of elements into phrasal constituents.

The question of whether prosody directs or assists syntactic parsing is addressed by Stirling and Wales (1996), who present data from a replication of Beach's (1991) off-line study of the use of prosody in determining the parse of closure ambiguities such as (30).

(30) Jay believed the gossip about the neighbours {right away/wasn't true}

Using two lengths of sentence fragment for continuation (up to *believed* or to *gossip*), these studies find that the relation between prosody and parsing is non-cumulative. In Beach's original study the additional information in long fragments does not improve subjects' correct judgements, whereas in Stirling and Wales' replication subjects become less well able to decide between the alternatives. A crucial difference between the two studies lies in Stirling and Wales' use of natural sentence recordings, as opposed to the synthesised utterances used by Beach. In the acoustic analysis of their speech materials, Stirling and Wales find that the early closure point (*believed*) is more clearly differentiated than the end of the longer fragment (*gossip*), which shows variation between speakers but no systematic differences according to the intended reading.

As pointed out earlier, variation in the realisation of prosodic features is unsurprising. In the context of their experiment, Stirling and Wales (1996) suggest that although the early cues result in some (albeit relatively weak) disambiguation, natural variation in the remaining material of the longer fragments increases variance and renders the prosody of the fragments less supportive of a particular syntactic interpretation. They subsequently suggest that this finding is compatible with a "cumulative integration" model of sentence processing, whereby the prosodic information that is available serves as one source of information in the parsing decision. Rather than directing the syntactic processor, prosody is claimed to support it.

This position is similar to recent proposals for integrating syntactic and other non-syntactic information sources during the parse (including for instance pragmatic plausibility and verb argument preferences). Such "constraint-based" models suggest an activation-type approach, with various information sources constraining the possible interpretation (MacDonald, 1994; McClelland, St. John, & Taraban, 1989; Spivey-Knowlton, Trueswell, & Tanenhaus, 1993). As Stirling and Wales (1996) point out, the "cue-trading" relationship observed by Beach (1991) for duration and F0 may also exist between prosody and other information sources, such as the relation between the verb and potential object noun phrase in (26). What is clear, at least, is that prosodic information early in the utterance does not subsequently exclude alternative structural interpretations.

An activation type approach, or at least a non-deterministic one, is supported also by off-line data reported by Marslen-Wilson et al. (1992) in their cross-modal naming study. To ensure that subjects attended to the prime fragment, a secondary task was carried out after each prime-probe presentation, in which subjects rated the appropriateness of the naming probe as a continuation of the auditory fragment. The rating data produced a pattern, across conditions, which differed from the on-line reaction time data. Whereas the latter showed clear effects of prosody on syntactic interpretation, the former failed to distinguish between prime conditions (while showing a clear effect in a control "anomaly" condition). In other words, subjects were still able to entertain a minimal attachment interpretation of stimulus fragments like (31), even though their reaction time data supported ambiguity resolution in favour of non-minimal attachment (the complement reading).

(31) The workers considered the last offer from the management.

It is clear that there are many unresolved issues in the consideration of where and when prosody is used in parsing. Variation in the realisation of prosody means that disambiguation may not always be possible, contributing to less clear findings for prosody in certain studies. However, many of the experimental results discussed in this section suggest that prosodic information is used as it becomes available, in an integrative or interactive manner. Clearly, there is a need for more explicit investigation of the precise time-course of the use of prosody.

CONCLUSION

This chapter has provided a review of research over the last 20 years or so into the relationship of prosody to language processing, particularly to syntax. It has probably left many stones unturned and questions unanswered (as well as answers unquestioned). Several themes have been recurrent, and should be borne in mind in future research. One is that the analysis of prosody as a set of separate phonetic features fails to capture the generalisations of a more abstract phonological analysis, in which the variable realisation of prosodic distinctions in different contexts and by different speakers can be more adequately portrayed. A second, related theme is the emphasis on clear and precise documentation of what it is that we are studying. A common transcription system, such as that developed under the ToBI framework, with its accessible tutorial materials, will provide a useful basis for greater comparability and accountability in future research.

Much has still to be learned about the precise role and position of prosody in relation to the parsing mechanism. It is clear that we still have a lot to discover, and a great deal of theorising and modelling to undertake. For instance, the discussion here of the point(s) in the input at which prosodic information helps to guide the parse has offered no definitive answers about the "granularity" of uptake of such information in sentence processing. Further research is needed in this as in other areas, possibly using experimental paradigms new to this area, such as the event-related potential studies of prosody being conducted at the University of Auckland (McAllister & Colrain, 1995).

Little of the research discussed here has addressed explicitly the broader architectural questions that are of great interest to psycholinguistic research, as revealed in other chapters in this volume. As we discover more about the relationship of prosodic and other structural aspects of language, and increase the range of prosodic contrasts investigated, so our questions should become more strongly focused on issues concerning how, when, and where prosodic information is used in language processing.

ACKNOWLEDGEMENTS

My thanks go to the editors of this volume, and to Janet Holmes, Allan Bell and Jan McAllister for helpful comments on an earlier draft of this chapter.

REFERENCES

Altmann, G.T.M., & Steedman, M.J. (1988). Interaction with context during human sentence processing. *Cognition*, *30*, 191–238.

Beach, C.M. (1991). The interpretation of prosodic patterns at points of syntactic structure ambiguity: evidence for cue trading relations. *Journal of Memory and Language*, *30*, 644–663.

Beckman, M. (1996). The parsing of prosody. *Language and Cognitive Processes*, *11*, 17–68.

Beckman, M.E., & Ayers, G.M. (1994). *Guidelines for ToBI labelling, ver. 2.0.* Unpublished manuscript, Ohio State University. (Materials available by writing to tobi@ling.ohio-state.edu)

Beckman, M.E., & Pierrehumbert, J.B. (1986). Intonational structure in Japanese and English. *Phonology Yearbook*, *3*, 266–309.

Brazil, D., Coulthard, M., & Johns, C. (1980). *Discourse intonation and language teaching.* London: Longmans.

Briscoe, E.J. (1987). *Modelling human speech comprehension: A computational approach.* New York: John Wiley & Sons.

Briscoe, E.J., & Warren, P. (1983). Dichotic switch monitoring: A technique for the experimental investigation of speech comprehension. *Cambridge Papers in Phonetics and Experimental Linguistics*, *1*, Department of Linguistics, University of Cambridge, UK.

Britain, D. (1992) Linguistic change in intonation: the use of HR terminals in New Zealand English. *Language Variation and Change*, *4*, 77–104.

Britain, D., & Newman, J. (1992). High rising terminals in New Zealand English. *Journal of the International Phonetic Association*, *22*, 1–11.

Chomsky, N. (1973). Conditions on transformations. In S.R. Anderson & P. Kiparsky (Eds.), *A festschrift for Morris Halle*. New York: Holt, Rinehart & Winston.

Chomsky, N., & Halle, M. (1968). *The sound pattern of English*. New York: Harper.

Cooper, W.E. (1976). Syntactic control of timing in speech production: A study of complement clauses. *Journal of Phonetics*, *4*, 151–171.

Cooper, W.E., & Paccia-Cooper, J. (1980). *Syntax and speech*. Cambridge, MA: Harvard University Press.

Cooper, W.E., & Sorensen, J.M. (1981). *Fundamental frequency in sentence production*. New York: Springer.

Cruttenden, A. (1997). *Intonation* (2nd ed.). Cambridge, UK: Cambridge University Press.

Cruttenden, A. (1995). Rises in English. In J. Windsor-Lewis (Ed.), *Studies in general and English phonetics: Essays in honour of Professor J.D. O'Connor* (pp. 155–173). London: Routledge.

Crystal, D. (1969) *Prosodic systems and intonation in English*. Cambridge: Cambridge University Press.

Cutler, A. (1990). Exploiting prosodic possibilities in speech segmentation. In G.T.M. Altmann (Ed.), *Cognitive models of speech processing: Psycholinguistic and computational perspectives*. Cambridge, MA: MIT Press.

Cutler, A., & Butterfield, S. (1992). Rhythmic cues to speech segmentation: evidence from juncture misperception. *Journal of Memory and Language*, *31*, 218–236.

Cutler, A., & Isard, S.D. (1980). The production of prosody. In B. Butterworth (Ed.), *Language production: Vol. 1. Speech and talk*. New York: Academic Press.

Cutler, A., & Ladd, D.R. (1983). Comparative notes on terms and topics in the contributions. In A. Cutler & D.R. Ladd (Eds.), *Prosody: Models and measurements*. Berlin: Springer.

Cutler, A., Mehler, J., Norris, D.G., & Segui, J. (1986). The syllable's differing role in the segmentation of French and English. *Journal of Memory and Language*, *25*, 385–400.

Cutler, A., & Norris, D.G. (1988). The role of strong syllables in segmentation for lexical access. *Journal of Experimental Psychology: Human Perception and Performance*, *14*, 113–121.

Danly, M., & Cooper, W.E. (1979). Sentence production: Closure vs. initiation of constituents. *Linguistics*, *17*, 1017–1038.

Dobroth, K.M., & Speer, S.R. (1995, March). A time course analysis of prosodic effects on the resolution of closure ambiguity. *Proceedings of the 8th annual CUNY meeting on sentence processing*, Tucson, AZ.

Durand, J. (1990). *Generative and non-linear phonology*. London: Longman.

Eefting, W., & Nooteboom, S.G. (1991). The effect of accentedness and information value on word durations: A production and a perception study. *Proceedings of the 12th International Congress of Phonetic Sciences*, *3*, 302–305.

Flores d'Arcais, G.B. (1978). The perception of complex sentences. In W.J.M. Levelt & G.B. Flores d'Arcais (Eds.), *Studies in sentence perception* (pp. 155–186). New York: John Wiley & Sons.

Fowler, C.A., & Housum, J. (1987). Talkers' signalling of "new" and "old" words in speech and listeners' perception and use of the distinction. *Journal of Memory and Language*, *26*, 489–504.

Frazier, L. (1979). *On comprehending sentences: Syntactic parsing strategies*. Bloomington, IN: Indiana University Linguistics Club.

Frazier, L. (1987). Theories of sentence processing. In J. Garfield (Ed.), *Modularity in knowledge representation and natural language processing* (pp. 291–307). Cambridge, MA: MIT Press.

Frazier, L. (1990). Exploring the architecture of the language-processing system. In G.T.M. Altmann (Ed.), *Cognitive models of speech processing: psycholinguistic and computational perspectives* (pp. 409–433). Cambridge, MA: MIT Press.

Frazier, L., & Rayner, K. (1982). Making and correcting errors during sentence comprehension: Eye movements in the analysis of structurally ambiguous sentences. *Cognitive Psychology, 14*, 178–210.

Gee, J.P., & Grosjean, F. (1983). Performance structures: a psycholinguistic and linguistic appraisal. *Cognitive Psychology, 15*, 411–458.

Giegerich, H. (1985). *Metrical phonology and phonological structure.* Cambridge: Cambridge University Press.

Goldman-Eisler, F. (1968). *Psycholinguistics: Experiments in spontaneous speech.* London: Academic Press.

Grabe, E., & Warren, P. (1995). Stress shift: Do speakers do it or do listeners hear it? In B. Connell & A. Arvaniti (eds.) *Phonology and phonetic evidence: Papers in laboratory phonology IV* (pp. 95–110). Cambridge: Cambridge University Press.

Grabe, E., Warren, P., & Nolan, F. (1994). Resolving category ambiguities—evidence from stress shift. *Speech Communication, 15*, 101–114.

Grosjean, F. (1985). The recognition of words after their acoustic offset: Evidence and implications. *Perception and Psychophysics, 38*, 299–310.

Grosjean, F., & Hirt, C. (1996). Using prosody to predict the ends of sentences in English and French: normal and brain-damaged subjects. *Language and Cognitive Processes, 11*, 107–134.

't Hart, J., Collier, R., & Cohen, A. (1990). *A perceptual study of intonation: An experimental-phonetic approach to speech melody.* Cambridge: Cambridge University Press.

Henderson, A.I. (1980). Juncture pause and intonation fall and the perceptual segmentation of speech. In H.W. Dechert & M. Raupach (Eds.), *Temporal variables in speech: Studies in honour of Frieda Goldman-Eisler* (pp. 199–207). The Hague, The Netherlands: Mouton.

Hogg, R., & McCully, C. B. (1987). *Metrical phonology.* Cambridge: Cambridge University Press.

Holst, T., & Nolan, F. (1995). The influence of syntactic structure on [s] to [ʃ] assimilation. In B. Connell & A. Arvaniti (Eds.), *Phonology and phonetic evidence: Papers in laboratory phonology* (Vol. IV, pp. 315–333). Cambridge: Cambridge University Press.

Kingdon, R. (1958). *The groundwork of English stress.* London: Longman.

Klatt, D.H. (1975). Vowel lengthening is syntactically determined in a connected discourse. *Journal of Phonetics, 3*, 129–140.

Ladd, D.R. (1980). *The structure of intonational meaning: Evidence from English.* Bloomington, IN: Indiana University Press.

Lehiste, I. (1970). *Suprasegmentals.* Cambridge, MA: MIT Press.

Lehiste, I. (1972). Timing of utterances and linguistic boundaries. *Journal of the Acoustical Society of America, 51*, 2018–2024.

Lehiste, I. (1973). Phonetic disambiguation of syntactic ambiguity. *Glossa, 7*, 102–122.

Liberman, M., & Prince, A. (1977). On stress and linguistic rhythm. *Linguistic Inquiry, 8*, 249–336.

MacDonald, M.C. (1994). Probabilistic constraints and syntactic ambiguity resolution. *Language and Cognitive Processes, 9*, 157–201.

Marcus, M., & Hindle, D. (1990). Description theory and intonation boundaries. In G.T.M. Altmann (Ed.), *Cognitive models of speech processing: Psycholinguistic and computational perspectives* (pp. 483–512). Cambridge, MA: MIT Press.

Marslen-Wilson, W.D. (1987). Functional parallelism in spoken word recognition. *Cognition, 25*, 71–102.

Marslen-Wilson, W.D., & Tyler, L.K. (1980). The temporal structure of spoken language understanding. *Cognition, 8*, 1–74.

Marslen-Wilson, W.D., & Tyler, L.K. (1987). Against modularity. In J. Garfield (Ed.), *Modularity in knowledge representation and natural language processing* (pp. 37–62). Cambridge, MA: MIT Press.

Marslen-Wilson, W.D., Tyler, L.K., & Seidenberg, M. (1978). Sentence processing and the clause boundary. In W.J.M. Levelt & G.B. Flores d'Arcais (Eds.), *Studies in the perception of language* (pp. 219–246). New York: Wiley.

Marslen-Wilson, W.D., Tyler, L.K., Warren, P., Grenier, P., & Lee, C.S. (1992). Prosodic effects in minimal attachment. *Quarterly Journal of Experimental Psychology, 45A*, 73–87.

McAllister, J., & Colrain, I. (1995). *Prosodic cues in the interpretation of spoken garden-path sentences: evidence from event-related brain potentials*. Unpublished manuscript.

McClelland, J.L., St. John, M., & Taraban, R. (1989). Sentence comprehension: A parallel distributed processing approach. *Language and Cognitive Processes, 4*, 287–336.

Mitchell, D.C. (1994). Sentence parsing. In M. Gernsbacher (Ed.), *Handbook of psycholinguistics* (pp. 375–409). London: Academic Press.

Nagel, H.N., Shapiro, L.P., Tuller, B., & Nawy, R. (1996). Prosodic influences on the resolution of temporary ambiguity during on-line sentence processing. *Journal of Psycholinguistic Research, 25*, 319–344.

Nespor, M.A., & Vogel, I. (1983). Prosodic structure above the word. In A. Cutler & D.R. Ladd (Eds.), *Prosody: Models and measurements*. Berlin: Springer.

Nespor, M.A., & Vogel, I. (1986). *Prosodic phonology*. Dordrecht, The Netherlands: Foris.

O'Connor, J.D., & Arnold, G.F. (1961). *Intonation of colloquial English*. London: Longman.

Perfetti, C.A. (1990). The co-operative language processor: semantic influences in an autonomous syntax. In D.A. Balota, G.B. Flores d'Arcais & K. Rayner (Eds.), *Comprehension processes in reading*. Hillsdale, NJ: Lawrence Erlbaum Associates Inc.

Pierrehumbert, J.B. (1980). *The phonology and phonetics of English intonation*. Dissertation. Cambridge, MA: Indiana University Linguistics Club.

Pierrehumbert, J.B., & Beckman, M.E. (1988). *Japanese tone structure*. Cambridge, MA: MIT Press.

Pierrehumbert, J.B., & Hirschberg, J. (1990). The meaning of intonational contours in the interpretation of discourse. In P.R. Cohen, J. Morgan, & M.E. Pollack (Eds.), *Intentions in communication* (pp. 271–311). Cambridge, MA: MIT Press.

Postal, P.M. (1974). *On raising: One rule of English grammar and its theoretical implications*. Cambridge, MA: MIT Press.

Price, P., Ostendorf, M., Shattuck-Hufnagel, S., & Fong, C. (1991). The use of prosody in syntactic disambiguation. *Journal of the Acoustical Society of America, 90*, 2956–2970.

Pynte, J., & Prieur, B. (1996). Prosodic breaks and attachment decisions in sentence parsing. *Language and Cognitive Processes, 11*, 165–192.

Rayner, K., & Frazier, L. (1987). Parsing temporarily ambiguous complements. *Quarterly Journal of Experimental Psychology, 39A*, 657–673.

Schafer, A., Carter, J., Clifton, C., & Frazier, L. (1996). Focus in relative clause construal. *Language and Cognitive Processes, 11*, 135–164.

Scott, D.R., & Cutler, A. (1984). Segmental phonology and the perception of syntactic structure. *Journal of Verbal Learning and Verbal Behavior, 23*, 450–466.

Selkirk, E.O. (1984). *Phonology and syntax: The relation between sound and structure*. Cambridge, MA: MIT Press.

Silverman, K., Beckman, M.E., Pitrelli, J., Ostendorf, M., Wightman, C., Price, P., Pierrehumbert, J., & Hirschberg, J. (1992, October). ToBI: A standard for labeling English prosody. *Proceedings of the 1992 International Conference on Spoken Language* (Vol. 2, pp. 867–870), Banff, Canada.

Speer, S.R., Crowder, R.G., & Thomas, L.M. (1993). Prosodic structure and sentence recognition. *Journal of Memory and Language*, *32*, 336–358.

Spivey-Knowlton, M., Trueswell, J., & Tanenhaus, M.K. (1993). Context and syntactic ambiguity resolution. *Canadian Journal of Experimental Psychology*, *47*, 276–309.

Steedman, M.J. (1991). Structure and intonation. *Language*, *67*, 260–296.

Stirling, L., & Wales, R. (1996). Does prosody support or direct sentence processing? *Language and Cognitive Processes, 11*, 193–212.

Streeter, L.A. (1978). Acoustic determinants of phrase boundary perception. *Journal of the Acoustical Society of America*, *64*, 1582–1592.

Tanenhaus, M.K., Carlson, G., & Trueswell, J. (1989). The role of thematic structures in interpretation and parsing. *Language and Cognitive Processes, 4*, 211–234.

Tyler, L.K., & Warren, P. (1987). Local and global structure in spoken language comprehension. *Journal of Memory and Language*, *26*, 638–657.

Wales, R., & Toner, H. (1979). Intonation and the perception of ambiguity in sentences. In W.E. Cooper & E.C.T. Walker (Eds.), *Sentence processing: Studies presented to Merrill Garrett* (pp. 135–158). New York: Lawrence Erlbaum Associates Inc.

Warren, P. (1984). On-line testing of prosodic disambiguation. *Cambridge papers in phonetics and experimental linguistics*, *2*. Department of Linguistics, University of Cambridge, UK.

Warren, P. (1985). *The temporal organisation and perception of speech.* Unpublished PhD thesis, University of Cambridge, UK.

Warren, P. (1995). The sound of "desert trains": Delay strategies and constraints in spoken sentence processing. *Wellington Working Papers in Linguistics*, *7*, 38–52.

Warren, P., Grabe, E., & Nolan, F. (1995). Prosody, phonology and parsing in closure ambiguities. *Language and Cognitive Processes*, *10*, 457–486.

Warren, P., Nolan, F., Grabe, E., & Holst, T. (1995). Post-lexical and prosodic phonological processing. *Language and Cognitive Processes*, *10*, 411–417.

Watt, S.M., & Murray, W.S. (1996). Prosodic form and parsing commitments. *Journal of Psycholinguistic Research*, *25*, 291–318.

PART THREE

Computational issues in language processing

CHAPTER SEVEN

Mechanisms for sentence processing

Matthew W. Crocker
Saarland University, Saarbrücken, Germany

INTRODUCTION

Sentence processing is the means by which the words of an utterance are combined to yield the interpretation of a sentence. It is a task which all people can do well: quickly, efficiently, effortlessly, and accurately. Unlike solving calculus problems or playing chess, we can hardly fail to be successful at understanding language. This wouldn't be surprising, were it not for the fact that language is not only extremely complex, but also highly ambiguous.

An interesting contrast can be made between lexical access and sentence processing. In the case of lexical access, we might simply imagine that the problem is one of matching the phonological or orthographic features of an input word or morpheme with an entry in our mental lexicon. Naively, this is simply a process of using the input as a key into a large database. This is simplifying things a great deal of course, but if we contrast this with sentence processing, we can quickly see that something very different is going on in the latter. While you have seen all the words in the previous sentence before, you have probably never seen the sentence itself before. Thus, we can easily imagine how one might retrieve the meanings of the individual words, but how does one understand the meaning of the sentence as a whole? You presumably have never seen a sentence with precisely that meaning before, yet you arrived at the intended interpretation effortlessly and immediately.

This chapter is concerned with how the task of sentence processing is accomplished, considering first the basic issues and then examining a number of proposals that have been advanced. In particular, the study of sentence processing touches on many of the interesting issues facing cognitive science more generally. These include: the nature of mental *representations*; the *algorithms* used to construct them; the extent to which the sentence processor is distinct or *modular*; what factors lead to increased processing *complexity*; what *strategies* are adopted; and why?

In our quest for a model of how people process the utterances they hear, we need first to consider two fundamental sources of information: An appropriate formal description of how the words of a sentence can be structured into a connected, interpretable representation, often characterised by a grammar, and also empirical evidence concerning people's behaviour when they process language. In this chapter we will provide a brief overview of grammar rules and representations, and then consider what kinds of mechanism might be used to build syntactic representations, or *analyses*, using such grammatical knowledge, with the aim of modelling the human sentence parsing mechanism (HSPM).

We will begin with a general discussion of the relationship between the grammar and a parser, since much of what follows relies on a clear understanding of these underlying topics. We then provide an overview of natural language ambiguity, a phenomenon which plagues the construction of artificial natural language parsing systems, while providing an important window into the nature of the human sentence processor. Finally, we turn our attention to the specific kinds of mechanism which might be used to characterise the human sentence processor. Here we consider a range of parsing algorithms and strategies for resolving ambiguity, and attempt to evaluate them with respect to their explanation of the data, their plausibility as psychological models, and their ability to make clear predictions.

Grammars and parsers

In building the representations of an utterance that allow us to interpret language, the sentence processor must bridge the automatic perceptual task of word recognition and lexical access with the more conscious, inferential processes of language understanding. Perhaps the most important aspect of sentence processing is that it is compositional; that is to say, the interpretation of a sentence is determined by the particular way its words can be combined. As we have noted already, this interpretation cannot simply be retrieved from our memory of previous sentences we have encountered, otherwise we would not be able to understand the novel utterances that make up most of our linguistic experience. Rather, an interpretation must be constructed when each new utterance is heard or read. Furthermore, current linguistic theories would suggest that it is indeed a very rich set of constraints, rules, representations, and principles which determine how words may be combined to yield structures which can be interpreted appropriately.

Linguistic theories have been developed with precisely the aim of (1) licensing for those utterances that are part of the language under investigation, and ruling out those that are not, and (2) providing an analysis of well-formed utterances, which can then serve as the basis for semantic interpretation.[1] To construct a syntactic analysis for a particular sentence, the linguist must show that the rules of grammar can be used to derive, or *generate*, the utterance in question. If there is no such analysis, then the grammar does not *generate* the utterance, and it is considered to be ungrammatical with respect to the grammar. Much work in computational linguistics has been devoted to the development of algorithms which can automatically construct such a syntactic analysis for a particular sentence, or *parse* it, given a particular grammar. As this corresponds closely to the task of the human sentence processor, as already sketched, it is useful to consider how parsers and grammars have been formalised within (computational) linguistics.

S	→	NP VP	Det	→	{*the, a, every*}
NP	→	PN	N	→	{*man, woman, book, hill, telescope*}
NP	→	Det N	PN	→	{*John, Mary*}
NP	→	NP PP	P	→	{*on, with*}
PP	→	P NP	V	→	{*saw, put, open, read, reads*}
VP	→	V			
VP	→	V NP			
VP	→	V NP PP			

FIG. 7.1 A simple phrase structure grammar.

To make our discussion more concrete, consider the phrase structure grammar and lexicon in Fig. 7.1, which covers a tiny fragment of English. The language defined by this grammar is, by definition, the complete set of sentences that are grammatical according to (or *generated* by) the rules provided. So, for example:

(1) the man saw the book.

[1] This is typically referred to as *descriptive adequacy*. In addition linguistic theories often seek to be *explanatory*, to the extent that they can shed light on, for example, how language might be acquired.

is in the language, as shown by the following phrase structure derivation:

(2)

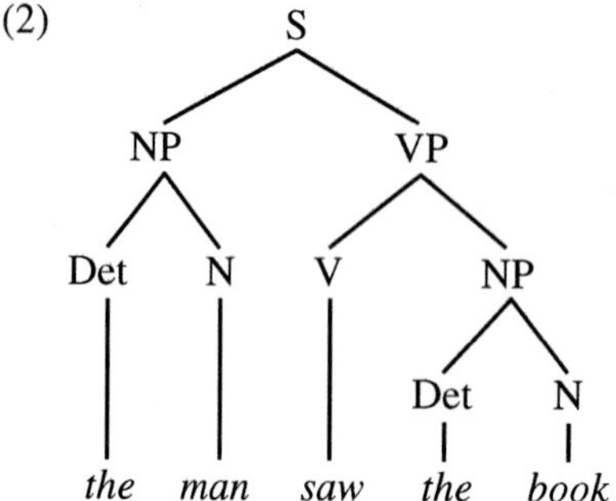

However, the following two sentences are excluded by this particular grammar:

(3a) The man saw the film.
(3b) The man saw the woman open the book.

Sentence (3a) is quite clearly out, for the simple reason that the word *film* is not in the lexicon, and (3b) because there is no derivation using the phrase structure rules in the given grammar. Despite the fact that this particular grammar is tiny, and not very representative of English, it is important to note that the language defined by this grammar is in fact infinite. This is because of the *recursive* rule NP → NP PP, which can in principle be used any number of times in generating a sentence, to produce sentences of arbitrary length (though these would be implausibly repetitive given the limited size of this grammar and lexicon). In this way, grammars of this sort represent a very powerful device, which have the potential to analyse, and therefore support the interpretation of, an infinite set of sentences.[2]

Ambiguity

Utterances may have more than one interpretation, and there can be several reasons for such ambiguities. If we first consider lexical ambiguity, we note that a given word may exhibit both semantic and part-of-speech ambiguities:

[2] Closer inspection of the grammar will also reveal that, although it only covers a tiny fragment of English, it still generates what we would consider ungrammatical sentences. For example, *The woman put* is permitted since, among other things, the grammar fails to account for the specific requirements of particular verbs (e.g. *put* must be followed by an NP and a PP).

(4a) I robbed the *bank*.
(4b) I fished from the *bank*.
(4c) I *bank* with Lloyds Bank.
(4d) *Bank* the plane to turn it.

Sentences (4a and 4b) demonstrate how *bank* is used as a noun, but with two distinct meanings; a semantic "sense" ambiguity. In (4c), *bank* is a verb, but has a meaning clearly related to that in (4a), but completely unrelated to (4b). Finally, (4d) demonstrates another verbal sense of *bank*, which is quite separate from the other uses, although possibly vaguely related to that in (4b), partially illustrating the range of possible category and sense ambiguities which can occur in the lexicon.

Another possibility, of particular interest to the present discussion is that sentences may have more than one possible grammatical structure associated with them. These are typically called structural, or syntactic, ambiguities. Consider, for example, the following sentence:

(5) John saw the moon with the telescope.

In this sentence, the prepositional phrase *with the telescope* might be considered a modifier of *the moon* (i.e. if there were a telescope on the moon), but it seems more likely that it is the instrument of *saw*, and therefore modifies the verb phrase, as shown in the following parse tree:

(6)

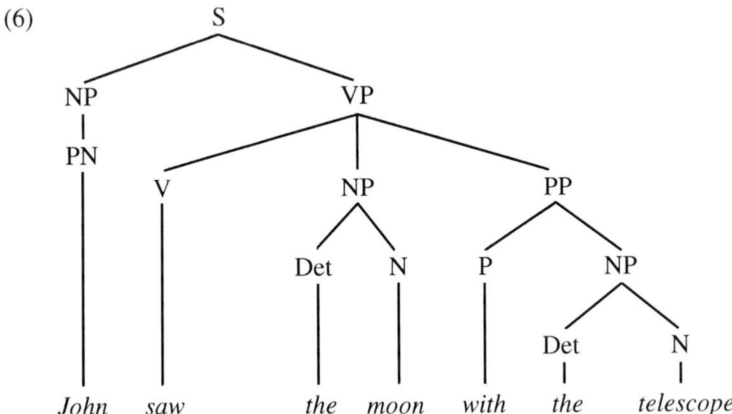

By changing just one word, however, the alternative structure becomes much more plausible (though not necessarily preferred). Consider:

(7) John saw the astronomer with the telescope.

In this sentence, the prepositional phrase may well be attached to the *the astronomer*, since it is reasonable that there may be several astronomers, and the sentence is referring to the one who owns a telescope. If this is the case, since it is *the astronomer* that's being modified, the parse tree would look as follows:

(8)

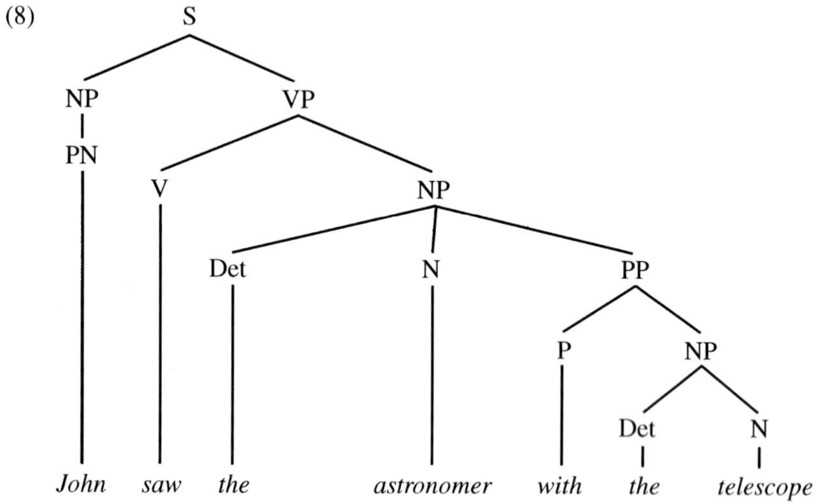

In these two examples, the sentences have two possible interpretations, and are said to be *globally* ambiguous. It is also possible, if we accept that sentences are processed incrementally and left-to-right, that we might encounter *local* ambiguities. That is, situations where there are a number of possible analyses for the current, initial sub-string of the utterance, but which are disambiguated by the end of the sentence, when the entire string has been processed.

(9) I knew the solution to the problem was incorrect.

In this sentence, the first ambiguity occurs as a result of *knew* being ambiguous as to the category of its complement: It may take either a noun phrase or a sentence. Thus, when the noun phrase *the solution to the problem* is encountered, we have two possible analyses: We can attach it directly as the object of *knew* or we can create a sentential complement with *the solution to the problem* as the embedded subject. In contrast with (7), however, the ambiguity is a temporary one, as only the sentential complement analysis is sustained when the remaining words *was incorrect* are encountered.

In fact, such sentences are only ambiguous if we assume *incremental* interpretation. Experimental evidence has demonstrated people do indeed have mild, but systematic, difficulty with such sentences (Frazier & Rayner, 1982), suggesting that they do analyse the sentence incrementally, and typically adopt the direct object analysis initially. Changing to the embedded sentence then causes an increase in reading complexity. This sort of effect is made even clearer by sentences like the following:

(10) The woman sent the letter was pleased.

If we again assume incremental processing, the most natural analysis to pursue for this sentence is to parse *sent* as the main verb, and *the letter* as its direct object. However the end of the sentence, *was pleased*, then leaves us with no way to continue. The verb *sent*, however, is ambiguous as either the simple past tense form or the past participle, so in fact the correct analysis is to parse *sent the letter* as a *reduced relative* clause, and *was pleased* as the main verb (cf. *The woman who was sent the letter was pleased*). Typically, people are unable to recover this alternative reading, and find the sentence to be ungrammatical unless the context is sufficiently biasing. Such examples of local ambiguities are often referred to as conscious "garden paths", since they have the apparent effect of leading the human parser towards one, ultimately wrong, analysis from which it is difficult or impossible to recover.

The competence hypothesis

We have outlined how grammars can be used to assign structural descriptions to sentences of a language, indeed, sometimes more than one if a particular sentence is ambiguous. We have tacitly assumed, here, that the sort of grammar proposed by linguists, similar in spirit to the one in Fig. 7.1 though much more complex, approximates the knowledge of language, or *competence*, that we as humans possess, and apply in our everyday use of language, our *performance*. This might not be the case. It is entirely possible that people make use of a completely different grammar. For example, while linguists typically pursue the simplest, most elegant theories about language, which capture as many generalisations and abstractions as possible, it may be the case that people make use of more specific grammatical knowledge tailored to cope more effectively with, say, frequent expressions and indeed certain "ungrammatical" sentences.

It is, however, commonly assumed by researchers that people do make use of grammatical knowledge that is approximated by our current theories of grammar, or minimally, that people recover equivalent representations: This assumption is referred to as the Competence Hypothesis and it will be assumed throughout this chapter (see Berwick & Weinberg, 1984) for a more thorough technical discussion of this point). Such an assumption is essential if linguistics is to shed light on the nature of language processes, since the linguistic theory is used to make predictions and shape the development of parsing models which can be tested empirically. That is, formal linguistic theory provides the common representational vocabulary linking computational and experimental psycholinguistics.

In the rest of this chapter we will consider two basic topics. The first concerns the range of possible mechanisms for constructing syntactic analyses, like the parse trees earlier. Second, we consider how people appear to cope with the problem of ambiguity when constructing such a parse for the utterances they hear.

PARSING ISSUES

If we assume that a theory of grammar approximates people's "knowledge" of their language's structure, then a theory of parsing must explain how people use that knowledge to construct an analysis or interpretation for the utterances they encounter. As mentioned previously, research in computational linguistics has led to numerous possible techniques and strategies for parsing natural language. Much of the theory behind these results has its origins in the study of formal and computer languages (see Aho, Sethi, & Ullman, 1986 for an overview), but other accounts have developed specifically to address problems involved in processing natural language as well.

In this section, we begin with a general discussion of parsing techniques, and introduce some standard parsing algorithms. We then consider some more specific proposals in the context of human language processing. Our aim is to consider how well current computational models of human sentence processing fare in explaining human language processing behaviour. In particular we are concerned with the following issues:

1. To what extent do the models process sentences incrementally, word-by-word in the manner in which people appear to process language?
2. How are structural ambiguities dealt with? Do parsing decisions reflect those of human processing?
3. Are increases in processing complexity predicted to occur in precisely those instances where people demonstrate processing difficulties?

Parsing algorithms

The task of a parser is to examine the string of words of an input sentence, and assign that string a well-formed syntactic structure, given a particular grammar. Crucially, there may be more than one analysis, if the sentence is syntactically ambiguous (as seen earlier), or there may be no analysis, if the sentence is not a member of the language defined by the grammar being used by the parser. The parsing algorithm specifies the procedures which are to be used to find the syntactic structure, or *parse tree*, for an utterance, and there are a number of different dimensions of variation for such algorithms.

For example, the parser might work through the string from left-to-right, as people presumably do, or from right-to-left. Also, it may use the grammar to "drive" the parsing process, first building structure and then matching it to the words of the string, or it may concentrate primarily on the words in the string, in an input-driven manner, and build structure "bottom-up". Algorithms also vary in how they handle ambiguities. Some, when faced with a situation where more than one structure could be built, will simply choose one. If that turns out to be incorrect, the parser will later "backtrack" to the point where it made that choice (called a *choice-point*), and try an alternative. On the other hand, some parsers will try all possibilities in parallel, then when one or more of the parallel analyses fail, such a parse simply forgets about them, secure in the knowledge that the successful analysis (if it exists) is also being pursued.

In the following sub-sections we consider two possible parsing algorithms in greater detail. We will then go on to some issues of parsing *complexity* that have been used to defend particular algorithms as good approximations of the human parser.

Bottom-up. Let us begin by considering a parser that is principally driven by the words in the sentence, using the grammar in Fig. 7.1 to combine them "bottom-up", into higher level constituents. In this case we consider the "shift-reduce" parser, which is the simplest instance of a bottom-up parser. It works by looking at the words of the sentence, and trying to combine them into constituents, using the rules of the grammar. As its name suggests there are two fundamental parsing operations: "shift", which moves the algorithm to the next word in the sentence, and "reduce", which tries to combine the constituents already found into new constituents. In (11), we illustrate a simple bottom-up parse for the sentence *the woman reads*.

As constituents are built up, we use a "stack" to keep track of what's been found so far. Thus, at step 1, we've found a determiner, so Det is

(11)

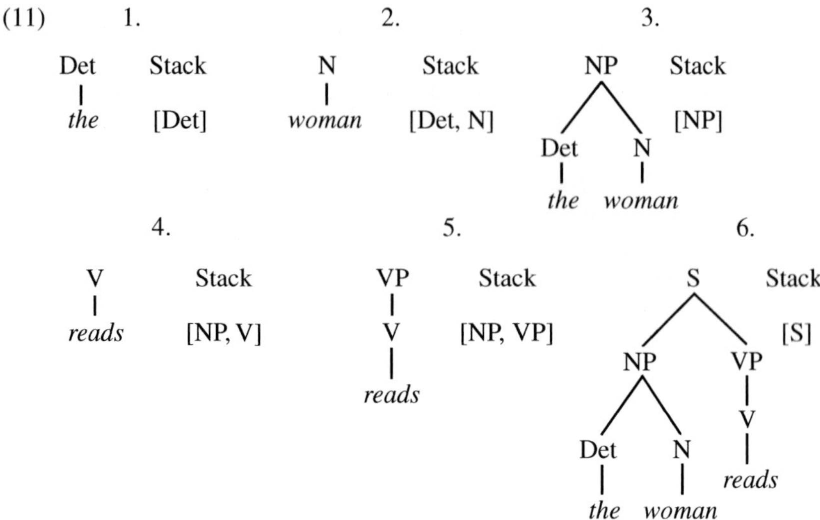

"pushed onto the stack". At step 2, we've also found a noun, so N is also "shifted" onto the stack, where the top of the stack is to the right. By keeping track of the categories found so far, the algorithm can then "reduce" two categories on the top of the stack, if there is a rule in which these categories appear on the right-hand-side. So, at step 3, the Det and N are replaced by NP. That is, they are combined using the NP → Det N rule. This continues until all the words have been processed, and the only category remaining on the stack is S, so we have found a sentence. The algorithm can be more explicitly stated as follows:

(12)
1. Initialise Stack = [ ] (empty)
2. Either *shift*:
   - Select the next word in the sentence (beginning with the first word)
   - Determine the category of the word in the lexicon
   - Push the category onto the top of the stack
3. Or *reduce*:
   - If the categories on the stack match those on the right-hand side of any grammar rule, then:
     —Remove those categories from the stack
     —Push the category on the left-hand side of the rule onto the top of the stack
4. If there are no more words in the sentence, then:
   - If the Stack = [S], then done
5. Go to step 2.

To be clear about what this algorithm is saying, consider each of the 5 steps. Step 1 simply initialises the algorithm's only data structure, the stack, to empty. That is, no constituents have been identified when the algorithm begins. Step 2 defines the *shift* operation, which simply looks at the next word in the sentence, beginning with the first word, moving left to right. It determines the category of the word, and pushes that category onto the top of the stack. For example in (11), Step 1, the word *the* is identified as a Det, and the category Det is put on the stack. Step 3 defines the *reduce* operation, which sees if the top of the stack matches the right hand side of any rule. If so, those categories are removed from the stack and replaced by whatever category was on the left-hand side of the rule. Thus, in (11), Step 3, the stack [Det, N] matches the right-hand side of the NP → Det N, so those categories are removed from the stack and replaced by the category NP. Step 4 is the termination case, which states that if the algorithm has consumed all the input words and reduced them to the single distinguished symbol, then it has successfully parsed the sentence and the algorithm finishes. This is precisely the case in (11), Step 6, when all the words have been consumed, and only the category S remains on the stack. If the algorithm is not done, then Step 5 causes the algorithm to continue by returning to Step 2.

It is important to note that Steps 2 and 3 are alternatives, and either may apply at any point, but not both, and neither has any priority. Within each step there may also be alternatives, if (for Step 2) a particular word has more than one preterminal category (e.g. *bank* might be both a verb and a noun), or (for Step 3) more than one phrase structure rule has a right-hand side that matches the categories on the top of the stack. This introduces an element of "choice" or *non-determinism* into the algorithm, a matter to which we shall return in the next section. Furthermore, if at some point in parsing, the algorithm can neither *shift* nor *reduce*, then the algorithm has blocked. This will occur if the sentence is ungrammatical, or if it is grammatical but we made an incorrect choice at some point. In the latter case, some additional mechanism is required to permit the algorithm to pursue an alternative, and we will consider this issue in greater detail later.

Top-down. A top-down parser constructs a parse tree by first assuming that there is a sentence, and then working its way down the tree to the words themselves. That is, it begins by establishing S as the root of the tree, then finds a rule with S on the left-hand side, and writes the categories on the right-hand side as the daughters of S in the parse tree. This step is then repeated for the first daughter, and so on, until the bottom of the tree is reached (i.e. a word, or *terminal*, is parsed). Then the parser looks back up the tree, and to the right, until it finds another node which it can similarly expand. So, for the grammar given in (1), the steps in the parsing process for the sentence *The woman read the book* would be as follows:

(13)

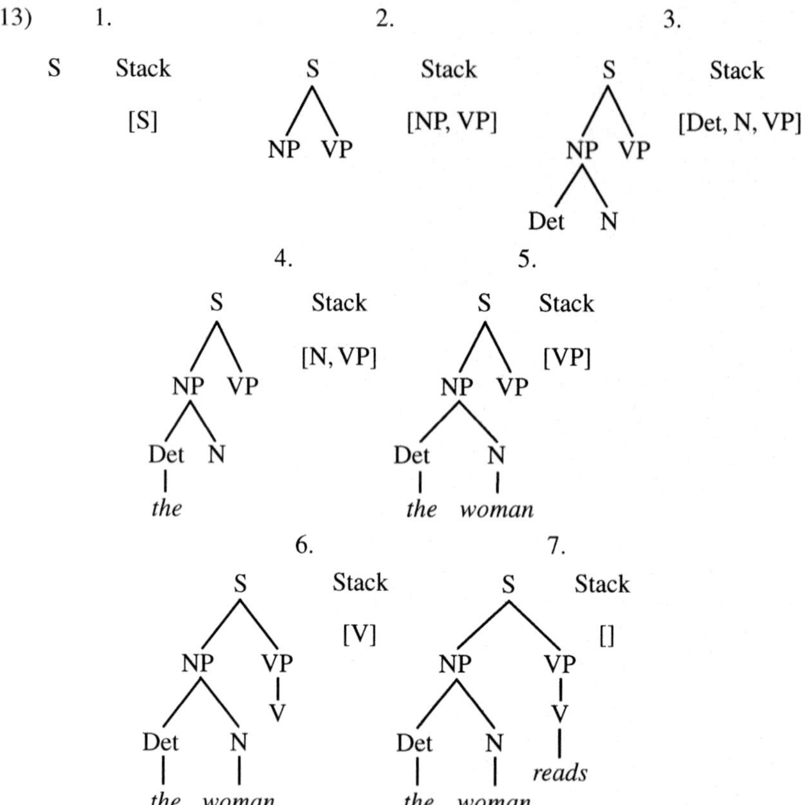

The top-down algorithm can be expressed as follows:

(14) 1. Initialise Stack = [S]
2. If top element of the stack is a non-terminal N, then:
   - Select a rule which rewrites N → R (where R is the symbol(s) on the right side of the rule)
   - Remove N from the stack
   - Add R to the top of the stack
3. If the top element of the stack is a pre-terminal P, then:
   - Find the next word W in the sentence
   - If there is a rule which rewrites P → W then: remove the pre-terminal from the stack
   - Else fail

4. If there are no more words to parse, then:
   - If the Stack = [ ], then done
5. Go to step 2.

Once again, let us consider the steps involved in this algorithm. In contrast with the bottom-up parser, the top-down algorithm uses a stack to keep track of categories that *need to be found*, rather than those that have *already been found*. As before, Step 1 initialises the stack, but since the algorithm is trying to find an S, the category S is put on the stack to represent this. Steps 2 and 3 constitute the two basic operations of the parser. Step 2 considers the case where the category on the top of the stack is a non-terminal (in fact, non-pre-terminal),[3] and finds a rule in the grammar which can expand this. In (13), Step 2, for example, the category S is expanded using the rule S → NP VP. The result is that S is removed from the stack and replaced by [NP VP]. Step 3 handles the case where the category on the stack is a pre-terminal (i.e. must dominate a word). At this step the parser must ensure that there is a rule in the grammar which rewrites the pre-terminal category as the next word in the sentence, otherwise the algorithm blocks. This occurs in (13), Step 5, when the pre-terminal N matches the input word "woman" via the grammar rule N → *woman*. Step 4 is the termination case, which states that if no more categories remain to be found (the stack is empty), and there are no more words to be parsed, then the algorithm has successfully parsed the sentence and finishes. Otherwise, Step 5 causes the algorithm to continue by returning to Step 2.

As with the bottom-up algorithm, the top-down algorithm also has an element of non-determinism. This does not occur between Steps 2 and 3, since the category on the stack will always be either a non-terminal or a pre-terminal. Within Step 2, however, there may be more than one way to expand a particular non-terminal. For example, the category NP can expand as either Det, N, or PN depending on which grammar rule is used. We return to discussion of this in the next section.

Properties of the parser

Let us suppose we wish to decide which of the two algorithms discussed earlier most closely resembles the procedures that people use to interpret

---

[3] To clarify, *non-terminals* are categories that can dominate other categories, whereas *terminals* can only appear at the leaves of the tree and dominate nothing else. The notion of *pre-terminals* is used for categories such as N, V, and P, which stand for sets of terminals (i.e. words), and thus only ever dominate a terminal.

sentences. What criteria might we apply? We have already argued that one of the most salient properties of the human sentence parser is that it appears to operate incrementally. Both of the algorithms are incremental in the sense that they process each word of the sentence one-by-one from left-to-right. But that only means they treat the *input* incrementally. If we assume, quite reasonably, that the *output* of the parser is a parse tree, and that this is to be used as the basis for subsequent semantic interpretation, then the two models differ substantially. In the case of the top-down parser there is a single "connected" parse tree for the sentence after each word is processed (although it is not complete, until the end of the parse). In the bottom-up parser, however, adjacent constituents may be left on the stack for an arbitrarily long period. For example, the NP subject of a sentence will not be reduced with the VP (via the rule S → NP VP) until after the entire VP has been parsed (in this example, the VP only contains the verb, but typically it will also contain a number of complements). Under the standard assumption that we cannot begin to evaluate the semantics and plausibility until these constituents are connected in the parse tree, the bottom-up parser will lead to a psychologically implausible delay in interpretation for all sentences (see Stabler, 1991 for discussion).

So from the standpoint of incrementality, the top-down parser fares much better than the bottom-up parser. The top-down parser, however, has problems of its own. To begin with, it attempts to construct large portions of the tree before even looking at the words in the sentence. In other words, given several (possibly dozens of) rules that expand a particular category, the parser simply has to choose one arbitrarily. Given that it makes such a guess at each node, the algorithm may fail numerous times before making the right sequence of guesses. The problem clearly is that the parser does not use the input to guide the decisions it makes. The bottom-up parser, on the other hand, is input-driven, but may leave large constituents sitting on the stack, and there fails to construct a single connected representation incrementally.

A psychologically plausible parser—The left-corner algorithm

The top-down and bottom-up algorithms represent two extremes of the vast range of possible parsing algorithms. One of the fundamental research goals in computational psycholinguistics has been to find the right parsing algorithm to meet the criteria of being both incremental and data-driven. An obvious strategy is to use a combined top-down/bottom-up algorithm. One now well-known instance of this is the "left-corner" parsing algorithm.

The central intuition behind the left-corner algorithm is to use the "left-corner" of a phrase structure rule (the left-most symbol on the right-hand side of the rule, i.e. the left-most daughter of a category), to project its mother category (the left-hand side of the rule), and predict the remaining categories on the right, top-down. Consider the parse sequence for the sentence fragment *John saw the*...:

(15)

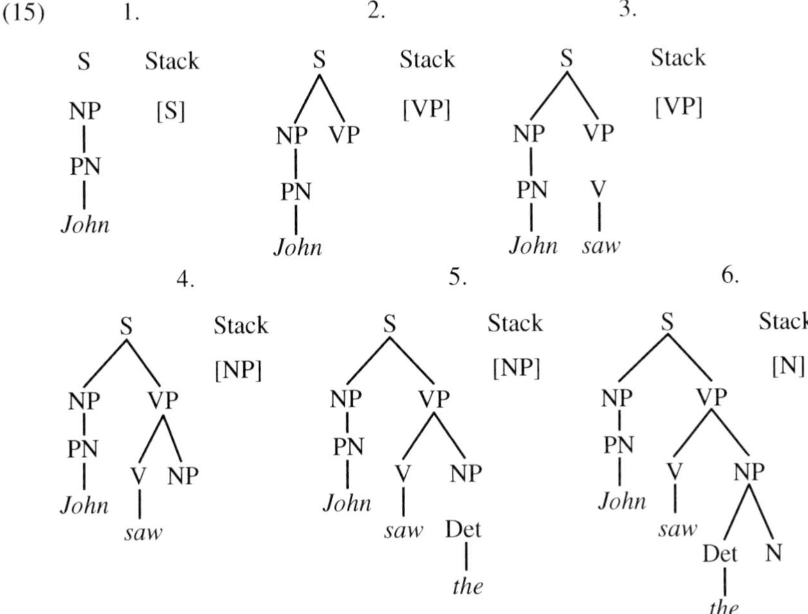

In Step 1, several things are happening: We make the top-down assumption that we are expecting to build a sentence, and S is placed on the stack. We also have found, bottom-up, a PN, and hence an NP. Step 2 illustrates the left-corner rule: Given that we are looking for an S (as it is on the stack), and have found an NP, we can use the rule S → NP VP to attach the NP as the left-corner of S, which is now removed from the stack, replaced by the VP we are now looking for. Step 3 simply shows that we have found a V, bottom-up, and in Step 4 we similarly use the left-corner rule to attach V to VP, and predict an NP (via the rule VP → V NP). Thus, VP is removed from the stack, replaced by newly predicted NP. We then continue by finding a Det, which is the left-corner of NP, and so on.

Incrementality. A quick inspection of the intermediate parse trees in (15) suggests that the algorithm builds up the tree incrementally, as each word is found. That is, as each word is encountered, it projects its structure bottom-up, and then uses the left-corner strategy to attach it to the structure we are trying to build top-down. In fact, while this algorithm is highly incremental, it is not guaranteed to be. That is, given some grammars and input strings, the parser will delay building a completely connected structure. A number of variations of this algorithm have pursued this problem in greater detail, and we will not digress further into the technical details here. The reader is referred to Crocker (1996), Shieber and Johnson (1993) and Stabler (1994) for more sophisticated discussion of related incremental parsing algorithms.

Memory load. Interestingly, it was not the issue of incrementality which initially brought the left-corner algorithm to the attention of psycholinguists; rather it was the issue of computational complexity. In looking at parsing algorithms so far, we have been principally concerned with how well they model the incrementality which is clearly demonstrated by the human sentence parser. There are, however, two other criteria which are commonly taken into consideration when motivating or evaluating particular parsing algorithms, and these concern their "computational complexity".

- Time. How quickly can the algorithm find a parse tree for an input sentence?
- Space. How much memory does the algorithm require to build a parse tree?

We will leave discussion of time complexity until later, and for the moment concentrate on space, or memory load, considerations. We have already seen examples of garden-path sentences, where the human parser finds it difficult to obtain the correct analysis. We noted this was particularly true for the so-called reduced relative sentence in (10), or this well-known, and more pathological, example:

(16) The horse raced past the barn fell.

Many people refuse to accept this is a grammatical sentence, unless they are assisted (again, cf. *The horse that was raced past the barn fell down*). There is, however, another type of sentence that is equally grammatical, and difficult to interpret, but for rather different reasons. Consider first the following sentence:

(17) The cat that the dog chased died.

This is called a *centre-embedded* sentence, since the clause about "the dog chasing" occurs in the middle of the clause about "the cat dying". This sentence may seem a little awkward, but presents no real difficulty. However, grammatically speaking, there is no reason why we cannot embed yet another clause, as in:

(18) The mouse that the cat that the dog chased bit died.

Suddenly the sentence becomes virtually uninterpretable, not because of any ambiguity in the sentence's structure, but because there is just something fundamentally difficult about constructing an interpretation for it. It has been suggested that one possible explanation for this is that processing the sentence may exceed the memory capacity of the human parser. That is, the space required by the parser to analyse such utterances exceeds the working memory available to the parser. Importantly, however, people only really have difficulty with centre-embedding, not left- or right-embedding constructions as in:

(19) [*S* [*S* That the dog chased the cat] bothered Ted]
(20) [*S* Ted believes [*S* that the dog chased the cat]]

In constructing the parsing algorithms, we have made use of a stack as an important data structure in each algorithm. Intuitively, the stack keeps track of what categories have been predicted and therefore need to be found in the case of top-down algorithms; or it keeps track of what categories have been found, and still need to be structured together, in the case of bottom-up algorithms. It therefore seems reasonable to consider the stack size as a possible metric for syntactic memory load (though see Frazier, 1985 for an alternative proposal), and to consider how various parsing algorithms compare with human performance. Beginning with the observation that people find left- and right-embeddings relatively easy, whereas centre-embeddings are difficult, Johnson-Laird (1983) observed that neither top-down nor bottom-up parsers correlate increasing stack size with centre-embeddings only. The left-corner algorithm, however, does exhibit the correct pattern of behaviour, and might therefore be considered to more accurately characterise human parsing and memory limitations.

Since this original work, there has been additional work in refining Johnson-Laird's idea (see Abney & Johnson, 1991; Resnick, 1992). Stabler (1994) in particular is concerned with formulating a parsing algorithm that both maximises incrementality, and continues to make the correct memory load predictions. The work of Gibson (1991) provides a more articulated account of precisely how memory load might be determined for syntactic structures. As we will see later, he goes on to suggest how such a memory-load account can also be used to explain a range of attachment preferences. In sum, although formulating an algorithm which accounts for all the relevant data is a difficult task, it is interesting that the simple empirical facts regarding incrementality and the difficulty of centre-embeddings can take us quite far in characterising the space of possible human parsing algorithms.

AMBIGUITY IN PARSING

We observed at the beginning of this chapter that sentences may have more than one potential syntactic analysis, either *locally* at some point during parsing, or *globally* when the utterance as a whole has several possible interpretations. In the previous discussion we did not discuss how this issue is to be addressed. For example, in (13, Step 3.), the NP was expanded using the NP → Det N, rule, which happened to be correct, but we could equally have chosen one of the other NP rules at that point, and then failed to reach a parse. In order to ensure that a parse is found (for grammatical sentences), some mechanism is needed to ensure that all possible parses can be considered. There are essentially three ways this can be achieved.

Backtracking. Pursue a single analysis. When more than one structure can be built, choose one, but mark that decision as a "choice point". If that analysis cannot be completed (i.e. it reaches an incomplete state where no further rules can be applied), undo everything up to the last choice point, select a different structure, and try again. Proceed until a parse is found.

Determinism. Give the parser sufficient information, such as looking ahead at the words to come, so that it can successfully decide which is the right rule to use at any given point. This means the parser won't make any "mistakes", so no parallelism or backtracking is required.

Parallelism. Pursue all possible parses in parallel, i.e. when more than one structure can be built, build all of them simultaneously, and simply discard those that don't lead to a valid parse.

Each of these techniques has its pros and cons when considered from the point of view of human sentence parsing. In the following subsections we consider each one in turn.

Serial, backtracking parsers

We observed above that in (13, Step 3.), the NP node was arbitrarily expanded using one particular rule instead of another (since the other would not have led to a successful parse). A serial parser, however, has no way of knowing which is the right rule to use at that particular point in the parse. It could equally well have used another rule, and subsequently failed to reach a parse. In the context of a complete language understanding model, it may be that a particular syntactic analysis, although perfectly grammatical, becomes semantically implausible as well; recall (5), and the relevant discussion. To accommodate such situations, we must augment the parser with a mechanism for *recovering* from such erroneous decisions. This is done by keeping track of the "choice points" during the parse, i.e. those points at which there were multiple rules which could have been used to expand a particular node.

This mechanism provides us with a course of action we can take should the parse become blocked. Thus, if we reach a point where we can no longer continue with the current parse (e.g. the current word cannot be grammatically attached), we assume that a wrong decision was made at some choice point. To continue parsing, the parser selects some choice point, and restarts the parse from that point, making sure to choose a different rule to expand the node at that point. Typically, in selecting a choice point, the parser begins with the most recent. There are several reasons for this strategy:

1. It seems likely that if earlier choices were indeed erroneous, they would have been discovered sooner. The fact that the parse successfully continued for some time, suggests they were good decisions. This assumes left-to-right, incremental processing.
2. All things being equal, this strategy will involve the least effort, since a smaller portion of the sentence will be reparsed.

This is the strategy used in the top-down parsers described earlier, but it is not necessary for us to restrict ourselves to this approach. A superficial consideration of human parsing performance suggests, however, that it may be a good first approximation. There is substantial evidence that reanalyses that are identified immediately (i.e. the choice point occurs just prior to the point of parse failure) are easier than cases where the appropriate choice point occurs "further back" in the parse. Consider, for example the following two parse fragments:

(21) The man saw the book was open.

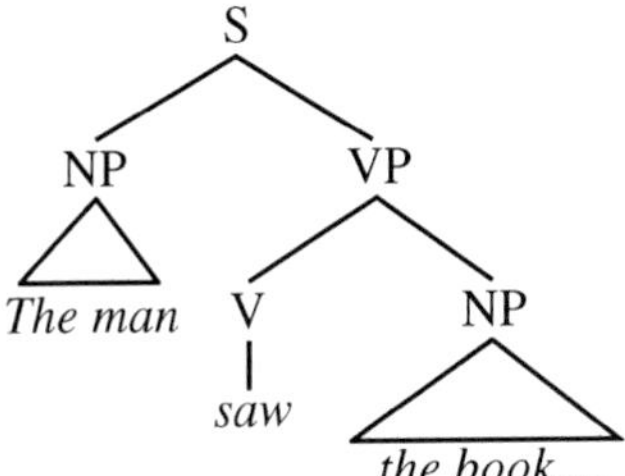

(22) The woman sent the letter was pleased.

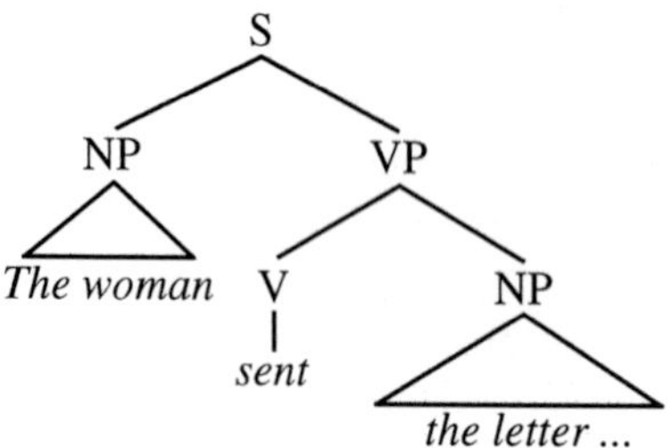

In (21), we need simply backtrack to the VP node, and reparse using the rule VP → V S, whereas in (22) it is necessary to reparse from the initial subject NP, using the rule NP → NP RelC, a choice point which involves substantially more reparsing. This might be accepted as an explanation for the fact that people find (21) much easier to process than (22). There are, however, counterexamples to this theory. Consider the sentence:

(23) After John left the shop closed.

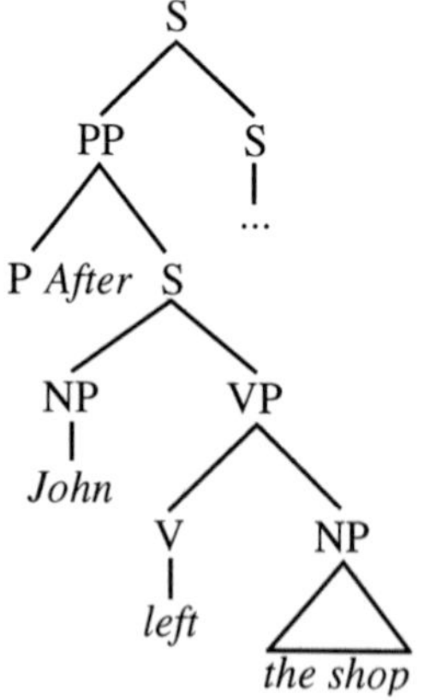

Here, it is necessary for *the shop*, initially attached at the direct object of *left*, to be reanalysed as the subject of the main clause. Although this should require no more reanalysis by the parser than (21), people find it much more difficult to process. Puzzles such as this have led to parsing models that either restrict the backtracking mechanism in such a way that it makes (22) and (23) both difficult to reparse, as in the parser of Abney (1989), and models that argue that the difficulty of reparsing, or *reanalysis*, is due to independent linguistic reasons, as suggested by Pritchett (1992). We will consider these models further later in the chapter.

Deterministic parsing: Time

One of the most striking of our intuitions about the nature of human sentence processing is the speed at which it takes place. For most utterances, people seem able to construct an interpretation in *real time*, at least without any perceptible delay, and without any conscious effort. This observation was the prime motivation for the deterministic parser developed by Marcus (1980). The reasoning was that since the human sentence processor is fast, it must be deterministic, i.e. build syntactic analyses only when there are sufficient grounds to guarantee it is the correct one, and thus avoid backtracking. This contrasts with the *non-deterministic* "guessing" which is the hallmark of the backtracking models discussed earlier. Such a deterministic parser will correspondingly *fail* if it encounters input that cannot be incorporated into the current analysis, since determinism prohibits *backtracking* to an alternative analysis. This approach has an added appeal in that it naturally predicts that failure on the part of the parser should occur for precisely those garden-path sentences that cause humans to have conscious difficulty, e.g. (22 and 23), if it is to be considered psychologically plausible. To achieve such a model, Marcus implemented an LR(3) parser—essentially a bottom-up, left-to-right parser, with three item look-ahead—for English.

As we observed earlier, the ability of a bottom-up parser to leave constituents, or phrases built up so far, "unstructured" on the stack violates the incrementality criterion established. The extent of the look-ahead mechanism compounds the implausibility of the algorithm itself. Finally, the reliance of the parser on lexical, subcategorisation information, although being quite natural for a head-initial language such as English, where verbs precede their objects, predicts serious problems for languages such as German, Dutch, and Japanese, where heads may follow their arguments, rendering even three constituent look-aheads inadequate. For these cases the parser would have to leave numerous, possibly large, constituents unstructured, or "buffered", until the sub-categorising verb was found, running counter to a variety of empirical evidence to the contrary (see Frazier, 1987 for data and discussion). Another serious criticism of the model is that it makes a rather black and white distinction between those sentences that are easy to process and those that are difficult. This seems too crude, as the experimental literature has demonstrated time and again that parsing difficulty is a matter of degree, with some sentences being only marginally difficult, e.g. (21). Others, although perfectly grammatical, become almost impossible to process, e.g. (22 and 23). Subtle manipulation of various factors, such as plausibility and discourse, both outside the domain of the parsing explanations offered thus far, can be used to either amplify or virtually nullify the so-called garden-path effect for reduced relative sentences such as (22) (Crain & Steedman, 1985; MacDonald, 1994; but see also Frazier & Clifton, 1996 and Sturt & Crocker, 1997 for discussion).

This early work has, however, inspired a number of more psychologically plausible models which focus upon "structural determinism" or, more accurately, structural monotonicity. Marcus, Hindle, and Fleck (1983) developed Description Theory (D-theory), which suggests that parse trees be characterised in terms of a set of dominance and precedence relations. By defining trees in this way, it is possible to allow certain structural revisions that only require adding such relations, and not removing any, which is why these models are considered "monotonic". Recall (21), repeated here, which was an instance of easy reanalysis:

(24) The man saw the book was open.

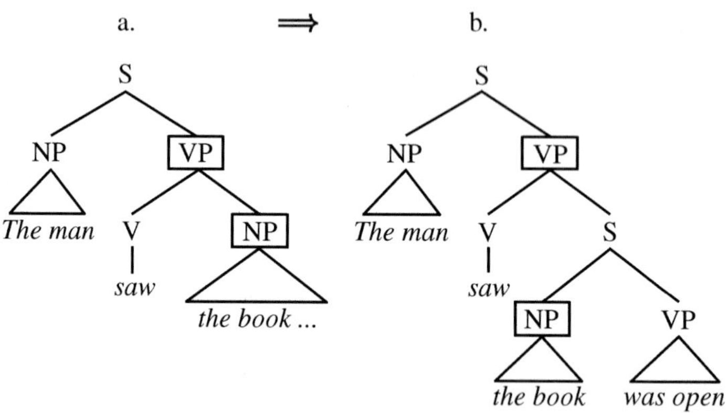

When the NP *the book* is parsed, we would assert that it is dominated by the VP node, and preceded by the V node. When the following VP is encountered, we must "lower" the NP into an embedded sentence. But this is predicted to be easy, since the NP node is still dominated by the VP (both shown in boxes), and is also still preceded by the V. The only change is that the NP is no longer *immediately* dominated and preceded by the VP and V nodes, respectively. But since such a revised structure represents a monotonic increase to the parser's knowledge about the current syntactic analysis, such revision of the structure does not entail full, destructive reanalysis. A full discussion of these models would take us rather too far afield here, but for further discussion the reader is referred to the work of Gorrell (1995), Weinberg (1994), and Sturt and Crocker (1996, 1997).

Parallel approaches

Up to this point, we have only considered parsing algorithms that pursue one syntactic analysis at a time, relying on backtracking to find different possible analyses. Such models have much to recommend them: (1) they are conceptually simpler, (2) they are computationally simpler, in that less processing and memory resources are required, and (3) if we assume that back-tracking, or *reanalysis*, correlates with increased processing complexity, then it makes strong, testable predictions about human behaviour.

There is, however, a perfectly coherent alternative, which suggests that people have the ability to construct alternative syntactic analyses in parallel, when an ambiguity is encountered. That is, rather than make some decision when a choice point is reached, simply pursue all (or perhaps some sub-set of) alternative parses in parallel. Thus, when one particular analysis fails, it can simply be eliminated from consideration. No backtracking is required, since we can be certain that the correct parse is taking place in parallel.

Bounded, ranked parallelism. It is important to note that full parallelism—where *every* analysis is pursued—is not psychologically possible. From a formal perspective, this is ruled out by the simple fact that there may potentially be an infinite number of such analyses, particularly if we insist on our criteria of building connected representations incrementally. Consider, for example, the following sentence initial fragment:

(25) I believe the ...

Each of the trees shown next is a possible partial parse for this fragment. It should also be clear that infinitely many other trees are possible:

(26)

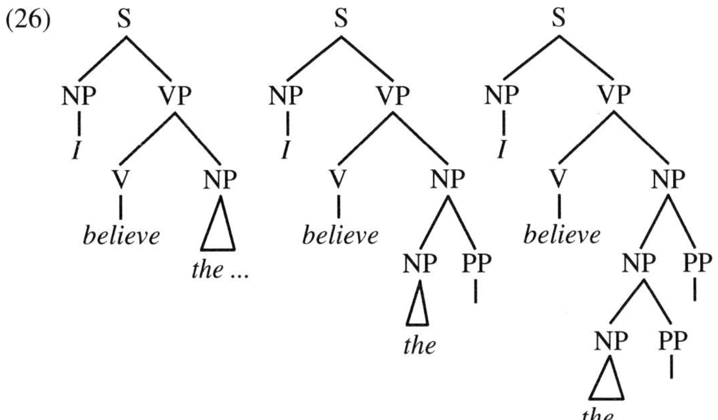

That is, for our grammar in (1), the *recursive* rule: NP → NP PP means that *the* could be infinitely deeply embedded within an NP. If we accept that the mind is finite, then it simply cannot represent all the alternatives in parallel. Even if we put some arbitrary limits on the depth of the possible recursion, say 10, then there is the added ambiguity of whether or not the NP is a direct object or an embedded sentence. Contrast the following two sentences:

(27a) I believe [*NP* the daughter of the sister of the colonel].
(27b) I believe [*S* [*NP* the daughter of the sister of the colonel] is my aunt].

If we combine, say, the 10 analyses due to the recursion, with the 2 further analyses, we now have 20. Indeed it is not difficult to introduce additional ambiguities which would multiply out the number of parallel alternatives even further. This suggests that the memory requirements of a fully parallel system would quickly exceed the short-term memory resources available. Note, a further criticism of such a fully parallel system is that it would not explain the existence of garden-path sentences, since in principle a parallel parser would have constructed the "dispreferred" analysis for such sentences, thereby predicting them to be straightforward.

The solution to these criticisms has been to propose bounded, ranked parallel parsing mechanisms. By bounded we mean simply that there exists an a priori limit on the number of analyses we can consider in parallel. By ranked we mean that the analyses are ordered in some way. Typically, the ordering reflects the extent to which an analysis is "preferred". This ranking in turn accounts for the preferred interpretations exhibited by people, as people are typically aware of only one interpretation both during and after parsing.

Ranking also crucially provides the mechanism for selecting which analyses are to be pursued in parallel and which are to be discarded. That is, since ranking usually reflects some notion of preference, a bounded parallel parser will typically pursue highly ranked structures, i.e. above some rank threshold, and discard any below the threshold. This directly predicts that analyses that are discarded will be difficult garden paths, if they ultimately turn out to be correct. In contrast, there will only be some relatively small cost associated with selecting one of the other parallel (but less preferred) analyses. One such parallel model is that of Gibson (1991), which ranks parallel structures according to a set of principles based on memory load, and discards any structures which have memory requirements that are too high.

A rather more restricted parallel mechanism is the *momentary* parallelism of Altmann (1988). In this model, all possibilities are considered at each choice point, but only one "survives" and is pursued. Altmann argued that this would permit the use of semantic and pragmatic knowledge to assist in resolving local ambiguity, while also limiting the explosion of multiple analyses that plagues full parallel models.

Competitive activation. Up to this point we have considered two basic parsing mechanisms, the first in which the parser pursues a single analysis, to the exclusion of all others, backtracking to alternatives as required. The second pursues a ranked and bounded set of parse analyses simultaneously. An additional possibility is a model which not only pursues multiple analyses in parallel, but crucially allows these structures to compete dynamically with each other in the ranking process. We might, for example, associate each competing analysis with an *activation level* where alternatives are ranked according to the strength of their activation. If we further assume some fixed total activation for all the analyses, then an increase in activation for one analysis will correspondingly entail a decrease in activation for its competitors, as in the models proposed by MacDonald, Pearlmutter, and Seidenberg (1994), Tanenhaus, Spivey, and Hanna (in press), and Trueswell and Tanenhaus (1994). In this way, one analysis might leapfrog several others in the ranking as the activation level for each analysis is adjusted during the course of parsing. Parallelism is then naturally bounded by simply dropping from consideration those analyses whose activation drops below some specified threshold.

There are numerous ways in which competitive activation might be realised in the HSPM. Stevenson (1994) proposes a hybrid parser which permits alternative syntactic attachments to compete with each other. Crucially, only a limited space of alternatives is allowed by the parser, and competition is based on syntactic information alone. In an alternative model, MacDonald et al. (1994) argue that syntactic representations and constraints interact freely with other levels of representation. The model is therefore relatively unconstrained with regard to the space of competing structures, and also the kinds of information brought to bear on the competition. So semantic and discourse constraints can directly influence competition between syntactic alternatives. We expand on this issue of "modularity" versus "interaction" in the next section.

STRATEGIES FOR DISAMBIGUATION

We noted at the beginning of this chapter that not only is language highly ambiguous, but that it is precisely how people cope with such ambiguity that gives us some insight into the workings of the mechanisms they employ. In the previous sections we have seen how a number of different parsing architectures deal with ambiguity in general. In the following sections we consider some specific strategies which have been proposed in the psycholinguistic literature, and ask which combination of general parsing mechanism and specific strategies might best account for, and explain, existing experimental findings.

Modularity versus interaction

In determining the strategies involved in disambiguation, a most fundamental question concerns what types of knowledge people recruit during parsing. There is no question that the process of language comprehension ultimately makes use of the vast range of linguistic and world knowledge in its efforts to arrive at an appropriate interpretation. Rather, the debate is concerned with how different knowledge sources are invoked during the time-course of language comprehension, from the initial moments of perception through to the final stages of full understanding. Possible models range from a highly modular architecture—in which lexical access strictly precedes parsing, which in turn strictly precedes semantic processing, and so on—to fully interactive models that claim there is a single process which combines lexical, syntactic, semantic, and world knowledge constraints without distinction. To our knowledge, neither of these extremist positions is occupied (though for a strongly interactive connectionist proposal see McClelland, St. John, & Taraban, 1989), but there are proposals which clearly tend towards either end of the spectrum. We will first consider some of the general architectures that have been proposed before turning our attention towards specific theories.

Modular models. Modularity draws its inspiration largely from the way linguists have carved up their theories: phonology, morphology, syntax, semantics, pragmatics, and so on have all been treated as independent phenomena. The result is that theories of each are extremely different from each other, not just in terms of the data they are concerned with, but in terms of the fundamental properties of the frameworks proposed. That is, the kinds of principle and representation that account successfully for phonological data are rather inappropriate for a treatment of semantics, whereas semantic formalisms are typically ill-suited for constructing grammars.[4] From a psychological perspective, it is a short (though not

---

[4] There has been recent work on developing more homogeneous sign-based linguistic theories within powerful unification-based frameworks, such as HPSG (Pollard & Sag, 1994). But despite sharing an overarching framework, the principles and representations instantiated within it still have important differences at each of the different levels of linguistic analysis.

necessarily correct) jump to suggest that the different systems proposed by linguists might correspond to distinct systems within the human language processor.

It is also generally held that some ordering of these components is necessary. For example, semantic interpretation of the sentence (or fragments of it) can only take place after a syntactic analysis is constructed. Were this not the case there would be no need for syntax. Thus, a traditional view of the language processor is one which includes a number of distinct sub-systems, which pass information in a particular direction, as illustrated in Fig. 7.2. The question which then arises naturally is, what is the nature of the communication between the modules? Is it "one-way"? This seems unlikely if the model is serial, since it would seem to preclude the kinds of semantically driven backtracking which are assumed by most models. Is it unrestricted and bi-directional? This is possible, but rather difficult to distinguish from the non-modular view.

Modular models have exploited the full range of parsing mechanisms from serial and parallel parsers, through to competitive activation. Perhaps the best-known instance of a modular model is that of Lyn Frazier, who proposes an architecture consisting of two basic modules: a *syntactic processor*, which constructs a constituent structure representation, and a *thematic processor*, which selects an appropriate assignment of semantic roles for the syntactic structure, on the basis of real-world knowledge (see Frazier, 1984 and Rayner, Carlson, & Frazier, 1983 for discussion and data supporting this view). The distinct stages of processing provide a potential explanation for the range of relative processing effects which occur due to variations in pragmatic plausibility: "... it follows automatically that a sentence will be easier to process when the frame chosen by the thematic processor is consistent with the initial

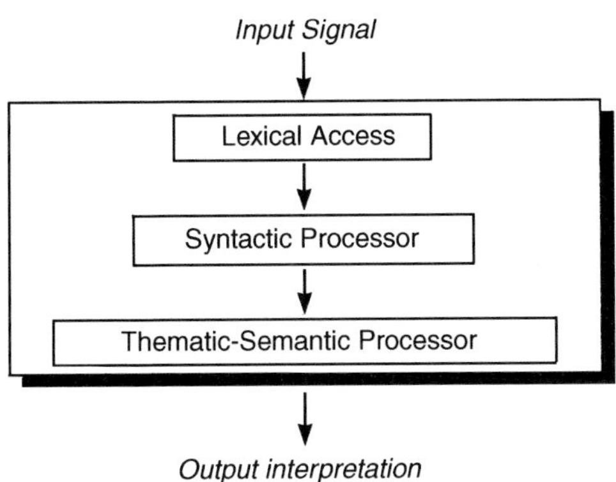

FIG. 7.2 The Modular HSPM

syntactic analysis of the input, than in cases where the two conflict" (Frazier, 1984, p. 134).

It is assumed that the thematic processor operates concurrently with the serial syntactic processor, permitting the rejection of inappropriate analyses immediately after they are proposed. Crucially, however, Frazier maintains that the *initial* decisions concerning constituent structure are made solely by the syntactic processor without "top-down" influence from the thematic processor. This is broadly representative of most modular models, and raises another important point. Modular models do *not* in practice assume or entail that one module must *complete* processing the utterance before it is passed to subsequent modules. Rather, they assume that each module makes its output available *incrementally* as the sentence is processed. Indeed, it seems that the principal computational advantage of a modular architecture is precisely that it enables multiple distinct, but related, processes to operate concurrently.

Interactive models. An alternative position is to suggest that there is no principled, a priori internal structure to the human language faculty, of the sort that modularists have proposed. Rather, we might begin with the observation that our linguistic knowledge consists of a variety of heterogeneous constraints, some concerned with phonology, some with syntax, some with pragmatics, and so on. Further, since we know that many different constraints are essential to resolving ambiguity and arriving at an ultimate interpretation, the constraints should simply be permitted to interact freely during this process. Typically this view is associated with a parallel parsing mechanism where different constraints combine to eliminate or support particular analyses. Indeed, the best examples of this approach, such as the work of Tanenhaus, MacDonald, and colleagues, assume a competitive architecture as discussed in earlier.

To exemplify the constraint-based, interactive approach, Trueswell and Tanenhaus (1994) consider the following pair of sentence fragments:

(28a) The fossil examined...
(28b) The archaeologist examined...

As discussed for (10), *examined* is ambiguous with respect to its form as either a past tense or past participle. If we assume the former, then it is attached as a main verb, and the NP is treated as the subject, and assigned the thematic role Agent. If it is the past participle, we must construct a reduced-relative clause, and the NP will be interpreted as the object, or Theme. The semantic fit of the NP with a particular role seems to successfully disambiguate these two fragments. In (28a), *the fossil* is most likely to be the Theme (the thing that was examined), thereby promoting the reduced-relative analysis. Whereas in (28b), *the archaeologist* is most likely to be the Agent (the entity doing the examining), thereby promoting the simple past reading of the verb, and the corresponding construction of a simple active sentence.

The interactive position is that such "semantic fit" constraints will combine directly with syntactic constraints to resolve such ambiguities immediately. Two-stage, modular models, on the other hand, maintain that the structurally preferred analysis (the main verb reading) will be constructed first. Then the thematic processor will accept it if the semantic fit is consistent, as in (28b), or reject it and force the construction of a reduced-relative in examples such as (28a). The predictions of the modular versus interactive models would therefore seem to be clear. The modular model predicts that the main clause reading will systematically be preferred to the reduced-relative, while the interactive position holds that there is no such systematic preference. Unfortunately, flexibility in both models, combined with contrasting interpretations of the empirical findings, mean that neither theory has been successfully refuted. Modularists point out that the semantic fit constraints, if strong enough and early enough, will force a rapid reanalysis into the parser, such that examples such as (28a) will be quickly reanalysed to the reduced relative. This may even happen so quickly that current experimental paradigms, such as eye-movement studies, will not successfully observe the slight increase in complexity is predicted. Furthermore, although some studies demonstrate that the garden-path effect can be eliminated, there remains a general bias towards constructing the simple active clause. The interactionists eschew this by suggesting that, though all constraints combine simultaneously, some—such as the preference to build an active over a reduced-relative clause—will have greater "weight".

Discussion. As we pointed out earlier, the real issue in the debate over the architecture of the human sentence processor, concerns *which* knowledge sources are used *when*. In its simplest form, the modular position is that constraints of a particular type (e.g. phonological, syntactic, or thematic) are "clustered together", and have some form of temporal priority. That is, syntactic constraints operate prior to semantic ones, since if this did not occur, the semantic processor would have to consider a vast array of possible interpretations, many of which would be syntactically impossible. A further computational advantage is that each module needs only pay attention to a relatively small knowledge base, rather than the vastness of everything known about language. In response to this last point, the constraint-based view holds that the relative priority of constraints will not be determined by their "type", but rather by their prior use and effectiveness, as determined by our linguistic experience. That is to say, the human sentence processor will give preference to constraints that are frequently applied, and that help in the interpretation process.

Interestingly, this view does not in principle exclude the modular position. Perhaps it is precisely the syntactic constraints which are most useful and most frequently applied, to such an extent that non-syntactic constraints are only brought to bear later. This would suggest that even if the system doesn't begin as a modular architecture, it may naturally develop into one. In the following sub-sections we consider some of the leading theories regarding the strategies for sentence processing. Considered from this constraint-based perspective, each may be seen as an attempt to identify which constraints have priority in the process of interpreting language, and their validity does not necessarily hinge on specific assumptions of modularity.

Structural strategies

Some of the most influential research on sentence processing has arisen from the work of Lyn Frazier and her colleagues. The underlying structure of the theory that has emerged assumes an organisation which is similar to that presented earlier. Frazier has concentrated on identifying the strategies operative at the syntactic level. Following the work of Kimball (1973), Frazier (1979) has suggested that the syntactic processor is guided by two basic principles of Minimal Attachment and Late Closure, defined as follows:

(29) Minimal Attachment (MA): Attach incoming material into the phrase marker being constructed using the fewest nodes consistent with the well-formedness rules of the language.
Late Closure (LC): When possible, attach incoming material into the clause or phrase currently being parsed.

This model of sentence processing is strictly incremental: Lexical items are incorporated into the current partial analysis as they are encountered. Where there is an ambiguity in the direction the analysis may take, the principles of MA and LC determine the parser's decision,[5] and if they contradict each other then MA has the higher priority of the two. If the analysis chosen turns out later to be incorrect—i.e. the parser has been

[5] Frazier does not actually assume that MA is a fundamental strategy; rather, she uses it to describe the behaviour of the human parser. Frazier assumes that there is a "race" to build a syntactic analysis for most recent input, and that it is the simplest analysis that will be found first, thus MA should be considered a descriptive, rather than causal, strategy.

led down the garden path—then the parser backtracks to pursue an alternative analysis. For this reason, Frazier's account has been dubbed the Garden-path Theory. It is important to note that the notion of garden path which Frazier adopts is very general, ranging from conscious garden paths, which are noticeably difficult to recover from, to unconscious garden paths, which can only be observed by experimental paradigms sensitive to subtle but systematic increases in complexity. This differs from the simple notion of garden-path phenomena assumed by Marcus's deterministic parser, i.e. just conscious examples.

The principles of MA and LC provide a reasonable account of the core attachment preferences in ambiguous constructions. Let's reconsider the PP attachment ambiguity, which we have simplified here:

Preferred VP attachment over NP adjunction.
(30a) I [*VP* saw [*NP* the girl] [*PP* with binoculars]].
(30b) I [*VP* saw [*NP* the girl [*PP* with flu]]].

These sentences illustrate that there are two possible attachments for the *with* PP, as either a complement of the verb, or a modifier of the NP *the girl*. Given incremental processing, the attachment of the preposition *with* must be performed before its object NP is encountered. Interestingly, this suggests that even recourse to semantic knowledge, e.g. the properties of the preposition's object, would be of no use in making this particular decision. The two possible phrase structures at this point are illustrated here:

(31)

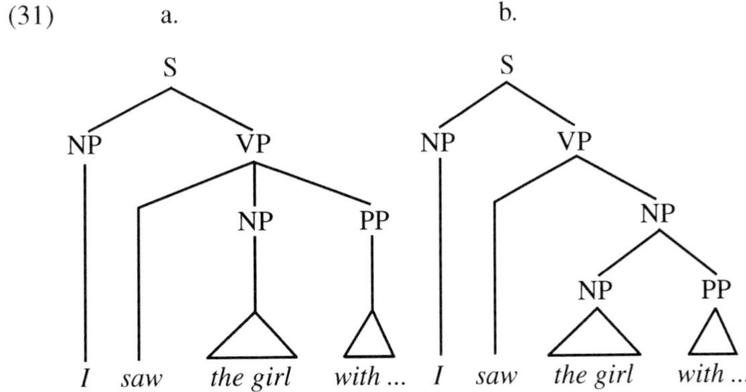

Minimal attachment dictates that the sentence processor will opt for the analysis (31a) over (31b) on the grounds that it involves postulating fewer nodes, namely the extra NP node. The prediction is that sentences where the PP continuation is consistent with the attachment into the VP (e.g.

such as *binoculars*) will be easier to process. This preference has been demonstrated using eye-movement studies by Rayner et al. (1983) and replicated by Ferreira and Clifton (1986) using a similar paradigm which also tested for possible contextual effects.

If we consider the reduced relative garden path discussed earlier (again based on data from Rayner et al., 1983 and Ferreira and Clifton, 1986), the minimal attachment analysis also applies:

Preferred active clause over reduced relative.
(32a) [*S* [*NP* The horse] [*VP* raced past the barn]] and fell.
(32b) [*S* [*NP* The horse [Rel [*VP* raced past the barn]]] fell].

Here we can see that when *raced* is encountered, the two available analyses vary widely in their syntactic complexity, regardless of the particular theoretical details. In the active analysis (32a), the verb *raced* projects to a VP which is then attached to the existing root S node. The complex-NP (32b) interpretation, however, requires the adjunction to the subject NP, of a relative-clause structure, a complex structure which we have abbreviated simply as Rel in (32b). Another example is possible local ambiguity of a complement as either NP or S:

Preferred NP vs. S complement.
(33a) The scientist knew [*S* [*NP* the solution to the problem] was trivial].
(33b) The scientist knew [*NP* the solution to the problem].

MA predicts the NP *the solution to the problem* will be initially analysed as the direct object (33b), since this avoids postulating the intervening S node. This prediction is borne out by the eye-movement experiment described in Frazier and Rayner (1982). That study also tested cases of clause boundary ambiguity illustrated by the following sentences:

Preferred object attachment where possible.
(34a) While Mary was [*VP* mending [*NP* the sock]] [*S* it fell off her lap].
(34b) While Mary was [*VP* mending] [*S* [*NP* the sock] fell off her lap].

There is a strong preference for attaching the sock as the object of mending, as in (34a), rather than as the subject of the main clause (34b), which results in a conscious garden path. Assuming, however, that the main clause S node is available for attachment, both analyses are equally minimal. To resolve this problem, LC prefers attachment to the VP, the most recent phrase considered by the parser, over the main S, which has yet to be analysed.[6]

Grammar-based strategies

Frazier's garden-path theory posits a pair of strategies[7] defined purely in terms of the *form* of syntactic structure, rather than their *content*. That is, the strategies simply count the number of nodes, or make reference to their parse tree positions, without consideration of the relations such nodes represent. Current linguistic theories, however, crucially distinguish various syntactic positions, with respect to their function and content. For example, some positions are potentially assigned case, other are reserved for constituents which can bear thematic roles, others are for modifying phrases, and so on. One might therefore imagine that not all aspects of the syntactic structure are treated equally.

In particularly influential work, Pritchett (1992) has suggested that the human sentence processor is principally concerned with satisfying the various syntactic constraints. Pritchett assumes a "principles and parameters" style of grammar, which has emerged from the Chomsky's *government-binding* (GB) theory (Chomsky, 1981). In addition to rules of phrase structure, such as we have been assuming, GB theory posits a number of additional contraints on syntactic structures. In particular, it assumes that each verb has a number of thematic roles which must be satisfied, such as Agent, Patient, or Theme as discussed earlier. The verb *mend*, for example, has a subject which is the Agent, and may also have an object following it, which is the Theme. The θ-criterion is simply a principle of grammar which insists that obligatory thematic roles must be assigned. Pritchett brings this principle into the parsing domain, by arguing that theta-role assignment be conducted as rapidly as possible (Pritchett, 1992):

(35) Theta Attachment: The θ-criterion attempts to apply at every point during parsing given the maximal θ-grid.

Roughly, this says attach constituents so as to receive the θ-roles of a given lexical item. The central assumption of this is that lexical entries of

[6] In most cases LC is used to explain the preferred "low attachment" of a constituent in multiple clause sentences. Consider, for example, *I told you John bought the car yesterday*. In this sentence, *yesterday* may modify either the main or embedded clause, but there is a general preference for the latter, which is accounted for by the LC strategy, since this is the clause currently being parsed.

[7] A more detailed specification of strategies is provided in Frazier and Rayner (1988), which advances a parameterised set of principles to account for certain cross-linguistic effects. However, for present purposes, we consider only the two core strategies.

verbs are fully specified for thematic roles, as already outlined, and that such information is immediately accessed and used to drive parsing.

In addition, Pritchett suggests the following principle, to account for the cost of reanalysis in the event that the parser makes an incorrect attachment:[8]

(36) On-line Locality Constraint: The target position (if any) assumed by a constituent must be governed or dominated by its source position (if any), otherwise attachment is impossible for the Human Sentence Processor.

Put simply, this states that once a constituent has been assigned a θ-role by some verb, it is difficult to move it out of that position. To make this more concrete, let's reconsider the example from (34), repeated for convenience:

(37a) While Mary was [*V P* mending [*NP* the sock]] [*S* it fell off her lap].
(37b) While Mary was [*V P* mending] [*S* [*NP* the sock] fell off her lap].

In (37a), at the point of processing *the sock*, it is attached as an object of *mending* since this means it can successfully discharge the Theme role for *mending*. However, should this attachment turn out to be incorrect, as in the continuation given in (37b), a garden path results and we must reanalyse *the sock* as the subject of *fell*, as shown in (37b). This reanalysis involves moving *the sock* out of the object position (and hence government domain) of *mending*, and into a new domain, i.e. of the subject position of the verb *fell*. The On-line Locality Constraint, therefore, correctly predicts a garden-path effect. In contrast, let's consider again example (33), repeated here:

(38a) The scientist knew [*S* [*NP* the solution to the problem] was trivial].
(38b) The scientist knew [*NP* the solution to the problem].

Pritchett argues that no garden path occurs in such sentences. As in Frazier's account, Pritchett suggests the NP *the solution to the problem* is originally licensed and attached as the direct object of *knew*, as in (38b). When the final VP is encountered in (38a), the NP is re-licensed as the

---

[8] In the original formulation of his theory, Pritchett defined the Θ-Reanalysis constraint, which required that a constituent remain in the Θ-Domain upon reanalysis—the On-line Locality Constraint effectively subsumes the original formulation.

subject of the embedded clause. Crucially, however, the NP remains governed by *knew*. This predicts the lack of a garden-path effect, contrary to the analysis of Frazier. This difference is due primarily to contrasting definitions of the term "garden path": while Frazier is concerned with characterising the broad range of processing phenomena, from subtle preferences to conscious garden paths, Pritchett's account is exclusively concerned with the latter.

A related proposal has been made by Abney (1989), who develops a deterministic LR parser which drives attachment decisions on the basis of the thematic roles required by particular verbs. He introduces a "steal-NP" operation to permit certain difficult, but possible, reanalysis operations as in (37), and predicts full garden paths to be unparseable. One problem shared by the models of both Pritchett and Abney derives from their reliance on verbal heads to drive the parsing process, which predicts that much of the processing in verb-final languages, such as German and Japanese, will be delayed, and therefore not incremental. To overcome this problem, Crocker (1996) proposes the following replacement for Theta Attachment:

(39) A-Attachment (AA): Attach incoming material, in accordance with $\bar{X}$ theory, so as to occupy (potential) A-positions.

where the simplified definition of A-position is roughly as defined in (Chomsky, 1981; see also Sells, 1985 for some discussion):

(40) A-Position: Those positions (e.g. subjects and objects) that are *potentially* assigned a θ-role, e.g. subject and complement positions.

This allows us to maintain the spirit of Pritchett's θ-Attachment strategy, while avoiding specific reference to thematic information which may not be available, particularly in verb-final languages. Specific evidence in support of this strategy (and Minimal Attachment) comes from Frazier (1987), who examines attachment preference in Dutch.

In related work, Gibson (1991) argues that unresolved thematic role assignments don't directly determine initial attachments, but rather affect the memory load associated with a particular analysis. A cost is associated with each unassigned theta role, and each NP position that has yet to receive a theta role. From this, a function is derived which ranks alternative parses: Roughly, the more unresolved role assignments, the greater the load. In the context of a bounded, parallel model, syntactic analyses with lower memory load are preferred, and those which exceed a specified threshold—as occurs in some centre-embeddings and reduced-relative clauses—are dropped from consideration by the parser. This approach has the interesting property of unifying the explanation of attachment preferences, garden-path effects, and memory load effects, within a single framework.

The important hallmark of all of these approaches is that they are grounded directly in the *content* of the syntactic relations posited by current linguistic theory, rather than on the more "artefactual" structural representations of such relations. For example, Frazier's Minimal Attachment strategy crucially relies on a rather peculiar phrase structure analysis to capture the preference in (30). That is, for MA to predict the attachment, Frazier has to stipulate that PP arguments are attached directly to the VP, whereas NP modifiers introduced an extra branching NP node. In the account presented here, this preference is accounted for directly, by claiming that theta (or argument) positions are preferred attachment sites, over modifier positions.

Experience-based strategies

It has long been accepted that statistical effects of some sort play a role in various aspects of linguistic perception. An obvious, though not necessary, assumption is that such statistical mechanisms are derived from the frequency with which particular lexical items and structures are encountered during our linguistic experience. Several well-specified theories of frequency effects exist at the sublexical and lexical levels: Cairns, Shillcock, Chater, & Levy (1997) suggest a statistical account of speech segmentation, Crocker and Corley (in press) argue for the role of statistical mechanisms in lexical disambiguation; Ford, Bresnan, and Kaplan (1982) for sub-categorisation preferences; and others for the role of frequency in accessing lexical meaning (see Duffy, Morris, & Rayner, 1988 and Kawamoto, 1993). More recently, theories concerning the role of statistical knowledge and strategies in syntactic processing have begun to emerge.

In most models, statistical mechanisms are taken as an *additional* factor, rather than a complete replacement, for the kinds of strategy we have discussed so far. The problem which faces researchers is: What rules, constraints, or processes are frequency-based in nature? In other words, when does the HSPM pay attention to statistical frequency effects, and when does it ignore them in favour of more general or fundamental principles? Or indeed, are there any such fundamental principles that are not simply statistical "generalisations"? The space of possible models is vast, and at present there is not enough empirical evidence for us to reasonably select among them, but it is worth looking briefly at the perspectives which are emerging.

Within the constraint-based architectures of MacDonald et al. (1994) and Trueswell and Tanenhaus (1994), it is envisaged that frequency effects will influence the likelihood or strength with which any particular constraint is applied, suggesting a vast number of statistical parameters. Broadly speaking, these theories argue that just as interactive, constraint-based behaviour can be naturally explained by connectionist architectures, so can the existence of frequency-based information. Indeed, within these architectures the influence of frequency is not so much strategic, as unavoidable—it is a fundamental property of the connectionist computational mechanism assumed. Precisely such frequency effects are used to explain, for example, the general bias toward the main clause versus the reduced-relative mentioned earlier, since people presumably encounter more simple active sentences than reduced relatives.

An alternative is to imagine a more strategic role for statistical mechanisms, where the HSPM invokes the use of frequency in only those cases where it improves performance, i.e. leads to the correct resolution of the ambiguity. The Tuning Hypothesis of Mitchell and Cuetos (1991) argues that a modular syntactic processor uses frequency information exclusively for the resolution of structural ambiguities (see also Mitchell, Cuetos, Corley, & Brysbaert, 1995). Thus, although a large statistical knowledge base is still required, it is substantially less than that of the interactionist models, where frequency effects are not limited to parsing. In contrast with both of these proposals, Gibson, Pearlmutter, Canseco-Gonzalez, and Hickok (1996) posit that a single statistical parameter is used to determine which of two attachment strategies has priority, to explain variation in high- versus low-attachment preferences across languages.

SUMMARY AND DISCUSSION

This chapter began by highlighting the problems faced by the human sentence processing mechanism in its task of constructing an interpretable representation for a given sentence or utterance. In particular, language is highly ambiguous at all levels of representation, including lexical, syntactic, and semantic forms. The fact that people appear to process language incrementally, essentially on a word-by-word (and perhaps even finer grained) basis, means that we are not only faced with global ambiguity, but also with the numerous local ambiguities which occur in mid-sentence. We formalised the problem of building syntactic analyses, and characterised the "choice points" that handle ambiguity, by considering several parsing algorithms: top-down, bottom-up, and the combined left-corner. Broadly speaking, the left-corner algorithm emerges as the most plausible model in that it is typically incremental, is highly bottom-up, and approximates certain general memory load restrictions. But it is important to note that it is far from perfect; memory load phenomena appear more complex than predicted by the left-corner algorithm, and incrementality is still not fully achieved in existing algorithms (unless certain restrictions are placed on the grammars used). Also, much of current work is based on English, where verbs precede their objects, making the job of incremental parsing much easier. Greater consideration of verb-final and free word order languages is necessary, if we are to arrive at satisfying models of sentence parsing (cf. Crocker, 1996; Cuetos & Mitchell, 1988; Frazier & Clifton, 1996; Frazier & Rayner, 1988 and Sturt & Crocker, 1996, as examples).

We then considered how the problem of ambiguity resolution might be dealt with by the parser, and considered deterministic, backtracking, parallel techniques for doing so. We noted that conclusive empirical data distinguishing between serial and parallel architectures has remained elusive. Of the two, the serial model has the appeal of lower memory requirements, and a generally simpler mechanism, which is probably to be preferred in the absence of evidence to the contrary. It is also worth noting that parallel models predict that alternative, though dispreferred, structures are represented by the language processor. As yet, direct psychological evidence for the existence of such parallel representations has not been forthcoming.

Finally we considered a range of theories about the kind of *information or strategies* that might then be used to inform this process. Do people systematically prioritise syntactic knowledge and strategies, as claimed by the modularists, or can all potentially useful linguistic (and possibly non-linguistic) knowledge contribute in an unorganised manner, as claimed by the constraint-based, interactionist camp. This polarisation of the modularity issue is probably not useful: If one begins from the assumption that language processing is simply a process of integrating a variety of constraints, then the modularist's position simply claims that syntactic constraints are "clustered" together, and typically apply prior to semantic constraints. The extent to which this is the case remains a matter of intense study, but increasingly there is consensus that the modularity versus interaction debate is really about the *degree* of modularity (or interaction), given that the extreme modular and interactionist positions are untenable.

In the last section, we noted that the interactive, constraint-based models of Tanenhaus, MacDonald, and colleagues draw much of their inspiration from work on connectionist architectures. In toy implementations, such networks have demonstrated good ability to combine different kinds of linguistic information, e.g. the system of McClelland et al. (1989), and naturally exhibit frequency effects. This, combined with the fact that they are modelled (sometimes rather loosely) on human neurons, makes such mechanisms appealing as cognitive models. Closer consideration raises a number of issues, however. To date, implemented models have yet to achieve sophisticated coverage of linguistic phenomena, and it is unclear if simple, non-modular connectionist architectures will scale up successfully.

More satisfactory connectionist parsing models make increased use of explicit symbolic representations, and exhibit rather less of the micro-level frequency and interaction effects of the simpler systems (Henderson, 1994). Finally, there is increasing support from the connectionist literature for modularised network models of perception (Jacobs, Jordan, & Barto, 1991; Miikkulainen & Dyer, 1991). In sum, it is largely the micro-level properties of connectionist systems that have promoted the constraint-based interactive approach, while we currently know very little about the macro-level properties that will undoubtably be more relevant to the necessarily large and complex models of language processing. This issue in turn bears on the question of statistical mechanisms. Simple connectionist architectures have an unavoidable frequency-based element, which may not be present at the macro-level of more complex neurally realised systems. In the latter, use of statistical knowledge may turn out to be more strategic, rather than simply automatic—a result that would be compatible with some of the alternative proposals concerning statistical mechanisms.

We have seen that the space of models of the human sentence processing mechanism abounds with a range of proposals. Each has its own appeal, and despite major differences, each can seemingly be made to account for empirical findings relatively well. Part of this stems from the fact that many models are only partially specified and implemented, if at all. Given the complexity of the accounts proposed, implementation is increasingly essential if the true predictions of a particular model are to be made, and potentially verified or falsified. The criteria for the success of a model are many: How well does it explain human behavioural data? Is there a "simpler" theory that can capture the same data (i.e. is the model over-complicated)? Can the model scale up to incorporate sophisticated linguistic knowledge and constraints, or is the model too naive? Is the model computationally and psychologically tractable? Does the fundamental architecture support the processing of the full range of possible human languages? Does the model make too many assumptions, or fail to account for known limitations of the HSPM?

REFERENCES

Abney, S. (1989). A computational model of human parsing. *Journal of Psycholinguistic Research*, *18*(1), 129–144.

Abney, S., & Johnson, M. (1991). Memory requirements and local ambiguities for parsing strategies. *Journal of Psycholinguistic Research*, *20*(3), 233–250.

Aho, A., Sethi, R., & Ullman, J. (1986). *Compilers: Principles, techniques, and tools.* Reading, MA: Addison Wesley.

Altmann, G. (1988). Ambiguity, parsing strategies, and computational models. *Language and Cognitive Processes, 3*, 73–97.

Berwick, R.C., & Weinberg, A.S. (1984). *The grammatical basis of linguistic performance.* Cambridge, MA: MIT Press.

Cairns, P., Shillcock, R.C., Chater, N., & Levy, J. (1997). Bootstrapping word boundaries: A bottom-up corpus-based approach to speech segmentation. *Cognitive Psychology, 33*, 111–153.

Chomsky, N. (1981). *Lectures on government and binding.* Dordrecht, The Netherlands: Foris Publications.

Crain, S., & Steedman, M. (1985). On not being led up the garden path: The use of context by the psychological syntax processor. In D.R. Dowty, L. Karttunen, & A.M. Zwicky (Eds.), *Natural language parsing* (pp. 320–358). Cambridge, UK: Cambridge University Press.

Crocker, M.W. (1996). *Computational psycholinguistics: An interdisciplinary approach to the study of language.* Dordrecht, The Netherlands: Kluwer Academic Publishers.

Crocker, M.W. & Corley, S. (in press). Modular architectures and statistical mechanism. The case from lexical category disambiguation. In P. Merlo & S. Stevenson (Eds.) *The lexical basis of sentence processing* John Benjamins.

Cuetos, F., & Mitchell, D.C. (1988). Cross-linguistic differences in parsing: Restrictions on the use of the late closure strategy in Spanish. *Cognition, 30*, 73–105.

Duffy, S.A., Morris, R.K., & Rayner, K. (1988). Lexical ambiguity and fixation times in reading. *Journal of Memory and Language, 27*, 429–446.

Ferreira, F., & Clifton, C. (1986). The independence of syntactic processing. *Journal of Memory and Language, 25*, 348–368.

Ford, M., Bresnan, J., & Kaplan, R. (1982). A competence-based theory of syntactic closure. In J. Bresnan (Ed.), *The mental representation of grammatical relations.* Cambridge, MA: MIT Press.

Frazier, L. (1979). *On comprehending sentences: Syntactic parsing strategies.* PhD thesis, University of Connecticut, CT.

Frazier, L. (1984). Modularity and the representational hypothesis. In *Proceedings of NELS 15* (pp. 131–144). Brown University, Providence, RI.

Frazier, L. (1985). Syntactic complexity. In D.R. Dowty, L. Karttunen, & A.M. Zwicky (eds.), *Natural language parsing* (pp. 129–189). Cambridge, UK: Cambridge University Press.

Frazier, L. (1987). Syntactic processing: Evidence from Dutch. *Natural Language and Linguistic Theory, 5*, 519–559.

Frazier, L., & Clifton, C. (1996). *Construal.* Cambridge, MA: MIT Press.

Frazier, L., & Rayner, K. (1982). Making and correcting errors during sentence comprehension: Eye movements in the analysis of structurally ambiguous sentences. *Cognitive Psychology, 14*, 178–210.

Frazier, L., & Rayner, K. (1988). Parameterizing the language processing system: Left- vs. right-branching within and across languages. In J. Hawkins (Ed.), *Explaining linguistic universals* (pp. 247–279). Oxford, UK: Basil Blackwell.

Gibson, E. (1991). *A computational theory of human linguistic processing: memory limitations and processing breakdown.* PhD thesis, Carnegie Mellon University, Pittsburgh, PN.

Gibson, E., Pearlmutter, N., Canseco-Gonzalez, E., & Hickok, G. (1996). Cross-linguistic attachment preferences: Evidence from English and Spanish. *Cognition, 59*, 23–59.

Gorrell, P. (1995). *Syntax and parsing.* Cambridge, UK: Cambridge Universiy Press.

Henderson, J. (1994). Connectionist syntactic parsing using temporal variable binding. *Journal of Psycholinguistic Research, 23*(5), 353–379.

Jacobs, R.A., Jordan, M.I., & Barto, A.G. (1991). Task decomposition through competition in a modular connectionist architecture: The what and where of vision tasks. *Cognitive Science*, *15*, 219–250.

Johnson-Laird, P.N. (1983). *Mental models*. Cambridge, UK: Cambridge University Press.

Kawamoto, A.H. (1993). Nonlinear dynamics in the resolution of lexical ambiguity: A parallel distributed processing account. *Journal of Memory and Language*, *32*, 474–516.

Kimball, J. (1973). Seven principles of surface structure parsing in natural language. *Cognition*, *2*(1), 15–47.

MacDonald, M.C. (1994). Probabilistic constraints and syntactic ambiguity resolution. *Language and Cognitive Processes*, *9*(2), 157–202.

MacDonald, M.C., Pearlmutter, N.J., & Seidenberg, M.S. (1994). Lexical nature of syntactic ambiguity resolution. *Psychological Review*, *101*(4), 109–134.

Marcus, M., Hindle, D., & Fleck, M. (1983). D-theory: Talking about talking about trees. In *Proceedings of 21st conference of the ACL* (pp. 129–136).

Marcus, M.P. (1980). *A theory of syntactic recognition for natural language*. Cambridge, MA: MIT Press.

McClelland, J., St. John, M., & Taraban, R. (1989). Sentence processing: A parallel distributed processing approach. *Language and Cognitive Processes*, *4*(3&4), 287–335.

Miikkulainen, R., & Dyer, M.G. (1991). Natural language processing with modular PDP networks and distributed lexicon. *Cognitive Science*, *15*, 343–399.

Mitchell, D.C., & Cuetos, F. (1991). The origins of parsing strategies. In *Current Issues in Natural Language Processing*. Houston, TX: Center for Cognitive Science, University of Houston.

Mitchell, D.C., Cuetos, F., Corley, M.M.B., & Brysbaert, M. (1995). Exposure-based models of human parsing: Evidence for the use of coarse-grained (non-lexical) statistical records. *Journal of Psycholinguistic Research*, *24*, 469–488.

Pollard, C., & Sag, I. (1994). *Head-driven phrase structure grammar*. Chicago: CSLI/University of Chicago Press.

Pritchett, B.L. (1992). *Grammatical competence and parsing performance*. Chicago: University of Chicago Press.

Rayner, K., Carlson, M., & Frazier, L. (1983). The interaction of syntax and semantics during sentence processing: Eye movements in the analysis of semantically biased sentences. *Journal of Verbal Learning and Verbal Behavior*, *22*, 358–374.

Resnick, P. (1992). Left-corner parsing and psychological plausibility. In *14th international conference on computational linguistics* (pp. 191–197).

Sells, P. (1985). *Lectures on contemporary syntactic theories*. Stanford, CA: Center for the Study of Language and Information.

Shieber, S., & Johnson, M. (1993). Variations on incremental interpretation. *Journal of Psycholinguistic Research*, *22*(2), 287–318.

Stabler, E.P. (1991). Avoid the pedestrians paradox. In R.C. Berwick, S.P. Abney, & C. Tenny (Eds.), *Principle-based parsing: Computation and psycholinguistics*. Dordrecht, The Netherlands: Kluwer Academic Publishers.

Stabler, E.P. (1994). *Syntactic preferences in parsing for incremental interpretation*. Unpublished manuscript, UCLA.

Stevenson, S. (1994). Competition and recency in a hybrid network model of syntactic disambiguation. *Journal of Psycholinguistic Research*, *23*(4), 295–322.

Sturt, P., & Crocker, M.W. (1996). Monotonic syntactic processing: A cross-linguistic study of attachment and reanalysis. *Language and Cognitive Processes*, *11*(6), 449–494.

Sturt, P., & Crocker, M.W. (1997). Thematic monotonicity. *Journal of Psycholinguistic Research*, *26*(3), 297–322.

Tanenhaus, M.K., Spivey, M.J., & Hanna, J.E. (in press). Modeling thematic and discourse context effects with a multiple constraints approach: Implications for the architecture of the language comprehension system. In M.W. Crocker, C. Clifton, & M. Pickering (Eds.), *Architectures and mechanisms for sentence processing*. Cambridge, UK: Cambridge University Press.

Trueswell, J.C., & Tanenhaus, M.K. (1994). Towards a lexicalist framework of constraint-based syntactic ambiguity resolution. In C.C. Clifton Jr., L. Frazier, & K. Rayner (Eds.), *Perspectives on sentence processing* (pp. 155–180). Hillsdale, NJ: Lawrence Erlbaum Associates Inc.

Weinberg, A. (1994). Parameters in the theory of sentence processing: Minimal commitment theory goes east. *Journal of Psycholinguistic Research*, *22*(3), 339–364.

CHAPTER EIGHT

Connectionism and natural language processing

Nick Chater
University of Warwick, Coventry, UK

Morten H. Christiansen
Southern Illinois University, Carbondale, USA

INTRODUCTION

Many of the chapters of this book are concerned with topics in language processing. This chapter is concerned, by contrast, with a particular method, connectionist computational modelling, which has been applied to a wide range of topics. It is, furthermore, a controversial method: Some have argued that natural language processing from phonology to semantics can be understood in connectionist terms; others have argued that *no* aspects of natural language can be captured by connectionist methods. And the controversy is particularly heated because of the *revisionist* claims of some connectionists: For many, connectionism is not just an additional method for studying language processing, but it offers an alternative to traditional theories, which describe language and language processing in symbolic terms. Indeed, Rumelhart and McClelland (1987, p. 196) suggest "that implicit knowledge of language may be stored among simple processing units organized into networks. While the behaviour of such networks may be describable (at least approximately) as conforming to some system of rules, we suggest that an account of the fine structure of the phenomena of language and language acquisition can best be formulated in models that make reference to the characteristics of the underlying networks." We shall see that the degree to which connectionism supplants, rather than complements, existing approaches to language is itself a matter of debate. Finally, the controversy over connectionist approaches to language is an important test case for the validity of connectionist methods in other areas of psychology.

In the next section, we describe the historical and intellectual roots of connectionism, then introduce the elements of modern connectionism, how it has been applied to natural language processing, and outline some of the theoretical claims that have been made for and against it. We then consider four central topics in connectionist research on language processing: word naming and visual word recognition, lexical processing during speech, morphological processing, and syntax.[1] These illustrate the range of connectionist research on language, give an opportunity to assess its strengths and weaknesses across this range, and allows the general debate concerning the validity of connectionist methods to be illustrated in specific contexts. We would argue that debates in each of these areas, although interrelated, should each be considered on their own merits: It may be that connectionist approaches are valuable in modelling some aspects of language processing, but not in others. Finally, in the Conclusions we sum up and consider the prospects for future connectionist research, and its relation to other approaches to understanding language processing and language structure.[2]

BACKGROUND

From the perspective of modern cognitive science, we tend to see theories of human information processing as borrowing from theories of machine information processing, i.e. from computer science. Within computer science, symbolic processing on general purpose digital computers has proved to be the most successful method of designing practical computational devices. It is therefore not surprising that cognitive science, including the study of language processing, has aimed to model the mind as a symbol processor.

Historically, however, theories of human thought inspired attempts to build computational devices, rather than the other way around. Mainstream computer science arises from the tradition that thought is a matter of symbol processing. This tradition can be traced to Boole's (1854)

[1] It should be noted that many connectionist models cut across this traditional division into different aspects of language. Thus, such a division may perhaps do injustice to connectionist models of language (Sharkey, 1991)—or even lead into an "incommensurability trap" (Christiansen & Chater, 1992). It is, however, merely meant to reflect the topics addressed in the rest of this book.

[2] For a survey of current research on connectionist natural language processing, see the Special Issue of the journal *Cognitive Science*, "Connectionist models of language processing: progress and prospects" (Christiansen, Chater, & Seidenberg, in press).

suggestion that logic and probability theory describe "Laws of Thought", and that reasoning in accordance with these laws can be conducted by following symbolic rules. It runs through Turing's (1936) argument that all human thought can be modelled by symbolic operations on a tape (the Turing machine), through von Neumann's design for the modern digital computer, to the development of symbolic computer programming languages, and thence to modern computer science, artificial intelligence, and symbolic cognitive science.

Connectionism (also known as "parallel distributed processing", "neural networks", or "neurocomputing") can be traced to a different tradition, which attempts to design computers inspired by the structure of the brain. McCulloch and Pitts (1943) provided an early and influential idealisation of neural function. In the 1950s and 1960s, Ashby (1952), Minsky (1954), Rosenblatt (1962), and many others designed various computational schemes based on idealisations of the brain. Aside from their biological origin, these schemes were of interest because they were able to learn from experience, rather than being designed. Such "self-organising" or learning machines therefore seemed prima facie plausible as models of the aspects of human cognition which are learned rather than innate, including many aspects of language processing (although Chomsky, e.g. 1965 was to challenge the extent to which languages are learned). Throughout this period connectionist and symbolic computation stood as alternative paradigms for modelling intelligence, and it was unclear which would prove to be the most successful. But gradually the symbolic paradigm gained ground, resulting in powerful models in the domains such as language (Chomsky, 1957, 1965) and problem solving (Newell & Simon, 1972). The connectionist approach was largely abandoned, particularly in view of the limited power of then current connectionist methods (see, e.g. Minsky & Papert, 1969, for an influential analysis). But some of these limitations have been overcome (Hinton & Sejnowski, 1986; Rumelhart, Hinton, & Williams, 1986), re-opening the possibility that connectionist computation constitutes an alternative to the symbolic model of thought.

So connectionism is inspired by the structure and processing of the brain. What does this mean in practice? At a coarse level of analysis, the brain can be viewed as consisting of a very large number of simple processors, neurons, which are densely interconnected into a complex network; and these neurons do not appear to tackle information processing problems alone—rather, large numbers of neurons operate co-operatively, and simultaneously, to process information. Furthermore, neurons appear to communicate numerical values (encoded by firing rate), rather than passing symbolic messages, and, to a first approximation at least, neurons can be viewed as mapping a set of numerical inputs (delivered from other neurons) onto a numerical output (which is then transmitted to other neurons). Connectionist models are designed to mimic these properties: Hence, they consist of large numbers of simple processors, known as *units* (or nodes), which are densely interconnected into a complex network, and which operate simultaneously and co-operatively to solve information processing problems. In line with the assumption that real neurons are numerical processors, units are assumed to pass only numerical values rather than symbolic messages, and the output of a unit is usually assumed to be a numerical function of its inputs. Typical connectionist networks do not amount to realistic models of the brain, however (see, e.g. Sejnowski, 1986), either at the level of the individual processing unit, which not only drastically oversimplifies, but knowingly falsifies, many aspects of the function of real neurons, or in terms of the structure of the neural networks, which bear little if any relation to brain architecture. One avenue of research is to seek increasing biological realism (e.g. Koch & Segev, 1989). In the study of aspects of cognition in which little biological constraint is available, most notably language, researchers have concentrated on developing connectionist models with the goal of accurately modelling human behaviour. They therefore take their data from cognitive psychology, linguistics, and cognitive neuropsychology, rather than from neuroscience. Here, they must compete head-on with symbolic models of language processing.

We noted earlier that the relative merits of connectionist and symbolic models of language are hotly debated. But should they be viewed as standing in competition at all? Advocates of symbolic models of language processing assume that symbolic processes are somehow implemented in the brain. Thus, they too are connectionists, at the level of *implementation*. They assume that language processing can be described at two levels: at the psychological level, in terms of symbol processing; and at the implementational level, in neuroscientific terms (to which connectionism approximates). If this is right, then connectionist modelling should proceed by taking symbol processing models of language processing, and attempting to implement these in connectionist networks. Advocates of this view (Fodor & Pylyshyn, 1988; Pinker & Prince, 1988) typically assume that it implies that symbolic modelling should be entirely autonomous from connectionism; symbolic theories set the goalposts for connectionism, but not the other way round. Chater and Oaksford (1990) have argued that, even according to this view, there will be two-way influence between symbolic and connectionist theories, since many symbolic accounts can be ruled out precisely because they could not be neurally implemented. But most connectionists in the field of language processing have a more radical agenda: not to implement, but to challenge, to varying degrees, the symbolic approach to language processing.

Before outlining and evaluating a range of specific connectionist models of language processing, it is useful to set out some of the recurring themes in discussion of the virtues and vices of the connectionist approach to language:

Learning. As discussed previously, connectionist networks typically, although not always, learn from experience,[3] rather than being fully specified by a designer. Symbolic computational systems, including those concerned with language processing, are typically, but not always, fully specified by the designer.

Generalisation. Few aspects of language are simple enough to be learnable by rote. The ability of networks to generalise to cases on which they have not been trained is thus a critical test for many connectionist models.

Representation. Because they are able to learn, the internal codes used by connectionist networks need not be fully specified by a designer, but are devised by the network so as to be appropriate for the task. Developing methods for understanding the codes that the network develops is an important strand of connectionist research. Whereas internal codes may be learned, the inputs and outputs to a network generally use a code specified by the designer. These codes can be crucial in determining network performance, as we shall see. How these codes relate to standard symbolic representations of language in linguistics is a major point of contention.

Rules versus exceptions. Many aspects of language can be described in terms of what have been termed "quasi-regularities"—regularities that are usually true, but which admit some exceptions. According to the symbolic descriptions used by modern linguistics, these quasi-regularities may be captured in terms of a set of symbolic rules, and sets of exceptions to those rules. Processing models often incorporate this distinction by having separate mechanisms to deal with rule-governed and exceptional cases. It has been argued that connectionist models provide a single mechanism, which can pick up general rules, while learning the exceptions to those rules. Although this issue has been, as we shall see, a major point of controversy surrounding connectionist models, it is important to note that attempting to provide single mechanisms for rules and exceptions is not

[3] Although important in many connectionist models, we will not provide a detailed account of connectionist approaches to language *acquisition* here. For an overview, see Plunkett (1995) and for discussion of possible consequences for traditional approaches to language acquisition, see Seidenberg (1994).

essential to the connectionist approach; one or both separate mechanisms for rules and exceptions could themselves be modelled in connectionist terms (Coltheart, Curtis, Atkins, & Haller, 1993; Pinker, 1991; Pinker & Prince, 1988). A further question is whether networks really learn rules at all, or whether they simply approximate rule-like behaviour. Opinions differ concerning whether the latter is an important positive proposal, which may lead to a revision of the role of rules in linguistics (Rumelhart & McClelland, 1986a; see also Smolensky, 1988), or whether it is a fatal problem with connectionist models of language processing (Pinker & Prince, 1988).

With these general issues in mind, let us consider some of the broad spectrum of connectionist models of language processing.

VISUAL WORD RECOGNITION AND WORD NAMING

The psychological processes engaged in reading are extremely varied and complex, ranging from early visual processing of the printed word, to syntactic, semantic, and pragmatic analysis, to integration with general knowledge. Connectionist models have concentrated on very simple aspects of the reading process: (1) recognising words from printed text, and (2) word "naming", i.e. mapping visually presented letter strings onto sequences of sounds (this may or may not involve word recognition). We focus on connectionist models of these two processes here.

One of the earliest connectionist models was McClelland and Rumelhart's "interactive activation" (1981) model of visual word recognition (see also Rumelhart & McClelland, 1982). The network is completely prespecified (i.e. it does not learn), and consists of a sequence of "layers" of units, as illustrated in Fig. 8.1. Units in the first layer are specific to particular visual *features* of letters (in particular positions within the word). Units in the second layer stand for particular letters (also in particular positions within the word). Units in the third layer stand for words. Within and between layers, there are inhibitory connections between units which stand for incompatible states of affairs. For example, there are inhibitory connections between units in the word layer, so that possible "candidate" words compete against each other. There are also excitatory connections between units which stand for mutually reinforcing states of affairs at different layers. For example, there is an excitatory connection between the unit standing for the word TAKE, the unit standing for the letter "T" (in the first position) as well as the particular letter features which make up "T". All excitatory connections of a given kind—for example, between the letter level and the word level units—have the same strength, but this strength varies depending on which two levels are involved. This is also the case with the inhibitory connections between

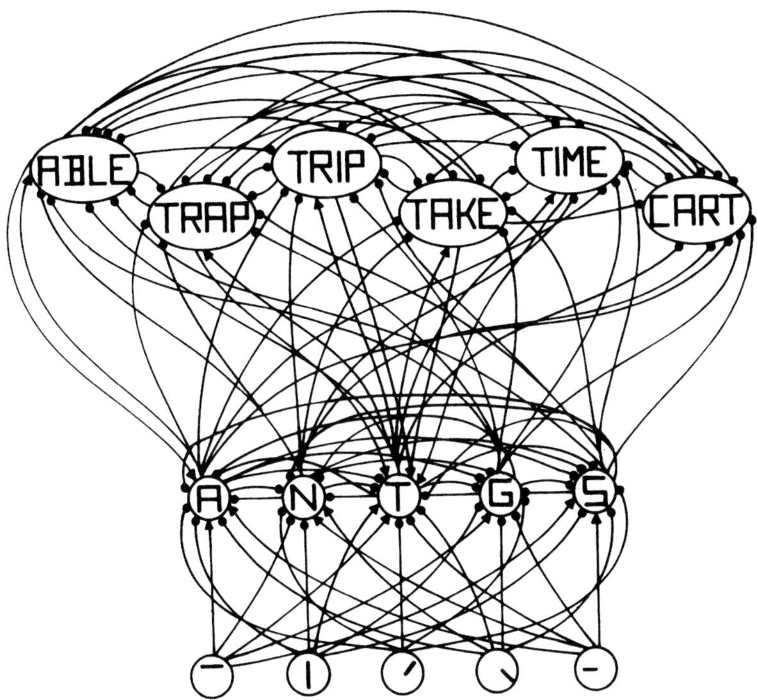

FIG. 8.1 The letter "T" in the first position of a word consisting of four letters, some of its neighbouring nodes, and their interconnections in the McClelland and Rumelhart (1981) interactive activation model of visual word recognition. Excitatory connections are shown as arrows, whereas inhibitory connections have circular ends. From "An interactive activation model of context effects in letter perception: Part 1. An account of basic findings" by J.L. McClelland and D.E. Rumelhart, 1981, *Psychological Review*, *88*, p. 380. Copyright © (1981) by the American Psychological Association. Reprinted with permission

and within unit levels. This defines the "architecture" of the network (shown in Fig. 8.1).

How do individual units behave? In interactive activation models such as this, the level of activity of a unit is determined by its previous level and its current input (as we shall see below, in more recent models, the state of a unit is typically determined only by its current input). If the input to a unit is 0, then all that happens is that the level of activity of the unit decays exponentially. The input to the unit is, as is standard, simply the weighted sum of the units which are inputs to that unit (where the weights correspond to the strengths of the connections). If the input is positive, then the level of activity is increased in proportion both to that input, and to the distance between the current level of activation and the maximum activation (conventionally set at 1); if the input is negative, the level of activity is decreased in proportion to the input, and to the distance between the current level of activation and the minimum activation (conventionally set at –1, but in the McClelland & Rumelhart, 1981, model it was set at –0.2 to allow rapid reactivation).

Although this behaviour sounds rather complex, the basic idea is simple. Given a constant input, the unit will gradually adjust to a stable level where the exponential decay balances with the boost from that input: Positive constant inputs will be associated with positive stable activation, negative constant inputs with negative stable activation; and small inputs lead to activations levels close to 0, whereas large inputs lead to activation values which tend to be near 1 or –1. An activation level near 1 corresponds to a high level of confidence that an item is present; an activation level near –1 corresponds to a high level of confidence that it is not.

Word recognition occurs as follows. A visual stimulus is presented, which activates in a probabilistic fashion the units in the first layer, standing for visual features. Depending on the particular experimental task being modelled (e.g. recognising a bright, high-contrast target followed by mask, or a degraded target), the probability of a feature being activated is set to 1.0 or below. As the features become activated, they send activation via their excitatory and inhibitory connections to the units at the letter level. Notice that so far only bottom-up flow of information has taken place—there is no inhibition between the feature units and no feedback from the letter level to the feature level. In addition, the weights of the inhibitory connections between the letter units (shown in Fig. 8.1) were set to 0, meaning that no inhibition takes place between the letters.[4] As the letter units become activated they, in turn, send excitatory and inhibitory activation to the word-level units. The words compete amongst each other via their inhibitory connections, and reinforce their component letter units via excitatory feedback to the letter level (there is no word-to-letter inhibition). At this point, an "interactive" process is thus occurring between the letter level and the word level: Bottom-up flow of information from the visual input is combined via the activation of the letter units with the top-down information flow from the word units. The entire process involves a cascade of overlapping and interacting processes: letter and word recognition do not occur one after the other as distinct processing stages, but rather are mutually constraining.

[4] The theoretical model, which motivated the simulation model described here, is meant to be fully "interactive", with mutual inhibition between competing units at the same level as well as bi-directional excitatory and inhibitory connections between the three levels, but this was not implemented.

The interactive character of McClelland and Rumelhart's model embodies a controversial theoretical claim about reading. Many researchers have assumed that reading involves the successive computation of increasingly abstract levels of representation, but that there is no feedback from more abstract to less abstract levels. This kind of account is sometimes known as "bottom-up" and can also be realised in connectionist networks, as we shall see later. The question of whether reading is bottom-up or interactive has been a major focus of debate. We shall see later that the same debate rages in the speech perception literature; and analogous issues arise throughout perception (e.g. Bruner, 1957; Fodor, 1983; Marr, 1982; Neisser, 1967).

This model proved able to account for a variety of phenomena, mainly concerning contextual effects on perception of single letters. For example, it captures the fact that letters presented in the context of a word are recognised more rapidly than letters presented individually, or in random letter strings (Johnston & McClelland, 1973). This is because the activation of the word containing a particular letter provides top-down confirmation of the identity of that letter, in addition to the activation provided by the bottom-up feature-level input. Moreover, it has been shown that letters presented in the context of pronounceable non-words (i.e. pseudowords, such as "mave", which are consistent with English phonotactics) are recognised more rapidly than letters presented singly (Aderman & Smith, 1971) or in contexts of random letter strings (McClelland & Johnston, 1977). In this case, the facilitation is caused by a "conspiracy" of partially activated similar words, which are triggered in the non-word context, but not in the random letter string context. These partially active words provide a top-down confirmation of the letter identity, and thus they "conspire" to enhance recognition. In a similar fashion, the model explains how degraded letters can be disambiguated by their letter context, and how occurring in a word context can facilitate the disambiguation of component letters even when they are all visually ambiguous. Moreover, it provides an impressively detailed demonstration of how interactive processing can account for a range of further experimental effects. As we shall see later, however, not all theorists agree that interactive processes are required to explain these and other phenomena in language processing.

Recent work on connectionist modelling of reading has had a somewhat different focus: on word naming rather than recognition. It has been concerned with the problem of learning the relationship between written word forms and their pronunciations, although, as we shall see, issues of word recognition also arise. The first such model was Sejnowski and Rosenberg's (1987) NETtalk—shown in Fig. 8.2—which learns to read aloud from written text.

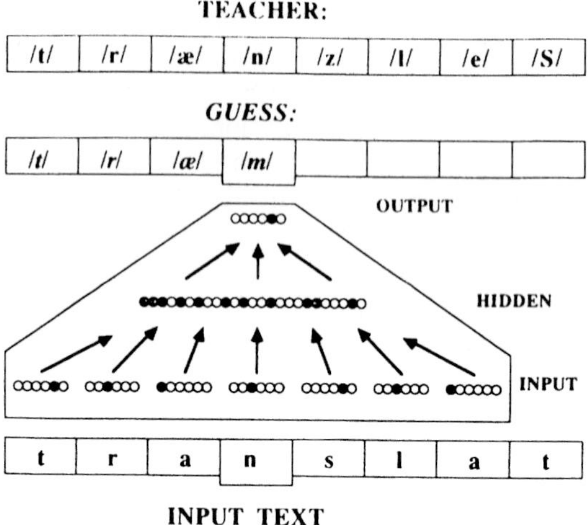

FIG. 8.2. Illustration of the NETtalk architecture. The input layer consists of 203 units divided into 7 groups, which each correspond to a particular letter position. Information from the inputs is fed forward via 80 hidden units to an output layer containing 26 units. During training the network's guess (the activation of the output units) is compared with the desired target provided by a teacher, and network weights are then subsequently altered so as to minimise any discrepancy. From "Neural representation and neural computation" by P.S. Churchland and T.J. Sejnowski in *Neural Connections, Mental Computations*, edited by L. Nadel, L. Cooper, P. Culicover and R.M. Harnish, 1989, MIT Press. Copyright © (1989) MIT Press. Reprinted with permission.

NETtalk uses a *feedforward*, rather than an interactive, network architecture. In a feedforward network, the units are, as before, divided into layers, but activation flows only in one direction through the network, starting at the layer of "input units", and finishing at the layer of "output units". The internal layers of the network are known as "hidden units". There may be several hidden layers in a feedforward network, but in NETtalk, as in many neural networks, there is just one. The input units represent a "window" of consecutive letters of text. The output units represent the network's suggested pronunciation for the middle letter. The network can be used to pronounce a written text by shifting the moving window across the text, letter by letter, so that the central letter to be pronounced moves onwards a letter at a time. In English orthography, there is not, of course, a one-to-one mapping between letters and phonemes. NETtalk uses a rather ad hoc strategy to deal with this: in clusters of letters realised as a single speech sound (e.g. "th", "sh", "ough") only one of the letters is chosen to be mapped onto the speech sound, and the others are not mapped onto any speech sound.

The behaviour of individual units is rather simpler than in the interactive activation network. The activation of each unit is determined by its current input (calculated as the weighted sum of its inputs, as before): Specifically, this input is "squashed", so that the activation of each unit lies between 0 and 1. As the input to a unit tends to positive infinity, the level of activation approaches 1; as the input tends to negative infinity, the level of activation approaches 0. With occasional minor variations, this description applies equally to almost all feedforward connectionist networks.

Whereas the interactive activation model was prespecified, NETtalk learns from exposure to text associated with the correct pronunciation. Specifically, the network is presented with inputs representing seven letter contexts through English texts; and with each input, it is given the "target" output, i.e. the output which corresponds to the correct pronunciation. The inputs use a "position-specific", letter level representation, i.e. the input units are divided into discrete banks, each corresponding to one of the seven letter positions, and within each bank, units correspond to specific letters. At the beginning of training, NETtalk's output bears no relation to the correct pronunciation; but after extensive training, its standard of pronunciation is good enough to be largely comprehensible when fed through a speech synthesizer.

How is learning achieved? Like many of the connectionist models we shall describe later, NETtalk is trained by "back-propagation" (Rumelhart et al., 1986, prefigured in Bryson & Ho, 1975; Werbos, 1974). When each input is presented, it is fed through the network, and the output is derived. The output is compared against the correct "target" value and the difference between the two is calculated for each output unit. The squared differences are summed over all the output units, to give an overall measure of the "error" that the network has made. The goal of learning is to reduce overall level of error, averaged across input/target pairs (in this context, this means averaging across typical texts). Back-propagation is a procedure which specifies how the weights of the network (i.e. the strengths of the connections between the units) should be adjusted in order to decrease the error. Training with back-propagation is guaranteed (within certain limits) to reduce the error made by the network. If everything works well, then the final level of error may be very small, meaning that the network produces the desired output. Notice that the network will produce an output not only for inputs on which it has been trained, but for any input. If the network has learned about regularities in the mapping between inputs and targets, then it should be able to *generalise* successfully to new items. NETtalk is able to pronounce letters in contexts that it has never before encountered reasonably successfully.

Back-propagation may sound too good to be true.[5] But note that back-propagation merely guarantees to adjust the weights of the network to *reduce* the error; it does not guarantee to reduce the error to 0, or a value anywhere near 0. Indeed, in practice, back-propagation can configure the network so that error is very high, but changes in weights in any direction lead to the same or a higher error level. This is known as the problem of local minima. Attempting to avoid this problem is a major day-to-day concern of connectionist researchers, as well as being a focus of theoretical research. Local minima can be avoided by judicious choice among the large number of variants of back-propagation, and by appropriate decisions on the numerous parameters involved in model building (such as the number of hidden units used, whether learning proceeds in small or large steps, and many more). Despite these problems, back-propagation is surprisingly successful in many contexts. Indeed, the feasibility of back-propagation learning has been one of the reasons for the renewed interest in connectionist research. Prior to the discovery of back-propagation, there were no well-justified methods for training multilayered networks. The restriction to single-layered networks was unattractive, since Minsky and Papert (1969) showed that such networks, sometimes known as "Perceptrons" have very limited computational power. It is partly for this reason that hidden units are viewed as having such central importance in many connectionist models; without hidden units, most interesting connectionist computation would not be possible.

What internal code on the hidden units is NETtalk using? This code is not prespecified by the designer, but is learned from experience by the network. Furthermore, it turns out that the pattern of hidden units does not have a transparent interpretation to the casual observer. Sejnowski and Rosenberg gained some insight into what their network is doing by first computing the average hidden unit activation given each of a total of 79 different letter-to-sound combinations. For example, the activation of the hidden unit layer was averaged for all the words in which the letter "c" is pronounced as /k/, another average calculated for words in which "c" corresponds to /s/, and so on. Next, the relationships among the resulting 79 vectors—each construed as the network's internal representation of a particular letter-to-sound correspondence—were explored via cluster analysis. Interestingly, all the vectors for vowel sounds clustered together, suggesting that the net had learned to treat vowels as different

[5] In fact, it is most likely not a biologically plausible learning algorithm. Still, back-propagation provides a convenient learning method which may result in networks with computational properties similar to those of real neural structures.

from consonants. Moreover, the net had learned a number of sub-regularities amongst the letter-to-sound combinations, evidenced for example by the close clustering of the labial stops /p/ and /b/ in hidden unit space.

NETtalk was intended as a demonstration of the power of neural networks, rather than as a psychological model. Seidenberg and McClelland (1989) provided the first detailed psychological model of reading aloud. They also used a feedforward network with a single hidden layer, but they represented the entire written form of the word as input, and the entire phonological form as output. This network implemented one side of a theoretical "triangle" model of reading in which the two other sides were a pathway from orthography to semantics and a pathway from phonology to semantics (these sides are meant to be bi-directional and, in fact, the implemented network also produced a copy of the input as a second output to attempt to model performance on lexical decision tasks, but we shall ignore this aspect of the model here). Seidenberg and McClelland restricted their attention to 2897 monosyllabic words of English, rather than attempting to deal with unrestricted text like NETtalk.

The orthographic and phonological representations used by Seidenberg and McClelland are rather complex, and we give just a sketch here. The most straightforward style of representation would be to use position-specific codes for each letter or phoneme. But this seems unattractive, partly because it fails to capture the fact that the mapping between letters and sounds is (roughly) the same wherever those letters or sounds occur on the word. Using a position-specific code, the network must learn afresh that the letter "t" often maps onto the phoneme /t/ for every position. This is because letters and sounds are represented by distinct units in each position. Indeed, the position-specific scheme does not seem just unattractive—it makes the absurd prediction that an orthographic system in which the correspondence between letters and sounds was different for every serial position should present no special problems. The network would learn this kind of "scrambled" mapping just as easily as normal English orthography; but the human learner would presumably be dramatically impaired. Another difficulty with position-specific encodings is that since, as discussed earlier, letters and phonemes do not stand in one-to-one correspondence, the network would have to solve a difficult "alignment" problem. As we noted, NETtalk finesses this problem by the designer prespecifying a particular alignment; we shall see later that it is also possible for the network itself to solve the alignment problems using a NETtalk style of position-specific representation (Bullinaria, 1994). But Seidenberg and McClelland sidestep the problem by using an ingenious strategy.

The idea is to decompose both the letter and phoneme strings into consecutive triples. Thus, the letter string FISH is decomposed into _FI, SH_, ISH, FIS. Notice that the triples are position-independent, but that the overall string can be pieced together again from the triples (in general, as Pinker & Prince, 1988 have noted, this piecing-together process cannot always be carried out successfully, but in this context it is adequate). The phonemic string is also decomposed into triples of phonemes. Rather than represent the phonemes directly, units are devoted to triples of features of phonemes. This style of representation, termed wickelfeatures (after Wickelgren, 1969, who employed triples in modelling memory for sequential material), was first used in Rumelhart and McClelland's (1986a) model of learning the English past tense, which we will discuss later in the section on morphological processing. In the orthographic layer, each unit is associated with a list of 1000 random letter triplets (10 possible first letters × 10 possible middle letters × 10 possible end letters) and is activated if one of the letter triplets in the input occurs in this list.

Seidenberg and McClelland trained their network to produce an output corresponding to wickel-representation of the pronunciation of a word, from a wickel-representation of its orthography given as input. The performance of the network captures a wide range of experimental data (on the reasonable assumption that network error can be roughly equated with response time in experimental paradigms). For example, frequent words are read more rapidly (with lower error) than rare words (Forster & Chambers, 1973); orthographically regular words are read more rapidly than irregulars, and the difference between regulars and irregulars is much greater on rare rather than frequent words (Seidenberg, Waters, Barnes, & Tanenhaus, 1984; Taraban & McClelland, 1987).

Seidenberg and McClelland's model uses a single mechanism to capture both the rules governing the pronunciation of English text and the exceptions to those rules. This contrasts with the standard view of reading, according to which the rules and the exceptions are treated separately. Indeed, it is standard to assume that there are two distinct routes in reading, a so-called "phonological route", which applies rules of pronunciation, and a so-called "lexical route", which is simply a list of words and their pronunciations. The idea is that regular words can be read using either route; that irregulars must be read by using the lexical route, to override the phonological route; and that non-words can be pronounced by using the phonological route (these will not be mentioned in the lexical route). Seidenberg and McClelland claim to have shown that this *dual-route* view is not necessarily correct, since a single route can pronounce both irregular words and non-words. Furthermore, they have provided a fully explicit computational model, whereas dual-route theorists have merely sketched the reading system at the level of "boxes and arrows" (though see Coltheart, Curtis, Atkins & Haller, 1993 for a recent exception).

A number of criticisms have been levelled at Seidenberg and McClelland's account, however, and we briefly consider some of these. First, can a single route really account for both non-word and exception word pronunciation? Besner, Twilley, McCann, and Seergobin (1990) have argued that the non-word reading performance of Seidenberg and McClelland's model is actually very poor compared with human readers (though see Seidenberg & McClelland, 1990 for a reply). Moreover, Coltheart et al. (1993) have argued that better performance at non-word reading can be achieved by symbolic learning methods, using the same word-set as Seidenberg and McClelland.

Another limitation of the Seidenberg and McClelland model is the use of frequency compression during training. Rather than present rare and frequent words equally often to the network, they presented words with a probability proportional to their log frequency of occurrence in English (using Kucera & Francis, 1967). Had they used raw frequency, rather than log frequency, the network could have encountered low frequency items too rarely to learn them at all; this must be counted as a difficulty for this and many other network models, since the human learner must deal with absolute frequencies. Recently, however, Plaut, McClelland, Seidenberg, and Patterson (1996) have demonstrated that a feedforward network can be trained successfully using the *actual* frequencies of words instead of their log frequency[6]—even to a level of performance similar to that of human subjects on both word and non-word pronunciation.

At a more technical level, Seidenberg and McClelland's model is limited in that it does not readily extend to deal with words with more than one syllable. Furthermore, the use of wickelfeatures creates a number of problems. One of the most important is that output from the network cannot readily be interpreted: There is no straightforward decoding from a muddle of partially activated output units representing wickelfeatures to a pronunciation, specified in a standard phonological format (or any sequential format that would seem to be required to drive speech). This meant that Seidenberg and McClelland had to assess the pronunciation intended by their network by considering various plausible pronunciations, converting these into wickelfeatures, and seeing which is the closest to the performance of the model. A better output code would code pronunciation explicitly, rather than burying it in a deeply encrypted form.

---

[6] Note that Plaut et al. (1996) used these (actual) frequencies to scale the contribution of error for each word during back-propagation training, rather than to determine the number of word presentations. As mentioned later, they also employed a different representational scheme (due to Plaut & McClelland, 1993) than Seidenberg and McClelland (1989).

Recently connectionist work on reading has attempted to take account of these difficulties. For example, Plaut and McClelland (1993) abandon wickelfeatures, and use a localist code, which is loosely position-specific, but which exploits some regularities in English orthography and phonology to avoid using a completely position-specific representation. This learns to read non-words very well—at levels comparable with human non-word reading. But it does so by building in a lot of knowledge into the representation, rather than having the network pick up this knowledge. One could plausibly assume (cf. Plaut et al., 1996) that this knowledge is acquired prior to reading acquisition; that is, children normally know how to pronounce words (i.e. talk) before they start learning to read. This hypothesis was tested by Harm, Altmann & Seidenberg (1994) who demonstrated how pretraining a network on phonology can facilitate the subsequent acquisition of a mapping from orthography to phonology.

One of the problems with this novel representational scheme is, however, that it only works for monosyllabic words. Bullinaria (1994), on the other hand, also obtains very high non-word reading performance, which applies to words of any length. To do so, he gives up the attempt to provide a single route model of reading, and aims only to model the phonological route: He uses a variant of NETtalk, in which orthographic and phonological forms are not prealigned by the designer. The rough idea is that, instead of having a single output pattern, the network has many output patterns corresponding to all possible alignments of the phonology with the orthography. All of these possibilities are considered, and the one that is nearest to the network's actual output is taken to be the correct output pattern, and used to adjust the weights. This approach, like NETtalk, uses an input window which moves gradually over the text, producing one phoneme at a time. Hence, a simple phoneme-specific code can be used; the order of the phonemes is implicit in the order in which the network produces them.

A further criticism of Seidenberg and McClelland's single-route model is that it does not appear to account for an apparent double dissociation between phonological and lexical reading in neuropsychological patients. On the one hand, surface dyslexics (e.g. Marshall & Newcombe, 1973) can read exception words, but not non-words; on the other, phonological dyslexics (e.g. Funnell, 1983) can pronounce non-words but not irregular words. The standard inference from double dissociation to modularity of function (e.g. Shallice, 1988) suggests that normal non-word and exception word reading are subserved by distinct systems—that is, to a dual-route model (Coltheart, 1985; Morton & Patterson, 1980)—although it is important to keep in mind that such double dissociations are never clear-cut. Acquired dyslexia can be simulated by damaging Seidenberg and McClelland's network in various ways (e.g. removing connections or units); although the results of this damage do have neuropsychological interest (Patterson, Seidenberg, & McClelland, 1989), they do not give rise to the double dissociation: an analogue of surface dyslexia is found (i.e. regulars are preserved), but no analogue of phonological dyslexia is observed. Furthermore, Bullinaria and Chater (1995) have explored a range of rule-exception tasks using feedforward networks trained by back-propagation, and concluded that, although double dissociations do occur with single-route models, this only occurs with very small-scale networks. With large networks, the dissociation in which the rules are damaged but the exceptions are preserved does not occur. It remains possible that some realistic single-route model of reading, incorporating factors that have been claimed to be important to connectionist accounts of reading such as word frequency and phonological consistency effects (cf. Plaut et al., 1996) might give rise to the relevant double dissociation.[7] However, Bullinaria and Chater's results indicate that modelling phonological dyslexia is potentially a major difficulty for any single-route connectionist model of reading. Perhaps for this reason, some of the most recent connectionist models of reading now implement an additional "semantic" route.[8]

Single- and dual-route theorists argue about whether non-word and exception word reading is carried out by a single system, but both believe in an additional semantic route for reading. In this route pronunciation is retrieved through accessing a semantic code from the orthographic form. The availability of this additional semantic pathway is evidenced by deep dyslexics, who make semantic errors in reading aloud, such as reading the word *peach* aloud as "apricot". Plaut et al. (1996) argue that this route also plays a role in normal reading. In particular, they suggest that a division of labour emerges between the phonological and the semantic pathway during reading acquisition: Roughly speaking, the phonological pathway moves towards a specialisation in regular (consistent) orthography-to-phonology mappings at the expense of exception words which become the main focus of the semantic pathway.

---

[7] Whereas "regularity" (the focus of the Bullinaria & Chater simulations) can be taken as indicating that the pronunciation of a word appears to follow a rule, "consistency" refers to how well a particular word's pronunciation agrees with other similarly spelled words. The magnitude of the latter depends on how many "friends" a word has (i.e. the summed frequency of words with similar spelling patterns and similar pronunciation) compared with how many "enemies" (i.e. the summed frequency of words with similar spelling patterns but different pronunciations) (Jared, McRae, & Seidenberg, 1990).

[8] Recall that the theoretical model, motivating the original Seidenberg and McClelland (1989) simulation model, included additional pathways from orthography to semantics and from phonology to semantics, but these were not implemented.

The putative effect of the latter pathway was simulated by Plaut et al. as extra input to the phoneme units in a feedforward network trained to map orthography to phonology. The strength of this external input is frequency dependent and gradually increases as learning progresses. As a result the network comes to rely on this extra phonological input. If eliminated (following a lesion to the semantic pathway), the network loses much of its ability to read exception words, but retains good reading of regular words as well as non-words. In this way, Plaut et al. provides a more accurate account of surface dyslexia than Patterson et al. (1989). In contrast, if the phonological pathway is selectively damaged the resulting deficit pattern should resemble that of phonological dyslexia: reasonable word reading but impaired non-word reading—but this hypothesis was not tested directly by Plaut et al.

Furthermore, the theoretical triangle model of Seidenberg and McClelland (1989)—as implemented in a recent (toy) model (Seidenberg & Harm, 1995)—offers an additional explanation of phonological dyslexia, but in the context of development, rather than as an acquired disorder. This first implementation of the full triangle model employs a so-called *recurrent* network (which, broadly speaking, is akin to a feedforward network, except that units in a particular layer are able to feedback onto units at the same layer).[9] The network thus implements the two "connectionist" routes to reading: either via the orthography–semantics pathway or via the orthography–phonology–semantics pathway. In this model, selective damage to the recurrent feedback connections in the phonological layer may provide an alternative explanation of phonological dyslexia. According to this view, in some kinds of development, and perhaps also acquired phonological dyslexia, *dyslexia* may (in some cases) simply be a misnomer—patients should encounter difficulty with *repeating* non-words, just as much as reading them.[10] Unfortunately, this hypothetical explanation has not been explored in simulations. So, while "lesioned" connectionist networks have been shown to model surface dyslexia quite successfully, no explicit simulations have been presented testing the connectionist explanations of phonological dyslexia.

We have considered connectionist models of reading in some detail, since they introduce the principal connectionist methods, and some of the key debates surrounding connectionist models. We have seen that a range

[9] That is, typically there is no feedback from higher to lower layers, as in an interactive architecture, but simply connections allowed within a layer (although there are a few specialised recurrent learning algorithms, e.g. Pearlmutter, 1989, allowing feedback connections between layers). A simple variant of these recurrent networks is discussed further in the next section.

[10] The empirical data concerning repetition abilities of putative dyslexics is highly controversial.

of connectionist accounts have provided a good fit with much of the data on normal and impaired reading, although points of controversy remain. Moreover, connectionist models have contributed to re-evaluation of core theoretical issues, such as whether reading is interactive or purely bottom-up, and whether rules and exceptions are dealt with separately or by a single cognitive mechanism. In subsequent sections we shall see these issues, and others that arise in models of reading, are also important sources of debate concerning connectionist models of other areas of language processing.

LEXICAL PROCESSING DURING SPEECH

Just as connectionist models in reading use two principal architectures, interactive activation, and feedforward networks trained by back-propagation, so with connectionist models of lexical processing during speech.

Speech perception

Interactive activation networks have been used to model both speech recognition and production. The early and very influential TRACE model of speech perception (McClelland & Elman, 1986) consists of a standard interactive activation architecture with layers of units standing for phonetic features, phonemes and words. There are several copies of each layer of units, standing for different points in time in the utterance, and the number of copies differs for each layer. At the featural level, there is a copy for each discrete "time slice" into which the speech input is divided. At the phoneme level, there is a copy of the detector for each phoneme centred over every three time slices. The phoneme detector centred on a given time slice is connected to feature detectors for that time slice, and also to the feature detectors for the previous three and subsequent three slices. Hence, successive detectors for the same phoneme overlap in the feature units with which they interact. Finally, at the word level, there is a copy of each word unit at every three time slices. The window of phonemes with which the word interacts corresponds to the entire length of the word. Here, again, adjacent detectors for the same word will overlap in the lower level units to which they are connected. In short, then, we have a standard interactive activation architecture, with an additional temporal dimension added, to account for the temporal character of speech input.

The debate between interactive and bottom-up models of speech perception parallels the debate between interactive and bottom-up accounts of reading. McClelland and Elman have two kinds of argument in favour of their position. First, and perhaps most important, is the broad coverage of the model in accounting for a range of empirical data on speech perception. For example, TRACE's interactive architecture nicely accounts for the apparent influence of lexical context on phoneme identification. Specifically, TRACE models Ganong's (1980) demonstration that the identification of a syllable-initial speech sound that was constructed to be between a /g/ and a /k/ was influenced by whether the rest of the syllable ended "iss" (making giss or kiss) or "ift" (making *gift* or *kift*). Specifically, the identification of the intermediate phoneme was biased towards the choice that completed a word rather than a non-word. This effect is particularly interesting since the identification of a phoneme appears to be affected by *subsequent* material. (Notice that this phenomenon is directly analogous to the facilitation of letter recognition in word or word-like contexts, discussed earlier.) TRACE captures this effect because phoneme and lexical identification occur in parallel and are mutually constraining. TRACE also captures experimental findings concerning various factors affecting the strength of the lexical influence (e.g. Fox, 1984), and aspects of the categorical aspects of phoneme perception (Massaro, 1981; Pisoni & Tash, 1974). TRACE also provides rich predictions concerning the time-course of spoken word recognition (e.g. Cole & Jakimik, 1978; Marslen-Wilson, 1973; Marslen-Wilson & Tyler, 1975), and lexical influences on the segmentation of speech into words (e.g. Cole & Jakimik, 1980). Although TRACE does account for an impressive range of phenomena, as in the case of reading, bottom-up connectionist models have been proposed which aim to account for a similar range of data (e.g. Norris, 1993; Shillcock, Lindsey, Levy, & Chater, 1992).

Second, McClelland and Elman can derive specific empirical predictions from their model which appear to be incompatible with any bottom-up model. Elman and McClelland (1988) conduct what is intended to be a crucial experiment between interactive and bottom-up approaches, and find the interactive view to be confirmed. The central theoretical question at issue is whether or not lexical effects on phoneme restoration are caused, as the interactive view supposes, by the feedback of information from the lexical to the phonemic level. At first glance, it might appear that these lexical effects simply directly demonstrate that this top-down feedback does occur. But there is an alternative explanation, which is entirely compatible with the modular view: that subjects' decisions concerning which phoneme was heard are influenced by both phonological and lexical representations of the stimulus. According to this view, the lexical level directly influences the subject's decision, without any top-down influence on the phoneme detection process itself.

Experimentally disentangling these two explanations is extremely difficult. But Elman and McClelland noticed a prediction of TRACE which appeared to suggest an appropriate crucial experiment. In natural speech, the pronunciation of a phoneme will to some extent be altered by the phonemes that surround it, in part for articulatory reasons: this phenomenon is known as coarticulation. This means that listeners should adjust their category boundaries depending on the phonemic context. Experiments confirm that people do indeed exhibit this "compensation for coarticulation" (Mann & Repp, 1980). For example, given a series of synthetically produced tokens between /t/ and /k/, listeners move the category boundary towards the /t/ following a /s/ and towards the /k/ following a /sh/. This phenomenon suggests a way of detecting whether lexical information really does feed back to the phoneme level. Elman and McClelland considered the case where compensation for coarticulation occurs across word boundaries, for example, a word-final /s/ influencing a word-initial /t/ as in *Christmas tapes*. If lexical-level representations feed back on to phoneme-level representations, the compensation of the /t/ should still occur when the /s/ relies on lexically driven phoneme restoration for its identity (i.e. in an experimental condition in which the identity of /s/ in *Christmas* is obscured, the /s/ should be restored and thus compensation for coarticulation proceeds as normal). Elman and McClelland noticed that the TRACE model does indeed produce this prediction; and that it is difficult to see how a modular account of speech perception could make the same prediction. They therefore decided to conduct the crucial experiment.

Subjects heard pairs of words such as *Christmas tapes* or *foolish capes*, where the last segment of *Christmas* or *foolish* was replaced by a synthetic segment midway between /s/ and /sh/. The first segment of *tapes*/*capes* was a synthetic segment drawn between /t/ and /k/. Subjects were required to report the identity of the second word. Their responses revealed that the restored identity of the ambiguous phoneme at the end of the first word affected the identification of the ambiguous phoneme at the beginning of the second word in a way which paralleled the compensation effect when unambiguous phonemes were present. Elman and McClelland's interpretation of this effect was that the final phoneme of the first word was being restored on the basis of lexical influences, and that the restored phoneme then triggered compensation for coarticulation, just as when the phoneme is unambiguous in the perceptual stimulus.

Advocates of bottom-up connectionist models have recently argued that, despite appearances, Elman and McClelland's (1988) results do not demonstrate top-down influence. Bottom-up connectionist models have been shown to be compatible with Elman and McClelland's results. For example, Norris (1993) presents results from a simulation involving a *simple recurrent network*, or SRN (introduced by Elman, 1988, 1990). As shown in Fig. 8.3, the SRN involves a crucial modification to a feedforward network: The current set of hidden unit values is "copied back" to

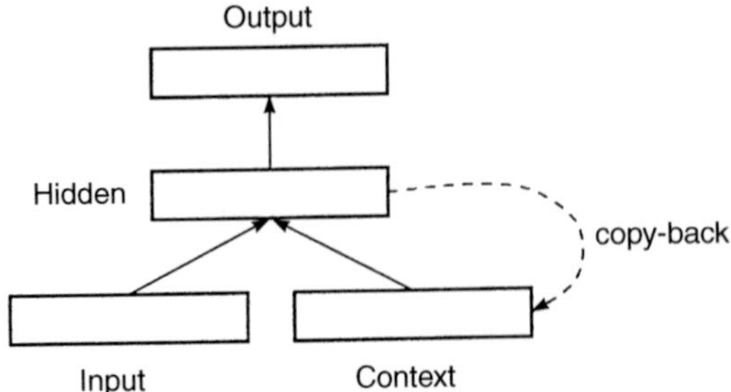

FIG. 8.3 Architecture of a simple recurrent network. This network is a conventional multi-layered feedforward network, except that there are additional input units into which the hidden unit activations from the previous time-step are copied.

a set of additional input units, and paired with the *next* input to the network. This means that the current hidden unit values can directly affect the next state of the hidden units; more generally, this means that there is a loop around which activation can reverberate over many time-steps. This gives the network a memory for past inputs, and therefore the ability to deal with integrated sequences of inputs presented successively. This contrasts with standard back-propagation networks, the behaviour of which is determined solely by the current input. This means that SRNs are able to tackle tasks such as language processing in which the input is revealed gradually over time, rather than being presented at once. For this reason SRNs have been widely used in connectionist models of language processing, as we shall see in subsequent sections, and there has also been some exploration of their computational properties (e.g. Chater & Conkey, 1992; Christiansen & Chater, in press; Cleeremans, Servan-Schreiber, & McClelland, 1989; Servan-Schreiber, Cleeremans, & McClelland, 1991).

Norris trained an SRN on input and output consisting of words (from a 12-word lexicon) presented one phoneme at a time. The input was represented in terms of phonetic features, which might have intermediate values, corresponding to ambiguous phonemes, and the output consisted of units, each detecting a particular phoneme. When input was presented to the trained network that had an ambiguous first word-final phoneme, and an ambiguous initial segment of the second word, a parallel to the compensation for coarticulation effect was observed, within the limits of the lexicon used: The percentages of /t/ and /k/ responses to the first phoneme of the second word depended on the identity of the first word, as in Elman and McClelland's original experiment. But the explanation for this pattern of results cannot be top-down influence from units representing words, since there are no units representing words in the network.

Norris's small-scale artificial example is no more than suggestive, however. The crucial question is: Would a network trained on natural speech, rather than on very small-scale artificial data, model Elman and McClelland's results? Shillcock et al. (1992) constructed such a network and found a close fit with Elman and McClelland's data. A recurrent network was trained on a corpus of phonologically transcribed conversational English, and inputs and outputs to the network were represented at the level of phonetic features. As in Norris's simulations, there is no lexical level of representation from which top-down information can flow. None the less, phoneme restoration follows the pattern that Elman and McClelland explain in terms of lexical influence.

Why is it that in the simulation purely bottom-up processes appear to mimic lexical effects? Shillcock et al. (1992) argue that restoration occurs in their network on the basis of statistical regularities at the phonemic level, rather than because of lexical influence. It just happens that the lexical items that Elman and McClelland used experimentally are more statistically regular at the phonemic level than the non-words with which they are contrasted. This is confirmed by a statistical analysis of the corpus of speech on which the network is trained. By carefully choosing stimulus items for which statistical regularities at the phonemic level have the opposite bias to that which would be provided by lexical status, it may be possible to experimentally distinguish between the interactive and bottom-up connectionist accounts. This experimental test is yet to be conducted, however.

The debate between interactive and bottom-up models of speech perception that we have just described is a good illustration of the way in which the introduction of connectionist models has led to unexpected theoretical predictions being derived (e.g. that bottom-up models can account for apparently lexically based phoneme restoration), as well as acting as a stimulus for empirical research.

Speech production

Throughout the field of language research as a whole, relatively little work has been done on the *production* of language. This general trend is also true of connectionist natural language processing. Thus, most connectionist language models address issues of processing and comprehension, rather than production. However, some steps have been taken towards the modelling of language production within a connectionist framework, most notably by Dell and colleagues (e.g. Dell, 1986; Dell, Juliano, & Govindjee, 1993; Dell & O'Seaghdha, 1991; Martin, Dell, Saffran, & Schwartz, 1994; Schwartz, Saffran, Bloch, & Dell, 1994).

Dell's (1986) spreading activation model of retrieval in sentence production constitutes one of the first connectionist attempts to account for speech production.[11] Although the model was presented as a sentence production model, only the phonological encoding of words was computationally implemented in terms of an interactive activation model. This lexical network consisted of hierarchically ordered layers of nodes, corresponding to the following linguistically motivated units: morphemes (or lexical nodes), syllables, rimes and consonant clusters, phonemes, and features. The individual nodes are connected bi-directionally to each other in a straightforward manner without lateral connections within layers, and with the exception of the addition of special null element nodes and syllabic position coding of nodes that correspond to syllables. For example, the lexical node for the word (morpheme) "spa" is connected to the /spa/ node in the syllable layer. The latter is linked to the consonant cluster /sp/ (onset) and the rime /a/ (nucleus). On the phoneme level, /sp/ is connected to /s/ (which in turn is linked to the features *fricative*, *alveolar*, and *voiceless*) and /p/ (which is connected to the features *bilabial*, *voiceless*, and *stop*). The rime /a/ is linked to the vowel /a/ in the phoneme layer (and subsequently is connected to the features *tense*, *low*, and *back*) and to a node signifying a null coda.

Processing begins with the activation of a lexical node (meant to correspond to the output from higher level morphological, syntactic, and semantic processing), and activation then gradually spreads downwards in the network. Activation also spreads upwards via the feedback connections. After a fixed period of time (determined by the speaking rate), the nodes with the highest activations are selected for the onset, vowel, and coda slots. Using this network model Dell was able to account for a variety of speech errors, such as substitutions (e.g. *dog* → *log*), deletions (*dog* → *og*), and additions (*dog* → *drog*). Speech errors occur in the model when an incorrect node becomes more active than the correct node (given the activated lexical node) and therefore gets selected instead. Such erroneous activation may be due to the feedback connections activating nodes other than those directly corresponding to the initial word node. Alternatively, other words in the sentence context as well as words activated as a product of internal noise may interfere with the processing of the network. This model also made a number of quantitative predictions concerning the retrieval of phonological forms during production, some of which were later confirmed experimentally in Dell (1988).

Dell's account of speech errors and the phonological encoding of words has had an impact on subsequent models of speech production, both the connectionist (e.g. Harley, 1993) as well as the more symbolic kind (e.g.

[11] A somewhat similar model of speech production was developed independently by Stemberger (1985). This model was inspired by the interactive activation framework of McClelland and Rumelhart (1981), whereas Dell's work was not.

Levelt, 1989). Nevertheless, Dell's model does suffer from a number of shortcomings, of which we mention a few here. As with the previously mentioned interactive activation models, the connections between the nodes on the various levels have to be hand-coded. This means that no learning is possible. In itself this is not a problem in principle if innate linguistic knowledge is assumed, but the information coded in Dell's model is language-specific and could not be innate. There is, however, a more urgent, practical side of this problem. It becomes very difficult to scale these models up, since every connection between each and every node has to be hand-coded. This shortcoming is alleviated by a recent recurrent network model presented by Dell et al. (1993). Their model learns to form mappings from lexical items to the appropriate sequences of phonological segments. The model consists of an SRN, as outlined earlier, with a small additional modification: The current *output*, as well as the current hidden unit state, was copied back as additional input to the network. This allowed both past activation states of the hidden unit layer as well as the output from the previous time-step to influence current processing.[12] When given an encoding of, for example, "can" as the lexical input the network was trained to produce the features of the first phonological segment /k/ on the output layer, then /æ/ followed by /n/, and then finally generate an end of word marker (null segment). Trained in this manner, Dell et al. were able to account for speech error data without having to build syllabic frames and phonological rules into the network (as was the case in Dell, 1986). Importantly, this recent connectionist model suggests that sequential biases and similarity may explain aspects of human phonology which have previously been attributed to separate phonological rules and frames. Furthermore, the model indicates that future speech production models may have to incorporate learning and distributed representations in order to accommodate the role that the entire vocabulary appears to play in phonological speech errors.[13] As with

---

[12] The idea of copying back output as part of the next input was first proposed by Jordan (1986).

[13] It should however be noted that despite the relative success of this feedforward learning model, Dell's (1986) interactive activation model is still a strong candidate as a model of speech production as it has a much wider empirical coverage. Moreover, it has been "lesioned" in 65 various ways to simulate language problems in aphasia. Schwartz et al. (1994) demonstrated that a reduction in connection strengths between nodes may provide a possible account of error patterns in jargon aphasia. Martin et al. (1994) showed that introducing an abnormally rapid decay rate for activated nodes allowed the model to simulate paraphasia in deep dysphasia, and that gradually changing this decay rate towards a normal level may simulate the pattern of recovery found in the longitudinal study of an aphasic patient. By changing connection strengths and/or the decay rate, Dell, Schwartz, Martin, Saffran, and Gagnon (1997) were in a similar manner able to fit the error patterns of 21 fluent aphasics as well as make a number of predictions that were subsequently confirmed.

reading, connectionist models of speech perception and production have modelled a wide range of empirical data on both normal and impaired performance. Moreover, they have contributed to a reassessment of fundamental theoretical issues and generated fresh experimental work on core theoretical questions, particularly on the question of whether speech perception and production are interactive or sequential. Connectionist research has greatly contributed to current thinking about speech perception and production. The validity of specific connectionist models, as well as the scope of connectionist approaches in general, will have an important role in shaping future research in this area.

MORPHOLOGICAL PROCESSING

One of the connectionist models that has created the most debate is Rumelhart and McClelland's (1986a) model of the learning of English past tense. This debate in many ways resembles the one following Seidenberg and McClelland's (1989) model of word recognition and naming discussed earlier. In particular, the debate has to a large extent focused on whether a single mechanism may be sufficient to account for the empirical data concerning the developmental patterns in English past-tense learning, or whether a dual-route mechanism is necessary. The discussion of the past-tense model also relates to the viability of the wickelfeature representation, which we have already described in the context of Seidenberg and McClelland's model of word naming. Here, we provide an overview of the current debate, as well as pointers to its wider ramifications.

Can a system without any explicit representation of rules account for rule-like behaviour? Rumelhart and McClelland's (1986a) model of the acquisition of the past tense in English was presented as an affirmative answer to this question. English past tense is an interesting test case because children very roughly appear to go through three stages during learning. In particular, children seemingly exhibit a pattern of U-shaped learning when acquiring English verbs and their past tenses. During the first stage, children only use a few verbs in past tense and these tend to be irregular words—such as *came*, *went*, and *took*—likely to occur with a very high frequency in the child's input. These verbs are furthermore mostly used in their correct past-tense form. At the second stage, children start using a much larger number of verbs in the past tense, most of these of the regular form, such as *pulled* and *walked*. Importantly, children now show evidence of rule-like behaviour. They are able to conjugate non-words, generating *jicked* as the past tense of *jick*, and they start to overgeneralise irregular verbs—even the ones they got right in stage 1—for example, producing *comed* or *camed* as the past tense of *come*. During the

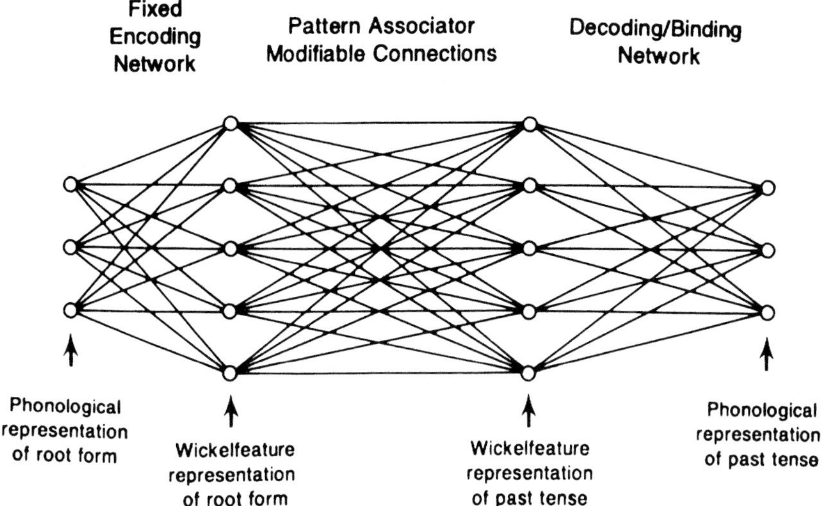

FIG. 8.4 The basic structure of the Rumelhart and McClelland (1986a) model for the learning of English past tense. Note that all learning takes place in the pattern associator. From "On learning the past tenses of English verbs" by D.E. Rumelhart and J.L. McClelland In J.L. McClelland and D.E. Rumelhart (Eds.), *Parallel Distributed Processing*, *Vol. 2* 1986b, MIT Press, p. 222. Copyright © (1986) MIT Press. Reprinted with permission.

third stage, the children regain their ability to correctly form the past tense of irregular verbs while maintaining their correct conjugations of the regular verbs. Thus, it appears prima facie that children (as in the case of reading, discussed earlier) learn to use a rule-based route for dealing with regulars as well as non-words and a memorisation route for handling irregulars. But how can such seemingly dual-route behaviour be accommodated by a single mechanism employing just a single route?

Rumelhart and McClelland (1986a) showed that by varying the input to a connectionist model during learning, important aspects of the three stages of English past-tense acquisition could be simulated using a single mechanism. As illustrated in Fig. 8.4, the model consists of three parts: a fixed encoding network, a pattern associator network with modifiable connections, and a competitive decoding/binding network. The encoding network is an (unspecified) network, which takes phonological representations of root forms (presumably represented as wickelphones) and transforms them into a set of wickelfeatures. In order to promote generalisation, additional incorrect features are randomly activated, specifically, those features that have the same central feature as well as one of the two other context features in common with the input root form. The focus of interest in this model is the pattern associator network. It has 460 input and output units, each representing a wickelfeature. This network is trained to produce past-tense forms when presented with root forms of verbs as input. During training, the weights between the input and the output layers are modified using the perceptron learning rule (Rosenblatt, 1962) (the back-propagation rule is not required for this network, since it has just one modifiable layer). Since the output patterns of wickelfeatures generated by the association network most often do not correspond to a single past-tense form, the decoding/binding network must transform these distributed patterns into unique wickelphone representations. In this third network, each wickelphone in the 500 words used in the study was assigned to an output unit. These wickelphones compete individually for the input wickelfeatures in an iterative process. The more wickelfeatures a given wickelphone accounts for, the greater its strength. If two or more wickelphones account for the same wickelfeature the assigned "credit" is split between them in proportion to the number of other wickelfeatures they account for uniquely (i.e. a "rich get richer" competitive approach). The end result of this competition is a set of more or less non-overlapping wickelphones which correspond to as many as possible of the wickelfeatures in the input to the decoder network.

The pattern associator was trained in the following manner, showing evidence of going through the three relevant stages whilst learning English past tense. First, the net was trained on a set of 10 high-frequency verbs (8 irregular and 2 regular) for 10 epochs. At this point the net reached a satisfactory performance, treating both regular and irregular verbs in the same way (as also observed in the first stage of human acquisition of past tense). Next, 420 medium-frequency verbs (about 80% of these being regular) were added to the training set and the net was trained for an additional 190 epochs. Early on during this period of training the net behaved as children at acquisition stage 2: The net tended to regularise irregulars while getting regulars correct. At the end of the 190 epochs, network behaviour resembled that of children in stage 3 of the past-tense acquisition process, exhibiting an almost perfect performance on the 420 verbs. The network was then subsequently tested on a set of 86 low-frequency verbs (of which just over 80% were regular). The net appears to capture the basic U-shaped pattern of the acquisition of English past tense. In addition, it was able to exhibit differential performance on different types of irregular and regular verbs, effectively simulating some aspects of similar performance differences observed in children (Bybee & Slobin, 1982; Kuczaj, 1977, 1978). Moreover, the model demonstrated a reasonable degree of generalisation from the 420 verbs in the training set to the 86 low-frequency verbs in the test set; for example, demonstrating that it was able to use the three different regular endings correctly (i.e. using /t/ with root forms ending with an unvoiced consonant, /d/ as suffix to forms ending with a voiced consonant or vowel, and /ˆd/ with verb stems ending with a "t" or a "d").

The merits and inadequacies of the Rumelhart and McClelland (1986a) past-tense model have been the focus of much debate, originating with Pinker and Prince's (1988) detailed criticism (and to a lesser extent by Lachter & Bever's 1988 critique). Since then the debate has flourished across the symbolic/connectionist divide (e.g. on the symbolic side: Kim, Pinker, Prince, & Prasada, 1991; Pinker, 1991; and on the connectionist side: Cottrell & Plunkett, 1991; Daugherty, MacDonald, Petersen, & Seidenberg, 1993; MacWhinney & Leinbach, 1991; Seidenberg, 1992; Daugherty & Seidenberg, 1992). Here, we focus on the most influential aspects of the debate.

As was the case with the Seidenberg and McClelland (1989) model of reading, the use of wickelphones/wickelfeature representations has been considered problematic (e.g. by Pinker & Prince, 1988). Perhaps for this reason, most of the subsequent connectionist models of English past tense (both of acquisition, e.g. Plunkett & Marchman, 1991, 1993, and of diachronic change, Hare & Elman, 1992, 1995) therefore use a position-specific phonological representation in which vowels/consonants are defined in terms of phonological contrasts, such as voiced/unvoiced, front/centre/back. Another, more damaging, criticism of the single-route approach is that the U-shaped pattern of behaviour observed in the model during learning appears essentially to be an artifact of suddenly increasing the total number of verbs (from 10 to 420) in the second phase of learning. Pinker and Prince (1988) point out that no such sudden discontinuity appears to occur in the number of verbs to which children are exposed. Thus, the occurrence of U-shaped learning in the model is undermined by the psychological implausibility of the training regime.

More recently, however, Plunkett and Marchman (1991) showed that this training regime is not required to obtain U-shaped learning. They trained a feedforward network with a hidden unit layer on a vocabulary of artificial verb stems and past-tense forms, patterned by regularities patterned on the English past tense. They held the size of the vocabulary used in training constant at 500 verbs. They found that the

[14] In this connection, type frequency refers to the number of different words belonging to a given class, each counted once (e.g. the number of different regular verbs). Token frequency, on the other hand, denotes the number of instances of a particular word (e.g. number of occurrences of the verb *have*).

net not only was able to exhibit classical U-shaped learning, but also had learned various selective micro U-shaped developmental patterns observed in children's behaviour. For example, given a training set with a type and token frequency[14] reflecting that of English verbs the net was able to simulate a number of sub-regularities between the phonological form of a verb stem and its past-tense form (e.g. *sleep* → *slept*, *keep* → *kept*).[15] In a subsequent paper, Plunkett and Marchman (1993) obtained similar results using an incremental, and perhaps more psychologically plausible, training regime. Following initial training on 20 verbs, the vocabulary was gradually increased until reaching a size of 500 verb stems. This training regime significantly improved the performance of the net (compared with a similarly configured net trained on the same vocabulary in Plunkett and Marchman, 1991). This approach also suggested that a critical mass of verbs is needed before a change from rote-learning (memorisation) to system-building (rule-like generalisation behaviour) may occur—the latter perhaps related to the acceleration in the acquisition of vocabulary items (or "vocabulary spurt") observed when a child's overall vocabulary exceeds around 50 words (e.g. Bates, Bretherton, & Snyder, 1988).

Most recently, the connectionist models of past-tense acquisition have been accused of being too dependent on the token and type frequencies of irregular and regular vocabulary items in English. Prasada and Pinker (1993) have argued that the purported ability of connectionist models to simulate verb inflection may be an artifact of the idiosyncratic frequency statistics of English. The focus of the argument is the *default* inflection of words; for example, the *-ed* suffixation of English regular verbs. The default inflection of a word is assumed to be independent of its particular phonological shape and occurs unless the root form corresponds to a specific irregular form. According to Prasada and Pinker, connectionist models are dependent on frequency and surface similarity for their generalisation ability. In English, most verbs are regular, that is, many regular verbs have a high type frequency but a relatively low token frequency, allowing a network to construct a broadly defined default category. Irregular verbs in English, on the other hand, have a low type frequency but a high token frequency, the latter permitting the memorisation of the irregular past tenses in terms of a number of narrow phonological sub-categories (e.g. one for the *i–a* alternation in *sing* → *sang*, *ring* → *rang*, another for the *o–e* alternation in *grow* → *grew*, *blow* → *blew*, etc.). Prasada and Pinker (1993) show that the default generalisation in Rumelhart and McClelland's (1986a) model is dependent on a similar frequency

[15] As pointed out by Pinker and Prince (1988), the Rumelhart and McClelland (1986a) model was not able adequately to accommodate such sub-regularities.

distribution in the training set. They furthermore contend that no connectionist model can accommodate default generalisation for a class of words that has both low type frequency and low token frequency. The default inflection of plural nouns in German appear to fall in this category and would therefore seem to be outside the capabilities of connectionist networks (Clahsen, Rothweiler, Woest, & Marcus, 1993; Marcus, Brinkmann, Clahsen, Wiese, Woest & Pinker, 1993). If true, such lack of cross-linguistic validity would render neural network models of past tense acquisition obsolete.

However, recent connectionist work has addressed this issue of minority default mappings with some success. Daugherty and Hare (1993) trained a feedforward network (with hidden units) to map the phonological representation of a stem to a phonological representation of the past tense given a set of verbs roughly representative of very early Old English (before about 870 AD). The training set consisted of five classes of irregular verbs plus one class of regular verbs—each class containing 25 words (each represented once in the training set). Thus, words taking the default generalisation /-ed/ formed a minority (i.e. only 17%) of the words in the training set. *Pace* Prasada and Pinker (1993) and others, the network was able to learn the appropriate default behaviour even when faced with a low-frequency default class. Indeed, it appears that generalisation in neural networks may not be strictly dependent on similarity to known items. Daugherty and Hare's (1993) results show that if the non-default (irregular) classes have a sufficient degree of internal structure, default generalisation may be promoted by the lack of similarity to known items. These results were corroborated by further simulations and analyses in Hare, Elman, and Daugherty (1995). Moreover, Forrester and Plunkett (1994) obtained similar results when training a feedforward model (with hidden units) to learn artificial input patterned on the Arabic plural. In Arabic, the majority of plural forms—called the Broken Plural—are characterised by a system of sub-regularities dependent on the phonological shape of the noun stem. In contrast, a minority of nouns takes the Sound Plural inflection which forms the default in Arabic. Forrester and Plunkett's net was trained to map phonological representations of the noun stems to their appropriate plural forms represented phonologically. Their results also indicate that connectionist models can learn default generalisation without relying on large word classes or direct similarity.

These positive results constitute important steps forward. Nevertheless, we presently have no detailed knowledge concerning the specific condition from which connectionist default generalisation can arise, nor do we know how it will scale when faced with the full complexity of language. On the other hand, rule-like and frequency-independent default generalisation may not be as pressing a problem for connectionist models as

Clahsen et al. (1993) and Marcus et al. (1993) claim. Via a reanalysis of the data concerning German noun inflection (in combination with additional data from Arabic and Hausa), Bybee (1995) showed that default generalisation is sensitive to type frequency and does not seem to be entirely rule-like. This kind of generalisation may fit better with the kind of default generalisation that connectionist models produce than with the rigid application of default rules in the symbolic models.

The issue of whether humans employ a single, connectionist-style mechanism for rule-like morphological processing is far from settled. Connectionist models can provide an impressive fit to a wide range of developmental and linguistic data. Even detractors of connectionist models of morphology typically allow that some kind of associative connectionist mechanism may explain the complex patterns found in the "irregular" cases. The controversial question is whether a single connectionist mechanism can simultaneously account both for regular and the irregular cases, or whether the regular cases can only be generated by a distinct route involving (perhaps necessarily symbolic) rules. The future is likely to bring further connectionist modelling of cross-linguistic data concerning morphology as well as a closer fitting of developmental micro patterns and distributional data to such models. As we shall see next, the question of whether language can be accounted for without the explicit representation of rules also plays an important part in connectionist modelling of syntactic processing.

SYNTAX

Syntactic processing is arguably the area of natural language which has the strongest ties to explicit rules as a means of explanation. Since Chomsky (1957), grammars have been understood predominately in terms of a set of generative phrase structure rules (often coupled with rules or principles for the further transformation of phrase structures). In early natural language research the central status of rules was directly reflected in the Derivational Theory of Complexity (Miller & Chomsky, 1963). This theory suggested that the application of a given rule (or transformation) could be measured directly in terms of time it takes for a listener/reader to process a sentence. This direct mapping between syntactic rules and response times was soon found to be incorrect, leading to more indirect ways of eliciting information about the use of rules in the processing of syntax. But can syntactic processing be accounted for without explicit rules? Radical connectionism aims to show that it can.

One way of dealing with syntax in connectionist models is to "hand-wire" symbolic structures directly into the architecture of the network. Much early work in connectionist processing of linguistic structure adopted this implementational approach; starting with Small, Cottrel, and Shastri's (1982) first attempt at connectionist parsing followed by Reilly's (1984) connectionist account of anaphor resolution and later by Fanty's (1985) connectionist context-free parser, Selman and Hirst's (1985) modelling of context-free parsing using simulated annealing, Waltz and Pollack's (1985) interactive model of parsing (and interpretation), McClelland and Kawamoto's (1986) neural network model of case-role assignment, and Miyata, Smolensky, and Legendre's (1993) structure-sensitive processing of syntactic structure using tensor representations (Smolensky, 1990). Such connectionist re-implementations of symbolic systems might have interesting computational properties and even be illuminating regarding the appropriateness of a particular style of symbolic model for distributed computation (Chater & Oaksford, 1990). On the other hand, there is the promise that connectionism may be able to do more than simply implement symbolic representations and processes; in particular, that networks may be able to *learn* to form and use structured representations. The most interesting models of this sort typically focus on learning quite limited aspects of natural language syntax. These models can be divided into two classes, depending on whether preprocessed sentence structures or simply bare sentences are presented as input.

The less radical class presupposes that the syntactic structure of each sentence to be learned is more or less given; that is, each input item is tagged with information pertaining the syntactic role of that item (e.g. the word *cat* may be tagged as Singular Noun). In this class we find, for example: connectionist parsers, such as PARSNIP (Hanson & Kegl, 1987) and VITAL (Howells, 1988); the structure dependent processing of Pollack's (1988, 1990) recursive auto-associative memory network subsequently used in Chalmers' (1990) model of active to passive transformation and in a model of syntactic processing in logic (Niklasson & van Gelder, 1994); Sopena's (1991) distributed connectionist parser incorporating attentional focus; and Stolcke's (1991) hybrid model deriving syntactic categories from phrase-bracketed examples given a vector space grammar. Typically, the task of these network models is to find the grammar (or part of thereof) which fits the example structures. This means that the structural aspects of language are not themselves learned by observation, but are built in. These models are related to statistical approaches to language learning such as stochastic context-free grammars (Brill, Magerman, Marcus, & Santorini, 1990; Jelinek, Lafferty, & Mercer, 1990) in which learning sets the probabilities of each grammar rule in a prespecified context-free grammar, from a corpus of parsed sentences.

The more radical models have taken on a much harder task, that of learning syntactic structure from strings of words, with no prior assumptions about the particular structure of the grammar. The most influential approach employs the earlier mentioned SRNs. It is fair to say that these radical models have so far reached only a modest level of performance. This may explain why the more radical connectionist attempts at syntax learning have not caused nearly as much debate as the earlier mentioned model of English past-tense acquisition (Rumelhart & McClelland, 1986a) and the model of reading aloud (Seidenberg & McClelland, 1989). Nevertheless, we focus on the radical connectionist models here because they potentially bear the promise of language learning without a priori built-in linguistic knowledge (*pace* e.g. Chomsky, 1965, 1986; Crain, 1991; Pinker, 1994; and many others).

Elman (1991, 1993) trained an SRN to predict the next word it will receive as input given sentences generated by a simple context-free grammar. This grammar involved subject noun/verb agreement, verbs with different argument structure (i.e. intransitive, transitive, and optionally transitive verbs), as well as subject and object relative clauses (allowing for multiple embeddings with complex long-distance dependencies). These simulations demonstrated that an SRN is able to acquire the grammatical regularities underlying a simple grammar. In addition, the SRN showed some behavioural similarities with human behaviour on centre-embedded structures (Weckerly & Elman, 1992). Christiansen (1994, in preparation) extended this work, training SRNs on more complex grammars involving prenominal genitives, prepositional modifications of noun phrases, noun phrase conjunctions, and sentential complements in addition to the grammatical features found in Elman's work. One of the grammars moreover incorporated cross-dependencies, a weakly context-sensitive structure found in languages such as Dutch and Swiss-German. Christiansen found that the SRNs were able to learn these more complex grammars, exhibiting the same kind of qualitative processing difficulties as humans do on similar sentence constructions (see also Christiansen & Chater, in press).

As we have seen, current models of syntax typically use "toy" fragments of grammar and small vocabularies. Aside from raising the question of the viability of scaling-up, this makes it difficult to provide detailed fits with empirical data. None the less, some attempts have more recently been made toward fitting existing data and deriving new empirical predictions from the models. For example, Tabor, Juliano, and Tanenhaus (1997) present a SRN-based dynamic parsing model that fits reading time data concerning the interaction between lexical and structural constraints in the resolution of temporary syntactic ambiguities (i.e. garden-path effects) in sentence comprehension. MacDonald and Christiansen (submitted) provide SRN simulations of reading time data concerning the differential processing of singly centre-embedded subject and object relative clauses by good and poor comprehenders. Finally, Christiansen (in preparation; Christiansen & Chater, in press) describes an SRN trained on recursive sentence structures, which fits grammaticality ratings data from several behavioural experiments. He also derives novel predictions about the processing of sentences involving multiple prenominal genitives, multiple prepositional modifications of nouns, and doubly centre-embedded object relative clauses, which have subsequently been empirically confirmed (Christiansen & MacDonald, in preparation).

These simulation results suggest that SRNs may be viable models of syntactic processing. However, connectionist models of language learning (i.e. Chalmers, 1990; Elman, 1990; McClelland & Kawamoto, 1986; Miyata et al. 1993; Pollack, 1990; Smolensky, 1990; St. John & McClelland, 1990) have recently been attacked for not affording the kind of generalisation abilities that would be expected from models of language. Hadley (1994a) correctly pointed out that generalisation in much connectionist research has not been viewed in a sophisticated fashion. The testing of generalisation is typically done by recording network output given a test set consisting of items not occurring in the original training set, but potentially containing many similar structures and word sequences. Hadley insisted that to demonstrate genuine, "strong" generalisation a network must be shown to learn a word in one syntactic position and then generalise to using/processing that word in another, novel syntactic position. He challenged connectionists to adopt a more rigorous training and testing regime in assessing whether networks really generalise successfully in learning syntactically structured material.

Christiansen and Chater (1994) addressed this challenge, providing a formalisation of Hadley's original ideas as well as presenting evidence that connectionist models are able to attain strong generalisation. In their training corpus (generated by the grammar from Christiansen, 1994), the noun *boy* was prevented from ever occurring in a noun phrase conjunction (i.e. noun phrases such as *John and boy* and *boy and John* did not occur). During training the SRN had therefore only seen singular verbs following *boy*. None the less, the net was able to predict correctly that a plural verb must follow *John and boy* as prescribed by the grammar. In addition, the net was still able to predict correctly a plural verb when a prepositional phrase was attached to *boy* as in *John and boy from town*, providing even stronger evidence for strong generalisation. This suggests that the SRN is able to make non-local generalisations based on the structural regularities in the training corpus (see Christiansen & Chater, 1994, for further details). If the SRN relied solely on local information it would not have been able to make correct predictions in either case. Christiansen (in preparation) demonstrated that the same SRN also was able to generalise appropriately when presented with completely novel words, such as *zorg*,[16] in a noun phrase conjunction by predominately activating the plural verbs. In contrast, when the SRN was presented with ungrammatical lexical items in the second noun position, as in *John and near*, it did not activate the plural nouns. Instead, it activated lexical items that were not grammatical given the previous context. The SRN was able to generalise to the use of known words in novel syntactic positions as well as to the use of completely novel words. At the same time, it was also able to distinguish items that were grammatical given previous context from those that were not. Thus, the network demonstrated sophisticated generalisation abilities, ignoring local word co-occurrence constraints, while appearing to comply with structural information at the constituent level. Additional evidence of strong generalisation in connectionist nets are found in Niklasson and van Gelder (1994; but see Hadley, 1994b for a rebuttal).

One possible objection to these models of syntax is that connectionist (and other bottom-up statistical) models of language learning will not be able to scale up to solve human language acquisition because of arguments pertaining to the purported poverty of the stimulus (see Seidenberg, 1994 for a discussion). However, there is evidence that some models employing simple statistical analysis may be able to scale up and even attain strong generalisation. When Redington, Chater, and Finch (1993) applied a method of distributional statistics (see also Finch & Chater, 1992, 1993) to a corpus of child-directed speech (the CHILDES corpus collected by MacWhinney & Snow, 1985), they found that the syntactic category of a new word could be derived from a single occurrence of that word in the training corpus. This indicates that strong generalisation may be learnable through the kinds of bottom-up statistical analysis that connectionist models appear to employ—even on a scale comparable with that of a child learning her first language. In this context, it is also important to note that achieving strong generalisation is not only a problem for learning-based connectionist models of syntactic processing. As pointed out by Christiansen and Chater (1994), most symbolic models cannot be ascribed strong generalisation since in most cases they are spoon-fed the lexical categories of words via syntactic tagging. The question of strong generalisation is therefore just as pressing for symbolic approaches as for connectionist approaches to language acquisition. The results outlined here suggest that connectionist models may be closer to solving this problem than their symbolic counterparts.

[16] In these simulations novel words corresponded to units that had not been activated during training.

Other aspects of language processing

There are a number of areas within connectionist natural language processing that have not received attention in this chapter. Amongst these are, for instance, models that deal with semantic aspects of language, models that address various issues at the level of discourse, and hybrid models seeking to combine the best of both the connectionist and the symbolic world. Unfortunately, space does not allow us to discuss such models here. Instead, we provide a few pointers for further reading.

Various aspects of semantic processing have been addressed in connectionist models, such as: word sense disambiguation (Cottrell, 1985); disambiguation of prepositional-phrase attachments using soft lexical preference rules (Sharkey, 1992); and incremental interpretation via the learning and application of contextual constraints in sentence comprehension (St. John & McClelland, 1990). Connectionist models of discourse and text comprehension include, for example, Allen's (1990) use of modified SRNs (called "connectionist language users") in a simple question answering task; Karen's (1990) modified SRN model of topic identification from written narrative discourse; and Sharkey's (1990) model of text comprehension involving four network modules (for respectively goals/plans, sequencing, knowledge, and the lexicon). Recent years have seen a surge in the number of hybrid connectionist/symbolic models of which we mention but a few examples: Bourlard and Morgan (1994) employ multi-layered feedforward networks to boost the performance of a state-of-the-art automatic speech recognition system based on hidden Markov models; Kwasny and Faisal (1990) implement a deterministic Marcus (1980) style parser in which a feedforward network is trained to suggest parsing actions given the state of a symbolic stack and buffer (see also Kwasny, Johnson, & Kalman, 1994, in which the feedforward net is replaced with an SRN); and Miikkulainen (1993) assembles modular networks dedicated to aspects of lexical, sentence, and story processing in a model of text comprehension inspired by symbolic script-based systems.

Overall, connectionist models of syntax and higher level aspects of language processing remain in early stages of development, and have not attained the level of sophistication of connectionist accounts of speech perception, production, reading, or morphology. Future research is required to decide whether promising, but limited, initial results can eventually be scaled up to deal with the complexities of real language input, or whether a purely connectionist approach is beset by fundamental limitations, and can only succeed to the extent that it rediscovers and reimplements the symbolic representations postulated by generative linguistics.

CONCLUSION

We have seen that controversy surrounds both the current significance of, and future prospects for, connectionist models of language processing. Current connectionist models involve over-simplifications with respect to the full complexity of human natural language processing, and only future research will determine the extent to which current models can be "scaled-up" successfully. Connectionism has, however, already influenced theoretical debates within the psychology of language processing in a number of ways, and we outline some of these influences here.

First, connectionist models have provided the first fully explicit and psychologically relevant computational models in a number of language processing domains, such as reading and past tense learning. Previous accounts in these areas consisted of "box-and-arrow" flow diagrams rather than detailed computational mechanisms. Whatever the lasting value of connectionist models themselves, they have certainly raised the level of theoretical debate in these areas, by challenging theorists of all viewpoints to provide computationally explicit accounts.

Second, the centrality of learning in connectionist models has brought a renewed interest in mechanisms of language learning (Bates & Elman, 1993), while Chomsky (e.g. 1986) has argued that although there are "universal" aspects of language that are innate, the vast amount of information specific to the language that the child acquires must be learned. Connectionist models provide mechanisms for how (at least some of) this learning might occur, whereas previous symbolic accounts of language processing have not taken account of how learning might occur. Furthermore, the attempt to use connectionist models to learn syntactic structure encroaches on the area of language for which Chomsky has argued innate information must be central. The successes and failures of this programme thus directly bear on the validity of this viewpoint.

Third, the dependence of connectionist models on statistical properties of their input has been one contributory factor in the upsurge of interest in the role of statistical factors in language learning (MacWhinney, Leinbach, Taraban, & McDonald, 1989; Redington et al. 1993) and language processing. This renewed interest in statistics is, of course, entirely compatible with the view that language processing takes account of structural properties of language, as described by classical linguistics. More radical connectionists have, as we have noted, also attempted to encroach on the territory of classical linguistics.

Finally, connectionist systems have given rise to renewed theoretical debate concerning what it really means for a computational mechanism to implement a rule, whether there is a distinction between "implicit" and "explicit" rules (see e.g. Davies, 1995 for discussions), and which kind should be ascribed to the human language processing system.

Connectionism has, we suggest, already had an important influence on the development of the psychology of language. But the final extent of that influence depends on the degree to which practical connectionist models can be developed and extended to deal with complex aspects of language processing in a psychologically realistic way. If realistic connectionist models of language processing can be provided, then the possibility of a radical rethinking not just of the nature of language processing, but of the structure of language itself, may be required. It might be that the ultimate description of language resides in the structure of complex networks, and can only be approximately expressed in terms of structural rules, in the style of generative grammar. On the other hand, it may be that connectionist models can only succeed to the extent that they build in standard linguistic constructs, or that connectionist learning methods do not scale up at all. The future development of connectionist models of language is therefore likely to have important implications for the theory of language processing and language structure, either in overturning, or reaffirming, traditional psychological and linguistic assumptions.

FURTHER READING

The suggested readings are grouped according to the general structure of the chapter.

Background. The PDP volumes (McClelland & Rumelhart, 1986; Rumelhart & McClelland, 1986b) provide a solid introduction to application of neural networks in cognitive models. Smolensky (1988) offers a connectionist alternative to viewing cognition as symbol manipulation, whereas Fodor and Pylyshyn (1988) is a classic criticism of connectionism.

Visual word recognition and word naming. For an early interactive activation model of visual word recognition, see McClelland & Rumelhart (1981). Seidenberg and McClelland (1989) is a classic paper on connectionist models of reading. Coltheart et al. (1993) provide a criticism of this model and a symbolic alternative. For the most recent advancement of this discussion, see Plaut et al. (1996).

Lexical processing during speech. The TRACE model of speech perception is described in McClelland and Elman (1986). The classic model of speech production and speech errors is Dell (1986).

Morphological processing. Rumelhart and McClelland (1986a) and Pinker & Prince (1988) define the two sides of the past-tense debate. See Plunkett and Marchman (1993) and Pinker (1991) for recent updates.

Syntax. Elman (1993) provides a recent update on an influential connectionist approach to the learning of syntactic regularities, but see Hadley (1994a) for a criticism of this and other connectionist models of syntax. For a survey of the most recent research on connectionist language processing—including discussions of its future prospects—see Christiansen et al. (in press).

ACKNOWLEDGEMENTS

We would like to thank Gary Dell, Joe Devlin, Kim Plunkett, and Ronan Reilly for commenting on an earlier draft of this chapter. NC is partially supported by the Joint Councils Initiative in Cognitive Science/HCI, Grant SPG 9029590. Part of the research presented here was carried out while MHC was a McDonnell Postdoctoral Fellow in the PNP Program at Washington University in St. Louis.

REFERENCES

Aderman, D., & Smith, E.E. (1971). Expectancy as a determinant of functional units in perceptual cognition. *Cognitive Psychology*, *2*, 117–129.

Allen, R.B. (1990). Connectionist language users. *Connection Science*, *2*, 279–311.

Ashby, W.R. (1952). *Design for a brain.* New York: John Wiley & Sons.

Bates, E., Bretherton, I., & Snyder, L. (1988). *From first word to grammar: Individual differences and dissociable mechanisms.* Cambridge: Cambridge University Press.

Bates, E.A., & Elman, J.L. (1993). Connectionism and the study of change. In M.J. Johnson (Ed.), *Brain development and cognition* (pp. 623–642). Cambridge, MA: Basil Blackwell.

Besner, D., Twilly, L., McCann, R.S., & Seergobin, K. (1990). On the association between connectionism and data: Are a few words necessary? *Psychological Review*, *97*, 432–446.

Boole, G. (1854). *The laws of thought.* London: Macmillan.

Bourlard, H.A., & Morgan, N. (1994). *Connectionist speech recognition: A hybrid approach.* Dordrecht, The Netherlands: Kluwer Academic Publishers.

Brill, E., Magerman, D., Marcus, M., & Santorini, B. (1990). Deducing linguistic structure from the statistics of large corpora. In *DARPA speech and natural language workshop.* Hidden Valley, PA: Morgan Kaufmann.

Bruner, J. (1957). On perceptual readiness. *Psychological Review*, *64*, 123–152.

Bryson, A.E., & Ho, Y.C. (1975). *Applied optimal control.* New York: Hemisphere.

Bullinaria, J.A. (1994). *Representation, learning, generalisation and damage in neural network models of reading aloud* (Tech. Rep.). Edinburgh, UK: University of Edinburgh, Department of Psychology.

Bullinaria, J.A., & Chater, N. (1995). Connectionist modelling: Implications for neuropsychology. *Language and Cognitive Processes*, *10*, 227–264.

Bybee, J. (1995). Regular morphology and the lexicon. *Language and Cognitive Processes*, *10*, 425–455.

Bybee, J., & Slobin, D.I. (1982). Rules and schemas in the development and use of the English past tense. *Language*, *58*, 265–289.

Chalmers, D.J. (1990). Syntactic transformations on distributed representations. *Connection Science*, *2*, 53–62.

Chater, N., & Conkey, P. (1992). Finding linguistic structure with recurrent neural networks. In *Proceedings of the 14th annual meeting of the Cognitive Science Society* (pp. 402–407). Hillsdale, NJ: Lawrence Erlbaum Associates Inc.

Chater, N., & Oaksford, M. (1990). Autonomy, implementation and cognitive architecture: A reply to Fodor and Pylyshyn. *Cognition*, *34*, 93–107.

Chomsky, N. (1957). *Syntactic structures*. The Hague, The Netherlands: Mouton.

Chomsky, N. (1965). *Aspects of the theory of syntax*. Cambridge, MA: MIT Press.

Chomsky, N. (1986). *Knowledge of language*. New York: Praeger.

Christiansen, M. (1994). *Infinite languages, finite minds: Connectionism, learning and linguistic structure*. Unpublished doctoral dissertation, University of Edinburgh, UK.

Christiansen, M.H. (in preparation). *Intrinsic constraints on the processing of recursive sentence structure*.

Christiansen, M.H., & Chater, N. (1992). Connectionism, meaning and learning. *Connection Science*, *4*, 227–252.

Christiansen, M., & Chater, N. (1994). Generalization and connectionist language learning. *Mind and Language*, *9*, 273–287.

Christiansen, M.H.M, & Chater, N. (in press). Toward a connectionist model of recursion in human linguistic performance. *Cognitive Science*.

Christiansen, M.H., Chater, N., & Seidenberg, M.S. (Eds.). (in press). Connectionist models of language processing: Progress and prospects. *Cognitive Science*.

Christiansen, M.H., & MacDonald, M.C. (in preparation). *Processing of recursive sentence structure: Testing predictions from a connectionist model*.

Churchland, P.S., & Sejnowski, T.J. (1989). Neural representation and neural computation. In L. Nadel, L. Cooper, P. Culicover & R.M. Harnish (Eds.), *Neural connections, mental computations*. Cambridge, MA: MIT Press.

Clahsen, H., Rothweiler, M., Woest, A., & Marcus, G.F. (1993). Regular and irregular inflection in the acquisition of German noun plurals. *Cognition*, *45*, 225–255.

Cleeremans, A., Servan-Schreiber, D., & McClelland, J. L. (1989). Finite state automata and simple recurrent networks. *Neural Computation*, *1*, 372–381.

Cole, R.A., & Jakimik, J. (1978). Understanding speech: How words are heard. In G. Underwood (Ed.), *Strategies of information processing*. New York: Academic Press.

Cole, R.A., & Jakimik, J. (1980). A model of speech perception. In R.A. Cole (Ed.), *Perception and production of fluent speech* (pp. 133–164). Hillsdale, NJ: Lawrence Erlbaum Associates Inc.

Coltheart, M. (1985). Cognitive neuropsychology and the study of reading. In M.I. Posner & O.S.M. Marin (Eds.), *Attention and performance, XI. Hillsdale, NJ: Lawrence Erlbaum Associates Inc.*

Coltheart, M., Curtis, B., Atkins, P., & Haller, M. (1993). Models of reading aloud: Dual-route and parallel-distributed-processing approaches. *Psychological Review*, *100*, 589–608.

Cottrell, G.W. (1985). *A connectionist approach to word sense disambiguation* (Tech. Rep. No. TR154). Rochester, NY: University of Rochester, Department of Computer Science.

Cottrell, G.W., & Plunkett, K. (1991). Learning the past tense in a recurrent network: Acquiring the mapping from meanings to sounds. In *Proceedings of the 13th annual meeting of the Cognitive Science Society* (pp. 328–333). Hillsdale, NJ: Lawrence Erlbaum Associates Inc.

Crain, S. (1991). Language acquisition in the absence of experience. *Behavioral and Brain Sciences*, *14*, 597–650.

Daugherty, K., & Hare, M. (1993). What's in a rule? The past tense by some other name might be called a connectionist net. In M. Mozer, P. Smolensky, D. Touretzky, J. Elman,

& A. Weigand (Eds.), *Proceedings of the 1993 connectionist models summer school* (pp. 149–156). Hillsdale, NJ: Lawrence Erlbaum Associates Inc.

Daugherty, K., MacDonald, M., Petersen, A.S., & Seidenberg, M.S. (1993). Why no mere mortal has ever flown out to center field, but often people say they do. In *Proceedings of the 15th annual meeting of the Cognitive Science Society* (pp. 383–388). Hillsdale, NJ: Lawrence Erlbaum Associates Inc.

Daugherty, K., & Seidenberg, M.S. (1992). Rules or connections? The past tense revisited. In *Proceedings of the 14th annual meeting of the Cognitive Science Society* (pp. 259–264). Hillsdale, NJ: Lawrence Erlbaum Associates Inc.

Davies, M. (1995). Two notions of implicit rules. In J.E. Tomberlin (Ed.), *Philosophical perspectives: Vol. 9: AI, connectionism, and philosophical psychology*. Atascadero, CA: Ridgeview Publishing Company.

Dell, G.S. (1986). A spreading activation theory of retrieval in language production. *Psychological Review, 93*, 283–321.

Dell, G.S. (1988). The retrieval of phonological forms in production: Tests of predictions from a connectionist model. *Journal of Memory and Language, 27*, 124–142.

Dell, G.S., Juliano, C., & Govindjee, A. (1993). Structure and content in language production: A theory of frame constraints in phonological speech errors. *Cognitive Science, 17*, 149–195.

Dell, G.S., & O'Seaghdha, P.G. (1991). Mediated and convergent lexical priming in language production: A comment on Levelt et al. (1990). *Psychological Review, 98*, 604–614.

Dell, G.S., Schwartz, M.F., Martin, N., Saffran, E.M., & Gagnon, D.A. (1997). Lexical access in aphasic and nonaphasic speakers. *Psychological Review, 104*, 801–838.

Elman, J.L. (1988). *Finding structure in time* (Tech. Rep. No. CRL-8801). San Diego, CA: University of California, Center for Research in Language.

Elman, J.L. (1990). Finding structure in time. *Cognitive Science, 14*, 179–211.

Elman, J.L. (1991). Distributed representation, simple recurrent networks, and grammatical structure. *Machine Learning, 7*, 195–225.

Elman, J.L. (1993). Learning and development in neural networks: The importance of starting small. *Cognition, 48*, 71–99.

Elman, J.L., & McClelland, J.L. (1988). Cognitive penetration of the mechanisms of perception: Compensation for coarticulation of lexically restored phonemes. *Journal of Memory and Language, 27*, 143–165.

Fanty, M. (1985). *Context-free parsing in connectionist networks* (Tech. Rep. No. TR-174). Rochester, NY: University of Rochester, Department of Computer Science.

Finch, S., & Chater, N. (1992). Bootstrapping syntactic categories by unsupervised learning. In *Proceedings of the 14th annual meeting of the Cognitive Science Society* (pp. 820–825). Hillsdale, NJ: Lawrence Erlbaum Associates Inc.

Finch, S., & Chater, N. (1993). Learning syntactic categories: A statistical approach. In M. Oaksford & G.D.A. Brown (Eds.), *Neurodynamics and psychology* (pp. 295–321). New York: Academic Press.

Fodor, J.A. (1983). *Modularity of mind.* Cambridge, MA: MIT Press.

Fodor, J.A., & Pylyshyn, Z.W. (1988). Connectionism and cognitive architecture: A critical analysis. *Cognition, 28*, 3–71.

Forrester, N., & Plunkett, K. (1994). Learning the Arabic plural: The case for minority mappings in connectionist networks. In *Proceedings of the 16th annual meeting of the Cognitive Science Society* (pp. 319–324). Hillsdale, NJ: Lawrence Erlbaum Associates Inc.

Forster, K.I., & Chambers, S. (1973). Lexical access and naming time. *Journal of Verbal Learning and Verbal Behavior, 12*, 627–635.

Fox, R.A. (1984). Effect of lexical status on phonetic categorization. *Journal of Experimental Psychology: Human Perception and Performance, 10*, 526–540.

Funnell, E. (1983). Phonological processing in reading: New evidence from acquired dyslexia. *British Journal of Psychology*, *74*, 159–180.

Ganong, W.F. (1980). Phonetic categorization in auditory word perception. *Journal of Experimental Psychology: Human Perception and Performance*, *6*, 110–115.

Hadley, R.F. (1994a). Systematicity in connectionist language learning. *Mind and Language*, *9*, 247–272.

Hadley, R.F. (1994b). Systematicity revisited: Reply to Christiansen & Chater and Niklasson & van Gelder. *Mind and Language*, *9*, 431–444.

Hanson, S.J., & Kegl, J. (1987). PARSNIP: A connectionist network that learns natural language grammar from exposure to natural language sentences. In *Proceedings of the 8th annual meeting of the Cognitive Science Society* (pp. 106–119). Hillsdale, NJ: Lawrence Erlbaum Associates Inc.

Hare, M., & Elman, J.L. (1992). A connectionist account of English inflectional morphology: Evidence from language change. In *Proceedings of the 14th annual meeting of the Cognitive Science Society* (pp. 265–270). Hillsdale, NJ: Lawrence Erlbaum Associates Inc.

Hare, M., & Elman, J.L. (1995). Learning and morphological change. *Cognition*, *56*, 61–98.

Hare, M., Elman, J.L., & Daugherty, K.M. (1995). Default generalization in connectionist networks. *Language and Cognitive Processes*, *10*, 601–630.

Harley, T.A. (1993). Phonological activation of semantic competitors during lexical access in speech production. *Language and Cognitive Processes*, *8*, 291–309.

Harm, M., Altmann, L., & Seidenberg, M. (1994). Using connectionist networks to examine the role of prior constraints in human learning. In *Proceedings of the 16th annual conference of the Cognitive Science Society* (pp. 392–396). Hillsdale, NJ: Lawrence Erlbaum Associates Inc.

Hinton, G.E., & Sejnowski, T.J. (1986). Learning and relearning in Boltzmann machines. In J.L. McClelland & D.E. Rumelhart (Eds.), *Parallel distributed processing*, Vol. 1. (pp. 282–317). Cambridge, MA: MIT Press.

Howells, T. (1988). VITAL, a connectionist parser. In *Proceedings of the 10th international conference on computational linguistics*, Stanford, CA.

Jared, D., McRae, K., & Seidenberg, M.S, (1990). The basis of consistency effect effects in word naming. *Journal of Memory and Language*, *29*, 687–715.

Jelinek, F., Lafferty, J.D., & Mercer, R.L. (1990). *Basic methods of probabilistic context free grammars* (Tech. Rep. No. RC 16374 72684). Yorktown Heights, NY: IBM.

Johnston, J.C., & McClelland, J.L. (1973). Visual factors in word perception. *Perception and Psychophysics*, *14*, 365–370.

Jordan, M. (1986). *Serial order: A parallel distributed approach* (Tech. Rep. No. 8604). San Diego, CA: University of California, San Diego, Institute for Cognitive Science.

Karen, L.F.R. (1990). Identification of topical entities in discourse: A connectionist approach to attentional mechanisms in language. *Connection Science*, *2*, 103–122.

Kim, J.J., Pinker, S., Prince, S., & Prasada, S. (1991). Why no mere mortal has ever flown out to center field. *Cognitive Science*, *15*, 173–218.

Koch, C., & Segev, I. (Eds.) (1989). *Methods in neuronal modeling: From synapses to networks*. Cambridge, MA: MIT Press.

Kucera, H., & Francis, W. (1967). *Computational analysis of present day American English*. Providence, RI: Brown University Press.

Kuczaj, S.A. (1977). The acquisition of regular and irregular past tense forms. *Journal of Verbal Learning and Verbal Behavior*, *16*, 589–600.

Kuczaj, S.A. (1978). Children's judgments of grammatical and ungrammatical irregular past tense verbs. *Child Development*, *49*, 319–326.

Kwasny, S.C., & Faisal, K.A. (1990). Connectionism and determinism in a syntactic parser. *Connection Science*, *2*, 63–82.

Kwasny, S.C., Johnson, S., & Kalman, B.L. (1994). Recurrent natural language parsing. In *Proceedings of the 16th annual meeting of the Cognitive Science Society* (pp. 525–530). Hillsdale, NJ: Lawrence Erlbaum Associates Inc.

Lachter, J., & Bever, T.G. (1988). The relation between linguistic structure and and theories of language learning: A constructive critique of some connectionist learning models. *Cognition*, *28*, 195–247.

Levelt, W.J.M. (1989). *Speaking: From intention to articulation.* Cambridge, MA: MIT Press.

MacDonald, M.C., & Christiansen, M.H. (submitted). *Individual differences without working memory: A reply to Just & Carpenter and Waters & Caplan.*

MacWhinney, B., & Leinbach, J. (1991). Implementations are not conceptualizations: Revising the verb learning model. *Cognition*, *40*, 121–157.

MacWhinney, B., Leinbach, J., Taraban, R., & McDonald, J. (1989). Language learning: Cues or rules? *Journal of Memory and Language*, *28*, 255–277.

MacWhinney, B., & Snow, C. (1985). The Child Language Data Exchange System. *Journal of Child Language*, *12*, 271–295.

Mann, V.A. & Repp, B.H. (1980). Influence of vocalic context of perception of the [s]–[d] distinction. *Perception and Psychophysics*, *28*, 213–228.

Marcus, M. (1980). *A theory of syntactic recognition for natural language.* Cambridge, MA: MIT Press.

Marcus, G.F., Brinkmann, U., Clahsen, H., Wiese, R., Woest, A., & Pinker, S. (1993). *German inflection: The exception that proves the rule* (MIT Occasional Paper No. 47). Cambridge, MA: MIT, Department of Brain and Cognitive Sciences.

Marr, D. (1982). *Vision.* San Francisco, CA: Freeman.

Marshall, J.C., & Newcombe, F. (1973). Patterns of paralexia: A psycholinguistic approach. *Journal of Psycholinguistic Research*, *2*, 175–199.

Marslen-Wilson, W.D. (1973). Linguistic structure and speech shadowing at very short latencies. *Nature*, *244*, 522–523.

Marslen-Wilson, W.D., & Tyler, L.K. (1975). Processing structure of sentence perception. *Nature*, *257*, 784–786.

Martin, N., Dell, G.S., Saffran, E.M., & Schwartz, M.F. (1994). Origins of paraphasia in deep dysphasia: Testing the consequence of decay impairment to an interactive spreading activation model of lexical retrieval. *Brain and Language*, *47*, 609–660.

Massaro, D.W. (1981). Sound to representation: An information-processing analysis. In T. Myers, J. Laver, & J. Anderson (Eds.), *The cognitive representation of speech* (pp. 181–193). New York: North-Holland.

McClelland, J.L., & Elman, J.L. (1986). Interactive processes in speech perception: The TRACE model. In J.L. McClelland & D.E. Rumelhart (Eds.), *Parallel distributed processing, Vol. 2* (pp. 58–121.) Cambridge, MA: MIT Press.

McClelland, J.L., & Johnston, J.C. (1977). The role of familiar units in the perception of words and non-words. *Perception and Psychophysics*, *22*, 249–261.

McClelland, J.L., & Kawamoto, A.H. (1986). Mechanisms of sentence processing. In J.L. McClelland & D.E. Rumelhart (Eds.), *Parallel distributed processing, Vol. 2* (pp. 272–325). Cambridge, MA: MIT Press.

McClelland, J.L., & Rumelhart, D.E. (1981). An interactive activation model of context effects in letter perception: Pt. 1. An account of basic findings. *Psychological Review*, *88*, 375–407.

McClelland, J.L., & Rumelhart, D.E. (Eds.). (1986). *Parallel distributed processing: Vol. 2. Psychological and biological models.* Cambridge, MA: MIT Press.

McCulloch, W.S., & Pitts, W. (1943). A logical calculus of ideas immanent in nervous activity. *Bulletin of Mathematical Biophysics*, *5*, 115–133.

Miikkulainen, R. (1993). *Subsymbolic natural language processing: An integrated model of scripts, lexicon and memory*. Cambridge, MA: MIT Press.

Miller, G.A., & Chomsky, N. (1963). Finitary models of language users. In R.D. Luce, R.R. Bush, & E. Galanter (Eds.), *Handbook of mathematical psychology, Vol. II* (pp. 419–491). New York: John Wiley & Sons .

Minsky, M. (1954). *Neural nets and the brain-model problem*. Unpublished doctoral dissertation, Princeton University, NJ.

Minsky, M., & Papert, S. (1969). *Perceptrons*. Cambridge, MA: MIT Press.

Miyata, Y., Smolensky, P., & Legendre, G. (1993). Distributed representation and parallel distributed processing of recursive structures. In *Proceedings of the 15th annual meeting of the Cognitive Science Society* (pp. 759–764). Hillsdale, NJ: Lawrence Erlbaum Associates Inc.

Morton, J., & Patterson, K.E. (1980). A new attempt at an interpretation, or, an attempt at a new interpretation. In M. Coltheart, K.E. Patterson & J.C. Marshall (Eds.), *Deep dyslexia*. London: Routledge.

Neisser, U. (1967). *Cognitive psychology*. New York: Appleton-Century-Crofts.

Newell, A., & Simon, H.A. (1972). *Human problem solving*. Englewood Cliffs, NJ: Prentice Hall.

Niklasson, L., & van Gelder, T. (1994). On being systematically connectionist. *Mind and Language*, *9*, 288–302.

Norris, D.G. (1993). Bottom-up connectionist models of "interaction". In G. Altmann & R. Shillcock (Eds.), *Cognitive Models of Speech Processing*. Hove, UK: Lawrence Erlbaum Associates Ltd.

Patterson, K.E., Seidenberg, M.S., & McClelland, J.L. (1989). Connections and disconnections: Acquired dyslexia in a computational model of reading processes. In R.G.M. Morris (Ed.), *Parallel distributed processing: Implications for psychology and neuroscience* (pp. 131–181). Oxford: Oxford University Press.

Pearlmutter, B.A. (1989). Learning state space trajectories in recurrent neural networks. *Neural Computation*, *1*, 263–269.

Pinker, S. (1991). Rules of language. *Science*, *253*, 530–535.

Pinker, S. (1994). *The language instinct: How the mind creates language*. New York: William Morrow & Company.

Pinker, S., & Prince, A. (1988). On language and connectionism: Analysis of a parallel distributed processing model of language acquisition. *Cognition*, *28*, 73–193.

Pisoni, D.B., & Tash, J. (1974). Reaction times to comparisons within and across phonetic categories. *Perception and Psychophysics*, *15*, 285–290.

Plaut, D., & McClelland, J.L. (1993). Generalization with componential attractors: Word and non-word reading in an attractor network. In *Proceedings of the 15th annual conference of the Cognitive Science Society* (pp. 824–829). Hillsdale, NJ: Lawrence Erlbaum Associates Inc.

Plaut, D., McClelland, J.L., Seidenberg, M., & Patterson, K. (1996). Understanding normal and impaired word reading: Computational principles in quasi-regular domains. *Psychological Review*, *103*, 56–115.

Plunkett, K. (1995). Connectionist approaches to language acquisition. In P. Fletcher & B. MacWhinney (Eds.), *The handbook of child language* (pp. 36–72). Cambridge, MA: Basil Blackwell.

Plunkett, K., & Marchman, V. (1991). U-shaped learning and frequency effects in a multilayered perceptron: Implications for child language acquisition. *Cognition*, *38*, 43–102.

Plunkett, K., & Marchman, V. (1993). From rote learning to system building. *Cognition*, *48*, 21–69.

Pollack, J.B. (1988). Recursive auto-associative memory: Devising compositional distributed representations. In *Proceedings of the 10th annual meeting of the Cognitive Science Society* (pp. 33–39). Hillsdale, NJ: Lawrence Erlbaum Associates Inc.

Pollack, J.B. (1990). Recursive distributed representations. *Artificial Intelligence, 46,* 77–105.

Prasada, S., & Pinker, S. (1993). Similarity-based and rule-based generalizations in inflectional morphology. *Language and Cognitive Processes, 8,* 1–56.

Redington, M., Chater, N., & Finch, S. (1993). Distributional information and the acquisition of linguistic categories: A statistical approach. In *Proceedings of the 15th annual meeting of the Cognitive Science Society* (pp. 848–853). Hillsdale, NJ: Lawrence Erlbaum Associates Inc.

Reilly, R.G. (1984). A connectionist model of some aspects of anaphor resolution. In *Proceedings of the 10th international conference on Computational Linguistics,* Stanford, CA.

Rosenblatt, F. (1962). *Principles of neurodynamics.* New York: Spartan Books.

Rumelhart, D.E., Hinton, G.E., & Williams, R.J. (1986). *Learning internal representations by error propagation.* In J.L. McClelland. & D.E. Rumelhart (Eds.), *Parallel distributed processing, Vol. 1* (pp. 318–362). Cambridge, MA: MIT Press.

Rumelhart, D.E., & McClelland, J.L. (1982). An interactive activation model of context effects in letter perception: Pt. 2. The contextual enhancement effects and some tests and enhancements of the model. *Psychological Review, 89,* 60–94.

Rumelhart, D.E., & McClelland, J.L. (1986a). On learning of past tenses of English verbs. In J.L. McClelland & D.E. Rumelhart (Eds.), *Parallel distributed processing, Vol. 2* (pp. 216–271). Cambridge, MA: MIT Press.

Rumelhart, D.E., & McClelland, J.L. (Eds.) (1986b). *Parallel distributed processing: Vol. 1. Foundations.* Cambridge, MA: MIT Press.

Rumelhart, D.E., & McClelland, J.L. (1987). Learning the past tenses of English verbs: Implicit rules or parallel distributed processing? In B. MacWhinney (Ed.), *Mechanisms of language acquisition* (pp. 195–248). Hillsdale, NJ: Lawrence Erlbaum Associates Inc.

Schwartz, M.F., Saffran, E.M., Bloch, D., & Dell, G.S. (1994). Disordered speech production in aphasic and normal speakers. *Brain and Language, 47,* 52–88.

Seidenberg, M.S. (1992). Connectionism without tears. In S. Davis (Ed.), *Connectionism: Advances in theory and practice* (pp. 84–122). Oxford, UK: Oxford University Press.

Seidenberg, M.S. (1994). Language and connectionism: The developing interface. *Cognition, 50,* 385–401.

Seidenberg, M.S., & Harm, M. (1995, November). *Division of labor and masking in a multi-component model of word recognition.* Paper presented at the 36th annual meeting of the Psychonomics Society, Los Angeles.

Seidenberg, M.S., & McClelland, J.L. (1989). A distributed, developmental model of word recognition and naming. *Psychological Review, 96,* 523–568.

Seidenberg, M.S., & McClelland, J.L. (1990). More words but still no lexicon: Reply to Besner et al. (1990). *Psychological Review, 97,* 447–452.

Seidenberg, M.S., Waters, G.S., Barnes, M.A., & Tanenhaus, M.K. (1984). When does irregular spelling or pronunciation influence word recognition? *Journal of Verbal Learning and Verbal Behavior, 23,* 383–404.

Sejnowski, T.J. (1986). Open questions about computation in the cerebral cortex. In J.L. McClelland & D.E. Rumelhart (Eds.), *Parallel distributed processing, Vol. 2* (pp. 372–389). Cambridge, MA: MIT Press.

Sejnowski, T.J., & Rosenberg, C.R. (1987). Parallel networks that learn to pronounce English text. *Complex Systems, 1,* 145–168.

Selman, B., & Hirst, G. (1985). A rule-based connectionist parsing system. In *Proceedings of the 7th annual meeting of the Cognitive Science Society*. Hillsdale, NJ: Lawrence Erlbaum Associates Inc.

Servan-Schreiber, D., Cleeremans, A., & McClelland, J. L. (1991). Graded state machines: The representation of temporal contingencies in simple recurrent networks. *Machine Learning*, *7*, 161–193.

Shallice, T. (1988). *From neuropsychology to mental structure*. Cambridge: Cambridge University Press.

Sharkey, N.E. (1990). A connectionist model of text comprehension. In D.A. Balota, G.B. Flores d'Arcais, & K. Rayner (Eds.), *Comprehension processes in reading*. Hillsdale, NJ: Lawrence Erlbaum Associates Inc.

Sharkey, N.E. (1991). Connectionist representation techniques. *AI Review*, *5*, 143–167.

Sharkey, N.E. (1992). Functional compositionality and soft preference rules. In B. Linggard & C. Nightingale (Eds.), *Neural networks for images, speech, and natural language*. London: Chapman & Hall.

Shillcock, R., Lindsey, G., Levy, J., & Chater, N. (1992). A phonologically motivated input representation for the modelling of auditory word perception in continuous speech. In *Proceedings of the 14th annual conference of the Cognitive Science Society* (pp. 408–413). Hillsdale, NJ: Lawrence Erlbaum Associates Inc.

Small, S.L., Cottrell, G.W., & Shastri, L. (1982). Towards connectionist parsing. In *Proceedings of the national conference on Artificial Intelligence*. Pittsburgh, PA.

Smolensky, P. (1988). On the proper treatment of connectionism. *Behavioral and Brain Sciences*, *11*, 1–74.

Smolensky, P. (1990). Tensor product variable binding and the representation of symbolic structures in connectionist systems. *Artificial Intelligence*, *46*, 159–216.

Sopena, J.M. (1991). *ERSP: A distributed connectionist parser that uses embedded sequences to represent structure* (Tech. Rep. No. UB-PB-1-91). Barcelona, Spain: Universitat de Barcelona, Departament de Psicologia Bàsica.

Stemberger, J.P. (1985). An interactive activation model of language production. In A.W. Ellis (Ed.), *Progress in the psychology of language, Vol. 1* (pp. 143–186). Hove, UK: Lawrence Erlbaum Associates Ltd.

St. John, M.F., & McClelland, J.L. (1990). Learning and applying contextual constraints in sentence comprehension. *Artificial Intelligence*, *46*, 217–257.

Stolcke, A. (1991). Syntactic category formation with vector space grammars. In *Proceedings from the 13th annual conference of the Cognitive Science Society* (pp. 908–912). Hillsdale, NJ: Lawrence Erlbaum Associates Inc.

Tabor, W., Juliano, C., & Tanenhaus, M.K. (1997). Parsing in a dynamical system: An attractor-based account of the interaction of lexical and structural constraints in sentence processing. *Language and Cognitive Processes*, *12*, 211–271.

Taraban, R., & McClelland, J.L. (1987). Conspiracy effects in word recognition. *Journal of Memory and Language*, *26*, 608–631.

Turing, A.M. (1936). On computable numbers, with an application to the Entscheidungsproblem. *Proceedings of the London Mathematical Society, Series 2*, *42*, 230–265.

Waltz, D.L., & Pollack, J.B. (1985). Massively parallel parsing: A strongly interactive model of natural language interpretation. *Cognitive Science*, *9*, 51–74.

Weckerly, J., & Elman, J. (1992). A PDP approach to processing center-embedded sentences. In *Proceedings of the 14th annual meeting of the Cognitive Science Society* (pp. 414–419). Hillsdale, NJ: Lawrence Erlbaum Associates Inc.

Werbos, P.J. (1974). *Beyond regression: New tools for prediction and analysis in the behavioral sciences*. Unpublished doctoral dissertation. Cambridge, MA: Harvard University.

Wickelgren, W.A. (1969). Context-sensitive coding, associative memory, and serial order in (speech) behavior. *Psychological Review*, *76*, 1–15.

PART FOUR

Semantic and discourse processing

CHAPTER NINE

Three models of discourse comprehension

Morton Ann Gernsbacher
Department of Psychology, University of Wisconsin-Madison, USA

Julie A. Foertsch
The LEAD Center, University of Wisconsin-Madison, USA

Over the last two decades, language processing researchers have proposed models to explain how it is that people come to understand connected text and spoken language, a medium known as discourse. Many questions arise, such as how do comprehenders build mental representations of discourse? How do comprehenders link the elements of discourse with information that they already know? How do comprehenders retrieve information from their representation of a discourse? In this chapter, we shall describe three models of discourse comprehension that have come to dominate the field of psycholinguistics: Kintsch and van Dijk's ever-evolving model of text comprehension (1978; van Dijk & Kintsch, 1983), presently under the name of the Construction–Integration Model (Kintsch, 1988; 1990); Sanford and Garrod's Memory-Focus Model (1981, 1994); and Gernsbacher's Structure Building Framework (1990; 1991; 1997). Because we are intimately familiar with the latter model, we shall spend more time reviewing it than the others.

KINTSCH AND VAN DIJK'S MODELS OF TEXT COMPREHENSION

One of the first attempts at developing a detailed model of discourse comprehension was made by Kintsch and van Dijk (1978). The Kintsch and van Dijk model combined Kintsch's earlier psychology-based work on units of meaning, which were called *propositions* (Kintsch, 1974, 1977), with van Dijk's functional linguistics-based work on the rules of discourse, which were called *macro-operators*, for transforming propositions (van Dijk, 1972, 1977). The resulting model of text comprehension proposed three basic steps: First, the meaningful elements of the text (the propositions) must be organised into a locally coherent whole (*a text base*). Due to the constraints of working memory, this is a cyclical process, usually dealing with only one sentence or clause at a time. Second, processing operations called *macro-operators* transform the propositions of the text base into a set of overarching *macro-propositions* that retain the gist of the text. These operations include deleting irrelevant propositions from the macro-structure (though not necessarily from memory), generalising across redundancies, and constructing new propositions to fill in logical gaps in the text (i.e. making *bridging inferences* at a global level). *Schemas* (structured frameworks representing typical events) retrieved from memory control the application of these macro-operators by determining which propositions are relevant—in other words, by deciding which text elements fit the constraints imposed by a comprehender's expectations about how the discourse should proceed. Macro-operators are also applied in cycles, with the relevance criteria becoming more and more stringent with each cycle.

The third and last set of operations in Kintsch and van Dijk's (1978) original model comes into play only when the text needs to be recalled from memory. When the comprehender is asked to recall or summarise the text, a *new* text base is generated from the memorial consequences of the original comprehension process. Some of the operations used to produce this text base are reproductive, whereas others are constructive. Both types of operations result from the inverse application of the macro-operators. Kintsch and van Dijk (1978) demonstrated how these three sets of operations could be used to understand a paragraph from a psychological research report and went on to suggest methods for testing the model empirically.

Some early criticisms of the original Kintsch and van Dijk model (e.g. Sanford & Garrod, 1981) focused on its use of propositional notation to represent meaning and the ambiguity of exactly how much information can be held in a single proposition. If, as Kintsch and van Dijk (1978) suggest, the propositions that represent nuggets of meaning within the text can be something *beyond* Kintsch's (1974) word-based notation, it becomes difficult to make any claims about the model's processing capacity. Kintsch and van Dijk (1978) had asserted that processing must be done in cycles because the working memory buffer that transforms propositions into a coherent text base can handle only a few propositions at a time. But if propositions comprise knowledge structures other than words (like event frames, for example), it is unclear what the capacity limits of the model really are. To illustrate, Sanford and Garrod (1981) questioned whether the concept of WOMAN-COOKING-CHIPS would be represented with one "pseudo-proposition" (as could be the case if propositions are event frames), or several formal propositions (as must be the case in Kintsch's (1974) propositional notation).

Kintsch and van Dijk's original model (1978) was also weakened by empirical results that suggested that a lot of discourse comprehension is done "on-line". A model that waits for an entire sentence or clause to be read into the working memory buffer before trying to figure out what that clause or sentence means was inconsistent with new data suggesting that attempts at local coherence are made *before* the ends of clauses are reached. In response to this shortcoming, van Dijk and Kintsch (1983) revised their model, making it more "strategic", dynamic, and on-line. In van Dijk and Kintsch's updated version (1983), the model attempts to establish local coherence as soon as possible instead of waiting for clause or sentence boundaries. This process was still conceived of as cyclical, but the length of the cycle had effectively shrunk from the size of a clause or sentence to that of a few words. Along the same lines, macro-operators were replaced by more flexible *macro-strategies*, which allow comprehenders to make inferences about the text and predictions about what will occur next before the entire text has been converted into a propositional text base.

Further modifications were soon to follow. After connectionist models became a popular way of explaining how memories might be stored and retrieved from the neural networks of the mind, Kintsch incorporated connectionist ideas into the model that he and van Dijk had developed. The result was Kintsch's (1988) Construction–Integration model of discourse comprehension, which was a hybrid between the symbolic systems used in the earlier Kintsch models and the connectionist systems used by computer modellers like Rumelhart and McClelland (1986).

Whereas the earlier Kintsch and van Dijk models (1978; van Dijk & Kintsch, 1983) suggested that discourse comprehension is driven by preformulated schemas in a top-down, expectation-based fashion, Kintsch's (1988) Construction–Integration model proposed that the initial processing is strictly data-driven and bottom-up. Such a change was needed to accommodate the late-1970s findings that the initial activation of meanings associated with a word occurs without regard to the context of that word (Swinney, 1979; Tanenhaus, Leiman, & Seidenberg, 1979). Priming experiments had shown that within the first several hundred milliseconds of presenting a word like *bat,* multiple meanings of that word become activated (both "a flying mammal" and "a club for hitting a ball"), even if only one of those meanings makes sense in the context of the sentence in which the word occurs. It is only after about 400 ms that the contextually appropriate meaning of the word is selected and the contextually inappropriate meaning is suppressed.

Taking such findings into account, Kintsch (1988) proposed a two-step comprehension process of acontextual *construction* followed by context-guided *integration*. During the first step of construction, word meanings are activated and propositions are formed without regard to the discourse context. This activation process is sloppy and weakly constrained so as to be maximally flexible (i.e. weak production rules can operate in many different contexts because they do not have to yield precise outputs, whereas more strongly constrained production rules do not work at all in novel or atypical situations). These weaker production rules tend to produce multiple candidates for later selection, some of which are bound to be wrong: They are powerful enough so that the right element is likely to be among those produced, but weak enough that some of the elements generated will be irrelevant or entirely inappropriate. Hence, the output of this initial phase of construction is somewhat incoherent and inconsistent.

Following the lead of Rumelhart and McClelland (1986), Kintsch proposed that the output of the construction phase's bottom-up activation process is in the form of an unstable network of associations. This network, corresponding to a text base, is formed through the following steps: (1) concepts and propositions directly corresponding to the verbal input are formed; (2) the concepts are elaborated by activating a small number of the most closely associated neighbours in the general knowledge net (background knowledge stored in memory); (3) inferences necessary for local—but not global—coherence may be generated; and (4) connection strengths or *weights* are assigned to all pair-wise interconnections.

It is only during the second step of integration that discourse context comes into play, and the model chooses between those elements that are appropriate for the discourse context and those that are not. During the integration phase, the construction phase's incoherent and unstable net of associations is transformed into a coherent and stable text base through the wonders of spreading activation. Briefly, this is a process whereby an activation vector passes through the network, and the weights on the interconnections are updated so that positively interconnected items (those that are a "good fit" with the other items) are boosted in activation strength, while unrelated items lose activation and drop out of the network, and implausible or inconsistent items become inhibited. (A detailed description of connectionist models and the algebraic principles by which they operate is beyond the scope of this chapter, but a good introduction to these models can be found in McClelland and Rumelhart,

1985. For a more formal and fully instantiated connectionist model of discourse comprehension than that attempted by Kintsch, see the models developed by Sharkey, 1990, and Golden and Rumelhart, 1993.)

As in earlier models, Kintsch (1988) proposed that the two-step construction-integration process occurs in cycles corresponding to short sentences or phases. In each cycle, a new net of associations is constructed from whatever was held over in working memory from the previous cycle. Once this net of associations is constructed, the integration process steps in and activation vectors are passed through the system until the weights on the interconnections stop changing and the system stabilises. The highly activated nodes that remain are the discourse representation that is then held over in working memory to aid in the construction processes of the next cycle. To clarify that these processes are still occurring "on-line", Kintsch (1988, p. 168) noted that integration does not necessarily need to wait for a clause or sentence boundary: "It would be quite possible to apply the relaxation procedure outlined here repeatedly in each cycle, as propositions are being constructed. This would allow for the disambiguation of word senses before the end of a cycle."

The latest instantiation of Kintsch's Construction–Integration model (1990) is very similar to the 1988 version, except that it incorporates the ideas of Givón (1979, 1992) about the role of grammar in discourse processing. Givón (1992) illustrates how the grammar of referentiality (e.g. the use of definite versus indefinite modifiers, the use of more explicit anaphors like full noun phrases versus less explicit anaphors like pronouns) provides "processing instructions" that guide the comprehender in producing a referentially coherent representation of a text. As Kintsch (1990, p. 5) states in his summarisation of Givón's ideas: "Syntactic cues signal to the reader what is likely to be important for the construction of the situation model, and some rather general semantic rules allow the reader to put these elements together into a weak or sloppy situation model ... The grammar tells the reader precisely where to look for what in the text". By allowing that grammar and some "general semantic rules" may guide processing and text base construction right from the start, Kintsch's (1990) model differs from his assertion (1988, p. 163) that "initial processing is strictly bottom-up. Word meanings are activated, propositions are formed, and inferences and elaborations are produced without regard to discourse context". This assertion does not entirely hold if the grammar of the sentence and the referential structure of the text are considered as part of a word's context, and indeed, Kintsch (1990) seems to be suggesting that grammar is used to "contextualise" discourse elements in reference to one another.

SANFORD AND GARROD'S MEMORY FOCUS MODEL

A parallel model of discourse comprehension has been proposed by Sanford and Garrod (1981; Garrod & Sanford, 1994). Whereas Kintsch and van Dijk's original (1978) model developed out of work on propositional transformations and the representation of meaning, Sanford and Garrod's (1981) Memory Focus model developed out of an interest in referential coherence and anaphoric resolution (Garrod & Sanford, 1977). Hence, although the latest versions of these two models are not inconsistent, they focus on different portions of what are essentially the same underlying processes. Kintsch and van Dijk have focused on how information from the text (in the form of propositions) is connected to and completed by information from long-term memory (schemas, general knowledge, and so forth), whereas Sanford and Garrod have focused most of their attention on a particular instantiation of that process: anaphoric resolution, or how the various referents in a text become associated with their antecedents in the text. For Kintsch and van Dijk, the primary question of interest during processing is "How does this new element change the scenario I am constructing?" For Sanford and Garrod, the primary question of interest is "Does this new element refer to something mentioned previously in the text, and if so, what?"

Sanford and Garrod's (1981) Memory Focus model has not gone through as many versions as the text comprehension model of Kintsch and van Dijk (1978), but it has been elaborated and updated by their continuing work in the field of anaphoric resolution (e.g. Garrod, Freudenthal, & Boyle, 1994; Garrod & Sanford, 1983, 1990; Sanford, Moar, & Garrod, 1988). The basic goal of their model—and of any discourse comprehension model—is to come up with a coherent interpretation of all of the text encountered thus far, a process that hinges on first establishing who or what is being talked about in a given text fragment and whether or not that element has been discussed before. This resolution process is influenced by three factors: (1) the discourse focus, which is whatever elements are the most highly activated at any one time, and which is constrained to only a few elements due to the limits of memory and attention; (2) the linguistic properties of the anaphors (whether the word that may refer back to an antecedent is in the form of a pronoun, common noun, or repeated name); and (3) pragmatic inference constraints, which reflect the need for global coherence.

The main assumptions of the Memory Focus model are as follows: First, the discourse focus clearly differentiates between different levels of activation in the discourse model. Information that is central to the discourse focus is the "current topic" and is highly active, while information that is on the periphery of the discourse focus (either due to prior mention or through close association with a current topic) is somewhat less active, but still readily retrievable. To capture this distinction, Garrod and Sanford (1990) propose two partitions of memory: the *explicit focus*, which corresponds to the text elements, or *tokens*, currently under discussion; and the *implicit focus*, which contains the somewhat less-active background information about the text scenario as it relates to the tokens.

As with Kintsch's (1988) model, the Memory Focus model distinguishes between immediate primary processing and subsequent secondary processing. Final resolution of a sentence occurs at a later stage than initial activation (which will include some options that are later rejected and deselected). Activation is immediate and automatic, whereas resolution (the choice that must be made prior to integration), and integration (the act of joining an element to its referent), are not. When the new element is a pronoun, activation, resolution, and integration are all immediate. This is because pronouns tap their tokens (the current topic) directly, and the downflow of activation from the token to the elements in the implicit focus is fast and easy. Alternatively, fuller, more explicit elements (like common nouns) tap into elements in the implicit focus. The reasoning is straightforward and guided by functional linguistics: If the discourse were talking about the explicit focus's token, it would clearly signal that by using a pronoun. Using a fuller noun suggests that something other than the current topic is being discussed.

According to the Memory Focus model, the immediacy of sentence resolution depends in every instance upon the costs and benefits that are associated with making an early commitment. Pronouns have a low probability of *not* being in the focus, so resolving them quickly is likely to be of much benefit and little cost. More explicit nouns tend to initiate a search for a referent in the implicit focus. If a referent that attaches to the token in the explicit focus is found, it takes another step to attach that referent to its token. (The *up*flow of activation from an implicit role slot to the explicit token is not fast and immediate.) If no referent is found in the implicit focus, the discourse focus is disrupted and a move to establish a new token as the discourse focus is made. More explicit anaphors are processing instructions that suggest either an old topic that has fallen out of focus is being reactivated or that an entirely new topic is being introduced. Thus, local cohesion is immediate, but coherence evaluation (resolution) and integration (structure updating) is not.

Although Kintsch's models of discourse comprehension have evolved over the years with regard to whether processing is top-down or bottom-up (top-down, Kintsch & van Dijk, 1978; van Dijk & Kintsch, 1983; bottom-up, 1988; both, 1990), Sanford and Garrod (1994) propose that some of the selectivity in their model is of a top-down nature. They argue that pragmatic mapping can sometimes override syntax (global coherence can sometimes predominate local coherence). Thus, the Memory Focus model aims for a satisfactorily high level of coherence, which in some cases can be obtained without detailed processing. When coherence is easily achieved due to the apparent fulfilment of expectations, sentences may be only shallowly analysed.

An example of a relatively shallow level of analysis is the Moses illusion: When subjects are asked, "How many animals of each sort did Moses put on the Ark?", they typically reply, "two", without commenting on the fact that it was Noah, and not Moses, who put animals on an ark. Sanford and Garrod (1994, p. 716) review numerous experimental data documenting their conclusion that "there is a considerable amount of evidence for partial or incomplete processing during the interpretation of sentences. In general, the effects appear to result from pragmatic aspects of interpretation dominating lower level semantic processing."

GERNSBACHER'S STRUCTURE BUILDING FRAMEWORK

Gernsbacher's (1990) Structure Building Framework is based on the assumption that language comprehension and language production draw on general, cognitive processes and mechanisms—processes and mechanisms that might underlie non-linguistic comprehension, as well. Therefore, the goal of her Structure Building Framework has been to identify these cognitive processes and mechanisms. She does so by observing discourse comprehension phenomena, such as those already discussed in the context of Kintsch and Garrod and Sanford's models, and then searching for common cognitive processes and mechanisms that enable those discourse comprehension phenomena.

Like each of Kintsch's models and Garrod and Sanford's (1990) Memory Focus model, the Structure Building Framework also proposes that the goal of comprehension is to build a coherent, mental representation or "structure" of the information being comprehended. According to the Structure Building Framework, building this mental structure involves several component processes. First, comprehenders lay foundations for their mental structures. Next, comprehenders develop their structures by mapping on information when that incoming information coheres or relates to previous information. But when the incoming information is less coherent or related, comprehenders employ a different process: They shift to initiate a new substructure. So, most representations comprise several branching substructures.

The building blocks of these mental structures are what Gernsbacher very loosely refers to as memory nodes. Memory nodes are activated by incoming stimuli. Initial activation forms the foundation of mental structures. Once the foundation is laid, subsequent information is often mapped on to a developing structure because the more the incoming information coheres with the previous information, the more likely it is to activate the same or connected memory nodes. In contrast, the less coherent the incoming information is, the less likely it is to activate the same or connected memory nodes. In this case, the incoming information might activate a different set of nodes, and the activation of this other set of nodes might form the foundation for a new substructure.

According to the Structure Building Framework, once memory nodes are activated, they transmit processing signals. These processing signals either enhance (boost) or suppress (dampen) other nodes' activation and thereby control the structure building processes. Presumably memory nodes are enhanced because the information they represent is necessary for further structure building. They are suppressed when the information they represent is no longer as necessary.

Gernsbacher's empirical research has been aimed at investigating these three sub-processes involved in structure building, namely, laying a foundation, mapping relevant information onto that foundation, and shifting to initiate a new sub-structure. She proposes these processes account for many language comprehension phenomena. For example, Gernsbacher and Hargreaves (1988) suggested that the processes of laying a foundation and mapping information onto that foundation accounts for a phenomenon they dubbed, the Advantage of First Mention. The advantage is this: Participants mentioned first in a sentence are more memorable than participants mentioned later. Gernsbacher and Hargreaves (1988) demonstrated that the Advantage of First Mention is not due to first-mentioned participants' tendency to be semantic agents; neither is the advantage due to the first-mentioned participants being literally the first words of their stimulus sentences (and possibly artificially highlighted by the warning signal that preceded each experimental trial). The advantage maintains even when both the first- and second-mentioned participants are syntactic subjects, and even when the first-mentioned participants are not the syntactic subjects. Gernsbacher and Hargreaves (1988) suggest that the Advantage of First Mention arises because comprehension requires laying a foundation and mapping subsequent information onto that foundation. First-mentioned participants are more accessible because they form the foundations for their sentence-level representations and because it is through them that subsequent information is mapped onto the developing representations.

The Advantage of First Mention has since been replicated numerous times in spoken (MacDonald & MacWhinney, 1990; McDonald & MacWhinney, 1995) and written English (Garnham, Traxler, Oakhill, & Gernsbacher, 1996; Gernsbacher, 1989; Neath & Knoedler, 1994; Schaibe

& McDonald, 1993) as well as Spanish (Carreiras, Gernsbacher, & Villa, 1995), Korean (Lee, 1992), Chinese (Sun, 1997), and American Sign Language (Emmorey, 1997). Gernsbacher and Hargreaves (1992) reviewed numerous languages whose preferred word order is both more and less constrained than English word order. Despite the greater or lesser constraints on word order in these languages, first-mentioned participants play a specific functional role. That is, speakers and writers specifically choose among the grammatical structures provided by their language so that they can purposely mention certain participants first. Indeed, Carreiras et al. (1995) demonstrated that the Advantage of First Mention occurs in Spanish, even though native Spanish speakers rely considerably less on word order for sentence comprehension than do English speakers (presumably because word order is less constrained in Spanish than it is in English). Carreiras et al. (1995) also demonstrated that the Advantage of First Mention occurs with first-mentioned inanimates as well as animates, semantic patients as well as semantic agents, and syntactic objects as well as syntactic subjects.

Gernsbacher, Hargreaves, and Beeman (1989) demonstrated how the processes of laying a foundation and shifting can account for another phenomenon, the Advantage of Clause Recency, which had been observed by other researchers. The Advantage of Clause Recency means that information in the most recently mentioned clause is more memorable than information from an earlier clause. The Advantage of Clause Recency obviously conflicts with the Advantage of First Mention. In a series of experiments, Gernsbacher et al. (1989) resolved this conflict by suggesting that comprehenders represent each clause of a two-clause sentence in its own mental sub-structure; while comprehenders are building a clause-level sub-structure, they have greatest access to the information that is represented in that sub-structure. Thus, the Advantage of Clause Recency occurs when comprehenders are building a mental sub-structure to represent the most recently comprehended clause. However, after comprehenders finish building the sub-structure to represent the most recently comprehended clause, information from the first clause becomes more accessible because the sub-structure representing the first clause serves as a foundation for the whole sentence-level representation (hence, the Advantage of First Mention). In this series of experiments, Gernsbacher et al. (1989) also demonstrated that the Advantage of First Mention is a relatively long-lived characteristic of the mental representation of a sentence.

The process of mapping

Another facet of Gernsbacher's research on the Structure Building Framework has been to investigate the cues in discourse that encourage comprehenders to employ the process of mapping (Gernsbacher, 1996). Gernsbacher and Robertson (in press) discovered that comprehenders use the definite article *the* as a cue for referential coherence; Deaton and Gernsbacher (in press) discovered that comprehenders use the conjunction *because* as a cue for causal coherence; Foertsch and Gernsbacher (1994) discovered that comprehenders use the explicitness of the referential device (from repeated noun phrases to definite noun phrases to pronouns) as a cue for referential coherence; Haenggi, Gernsbacher, and Bolliger (1993) discovered that comprehenders draw inferences about the implied location of protagonists in narratives, and comprehenders use those inferences as cues for mapping during discourse comprehension; and Gernsbacher, Goldsmith, and Robertson (1992; see also Gernsbacher & Robertson, 1992; Gernsbacher, Hallada, & Robertson, 1998) discovered that comprehenders draw inferences about the implied emotional states of protagonists in narratives, and comprehenders use those inferences as cues for mapping during discourse comprehension.

The process of shifting

Gernsbacher (1985) claimed that the process of shifting explained why comprehenders rapidly forget recently comprehended information (in particular, information that is typically considered "superficial" or "surface" information). These experiments demonstrated that comprehenders rapidly forget recently comprehended information when they are comprehending non-verbal picture stories; so, the phenomenon is not unique to language. Furthermore, this rapid forgetting was most likely to occur when comprehenders encountered a structural boundary, for instance, when they encountered a new clause, a new sentence, or—as in Gernsbacher's (1985) picture story experiments—a new episode. Because the phenomenon occurs with non-verbal picture stories, it is probably not due to the traditional psycholinguistics explanation. Moreover, because the structure of the information, rather than the amount, affects comprehenders' memory, the phenomenon is probably not due to the limitations of a short-term memory. Gernsbacher (1985) empirically demonstrated that the phenomenon is not due to another popular explanation, namely, that comprehenders lose access to information—in particular verbatim information—because it is recoded into "gist". Instead, Gernsbacher (1995) empirically demonstrated that comprehenders rapidly forget information because comprehension involves the cognitive process of shifting. Once comprehenders have shifted to initiate a new sub-structure, information represented in a previous sub-structure is more difficult to access. Surface information is least likely to remain accessible because it is least likely to be represented in multiple substructures.

The mechanisms of suppression and enhancement

According to the Structure Building Framework, mental structures are built of memory nodes; once activated, two cognitive mechanisms control memory nodes' activation levels: suppression and enhancement. Gernsbacher and her students have also investigated these two mechanisms and identified many of the roles they play in comprehension. For example, Gernsbacher and Faust (1991b) demonstrated the role the mechanism of suppression plays in how comprehenders understand the meanings of words. As a test case, Gernsbacher and Faust (1991b) investigated how comprehenders understand the contextually appropriate meanings of words that have diverse meanings, namely, homographs. As described earlier, when comprehenders encounter homographs (such as *spade*), multiple meanings are often immediately activated, even though one meaning is clearly implied by the context (as in *He dug in the garden with the spade*). However, within a half second, only the contextually appropriate meaning (e.g. the garden tool meaning) remains activated. What happens to the contextually inappropriate meanings? Gernsbacher and Faust (1991b) discovered that the contextually inappropriate meanings do not become less activated through a mechanism they dubbed mutual inhibition (i.e. the contextually inappropriate meanings do not decrease in activation simply because the contextually appropriate meanings increase, as in a see-saw effect). They also discovered that the contextually inappropriate meanings do not become less activated simply because they decay. Rather, inappropriate meanings become less activated through an active dampening of activation; they are suppressed by signals transmitted by memory nodes representing the semantic, pragmatic, and syntactic context (see also Gernsbacher & St. John, in press).

Gernsbacher (1989) demonstrated the role that both the mechanisms of suppression and enhancement play in how comprehenders understand anaphoric devices. Through enhancement and suppression, the anaphor's antecedent becomes the most activated concept. Furthermore, the more explicit the anaphor is, the more likely it is to trigger the mechanisms of suppression and enhancement. Very explicit anaphors, such as repeated names, immediately enhance the activation of their antecedents and immediately suppress the activation of other concepts. Less explicit anaphors, such as pronouns, take longer to trigger suppression, and they trigger enhancement less powerfully.

Gernsbacher and Shroyer (1989) demonstrated that just as anaphoric devices mark concepts that have been mentioned before, cataphoric devices mark concepts that are likely to be mentioned again. For example, two cataphoric devices typically found in spoken English are spoken stress and the indefinite article *this* ("I know *this* guy who ...").

Gernsbacher and Jescheniak (1995) demonstrated how the mechanisms of suppression and enhancement make the concepts to which cataphoric devices refer more accessible: Concepts marked by cataphoric devices are enhanced; concepts marked by cataphoric devices are better at suppressing the activation of other concepts; and concepts marked by cataphoric devices better resist being suppressed by other concepts.

Individual differences in structure building

According to the Structure Building Framework, many of the cognitive processes and mechanisms underlying language comprehension are general cognitive processes and mechanisms; therefore, some of the bases of individual differences in comprehension skill might not be language specific. Gernsbacher and her colleagues have tested this prediction and found substantial support for it. For example, Gernsbacher, Varner, and Faust (1990) demonstrated that skill at comprehending linguistic media (written and auditory stories) is highly correlated with skill at comprehending non-linguistic media (picture stories). In a second experiment, they discovered that less-skilled comprehenders lose access to recently comprehended information more rapidly than more-skilled comprehenders do, and this difference occurs regardless of whether they are comprehending written, auditory, or picture stories. According to the Structure Building Framework, all comprehenders lose access to recently comprehended information when they shift from actively building one substructure and initiate another. So, less-skilled comprehenders might be worse at remembering recently comprehended information because they shift too often. In Gernsbacher et al.'s (1990) third experiment, they found evidence to support this hypothesis. In their last experiment they discovered why a greater tendency towards shifting might characterise less-skilled comprehenders: Less-skilled comprehenders are less able to suppress inappropriate information, such as the contextually inappropriate meanings of ambiguous words (e.g. the playing card meaning of *spade* in the sentence *He dug in the garden with the spade*). Because inappropriate information cannot be easily mapped onto an existing substructure, its activation could trigger the development of a new substructure, leading to an increased amount of shifting, and poorer access to previously comprehended information.

Gernsbacher and Faust (1991a; see also Gernsbacher, 1993; Gernsbacher & Faust, 1995) provided more evidence to support the hypothesis that less-skilled comprehenders have less-efficient suppression mechanisms. Gernsbacher and Faust (1991a) discovered that less-skilled comprehenders are also less able to suppress the incorrect forms of homophones (e.g. the word *rose* when they read *rows*); less-skilled comprehenders are less able to suppress the typical-but-absent members of visual scenes (e.g. a picture of a *tractor* in a farm scene); and less-skilled comprehenders are less able to ignore words superimposed on pictures or pictures surrounding words. However, Gernsbacher and Faust (1991b) also discovered that less-skilled comprehenders are not less appreciative of context (see also Gernsbacher & Robertson, 1995); in fact, they often activate contextually appropriate information more strongly than more-skilled comprehenders do. Therefore, Gernsbacher and her colleagues have concluded that less-skilled comprehenders' suppression mechanisms, but not their enhancement mechanisms, are less efficient.

BRIEF COMPARISON AMONG MODELS

Clearly, these three models are alike. For instance, the general, cognitive process of laying a foundation proposed by Gernsbacher's Structure Building Framework is akin to the process by which tokens are used "an anchor for attaching information" in Garrod and Sanford's Memory Focus model. Similarly, the general, cognitive process of mapping proposed by Gernsbacher's Structure Building Framework resembles the following phenomenon in Garrod and Sanford's Memory Focus model: If a referent that attaches to the token in the explicit focus is found, it takes another step to attach (map) that referent. Furthermore, Garrod and Sanford's proposal that if no referent is found in the implicit focus, the discourse focus is disrupted and a move to establish a new token as the discourse focus is made sounds quite similar to Gernsbacher's general cognitive process of shifting.

The general cognitive mechanism of suppression found in Gernsbacher's Structure Building Framework resembles the process of integration found in Kintsch's (1988) Construction–Integration model. Recall that in Kintsch's (1988) model, two processes build mental representations during language comprehension: The process of *construction* builds a propositional network (a text base), and the process of *integration* edits that network. Like the Structure Building Framework's mechanism of enhancement, Kintsch's (1988) process of integration increases the activation of contextually relevant information. And, like the Structure Building Framework's mechanism of enhancement, Kintsch's process of integration operates after concepts have been initially activated.

We end this chapter by posing a challenge to those involved in researching discourse comprehension: Generate testable hypotheses from these models that make clearly *different* predictions about what will or will not occur, and then perform a critical experiment to see which of the models is correct. Those who take us up on the challenge may well find that the models do *not* make different predictions a vast majority of the time. If that is the case, and if the models merely describe the same basic processes using different terms, then we must do what our brains compel us to do: We must lump all the models together into one.

REFERENCES

Carreiras, M., Gernsbacher, M.A., & Villa, V. (1995). The advantage of first mention in Spanish. *Psychonomic Bulletin and Review, 2*, 124–129.

Deaton, J.A., & Gernsbacher, M.A. (in press). Causal conjunctions and implicit causality cue mapping in sentence comprehension. *Journal of Memory and Language*.

Emmorey, K. (1997). Non-antecedent suppression in American Sign Language. *Language and Cognitive Processes, 12*, 103–119.

Foertsch, J., & Gernsbacher, M.A. (1994). In search of complete comprehension: Getting "minimalists" to work. *Discourse Processes, 18*, 271–296.

Garnham, A., Traxler, M.J., Oakhill, J.V., & Gernsbacher, M.A. (1996). The locus of implicit causality effects in comprehension. *Journal of Memory and Language, 35*, 517–543.

Garrod, S., Freudenthal, D., & Boyle, E. (1994). The role of different types of anaphor in the on-line resolution of sentences in a discourse. *Journal of Memory and Language, 33*, 39–68.

Garrod, S., & Sanford, A.J. (1977). Interpreting anaphoric relations: The integration of semantic information while reading. *Journal of Verbal Learning and Verbal Behavior, 16*, 77–90.

Garrod, S.C., & Sanford, A.J. (1983). The mental representation of discourse in a focused system: Implications for the representation of anaphoric noun-phrases. *Journal of Semantics, 1*, 21–41.

Garrod, S.C., & Sanford, A.J. (1990). Referential processing in reading: Focusing on roles and individuals. In D.A. Balota, G.B. Flores d'Arcais, and K. Rayner (Eds.), *Comprehension processes in reading* (pp. 465–486). Hillsdale, NJ: Lawrence Erlbaum Associates Inc.

Garrod, S.C., & Sanford, A.J. (1994). Resolving sentences in a discourse context: How discourse representation affects language understanding. In M.A. Gernsbacher (Ed.), *Handbook of psycholinguistics* (pp. 675–698). San Diego, CA: Academic Press.

Gernsbacher, M.A. (1985). Surface information loss in comprehension. *Cognitive Psychology, 17*, 324–363.

Gernsbacher, M.A. (1989). Mechanisms that improve referential access. *Cognition, 32*, 99–156.

Gernsbacher, M.A. (1990). *Language comprehension as structure building*. Hillsdale, NJ: Lawrence Erlbaum Associates Inc.

Gernsbacher, M.A. (1991). Cognitive processes and mechanisms in language comprehension: The structure building framework. In G.H. Bower (Ed.), *The psychology of learning and motivation* (pp. 217–263). New York: Academic Press.

Gernsbacher, M.A. (1993). Less skilled readers have less efficient suppression mechanisms. *Psychological Science, 4*, 294–298.

Gernsbacher, M.A. (1995). The Structure Building Framework: What it is, what it might also be, and why. In B.K. Britton & A.C. Graesser (Eds.), *Models of text understanding* (pp. 289–311). Hillsdale, NJ: Lawrence Erlbaum Associates Inc.

Gernsbacher, M.A. (1996). Coherence cues mapping during comprehension. In J. Costermans & M. Fayol (Eds.), *Processing interclausal relationships in the production and comprehension of text* (pp. 3–21). Hillsdale, NJ: Lawrence Erlbaum Associates Inc.

Gernsbacher, M.A. (1997). Two decades of structure building. *Discourse Processes, 23*, 265–304.

Gernsbacher, M.A., & Faust, M. (1991a). The mechanism of suppression: A component of general comprehension skill. *Journal of Experimental Psychology: Learning, Memory, and Cognition, 17*, 245–262.

Gernsbacher, M.A., & Faust, M. (1991b). The role of suppression in sentence comprehension. In G.B. Simpson (Ed.), *Comprehending word and sentence* (pp. 97–128). Amsterdam: North-Holland.

Gernsbacher, M.A., & Faust, M. (1995). Skilled suppression. In F.N. Dempster & C.N. Brainerd (Eds.), *Interference and inhibition in cognition* (pp. 295–327). San Diego, CA: Academic Press.

Gernsbacher, M.A., Goldsmith, H.H., & Robertson, R.R.W. (1992). Do readers mentally represent fictional characters' emotional states? *Cognition and Emotion, 6*, 89–111.

Gernsbacher, M.A., Hallada, B.M., & Robertson, R.R.W. (1998). How automatically do readers infer fictional characters' emotional states? *Scientific Studies of Reading, 2*, 271–300.

Gernsbacher, M.A., & Hargreaves, D. (1988). Accessing sentence participants: The advantage of first mention. *Journal of Memory and Language, 27*, 699–717.

Gernsbacher, M.A., & Hargreaves, D. (1992). The privilege of primacy: Experimental data and cognitive explanations. In D.L. Payne (Ed.), *Pragmatics of word order flexibility* (pp. 83–116). Philadelphia: John Benjamins.

Gernsbacher, M.A., Hargreaves, D., & Beeman, M. (1989). Building and accessing clausal representations: The advantage of first mention versus the advantage of clause recency. *Journal of Memory and Language, 28*, 735–755.

Gernsbacher, M.A., & Jescheniak, J. (1995). Cataphoric devices in spoken discourse. *Cognitive Psychology, 29*, 24–58.

Gernsbacher, M.A., & Robertson, R.R.W. (1992). Knowledge activation versus sentence mapping when representing fictional characters' emotional states. *Language and Cognitive Processes, 7*, 353–371.

Gernsbacher, M.A., & Robertson, R.R.W. (1995). Reading skill and suppression revisited. *Psychological Science. 6*, 165–169.

Gernsbacher, M.A., & Robertson, R.R.W. (in press). The definite article "the" as a cue to map thematic information. In W.v. Peer & M. Louwerse (Eds.), *Thematics: Interdisciplinary studies.*

Gernsbacher, M.A., & Shroyer, S. (1989). The cataphoric use of the indefinite *this* in spoken narratives. *Memory and Cognition, 17*, 536–540.

Gernsbacher, M.A., & St. John, M.F. (in press). Modeling the mechanism of suppression in lexical access. In R. Klein & P. McMullen (Eds.), *Converging methods for studying reading and dyslexia.* Cambridge, MA: MIT Press.

Gernsbacher, M.A., Varner, K.R., & Faust, M. (1990). Investigating differences in general comprehension skill. *Journal of Experimental Psychology: Learning, Memory, and Cognition, 16*, 430–445.

Givón, T. (1979). From discourse to syntax: Grammar as a processing strategy. In T. Givón (Ed.), *Discourse and syntax, syntax and semantics.* New York: Academic Press.

Givón, T. (1992). The grammar of referential coherence as mental processing instructions. *Cognitive Science, 30*, 5–55.

Golden, R.M., & Rumelhart, D.E. (1993). A parallel distributed processing model of story comprehension and recall. *Discourse Processes, 16*, 203–237.

Haenggi, D., Gernsbacher, M.A., & Bolliger, C.M. (1993). Individual differences in situation-based inferencing during narrative text comprehension. In H. van Oostendorp & R. A. Zwaan (Eds.), *Naturalistic text comprehension: Vol. LIII. Advances in discourse processing* (pp. 79–96). Norwood, NJ: Ablex.

Kintsch, W. (1974). *The representation of meaning in memory.* Hillsdale, NJ: Lawrence Erlbaum Associates Inc.

Kintsch, W. (1977). On comprehending stories. In M.A. Just & P. Carpenter (Eds.), *Cognitive processes in comprehension* (pp. 33–62). Hillsdale, NJ: Lawrence Erlbaum Associates Inc.

Kintsch, W. (1988). The role of knowledge in discourse comprehension: A construction–integration model. *Psychological Review, 95*, 163–182.

Kintsch, W. (1990, January). *How readers construct situation models: The role of syntactic cues.* Paper presented at the First Winter Text Conference, Jackson Hole, WY.

Kintsch, W., & van Dijk, T.A. (1978). Toward a model of text comprehension and production. *Psychological Review, 85*, 363–394.

Lee, J. (1992). *On-line processing of pronoun resolution in reading.* Unpublished doctoral dissertation, Korea University, Seoul.

MacDonald, M.C., & MacWhinney, B. (1990). Measuring inhibition and facilitation effects from pronouns. *Journal of Memory and Language, 29*, 469–492.

McClelland, J.L., & Rumelhart, D.E. (1985). Distributed memory and the representation of general and specific information. *Journal of Experimental Psychology: General, 114*, 159–188.

McDonald, J.L., & MacWhinney, B. (1995). The time course of anaphor resolution: Effects of implicit verb causality and gender. *Journal of Memory and Language, 34*, 543–566.

Neath, I., & Knoedler, A. (1994). Distinctiveness and serial position effects in recognition and sentence processing. *Journal of Memory and Language, 33*, 776–795.

Rumelhart, D.E., & McClelland, J.L. (1986). *Parallel distributed processing: Explorations in the microstructure of cogntion: Vol. 1. Foundations.* Cambridge, MA: MIT Press.

Sanford, A.J., & Garrod, S.C. (1981). *Understanding written language: Explorations of comprehension beyond the sentence.* Chichester, UK: John Wiley & Sons.

Sanford, A.J., & Garrod, S.C. (1994). Selective processing in text understanding. In M. A. Gernsbacher (Ed.), *Handbook of psycholinguistics* (pp. 699–723). San Diego, CA: Academic Press.

Sanford, A.J., Moar, K., & Garrod, S.C. (1988). Proper names as controllers of discourse focus. *Language and Speech, 31*, 43–56.

Shaibe, D.M., & McDonald, J.L. (1993, November). *Why is the president less accessible than Hillary?* Paper presented at the annual meeting of the Psychonomic Society, Washington, DC.

Sharkey, N.E. (1990). A connectionist model of text comprehension. In D.A. Balota, G.B. Flores d'Arcais, & K. Rayner (Eds.), *Comprehension processes in reading* (pp. 487–513). Hillsdale, NJ: Lawrence Erlbaum Associates Inc.

Sun, Y. (1997). *The immediacy effects in pronoun resolution in Chinese comprehension.* Diploma thesis, Beijing Normal University, Beijing, China.

Swinney, D.A. (1979). Lexical access during sentence comprehension: (Re)consideration of context effects. *Journal of Verbal Learning and Verbal Behavior, 18*, 645–659.

Tanenhaus, M.K., Leiman, J.M., & Seidenberg, M.S. (1979). Evidence for multiple stages in the processing of ambiguous words in syntactic contexts. *Journal of Verbal Learning and Verbal Behavior, 18*, 427–440.

Van Dijk, T.A. (1972). *Some aspects of text grammars.* The Hague, The Netherlands: Mouton.

Van Dijk, T.A. (1977). Semantic macro-structures and knowledge frames in discourse comprehension. In M.A. Just & P. Carpenter (Eds.), *Cognitive processes in comprehension* (pp. 3–32). Hillsdale, NJ: Lawrence Erlbaum Associates Inc.

Van Dijk, T.A., & Kintsch, W. (1983). *Strategies of discourse comprehension.* New York: Academic Press.

CHAPTER TEN

Word meaning and discourse processing: A tutorial review

Anthony J. Sanford
Human Communication Research Center, Department of Psychology, University of Glasgow, UK

INTRODUCTION

The focus of this chapter is on the role of meaning in the comprehension of text. Our concern is almost entirely restricted to listening to or reading text, rather than with interactive dialogue. To the extent that meaning depends upon word meaning, we discuss some of the literature on accessing word meaning, but with an emphasis on how access relates to the processing of discourse. In this way, the treatment is meant to complement that of Moss and Gaskell (Chapter 3). Similarly, meaning in discourse is closely related to discourse processing, as discussed by both Garnham (on reference) and Gernsbacher (on integration). Our course will be between these two approaches.

OPEN- AND CLOSED-CLASS WORDS

It is important to distinguish between open- and closed-class words. Open-class words, sometimes called content words, include terms of substance such as nouns, verbs, and adjectives, while closed-class words, sometimes called function words, include prepositions, connectives, and other function terms. Essentially, although the number of closed-class words in a language remains constant, new open-class words may be introduced at any time. Open-class words can *refer* to things (nouns) and attributes of things (adjectives), and to actions, events, or states (verbs), and to the manner and intensity of these (adverbs). In contrast, closed-class words do not refer to anything. For instance, *but* and *and* cannot refer. Rather, what they do is to give us tools to set up different arguments in relation to each other. This distinction is not new, going back to Aristotle's distinction between material and formal meanings (Lyons, 1968, p. 435). Linguists sometimes even refer to closed set items as grammatical items and open set as lexical items.

From a processing perspective, we shall pursue the idea that open- and closed-class words function differently in the process of understanding discourse. Specifically, open-class words provide pointers to world knowledge, and it is this world knowledge which is manipulated in the mind of the reader during understanding. In contrast, closed-class words (like syntax) contribute to the *way* in which knowledge is manipulated. An extreme form of this argument is that closed-class words serve primarily, if not wholly, as instructions for mental operations to be carried out, whereas open-class words serve as cues as to which pieces of knowledge are to be operated upon.

Meaning, pragmatics, and significance

When we hear a sentence and say that we know what it means, we appreciate both the meaning of the sentence (semantics), and what the speaker intended it to mean. We also appreciate how it fits into a wider intended context. That is, we appreciate its significance. If we do not appreciate the significance of an utterance, we may end up by saying things such as "I know what you are saying but I don't see what you mean". Meaning and significance are separable concepts, and are typically illustrated by means of the distinction between a true utterance and an utterance which is both true and informative. Suppose that somebody tells you that *Nobody passed the psychology finals at the Rob Roy University in 1970*. A search for records of passes in 1970 does indeed yield no examples of passes. It is then *true* that nobody passed. But now suppose that you discover that there was no psychology course at the Rob Roy in 1970. It is still true that nobody passed, but the utterance is clearly misleading, since it led you to suppose that there was such a course even though there wasn't, and the significance you gave to the utterance was therefore wrong. The utterance wasn't sufficiently informative, and was therefore misleading.

This simple illustration shows the difference between sentence meaning (what is true or false given a statement) and significance, and shows the importance of the intention we attribute to the speaker (or "speaker meaning") in establishing significance. Sentence meaning (semantics) is concerned with what is necessarily true. If there was no course in psychology in our example, then nobody passed it! But beyond what is necessary is what is implied (pragmatics): The implication is that if I say nobody passed a course, then that course was on offer. But this implication is *defeasible*: it can be falsified without affecting the truth of the sentence, as we have seen. Obviously, in communication we assume that a speaker or writer will not signal false implications (Grice, 1975).

As we have indicated, the distinction is one between the meaning of a sentence and the meaning of an utterance, which includes the intended meaning of the speaker. The meaning of an utterance includes the pragmatic implicatures intended by the speaker, whereas the meaning of a sentence does not. Sentence meaning and utterance meaning are thus just other terms signalling the inclusion or exclusion of pragmatics respectively. Although it might be argued that sentence meaning could be derived from the meanings of the words of a sentence, speaker meaning requires an interpretation in which the intention, the goals, of the speaker are inferred by the listener.

Although much work on language comprehension has treated the processing of meaning simply as retrieving the meaning of words, in this chapter we shall take a broader view of the processing problem by including a number of phenomena which bring in pragmatics and speaker meaning, such as metaphor and indirect speech acts.

Compositionality

One view of meaning, that it is compositional, assumes that each word (or more strictly, morpheme) in a sentence contributes its meaning to the total meaning of a sentence, and that the meanings of words are made up of aggregates of simple, primitive, features. The meaning of a sentence is the sum of the meanings of the words making it up. From a processing perspective, this suggests that when a word is encountered, there is a process of lexical access during which its meaning is retrieved. Then follows a process of lexical integration, during which the meaning of the word is incorporated into the meaning representation of the sentence. Finally, the entire sentence might be incorporated into the discourse to date (corresponding to significance establishment). This stagewise sequence is superficially attractive for a number of reasons. First, it keeps word meanings modular. Meanings are accessed and utilised when words are encountered. Second, it follows compositionality. By putting together the meanings of words, the meaning of a sentence is established.

There are questions raised by such a scheme, however. For instance, when an ambiguous word such as *bank* is read, are both meanings retrieved and later sorted out by context, or does prior context bias what is retrieved? When we read a metaphor, like *John's wife is a tiger*, do we first discover that it is literally nonsense and then go on to interpret it as a metaphor? These questions are amongst those addressed in the present chapter.

Incrementality and partial processing

Are the words of a discourse semantically interpreted as they are read or heard, or is there a delay in interpretation until, say, a complete sentence is encountered? There are obvious advantages to interpreting each word as it is encountered: There is less load on memory, for instance. On the other hand, immediate interpretation may lead to error. Examples of problems due to early interpretation are well-recognised. Compare the following pair of sentences:

(1) The steel ships are transporting is heavy.
(2) The granite carpets are covering up is ugly.

Intuitively there is a problem with (1) that is absent in (2), borne out by performance data (Kramer and Stevens, described in Rumelhart, 1977) and this is because *the steel ships* forms a coherent semantic structure, whereas *the granite carpets* does not. The result is that *the steel ships* comes (erroneously) to be treated as a noun-phrase, whereas *the granite carpets* (correctly) does not. Semantic analysis is being used in parsing here, but the outcome of such possibly incremental processing is that a garden path is created.

Coherence and meaning

The objective during reading or listening is to achieve a coherent mental representation of what is being said. Theories of discourse processing have evolved around accounts which might specify how coherence is achieved. From a linguistic perspective, there has been considerable emphasis on what it is about the structure of a *text* which makes it coherent. For instance, there are many devices in text which cue semantic relations, such as connectives like *because* (signalling causality) and *then*, signalling succession. These and other devices are called cohesion markers (e.g. Halliday & Hasan, 1976). But coherence is not simply determined by what is in a text. Indeed, work from artificial intelligence in the 1970s emphasised the role that world knowledge played in the establishment of coherence. A simple example is: *John fell over the cliff. The path was eroded.* Here, the inference that John had been walking on an eroded path is made, and the knowledge that eroded paths can be dangerous is utilised. It is easy to acknowledge the role of world knowledge on coherence establishment, but it is quite another thing to model how it is utilised. One of the major challenges of discourse processing is to work out how context and world knowledge is used to enable the significance of utterances to be established. From the point of view of a semantic representation, world knowledge can fill in semantic relations that are not explicit. Not all semantics derive from the text.

The organisation of this chapter

In the next section we ask when meaning is accessed. Is it accessed immediately, as each word is encountered? Does context influence how word meanings are accessed, and do the influences take place as soon as the word is encountered? In fact, in the case of ambiguous words, we can ask how context determines which sense of the word is selected. These issues are addressed in the second section. In the third section we tackle a related but different question: To what extent is the whole meaning of a word recruited during interpretation, or are only aspects of the meanings of words accessed, as determined by context. In sum, these sections concern the immediacy with which meaning and significance is established, and the contribution that lexical semantics makes to the meaning of sentences.

Next, we go on to consider cases in which interpretations are non-literal, including indirect speech acts, and metaphors. In fact, the problem of non-literal meaning relates very directly to the question of the role of context in interpretation, and we end with some discussion of how this section links with evidence presented in the preceding sections.

The final section is concerned with a discussion of how function words and expressions serve the interpretation of discourse.

MEANING ACCESS: TIME-COURSE AND CONTEXT

Detection of violations of meaning and significance

The idea that meanings are accessed rapidly is related to the notion of incremental interpretation. According to this idea, fragments of language are processed as soon as they are encountered. One question is whether word meaning is accessed as soon as the word in question is encountered, that is, whether word meaning is accessed incrementality. Several studies have suggested it might be, Thus, using shadowing of continuous speech, Marslen-Wilson (1973, 1975) found evidence for incremental processing. In reading, one of the most compelling recent studies showed effects of word plausibility as a function of context on the very first fixations made during reading. Traxler and Pickering (1996) monitored subjects' eye-movements while they read sentences like those in (3a)–(3d):

(3a) That's the pistol with which the man shot the gangster yesterday afternoon.
(3b) That's the garage with which the man shot the gangster yesterday afternoon.
(3c) That's the pistol in which the man shot the gangster yesterday afternoon.
(3d) That's the garage in which the man shot the gangster yesterday afternoon.

Sentences (3a) and (3d) are plausible, but (3b) and (3c) are not. The very first fixations on the word *shot* were longer in the implausible conditions than in the plausible conditions, and very first fixations clearly indicate very early discovery of those cases in which the word *shot* was anomalous. These studies all demonstrate that meaning of a word becomes available, at least to some extent, as soon as the word is encountered, and that the meaning is evaluated against a representation of the preceding context.

Results of studies by Garrod and Sanford (1985) and Garrod, Freudenthal, and Boyle (1993) with written texts show a checking of the meaning of a word at the level of discourse-based significance at the point where that word appears. Specifically, the experiments used materials that introduced characters who carried out various actions. Later in the materials, further actions were introduced that were either consistent with or at odds with the earlier actions. To understand that the verb of the new action was not appropriate, the verb meaning must be compared with the goals or states of the appropriate individual. In this way, the significance of the new action is established as coherent or incoherent. Using an error detection paradigm (Garrod & Sanford, 1985) and an eye-tracking analysis (Garrod et al., 1993) it was shown that inconsistencies were detectable on the target verb itself, rather than downstream of this point.

The work just discussed has the merit of relying upon a relatively natural mode of presentation, but the general findings are supported by word-by-word procedures, including studies of brain electrophysiological responses. The averaged event-related potential obtained to words that do not fit the preceding context for semantic reasons show an enhanced negative deflection, relative to a mastoid reference, over control words at around 400 ms after word onset (hence the name N400 for the deflection) (Kutas & Hillyard, 1980a, 1980b; Neville, Nicol, Barss, Forster, & Garrett, 1991). Insofar as word-by-word presentation is an acceptable approximation to normal reading, these results show that anomalies have a cortical effect within 400 msec of word onset, indicating that some aspect of meaning has been accessed within that time, and related to prior context.

Ambiguity resolution and the access of meaning

In order to obtain a satisfactory representation of sentence meaning, the processor must select the correct sense of a word when that word has multiple senses. For instance, the word *bank* in (4a) has the sense of a financial instituion, whereas in (4b) it has the sense of the side of a river:

(4a) Mary needed to buy some presents, so she went to the bank.
(4b) Mary found the river cold, so she swam to the bank.

The fact that these sentences are intelligible relies upon a process of sense selection, based on surrounding context. Note that sense selection can take place without difficulty even when the disambiguating context is some way downstream:

(5) Harry made for the bank because the water in the river was flowing too quickly for his canoeing skills to cope with.

The fact that (5) is quite intelligible raises the question of whether disambiguation takes place as soon as possible with prior context, as in (4a).

In fact, particular attention has been paid to how disambiguation takes place with the context-first case. This emphasis is useful for two reasons. First, it enables one to discover the time-course of interpretation, and second, it has a bearing on the question of whether the lexicon, and its access, is modular. There are two rather different processes that could take place when the ambiguous word (*bank*) is encountered: Either both lexical entries could be made active, and the appropriate one selected later, or just one could be made active, determined by prior contextual guidance. These perspectives underlie two theoretical positions. First, the modular position which assumes a separate module for the lexicon (Fodor, 1983), and so claims that when a word is read the lexicon is first addressed, and only after that does context play a role in selecting the appropriate meaning. Second is the interactive position (McClelland & Rumelhart, 1981; Morton, 1969), which supposes that context and lexical access interact directly. Interest in these issues is tied to the general problem of identifying that which is modular and that which is interactive in cognition.

Swinney (1979) carried out important early work in this area, using the cross-modal priming paradigm. He presented subjects with spoken passages like (2), and, immediately after the auditory presentation of the ambiguous word, he presented a single letter-string on a screen. Subjects had to decide whether the letter string was a word or not (lexical decision). When the string was a word, it could either be related to the intended sense of the ambiguous word (e.g. *money*), related to the other sense (e.g. *mud*), or unrelated to either. It has long been known that the time to recognise a letter string is less if that string is related in meaning to a previous word (e.g. Meyer & Schvaneveldt, 1971). In Swinney's case, the question was whether there would be a response time advantage for the intended-sense associate alone, or whether there would also be an advantage for the other-sense associate. It turned out that there was equal advantage (priming) for both senses. So, context did not appear to affect initial sense selection. However, if there was a delay of only 300 ms between hearing the ambiguous word and reading the letter string, then the priming effect remained only with the intended (contextually cued) sense.

These data suggest that both senses of an ambiguous word are activated when the word is first read, but that prior context quickly inhibits the "wrong" meaning. Other studies have replicated this result (e.g. Onifer & Swinney, 1981; Seidenberg, Tanenhaus, Leiman, & Bienkowsi, 1982), and offered apparent support for the modular position. But subsequent work has called this earlier interpretation into question, and provided evidence which is not compatible with the strictly modular account. For instance, McClelland (1987) examined the now classic data from Swinney (1979), Tanenhaus, Leiman, and Seidenberg (1979), and Seidenberg et al. (1982) and found that, overall, there was a priming advantage for the contextually appropriate targets over the contextually inappropriate ones. An extensive meta-analysis by St. John (1991) concluded that there was an immediate bias towards the contextually appropriate sense. This appears to be at odds with the modular position, but there is a complication in that it can always be argued that the targets were being presented after enough of a delay for the influence of context to come in after initial lexical access. In fact, the whole issue could easily be construed as one of how to define what "immediately after" means in terms of neural mechanisms.

Happily, there are other ways of tackling the problem. For instance, Van Petten and Kutas (1987) used a single-mode priming paradigm, with visual presentation, and required subjects to name the targets, and they also measured ERP responses to the targets. In the first (priming) experiment, they produced data very like the original Swinney data: At 200 ms SOA, there was facilitation of the targets related to both the contextually appropriate and the inappropriate meaning; at 700 ms SOA, there was priming only of the associate of the appropriate sense.

A further experiment showed a more interesting pattern. In this study, they recorded event-related potentials (ERPs) from the subjects as they did the priming task. The idea was that if both senses are selected at a 200 ms SOA, then the N400, indicating semantic mismatch, should be the same for both the associates of both senses. This did not happen. At 200 ms, the N400 response to the appropriate meaning began some 200 ms before the response to the inappropriate meaning. Van Petten and Kutas say this shows that the contextually inappropriate meanings are accessed *later* than the appropriate one. This experiment is good because there is no question of whether there is some vanishingly small influence of context on the sense-selection process; the activation of the inappropriate meaning is simply delayed. The ERP findings are more consistent with the interactive type of account than with any other. What of the priming results in general? It is possible that the results of the naming and more particularly lexical decision experiments reflect a process in which the processor attempts to integrate the target word into the text, and in so doing, the inappropriate sense will be activated, but not because it was active before the target word came along. This effect, so-called backwards integration, is a general problem for the priming paradigm in the present and other applications (see e.g. Glucksberg, Kreuz, & Rho, 1986 and Burgess, Tanenhaus, & Seidenberg, 1989 for counter-arguments).

At the time of writing, research on the time-course of sense selection is at a point where neither the simple selective access model (in which context activates the appropriate meaning only), or multiple access (in which all meanings of a word are activated equally prior to the operation of context) appears adequate. Much of the problem arises from the fact that dominant senses of words become active before non-dominant meanings. Thus, more recent work (e.g. Sereno, 1995) shows that both of these positions would need to be modified to account for the data. In the reordered access model, for instance, it is assumed that alternative senses of an ambiguous word are activated in order of their meaning frequency, and context can "boost" the activation of the appropriate sense. This amounts to a softened version of the selective access account to take account of dominant sense effects. Relaxing the multiple access account gives rise to the Integration Model, in which again alternative senses are activated in order of their meaning frequency again, but context operates on these meanings as they become available. It is assumed that successful integration of one meaning might terminate incomplete access procedures of other meanings. Although this latter account preserves the modularity of the lexicon, it produces results which are difficult to discriminate from the reordered access model. Experimental work by Sereno (1995) using a fast-priming procedure associated with eye-tracking measures found evidence offering marginal support to the reordered access model.

Contextual effects with unambiguous words

A similar set of questions to those raised by ambiguity resolution can be raised with respect to unambiguous words. For instance, with the sentence *The men lifted the piano*, the aspect of *piano* to do with its *weight* is important, whereas with *The woman played the piano*, it is its function that is important. It has been amply demonstrated that listeners use contextual information to sharpen their interpretations of words. Thus using a cued recall task, Garnham (1979) showed that the word *fried* was a better recall cue for the sentence *The housewife cooked the chips* than is the word *cooked*, even though the latter actually occurred in the sentence. Thus, the context of making chips specifies a certain type of cooking, and it is possible to think of the resulting effect as being a specification on the concept of *cook*. Such off-line investigations as these do not address the issue of when and how context might influence the selection of different aspects of the meaning of expressions, however. Tabossi (1988) carried out an experiment to test when context had an effect on selecting aspects of meaning. She examined the effect of context sentences on word recognition in a lexical decision context. For instance, consider the test word YELLOW. Three types of context were used, a neutral context, one biasing yellow, and one biasing some other aspect:

- At the lecture the good teacher spoke at length about gold. (Neutral: no aspect of gold is cued)
- In the light the blond hair of the little girl had the lustre of gold. (Facilitating: cues gold is *yellow*)
- In the shop the artisan shaped with ease the bar of gold. (Irrelevant: cues gold is *malleable*)

Using a cross-modal priming paradigm, with a spoken context and a visual test string, Tabossi found that decision times were fastest for the facilitating context, and slowest for the irrelevant. She interpreted her results as showing that contextual constraint causes an immediate boosting of the relevant aspects of a word. She views this as evidence against the modular view in which word meaning is first retrieved, and then context operates on the product of retrieval. But the same problems arise here as with the studies of lexical disambiguation: The results may be due to backwards integration. A further problem is that, with spoken words, there is evidence that a word is identified (i.e. its semantics become accessible) at the point where there is enough acoustic information to uniquely identify it (Marslen-Wilson, 1987; see also Moss & Gaskell, Chapter 3), Consequently, with Tabossi's study, it may be the case that context influences the word after it has been uniquely identified. With such critical timing questions being involved, it is difficult to accept any hard-and-fast claims about precisely when context exerts an influence beyond noting the extremely important fact that it seems to be a prompt process indeed. From a broader perspective, the fact that aspects of the meanings of a noun can be favoured over others as a result of context in the powerful way demonstrated earlier raises the question of how selective semantic processing might enter into discourse processing proper.

To summarise, there is evidence for early access to word meaning upon encountering a word, and there are early influences of context on the access process, both in terms of sense selection, and in terms of selecting aspects of meaning for single-sense words. Regardless of the modularity issue, the important things are that there is selective activation of aspects of word meaning as a function of context, and that this selectivity operates very rapidly. Semantic information certainly becomes available very soon after a word is encountered during reading or listening, and may be influenced by context from the outset.

The sense-selection work indicates a selectivity of aspects of meaning associated with a particular grapheme string which survive for subsequent processing, and work like that of Tabossi (1988) on unambiguous words suggests that context may highlight or inhibit various aspects of word meaning quite early on during processing. This relates to the more general question of just how much semantic information becomes available when a word is encountered during reading or listening, a topic tackled in the next section.

THE EXTENT OF SEMANTIC ANALYSIS IN DISCOURSE PROCESSING

How much information is retrieved when the meaning of a word enters into processing? Just what is the contribution of each word to the meaning of a sentence or larger piece of text? Moss and Gaskell (Chapter 3) argue on the basis of priming studies that a very wide range of semantic information becomes available when a word is encountered. But some very recent work on priming suggests that there is a differential time-course for the retrieval of different kinds of semantic information from words in isolation (e.g. Moss, McCormick, & Tyler, 1995). In particular, for artificial objects at least, aspects of objects to do with their function seems to be accessible more readily than do aspects concerned with their visual form. During a dynamic process such as reading or listening, it may well be that not all aspects of the meaning of a word are accessed. In this section, we examine what work on failures to detect anomalies tells us about partial, or incomplete, processing.

The recruitment of word meanings allows anomalies to be detected. For instance, the sentence *John was feeling hungry so he ate his hat* is spotted as anomalous because hats do not fit the specification of something normally considered edible. However, there are circumstances under which it can be shown that semantic analysis can be very shallow indeed, and may typically be so. The primary data for this come from *failures* to detect anomalies.

The Moses illusion

Erickson and Mattson (1981) asked subjects to answer the question: *How many animals of each sort did Moses put on the Ark?* The typical answer was "two". What is going on here? Although this is the typical answer it is incorrect: it was not Moses who put the animals on the Ark, but Noah. Subjects typically fail to notice the anomaly, producing the effect that is now dubbed the Moses Illusion. Reder and Kusbit (1991) have shown that not only is the phenomenon easy to reproduce with different materials, it turns out that subjects will miss the anomalies even when they are explicitly instructed to watch out for them.

Several factors determine whether or not an anomaly is likely to be detected. First, to be missed, the anomalous word has to be semantically related to the non-anomalous word one would normally use. For instance, if *Nixon* is used instead of *Moses*, it will not be missed. Also, if *Adam* is used instead of *Moses*, it will be less likely to be missed. *Nixon* is not semantically similar to *Noah*; and *Moses* is judged more similar to *Noah* than is *Adam* (Erickson & Mattson, 1981; van Oostendorp & de Mul, 1990; van Oostendorp & Kok, 1990). So, it is not the case that the effect results from people simply failing to process the critical words.

The data suggest that the phenomenon is plainly semantic; experiments show that it is not phonological in that phonological similarity between an anomalous term and the corresponding correct term does not influence error rates (Erickson & Mattson, 1981). Erickson and Mattson suggested an account related to a feature-theory of meaning. They propose that substantive things denoted by proper nouns will have very large numbers of features, but that most of these will be irrelevant in any particular context. For this reason, an exhaustive test of the match of all features to the context will not take place (and may not be possible, even in principle). So, a few dominant and initially available features are tested, and if the fit to context is good, then further tests are not carried out. In this way, an anomalous item which fits well on the basis of initial tests may be missed. A similar case may be made in terms of other types of processing mechanism.

The idea of incomplete feature processing is not new. In the earlier semantic memory literature, the pattern of response latencies obtained for verifying statements of the type *a robin is a bird*, and *a whale/robin is a fish* has been explained in terms of how long it takes to obtain a criterion number of feature matches or mismatches between the proposed exemplar and the category (see Smith, Shoben, & Rips, 1974). The criterion may be considered to be under subjective control, and the fact that in the "Moses" type of task, explicit instructions to look for anomalies result in a higher detection rate than with no such instructions suggests that the evaluation process behind the Moses Illusion may be similarly under subjective control to some extent (compare Erickson & Mattson, 1981, with Reder & Kusbit, 1991).

A study of the Moses Illusion by Bredart and Modolo (1988) showed that the amount of processing given to a word depends upon linguistic factors. They compared the probability of detection of the error with a sentence in which Moses was the topic (6a), with one in which he was not (6b). Subjects had to say whether the sentence was true or false:

(6a) It was Moses who put two of each kind of animal on the Ark.
(6b) Moses put two of each kind of animal on the Ark.

Sentence (6a) is an answer to the question *Who put two of each kind of animal on the Ark?*, the focus being on *Moses*. In this case, detection was high. In contrast, *Moses* is not in linguistic focus in (6b), and anomaly detection was much lower. So, such as it is the evidence suggests that the amount of semantic analysis afforded a word appears to depend upon whether that word is part of the linguistic focus of the sentence. Analysis is thus not uniformly deep, and is correlated with linguistic focus. More substantial demonstrations of this idea are required.

In discourse understanding more generally, coherence depends upon a good fit of each part of a sentence to the role-slot to which it is to be assigned. For instance, to say *Jack had some pitch for tea* is incoherent, because *pitch* is not edible. In this case, the fit is very poor and detection takes place. Barton and Sanford (1993) explored anomaly detection with this example:

> There was a tourist flight travelling from Vienna to Barcelona. On the last leg of the journey, it developed engine trouble. Over the Pyrenees, the pilot started to lose control. The plane eventually crashed right on the border. Wreckage was equally strewn in France and Spain. The authorities were trying to decide where to bury the survivors.
>
> *What is your solution to the problem?*

Not all subjects notice that it is not appropriate to bury survivors! Using this as a single case for study, Barton and Sanford uncovered what factors influence detection. First, it appeared that the core meaning of a word plays a greater role than what the use of the word presupposes. For example, the word *survived* has as its core meaning "alive after a life-threatening event", while the word *injured* has as its core meaning "body is damaged". However, we would only use the term injured to describe people when they are alive—in other words, *injured* presupposes being alive, whereas being alive is part of the core meaning of *survived*. Barton and Sanford showed that when the word *injured* was substituted for *survivors* in their passage, the anomaly detection rate fell even further. This they attributed to the core meaning becoming active prior to any presuppositions.

Other findings from this case study included it being easier to detect the term *survivors* as anomalous when the term fits the general scenario less well. So, when the event was a crash between bicycles, death was judged as less likely to result, and it turned out that the anomalous use of *survivors* was more readily detected. On the basis of these and other experiments, Barton and Sanford (1993) suggested that the sentences of a text call up background knowledge specific to the situation being depicted. If the anomalous word readily fits into this scenario, then this early good-fit reduces further analysis, and the anomaly may be missed. The probability of the anomaly being missed depends upon whether the inconsistent information is part of the lexical-semantic information first accessed (the core meaning in the example described here).

All of these observations show that the analysis of the meaning of words in discourse can be quite shallow. This may seem like a fault but we have already suggested that there is no such thing as a *complete* semantic analysis, so the question becomes one of where the processor draws the line. There are other advantages to shallow processing: Much of natural speech is technically ungrammatical, full of errors of one sort or another, so the comprehension system has to be tolerant of errors. The comprehension system requires that speakers try to be co-operative with the listener in making the contributions appropriate (Grice, 1975), and it is precisely this which enables the system to get by with a shallow analysis. For instance, *where one might bury survivors* is a good question provided *survivors* is only analysed to give something like *Where might one bury people involved in the accident who need to be buried.* An obvious step in future research is to use other techniques, such as priming or eye-tracking, to investigate the dynamics of shallow processing in more detail.

NON-LITERAL INTERPRETATION

Up to now we have treated the processing of meaning in a relatively simplistic way, dealing with what is essentially sentence meaning. But it is often the case that sentence meaning does not equate with the speaker's intended meaning, and that what is conveyed by a sentence's meaning may be literally false. Two good examples of this are indirect speech acts and metaphors. These are commonplaces of communication, and show how an understanding of the computation of literal, or sentence meaning, is far from adequate to characterise the processing of meaning. The fact is that the literal meaning of indirect speech acts does not correspond to speaker meaning. For instance, consider asking for the salt by saying *Can you pass the salt?*, or asking *Can you tell me the time?*. As every junior schoolchild knows, the literal answer might well be *yes*, but that is not likely to be what the speaker intended. The problem then arises as to what role literal meaning plays in these examples, and how speaker meaning is derived.

Similar problems arise with metaphors. Although statements of similarity, such as *John is like his mother*, might be taken as literal assertions having truth values which may in principle be true, most metaphors are just literally false. For instance, *Some jobs are jails* cannot be true, yet as a metaphor it may be quite powerful; the same applies to *Adolf Hitler was a butcher*. Unless Adolf Hitler was in fact a butcher, the statement is literally false; it is simply the case that Adolf Hitler had certain attributes that might be said to be characteristic of a butcher, such as being responsible for large numbers of killings. This raises the question of what kind of processing underlies the comprehension of metaphors. As we shall see, the question is an important one, since there is some evidence that metaphorical thinking is pervasive in our use of language.

The traditional view of the processing of both indirect speech acts and metaphor, from philosophy and linguistics, is that the processor attempts to derive a literal (sentence-meaning) interpretation of the utterance, and when this proves impossible, meaningless, or inappropriate, looks for a meaning that differs from the literal sentence-meaning (Bach & Harnish, 1979; Searle, 1975, 1979; see Ortony, 1979). In terms of a series of processing operations, this may be formulated as follows (from Glucksberg & Keysar, 1990):

(a) Derive a literal interpretation of the utterance
(b) Assess the interpretability of that interpretation against the context of that utterance, and
(c) If that literal meaning cannot be interpreted, then and only then derive an alternative non-literal interpretation.

This formulates the idea that, in order to make an appropriate interpretation of a statement, we need to know whether it is meant to be literally true or not. But it makes strong assumptions about the processes underlying comprehension, which subsequent work has suggested may be incorrect.

Indirect speech acts

Although early work by Clark and Lucy (1975) seemed to provide preliminary support for this sort of model, in a later and extensive series of studies, Gibbs (1979, 1983) presented evidence to the contrary. Gibbs (1979) showed that people take no longer to process indirect requests, such as *Must you open the window?*, meaning *Do not open the window*, presented in story contexts, than to understand literal uses of the same expressions (in the present case, meaning *Need you open the window?*). These data suggest that people do not need to obtain a literal meaning first in order to comprehend an indirect speech act, which runs against the traditional model.

However, Clark (1979; Clark & Schunk, 1980) suggested that although there is no need for a literal interpretation to be made first, to recognise the speech act as indirect requires that a literal meaning is established at some point, and that it is established at the same time as a non-literal interpretation. The argument is based on the view that there is often good reason for listeners to take into account literal meaning during dialog. For instance, Clark and Schunk (1980) showed that the more the hearer is benefitted by the literal meaning of an utterance, the more polite that utterance is perceived to be. So, *May I ask you what the time is?* literally offers the speaker authority to say no, and is considered polite. On the other hand, *Shouldn't you tell me what the time is?* asks whether the speaker is under some obligation, and is considered less polite. Yet these two utterances have the same non-literal force (*Tell me what the time is*). If listeners compute politeness, then, according to this view, they have to compute literal meaning.

Although conceding that literal meanings may sometimes be established for indirect speech acts, Gibbs (1983) claimed that the literal meaning is not necessarily computed, particularly if the indirect request is "conventional". On the surface, to establish this would be to provide a further bit of evidence against the traditional model, since it specifies that literal meanings are necessarily established. Gibbs had subjects read stories that ended with critical sentences such as *Can't you be friendly?* In different stories, such a sentence was given a literal meaning (*Are you unable to be friendly?*) or an indirect interpretation (*Please be friendly*). After reading a passage, subjects performed a sentence judgment task: They had to decide whether a string of words was a grammatical sentence or not. Some of the strings were either the literal or the non-literal interpretation of the critical sentence. Gibbs prediction was that the literal context would prime the literal interpretation, and the non-literal context the non-literal interpretation, but *not* the literal interpretation. These results should be reflected in a priming effect on the sentence judgement. In two experiments, the results confirmed Gibbs's expectations. When the context biased the interpretation of the critical sentence towards a non-literal interpretation, then there was no priming of the literal interpretation.

These findings show that the applicability of the standard account is at best limited, although it must be noted that the comprehension of sentences in stories (reported speech) and actual interactions in dialog, are very different situations, so one should guard against simplistic comparisons of Clark's views and Gibbs's investigations. Nevertheless, work on metaphor comprehension reinforces the view that literal interpretation is not always necessary.

Metaphors and idioms

If metaphors (like any other utterance) were checked for literal truth first, then metaphors should take longer to process than literal statements. Also, if there is no need to take metaphorical meaning into account (for instance, in a task of deciding whether something is literally true), then the processor should not go on to the second stage of generating metaphorical interpretations.

Both of these predictions have been investigated and found to be false. First, Glucksberg, Gildea, and Bookin (1982) had subjects decide whether simple statements were literally true or false. For example, take *Some desks are junkyards*. This is literally false, and so the obvious metaphorical interpretation should not interfere with processing and the production of a "no" response. Yet it does. Compared with false sentences that have no obvious figurative meaning, such as *Some desks are roads*, they took longer to process, yielding a slower "no" response. Glucksberg et al. suggested that metaphorical meaning is computed automatically and that it can interfere with literal meaning computation, so testing literal meaning cannot be a prior, modular stage.

Dascal (1987) criticised this study, on the basis that the determination of something being literally false is difficult, and that in the face of the difficulty of trying to determine a literal meaning for the "false" cases, subjects encountered the metaphorical possibilities. Dascal thus argued that the results have no bearing on the processing of literally true sentences.

This criticism was met by Keysar (1989), who added additional evidence. His studies utilised a verification paradigm and also a reading time paradigm, and results from both of these suggested that the interpretation of Glucksberg et al. (1982) was justified. He created passages in which a context was generated that could provide support for a later target statement being literally true or literally false, and metaphorically true or metaphorically false, literal truth and metaphorical truth being orthogonal. In one experiment he created texts in which the crucial target sentences were either consistent (literally true and metaphorically true, or literally false and metaphorically false), or inconsistent (e.g. literally true but metaphorically false), Keysar found that in a verification task, verification times were longest for the inconsistent items.

In another experiment, Keysar investigated the time taken to read the target sentences as a continuation of the context sentences. Reading times were shortest when both literal and metaphorical meanings were plausible in context. Both results suggest that non-literal meanings were automatically generated, and were not constructed only after a literal interpretation had been found wanting. Readers appear to compute multiple contextually plausible interpretations, whether they are metaphorical or literal. Furthermore, discovery of a metaphorical meaning is not blocked even if a literal meaning *is* derivable. In short, the traditional theory is an incorrect specification of processing.

A processing account of metaphor

The traditional view also assumes a way in which a metaphor is treated when the sentence conveying it is found to be literally false. It is supposed that *My job is a jail* is understood by seeing it as a statement of similarity, that is, it means *My job is like a jail.* The idea that once literal meaning has failed, the statement is evaluated as portraying similarity is motivated by the idea that listeners assume that speakers assert the truth, so literal falsehood leads to a search for some way in which the statement is true. A statement of similarity is invariably true in some respect (Davidson, 1978).

Glucksberg and his colleagues (especially Glucksberg & Keysar, 1990) propose an account which is quite different. They suggest that metaphors are treated as slightly complex class-inclusion statements during processing. Thus, if someone asserts that *My surgeon is a butcher*, that is precisely what is meant. First, there are good reasons to reject the idea of converting a metaphor into a similarity assertion. Glucksberg (1991) uses the example of *My dog is an animal.* Although literally true, this, he claims, makes metaphorical sense in the same way *Rambo is an animal* makes sense. On the other hand, *My dog is like an animal* makes no sense at all, since a dog *is* an animal. Glucksberg says that if people want to make a similarity assertion, they can do so directly. Second, the idea that a metaphor is processed as a class inclusion statement makes sense if it is assumed that the vehicle of the metaphor defines an exemplar of a category. So, with *My dog is an animal, animal* stands for the category of things that are rough, violent, has antisocial qualities, etc. Glucksberg and Keysar suppose that what is being asserted is that *My dog* also belongs to this class.

Part of this argument has to do with the fact that not all categories have names, and that it is typical to refer to such classes by means of exemplars. For instance, in North American Sign Language, only basic categories (e.g. *chair*, *table*) have names; superordinates such as *furniture* do not, and are referred to by picking out a good exemplar or two during dialog. Viewed in this way, metaphors create the means to assign things to categories which may not themselves have names. Glucksberg and Keysar show that many phenomena which discriminate between good metaphors and unsuccessful ones can be explained by this theory. They also provide interesting evidence in support of the view that metaphors are not processed as indirect similarity statements.

Metaphorical structuring of concepts

It is important to stress that the processing of metaphor should not be considered abnormal in any way, to be treated as a special case compared to the processing of literal meanings. Metaphors are certainly much more prevalent than is normally realised (Cacciari & Glucksberg, 1994). Far from being restricted to specialist literary uses, they permeate our language in such a way that they surely must reflect something about the way our conceptual structures support understanding in general. A recent champion of this approach is the linguist George Lakoff (e.g. 1987; Lakoff & Johnson, 1980; see also Gibbs, 1994). Lakoff suggests that there are certain fundamental ways we adopt for thinking about other things. This kind of analogical thinking finds its way into our languages in striking ways. For example, Lakoff (1987) considers the concept of anger. There are many expressions relating to anger which if taken literally make no sense at all:

- John was so angry, he hit the ceiling.
- Mary blew her stack when she heard the news.
- When John broke the news, Mary exploded.
- The next thing we knew, there was steam coming out of his ears.

Lakoff claims that one way in which we conceptualise anger is in terms of heat being applied to a container which may contain a liquid (e.g. *She was boiling/seething*). He suggests that such an analogy is reasonable, because when we are angry we get hot and flushed, blood pressure goes up, and so on. The results of this are boiling, steaming, etc. Put a lid on the container (*Contain your anger*, *Put a lid on it*) and there is the possibility of increased pressure, the lid coming off (*he flipped his lid*) and ultimate explosion! In his case study of anger, Lakoff suggests many metaphors may be produced on this well-known, simple basis. Furthermore, it is possible to understand statements like *I thought he was going to erupt* because of these well-worn conceptual connections. If one overheard this statement in a conversation, one would be more likely to infer a conversation about anger than one about a spotty face, even though the statement could be literally true in the case of the spots.

Lakoff and his supporters have produced an interesting case for the role of generative metaphorical systems in structuring descriptions of many different things, some of them seeming a lot more innocuous than the anger example. For example, *up* standing for *good* and *down* standing for *bad*:

- I'm feeling down today.
- I feel low.
- I feel on top of everything.
- Everything is on top of me.
- John thought things were looking up.

None of these make any literal sense, but they are easy enough to understand. Many intriguing examples have been highlighted, using *container*, *journey*, *argument*, and *machine* as bases for many everyday constructions.

Some of these expressions are *idioms*, having no apparent connection to what they denote, even if they did at some time in the past. Other examples include *Kick the bucket*, *Pop the question*, and *Spill the beans*. The origins of these are for most people quite opaque, and so they appear to be arbitrary, and to have little if anything to do with literal meaning. Indeed, one prevalent view of idioms is that they are really just like single, complex, lexical items (e.g. Swinney and Cutler, 1979). This view is problematic because it does not explain why some things can be successfully changed in an idiom, whereas others cannot. For instance, instead of *break the ice*, one can say *crack the ice*, or even *shatter the ice* (Cacciari & Glucksberg, 1991). For instance, *The party was not going at all well; people were just sitting around talking to people they already knew. John got out his Fender Stratocaster. It was time to shatter the ice*. Gibbs (1991) suggests that although some idioms, like *kick the bucket*, may not be decomposable, others, like *crack the ice*, are. He argues that those which are decomposable allow a limited range of substitutions, whereas undecomposable ones do not. Why should some idioms be decomposable and others not? Gibbs suggests that decomposability results from the elements of the idiom mapping onto an underlying metaphorical-conceptual structure, rather like expressions about anger mapping onto ideas of heated liquids in a container. In support of this idea, Nayak and Gibbs (1990) and Gibbs (1992) report studies showing that an expression like *blew her stack* is more comprehensible in a story about the woman's anger being like heat in a pressurised container, whereas *she bit his head off* is more comprehensible in a context where anger is likened to causing the person to become a wild animal.

Lakoff believes that the conceptual system itself is fundamentally metaphorically structured, and that containers, journeys, arguments, and other universal human experiences provide a rich background into which all kinds of new things can be mapped. He tries to explain the widespread occurrence of metaphors related to these concepts in terms of their ubiquity in human experience. For instance, *up is good* may be related to the fact that in a fight, to be above an adversary is to be in a positive position.

It is fair to say that although Lakoff's views offer a potentially interesting way of developing accounts of human understanding, there is much need for rigorous experimentation in order to establish the processing consequences of his ideas. There has been some activity in this direction, particularly in the work of Gibbs and his associates, reviewed in Gibbs (1991). The relation of Lakoff's views to the Glucksberg category statement theory is not clear. In some ways, a Lakovian account of the conceptual system is not necessary for Glucksberg and Keysar's account, since no mechanism is offered by them through which the implicit categories might be identified, and no processing mechanism is offered by Lakoff to explain the means through which the conceptual system is utilised during comprehension. The accounts are not incompatible either, however (see Gibbs, 1992; Glucksberg, Keysar, & McGlone, 1992). Glucksberg and his colleagues do not deny the systematicity in metaphors, but they do question how much of it is involved in normal metaphor comprehension.

Non-literal meaning, schemata, and the broader processing framework

Work on metaphor and other forms of non-literal interpretation is just the tip of an iceberg. Although metaphors are rife in language, many other aspects of interpretation raise similar problems (Recanati, 1995). For instance, if someone in a restaurant orders a ham sandwich, a waitress may well tell a colleague, *The ham sandwich wants a coffee*. The term *The ham sandwich* refers to the person who will eat the sandwich. Other examples are less obviously problematic at first sight. For example, *John finished the book* could mean many things (finished reading it, finished tearing it up, finished writing it), with context providing the disambiguating cue, as it would with senses of *bank*. But more than that, the problem is that *finish* applies to a process, and *book* is not a process. So, in this case, it could be argued that if *finished* has its standard sense, then *the book* must be interpreted non-literally. On the other hand, if the book is interpreted literally, then *finished* could be taken as meaning *finished reading*.

Other examples from Recanati include *The city is asleep*, which would normally be taken as meaning *the inhabitants of the city are asleep*, in which case it is the term the city which has to receive a nonliteral interpretation. But if *asleep* is given a non-literal interpretation, then it could mean that the city itself shows little sign of activity. Which sentence constituent is taken as being non-literal and which literal must be under contextual control, albeit a default context? This latter example shows that sometimes which constituent is taken as literal and which as non-literal may influence meaning (unlike the case of *John finished the book*). This, claims Recanti, shows that the relation between literal and non-literal meaning is more complex than is normally acknowledged, and he claims that such problems are best solved through schema-based interpretation.

Precisely how context and existing biases operate with such examples is unclear, but it should be emphasised that these are very commonplace types of problem. Recanati makes an argument that computing literal meaning is of little help in many of these cases, and instead, he suggests that the constituents of a sentence map onto schemata in long-term memory (insofar as a suitable one can be retreived) (see e.g. Ortony, 1977, Sanford, 1987, and Sanford & Garrod, 1981 for a discussion of schema-based accounts of comprehension). A recovered schema then provides the full means for interpreting the sentence in question. He also suggests that context can influence the availability of schemata and so determine interpretation patterns.

The essence of schema-based understanding is that knowledge structures are activated by discourse as soon as possible, and are used for subsequent interpretation. Because they serve to "contextualise" utterances, schemata provide a general means of disambiguation. In fact, insofar as the sources of metaphors are schemata, it is easy to see that schema-based comprehension can encompass the processing of metaphors, as well as offering a principled treatment of disambiguation. These issues lead us towards the interface between the theories of discourse comprehension *per se* and semantics, and further exploration is beyond the scope of the present chapter.

FUNCTION WORDS AND CUE PHRASES IN SEMANTICS AND COHERENCE

We now move away from the semantics of content words and expressions to another issue raised in the introduction: function word semantics.

Function words play a vital role in determining meaning, they comprise an extremely heterogeneous group of words, and can even be combined to form complex expressions. A major function of these expressions is to indicate the ways in which the propositions of a text relate to one another, and how larger aspects of a text may fit together. One major class of semantic functions is *conjunctions*, which join propositions, and form two place predicates, as in examples such as *and (x, y)*, *but(x, y)*, *although (x, y)*. The other is *negation*, the most obvious of which is the simple one place predicate *not (x)*. We shall restrict our discussion here to some aspects of how conjunction and negation might work in processing terms.

General considerations

There have been attempts to make classifications of coherence relations. Since many function words trigger coherence relations, these taxonomies are ultimately relevant to the processing story, even though the classifications are not concerned with processing *per se*. One of the best known is Rhetorical Structure Theory (Mann & Thompson, 1986; 1988). This amounts to an attempt to describe possible relations holding between parts of text, and is based entirely on linguistic observation. There is a tacit assumption that each of the many relations they discuss have a cognitive reality, but no proof of this is offered. More recently, a genuine taxonomy was offered by Sanders, Spooren and Noordman (1992), with claims of psychological reality. Sanders et al.'s paper illustrates something of the richness of rhetorical relations and connectives which any processing account of meaning must ultimately address. In the same vein, Knott and Dale (1996) give a global consideration of what they term *cue phrases*, which range from connectives like *because* and *furthermore*, to other phrases indicating the general status of parts of a text, such as *at the outset*, *above all*, *eventually*, etc. These accounts must offer the discourse psychologist a happy hunting ground, the question being the manner in which such expressions influence the course of text processing, and when these influences come into play. The suggestion here is that, at the most basic level, they work by manipulating the operations carried out on the content part of the propositions of a text.

In the remainder of this section, we do no more than scratch the surface of some of the processing issues.

Connectives as processing aids

Connectives make explicit the kinds of relationships which hold between propositions, and they have been considered as fundamental to the coherence of a text (e.g. Halliday & Hasan, 1976). Yet, often a connective relation can be inferred between two statements even when no explicit connective is present. For example, with the sentence pair—*John walked out onto the thin ice. He drowned.*—readers will assume that being on the thin ice caused his death. One view of connectives, therefore, is that they serve as cues to help the construction of a suitable semantic representation linking together the assertions in a discourse.

This is perhaps the most general idea about connectives which is empirically testable, and has received some attention, most explicitly by Murray (1995), who investigated whether connectives facilitated interpretation.

To begin, consider causal connectives. There are many ways of expressing a fact such as *A causes B*, *B because A*, *On account of A, B*, *A so B*, *A therefore B*, *A hence B*, and so on. Causality is considered to be one of the major ways in which discourse attains coherence, and it has been suggested that during comprehension, particularly of narratives, the processor tries actively to produce a causal chain (e.g. Fletcher & Bloom, 1988; Keenan, Baillet, & Brown, 1984; Myers, Shinjo, & Duffy, 1987). It has been argued that, in general, discourse with a soundly perceived causal structure is easier to understand and recall than is discourse with weaker forms of connectedness (Caron, Micko, & Thuring, 1988; Haberlandt, 1982; Townsend, 1983). Specifically, Caron et al. (1988) reported that the presence of the causal connective *because* between two unrelated sentences led to better memory for these sentences than either *and* (an additive connective), *but* (an adversarial), or no connective, suggesting that *because* served to trigger a better integration of the material. However, Millis, Graesser, and Haberlandt (1993) reported results showing that causal connectives can actually inhibit memory compared to a no-connective condition if the sentences are easily integrated without the causal connective.

Murray carried out a series of experiments in which he looked for advantages of using an explicit connective. For instance, for the causal material in (7), the connective therefore was either present or absent during reading. The brackets contain the alternatives:

(7) Rudy and Tom fought with each other on the bus to the amusement park. {Therefore they/They} didn't speak to one another for the rest of the day.

He used materials with additive (e.g. *and*), causal (e.g. *because*), and adversative (e.g. *but*) connectives, and examined the reading times for the second sentences with the connective either absent or present. Only for the adversative relation did the presence of a connective speed up reading time. For the causal materials, the presence of a connective appeared to increase reading times. Furthermore, the presence of connectors did not influence memory at all. These results are interesting because they run counter to the simple claim that connectives facilitate integration by making the manner of integration explicit.

Other research has focused on how connectives bring about integration. For instance, Millis and Just (1994) propose the connective integration model, the basis of which is that when readers encounter a connective in statements of the form *A connective B*, they close processing on the first clause, holding information about this in a memory buffer, then process the second clause, and then integrate the two clauses, possibly at sentence wrap-up. As evidence, they cite a study in which subjects read either two single-clause sentences, or the same pairs of clauses combined by a connective (*because* or *although*) into single, complex sentences. The subject's task was to read the sentences, and decide whether a word probe presented at the end or beginning of the second clause or sentence had in fact been presented in the text itself. When they were positive probes, which had been in the text, they were either the main verb from the first sentence/clause, or the main verb from the second sentence/clause. When the probes were at the end of the second sentence/clause, readers responded more rapidly to the main verb of the first clause when the connective was present. When the probes were at the start of the second sentence/clause, no such facilitation occurred. This Millis and Just take as evidence that the first clause is reactivated after the second clause is processed in order to integrate the two. In effect, the connective acts as an instruction to the processor to put the first clause in a store, process the next clause, and then attempt an integration with the first clause.

Although this theory nicely illustrates the idea of how a class of function words (connectives) might serve as control intructions, there are problems with the account (Traxler, Bybee, & Pickering, 1996). Note that despite the earlier presented evidence for incremental interpretation effects, the connective integration model assumes that the first clause has no effect on the interpretation of the second clause until the second clause has received a preliminary interpretation—a kind of delayed integration. Traxler et al. show that the first clause does have an effect on the interpretation of the second clause, which is more consistent with the incremental account.

The materials rely on the finding that it is more difficult to read the second clause of (8a) than (8b) (Traxler, Sanford, Aked, & Moxey, 1997). This is essentially because in (8b) it has to be inferred that the second clause is evidence, rather than a cause, of what is portrayed in the first clause:

(8a) Mary felt cold when she went outside because her jumper had a big hole in it.
(8b) Mary had moths in her cupboard because her jumper had a big hole in it.

Traxler et al. (in press) were interested in whether the second clause of (8b), being slower to read, shows difficulties before the end of the clause is reached, or whether the difficulties are confined to the end (as the Millis and Just model would predict). Using an eye-tracking procedure, Traxler et al. were able to demonstrate that difficulties emerged on first pass eye-movements and regressions with sentences like (8b), so deferred integration was not supported. A more plausible theory is that, although connectives might trigger closure on the first clause, they also trigger incremental interpretation of the second clause with respect to the first. How these arguments apply to a full range of connectives remains to be established.

Processing negation and related phenomena

The bulk of psychological work on negation has been concerned with the logic of negation, and in particular with the way that negative sentences are processed during verification (truth-establishment) tasks. One fundamental finding is that negative statements take longer to process than positive findings. For instance, given a display of black dots, subjects are slower to evaluate the truth of the statement *The dots aren't red* than they are the statement *The dots are black* (Chase & Clark, 1972; Gough, 1966). Similar results hold with dual-clause sentences of the type *If John did not remember to put the dog out, then the dog is in.* If the first clause is negative, evaluating that the sentence is reasonable takes longer (Just & Clark, 1973). In general, it is supposed that the processing of sentences containing a negation marker takes longer because sentences are coded primarity in terms of a positive assertion. Negating this, through a marker, is a time consuming extra process.

This account, Clark's "True" model (Clark, 1976), is part of a more general framework for understanding how negation works. It is thought that negative statements are made when there is reason to suppose that what is being negated might have been the case. For instance, if I say *John did not go to the meeting*, I do so only if there was reason to suppose that he might have gone. Effectively, the negation denies the supposition that John went to the meeting, and its mental representation might be expressed as *false (John went to the meeting)*.

A direct test of this idea was carried out by Moxey and Sanford (1993a) using negative and positive quantifiers. Using a sentence like *Not many of the residents enjoyed the party*, they asked different groups of subjects to indicate:

(a) what percentage of residents the speaker might have expected to enjoy the party before he learned the facts
(b) what percentage of residents the speaker might have thought the *listener* would have expected before learning the facts.

A comparison was made with a positive sentence like *A few of the residents enjoyed the party*. The results showed that what was expected was higher for the negative *not many* than for the positive *a few*, consistent with the supposition denial position explicated by Clark.

Discourse comprehension does not normally involve the explicit testing of truth-values, and there is some evidence of how negation influences discourse processing when explicit evaluation is not required. First, negation affects the activation level of concepts. MacDonald and Just (1989) used a probe recognition task to test the activation of concepts after negation. For instance, subjects read a sentence like *Elizabeth baked some bread but no cookies*, and were asked whether the word *bread* (or *cookies*) had appeared in the text. They took longer to respond "yes" to the probe word corresponding to the negated concept (cookies) than to the un-negated one. When asked to read the probe word out loud instead of make a recognition judgement, essentially identical results were obtained. Thus, activation levels of recently negated concepts are lower than those not negated. This activation reduction appears to be restricted to the negated concept itself, in that associates of negated terms do not have reliably lower activation levels.

MacDonald and Just (1989) attribute these effects to the shifting of the negated concepts out of discourse focus; negation is functioning as an instruction not to pay attention to the negated concept. Further evidence of a focus-control function of negation comes from work on quantifiers reported by Moxey and Sanford (1987, 1993b). Whereas MacDonald and Just used activation level as an index of what is in focus, Moxey and her colleagues used ease of pronominal reference, arguing that a good test of which set is most accessible is to see which set is most easily referred to by means of a pronoun. Since nominal pronouns carry very little information, specifying only number and perhaps gender, in order to use one felicitously, it is necessary that a representation of the thing to which it will refer is unambiguously highlighted. Such a highlighting has been called foregrounding (e.g. Chafe, 1972) or focusing (e.g. Sanford & Garrod, 1981; see also Garnham, Chapter 11). So, if an entity is most easily refered to by a pronoun, we assume it has a special high-accessibility status. They tested examples like (9a) and (9b):

(9a) Many of the football fans went to the match.
(9b) Not many of the football fans went to the match.

Subjects were invited to write continuation sentences to examples such as these, starting with the pronoun *They*. Whereas the positives such as (9a) almost always gave continuations in which *they* referred to the fans who did go to the match (e.g. *They enjoyed the first half best*) the negatives (9b) gave a high proportion of continuations in which *They* referred to the fans who did not go to the match (e.g. *They stayed at home instead because the weather was atrocious*). A reading time experiment also showed that sentences referring back to the fans who were at the match gave the faster reading times for positives, and sentences referring back to fans who did not go to the match was best for negatives (Sanford, Moxey, & Paterson, 1996). Sanford et al. (1996) offered an explanation in which negatives are seen as first violating a supposition (Clark, 1976), which causes the start of a search for plausible reasons why the supposition was violated. This in turn leads to focus on the actions of the set of people who did not go the match. So they are favoured in continuations and in subsequent comprehension.

The processing of negation offers a good example of how function words can be construed as instructions to the processor to control focus and inference.

Incomplete and partial processing of semantic relations

In the case of content words, the Moses Illusion demonstrates how semantic processing is partial or shallow, and is under the control of a number of text variables. There is also evidence of incomplete processing of the semantic relations that make a text coherent. This is often obvious with sentences heavily laden with implicit and explicit negatives. The following example comes from Wason and Reich (1979):

(10) No head injury is too trivial to be ignored.

As they show, this is normally interpreted as meaning something like *However trivial a head injury is, it should not be ignored.* But in fact what it actually asserts is *However trivial a head injury, it should be ignored.* The reader can confirm this by noting that (10) has the same form as (11), and clearly means *however small a missile, it still should be banned*:

(11) No missile is too small to be banned.

Here is a failure of determination of the sentence's local semantic structure, which relies on utilising the implicit negativity in *ignored.* Wason and Reich present evidence showing that the interpretation given is more determined by what is pragmatically plausible than by anything else. Such examples clearly show incomplete processing at a local semantic level, and may well parallel lexical effects such as the Moses Illusion. In the case of the Moses Illusion, the fit of the word to the general background scenario was found to be a major determinant of the probability of detecting an error. In the case of Wason and Reich's example, the situation to which the sentence seems to refer (How small a head injury should be before it is ignored) lends ready top-down support for a particular interpretation, which leads to shallow semantic processing of semantic relationships, which would ultimately indicate an anomaly. This raises the very general question of whether the relationships that hold between all the aspects of a sentence are computed, and, if not, what is it that controls which ones are.

SUMMARY AND CONCLUSIONS

The principal points made in this review are as follows.

1. Incrementality. With content words, the evidence suggests that words are evaluated against prior context for how well they fit that context. Since this involves access to at least part of the meaning of those words, it suggests that at least some of the meaning of a word is accessed as soon as it is encountered in a sentence.

2. Early sense selection. When words are ambiguous, there is evidence to suggest that both meanings are initially retrieved, though this is complicated by which sense is dominant. After only a very short delay, the unwanted meaning is suppressed. Other evidence, notably from ERP data, suggests that only the contextually relevant meaning may be initially activated.

3. Partial processing. With unambiguous words, context can cause certain aspects of the word's meaning to become active, whereas others remain inactive. This appears to be an early process, and shows selective (or partial) availability of semantic information as a function of context. Perhaps more dramatically, when the context is strong enough, anomalous words may be missed. This shows that semantic processing can be shallow or incomplete. If a content word fits the context well, only the earliest available information is accessed. A major question for the role of semantic information in processing is what factors control the contribution made by each word, There is some evidence that linguistic focus leads to more extensive analysis. The fact that polarity appears to be unprocessed in some contexts opens up the very general question of how much specification is required in the mental representation of discourse for it to seem coherent.

4. Non-literal meaning. Although the simplest view of meaning would suppose that the meanings of each word in a sentence are combined to achieve an overall sentence meaning, indirect speech acts and metaphors pose problems for theories that only explain literal meaning establishment. The evidence suggests that literal meaning is not necessarily computed prior to non-literal interpretation, and that it may not be computed at all. Rather, meaning may be established by mapping expressions straight onto background knowledge that supports the metaphor. Since so much of our language seems to be metaphorical in nature (Lakoff, 1987), this may be a very general and widespread process. In this chapter, we have suggested that the mapping process might be a very fundamental one in the comprehension process. There has been little work to date on the time-course of processing non-literal meaning, but the issue is quite clearly related to the partial processing and lexical disambiguation questions.

5. Function words and cue-phrases. These serve to instruct the processor as to how aspects of content should be brought together. Function words signal relationships between propositions and utterances, although the presence of connectives, for instance, does not always facilitate speed of understanding. This may be because an explicit connective specifies a semantic relation at a level of detail which the processor may not require. Turning to negation, this may be signalled in a number of ways, including words that are explicitly or implicitly negative. There is evidence that negation influences the activation levels of concepts, and the kinds of inference which people make. Thus, negatives seem to have a selective function on processing.

In summary, traditional thinking about meaning portrays text as composed of the individual meanings of the words (or morphemes) that make it up. Consideration of both content and function words shows that a major problem is that only aspects of the potential meanings of expressions are in fact computed. The interest is in what *is* computed and under what circumstances.

In this chapter we have studied the role of meaning only with respect to discourse. Much is known about the semantics of a broad spectrum of words, but in many cases the effect in a discourse context has not been studied, leaving open a very interesting field of enquiry. Our efforts have been aimed at some of the more obvious problems of bringing together the fields of discourse processing and word meaning.

REFERENCES

Bach, K., & Harnish, R. (1979). *Linguistic communication and speech acts*. Cambridge, MA: MIT Press.

Barton, S., & Sanford, A.J. (1993). A case-study of pragmatic anomaly-detection: Relevance-driven cohesion patterns. *Memory and Cognition, 21*, 477–487.

Bredart, S., & Modolo, K. (1988). Moses strikes again: Focalization effects on a semantic illusion. *Acta Psychologica, 67*, 135–144.

Burgess, C., Tanenhaus, M.K., & Seidenberg, M.S. (1989). Context and lexical access: Implications of non-word interference for lexical ambiguity resolution. *Journal of Experimental Psychology: Learning, Memory, and Cognition, 15*, 620–632.

Cacciari, C., & Glucksberg, S. (1990). Understanding figurative language. In M.A. Gernsbacher (Ed), *Handbook of psycholinguistics*. New York: Academic Press.

Caron, J., Micko, H.C., & Thuring, M. (1988). Conjunctions and recall of composite sentences. *Journal of Memory and Language, 27*, 309–323.

Chafe, W. (1972). Discourse structure and human knowledge. In J.B. Carroll & R.O. Freedle (Eds.), *Language comprehension and the acquisition of knowledge*. Washington, DC: Winston.

Chase, W.G., & Clark, H.H. (1972). Mental operations in the comparison of sentences and pictures. In L. Gregg (Ed.), *Cognition in learning and memory* (pp. 205–232). New York: John Wiley & Sons.

Clark, H. (1976). *Semantics and comprehension*. The Hague, The Netherlands: Mouton.

Clark, H. (1979). Responding to indirect speech acts. *Cognitive Psychology, 11*, 430–477.

Clark, H., & Lucy, P. (1975). Understanding what is meant from what is said: A study in conversationally conveyed requests. *Journal of Verbal Learning and Verbal Behavior, 14*, 56–72.

Clark, H., & Schunk, D. (1980). Polite responses to polite requests. *Cognition, 8*, 111–143.

Dascal, M. (1987). Defending literal meaning. *Cognitive Science, 11*, 259–281.

Davidson, D. (1978). What metaphors mean. In S. Sacks (Ed.), *On metaphor* (pp. 29–45). Chicago: University of Chicago Press.

Erickson, T.A., & Mattson, M.E. (1981). From words to meaning: A semantic illusion. *Journal of Verbal Learning and Verbal Behavior, 20*, 540–552.

Fletcher, C.R., & Bloom, C.P. (1988). Causal reasoning in the comprehension of simple narrative texts. *Journal of Memory and Language, 27*, 235–244.

Fodor, J.A. (1983). *The modularity of mind*. Cambridge, MA: MIT Press.

Garnham, A. (1979). Instantiation of verbs. *Quarterly Journal of Experimental Psychology, 31*, 207–214.

Garrod, S.C., Freudenthal, D., & Boyle, E. (1993). The role of different types of anaphor in the on-line resolution of sentences in a discourse. *Journal of Memory and Language, 32*, 1–30.

Garrod, S.C., & Sanford, A.J. (1985). On the real-time character of interpretation during reading. *Language and Cognitive Processes, 1*, 43–61.

Gibbs, R. (1979). Contextual effects in understanding indirect requests. *Discourse Processes, 2*, 1–10.

Gibbs, R. (1983). Do people always process the literal meanings of indirect requests? *Journal of Experimental Psychology: Learning, Memory, and Cognition, 9*, 524–533.

Gibbs, R. (1991). Semantic analyzability in children's understanding of idioms. *Journal of Speech and Hearing Research, 34*, 613–620.

Gibbs, R. (1992). Categorisation and metaphor comprehension. *Psychological Review, 99*, 572–577.

Gibbs, R. (1994). Figurative thought and language. In M.A. Gernsbacher (Ed.), *Handbook of psycholinguistics* (pp. 411–446). New York: Academic Press.

Glucksberg, S. (1991). Beyond literal meanings: The psychology of allusion. *Psychological Science, 2*, 146–152.

Glucksberg, S., Gildea, P., & Bookin, H. (1982). On understanding nonliteral speech: can people ignore metaphors? *Journal of Verbal Learning and Verbal Behavior, 21*, 85–98.

Glucksberg, S., & Keysar, B. (1990). Understanding metaphorical comparisons: Beyond similarity. *Psychological Review, 97*, 3–18.

Glucksberg, S., Keysar, B., & McGlone, M.S. (1992). Metaphor, understanding, and accessing conceptual schema: A reply to Gibbs. *Psychological Review, 99*, 578–581.

Glucksberg, S., Kreuz, R.J., & Rho, S.H. (1986). Context can constrain lexical access: Implications for models of language comprehension. *Journal of Experimental Psychology: Learning, Memory, and Cognition, 12*, 323–335.

Gough, P.B. (1966). The verification of sentences: The effects of delay on evidence and sentence length. *Journal of Verbal Learning and Verbal Behavior, 5*, 492–496.

Grice, L.P. (1975). Logic and conversation. In P. Cole & J.L. Morgan (Eds.), *Syntax and semantics: Vol 3. Speech acts* (pp. 41–58). New York: Academic.

Haberlandt, K. (1982). Reader expectations in text comprehension. In J.F. Le Ny, & W. Kintsch (Eds.), *Language and comprehension*. The Netherlands: North-Holland.

Halliday, M.A.K., & Hasan, R. (1976). Cohesion in English. London: Longman.

Just, M.A., & Clark, H.H. (1973). Drawing inferences from the presuppositions and implications of affirmative and negative sentences. *Journal of Verbal Learning and Verbal Behavior, 19*, 668–682.

Keenan, J.M., Baillet, S.D., & Brown, P. (1984). The effects of causal cohesion on comprehension and memory. *Journal of Verbal Learning and Verbal Behavior, 23*, 115–126.

Keysar, B. (1989). On the functional equivalence of literal and metaphorical interpretation in discourse. *Journal of Memory and Language, 28*, 375–385.

Knott, A., & Dale, R. (1996). Using linguistic phenomena to motivate a set of coherence relations. *Discourse Processes, 18*, 35–62.

Kutas, M., & Hillyard, S.A. (1980a). Event related brain potentials to semantically inappropriate and surprisingly large words. *Biological Psychology, 11*, 99–116.

Kutas, M., & Hillyard, S.A. (1980b). Reading senseless sentences: Brain potentials reflect semantic incongruity. *Science, 207*, 203–205.

Lakoff, G. (1987). *Women, fire and dangerous things*. Chicago: University of Chicago Press.

Lakoff, G., & Johnson, M. (1980). *Metaphors we live by*. London: University of Chicago Press.

Lyons, J. (1968). *Introduction to theoretical linguistics*. Cambridge: Cambridge University Press.

MacDonald, M.C., & Just, M.A. (1989). Changes in activation level with negation. *Journal of Experimental Psychology: Learning, Memory, and Cognition, 15*, 633–642.

Mann, W.C., & Thompson, S.A. (1986). Relational propositions in discourse. *Discourse Processes, 9*, 57–90.

Mann, W.C., & Thompson, S.A. (1988). Rhetorical structure theory: A theory of text organisation. *Text, 8*, 243–281.

Marslen-Wilson, W.D. (1973). Linguistic structure and speech shadowing at very short latencies. *Nature, 244*, 522–523.

Marslen-Wilson, W.D. (1975). Sentence perception as an interactive parallel process. *Science, 189*, 226–228.

Marslen-Wilson, W.D. (1987). Functional parallelism in spoken word-recognition. *Cognition, 25*, 71–102.

McClelland, J.L. (1987). The case for interactionism in language processing. In M. Coltheart (Ed.), *Attention and performance XII: The psychology of reading* (pp. 1–36). Hove, UK: Lawrence Erlbaum Associates Ltd.

McClelland, J.L., & Rumelhart, D.E. (1981). An interactive activation model of context effects in letter perception: Pt. 1. An account of the basic findings. *Psychological Review, 88*, 375–407.

Meyer, D.E., & Schvaneveldt, R.W. (1971). Facilitation in recognizing words: Evidence of a dependence on retrieval operations. *Journal of Experimental Psychology, 90*, 227–234.

Millis, K.K., Graesser, A.C., & Haberlandt, K. (1993). The impact of connectives on memory for expository texts. *Applied Cognitive Psychology, 7*, 317–339.

Millis, K.K., & Just, M.A. (1994). The influence of connectives on sentence comprehension. *Journal of Memory and Language, 33*, 128–147.

Morton, J. (1969). Interaction of information in word recognition. *Psychological Review, 76*, 165–178.

Moss, H.E., McCormick, S., & Tyler, L.K. (1995, September). *The time-course of activation of semantic information during spoken word recognition.* Paper presented at the conference on Cognitive Models of Speech Processing, Sperlonga, Italy.

Moxey, L.M., & Sanford, A.J. (1987). Quantifiers and focus. *Journal of Semantics, 5*, 189–206.

Moxey, L.M., & Sanford, A.J. (1993a). Prior expectation and the interpretation of natural language quantifiers. *European Journal of Cognitive Psychology, 5*, 73–91.

Moxey, L.M., & Sanford, A.J. (1993b). *Communicating quantities: A psychological perspective.* Hove, UK: Lawrence Erlbaum Associates Ltd.

Murray, J.D. (1995). Logical connectives and local coherence. In R.F. Lorch & E.J. O'Brien (Eds.), *Sources of coherence in reading* (pp. 107–125). Hillsdale, NJ: Lawrence Erlbaum Associates Inc.

Myers, J.L., Shinjo, M., & Duffy, S.A. (1987). Degree of causal relatedness and memory. *Journal of Memory and Language, 26*, 453–465.

Nayak, N., & Gibbs, R. (1990). Conceptual knowledge in the interpretation of idioms. *Journal of Experimental Psychology: General, 119*, 315–330.

Neville, H.J., Nicol, J.L. Barss, A., Forster, K.I., & Garrett, M.F. (1991). Syntactically based sentence processing classes: Evidence from event-related brain potentials. *Journal of Cognitive Neuroscience, 3*, 151–165.

Onifer, W., & Swinney, D.A. (1981). Accessing lexical ambiguities during sentence comprehension: Effects of frequency of meaning and contextual bias. *Memory and Cognition, 23*, 87–101.

Ortony, A. (1979). Beyond literal similarity. *Psychological Review, 86*, 161–180.

Recanati, F. (1995). The alleged priority of literal interpretation. *Cognitive Science, 19*, 207–232.

Reder, L.M., & Kusbit, G.W. (1991). Locus of the Moses illusion: Imperfect encoding, retreival, or match? *Journal of Memory and Language, 30*, 385–406.

Rumelhart, D.E. (1977). *An introduction to human information processing.* New York: John Wiley & Sons.

Rumelhart, D.E., & Ortony, A. (1977). The representation of knowledge in memory. In R.C. Anderson, R.J. Spiro, & W.E. Montague (Eds.), *Schooling and the acquisition of knowledge.* Hillsdale, NJ: Lawrence Erlbaum Associates Inc.

Sanders, T.J.M., Spooren, W.P.M., & Noordman, L.G.M. (1992). Towards a taxonomy of coherence relations. *Discourse Processes, 15*, 1–35.

Sanford, A.J. (1987). *The mind of man.* New Haven, CT: Yale University Press.

Sanford, A.J., & Garrod, S.C. (1981). *Understanding written language*. Chichester, UK: John Wiley & Sons.

Sanford, A.J., Moxey, L.M., & Paterson, K.B. (1996). Attentional focusing with quantifiers in production and comprehension. *Memory and Cognition*, *24*, 144–155.

Searle, J. (1975). Indirect speech acts. In P. Cole & J. Morgan (Eds.), *Syntax and semantics, Vol. 3* (pp. 59–82). New York: Academic Press.

Searle, J. (1979). Metaphor. In A. Ortony (Ed.), *Metaphor and thought* (pp. 92–123). Cambridge: Cambridge University Press.

Seidenberg, M.S., Tanenhaus, M.K., Leiman, J.M., & Bienkowsi, M. (1982). Automatic access of the meanings of ambiguous words in context: Some limitations of knowledge-based processing. *Cognitive Psychology*, *14*, 489–537.

Sereno, S.C. (1995). Resolution of lexical ambiguity: Evidence from an eye movement priming paradigm. *Journal of Experimental Psychology: Learning, Memory, and Cognition*, *21*, 582–595.

Smith, E.E., Shoben, E.J., & Rips, L.V. (1974). Structure and process in semantic memory: A featural model for semantic decision. *Psychological Review*, *81*, 214–241.

St. John, M.F. (1991). *Hitting the right pitch: a meta-analysis of the effect of context on lexical access*. Research Rep. 5:6. Department of Cognitive Science, University of California, San Diego.

Swinney, D., & Cutler, A. (1979). The access and processing of idiomatic expressions. *Journal of Verbal Learning and Verbal Behavior*, *18*, 523–534.

Swinney, D.A. (1979). Lexical access during sentence comprehension: (Re)consideration of context effects. *Journal of Verbal Learning and Verbal Behavior*, *18*, 545–567.

Tabossi, P. (1988). Effects of context on the immediate interpretation of unambiguous nouns. *Journal of Experimental Psychology: Learning, Memory, and Cognition*, *14*, 153–162.

Tanenhaus, M.K., Leiman, J.M., & Seidenberg, M.S. (1979). Evidence for multiple stages in the processing of ambiguous words in syntactic contexts. *Journal of Verbal Learning and Verbal Behavior*, *18*, 427–440.

Townsend, D.J. (1983). Thematic processing in sentences and texts. *Cognition*, *13*, 223–261.

Traxler, M.J., Bybee, M.D., & Pickering, M.J. (1996). *Incremental interpretation of connected text: A reply to Millis and Just*. Unpublished manuscript.

Traxler, M.J., & Pickering, M.J. (1996). Plausibility and the processing of unbounded dependencies: An eye-tracking study. *Journal of Memory and Language*, *35*, 454–475.

Traxler, M.J., Sanford, A.J., Aked, J.P., & Moxey, L.M. (1997). Processing causals and diagnostics in discourse. *Journal of Experimental Psychology: Language, Memory, and Cognition*, *23*, 87–101.

Van Oostendorp, H., & de Mul, S. (1990). Moses beats Adam: A semantic relatedness effect on a semantic illusion. *Acta Psychologica*, *74*, 35–46.

Van Oostendorp, H., & Kok, I. (1990). Failing to notice errors in sentences. *Language and Cognitive Processes*, *5*, 105–113.

Van Petten, C., & Kutas, M. (1987). Ambiguous words in context: An event related potential analysis of the time-course of meaning activation. *Journal of Memory and Language*, *26*, 188–208.

Wason, P., & Reich, S.S. (1979). A verbal illusion. *Quarterly Journal of Experimental Psychology*, *31*, 591–597.

CHAPTER ELEVEN

Reference and anaphora

Alan Garnham
Laboratory of Experimental Psychology, University of Sussex, UK

INTRODUCTION

"I don't know what you are talking about" is a common lament from the uncomprehending. It points to a fact about language that has rarely been at the forefront of psychological research on language processing: People talk and write about other people and things, and the events, states, and processes in which they take part. Language conveys information. It may convey that information via complex systems of phonetics and phonology (or orthography), morphology, syntax, semantics, and pragmatics, but except in writings about language itself it does not convey information about those systems. Similarly, even if the mental mechanisms that underlie our ability to understand language make use of phonetic and phonological (or orthographic), morphological, syntactic, semantic, and pragmatic representations, these representations can only be intermediaries in the process of conveying information about individuals and their interactions. It is the individuals and interactions that are represented in the products of comprehension we have conscious access to, and those mental representations are representations of situations (they are what have been called mental models), not representations of language. From the perspective of language production, a speaker or writer will want to convey information about a particular situation (in the broadest sense) and will need to find appropriate ways to talk about the individuals in that situation and the relations between them. From the perspective of language perception, a hearer or reader must determine what individuals and relations the speaker or writer is talking about. To put it simply: Speakers and writers *refer*, and hearers and readers must work out to whom or to what they are referring.

I am not, of course, saying that referring is the only thing that speakers and listeners do, or that conveying information about situations in the world is the only, or even the primary, function of linguistic interchange. That would be an over-intellectualised view of everyday conversation, in particular. Nevertheless, even in social chit-chat there are fixed points of reference: To common acquaintances, to mutually known places, and to salient events, for example. A "theory of language processing" that does not take reference seriously is not a theory of language processing at all.

Why are these common-sense facts about language processing so manifestly downplayed in many of the best-known theories of language processing? One reason is that there are other facts to be explained. Facts, for example, about the identification of words, which have little, if anything, to do with reference. Even at "higher" levels there are other processes to be modelled. Nevertheless, if a broad and consistent framework for the study of language processing is to be established, it must recognise that the computation of appropriate referring expressions is a crucial part of language production, and that the computation of the referents of those referring expressions is a crucial part of comprehension. Indeed, according to David Marr's (1982) ideas, which have proved seminal in research on vision, the study of a complex system, such as the human language processor, should start with an analysis of the task or tasks that the system performs.

Another set of reasons why modern psycholinguistics has downplayed referential matters is historical. Questions of reference figured hardly at all among the initial concerns of the discipline. On the one hand, psycholinguistics grew out of Chomskyan linguistics, with its primary emphasis on syntax. Questions about syntax—deep structure, surface structure, and transformations—loomed large in early psycholinguistic research, and much subsequent work was directed at showing that transformationally based accounts of language processing were incorrect. On the other hand, the cognitive psychologists who tried to wrench control of the psychology of language away from the generative grammarians were primarily concerned with processes such as encoding, storage, and retrieval of information. And partly because they were not trained in linguistics, they tended to be less sensitive to the subtleties and complexities of natural languages.

MENTAL MODELS OF DISCOURSE

The advent of "cognitive science" in the late 1970s witnessed a new set of interactions between psychologists interested in language and linguists, which led to modern theories of discourse processing. By this time, there was a serious interest in formal questions about semantics in the linguistic community, and a recognition that the sentence-by-sentence approach to semantics, which worked for logical systems such as predicate calculus, was inappropriate for natural language. Thus, the late 1970s saw the development of new approaches to the semantics of discourse, such as *situation semantics* (e.g. Barwise & Perry, 1983) and *discourse representation theory* (Kamp, 1981). The interaction of these ideas with those of certain psychologists led to the formulation of the notion of a *mental model of discourse* (e.g. Johnson-Laird & Garnham, 1980), and to theories of how such models might be constructed by readers and listeners. Such mental models are representations of situations in the world. They are built up incrementally as a discourse is processed, and they contain representations of individuals, properties, and events that can be referred to in the upcoming discourse. They also contain information on what the participants know about each other, and this information is used to select appropriate, comprehensible, referring expressions. However, this aspect of mental models of discourse has received little attention in later work.

Mental models contain representations of the types of things we take the world to be made up of. So, mental models of ordinary conversations contain representations of individuals, events, and properties of those individuals and events. For technical or other specialist texts the ontology may be different. For example, texts about language comprehension make reference to abstract objects such as mental models (see Garnham & Oakhill, 1996 for further discussion).

WHAT IS REFERENCE?

If psychologists have not worried about what it means to refer, philosophers have. Many of the crucial ideas were developed in the context of formal logic, and can be traced back to the work of Gottlob Frege in the late 19th century. Frege formalised the notion that the meaning of an expression should be thought of as the way it contributed to the meaning of larger expressions of which it could be part. From a psycholinguistic point of view, this idea implies that meanings can be computed by a compositional process that puts meanings of smaller expressions together to make meanings of larger expressions.

Focusing, at least initially, on the language of mathematics, Frege argued that the significance of a "sentence" consisted in its being either true (as for "2 + 2 = 4") or false (as for "2 + 2 = 5"). He further argued that the significance of proper names, or *singular terms* as they are often called, was that they stood for, or referred to, objects. In mathematics, a typical proper name would be "two" and the object it stands for is the number two, which, for a Platonist such as Frege, is an abstract object.

Later, Frege (1892/1952) distinguished between two aspects of meaning, which he called, in German, "Sinn" and "Bedeutung". "Sinn" is usually translated as "sense" and "Bedeutung" as "meaning", "reference", or "denotation". The notion of sense, which Frege glossed as a "mode of presentation" of the referent, is usually explained by a non-mathematical example. The expression "the morning star" presents an object as unique ("the"), and shining in the night sky ("star"), and as appearing towards the end of the night ("morning"). The expression "the evening star" presents an object in a similar way, but with a crucial difference in the time at which it appears. For the purposes of language comprehension, the sense of an expression can be thought of as providing a way working out what the referent is. As it turns out, astronomical discovery showed that the referents of the two expressions "the morning star" and "the evening star" were one and the same. Both expressions refer to the planet Venus (which, of course, is not a star at all).

The reference of an expression, in the Fregean sense, is, the object, or other real world entity, that it stands for. Sentences stand for Truth and Falsity, which Frege regarded as abstract Platonic objects, and their senses (e.g. about the sum of two and two being four) are modes of presentation of these objects. For sentences, the notion of sense as a mode of presentation of a denoted object is much less intuitively appealing than it is for proper names. Nevertheless, Frege's assumptions about sentences are crucial to the operation of his system.

Frege's ideas cannot be applied straightforwardly to ordinary language. Part of the difficulty is that Frege paid no attention to the role of context. Nor did he need to in the domain of arithmetic. "Two" always refers to the number two. "2 + 2 = 4" is always true regardless of the context in which it is considered. Thus, in the domain of mathematical proof, the notion of a Fregean proper name is unproblematic. However, a proper name in ordinary language, such as "John", refers to different people on different occasions, and a sentence such as "the man came into the room" cannot be designated true or false until we know what situation it describes, and hence which man and which room the sentence is about. Only with information about the context can we fix the reference of "the man" and "the room", and determine whether an event of the type that the sentence is about (a man entering a room) took place before the time of utterance, since the sentence is about an event that happened before that time.

Despite using ordinary language examples, as with the morning star and the evening star, Frege had some harsh things to say about the semantic coherence of natural languages. Our concern as psycholinguists is, however, with the processing of such languages, and we must take their operation seriously. If proper names refer to objects, and sentences denote truth values, how do proper names contribute to the truth values of sentences in which they occur? The simplest case is a sentence such as "John sleeps", in which a property (sleeping) is predicated of an individual (John). If we take Frege's notion of contribution to significance seriously, then the meaning of "sleeps" must be the sort of thing that can combine with something whose meaning (Bedeutung) is an object to produce something whose meaning is a truth value: In technical terms, it must be a function from individuals to truth values. In other words, the meaning of "sleep", when given an individual (the meaning of a proper name) will produce the value either true (if the individual is asleep) or false (if the individual is not asleep). This *functional* analysis points both to how meanings of words might be represented and to how they might be combined during comprehension.

VARIETIES OF REFERENCE

We are constantly referring to individuals, but do all types of referring expression work in the same way? Formal logicians tell us that they do not. Indeed, a tradition going back to Russell (and arguably to Frege, too, see Evans, 1982), claims that *definite descriptions* (i.e. definite noun phrases), such as "the present king of France", are not referring expressions in the strict sense, despite their typical use to refer to individuals, because they can fail to refer (France is a republic, and has no monarch). Indeed, Russell claimed that there are few genuine referring expressions (or singular terms). This claim was based on his distinction between knowledge by acquaintance and knowledge by description, and the idea that genuine reference could only be to individuals of whom one had knowledge by acquaintance.

Whether Russell's claims are correct or not, there is a distinction between definite descriptions and other expressions used to refer to individuals: Proper names, pronouns, and demonstratives. Furthermore, this distinction is relevant to theories of language processing, because it determines whether certain sentences have one interpretation or two, and hence whether there is a need for disambiguation of meaning. For example, Evans (1982) considers the sentence:

(1) The first man in space might have been an American.

This sentence has two possible interpretations. One is that Yuri Gagarin, the Soviet astronaut who was the first man in space, might have been an American. The other is that, in another universe, America might have won the space race. Context should determine which interpretation is intended. The corresponding sentence with a proper name:

(2) Yuri Gagarin might have been an American.

shows no such ambiguity. In technical terms, a definite description shows a scope ambiguity with respect to a modal verb such as "may", whereas a proper name does not. "Yuri Gagarin" always refers to a person in the real world, but "the first man in space" can either take its reference in the real world (Yuri Gagarin), and hence be outside the scope of "might", as in the first reading of sentence (1), or it might be interpreted within the "world" defined by counterfactual supposition introduced by "might", and hence give the second reading.

According to Evans, the conclusion that should be drawn from these observations is that definite descriptions, at least in one use, are quantifier expressions, and not referring expressions, since only quantifier expressions show scope ambiguities. For example, (3):

(3) Every woman loves some man.

with the quantifier expressions "every woman" and "some man", has two interpretations, one in which all the women love the same man, and one in which they love different men. This idea, that definite noun phrases are quantifier expressions, has also been mooted by linguists such as Chomsky (1975) and Hawkins (1978). It originates in Russell's theory of descriptions, in which a statement containing a definite description, such as "the present King of France is bald", asserts the existence of a unique object that has the property denoted by the body of the description (informally: There is one and only one individual that has the property of being the present King of France [and that individual is bald]).

If this idea is applied to everyday language, as opposed to the language of mathematics that Russell originally had in mind, a problem immediately arises. The use of a definite description, such as "the chair", does not commit a speaker to the view that there is only one chair in the world, merely that some object in a contextually relevant set of objects uniquely has the property of being a chair. To understand such a definite noun phrase, a listener or reader must be able to identify the appropriate set of objects, and the appropriate individual object within it. Ordinary language utterances are interpreted in contexts that severely restrict the parts of the world that are relevant to their interpretation. The theory of mental models here makes an important contribution to questions about how such expressions are understood. If part of the world (described in the text so far) is represented in a mental model, that model may contain, for example, a representation of just one chair, and hence an expression such as "the chair" may be interpreted as referring to that chair, even though, in the world as a whole there are many chairs.

DISCOURSE: SUBSEQUENT REFERENCE AND ANAPHORA

Much work in formal logic has focused on individual sentences, whose interpretation was assumed to be independent of the context in which they occur. This assumption has some plausibility in the domain of mathematical proof, with which Frege and Russell were primarily concerned. But even in that domain it is questionable (the expression "angle ABC", for example, means different things in different geometrical proofs, and its referent is determined by the particular diagram used to represent the given information). In the domain of everyday language, the assumption in untenable.

As has already been mentioned, context-dependent interpretation is a ubiquitous feature of ordinary language. Another example of this phenomenon, and one that is particularly important for psycholinguists, is the use of (apparently) indirect *anaphoric* references. Anaphoric references to individuals are apparently indirect, because on traditional accounts they depend on a prior *antecedent* reference (see Bosch, 1983, chapter 1, for a historical survey of anaphora). On this account, the anaphoric reference of the pronoun "it" in (4):

(4) The vase fell from the shelves and it broke.

depends on the reference to "the vase" earlier in the sentence. A theory of comprehension based on this idea might assume that the interpretation of an anaphor requires a search for the antecedent expression.

Modern analyses, such as that of Hankamer and Sag (1976) and Cornish (1996), suggest that the traditional idea that an anaphoric pronoun is interpreted by linking it to a preceding textual expression is incorrect. Rather, the pronoun refers to an element in a conceptual representation (mental model), and the importance of the antecedent expression is that it introduced the appropriate element into the conceptual representation, or singled it out in some other way, by acting as an *antecedent trigger* in Cornish's terminology. On this view, the function of the antecedent expression can be replaced, and the anaphoric element placed under *pragmatic control*. Thus, in conversation, a deictic or pointing gesture can single out an appropriate referent for a pronoun, and the pronoun can be used without any linguistic antecedent. On this view the distinction between anaphoric reference and deictic reference is less clear cut than in traditional accounts, though if an antecedentless pronoun can be used without specially marked prosody or an overt pointing gesture, it can be argued that it is not truly deictic, because it does not serve the function of directing attention to its (already salient) referent. In any case, anaphors (or at least identity of reference anaphors, such as definite pronouns in their most typical uses) are interpreted by searching for a representation of their referent in a mental model, *not* by searching for an antecedent, co-referring, expression.

Varieties of anaphoric reference

As I have already indicated, a paradigm example of anaphoric reference is the use of third person definite pronouns (in English, "he", "she", "it", "they", and cognate forms, such as "him" and "her"). It is with anaphoric definite pronouns that I will be primarily, though not exclusively, concerned in the rest of this chapter. In the most straightforward cases, as in the "vase" example in (4), the pronoun refers to the same entity (person or object) as its antecedent expression ("it" refers to the earlier mentioned vase). However, not all uses of definite pronouns are so straightforward. For example, when pronouns follow quantifier expressions, such as "every man", or "few congressmen", they may have a different interpretation. Traditionally, pronouns following quantifier expressions were said to function as *bound variables*. So, for example, a sentence such as (5a):

(5a) Every man loves his mother.

has a quasi-logical analysis of the form (5b):

(5b) For any man (call him x), x loves x's mother.

In this analysis, the pronominal form "his" translates into a variable x, and that variable is *bound* by the quantifier expression "every man", so that the relation between x and x's mother is stated to hold whenever the name of a man is substituted for x. However, not all pronouns following quantifier expressions function as bound variables. Gareth Evans (1980) contrasted sentences of the following kinds:

(6a) Few congressmen admire only the people they know.
(6b) Few congressmen admire Kennedy, and they are very junior.

The first of these *does* state that the relationship of admiring only people they know is true only in a few cases when the person is a congressman, and hence the pronoun "they" can be analysed as a bound variable. But (6b) does not say that admiring Kennedy and being very junior hold of only a few congressmen, which it would have to if its "they" were a bound variable. It says that admiring Kennedy holds of only a few congressmen, and that when those congressmen have been identified they are found to be junior. It is not, for example, compatible with many congressmen admiring Kennedy, only a few of whom are junior, which it would have to be on the standard bound variable interpretation. Evans called pronouns such as "they" in the second of these sentences *E-type pronouns* (see later for further discussion). From a psycholinguistic point of view, what such examples show is that the procedures for producing and interpreting definite pronouns must be complex.

In other cases, pronouns refer not to the same person or thing as was previously mentioned, but to something of the same type. This interpretation is the standard one for indefinite pronouns, such as "one" and "some". For example, in (7a):

(7a) My sister has a new pair of roller skates, and I want some, too.

"some" means "roller skates", but it does not mean the same pair that my sister has. Contrast (7b):

(7b) My sister has a new pair of roller skates, and I want them.

It is also possible to use definite pronouns in this way, for example in so-called *paycheck* sentences (Karttunen, 1969), as in (8):

(8) The man who gives his paycheck to his wife is wiser than the man who gives it to his mistress.

In (8), the definite pronoun "it" refers to a paycheck, but clearly not the same paycheck that was mentioned earlier in the sentence.

Apart from pronouns, the other major class of anaphoric expressions is elliptical verbal constructions of various kinds, though this class is far from homogeneous. Neither is it entirely separate from pronominal anaphora, since it includes both predicational and sentential forms of "it" anaphora, for example see (9), which has a predicational "do it" = wash up), and (10), which has a sentential "it" = Bill has left his wife:

(9) I don't like washing up, but I suppose I'll have to do it.
(10) John says Bill has left his wife, but I don't believe it.

In English, the most familiar of these constructions is probably *verb-phrase ellipsis*, in which an entire verb phrase (or predicate) is omitted, if it would have been identical to a previous one, as in (11):

(11) I don't want to go out in the rain, but I have to.

If the ellipsis leaves a finite clause without a verb, a corresponding form of the auxiliary verb "to do" usually stands in:

(12) I went on a ski-ing holiday. My sister did, too.

As we will see later, ellipses and pronouns have different properties, and may be interpreted by different types of procedure during comprehension.

The complexities of anaphoric reference

Psychologists are concerned primarily with psychological questions about how anaphoric references are produced and understood. However, these questions cannot be addressed independently of linguistic questions about anaphora, questions about where and when (in discourse or text) anaphoric references are permissible, and what form they take. These questions may receive descriptive or (preferably) explanatory answers. The principal difference between linguistic and psychological approaches to anaphora is that the former typically make no direct reference to the mental mechanisms, representations, and processes that underlie the production and comprehension of anaphoric reference. They are based on data about what forms of anaphoric reference are appropriate at what points in a text, and what interpretation(s) they have. In particular they make no use of standard psychological measures such as the time taken to understand an anaphor, or the mistakes made in interpreting it, or in answering questions following a text containing anaphoric references. Nevertheless, linguistic ideas about anaphora play a crucial role in the formulation of processing theories.

In English (and many other languages) anaphoric expressions are morphologically marked. Considering just third person definite pronouns, English distinguishes singular from plural ("he", "she", "it", versus "they"), masculine, feminine, and neuter (among the singulars), and nominative and accusative (in the masculine and feminine singular: "he" versus "him", "she" versus "her"). The choice of nominative or accusative form is determined by the role of the pronoun within its own clause (subjects are nominative, objects of various kinds are accusative). However, the choice between masculine and feminine forms and between singular and plural forms is determined largely by what the pronoun refers to. There are, however, some complications, so that in some contexts for example, certain types of vehicle can be referred to as "she" rather than "it". In addition, there is a question of whether number and gender are determined directly by the object or objects referred to, or whether the choice is linguistically mediated. In a case such as "the boy ... he..." these two factors cannot be separated, since the person referred to is (presumably) male, and the English word "boy" is typically used to refer to males. However, other cases show that linguistic mediation is crucial. In English, one says "the pants ... they ..." not "the pants ... it...", even though a pair of pants is a single object (and, indeed, one can say "a pair of pants ... it..."). Furthermore, in languages in which words for objects have arbitrary genders, the gender of a pronoun referring to an object is determined by the name of that object, even if the name has not been explicitly used (Tasmowski-de Ryck & Verluyten, 1982).

There are also rules governing anaphoric relations between expressions in different parts of a sentence. One rule distinguishes between ordinary definite pronouns and reflexives and reciprocals. So, in certain positions in a sentence, an ordinary pronoun cannot be co-referential with another noun phrase, but a reflexive is permitted. Compare (13) and (14):

(13) John wrote about him.
(14) John wrote about himself.

In (13), "him" ≠ John, whereas in (14) "himself" = John. Bosch (1983) argues on both analytic and historical grounds that reflexives are not referential, but are agreement markers. He argues that pronouns that appear in positions where they can be interpreted as bound variables if they follow quantifiers, are also agreement markers, as in (15) and (16).

(15) No one thought he would win.
(16) John thought he would win.

A second general constraint on anaphoric reference is the so-called *backwards anaphora constraint*. Within a sentence, an anaphor usually follows its antecedent. In English and many other languages anaphors may, under certain conditions, precede their antecedents, and when they do they are sometimes called *cataphors*. However, the use of backwards anaphora is greatly restricted compared with the more usual forwards anaphora. Solan (1983) argues that all languages incorporate a constraint on backwards anaphora. Some rule it out altogether, others permit it under restricted circumstances. According to Solan, there are a limited number of versions of the backwards anaphor constraint, and children start off by assuming that the language they are learning incorporates the most restrictive version. Then they relax this constraint if they encounter sentences that can only be sensibly interpreted on the assumption that they contain backwards anaphora. English allows backwards anaphora in sentences such as (17a) and (18a):

(17a) Near him, John saw a snake.
(18a) After Bill did, John took a cake.

The restriction is that the early anaphor has to be sufficiently buried in the syntactic structure. If it is not, then backwards anaphora is not possible, as in (17b), where "he" ≠ John, and (18b), where "did" ≠ took a cake:

(17b) He saw a snake near John.
(18b) Bill did, after John took a cake.

Morphological and syntactic constraints on anaphora are relatively easy to describe, even if, for the morphological constraints, there are important questions about when they are violated (see later for further discussion). Discourse-level constraints on anaphora are more difficult to specify. They clearly exist, but the theoretical constructs required to explain them are not altogether obvious. A major issue in referring to entities is what type of expression to choose (e.g. null, definite pronoun, full definite noun phrase, proper name). These expressions vary in the extent to which their interpretation is dependent on context and, conversely, in the extent to which their own content specifies what they refer to. Thus, pronouns are highly dependent on context for their interpretation, as their own semantic content is limited. A definite pronoun, such as "she" can only be used felicitously when context (in a broad sense) makes one (presumably) female individual most salient. Given the number of female individuals (real and imaginary) that could in principle be under discussion, context must play a major role in these cases.

The role of context is sometimes described as the *focusing* of a particular individual or set of individuals. Obviously, a pronoun has not been used felicitously if its own content, plus contextual information, which may occur after the pronoun as well as before it, does not determine its referent. A more extreme view is that, regardless of the actual occurrence of pronouns, a well-written text always keeps a single entity in focus, and that entity is the default referent for any pronoun that is encountered. In language production, these sorts of consideration clearly influence the choice of referential forms. For example, Marslen-Wilson, Levy, and Tyler (1982) found that the choice of referential form (e.g. pronoun versus full noun phrase) depended on whether the antecedent was close, and hence likely to be focused, or distant in the discourse structure. Vonk, Hustinx, and Simons (1992) showed, in addition, that the use of particular forms can act as signals to text structure. For example, the use of a fuller form, when a pronoun would be perfectly comprehensible, can signal a change of topic.

EMPIRICAL STUDIES OF ANAPHORIC REFERENCE

Representations used to interpret anaphoric expressions

Hankamer and Sag (1976) identified two broad classes of anaphoric expressions, which they labelled *deep* and *surface anaphors*. Sag and Hankamer (1984) later relabelled these two types of anaphor as *model-interpretive anaphors* and *ellipses*, and sketched a processing theory in which the two types of anaphor are interpreted using different mental representations. Deep or model-interpretive anaphors can occur with or without linguistic antecedents. For example, pronouns, which are deep anaphors, can be used *exophorically* to refer to salient entities in the context that have not been explicitly mentioned. Ellipses need linguistic antecedents. Furthermore, ellipses need antecedents that parallel their own *form*, as it would be if the anaphor was expanded, whereas model-interpretive anaphors do not. So, Hankamer and Sag claim that a model-interpretive anaphor, such as "do it", is indifferent to an alternation between, for example, active and passive forms in the antecedent, as is (19a):

(19a) The rubbish must be taken out, so I may as well do it.

Here, "do it" = take the rubbish out. They claim, however, that ellipses with similar meanings cannot tolerate such alternations, as in (19b), where "do so" ≠ take the rubbish out.

(19b) The rubbish must be taken out, so I may as well do so.

Without the active/passive alternation, the sentence is perfectly acceptable, as in (19c), where "do so" = take the rubbish out.

(19c) Someone must take the rubbish out, so I may as well do so.

Sag and Hankamer suggest that model-interpretive anaphors are interpreted directly from a representation of content, or mental model. They refer to things that are represented in that model. Those individuals may or may not have been introduced into the model because they were mentioned in the text, and how they are represented in the model is, to some extent, independent of the form of the text that introduced them, if they were so introduced. Surface anaphors, on the other hand, are interpreted by copying a piece of a superficial representation of the surrounding text (Sag and Hankamer suggest Chomskyan Logical Form, or LF) and then interpreting the fleshed out form of the ellipsis. Hence, the need for a linguistic antecedent, and the need for parallelism of form—LF preserves many of the surface features of a text. Sag and Hankamer's suggestion fits with a long-standing distinction in psycholinguistics between representations of content and representations of the superficial form of texts.

The considered linguistic judgements on which Hankamer and Sag's distinctions are based are not, for the most part, to be disputed, though those authors' characterisation of the distinction between deep and surface anaphora has sometimes been questioned (e.g. Murphy, 1985b). Furthermore, although their suggested processing theory is both plausible and elegant, plausibility and elegance do not, of themselves, guarantee correctness. A strong form of the theory claims that superficial representations play no role in interpreting deep anaphors, and that surface anaphors are interpreted by a copying process, so that considerations of meaning are only important in interpreting them because their meaning has to be recomputed. This strong version of the theory has been shown empirically to be incorrect. It does not, however, follow that deep and surface anaphors cannot be distinguished from a processing point of view.

The argument against the strong form of Hankamer and Sag's hypothesis is that superficial representations are involved in the interpretation of deep anaphors, and that the representation of the content of the preceding text influences the interpretation of surface anaphors. Murphy (1985a) argues that effects of parallelism between anaphor and antecedent for deep anaphors suggest an involvement of a superficial representation in the interpretation of deep anaphors. However, Tanenhaus and Carlson (1990) have suggested an alternative explanation for this finding in terms of focus switching. In the example about taking out the rubbish, repeated here in (20):

(20) The rubbish must be taken out, so I may as well do it.

there is a switch of focus from the rubbish to the narrator in the non-parallel form, which is not found in the parallel form, and this switch may have a processing cost, which is independent of questions about parallelism.

Garnham, Oakhill, Ehrlich, and Carreiras (1995) provide a different type of evidence for the involvement of superficial representations in the interpretation of deep anaphors. They found that morphological cues (in this case gender) to the referents of pronouns speeded their resolution, even when those cues were purely formal. The pronouns referred to objects in French and Spanish, and there was no semantic link between the objects referred to and the gender of the nouns used to refer to them.

The other part of the argument against Sag and Hankamer is that ellipses can be assigned interpretations that are made plausible by context, but that cannot be explained by the copy-and-interpret strategy of Hankamer and Sag. Garnham and Oakhill (1987) showed that (21a) and (21b):

(21a) The patient had been examined by the doctor during the ward round.
(21b) The nurse had, too.

were often interpreted to mean that the nurse had examined the patient (plausible in the context), whereas linguistically it ought to mean that the nurse had been examined by the doctor.

If the strong form of Hankamer and Sag's theory does not hold up, there is evidence, though somewhat mixed, that deep and surface anaphors are treated psychologically in different ways. Murphy (1985a) has emphasised the similarity in the processing of deep and surface anaphors. He finds that both are affected by the distance between antecedent and anaphor, and both are affected by parallelism between antecedent and anaphor. Tanenhaus and Carlson (1990) however, do find differences, particularly in judgements of acceptability, between deep and surface anaphors with parallel and non-parallel antecedents. And in a recent study, Mauner, Tanenhaus, and Carlson (1995) have identified a set of cases (truncated rather than full passive antecedents) where deep anaphors are not affected, in processing time, by (non-)parallelism whereas surface anaphors are.

What's in a mental model?

Pronouns refer to things represented in mental models. In the most straightforward cases, a noun phrase introduces a referent into a mental model of what a text is about, and a definite pronoun makes a second reference to that object. Hence, the traditional theory that anaphors are interpreted by mapping them onto their antecedents. However, not all uses of definite pronouns are so simple. Setting aside cases in which the pronoun is not referential (see earlier, and Bosch 1983 for a fuller account), there are many cases in which pronouns have their referents introduced indirectly. Some of these cases have attracted particular attention in the literatures of philosophical logic and linguistic semantics, whereas others have been investigated by psychologists. Bosch (1983, pp. 128–141), writing from the first of these perspectives, discusses four main categories: E-type pronouns, *donkey sentences*, *examination sentences*, and inferred referents (of which his main example is reference into anaphoric islands, see later). As Bosch (1983, p. 137) points out, given that these pronouns are referential, the principal question to be asked is "Where do the referents for pronouns in these sentences come from?" His answer is that, in various ways, they are introduced into context models, which provide some of the material needed to interpret the pronoun, and which are similar in many ways to mental models.

As pointed out earlier, in (22):

(22) Few congressmen admire Kennedy, and they are very junior.

the pronoun does not act as a bound variable, as a pronoun following a quantifier expression might be expected to, but as an E-type pronoun. However, the quantifier expression "few congressmen" is not itself referential. So, although the pronoun "they" is referential, and it refers to those few congressmen that admire Kennedy, it cannot be co-referential with the quantifier phrase, even though in (23):

(23) Fred and Bill admire Kennedy, and they are very junior.

"they" is co-referential with "Fred and Bill". Donkey sentences were first discussed by Geach (1962). The original donkey sentence is given in (24):

(24) If any man owns a donkey, he beats it.

but there are many others. Evans had pointed out some similarities between pronouns in donkey sentences and E-type pronouns, but the parallels do not hold up across the full range of donkey sentences. Examination sentences such as (25) also contain quantifiers followed by pronouns that cannot be interpreted as bound variables, but they are farther still from being amenable to an E-type analysis:

(25) No one will be admitted to the examination unless they have registered four weeks in advance.

Bosch argues that, despite their differences, all these sentences introduce indirectly (i.e. by inference) things for the pronouns to refer to (the small number of congressmen that admire Kennedy, men that own donkeys, people who will be admitted to the examination).

Psychologists have also studied cases of indirect reference that can be picked up by pronouns. One example is that of *conceptual pronouns* (Gernsbacher, 1991). Conceptual pronouns are additionally interesting in that they may mismatch (in number, in the cases considered by Gernsbacher) the morphological form of their apparent antecedent. For example, in (26):

(26) I need a plate. Where do you keep them?

the plural pronoun "them" follows the singular noun phrase "a plate". However, "a plate" is not used referentially in this sentence, and the referent of "them" is the set of plates that the addressee is assumed to have. This set of plates is not the previously mentioned plate, but is conceptually related to it. Hence the name conceptual pronoun. The existence of the set of plates is an inference from the text, and one question is when the set of plates is represented in the mental model of the text. Gernsbacher found that conceptual pronouns are easily understood, and are preferred to linguistically "matching" pronouns, as in (27):

(27) I need a plate. Where do you keep it?

However, they are not always as readily understood as comparable references to the same sets of objects, explicitly introduced (Oakhill, Garnham, Gernsbacher, & Cain, 1992). This finding suggests that an inference may be needed *when the pronoun is read*, so that the set of plates may be introduced into the mental model only at this point.

Another kind of indirect reference, both mentioned by Bosch (1983) and studied by psychologists (e.g. Garnham & Oakhill, 1988), is reference into anaphoric islands. In (28):

(28) Jim reviewed that book and it will be published in *Linguistic Inquiry*.

Corum (1973), "it" refers to the review, but the review has not been explicitly mentioned, only the act of reviewing. The existence of the review, as a product of that act, can, however, be inferred. Corum's discussion of such cases, which was from a linguistic perspective, was to point out that such indirect pronominal references were much more acceptable when the expression that triggered the inference was morphologically related to the inferred form ("reviewed", "review"). Postal (1969) had earlier pointed out that, in the absence of such a relation, such references were unacceptable, and that lexical items were *anaphoric islands*, in the sense that components of their meaning were not available as antecedents of anaphors. In one of his classic examples, "them" cannot mean Max's parents in (29):

(29) Max is an orphan and he deeply misses them.

even though parent is a component of the meaning of orphan. As with conceptual pronouns, Garnham and Oakhill's (1988) psychological studies suggested that the required inference was only made when the pronoun itself had to be interpreted.

Issues of focus

Another set of issues about the structure of mental models, and hence the structure of the representations in which pronoun antecedents are found, can be loosely grouped under the head of focus. Issues of focus are sometimes divided into those about global focus and those about local focus, which are related to questions about local and global topics. Focused elements are more readily available for reference than non-focused elements, and the general problem is to describe how focus partitions a mental model, and how the partitions affect both the production and the comprehension of anaphoric references. A good example of global focus is produced by the episodic structure of texts. In texts of any length there are shifts between episodes, which are reflected in the mental representation of texts (see e.g. Garnham & Mason, 1987). Following an episode shift, a pronominal reference to an episode-dependent character, such as a waiter in a description of a visit to a restaurant, is difficult to understand, but a pronominal reference to a main character, who can be expected to appear in several episodes, is not (Anderson, Garrod, & Sanford, 1983). More generally, people and things mentioned in texts can be either foregrounded or backgrounded, and foregrounded items are more acceptable antecedents for pronouns than backgrounded ones (Morrow, 1985).

The question of local focus is more complex. The most favoured pattern of reference is that a pronoun which is the subject of its own clause is co-referential with the subject noun phrase of the immediately preceding clause. The preference for the pronoun to be a subject reflects the fact that the information conveyed by the pronoun should be given information (its referent is usually already known in the context of the current discourse), and given information usually comes before new information in a clause. Whether the overall pattern reflects a preference for antecedents in parallel grammatical position to the pronouns, a preference for subject antecedents (e.g. Crawley, Stevenson, & Kleinman, 1990), a preference for first mentioned antecedents (Gernsbacher & Hargreaves, 1988), or whether it needs a more complex explanation in terms of

"Centering" (Gordon & Chan, 1995; Gordon, Grosz, & Gilliom, 1993) is not yet fully resolved. In addition, the way that the antecedent is introduced can affect how strongly it is focused, independent of the sentential role of the antecedent. Proper names produce stronger focus than definite descriptions (Sanford, Moar, & Garrod, 1988).

Questions about focus also arise for indirectly introduced antecedents, for example, with E-type pronouns. In (30), the quantifier phrase, "some people", is not referential:

(30) Some people are asleep. They should not be disturbed.

However, the first sentence implies the existence of some people that are asleep, and this is the set that "they" refers to. Moxey and Sanford (1993) point out that there are some quantifier expressions, such as "hardly any", that appear to make a different set available for pronominal reference, as in (31):

(31) Hardly any people are asleep. They couldn't settle because of the noise.

In this brief text, "they" refers to the people who are *not* asleep, the *complement* of the set referred to in the earlier sentence pair. Thus, different quantifiers appear to focus on different sets (the REFSET and the COMPSET in Moxey and Sanford's terminology). Moxey and Sanford show that this difference in focus is correlated with logical properties of quantifiers (being monotone increasing versus being monotone decreasing) that have been identified in general quantifier theory (e.g. Barwise & Cooper, 1981).

Although there are preferences for taking pronouns to refer to particular items, they are only preferences and they can be overturned. For example, the preference for subject antecedent (or first mentioned antecedent, or favoured forward-looking discourse centre as antecedent) is met in (32):

(32) Max confessed to Bill because he wanted a reduced sentence.

However, it is overturned in both (33) and (34):

(33) Max confessed to Bill because he offered a reduced sentence.
(34) Sue blamed Pam because she had been careless.

In (33), pen and paper sentence completion studies have shown that the subject antecedent is indeed preferred, and that the content of the second version overrides this preference. However, in (34) there is a preference for the object antecedent in completions (which can also be overturned by appropriate content in the "because" clause, e.g. "because she needed a scapegoat"). The factor at work here is the *implicit causality* of the verb (Garvey & Caramazza, 1974). Actions of blaming are usually provoked by the person who gets blamed, so an explicit statement of what provoked the action, in a "because" clause, will usually refer to that person. However, in a main clause describing the action, the person blamed is the direct object of the verb "blame". In this respect, "blame" contrasts with "confess". Acts of confession are usually instigated by the confessor, who is the subject of a simple main clause describing the action. It has been known for some time that, in relatively coarse on-line measures, an explicit cause that is congruent with the implicit cause (e.g. "because he wanted a reduced sentence") can be understood more rapidly than one that is incongruent (e.g. "because he offered a reduced sentence") (e.g. Caramazza, Grober, Garvey, & Yates, 1977; Vonk, 1985). However, Garnham, Traxler, Oakhill, and Gernsbacher (1996) have shown that this is not a focusing effect, in which the implicit cause is foregrounded. It is an effect that arises only when the implicit cause is integrated with the explicit clause, typically after the "because" clause has been read. By contrast, the preference for subjects or first-mentioned protagonists can be picked up at any point in the sentence, and does appear to be a focusing effect.

Implicit causality does not appear to add information into the mental model in the first instance. A different case, in which we have argued that inferential information *is* incorporated into a mental model (and subsequently influences pronoun resolution) is social stereotyping. A masculine pronoun ("he") is resolved more quickly than a feminine pronoun ("she") if it refers to a person whose occupation or role is stereotypically masculine (e.g. engineer). The reverse is true if the role is stereotypically feminine (e.g. secretary). In English, this effect could arise because people's genders are immediately encoded from their role names, or only when an attempt is made to link the pronoun to the role name. Carreiras, Garnham, Oakhill, and Cain (1996) have shown a similar effect arises early in Spanish, where it can be detected by a match or mismatch with the gender of a definite article (e.g. "el futbolista", the male footballer versus "la futbolista", the female footballer). They argue that if the effect is early in Spanish it is likely to be early in English, too.

The mechanism and time-course of pronoun resolution

Although mental models greatly restrict the number of possible referents for pronouns, the strong theory that they provide a default referent for any pronoun is incorrect. Studies using probe word techniques have shown that, in a sentence such as (35):

(35) Jack threw a snowball at Phil, but he missed.

both potential antecedents of the pronoun "he" (Jack and Phil) are activated at the end of the sentence. Responses to "Phil" were quicker than when the pronoun was replaced with the proper name "Jack" (Corbett & Chang, 1983). In addition, and as expected, responses to "Jack" were quicker than responses to "Phil" in both the pronoun and the proper name conditions. Gernsbacher (1989) pointed out that these results could be explained either in terms of activation of the (name of the) antecedent or suppression of the name of the non-antecedent. The results of her experiments suggested that suppression of the non-antecedent was by far the more important of the two mechanisms. Furthermore, Gernsbacher found that for pronouns, but not for proper names, the effects were not immediate, but were delayed to the end of the clause containing the pronoun.

This result points to the fact that, if there is a choice to be made between potential referents for an anaphor, that work may take time to complete. Indeed, even if the choice is resolved by the morphological form of the pronoun, resolution may not be immediate. Gernsbacher found the same delay of suppression of the non-antecedent when the pronouns referred unambiguously, on the basis of their gender (1989, Exp. 5). An earlier eye-tracking study by Ehrlich and Rayner (1983) also provided evidence for delayed resolution, at least in some cases. When a pronoun had a distant, and no longer strongly foregrounded, antecedent, the processes that resolved its reference were delayed compared to the case of a near antecedent. On the basis of this result, and subsequent studies of their own, Garrod and Sanford (1985; Garrod, Freudenthal, & Boyle, 1993) have suggested that pronouns are resolved immediately when they refer unambiguously to (focused) main characters, but not otherwise.

Activation or suppression of the name of a referent is not the same as assigning a referent to a pronoun. It may be for this reason that the results of Garrod et al. (1993), who used an eye-movement monitoring technique, differ from those of Gernsbacher (1989), who never found evidence for immediate resolution of pronouns. Garrod et al.'s subjects read sentences such as (36):

(36) Right away she ordered/poured a large glass of coke.

Each sentence appeared in a context in which the pronoun either referred unambiguously, on the basis of its gender, or it did not. If it referred unambiguously, it could be to either a focused or a non-focused character. The different verbs denoted actions that were either consistent with reference to the focused character (passenger *ordered* a drink) or to the nonfocused character (steward[ess] *poured* a drink). In this study Garrod et al. found evidence for immediate resolution of the pronoun, but only when it referred unambiguously to the focused referent. In these circumstances, reading of the incongruent verb ("poured") was slowed compared with reading of the congruent verb ("ordered"). In a second study, Garrod et al. found no such effects when the pronouns were replaced by proper names or definite noun phrases, again in apparent contrast with Gernsbacher's results. Sanford and Garrod (1989) distinguish between initiating the process of anaphor resolution, which they claim is almost always immediate, and completing it, which they claim is not. However, although this distinction is an important one, it cannot reconcile the results of Garrod et al. (1993) and of Gernsbacher (1989), since Garrod et al. used a technique that reflects resolution more directly, rather than processes that ought to be prior to resolution, but they found evidence for early completion of the process, at least for pronouns. Two further possibilities are (a) that, because Gernsbacher did not use contexts, her sentences never referred to characters that were focused in the sense of Garrod et al., and (b) that suppression of non-antecedents is a process that occurs primarily *after* a pronoun has been resolved.

If pronoun resolution takes time, it need not be an all or not process. Several observations are consistent with this idea. One is the phenomenon of false bonding (Sanford, Garrod, Lucas, & Henderson, 1984). In (37a), subjects experience a difficulty in reading the second sentence and a subjective impression that they have considered (and rejected) the possibility that "it" refers to Ireland. (37b) does not produce this effect.

(37a) Harry was sailing to Ireland. It sank without trace.
(37b) Harry was sailing to Ireland. It was a beautiful day.

This finding suggests that, if the *bonding* of the pronoun to the potential antecedent is immediate, the difficulty only arises when later material is used to develop this link into a referential one (see Sanford & Garrod, 1989, pp. 254–256 for discussion), and that if a referential interpretation of the "it" is ruled out by later material, this type of link is never developed, and false bonding does not manifest itself in processing difficulties. On this view, resolution of the pronoun is delayed, as it is not completed until the referential link is established.

Another possible case of partial resolution is implicit in Oakhill, Garnham, and Vonk's (1989) distinction between role-to-role and role-to-name mapping of pronouns. In a sentence such as (38):

(38) Max confessed to Bill because he wanted a reduced sentence.

the role of the pronoun's referent (the person doing the wanting) can be mapped to either the role of the antecedent (the confessor) or to the name of the antecedent (Max). Full interpretation requires both. But Oakhill et al. point out that the two types of mapping can be carried out separately, and that there are circumstances in which one may well be performed without the other. For example, if Bill were replaced by Jill (38), the pronoun could be resolved on this basis of its gender, so role-to-name mapping would be possible without role-to-role mapping.

Reference and syntactic processing

In well-written texts references should eventually be resolved as the author intended. If a sentence is structurally ambiguous, either globally or locally, referential considerations may determine which analysis is preferred. So, in a context in which there are two women, one of whom has been rescued by a fireman, the "that" clause in a sentence beginning:

(39) The fireman told the woman that he had rescued...

might have to be interpreted as a relative clause so that it is clear which woman the sentence is about. This interpretation would run counter to the normal preference to interpret "that" clauses, where possible, as complements rather than relatives, because (the initial part of a) complement clause is structurally simpler than (the initial part of a) relative clause. It is agreed by all parties that readers and listeners usually do produce the correct interpretation of such sentences eventually. However, there has been a debate about whether the *failure* of the simple noun phrase "the woman" to refer in such a context can prevent the initial (mis)analysis of the (beginning of the) "that" clause as a complement. According to the garden-path theory (e.g. Frazier, 1987), only syntactic information can guide initial parsing decisions. Referential considerations can only *overturn* the incorrect initial decision that favours a complement reading of a "that" clause over a relative reading. They cannot prevent that decision from being made.

The strongest evidence for the initial misanalysis of relative clauses as complement clauses comes from experiments in which subjects' eye movements are monitored as they read sentences with ambiguous "that" clauses that turn out to be either complements or relatives, for example:

(40a) The fireman told the woman that he had rescued many people in similar fires.

(40b) The fireman told the woman that he had rescued to install a smoke detector.

Readers slow down and/or look back when they reach the so-called disambiguating region of the sentence, if that disambiguation shows that the "that" clause is a relative clause ("to install" is harder than "many people"). This is not simply an effect of different content, since "to install" is read without difficulty when there is no ambiguity, as in (41):

(41) The fireman asked the woman that he had rescued to install a smoke detector.

("asked" cannot have a complement beginning with "that", so there is no complement/relative ambiguity in this sentence).

Altmann, Garnham, and Dennis (1992) showed that, at least in the majority of cases, *referential failure* of a simple noun phrase (such as "the woman" in the previous examples) resulted in an immediate preference for interpreting the "that" clause as a relative. Altmann, Garnham, and Henstra (1994) reported similar findings when the ambiguity was resolved earlier (because the relative clause was a subject relative, not an object relative, and a complement clause cannot have a missing subject).

(42) He told the woman that had been waiting for him...

Thus, if a simple noun phrase fails to refer, following material is preferably analysed as a modifier that provides more specific information, and that, if the text is felicitous, will resolve the reference. Relative clauses are modifiers, but complement clauses are not. Our results contrast sharply with an attempt to manipulate referential factors by a focusing manipulation (Rayner, Garrod, & Perfetti, 1992), in which default structural preferences were not overturned. They are also difficult to reconcile with the results of Garrod et al. (1993) who found no evidence that definite noun phrase anaphors were linked immediately to their antecedents.

SUMMARY AND CONCLUSIONS

Psycholinguists are primarily concerned with what goes on in people's heads when they produce and understand language. Nevertheless, much of our linguistic mental machinery is there to let us talk about things that happen in real and imaginary worlds. Reference is crucial to language, and theories of language processing must explain how our mental machinery allows us to refer to things external to us. Linguists and philosophers have shown that, despite the apparent transparency of simple cases (e.g.

reference to the author of this chapter using the proper name "Alan Garnham"), questions about how linguistic expressions refer are complex. A fully worked-out theory of language processing is likely to be correspondingly complex.

A common phenomenon in ordinary discourse and text is repeated reference to the same entity. Second and later references typically use anaphoric devices, such as definite pronouns. These devices usually refer successfully in context, even though it would be impossible to guess at the referent of a pronoun such as "it" if its context were not known. The theory of mental models provides a framework within which the narrowing down of the set of possible referents for an anaphoric expression can be described. However, the existence of this framework leaves many questions about the detailed mechanisms of anaphor resolution unanswered. A substantial body of empirical work in psycholinguistics has been devoted to answering these questions, and some of it has been described in this chapter. Finally, although these processes are semantic, or meaning-based, processes, there is some indication that they can interact with syntactic processes in assigning referents to noun phrases.

ACKNOWLEDGEMENTS

The author's work described in this chapter has been supported by grants RC00232439 "Mental Models and the Interpretation of Anaphora", and R000236481 "Mental Models in Text Comprehension: Constraints on Inference" to Alan Garnham and Jane Oakhill from ESRC, by grant SPG8920151 "Parsing in Context: Computational and Psycholinguistic Approaches to Resolving Ambiguity during Sentence processing" to Gerry Altmann and Alan Garnham from the Joint Research Councils Initiative on Cognitive Science and Human Computer Interaction, by NATO Collaborative Research Grant CRG.890527, and by Acción Integrada MDR/980/2/(1994/5)/532 from the British Council and the Spanish Ministry of Education and Science.

REFERENCES

Altmann, G.T.M., Garnham, A., & Dennis, Y. (1992). Avoiding the garden path: Eye movements in context. *Journal of Memory and Language*, *31*, 685–712.

Altmann, G.T.M., Garnham, A., & Henstra, J.-A. (1994). Effects of syntax in human sentence parsing: Evidence against a structure-based proposal mechanism. *Journal of Experimental Psychology: Learning, Memory, and Cognition*, *20*, 209–216.

Anderson, A., Garrod, S.C., & Sanford, A.J. (1983). The accessibility of pronominal antecedents as a function of episode shift in narrative text. *Quarterly Journal of Experimental Psychology*, *35A*, 427–440.

Barwise, J., & Cooper, R. (1981). Generalized quantifiers and natural language. *Linguistics and Philosophy*, *4*, 159–219.

Barwise, J., & Perry, J. (1983). *Situations and attitudes*. Cambridge, MA: MIT Press.

Bosch, P. (1983). *Agreement and anaphora: A study of the role of pronouns in syntax and discourse*. London: Academic Press.

Caramazza, A., Grober, E., Garvey, C., & Yates, J. (1977). Comprehension of anaphoric pronouns. *Journal of Verbal Learning and Verbal Behavior, 16*, 601–609.

Carreiras, M., Garnham, A., Oakhill, J.V., & Cain, K. (1996). The use of stereotypical gender information in constructing a mental model: Evidence from English and Spanish. *Quarterly Journal of Experimental Psychology, 49A*, 639–663.

Chomsky, N. (1975). Questions of form and interpretation. *Linguistic Analysis, 1*, 75–109.

Corbett, A.T., & Chang, F.R. (1983). Pronoun disambiguation: Accessing potential antecedents. *Memory and Cognition, 11*, 283–294.

Cornish, F. (1996). "Antecedentless" anaphors: Deixis, anaphora, or what? Some evidence from English and French. *Journal of Linguistics, 32*, 19–41.

Corum, C. (1973). Anaphoric peninsulars. *Chicago Linguistics Society, 9*, 89–97.

Crawley, R.A., Stevenson, R.J., & Kleinman, D. (1990). The use of heuristic strategies in the interpretation of pronouns. *Journal of Psycholinguistic Research, 19*, 245–264.

Ehrlich, K., & Rayner, K. (1983). Pronoun assignment and semantic integration during reading: Eye movements and immediacy of processing. *Journal of Verbal Learning and Verbal Behavior, 22*, 75–87.

Evans, G. (1980). Pronouns. *Linguistic Inquiry, 11*, 337–362.

Evans, G. (1982). *The varieties of reference*. Oxford, UK: Oxford University Press.

Frazier, L. (1987). Sentence processing: A tutorial review. In M. Coltheart (Ed.), *Attention and performance XII: The psychology of reading* (pp. 559–586). Hove, UK: Lawrence Erlbaum Associates Ltd.

Frege, G. (1952). On sense and meaning. (M. Black, Trans.). In P. Geach & M. Black (Eds.), *Translations from the philosophical writings of Gottlob Frege* (pp. 56–78). Oxford, UK: Basil Blackwell. (Reprinted from Über Sinn und Bedeutung, *Zeitschrift für Philosophie und philosophische Kritik*, 1852, *100*, 25–50).

Garnham, A., & Mason, J.L. (1987). Episode structure in memory for narrative text. *Language and Cognitive Processes, 2*, 133–144.

Garnham, A., & Oakhill, J.V. (1987). Interpreting elliptical verb phrases. *Quarterly Journal of Experimental Psychology, 39A*, 611–627.

Garnham, A., & Oakhill, J.V. (1988). "Anaphoric islands" revisited. *Quarterly Journal of Experimental Psychology, 40A*, 719–735.

Garnham, A., & Oakhill, J.V. (1996). The mental models theory of language comprehension. In B.K. Britton & A.C. Graesser (Eds.), *Models of understanding text* (pp. 313–339). Mahwah, NJ: Lawrence Erlbaum Associates Inc.

Garnham, A., Oakhill, J.V., Ehrlich, M.-F., & Carreiras, M. (1995). Representations and processes in the interpretation of pronouns: New evidence from Spanish and French. *Journal of Memory and Language, 34*, 41–62.

Garnham, A., Traxler, M., Oakhill, J.V., & Gernsbacher, M.A. (1996). The locus of implicit causality effects in comprehension. *Journal of Memory and Language, 35*, 517–543.

Garrod, S.C., Freudenthal, D., & Boyle, E. (1993). The role of different types of anaphor in the on-line resolution of sentences in a discourse. *Journal of Memory and Language, 32*, 1–30.

Garrod, S.C., & Sanford, A.J. (1985). On the real-time character of interpretation during reading. *Language and Cognitive Processes, 1*, 43–59.

Garvey, C., & Caramazza, A. (1974). Implicit causality in verbs. *Linguistic Inquiry, 5*, 459–464.

Geach, P. (1962). *Reference and generality*. Ithaca, NY: Cornell University Press.

Gernsbacher, M.A. (1989). Mechanisms that improve referential access. *Cognition, 32*, 99–156.

Gernsbacher, M.A. (1991). Comprehending conceptual anaphors. *Language and Cognitive Processes*, *6*, 81–105.

Gernsbacher, M.A., & Hargreaves, D. (1988). Accessing sentence participants: The advantage of first mention. *Journal of Memory and Language*, *27*, 699–717.

Gordon, P.C., & Chan, D. (1995). Pronouns, passives, and discourse coherence. *Journal of Memory and Language*, *34*, 216–231.

Gordon, P.C., Grosz, B.J., & Gilliom, L.A. (1993). Pronouns, names, and the centering of attention in discourse. *Cognitive Science*, *17*, 311–347.

Hankamer, J., & Sag, I.A. (1976). Deep and surface anaphora. *Linguistic Inquiry*, *7*, 391–428.

Hawkins, J.A. (1978). *Definiteness and indefiniteness: A study in reference and grammaticality prediction*. London: Croom Helm.

Johnson-Laird, P.N., & Garnham, A. (1980). Descriptions and discourse models. *Linguistics and Philosophy*, *3*, 371–393.

Kamp, H. (1981). A theory of truth and semantic representation. In J.A.G. Groenendijk, T.M.V. Janssen, & M.B.J. Stockhof (Eds.), *Formal methods in the study of language* (pp. 227–322). Amsterdam: Mathematical Centre Tracts.

Karttunen, L. (1969). Pronouns and variables. *Chicago Linguistics Society*, *5*, 108–116.

Marr, D. (1982). *Vision: A computational investigation into the human representation and processing of visual information*. San Francisco: Freeman.

Marslen-Wilson, W.D., Levy, E., & Tyler, L.K. (1982). Producing interpretable discourse: The establishment and maintenance of reference. In R.J. Jarvella & W. Klein (Eds.), *Speech, place and action* (pp. 339–378). Chichester, UK: John Wiley & Sons.

Mauner, G., Tanenhaus, M.K., & Carlson, G.N. (1995). A note on parallelism effects in processing deep and surface verb-phrase anaphora. *Language and Cognitive Processes*, *10*, 1–12.

Morrow, D.G. (1985). Prominent characters and events organize narrative understanding. *Journal of Memory and Language*, *24*, 304–319.

Moxey, L.M., & Sanford, A.J. (1993). *Communicating quantities: A psychological perspective*. Hove, UK: Lawrence Erlbaum Associates Ltd.

Murphy, G.L. (1985a). Processes of understanding anaphora. *Journal of Memory and Language*, *24*, 290–303.

Murphy, G.L. (1985b). Psychological explanations of deep and surface anaphora. *Journal of Pragmatics*, *9*, 785–813.

Oakhill, J.V., Garnham, A., Gernsbacher, M.A., & Cain, K. (1992). How natural are conceptual anaphors? *Language and Cognitive Processes*, *7*, 257–280.

Oakhill, J.V., Garnham, A., & Vonk, W. (1989). The on-line construction of discourse models. *Language and Cognitive Processes*, *4*, 263–286.

Postal, P. (1969). Anaphoric islands. *Chicago Linguistics Society*, *5*, 205–239.

Rayner, K., Garrod, S.C., & Perfetti, C.A. (1992). Discourse influences during parsing are delayed. *Cognition*, *45*, 109–139.

Sag, I.A., & Hankamer, J. (1984). Toward a theory of anaphoric processing. *Linguistics and Philosophy*, *7*, 325–345.

Sanford, A.J., & Garrod, S.C. (1989). What, when and how: Questions of immediacy in anaphoric reference resolution. *Language and Cognitive Processes*, *4*, SI235–262.

Sanford, A.J., & Garrod, S.C., Lucas, A., & Henderson, R. (1984). Pronouns without antecedents? *Journal of Semantics*, *2*, 303–318.

Sanford, A.J., Moar, K., & Garrod, S.C. (1988). Proper names as controllers of discourse focus. *Language and Speech*, *31*, 43–56.

Solan, L. (1983). *Pronominal reference: Child language and the theory of grammar*. Dordrecht, The Netherlands: Reidel.

Tanenhaus, M.K., & Carlson, G.N. (1990). Comprehension of deep and surface anaphors. *Language and Cognitive Processes*, *5*, 257–280.

Tasmowski-de Ryck, L., & Verluyten, P. (1982). Linguistic control of pronouns. *Journal of Semantics*, *1*, 323–346.

Vonk, W. (1985). The immediacy of inferences in the understanding of pronouns. In G. Rickheit & H. Strohner (Eds.), *Inferences in text processing* (pp. 205–218). Amsterdam: North-Holland.

Vonk, W., Hustinx, L.G.M.M., & Simons, W.H.G. (1992). The use of referential expressions in structuring discourse. *Language and Cognitive Processes*, *7*, 301–333.

PART FIVE

Language production and dialogue processing

CHAPTER TWELVE

Language production

Kathryn Bock and John Huitema
Beckman Institute for Advanced Science and Technology, University of Illinois, Urbana, USA

Language production—talking—is a facet of language performance. Its special properties may be set in relief against the backdrop of Noam Chomsky's (1965, p. 3) famous definition of the subject matter of linguistics:

> Linguistic theory is concerned primarily with an ideal speaker-listener, in a completely homogeneous speech-community, who knows its language perfectly and is unaffected by such grammatically irrelevant conditions as memory limitations, distractions, shifts of attention and interest, and errors (random or characteristic) in applying his knowledge of the language in actual performance.

By contrast, psycholinguistic theory is concerned with *real* speakers who are *vulnerable* to memory limitations, distractions, shifts of attention and interest, and errors (random or characteristic) in applying their knowledge of the language. Regarding language production in particular, the goal of psycholinguistics is to explain how real speakers in real time retrieve and assemble elements of language from long-term memory in order to communicate their ideas.

The chief issues in language production centre on information processing, and include how and when the processing system retrieves different kinds of linguistic knowledge, how the system uses the knowledge once it has been retrieved, how the system interrelates linguistic and non-linguistic knowledge, and how the system is organised within and constrained by human cognitive capacities. In this chapter we will survey the kinds of phenomena that serve as focal points for research on production, present an overview of the cognitive processes that take place in the course of creating an utterance, and summarise some of the psycholinguistic findings that illuminate the workings of these processes. At the end we will consider how language production fits into the broader framework of psycholinguistic research.

PHENOMENA OF LANGUAGE PRODUCTION

The facts that a theory of language production should explain are not immediately obvious, because—intuitively—talking isn't hard. In a lecture delivered at the University of Illinois in 1909, a famous founder of American psychology claimed to be able to "read off what I have to say from a memory manuscript" (Titchener, 1909, p. 8). This caricatures one's usual experience when speaking, but perhaps not by much. Talking seems just too easy to pose any problems worth explaining.

Because of this, the challenges of production are more readily appreciated in terms of talk's typical failures. The failures range widely. One sort is illustrated by a psychology professor's experience during a transient neurological episode. During the attack, the professor was able to form perfectly coherent messages, but could not express them (Ashcraft, 1993, pp. 49, 54):

> The thoughts can only be described in sentence-like form, because they were as complex, detailed, and lengthy as a typical sentence. They were not sentences, however. The experience was not one of merely being unable to articulate a word currently held in consciousness. Instead, it was one of being fully aware of the target idea yet totally unable to accomplish what normally feels like the single act of finding-and-saying-the-word ... The idea ... was as complete and full as any idea one might have normally, but was not an unspoken mental sentence ... It was the unusual "gap" in this usually seamless process [of sentence production], a process taken completely for granted in normal circumstances, that amazes me.

More than a century earlier, William James (1890, pp. 251–252) described another type of failure during speech, the common tip-of-the-tongue experience, in which a single circumscribed meaning comes to mind but the corresponding word does not:

> Suppose we try to recall a forgotten name. The state of our consciousness is peculiar. There is a gap therein: but no mere gap. It is a gap that is intensely active. A sort of wraith of the name is in it, beckoning us in a given

> direction, making us at moments tingle with the sense of our closeness, and then letting us sink back without the longed-for term. If wrong names are proposed to us, this singularly definite gap acts immediately so as to negate them. They do not fit into its mould. And the gap of one word does not feel like the gap of another, all empty of content as both might seem necessarily to be when described as gaps.

These introspections allude to gaps in the process of putting ideas into words, but gaps of different kinds. Ashcraft experienced an unbridgeable gap between the thought he wanted to convey and the cognitive processes that normally create the linguistic form to express that thought. The tip-of-the-tongue state that James described reveals a gap between a single concept and the word that expresses it.

In addition to such problems of omission, there are problems of commission. Table 12.1 presents a selection, drawn from our own observations, of the many kinds of speech errors that have been studied in research on language production. The first two examples are anticipations—saying too early a word or a sound that is supposed to come later in the utterance. The next two are perseverations—repeating a word or a sound from earlier in the utterance. Sometimes two linguistic elements exchange places in an utterance, as illustrated in examples 5–8. Still

TABLE 12.1
Sample Speech Errors

Type of Error	*Intended Utterance*	*Error*
1. Word anticipation	bury me right with him	bury him right with him
2. Sound anticipation	the lush list	the lust list
3. Word perseveration	evidence brought to bear on representational theories	evidence brought to bear on representational evidence
4. Sound perseveration	President Bush's budget	President Bush's boodget
5. Word exchange	the head of a pin	the pin of a head
6. Sound exchange	occipital activity	accipital octivity
7. Stranding exchange	the dome doesn't have any windows	the window doesn't have any domes
8. Phrase exchange	the death of his son from leukaemia	the death of leukaemia from his son
9. Semantically related word-substitution	I like berries with my cereal	I like berries with my fruit
10. Phonologically related word-substitution	part of a community	part of a committee
11. Sound substitution	the disparity	the disparigy
12. Word blend	it really stood/stuck out	it really stook out
13. Phrase blend	at large/on the loose	at the loose

another type of error, called a substitution, is to say a word or sound other than the one that was intended, as shown in examples 9–11. The final sort of error illustrated in the table is when a speaker blends two words or phrases together, as in the last two examples.

The most common problem in production is disfluency: Speakers commit false starts, they pause silently or noisily (saying "uh" or "um") in the course of an utterance, and they retrace their verbal steps. They do these things very often. Considering only filled pauses ("uh", "um", and "er"), the average rate in the lectures of 45 professors from 10 different disciplines has been clocked at one pause every 18 seconds (Schachter, Christenfeld, Ravina, & Bilous, 1991). Some of these disfluencies reflect simple indecision about what to say next, but others stem from momentary disruptions in specific language processes, such as retrieving a particular word or constructing an expression.

Speech errors and disfluencies both provide clues about the nature of information processing in language production. A schematic view of what they suggest about the processes and their organisation is shown in Fig. 12.1. In the next section we will explain how the components of the figure relate to the errors that people commit when they talk.

THE COGNITIVE COMPONENTS OF LANGUAGE PRODUCTION

Production begins with an intention to communicate an idea. The idea is called a *message*, and we assume that it is a thought, largely unadorned by the trappings of language. At this level, the messages of a French speaker may not be much different from those of an English speaker, or a Japanese speaker, or a speaker of any language. Returning to Ashcraft's description of his transient neurological episode, it appears that he was able to formulate messages but was momentarily unable to express them in language.

In terms of the model in Fig. 12.1, what was missing was the ability to carry out the cognitive work that is needed for finding words and putting them together (grammatical encoding) or for finding sounds and putting them together (phonological encoding). Notice in the figure that these processes are separated into two different components. There are several reasons for this separation. We will briefly survey four of them.

First, consider the frequency with which different kinds of elements are involved in errors, shown in Fig. 12.2. Two kinds of units stand out. Among the meaningful units, words are more frequently implicated than any others, and among the sound units, phonemes (single sounds) are by far the most frequently involved. This would not be surprising if words and phonemes were the most common units in speech overall, but they

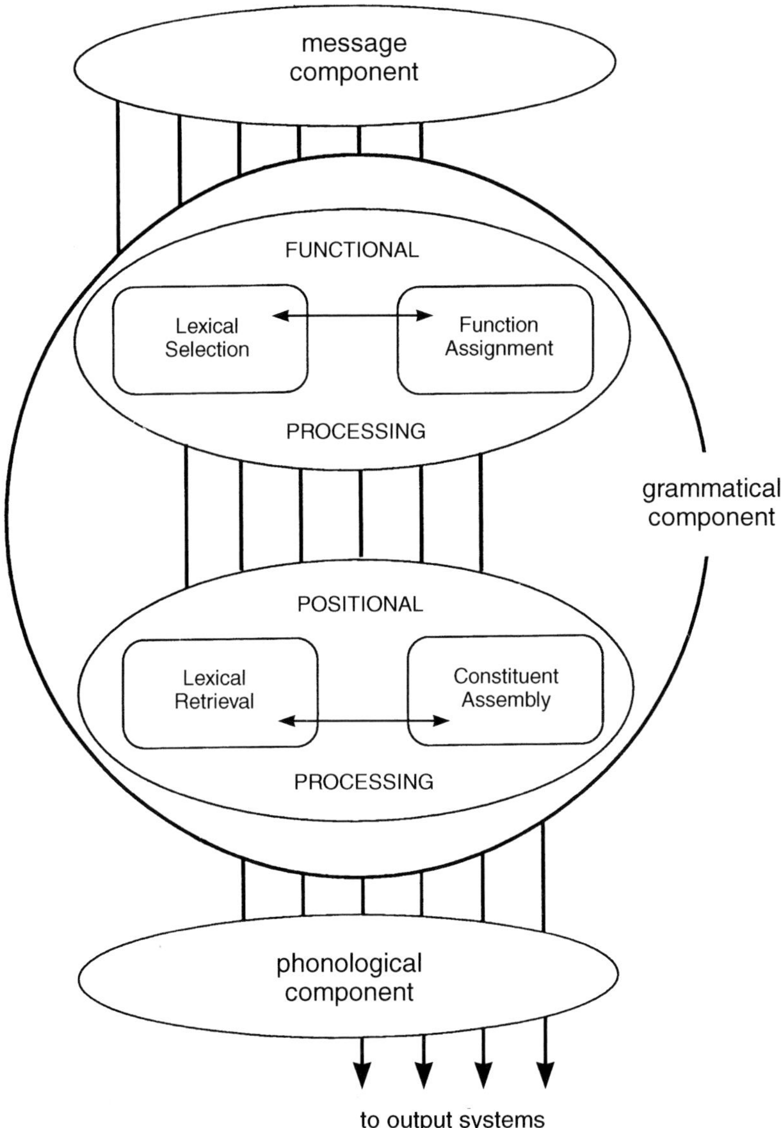

FIG. 12.1 The organisation of processing components in normal language production (from Bock, 1995). Copyright © (1995) Academic Press. Reprinted with permission.

are not: Words are less common than morphemes (units of meaning like *un-* and *-happy* in the word *unhappy*), and phonemes are less common than features (articulatory components of sounds, such as voicing). The implication is that there is a set of processes that deal mainly with finding

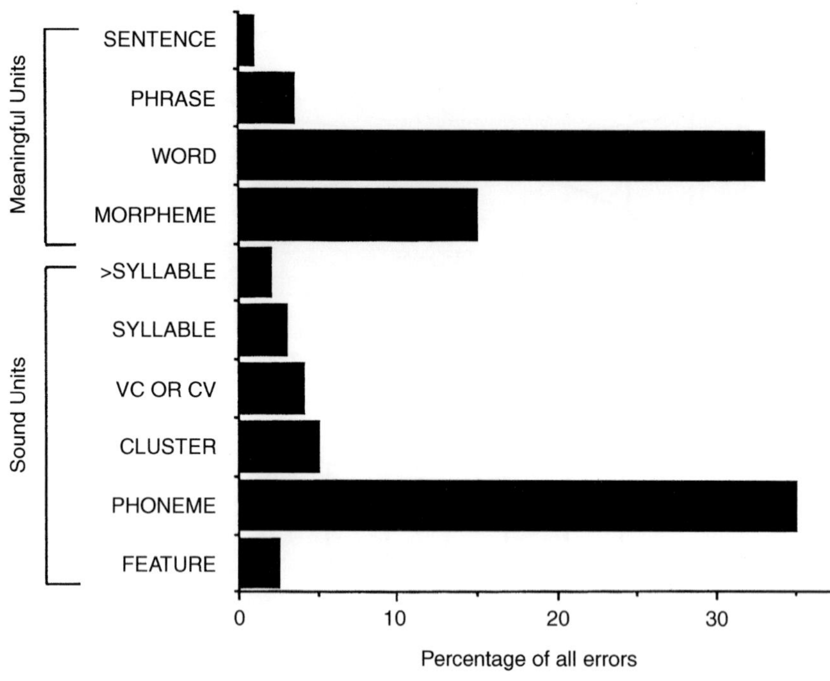

FIG. 12.2 The frequency of different types of linguistic units in exchange errors (from Dell, 1995). Copyright © (1995) MIT Press. Reprinted with permission.

and arranging words (grammatical encoding) and a set of processes that deal mainly with finding and arranging phoneme segments (phonological encoding).

A second reason for separating the grammatical and phonological components can be seen in another feature of exchange errors. The words in exchanges usually represent the same grammatical category: Nouns exchange with nouns, verbs with verbs, and so on. By contrast, when a phoneme exchanges with another phoneme, there is no obvious grammatical similarity between the words in which the exchanging phonemes originated. So, counter to what one would expect if syntactic categories constrained all production processes, the syntactic categories of the containing words are irrelevant to sound exchanges. However, the exchanging sounds themselves tend to come from similar phonological categories: Consonants exchange with other consonants, whereas vowels exchange with other vowels. The implication again is that one component of the production system attends to the syntactic category of words in order to arrange them grammatically, while another component attends to the sounds of words and is oblivious to their syntactic functions.

A third piece of evidence for the separation of grammatical and phonological processes comes from yet another property of word and sound exchanges. Words that exchange are typically separated by a phrase or two, whereas sounds that exchange usually come from adjacent words in the same phrase (Garrett, 1980a). This observation suggests that grammatical processes and phonological processes differ in the range over which they operate, with grammatical encoding having a longer view of the eventual utterance than phonological processes.

The model's division into grammatical and phonological processes can also help to explain the features of certain complex errors, such as "The skreaky gwease gets the wheel". The speaker intended to say "The squeaky wheel gets the grease", implying that someone who whines and complains is more likely to get attention than someone who suffers in silence. According to the model in Fig. 12.1, the erroneous utterance occurred because of two distinct disruptions. First, in arranging the words, the grammatical component misplaced the nouns *wheel* and *grease*, setting the stage for the utterance "The squeaky grease gets the wheel". But then something else went wrong. Since *squeaky* and *grease* became next-door neighbours as a result of the word-exchange error, they were close enough for their sounds to exchange, and two of them did. So, while ordering the words' phonemes, the /r/ and /w/ sounds exchanged, leading to "skreaky gwease".

GRAMMATICAL ENCODING

Now we will look inside the grammatical component at the processes that retrieve and arrange words. There are two sets of operations, divided into functional processing and positional processing. In describing these operations, we will make use of an analogy to a mental dictionary with entries arranged like the one in the left panel of Fig. 12.3, and a mental sentence skeleton constructed like the one in the right panel. Notice that the lexical entry works like one in a reverse dictionary, or Roget's (1852) original thesaurus, a dictionary in which entries must be consulted according to their meanings rather than their letters or sounds.

Functional processing

Functional processing is concerned with selecting words from the mental lexicon (lexical selection) and assigning syntactic functions to them (function assignment). Lexical selection can be likened to locating an entry with the right meaning in the mental reverse dictionary, prior to finding a pronunciation for it (unlike a real dictionary entry). Function assignment is deciding which message element is going to be the grammatical subject, which the direct object, and so on.

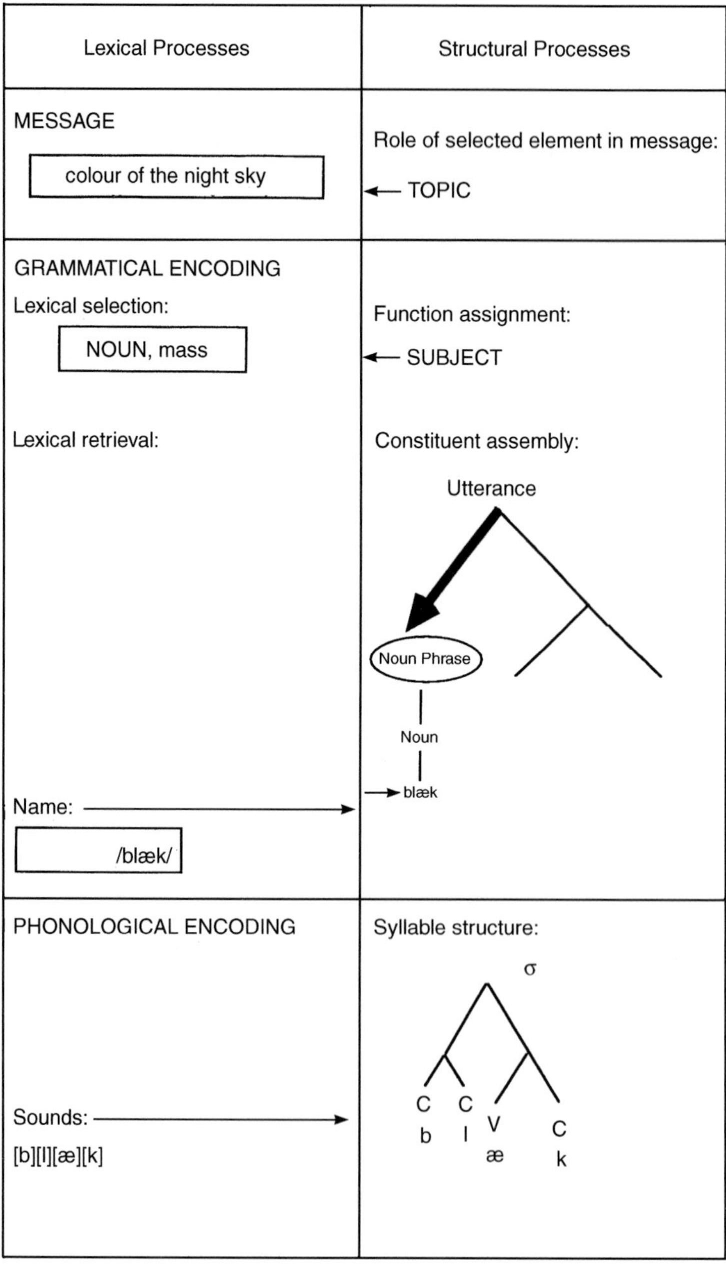

FIG. 12.3 Retrieving a word (*black*) for production in the utterance *Black is my favourite colour*.

The operation of lexical selection is discernible in the tip-of-the-tongue (TOT) state. This is the annoying condition that William James described, in which one is quite sure of knowing a word to express a particular meaning, while being unable to retrieve the word's sounds. Some evidence that speakers in this state have in fact selected a particular word, rather than just a concept, comes from a speaker of Italian who suffered brain damage, making it very difficult for him to name pictures of everyday objects. Even when he could only guess at what the first or last sound of the name was, he was almost perfect at choosing the appropriate masculine or feminine article (Badecker, Miozzo, & Zanuttini, 1995). The concepts expressed by these words were not inherently male or female: For example, the Italian word for dessert, *dolce*, is masculine, and the word for hand, *mano*, is feminine. The concept alone is not enough to determine the gender of the word. Therefore, the speaker must have been using information about the word itself to make his judgement, showing that he had indeed selected a particular word, even though he was not able to retrieve the sounds of that word.

Lexical selection can go astray in a different way, as in the error "I like berries with my fruit" (produced instead of "I like berries with my cereal", see in Table 12.1). In such semantic substitutions, an incorrect but related word is selected to express a concept. The problem is analogous to mistakenly picking an entry next to the intended word in the reverse dictionary. The result is a substitution that is similar in meaning to the intended word but not usually similar in sound.

The other component of functional processing is function assignment. Function assignment determines the syntactic role that message elements will play in an utterance. Errors involving the exchange of pronouns are particularly informative about the process. This is because pronouns in English overtly mark syntactic functions like subject (nominative case), object (objective case), possessive (genitive case), and so on, as seen in the respective forms of the masculine singular pronoun in "*He* liked *him* and *his* family". An illustrative mistake was reported by Garrett (1980b). A speaker intended to say "She offends his sense of how the world should be", but what came out was "He offends her sense of how the world should be". This is an exchange of pronouns, but the thing to notice is that it is not a simple exchange of the pronoun forms: The error is not "His offends she sense of how the world should be". What happened? Apparently, the syntactic function of subject was erroneously assigned to the masculine player in the event, while the possessive function was assigned to the feminine player. In other words, something went wrong during function assignment, causing the message elements to be mapped to the wrong syntactic roles.

The product of functional processing is a representation that indicates for each message element its syntactic role and the words to be used for expressing it. Two important properties of utterances are yet to emerge: The actual order of the phrases and specifications for the sounds of words. These are part of positional processing.

Positional processing

Like functional processing, positional processing involves both a syntactic and a lexical sub-component. The syntactic sub-component is called *constituent assembly*. It puts phrases, words, and grammatical inflections in order, arranging them in accordance with the grammatical patterns of the language. One error feature that is associated with constituent assembly is termed *stranding* (see Table 12.1), which reliably accompanies any exchange of inflected words. The occurrence of stranding implies that the stems and affixes of words are positioned separately during processing, even though they eventually surface together in speech. This is illustrated in the utterance of a speaker who intended to say "The dome doesn't have any windows" and instead said "The window doesn't have any domes". Despite the exchange of the word stems *dome* and *window*, the plural *-s* suffix stayed put: It was stranded in the direct object position and affixed itself to *dome*. The error suggests that function assignment was correctly carried out: The intended subject was singular and the subject remains singular in the error, though the subject noun is the wrong one. Similarly, the intended direct object was plural and the direct object remains plural in the error, though the noun is wrong. Evidently, the problem arose when the processes of constituent assembly positioned the retrieved word forms, putting them into phrase slots like the one shown on the right in Fig. 12.3.

The lexical sub-component of positional processing, lexical retrieval, is concerned with retrieving abstract word forms, like the one shown on the left in Fig. 12.3. More precisely, the outcome of lexical retrieval is a description of a word's morphology to be filled out in more detail during phonological encoding. Continuing the analogy to the reverse-dictionary entry, lexical retrieval involves finding the part of the entry that indicates the word's structure and alphabetic spelling (which is likewise a description of a word's sounds, albeit a different sort of description than one envisions for the mental lexicon). One type of error that may be attributable to disruptions in lexical retrieval is the phonological word-substitution, sometimes termed a malapropism. The substituted word sounds similar to the intended word (e.g. "committee" instead of "community"; see Table 12.1) but need not be related to it in meaning. This indicates that similar-sounding word forms can interfere with one another during retrieval, despite being different in meaning, and can be explained as another consequence of the separation of lexical retrieval from lexical selection.

PHONOLOGICAL ENCODING

Whereas grammatical encoding manipulates words or morphemes as wholes, phonological encoding manipulates the components of words, the speech sounds. It is responsible for putting phonemes and syllables in order, within representations that carry the rhythmic and intonational qualities of the language. It determines how the individual sounds of a word are pronounced, how they should be ordered, where syllable boundaries are, and so on. At the bottom of Fig. 12.3, the sounds of the word *black* are spelled out in preparation for assignment to slots in a syllabic frame that helps to control the articulation of speech.

Failures of phonological encoding are revealed in such errors as sound exchanges, perseverations, and anticipations (see Table 12.1). These errors show that phonological encoding is, like grammatical encoding, tightly constrained. Phoneme exchanges almost always involve sounds from the same class (consonant or vowel; MacKay, 1970). Elements are more likely to exchange when the sounds that precede or follow them are phonetically similar (Garrett, 1975). There is a positional constraint, as well, such that errors tend to implicate the same parts of different syllables. For example, in the error "lust list" (in Table 12.1), the cluster of syllable-final consonants (or *coda*) in the intended word "lush" was replaced by the coda of the following word, "list". Errors in which different parts of successive syllables interact (e.g. "stush list") are rare.

The product of phonological encoding serves as input to the articulatory processes that actually give voice to the utterance. Although not the focus of this chapter, articulation is itself a complex skill: Producing the roughly 15 sounds per second that make up fluent speech requires the rapid co-ordination of more groups of muscles than are involved in any other mechanical performance of the human body (Fink, 1986).

AN ALTERNATIVE PERSPECTIVE ON SPEECH ERRORS?

The information-processing approach exemplified by the model in Fig. 12.1 stands in stark contrast to a more famous theory of the origin of speech errors, that of Sigmund Freud. Freud formulated his views in reaction to the work of an Austrian linguist of the late 1800s named Rudolf Meringer (Meringer & Mayer, 1895/1978). Meringer recorded the speech errors he heard, and noticed that errors often involved linguistic elements that are similar to one another. He suggested that errors might come about because of transient changes in the memory strength of words or sounds that cause them to appear in places where they do not belong. This is reminiscent of claims in some contemporary production theories (e.g. Dell, 1986), close relatives of the model we have sketched in this chapter.

Freud, in contrast, speculated that the true sources of errors lie beyond the mundane linguistic similarities that Meringer emphasised. As almost everyone knows, Freud proposed that errors were the result of unconscious intentions that coloured or played havoc with the consciously intended message. He offered the instance of a professor who said "In the case of the female genital, in spite of the tempting ... I mean, the attempted..." (Freud, 1924/1935, p. 38). Another of Freud's examples was analysed as originating in the underlying ill-feeling of a worker toward his boss. The worker called on his colleagues before a meal to "burp [*aufzustossen*] to the health of our chief" instead of "drink a toast [*anzustossen*] to the health of our chief" (Freud, 1924/1935, p. 38).

Freud's idea that speech errors reveal unconscious motives was clearly more provocative than Meringer's. It was so provocative, in fact, that there was very little work on speech errors from a cognitive or linguistic perspective for many years after Freud produced his psychodynamic analysis.

Yet there are fundamental weaknesses in the Freudian account. One is that hardly any speech errors have a clear Freudian interpretation. Most errors are at best innocuous and at worst downright boring, as the examples in Table 12.1 testify. Freud may have been misled by the properties of the sample of speech errors he observed or, more likely, he overemphasised the most interesting of the mistakes that he encountered. Ellis (1980) showed that Freud's collection of errors is indeed unrepresentative of the distribution that arises in everyday speaking.

A second problem with the Freudian account is also apparent in Table 12.1. Almost all speech errors show a strong influence of purely linguistic factors. Consider the "toasting/burping" example again, in the original German form: "Ich fördere sie auf, auf das wohl unseres chefs aufzustossen." The substituted word *aufzustossen* is very similar to the intended word *anzustossen*, and the word *auf* appeared twice prior to its erroneous appearance, suggesting that it was very strongly primed. Freud considered this and dismissed it out of hand (Freud, 1924/1935, pp. 53–54), embracing as the only possibility that the production of a word or phrase entails the representation of a relevant meaning within what we have termed the speaker's message. The linguistic constraints on errors, their most prominent characteristics, have no satisfactory explanation in this framework.

None of this means that Freud was demonstrably wrong in his hypotheses about the causes of errors. None the less, his hypotheses explain very little about most mistakes in speech, overlooking or omitting most of the data. The study of speech errors therefore returned to Meringer's original interest in what errors can tell us about how people talk, instead of what they might reveal about the darker recesses of people's thought. Building from this work on errors, experimental research has begun to uncover a variety of facts about the kinds of processes that are involved in speaking.

EXPERIMENTAL RESEARCH ON LANGUAGE PRODUCTION

Although analyses of errors in spontaneous speech served as the starting point for the contemporary study of language production, there is much more for a theory to explain. Errors are rare events, particularly when we consider them in light of ordinary speech achievements. Measurements of normal speech rates give average values of about 150 words per minute (Maclay & Osgood, 1959) or 5.65 syllables per second (Deese, 1984). Although this speech is liberally sprinkled with pauses and false starts, outright error is very uncommon. For example, in a tape-recorded corpus of nearly 15,000 utterances, Deese (1984) counted only 77 syntactic anomalies—roughly one in every 195 utterances. Heeschen (1993) reported a similarly low incidence of syntactic errors in spoken German. Errors of lexical selection and retrieval (such as semantic and phonological word-substitutions) are even less common, with attested rates averaging under one per 1000 words (Bock & Levelt, 1994). Sound errors are rarest of all, occurring less than once in every 2000 words. The implication is that the most challenging facts about speaking stem from its general accuracy and fluency.

These normal levels of speech performance reflect the workings of an information-handling system of great complexity and considerable efficiency. To discover the system's properties, we must rely on subtle but powerful experimental techniques that can reliably detect the fleeting cognitive operations that give rise to speech. These techniques make it possible to examine the details of production processes in rigorous and systematic ways. To illustrate the experimental study of language production, we will present experiments designed to illuminate the workings of the components of the model in Fig. 12.1.

Message creation

Processing in the message component is responsible for determining the communicative content of the intended utterance. One thing a message should do, if it is to succeed in communication, is ensure that the expressions that are used to refer to things will be understandable to the listener. For instance, if one wants a listener to pick out a particular photograph from among a set of photographs of buildings in New York City, one must choose a referring expression that makes contact with what the listener knows. A particular building could be referred to in any of several ways, such as "the Citicorp building" or "the building with the slanty roof". The first expression will work well if the person one is talking to is familiar with the names of buildings in New York City; otherwise, the second expression will work better. The decision about which expression to use is a decision about what to put in one's message.

Isaacs and Clark (1987) studied exactly this situation. In their experiment, one person (the director) viewed a display of postcards depicting landmarks in New York City. The second person in the experiment (the matcher) viewed a display that had the same postcards in a different order. Neither participant could see the other's display. The only task was to get the matcher's postcards into the same order as the director's. However, none of the pictures were visibly labelled, so the partners had to come up with their own expressions to refer to them. So the director could say something along the lines of "The first picture is the Citicorp Building" or "The first picture is a building with a slanty roof".

The twist in the experiment was that some of the directors and matchers were knowledgeable about New York City, and some were not. Isaacs and Clark found that the participants quickly determined whether their partners could successfully identify pictures based on proper names (*Citicorp Building*) or needed more descriptive expressions (*building with a slanty roof*). The directors adapted their subsequent utterances appropriately, using more descriptive expressions when their listeners were unfamiliar with New York City landmarks and more proper names when directors and matchers both were knowledgeable.

This is an example of just one factor that enters into determining the substance of an utterance. It may seem obvious, but its implications are far-ranging. The content of a message typically includes more than "just the facts" that the speaker intends to convey, going beyond them to incorporate information specifically tailored to the communicative context (Clark & Bly, 1995). Message formulation can demand a great deal of problem solving, much more so than the rather mechanical operations of the encoding processes. One upshot is that speakers frequently fail to plan their messages adequately, and communication may suffer as a result (Horton & Keysar, 1996).

In addition to specifying the content of an utterance, a message must also signal the relative prominence of its components. Most important, it must indicate which element is the topic of the utterance, what the

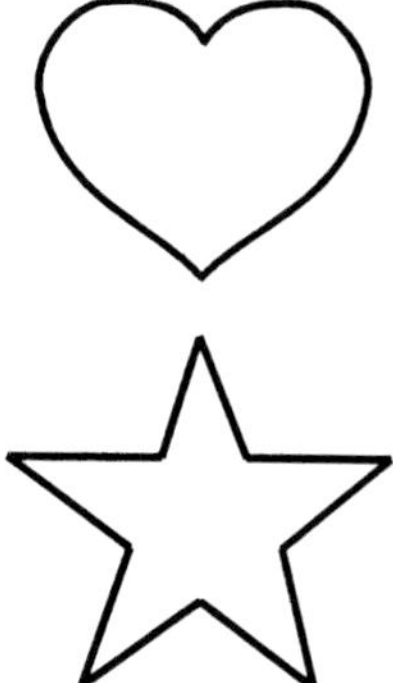

FIG. 12.4 Which component of this display is more prominent?

utterance is about. Things can become topics by attracting attention, a process illustrated in a study by Forrest (1993). In Forrest's experiments, speakers watching a computer screen had to describe the physical relation between two pictured objects like those shown in Fig. 12.4.

Immediately before the pair of objects was displayed, a cue was presented at the screen location where one of the objects would appear, drawing the speaker's attention to that location. Forrest found that this attentional manipulation strongly influenced how speakers described the scenes. Speakers were more likely to say "The heart is above the star" when their attention was directed to the heart than when it was directed to the star, and more likely to say "The star is below the heart" when their attention was directed to the star than when it was directed to the heart. Thus, it appears that an element that a speaker is attending to, an element that constitutes the intended topic, is likely to be given a prominent position in the utterance.

Grammatical encoding: Structural processes

Grammatical encoding is responsible for translating the message into a series of words, and comprises assigning syntactic functions (like subject) and arraying words in a grammatical order. Consider how one might describe the event pictured in Fig. 12.5. One could say, "The boy is being awakened by the alarm clock"—a passive sentence with "the boy" as subject—but one could also say, "The alarm clock is awakening the boy"—an active sentence with "the alarm clock" as subject. The idea is virtually the same in either case. What determines which noun is assigned the syntactic function of subject? Forrest's (1993) results suggest that function assignment takes the most prominent message element, the topic, and

FIG. 12.5 A target picture adapted from Figure 5 in Bock, Loebell, and Morey (1992).

assigns it the role of subject. Since animate objects (humans and animals especially) tend to attract attention in events, a likely subject is *the boy*.

Bock, Loebell, and Morey (1992) relied on this tendency to examine the relationship between function assignment and constituent assembly. In their experiment, subjects were presented with a series of spoken sentences and pictures, one by one. The subjects repeated each sentence and described each picture. The critical manipulation in the experiment lay in the properties of the sentences that preceded the target pictures (the "prime" sentences). The sentences varied on two dimensions, as illustrated in Table 12.2. One dimension was the animacy of the subject and object noun phrases: The subject of the prime sentence was either an animate noun phrase ("five people") or an inanimate noun phrase ("the boat"). The goal of the animacy variation was to prime the function assignment process: The type of assignment pattern used in one sentence (that is, in

TABLE 12.2
Sample Priming Sentences

Priming Condition	*Example Sentence*
Active, animate subject	Five people carried the boat.
Active, inanimate subject	The boat carried five people.
Passive, animate subject	Five people were carried by the boat.
Passive, inanimate subject	The boat was carried by five people.

the priming sentence) should tend to be repeated in a subsequent sentence (the sentence used to describe the target picture). For example, if the subject of a prime sentence was inanimate (either "The boat carried five people" or "The boat was carried by five people"), there may be a tendency to try to assign the inanimate entity in the target picture to the subject function (saying "The alarm clock wakened the boy"). The events depicted in the target pictures always included one animate and one inanimate entity, either of which could serve as the sentence subject (as in "The alarm clock wakened the boy" or "The boy was wakened by the alarm clock"). However, with function priming, there should be more sentences with inanimate subjects after primes with inanimate subjects than after primes with animate subjects.

The second variation in the priming sentences was in their syntactic form: They could be in the active voice ("Five people carried the boat"; "The boat carried five people") or in the passive ("Five people were carried by the boat"; "The boat was carried by five people"). The goal of this manipulation was to prime the constituent assembly process. Having used a particular syntactic structure for the prime sentence, the constituent assembly process may tend to repeat that structure in describing the target picture. So, active descriptions of the target picture should be more likely following active prime sentences than following passive prime sentences.

Both of these manipulations affected speakers' descriptions: First, inanimate subjects were more likely following primes with inanimate subjects, showing that function assignment tends to repeat the previous mapping of animacy to syntactic function. Second, active sentences were more likely following active primes than following passive primes, showing a tendency for constituent assembly to encore a recently produced structure. This argues that function assignment and constituent assembly are separable processes.

Grammatical encoding: Lexical processes

Recall that lexical selection is the process of identifying an entry from the mental lexicon for conveying the intended meaning. Earlier, we described the case of a brain-damaged speaker, which showed that a word can be selected and its grammatical properties accessed without its sounds becoming available. Is this true for normal speakers? This seems to be what happens when one is in a tip-of-the-tongue state: One has a word in mind but the sounds of the word are inaccessible. To find out whether speakers in a TOT state have in fact selected a particular word (rather than a concept), Vigliocco, Garrett, and Antonini (1997) asked speakers of Italian who were having a TOT experience to identify the gender of the word that they were unable to retrieve. Even when they knew nothing about how the word sounded, the speakers were able to identify the gender over 80% of the time. Because the *concepts* expressed by these nouns were neither masculine nor feminine, the ability of the Italian speakers to identify the gender of a wayward noun must be due to their having selected a particular word. This argues that word meanings and word forms are separately represented, and that lexical retrieval is a necessary component of the production process.

Phonological encoding

When the form of a word is retrieved, its sounds must be individually encoded in preparation for ordered production. We pointed out earlier that sound exchanges seem to involve phonemes of the same phonological category (consonant or vowel), in similar phonetic environments, and in similar syllable position. For example, in the vowel exchange "accipital octivity" (see Table 12.1), the exchanging vowels were both followed by the consonant /k/ and occurred in the same syllable position.

Dell (1984) tested this observation experimentally, using a procedure developed by Baars, Motley, and MacKay (1975). In this procedure, the speaker is presented visually with pairs of words, like the following:

bid meek
bud meek
big men
mad back

After certain pairs, the speaker is cued to say the words out loud. Sometimes speakers make errors when saying the words, and these are recorded. In order to increase the likelihood of an error, the target trials are preceded by several trials that are designed to bias the subject to make a slip. For example, if the target trial is the pair *mad back*, the three preceding trials would all have pairs in which the first word started with a /b/ sound and the second with an /m/ sound, biasing the subject to slip on the target pair and mistakenly say *bad mack*. Dell compared the likelihood of a slip occurring for pairs like *mad back*, in which both words have the same vowel, and pairs like *mad bake*, in which the words have different vowels. He found that exchanges of word-initial phonemes (*bad mack* or *bad make*) were more likely when the words contained the same vowel, confirming the pattern hinted at in naturalistic errors.

An important aspect of phonological encoding is placing sounds in syllable frames, as illustrated at the bottom of Fig. 12.3. This helps to ensure the correct ordering of phonemes, because syllable frames specify the order of consonants and vowels within the syllable. Syllables with different orderings are said to have different consonant-vowel (CV) structures. So, for example, the syllables "kem" and "til" have the same structure—both are consonant-vowel-consonant (CVC)—even though they are made up of different phonemes. The syllable "tilf" has a different structure (CVCC).

To test experimentally whether the phonological component represents the consonant-vowel structure of syllables during production, Sevald, Dell, and Cole (1995) asked speakers to repeat a pair of nonsense words as often as they could in a four-second interval. The two words had either the same or different CV structures. In the shared-structure conditions, the first two syllables of the pair had the same structure, e.g. "kem tilfer" (note that the second word is made up of the syllables "til" and "fer"). In the different-structure conditions, the two syllables differed in structure, e.g. "kem tilfner" (the second word is made up of "tilf" and "ner"). If the phonological component represents the CV structure of syllables, and this structure can be re-used from one syllable to the next, then speakers should be able to say "kem tilfer" more often in four seconds than "kem tilfner". Of course, the pair that has the most phonemes would be expected to take longer to say, regardless of structure, so Sevald et al. also compared utterances like "kemp tilfner" and "kemp tilfer", where the shared-structure pair had more phonemes than the non-shared pair.

The results showed that speakers could say the shared-structure pairs more quickly than the non-shared pairs. Even more strikingly, repeating the exact same phonemes as well as the structure ("til tilfer" or "tilf tilfner") did not speed production any more than just repeating the structure. So the study suggests that part of phonological processing is representing syllables in terms of their CV structure, independent of the particular sounds that instantiate that structure.

The experimental approach to the study of language production has largely confirmed the picture developed through analysis of spontaneous speech errors, but there are a number of advantages of experimental methods over purely observational investigations. First, experiments avoid some of the biases inherent in the collecting of errors. Some speech errors are simply more noticeable or more easily remembered than others. Experiments can investigate the full range of errors and so give a more accurate picture of production failures. Just as important, experiments extend the investigation of language production to include aspects of normal error-free production that cannot be investigated adequately through naturalistic observation. For instance, because speakers often talk about animate entities (such as other people), in naturally occurring speech the subjects of sentences are often animate. It is only through experimental manipulation that this normal correlation of animacy and subjecthood can be teased apart in order to investigate (for example) the process of function assignment. Experimental approaches to the study of language production therefore promise to shed new light on the workings of the language production system, going well beyond the understanding provided by the analysis of speech errors.

THE IMPORTANCE OF LANGUAGE STRUCTURE

We have already alluded to one of the most striking facts about language production, but it deserves explicit mention. At every level of processing, there are powerful structural constraints that govern the arrangements of elements. In speech errors, this shows up as restrictions on the elements that interact with one another. When words interact with one another, they come from the same grammatical class. When sounds interact with one another, they come from the same phonological (vowel or consonant) class. The consequence is that the basic structural patterns of the utterances are preserved even in errors.

This principle is vividly clear in stranding errors. In "you ordered up ending some fish dish" (said instead of "you ended up ordering some fish dish"; Garrett, 1993), the past tense and progressive affixes (*-ed* and *-ing*) occurred in the correct locations. Had they moved along with the word stems, the sentence would have become ungrammatical: "You ordering up ended some fish dish." But the inflections generally do not move, and the syntactic structure remains intact.

Notice that the structure is stable in the face of radical distortions of the speaker's intended meaning. Errors such as "dinner will be served at wine" (Fromkin, 1973) and "a room in your phone" are abysmal failures as vehicles for the speaker's communicative intention. (Take a moment to work out what the speakers of these errors actually intended. Both errors involve word exchanges.) Yet the utterances observe normal grammatical constraints. The rarity with which errors make sense, hidden or otherwise, is a challenge not only to claims like Freud's but also to any theory that overlooks the complex information processing system that mediates the translation of thoughts into language.

Considerations such as these have led contemporary theories of language production to emphasise the structural and information-processing constraints on speech, rather than the processes determining what the speaker means to convey. As one of the contemporary pioneers of language production research pointed out (Garrett, 1980a, p. 216), "The production system must get the details of form 'right' in every instance, whether those details are germane to sentence meaning or not". For example, verbs in English agree in number with their subjects ("She sneezes" vs. "They sneeze"), and this agreement operates in virtually every utterance that a speaker produces. Yet number agreement affects meaning hardly at all. If number inflection is omitted by mistake, the sentence is still understandable. In the past tense, number is completely unmarked on most verbs ("She sneezed" and "They sneezed"). Even so, when number marking is required, speakers almost always get it right. Thus, the creation of linguistic structure is central to any account of what people do when they talk.

LANGUAGE PRODUCTION IN PSYCHOLINGUISTICS

Speaking is only one part of what we do with language, because speakers are also listeners. Neither speaking nor listening can be fully explained without the other, so the relationship between language production and language comprehension is a natural target of curiosity. Both put our knowledge of language to work. But they put it to work in different ways, inasmuch as they differ in their goals. Production starts from a meaning to be conveyed and then works to convert that message ultimately into a series of speech sounds. Comprehension, by contrast, starts with speech sounds (or written letters) and works toward determining the meaning conveyed by those sounds.

As a consequence of this fundamental difference in the problems that the two systems must solve, we might expect them to differ considerably in their operation. For instance, the comprehension system must have ways to deal with ambiguous input, because natural language is rife with ambiguities. When one hears a sentence such as *The spy observed the man with binoculars*, one must decide whether the spy is using the binoculars to observe the man, or whether the spy is observing a man who is carrying binoculars. There is presumably no ambiguity in the mind of the speaker of the sentence, though, about which message is intended. Conversely, it is possible that comprehension of some sentences does not require a complete syntactic analysis of the sentence; the meanings of the words might be enough to give the listener a good idea of the meaning of the sentence as a whole. If one hears a sentence containing "villagers," "soldiers", and "massacred", one can understand that the soldiers massacred the villagers without having to decide which noun was the subject of the sentence and which the direct or indirect object. Of course, one might be wrong—the villagers may actually have massacred the soldiers—but there may be times when just knowing the words in their context is enough to understand the speaker, without a complete syntactic analysis of the utterance. But in producing a sentence, a speaker necessarily assigns syntactic functions to every element of the sentence; it is only by deciding which phrase will be the subject, which the direct object, and so on that a grammatical utterance can be formed—there is no way around syntactic processing for the speaker.

Although there is reason, then, to believe that production and comprehension may operate in different ways, there is also reason to believe that at some level they draw on the same linguistic knowledge. After all, every one of us both speaks and understands our native language. Communication occurs because speakers and listeners know the same code, a code that governs how arrangements of sounds and words convey meaning, allowing us (Pinker, 1994, p. 15):

> to shape events in each other's brains with exquisite precision. I am not referring to telepathy or mind control or the other obsessions of fringe science; even in the depictions of believers these are blunt instruments compared to an ability that is uncontroversially present in every one of us. That ability is language. Simply by making noises with our mouths, we can reliably cause precise new combinations of ideas to arise in each other's minds.

CONCLUSION

Titchener's (1909) introspection failed him when he claimed that talking is as easy as reading from a memory manuscript. The errors that people make reveal that speech is the product of a complex information-processing system that must piece together words and sounds to convey messages. We have sketched an outline of that system and showed how the workings of its components are being explored through experimental research. As this research proceeds, our sketch will come closer to a blueprint of how normal speakers draw on their linguistic knowledge to formulate utterances. The confluence of this explanation with models of normal comprehension, with accounts of the development of fluent speaking ability in children, and with descriptions of the disintegration of speech due to brain injury and the diseases of ageing, should offer a better understanding of the cognitive architecture of human language and its contribution to human communication.

ACKNOWLEDGEMENTS

This chapter is abridged and adapted from Bock (1995). Its preparation was supported in part by grants from the National Institutes of Health (R01 HD21011, F32 DC00141) and the National Science Foundation (SBR 94-11627). We thank David Huitema for comments on an early draft of the manuscript.

REFERENCES

Ashcraft, M.H. (1993). A personal case history of transient anomia. *Brain and Language*, *44*, 47–57.

Baars, B.J., Motley, M.T., & MacKay, D.G. (1975). Output editing for lexical status from artificially elicited slips of the tongue. *Journal of Verbal Learning and Verbal Behavior, 14*, 382–391.

Badecker, W., Miozzo, M., & Zanuttini, R. (1995). The two-stage model of lexical retrieval: Evidence from a case of anomia with selective preservation of grammatical gender. *Cognition, 57*, 193–216.

Bock, K. (1995). Sentence production: From mind to mouth. In J.L. Miller & P.D. Eimas (Eds.), *Handbook of perception and cognition: Vol. 11. Speech, language, and communication* (pp. 181–216). Orlando, FL: Academic Press.

Bock, J.K., & Levelt, W.J.M. (1994). Language production: Grammatical encoding. In M.A. Gernsbacher (Ed.), *Handbook of psycholinguistics* (pp. 945–984). San Diego, CA: Academic Press.

Bock, K., Loebell, H., & Morey, R. (1992). From conceptual roles to structural relations: Bridging the syntactic cleft. *Psychological Review, 99*, 150–171.

Chomsky, N. (1965). *Aspects of the theory of syntax.* Cambridge, MA: MIT Press.

Clark, H.H., & Bly, B. (1995). Pragmatics and discourse. In J.L. Miller & P.D. Eimas (Eds.), *Handbook of perception and cognition. Vol. 11: Speech, language, and communication* (pp. 371–410). Orlando, FL: Academic Press.

Deese, J. (1984). *Thought into speech: The psychology of a language.* Englewood Cliffs, NJ: Prentice-Hall.

Dell, G.S. (1984). Representation of serial order in speech: Evidence from the repeated phoneme effect in speech errors. *Journal of Experimental Psychology: Learning, Memory, and Cognition, 10*, 222–233.

Dell, G.S. (1986). A spreading-activation theory of retrieval in sentence production. *Psychological Review, 93*, 283–321.

Dell, G.S. (1995). Speaking and misspeaking. In L.R. Gleitman & M. Liberman (Eds.), *An invitation to cognitive science: Language* (Vol. 1, pp. 183–208). Cambridge, MA: MIT Press.

Ellis, A. (1980). On the Freudian theory of speech errors. In V.A. Fromkin (Ed.), *Errors in linguistic performance: Slips of the tongue, ear, pen, and hand* (pp. 123–131). New York: Academic Press.

Fink, B.R. (1986). Complexity. *Science, 231*, 319.

Forrest, L.B. (1993). *Syntactic subject and focus of attention.* Unpublished masters thesis, University of Oregon, Eugene, OR.

Freud, S. (1924/1935). *A general introduction to psychoanalysis.* New York: Washington Square Press.

Fromkin, V.A. (Ed.). (1973). *Speech errors as linguistic evidence.* The Hague, The Netherlands: Mouton.

Garrett, M.F. (1975). The analysis of sentence production. In G.H. Bower (Ed.), *The psychology of learning and motivation* (pp. 133–177). New York: Academic Press.

Garrett, M.F. (1980a). Levels of processing in sentence production. In B. Butterworth (Ed.), *Language production* (pp. 177–220). London: Academic Press.

Garrett, M.F. (1980b). The limits of accommodation: Arguments for independent processing levels in sentence production. In V.A. Fromkin (Ed.), *Errors in linguistic performance: Slips of the tongue, ear, pen, and hand* (pp. 263–271). New York: Academic Press.

Garrett, M.F. (1993). Errors and their relevance for models of language production. In G. Blanken, J. Dittmann, H. Grimm, J. Marshall, & C.-W. Wallesch (Eds.), *Linguistic disorders and pathologies* (pp. 72–92). Berlin: Walter de Gruyter.

Heeschen, C. (1993). Morphosyntactic characteristics of spoken language. In G. Blanken, J. Dittman, H. Grim, J. Marshall, & C. Wallesch (Ed.), *Linguistic disorders and pathologies* (pp. 16–34). Berlin: Walter de Gruyter.

Horton, W.S., & Keysar, B. (1996). When do speakers take into account common ground? *Cognition, 59*, 91–117.

Isaacs, E.A., & Clark, H.H. (1987). References in conversation between experts and novices. *Journal of Experimental Psychology: General, 116*, 26–37.

James, W. (1890). *The principles of psychology, Vol. 1.* New York: Dover.

MacKay, D.G. (1970). Spoonerisms: The structure of errors in the serial order of speech. *Neuropsychologia, 8*, 323–350.

Maclay, H., & Osgood, C.E. (1959). Hesitation phenomena in spontaneous English speech. *Word, 15*, 19–44.

Meringer, R., & Mayer, K. (1895/1978). *Versprechen und Verlesen.* Amsterdam: John Benjamins. (Original work published 1895)

Pinker, S. (1994). *The language instinct.* New York: Morrow.

Roget, P.M. (1852). *Thesaurus of English words and phrases, classified and arranged so as to facilitate the expression of ideas and assist in literary composition.* London: Longman, Brown, Green, & Longmans.

Schachter, S., Christenfeld, N., Ravina, B., & Bilous, F. (1991). Speech disfluency and the structure of knowledge. *Journal of Personality and Social Psychology, 60*, 362–367.

Sevald, C.A., Dell, G.S., & Cole, J.S. (1995). Syllable structure in speech production: Are syllables chunks or schemas? *Journal of Memory and Language, 34*, 807–820.

Titchener, E.B. (1909). *Lectures on the experimental psychology of the thought-processes.* New York: Macmillan.

Vigliocco, G., Antonini, T., & Garrett, M.F. (1997). Grammatical gender is on the tip of Italian tongues. *Psychological Science, 8*, 315–317.

CHAPTER THIRTEEN

The challenge of dialogue for theories of language processing

Simon Garrod
Human Communication Research Centre, University of Glasgow, UK

INTRODUCTION

Most of the evidence used to support or reject theories of language processing, whether about *word recognition*, *lexical processing during speech*, *syntactic parsing*, or even *discourse processing*, comes from the study of monologue. When investigating comprehension, researchers typically concentrate on people reading a piece of text or listening to someone reading a piece of text. When investigating production they typically concentrate on analysis of spoken monologue or citation speech. This is because dialogue presents such a challenge to established treatments of language and language use. Dialogue is inherently interactive and complex: Each party to a conversation both speaks and tries to understand speech during the course of the interaction; each interrupts the other and herself; on occasion two or more speakers even collaborate in producing the same sentence. So it is not surprising that it is commonly viewed as marginally grammatical, contaminated by complexities beyond theoretical consideration and outside the scope of rigorous psycholinguistic investigation. However, in recent years there has been an increasing interest in the psycholinguistic study of dialogue and in what it can contribute to theories of processing. This chapter considers some of these developments and looks into the question of whether its study can tell us anything new about language processing.

There are a number of reasons why dialogue is worth investigating. Some language processes are inherently interactional, such as answering a question or collaborating to establish precisely what is being referred to by the speaker, and it is difficult to see how these can be effectively investigated without reference to dialogue. Other aspects of processing, relevant to monologue, may be better understood in relation to dialogue. One candidate, which I shall consider briefly at the end of the chapter, is intonation; another is lexical ambiguity. But perhaps the principal reason for investigating dialogue is that conversation represents language use in its most untutored form. Everyone who speaks can converse, yet the large majority of the world's adult population have not learned to read. So any account of language processing which does not confront the challenge of dialogue is going to be incomplete.

The chapter is organised into three main sections. In the first, Background, I start out by considering what is systematic about dialogue and the special issues that that raises for processing accounts. The second section, Psychological Studies of Dialogue Processing, forms the main body of the chapter and takes up a number of these issues in relation to experimental approaches to dialogue. The third section of the chapter looks at the implications of these findings for standard models of communication and suggests an alternative framework more appropriate for the kind of language processing seen in dialogue. Finally, I shall consider outstanding problems and where the research might be expected to go over the next few years.

BACKGROUND

First, let us examine a short stretch of dialogue. The example shown here comes from a transcript of two players in a co-operative maze game where one player *A* is trying to describe his position to his partner *B* who is viewing the same maze on a computer screen in another room. (An example of the speaker's mazes is shown schematically in Fig. 13.1.)

(1) **B:** . . . Tell me where you are?
(2) **A**: Ehm: Oh God *(laughs)*
(3) **B:** *(laughs)*
(4) **A:** Right: **two along from the bottom one up**:
(5) **B:** Two along from the bottom, which side?
(6) **A:** The left: going from left to right in the second box.
(7) **B:** You're in the second box.
(8) **A:** One up: *(1 sec)* I take it we've got identical mazes?
(9) **B**: Yeah well: right, starting from the left, **you're one along:**
(10) **A:** Uh-huh:

(11) **B: and one up?**
(12) **A:** Yeah, and I'm trying to get to ... *etc.*

[*28 utterances later*]

(41) **B:** You are starting from the left, **you're one along, one up?** *(2 sec)*
(42) **A: Two along**: I'm not in the first box, I'm in the second box:
(43) **B:** You're **two along**:
(44) **A: Two up** *(1 sec)* counting the: if you take: the first box as being one up:
(45) **B:** *(2 sec)* Uh-huh:
(46) **A:** Well: I'm **two along, two up:** *(1.5 sec)*
(47) **B:** Two up?:
(48) **A:** Yeah *(1 sec)* so I can move down one:
(49) **B:** Yeah I see where you are:

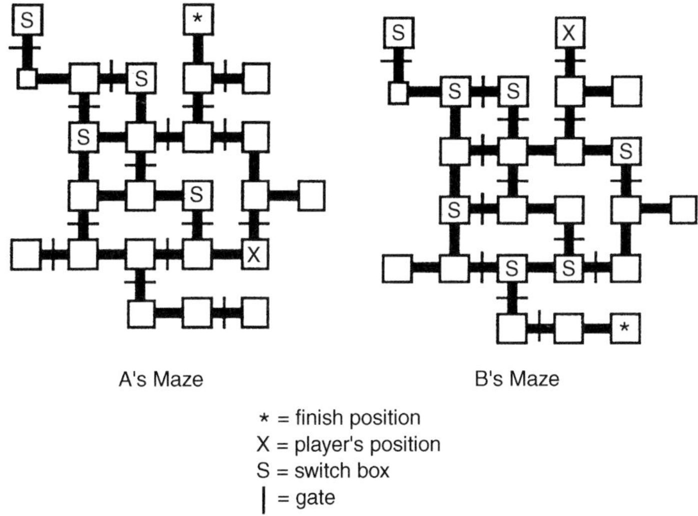

FIG. 13.1 A schematic representation of the kind of mazes used in Garrod and Anderson's (1987) maze game experiments.

At first glance the language looks disorganised. Strictly speaking many of the utterances are ungrammatical—only one of the first six contains a verb. There are occasions when production of the same sentence is shared between the speakers, as in utterances (7–8) and (43–44), and it often seems that they do not know what they want to say—in this short extract, *A* describes his position quite differently in utterance (4), "two along from the bottom **one up**", and utterance (46), "two along, **two up**". Yet, as we shall see, the sequence as a whole is, in fact, quite orderly.

The orderliness of dialogue comes from the fact that conversation is about establishing *consensus* and this in turn imposes *co-ordination* constraints on the language users.

Dialogue and consensus

In a piece of written text, whether it be a newspaper article or the chapter of a learned volume, the meaning is there on the page waiting to be extracted. If it is well written and you are a competent reader, then you should be able to come to an interpretation which matches roughly what the writer intended. However, this does not depend on establishing any kind of consensus with the author. After all he may well be long dead and gone.

In dialogue the situation is very different. Take for example utterances (4–11) in the earlier fragment. In utterance (4) player *A* describes his position as "Two along from the bottom and one up", but the final interpretation is only established at the end of the first exchange where consensus is reached on a rather different description by *B* (9–11) "You're one along—one up". As Clark and Brennan (1991) point out, conversation is organised around establishing consensus, but what follows from this?

Looking first at the structure of dialogue it is clear that utterances do not stand alone. They form pairs of turns, sometimes referred to as *adjacency pairs* (Schegloff & Sacks, 1973). Thus, a question, such as (1) "Tell me where you are?", calls for an answer, such as (4) "Two along from the bottom and one up". Similarly greetings like "Good morning" call for responses such as "Fine, thank you". This is all part of the business of establishing consensus between the participants. In dialogue, not even a bland statement, such as (4) "Right, two along from the bottom one up" can stand alone. It requires either an affirmation or some form of query, such as (5) "Two along from the bottom, which side?". So at the most basic level of utterance planning dialogue forces the participants to co-ordinate their processing to produce coherent utterances (Garrod & Doherty, 1995).

The second way that dialogue requires co-ordinated processing relates to the general problem of ambiguity. In the extract shown, the participants spend most of the time trying to work out a mutually acceptable and unambiguous description for *A*'s location on the maze. As we shall see later, this is achieved through a process of co-ordinating outputs with inputs: Speakers always attempt to generate utterances which correspond semantically to the utterances which they have recently had to comprehend. As a result the same expression will tend to take on the same meaning within any stretch of dialogue.

Finally, dialogue participants try to establish a co-ordinated conception of their topic. In the case of the maze game illustrated previously this amounts to converging on a common spatial concept. Thus, some people playing this game will refer to their locations by reference to *right indicators*, *upside down T shapes*, or *Ls on their sides*. These speakers, unlike the pair responsible for the dialogue illustrated, conceive of the maze as a conglomeration of patterns or shapes each with a different name. As we shall see later, conversational partners often establish quite idiosyncratic conceptions of the topic, but in well-managed dialogues they will always co-ordinate on the same idiosyncratic conception. Again, this process supports consensus which is the fundamental goal of dialogue.

One of the reasons why dialogue presents such a challenge to processing accounts is that these interactional characteristics are difficult to reconcile with the standard view of communication as a one-way process of *information transfer*. And it is just such a view that underpins much of the work in psycholinguistics. I will argue that a more useful processing framework for dialogue is based on the notion of *information co-ordination*, and it is against this background that the experimental work needs to be evaluated.

The next section of the chapter will consider in more detail experimental investigations of dialogue which relate to these notions of consensus and co-ordination. Although this will serve as a selective review, its real aim is to establish what (if any) implications these studies may have for the various accounts of language processing described in other chapters of the book.

PSYCHOLOGICAL STUDIES OF DIALOGUE PROCESSING

As in other areas of psycholinguistics, the study of dialogue has developed around a relatively small number of experimental situations. Here again it presents something of a challenge. The experimenter cannot readily control the language being processed, because it is in the nature of conversation that it be spontaneous. So, instead, experimenters have designed ways of eliciting semi-spontaneous dialogue in situations where there is some degree of control over the topic of conversation and even on occasion the lexical items likely to be used.

The first such paradigm was developed by Krauss and Weinheimer (1964) and involved pairs of subjects describing to each other a sequence of abstract shapes, what they called nonsense figures. Despite the rather stilted dialogue produced in this referential communication paradigm, early studies led to a number of important discoveries about interaction and reciprocity in language processing (Krauss & Weinheimer, 1964,

1966, 1967). In particular they noticed a dramatic reduction in the length of descriptions as the task proceeded, which seemed to be related to listener feedback. Hence, if feedback was delayed or disrupted in other ways it greatly affected the degree of abbreviation (Krauss & Bricker, 1966; Krauss & Weinheimer, 1966). This suggested that the referential process depended on co-ordination between communicators.

Some years later the referential communication paradigm was taken up again by Herb Clark and his colleagues, and this has led to a more explicitly interactional model of reference, something which is very much in contrast with accounts based, for example, on referential processing during reading (see Chapter 11, this volume).

Studies using the referential communication paradigm

Referential communication studies challenge standard processing accounts to the extent that they clearly demonstrate the inherently collaborative nature of reference. Take, for instance, the explanation of why references tend to become increasingly abbreviated as a discourse unfolds. The standard account attributes this to the speaker expending the least amount of processing effort consistent with enabling their addressee to pick out a referent from all potential alternatives in that context (Brown, 1958; Olson, 1970). Thus, initial references will be maximally differentiating but when repeated can become increasingly elliptical because the context now facilitates differentiation: "a dog standing in the corner" becomes "the dog" and then "it". However, this account tacitly assumes that speakers work alone.

Clark and Wilkes-Gibbs (1986) developed a variant of the Krauss and Weinheimer (1964) task using Tan-Gram figures and analysed in some detail how successive descriptions changed as a result of the interactions. The first thing they noted was that the references tend to be built up by both participants during an extended exchange. For example:

A. Uh, person putting a shoe on.
B. Putting a shoe on?
A. Uh huh. Facing left. Looks like he's sitting down.
B. Okay.

This led them to propose an alternative account of processing economy based on what they called the principle of least *Collaborative Effort*. The idea behind this is simple: Communicators act so as to minimise the overall effort of initiating a reference and refashioning it during the subsequent exchange. They suggested three reasons why speakers do not necessarily start out with an optimal description (at least according to the standard account). First, there is time pressure in dialogue: Properly managed conversations have to flow. So a speaker may not find the time to fashion the optimal description. Second, there is the problem of complexity. A description may be too complex for a single turn in the dialogue and have to be broken up into simpler components. Finally, there is the problem of ignorance. In the heat of real conversation a speaker may simply not know enough about the addressee's view of the context to formulate the maximally differentiating reference. All of these constraints motivate a collaborative process where both parties contribute to establishing the reference and Clark and Wilkes-Gibbs (1986) were able to find many examples of exchanges reflecting each of the constraints.

However, the most striking empirical evidence for the importance of interaction comes from a subsequent series of experiments by Schober and Clark (1989). These experiments used the same Tan-Gram communication task, but included a third party who overheard the conversation without directly participating in it. The overhearer then had to try to identify the figures in the same way as the addressee and it turned out that they did systematically less well. Although the performance of both addressee and overhearer improved over time, overhearers never managed to catch up. The simple conclusion is that you need to actively participate in the referential process in order to interpret what is being said. But it is possible to go further than that. As we can see in our example dialogue shown earlier, addressees control the referential process in a number of ways. They can elicit what to them is missing detail (as in utterance 5), or supply an alternative description (as in utterances 9–11), and most importantly they can terminate the exchange when they are satisfied that the reference has been established (utterance 49). Schober and Clark argued that it is being in this kind of control which gives an addressee a big advantage over an overhearer.

To test the idea they examined exactly when subjects physically picked the card being referred to. For addressees the card was picked at or before the point of verbal completion of the exchange on 99% of occasions, whereas for the overhearers it was only chosen 63% of the time. However, when the overhearers did choose the card before the verbal completion point they were almost as accurate as the addressees. So this suggests that being able to participate in the interaction enables communicators to convey just the right amount of joint information to establish what is intended, whereas overhearers get access either to more than they require or not enough.

It is apparent that even with the rather stilted dialogue of the referential paradigm interactional factors play an important role in the language processing. Quite apart from local co-ordination between the different dialogue moves, question-answer, statement-confirmation, and so on, there seems to be a more global process of establishing a co-ordinated understanding of what communicators are trying to say.

However, it is still not clear whether this kind of co-ordinated understanding has direct consequences for the more detailed analysis of language processing at the levels considered in the other chapters of this volume. Co-ordinated understanding may come about as a result of rather general inferential processes of the kind used in other non-linguistic activities such as performing a symphony or playing your part in a football team where participants have to act in a concerted way (Clark, 1985). So we are still left with the question of whether dialogue has intrinsic bearing on how we process language in lexical, syntactic, or semantic terms. Next we turn to experiments using a somewhat richer dialogue task, which suggest that the language processing system may well have constraints built into it in relation to the organisation of these processes which reflect the reciprocal co-ordinated nature of dialogue. The task has been called the maze game and is responsible for the dialogue illustrated earlier.

Maze game studies

The maze game was designed as a more interactive task than the standard referential communication paradigm. Two players sit in different rooms confronted with a maze displayed on a computer screen (see Fig. 13.1) and they have the task of moving their position markers alternately through the mazes until they reach their respective goals. There are two features of the game which make it co-operative. First, at any time about half of the paths that link the boxes on the maze are blocked with gates. So when a subject tries to move along the path their position marker bounces off the gate and returns to its original position at the cost of a penalty point. Second, a small number of the boxes on each maze are marked as "switch boxes". When one of the players, say player *A*, lands in a switch box this has the effect of opening all of *B*'s gated paths and gating all of his open paths. When *B* lands where *A* has a "switch box" *A*'s paths are switched in the same way.

The players, who are in audio contact with each other, therefore have to negotiate a strategy of moving to positions where their partner has the appropriate "switch boxes" in order to allow them a free route to goal. As a result, the game elicits free dialogue interspersed with repeated location descriptions and it is the analysis of how these descriptions develop during the course of the game which has led to a number of insights about co-ordinated language use and interpretation.

In the original studies (Anderson & Garrod, 1987; Garrod & Anderson, 1987) a number of adult pairs played a couple of games each. The

TABLE 13.1
Different Types of Location Description in the Maze Task (Point marked X in A's Maze in Fig. 13.1)

(1) Figural scheme:

Model:	Maze is broken down into a set of different figural patterns and the position is described in relation to these.
Example:	"See that right-turn indicator. Well I'm in the box immediately below it."

(2) Path scheme:

Model:	Maze is treated as made up of a series of paths linking the nodes and positions are described in relation to such paths.
Example:	"See the bottom right well go along two then up one and go along to the end on the right. That's where I am."

(3) Line scheme:

Model:	Maze is broken down into a set of lines of nodes in the same plane and the position is described in relation to these.
Example:	"I'm on the second row from the bottom at the end on the right."

(4) Matrix scheme:

Model:	A square matrix is imposed on the maze and positions are described as at the appropriate co-ordinates in the matrix.
Example:	"I'm at E5."

location descriptions in the resulting dialogues turned out to be extraordinarily varied across the sample of players. However, each description could be classified according to one of the four basic schemes illustrated in Table 13.1, where a scheme corresponds to some combination of spatial conception of the maze configuration together with a description lexicon. For example, in the most commonly used scheme, the PATH scheme, speakers conceive of the maze configuration as a set of boxes or nodes linked by the actual path links on the maze. A position can then be described by first establishing a prominent starting point on the maze and then recounting the path route which links that point to the one being referred to. In this case the conception or model is of a path network kind (similar to that underlying underground or subway maps) and the description lexicon may include terms such as *box*, *node*, or *link* used together with cardinals or ordinals to count the number of elements traversed in the route. For the other schemes, LINE, FIGURAL, and MATRIX, the form of model and example lexica are shown in the table.

Having established a means for classifying these descriptions it is possible to analyse how the content of the references develops during the course of the dialogues. Garrod and Anderson (1987) initially found two things. First, against the background of variation across the whole corpus any pair of communicators were very consistent in their choice of descriptions in any stretch of dialogue. Thus, by the time they had played one game together communicators had adopted the same scheme and even co-ordinated on a particular, often idiosyncratic, variant of that basic scheme. The second observation concerned how the schemes developed across the whole corpus of dialogues. In general, communicators began by using descriptions that reflected a salient concrete spatial model of the maze configuration. Hence, in the first game speakers were more likely to use FIGURAL or PATH descriptions depending on models which reflect quite directly what is being seen on the maze (e.g. figural patterns of nodes) or how the players interact with it as part of the primary task (e.g. representing the actual paths along which the players can move their tokens). However, by the time they have played two games players typically end up using a more abstract description scheme such as MATRIX or LINE where the model can be extended to positions not actually represented in the maze itself (e.g. it is possible to describe "missing" nodes according to either MATRIX or LINE schemes). These more abstract schemes also tend to produce more ambiguous descriptions than the concrete PATH and FIGURAL schemes. The centre of a 5×5 maze can be described as "Three, three" according to at least eight distinct co-ordinate organisations, depending upon different origins and different order of mention of co-ordinates.

Garrod and Anderson (1987) drew two main conclusions from these initial observations. First, they argued that conversationalists not only collaborate in establishing isolated references but also collaborate in formulating local "description languages" and dialogue lexica in order to support sustained communication about a particular topic. Furthermore, a more detailed analysis of the sub-schemes being used (i.e. the particular versions of the scheme a pair would be using at any time) indicated that these local "description languages" were formulated to be unambiguous in that context. Thus, a single element in a model such as a line in the LINE scheme would always be given the same name (e.g. *line*, *row*, *layer*, *level*, or whatever) as long as it was being referred to in exactly the same way. However, if for some reason a speaker wanted to refer to it outside the particular sub-scheme then a new lexical item would be introduced. For example, in a scheme where speakers referred to rows as ordered elements with descriptions like "the third row", when they wanted to describe the bottom one they would refer to this as "the bottom *line*" but not "the bottom row"; the latter term would only be used with the alternative "the first row" (see Garrod & Anderson, 1987, for a more detailed analysis and discussion).

The second main conclusion was that co-ordinating on a common "description language" was not simply a matter of sticking with the first reasonable scheme that emerged. It seemed to involve a much more extended history of development whereby speakers would explore different schemes in a co-ordinated fashion over a period of time. This is important because it suggests a more complex underlying mechanism than one which simply sticks with the first mutually acceptable scheme encountered. The final point Garrod and Anderson (1987) made relates to the degree of explicit inference involved in this kind of language co-ordination.

According to the standard account collaboration is made possible through explicit negotiation between communicators (Clark & Wilkes-Gibbs, 1986; Rommetveit, 1983). Thus, in the context of the maze game a particular common scheme should be established as a result of agreement between the speakers about how they are to go about describing where they were. In fact, Garrod and Anderson (1987) report a limited amount of explicit negotiation of this kind in the games. However, it did not seem to play an important role in either establishing a common "description language" or in fixing the language over the subsequent dialogue. Thus, in dialogues where explicit negotiation was observed it occurred most of the time only in the second game rather than the first (i.e. on 66% of occasions). This is inconsistent with negotiation as a mechanism for setting up a co-ordinated scheme. But perhaps more strikingly, when negotiation did occur the scheme agreed upon only predicted 59% of subsequent descriptions in that dialogue, which is at about chance level as compared to the prediction from any other description used by that pair. So this is quite inconsistent with negotiation as a means of fixing the scheme to be used. Whatever role it plays in these dialogues it does not seem to be instrumental in determining the underlying description languages.

On the basis of these observations Garrod and Anderson (1987) argued that conceptual and semantic co-ordination follows from a basic processing constraint which they termed the output/input co-ordination principle. When producing an utterance (output) the processor will where possible make the same choices at the lexical, syntactic, semantic, and pragmatic level as were required in interpreting the most recent relevant utterance from their interlocutor (input). So output processes will be co-ordinated with input processes. They argued that following such a principle leads to processing benefits both at the level of the individuals and for the dialogue pair as a whole.

For the individuals there are clear advantages in using the same background knowledge to support both the production and the comprehension process. If, as a listener, you have already interpreted an utterance in a certain way, you will have been forced to take a particular perspective on the topic and to adopt a particular interpretation for the words in the utterance. Hence, when it is your turn to speak, many of the background decisions required in formulating the utterance have, in a sense, already been taken for you. All you have to do is run the generation process over the relevant parts of the decision tree used to interpret recent utterances from your interlocutor (see Garrod, Anderson, & Sanford, 1984 for a discussion of a computer simulation which works along these lines). This would explain the well-established tendency to repeat materials from previous talk (Levelt & Kelter, 1982).

Quite apart from these individual processing benefits, co-ordinating output with input is also efficient in terms of reducing the overall collaborative effort in dialogue (Clark & Wilkes-Gibbs, 1986). This is because it helps to establish the common ground (Clark & Marshall, 1981). When you interpret an utterance successfully, you can presume that your interpretation matches how the speaker would have interpreted the utterance in that same context. So if you want to facilitate their understanding when next speaking on that topic, your best bet is to match their previous utterance as closely as possible. The co-ordination of comprehension with production processes within individual conversationalists therefore promotes mutual understanding between them. Furthermore, the whole process does not require that a speaker model his or her partner's knowledge state directly, in the sense of having to hold a distinct model of the other, it simply requires that they each hold a representation of the current state of the discourse as a whole.

Now if the output/input co-ordination constraint is accounting for a large part of the co-ordinated language processing that occurs in dialogue then this does have consequences of a more general nature for the organisation of the language processing system. In the first place it would suggest that in natural conversation problems of ambiguity may be much less marked than one would expect. This is important because ambiguity resolution of one kind or another is one of the major issues in understanding processing at almost any level from word to discourse. It is inherent in lexical processing (see Chapters 2 and 3), in syntactic processing (Chapters 5 and 7), and, as we have seen in this chapter, in reference resolution. This then leads to the second processing implication which concerns the more general relationship between production and comprehension processes.

One of the main motivations behind output/input co-ordination is that language generation is facilitated in various ways by interpretation of prior discourse (cf. Levelt & Kelter, 1982; Bock & Huitema, Chapter 12). The generation process involves choosing appropriate formulations of an utterance from a very large set of alternatives at the lexical, syntactic, semantic, and conceptual levels. And, because of the inherently ambiguous nature of language, comprehension also involves choosing particular interpretations at all these levels. But for the two processes to benefit from each other they must both have access to the same kind of underlying representations. In other words, the extent that output/input co-ordination operates effectively and automatically in dialogue contexts would suggest that generation and comprehension processes access a common set of representations associated in some way with the current dialogue (see Garrod & Doherty, 1994 for more detailed suggestions about how this might work).

The maze game has also been used to examine how co-ordination between isolated conversational partners may have broader ranging consequences for inter-speaker co-ordination in larger communities. Although this issue of interactional influences on larger groups is strictly speaking beyond the scope of the present volume, I will consider it briefly next, because it illustrates that dialogue processes may have an important bearing on how languages develop within speech communities.

Dialogue processes and establishing a speech community

One of the questions raised by Garrod and Anderson's maze game results concerns the extent to which inter-speaker co-ordination is a local process associated just with the particular interaction under way. This is an interesting issue because certain speech communities can also be viewed as supporting particular languages. For example, congregations of scientists, farmers, doctors, or lawyers all use language which is at times incomprehensible to those outside their group. Are these "languages" supported by interactions between members of those communities in the same fashion?

To test this Garrod and Doherty (1994) designed a community version of the maze game experiment. The basic idea was to have a group of players interacting not with just one partner but with all the other members of the group in turn, so they would come to be a kind of small speech community. Their performance could then be compared with other groups who interacted over the same number of games either with the same partner (isolated pairs) or with fresh partners not drawn from the same group (non-community pairs). The question is whether the community group manage as a whole to converge on a single language of description simply by virtue of interacting one to one with different potential members of a new community.

Garrod and Doherty's results are very striking. They show: first, that such inchoate communities do rapidly converge onto one scheme; second, that they do so even more dramatically than isolated pairs with the same level of experience; and, third, that non-communities become increasingly discoordinated as speakers are exposed to more "fresh" partners. A

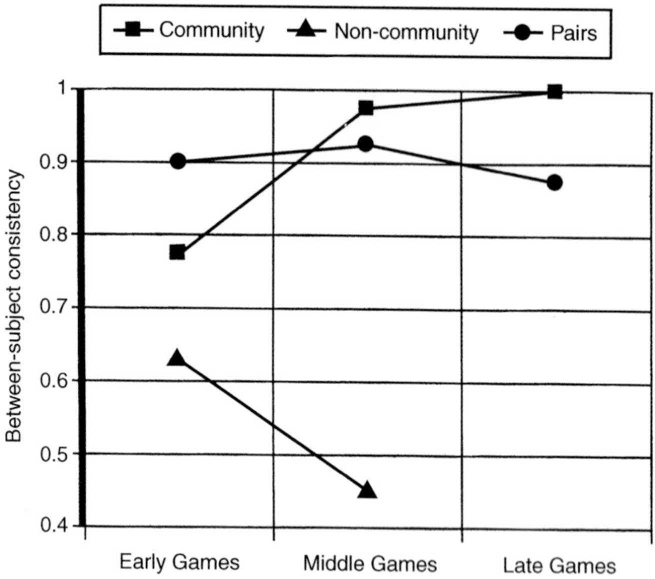

FIG. 13.2 Measures of the degree to which each player's description scheme on turn $n + 1$ is predicted by their partner's description on turn n. The data are pooled for early games (1–3), middle games (4–6) and late games (7–9). The data are shown for isolated pairs (pairs), virtual community pairs (Community) and non-community pairs (Non-community).

comparison of the degree of inter-speaker co-ordination in language use is illustrated in Fig. 13.2.

These results strongly suggest that processes whereby individuals co-ordinate their language use during conversation could play a role in establishing and supporting local languages within speech communities. Garrod and Doherty considered a number of possible mechanisms which could account for emergence of the community-wide language scheme. The details of their discussion are beyond the scope of this chapter, but an interesting conclusion they come to is that the process does not rely on speakers adopting a conscious strategy of convergence. Rather it emerges out of constraints on the language-processing system of the kind described earlier in the context of convergence between isolated conversational pairs. To the extent that this analysis proves correct, it points to an important way in which language processing in the context of interactive dialogue may play a role in language change.

The maze game experiments have highlighted some of the ways in which the immediate processing of language affects and is affected by the consensus imperative in dialogue. The final dialogue elicitation technique that I am going to consider is called the Map Task. This was originally devised by Brown, Anderson, Shillcock, and Yule (1984) to explore properties of effective versus ineffective communication in dialogue. However, it has been used more recently to look at a whole range of dialogue-processing issues from reference to speech articulation.

Map Task studies

The Map Task was designed to elicit more coherent referential dialogue than that seen with the standard referential communication task of Krauss and Weinheimer (1966). Each participant has a map of an imaginary island containing a number of labelled landmarks. One participant has a route marked across the island, whereas the other just has the map containing the landmarks. The goal is for the first player, the instruction giver, to communicate the route to the second player, the instruction follower, so that she can then draw the route on her map.

This task allows for a number of interesting manipulations. For example, the landmark labels can be chosen to highlight potentially interesting phonological contrasts. When a name such as "Crane Bay" is spoken in a relaxed manner the final consonant of *crane* may be assimilated into the initial consonant of *bay* to produce something which sounds like *cramebay*. By labelling the landmarks appropriately it is possible to explore the incidence of phonological reductions and assimilations in a corpus of naturalistic speech. One can also examine how reductions relate to the state of the dialogue: Are repeated references treated differently when the repeat occurs across the two speakers, for example? Do speakers modulate the intelligibility of what they say depending on whether or not they can see and be seen by their partner?

Another manipulation relates to introducing discrepancies between the landmarks shown on the two maps. Players are informed that their maps are of the same island but created by two different explorers so that they might contain certain discrepancies: A landmark shown on one map may be missing on the other and vice versa. This latter kind of manipulation makes it possible to vary the degree of overlapping knowledge between communicators and thereby explore how they use different referential forms to signal their relative knowledge states.

Yet another kind of manipulation concerns the relationship between communicators: They can be familiar acquaintances or strangers; they can see each other's faces while conversing or be separated by a screen. Finally, the task has the advantage, shared by the standard referential communication paradigm, of producing an independent measure of communicative success. One can make a direct comparison between the route given on the instruction giver's map with that drawn by the instruction follower.

Here, I am going to concentrate on the findings that have emerged from analysis of the map task dialogues in relation to reference and speech articulation. I will leave the preliminary results on intonational aspects of the dialogues to the final section where we consider future directions. The map task has contributed in two ways to our understanding of referential communication. First, in terms of how speakers deploy different linguistic devices to communicate about shared and unshared information, and, second, in terms of how speakers fuse auditory linguistic and visual gestural information in co-ordinating their interpretations and productions.

One of the ways in which languages express the referential status of a description is through the definiteness of noun phrases (see Chapter 11, this volume). Halliday (1967) produced an influential account of this in terms of what he called the informational structure of the utterance. He argued that definites (e.g. phrases like "the man" or "he") are used to refer to Given information—information that is in some way shared by the two communicators. Thus, according to his account speakers use indefinite descriptions to introduce items New to the discourse and definites to mark items already Given. More recently, Clark and Marshall (1981) refined this notion by suggesting that the interpretation of definite descriptions depends crucially on what they called *mutual knowledge*, which means knowledge that is both shared between communicators and *known* to be shared between them. So, conversationalists should come up with different interpretations of definite versus indefinite noun phrases according to how they construe their mutual knowledge state at the time.

Anderson and Boyle (1994) used the map task to examine these claims. They took advantage of the landmark discrepancy manipulation to make predictions about when participants should be using different referential devices according to their relative states of knowledge. On the assumption that a proportion of the landmarks were not shared, initial mentions should be marked with indefinites and subsequent mentions marked with definites. In fact, they discovered a much more complex pattern of usage.

On the basis of 64 map dialogues they found that use of definites and indefinites was obscured by a variety of other factors. First, it was apparent that speakers were in general no more likely to use the indefinite than the definite description when introducing a landmark for the first time. However, it was also clear that communicators did take into account mutual knowledge. So the more successful ones would typically probe their interlocutor's knowledge with explicit questions about the landmarks. In this case indefinite descriptions were more likely (about 60% of the descriptions in the questions were indefinite) but still did not seem to be playing a very crucial role *vis-a-vis* either Givenness or Mutual Knowledge. To understand what was actually happening, Anderson and Boyle had to examine in more detail the interactions associated with each introduction.

They started by classifying the appropriateness of the listener's response. When a new landmark is introduced it is obviously important that the listener check whether it is actually present on their map. This process can be established on the basis of the transcriptions and responses coded accordingly. Examining the incidence of such responses, Anderson and Boyle found that they were far more likely to occur when the speaker used a question introduction and in particular when this was combined with the use of the indefinite article. Asking your partner if they have *an X* is better than asking if they have *the X* and this is far more satisfactory than simply referring to either *an X* or *the X* in a standard description.

One interesting explanation for the apparent failure of the simple definite/indefinite contrast as a reliable cue to mutual knowledge is that in real conversational speech the acoustic distinction between the two forms *a* and *the* is often just missing (see e.g. Bard & Anderson, 1994). So, speakers who rely solely on this distinction to mark the status of referential knowledge will often be unsuccessful.

This leads to a second way in which the map task has contributed to our understanding of referential communication which concerns the distribution of information between the spoken and visual channels during face to face dialogues. Initial interest came from the finding that communicators who could see each other only needed about 75% of the speech to convey the same amount of information as those who could not (Boyle, Anderson, & Newlands, 1994). In turn, this motivated a much more detailed analysis of the relationship between the dialogue situation and speech articulation.

It has long been known that speakers control the intelligibility of the words they produce as a function of contextual predictability (Bard & Anderson, 1983; Fowler & Housum, 1987; Hunnicut, 1985). The more predictable the word the more degraded the articulation. Typically this relates to shortening of word tokens and as a result systematic phonological reduction and assimilation both within and across word boundaries. Furthermore speakers seem to take into account contextual predictability in adjusting articulation in a number of ways. For example repeated tokens of the same word tend to be less intelligible (Fowler & Housum, 1987), but interestingly this effect does not emerge when the repetitions refer to different entities or events (Bard, Lowe, & Altmann, 1989). Similarly, when the referent is physically co-present for speaker and addressee this produces reductions in intelligibility (Bard & Anderson, 1994). So it seems that there are a variety of ways that speakers take into account the context in controlling the rate and intelligibility of their speech and this includes some considerations of context from the listener's point of view (see Bock & Huitema, Chapter 12 for another example of this phenomenon in relation to referential choice).

Anderson, Bard, Sotillo, Newlands and Doherty-Sneddon (1997) used the map task to investigate how such speech adaptations reflect the speaker's model of the listener. First, they examined the intelligibility of matched word tokens in dialogues where communicators could see each others' faces versus dialogues where they could not. Reductions in intelligibility were estimated from comparing words excerpted from the speech stream of the normal dialogue with citation word forms from the same speaker collected at the end of the experiment. The result was a clear pattern of both reduced intelligibility and associated length reductions for word tokens in the visible condition over the non-visible. So this suggested that speakers were taking into account the differences in the communicative situation in articulating their speech.

Being able to see a speaker offers potentially helpful information in processing speech. First, there is information from the lip movements, which can be systematically combined with acoustic information to produce a phonological percept (McGurk & MacDonald, 1976). Perhaps less obvious is the role that looking can play in helping to monitor the interpretation of what is being said. Boyle et al. (1994) found that communicators often looked at each other during segments of dialogue where they were having problems communicating, typically places where there was some discrepancy between the two maps. Apparently being able to monitor your listener's face, and vice versa, can help in the management of the exchange. However, this still leaves the question of the degree to which modulating the intelligibility of the speech reflects a precise modelling of the listener's actual use of the visual channel.

To address the issue Anderson et al. (1997) separated out spoken word tokens where the listener was actually looking at the speaker from those where she was not. They reasoned that a close modeller would modulate the intelligibility of their speech in relation to listener's patterns of gaze. So they compared the reductions in intelligibility for word tokens produced when the listener was looking at the speaker with matched tokens where the listener was not. In two studies they could find no evidence for greater reductions when the listener was actually looking at the speaker. In fact the only difference they discovered was in length of tokens and that was in the opposite direction to the prediction. If anything speakers increased the intelligibility of their speech when the listener was looking at them. This result may seem somewhat surprising, but it does make sense in relation to the earlier observation that conversationalists tend to look at each other when they are having trouble understanding what is being said. Thus, gaze will tend to coincide with communication difficulty and presumably that is when speakers will also tend to articulate more clearly.

So it seems that, whereas speakers will reduce the intelligibility of their speech in general when the listener has the opportunity to use the visual channel, the reductions do not reflect a moment-by-moment modelling of the listener's actual use of the channel. Rather, it seems to reflect a more general assessment of the state of the mutual intelligibility of the conversation at that time. Being able to look at your partner and be seen improves the overall mutual intelligibility of the dialogue and so elicits faster and less intelligible speech. In certain respects this result is consistent with Garrod and Anderson's findings from the maze game, where communicators collaborate to establish a mutually acceptable description scheme but without explicitly modelling their partner's knowledge state.

Summary of the main experimental findings

The experiments which I have discussed illustrate various ways in which language processing is sensitive to the special kinds of constraints imposed by interactive dialogue. The original work using Krauss and Weinheimer's referential communication paradigm highlighted the importance of feedback in generating referential descriptions. Feedback and interaction also play a central role in explaining the results from the subsequent studies using this paradigm reported by Clark and his colleagues. The process of referring is governed by principles of collaborative effort and effective referential communication depends on actively participating in the dialogue rather than just being exposed to the linguistic material.

One of the things that follows from this work is that in dialogue production and comprehension processes are very tightly coupled. What we say and how we say it is conditioned by what we have just heard. How we interpret what we are hearing is conditioned by what we have just said. In fact, it is quite often the case that a listener takes over producing an utterance from the current speaker or overlaps in producing the same utterance.[1] The tight coupling of production and comprehension is the basis for Garrod and Anderson's "output/input co-ordination" principle which they use to explain the way in which pairs of communicators come to converge on common referential schemes. Like the earlier

[1] Recent analyses of the map task corpus indicate that there can be as much as 20% overlap in the dialogue and it is not uncommon to find cases where speaker B shadows part of A's contribution with a lag as little as 100 ms (Henry Thompson, personal communication).

observations it seems that the form and content of the language is subject to interactional constraints between communicators.

Finally, the map task studies throw light on some of the details of the adaptations that dialogue participants make to each other. Whereas the studies that look at referential forms suggest that communicators are sensitive to aspects of mutual knowledge as predicted from Clark and Marshall (1981) they also indicate that there is more to this than choice of referential form. Effective communicators rely more on establishing directly the shared information by taking advantage of the interaction (i.e. querying the information) than they do on the form of the reference itself. In this respect, studies of dialogue force us to consider how speakers deploy and listeners construe different linguistic devices in these interactional contexts. In the case of the articulation reduction studies, the results indicate a degree of special sensitivity to mutual intelligibility in terms of a quite subtle tuning of the speech process.

We are now in a position to consider the question raised at the beginning of this chapter about the degree to which studies of dialogue should make us reconsider accounts of language processing. The key conclusion that comes from the experimental work is that language processing in dialogue directly reflects interaction between participants. In this section I argued that it is this inherently interactional character of dialogue that is difficult to represent in a model of communication based solely on the notion of information transfer. In the final section of the chapter I will consider an alternative framework for conversational communication based on the notion of information co-ordination.

INFORMATION CO-ORDINATION VERSUS INFORMATION TRANSFER

To the extent that psycholinguists place language processing within a communication framework they do so with respect to what is often called the information transfer model. According to this model, which has its origins in communication engineering, a sender encodes his message into a signal, which then enables information to be transferred to a receiver who decodes that signal back into the original message (Cherry, 1956; see Fig. 13.3). In the case of linguistic communication the intended meaning of an utterance corresponds to the message, and the language being used corresponds to the code. Hence, language production is treated as a process of constructing utterances that encode a speaker's meaning, and comprehension is treated as a process of extracting that meaning from the code.

The information transfer model has been responsible for many insights into how language is structured and processed and this is clearly

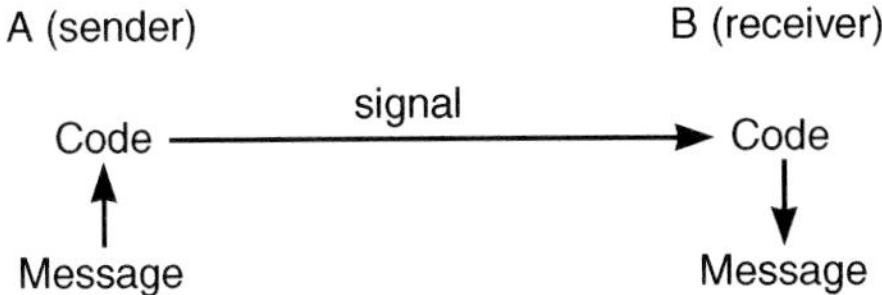

• sender encodes message
• receiver decodes message
• communication = encoding/decoding processes

FIG. 13.3 The information transfer model of communication.

illustrated in most of the other chapters in the present volume. However, it presumes an individualistic and one-way communication process which does not really do justice to conversation. The great strength of the model from an engineering point of view was how it drew on the mathematical theory of information and its quantification in terms of uncertainty reduction (Shanon & Weaver, 1949; Weiner, 1948). However, as Krauss and Fussel (1996, p. 661) point out:

> information theory has not contributed importantly to the study of human communication. The aspect of the theory that has had greatest scientific impact is its ability to characterize information in an abstract, quantitative way. And a major impediment in using the theory to describe human communication is that for a particular message transmitted at a particular time to a particular receiver, more often than not we are at a loss to specify just what uncertainty (if any) has been reduced.

What we require for conversation is a framework which more directly reflects its dialogic character. The one proposed here is based on the idea of *information co-ordination* (Garrod & Doherty, 1995). It builds on the assumption that communicators are always engaged in attempting to co-ordinate their respective actions and states. For communication in its most general form, the states may correspond to emotions, beliefs, plans, intentions and such like (see Fig. 13.4).

However, when it comes to language processing we are mainly concerned with beliefs, plans and intentions; what I shall call *information states*. Within this framework, language processing can be characterised as an attempt to co-ordinate interpretations at a number of levels (see Fig. 13.5 for a schematic representation).

Whereas the information transfer model only recognises communication failures with respect to either noise in the signal or breakdown in the encoding/decoding process, information state co-ordination can fail at

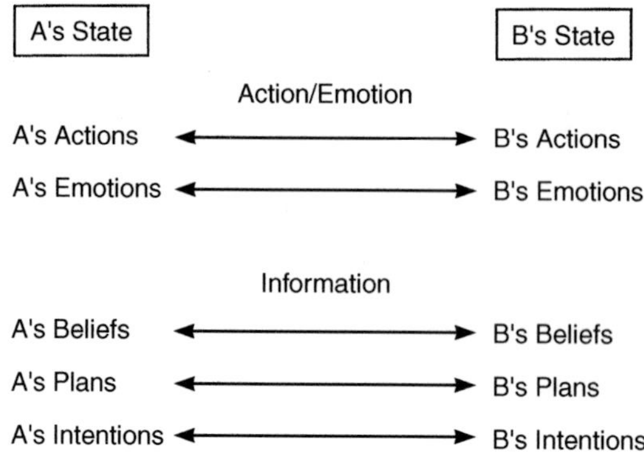

FIG. 13.4 State co-ordination model.

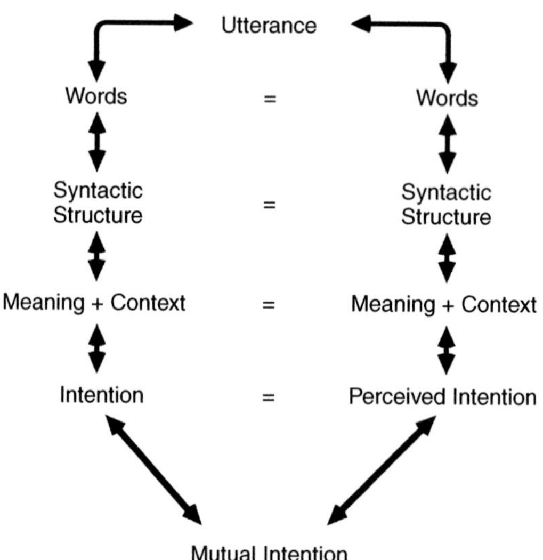

FIG. 13.5 Communication cycle diagram.

any level. At the most superficial we can fail to co-ordinate on the same utterance. To use a famous example from the literature on machine speech recognition, someone says "I recognise speech" and the machine comes up with " I wreck a nice beach" or " I reckon ice peach". Bizarre though these mechanical errors may seem, human subjects can only accurately identify about 60% of spoken words excerpted from normal conversational speech (Bard & Anderson, 1983). So, in principle, conversationalists are always at risk of making an utterance co-ordination error and think that they are dealing with a different set of words.

At the next level of establishing co-ordinated syntactic interpretations we have seen in previous chapters (Crocker, Chapter 7; Pickering, Chapter 5) that sentences are inherently ambiguous syntactically and this also presents communicators with potential co-ordination problems. Failures at the next level of semantic interpretation are especially common. The dialogue at the beginning of the previous section contains many examples of this kind. Consider for instance utterances (9–12) in the light of the subsequent exchange (41–44). It is clear that *A*'s interpretation of "One along, one up" does not correspond to *B*'s, since the two exchanges are about exactly the same position on the maze. Finally, at the lowest level of the diagram conversationalists regularly fail to co-ordinate on the intention of a particular utterance: "Can you open the window?" can be taken as a request to do so, or in other contexts as a request for information—consider a joiner refurbishing an old house and trying to find out which windows can be opened.

The basic principle behind this alternative communication framework is that of co-ordinating the interpretation process at all levels. However, it also goes further than this in treating communication as a reciprocal two-way process, where one party proposes and the other accepts or modifies or counters that proposal. Hence, the two-way flow of information in Fig. 13.5.

Reciprocity is central to a number of psychological and sociological accounts of dialogue. Clark and Schaefer (1989) capture it by reference to what they call the *grounding process*, whereby any dialogue contribution is seen as having two phases: "presentation" and "acceptance" (see also Clark and Wilkes-Gibbs, 1986). In turn, their account derives from the earlier sociological treatments in terms of adjacency pairs mentioned earlier (Schegloff & Sacks, 1973). Thus, the present framework highlights two important processing features of dialogue: co-ordination of information states and its achievement through reciprocal actions on the part of the communicators (see Krauss & Fussel, 1996 for a more extensive review of communication models).

How does this framework accommodate the experimental findings described previously? Consider first the findings on speech processing in dialogue. The main observation was that speakers modulate the intelligibility of their speech according to its interpretability in the particular dialogue context. Notice that it is not simply a generalised response to the overall predictability of the message but takes into account the feedback opportunities of the interlocutor and how they relate to the availability of different channels of communication. So it demonstrates a processing sensitivity to the reciprocal and interactive nature of dialogue. In effect, production and comprehension processes are adapted to establishing a co-ordinated representation of the utterance.

The findings from the earlier research on establishing reference in conversational context are again quite consistent with information state co-ordination framework. As Clark and his colleagues so clearly demonstrate, references are not established as a result of one-way information transfer between reference maker and reference interpreter. Rather, the whole process is distributed between the two until they are satisfied that both agree as to what is being referred to. Even more problematic for the information transfer model are the findings from Garrod, Anderson, and Doherty. Their results highlight in a very direct way the reciprocal and co-ordinated nature of language processing in dialogue. Not only do communicators collaborate in establishing the reference of what they are saying, but also they collaborate on defining interpretations for the language being used in the conversation. So it seems that language processing in dialogue is co-ordinated at every level and this is difficult to accommodate within the traditional one-way information transfer model.

Whether this new framework will prevail is yet to be seen, but the results from current studies of dialogue clearly test the standard model. However, this should not lead us to completely reject the information transfer account. Rather we should consider it as the special case where communicators are operating within an already co-ordinated framework. We also have to recognise that research in this area is still in its early stages as is theory. So, to finish the chapter I am going to consider some of the consequences of the current work and speculate about where research might be expected to go over the next few years.

Conclusion and future directions

In comparison with many of the topics covered in this book research on dialogue processing is still relatively underdeveloped. For the most part the experimental studies are only at the stage of demonstrating where the interesting questions are to be sought. However, even at this early stage it is clear that dialogue does present an important challenge for language processing accounts; if for no other reason than it forces us to consider how speech production and speech comprehension processes can be so closely coupled during the normal course of language use. And there are a number of promising areas for development. One in particular concerns intonation. Although there have been considerable advances in the linguistic and psycholinguistic understanding of prosody and intonation (see Warren, Chapter 6 this volume), there is still relative ignorance of how it functions. On the one hand, intonation seems to be that quality of speech which convinces us that a speaker "means what he says". On the other hand, it has proved difficult to establish how it does so. One approach is to consider how intonational tune may relate to the role of an utterance within a dialogue.

To take an example proposed by Isard,[2] the two answers (51 and 52) to the following question have a very different intonation:

(50) A: Do you know where John is?
(51) B: He's in his office.
(52) B: He's not in his office.

Whereas utterance (51) represents the standard dialogue move of supplying a straightforward answer to the question in (50), utterance (52) does not. However, the respondent is trying in (52) to give as much useful information as possible while indicating that this is not the standard or default move. Isard argues that it is just such information that may be carried by intonation. If this proves correct, understanding the semantics of intonation may well depend upon deeper analysis of dialogue and dialogue moves.

Another aspect of language processing likely to be illuminated by the study of dialogue is speech production and planning processes (see Bock & Huitema, Chapter 12, this volume). Because dialogue needs to flow at a reasonable rate, particularly when there is competition for the floor in a larger group, it imposes real time pressure on the production and speech planning process. This is probably the reason why so many dialogue utterances contain false starts and repairs. Again, I would expect to see the more detailed study of speech production in dialogue to begin to throw further light on exactly how the planning process operates under strong time constraints.

REFERENCES

Anderson, A.H., Bard, E.G., Sotillo, C., Newlands, A., & Doherty-Sneddon, G. (1997). Limited visual control of the intelligibility of speech in face-to-face dialogue. *Perception and Psychophysics*, *59*, 580–592.

Anderson, A.H., & Boyle, E. (1994). Forms of introduction in dialogues: their discourse contexts and communicative consequences. *Language and Cognitive Processes*, *9*, 101–122.

Anderson, A., & Garrod, S. (1987). The dynamics of referential meaning in spontaneous dialogue: some preliminary studies. In R.G. Reilly (Ed.), *Communication failure in dialogue and discourse* (pp. 161–183). Amsterdam: Elsevier Science Publishers.

Bard, E.G., & Anderson, A.H. (1983). The intelligibility of speech to children. *Journal of Child Language*, *10*, 265–292.

Bard, E.G., & Anderson, A.H. (1994). The intelligibility of speech to children: Effects of referent availability. *Journal of Child Language*, *21*, 623–648.

[2] Personal communication.

Bard, E.G., Lowe, A., & Altmann, G. (1989). The effects of repetition on words in recorded dictations. *Proceedings of EUROSPEECH '89, 2*, 573–576.

Boyle, E., Anderson, A.H., & Newlands, A. (1994). The effects of visibility on dialogue performance in a co-operative problem solving task. *Language and Speech, 37*, 1–20.

Brown, R. (1958). *Words and things*. New York: Free Press.

Brown, G., Anderson, A.H., Shillcock, R., & Yule, G. (1984). *Teaching talk*. Cambridge: Cambridge University Press.

Cherry, E.C. (1956). *On human communication*. Cambridge, MA: MIT Press.

Clark, H.H. (1985). Language and language users. In G. Lindzey & E. Aronson (Eds.), *The handbook of social psychology* (3rd ed.; pp. 179–231). New York: Harper Row.

Clark, H.H., & Brennan, S.E. (1991). Grounding in communication. In L.B. Resnick, J.M. Levine, & S.D. Teasley (Eds.), *Perspectives on socially shared cognition*. Washington, DC: American Psychology Association.

Clark, H.H., & Marshall, C.R. (1981). Definite reference and mutual knowledge. In A.K. Joshi, I.A. Sag, & B.L. Webber (Eds.), *Elements of discourse understanding* (pp. 10–46). Cambridge: Cambridge University Press.

Clark, H.H., & Schaefer, E.F. (1989). Contributing to discourse. *Cognitive Science, 13*, 259–294.

Clark, H.H., & Wilkes-Gibbs, D. (1986). Referring as a collaborative process. *Cognition, 22*, 1–39.

Fowler, C., & Housum, J. (1987). Talker's signalling of "new" and "old" words in speech and listener's perception and use of the distinction. *Journal of Memory and Language, 26*, 489–504.

Garrod, S., & Anderson, A. (1987). Saying what you mean in dialogue: A study in conceptual and semantic co-ordination. *Cognition, 27*, 181–218.

Garrod, S., Anderson, A., & Sanford, A.J. (1984). *Semantic negotiation and the dynamics of conversational meaning* (Tech. Rep. No. 1). Glasgow, UK: Glasgow University Psychology Department.

Garrod, S., & Doherty, G. (1994). Conversation, co-ordination and convention: an empirical investigation of how groups establish linguistic conventions. *Cognition, 53*, 181–215.

Garrod, S., & Doherty, G. (1995). Special determinants of coherence in spoken dialogue. In C. Habel & G. Rickheit (Eds.), *Focus and coherence in discourse processing* (pp. 97–115). Berlin: de Gruyter.

Halliday, M.A.K. (1967). Notes on transitivity and theme in English. *Journal of Linguistics, 3*, 199–244.

Hunnicut, S. (1985). Intelligibility vs. redundancy—conditions of dependency. *Language and Speech, 28*, 47–56.

Krauss, R.M., & Bricker, P.D. (1966). Effects of transmission delay and access delay on the efficiency of verbal communication. *Journal of the Acoustical Society of America, 41*, 286–292.

Krauss, R.M., & Fussel, S.R. (1996). Social psychological models of interpersonal communication. In E.T. Higgins & A. Krugasnki (Eds.), *Social psychology: Handbook of basic principles* (pp. 655–701). New York: Guilford Press.

Krauss, R.M., & Weinheimer, S. (1964). Changes in reference phrases as a function of frequency of usage in social interactions: A preliminary study. *Psychonomic Science, 1*, 113–114.

Krauss, R.M., & Weinheimer, S. (1966). Concurrent feedback, confirmation and the encoding of referents in verbal communications. *Journal of Personality and Social Psychology, 4*, 343–346.

Krauss, R.M., & Weinheimer, S. (1967). Effects of referent similarity and communication mode on verbal encoding. *Journal of Verbal Learning and Verbal Behaviour, 6*, 359–363.

Levelt, W.J.M., & Kelter, S. (1982). Surface form and memory in question answering. *Cognitive Psychology*, *14*, 78–106.

McGurk, H., & MacDonald, J.W. (1976). Hearing lips and seeing voices. *Nature*, *264*, 746–748.

Olson, D. (1970). Language and thought: Aspects of a cognitive theory of semantics. *Psychological Review*, *77*, 257–273.

Rommetveit, R. (1983). In search of a truly interdisciplinary semantics: A sermon on hopes and salvation from hereditary sins. *Journal of Semantics*, *2*, 1–28.

Schegloff, E.A., & Sacks, H. (1973). Opening up closings. *Semiotica*, *8*, 289–327.

Schober, M.F., & Clark, H.H. (1989). Understanding by addressees and overhearers. *Cognitive Psychology*, *21*, 211–232.

Shanon, C.E., & Weaver, W. (1949). *The mathematical theory of communication*. Champaign-Urbana, IL: University of Illinois Press.

Weiner, N. (1948). *Cybernetics*. New York: John Wiley & Sons.

Author Index

Subject Index